SISTER BROTHER
Gertrude and Leo Stein

SISTER BROTHER
Gertrude and Leo Stein

BRENDA WINEAPPLE

G. P. PUTNAM'S SONS · NEW YORK

Published by G. P. Putnam's Sons
200 Madison Avenue
New York, NY 10016
Published simultaneously in Canada

A list of permissions appears on pages 418–20.

The text of this book is set in Fairfield Light.
Book design by Iris Weinstein

Library of Congress Cataloging-in-Publication Data

Wineapple, Brenda.
Sister brother: Gertrude and Leo Stein / Brenda Wineapple.
p. cm.
Includes bibliographical references and index.
ISBN 0-399-14103-0
1. Stein, Gertrude, 1874–1946—Family.
2. Women authors, American—20th century—Family relationships.
3. Stein, Leo, 1872–1947—Family.
4. Art—Collectors and collecting—France—Paris—Biography.
5. Paris (France)—Intellectual life—20th century.
6. Americans—France—Paris—History—20th century.
7. Brothers and sisters—France—Paris—Biography.
8. Stein family.
I. Title.
PS3537.T323Z96   1996   95-19523 CIP
818′.5209—dc20
[B]

Printed in the United States of America
1   3   5   7   9   10   8   6   4   2

This book is printed on acid-free paper. ∞

CONTENTS

TO HELENE WINEAPPLE AND IRVING WINEAPPLE

And they were not wrong in believing that the thoughts and loves of these first years would always make part of their lives.

GEORGE ELIOT, *THE MILL ON THE FLOSS*

SISTER BROTHER

Gertrude and Leo Stein

PROLOGUE: AND THEY WERE NOT WRONG

GERTRUDE I never saw after 1920," said her brother Leo Stein in February 1947, five months before his death. One day in Paris when they might have passed each other on the street, Gertrude Stein and Alice Toklas crossed to the other side. "It was she who avoided me," he remarked.

If this incident occurred, and probably some version of it did, Alice Toklas remembered it quite differently. She and Gertrude were sitting in traffic in their two-seater Ford, acquired in December 1920, on the boulevard Saint-Germain near the old church of Saint-Germain-des-Prés. Not moving in either direction, the traffic was the worst they'd ever seen. "Everybody had a car," Toklas recalled, army cars, secondhand cars, the cars foreigners were driving. And because all the traffic police had been killed at the front, she decided, leaving only a few ill-trained security police, she and Gertrude would just have to sit and listen to the honking and shouts. "Three centimeters back and I can get through," someone yelled, and some of the smaller cars, but not the Ford, moved forward.

Gertrude Stein suddenly stood and bowed, ever so slightly, in recognition of a man doffing his hat. Who was that? Toklas asked. That was Leo, Gertrude answered. Nothing further was said. But the look on Gertrude's face, Toklas observed, was "compounded of something sardonic yet affectionate, and containing some regret . . . and a little love."

Toklas concluded the story by contending that Gertrude Stein wrote "How She Bowed to Her Brother" that night in their apartment on the rue de Fleurus. The apartment was the same one, albeit renovated, that Leo took in 1903 and into which his sister, visibly unsure of herself, moved shortly thereafter. It was also the apartment where so many celebrated their "freedom," the freedom to see, to talk, to explore; this was "a place where genuine ideas thrive and mediocrity walks away with discretion," or so Marsden Hartley exclaimed long before the rue de Fleurus became synonymous with the expatriate Paris of the glittering twenties.

But in the first years of the century, painters and talkers and hangers-on had gathered there to look at the Steins' collection of modern art: odd, incendiary canvases hung all the way to the ceiling, by artists whose names no one could yet know how to spell. And in their midst was Leo, passionately declaiming in the most ephemeral of all media: talk. Excited, he paced to and fro. His knowledge seemed encyclopedic, his mind quick and alert. Opinionated, lively, egocentric, Leo Stein was, according to the first director of the Museum of Modern Art, Alfred H. Barr, Jr. (a man chary of compliments), "possibly the most discerning connoisseur of twentieth-century painting in the world."

Gertrude and Leo Stein lived together among these canvases until 1914, arguing philosophy and psychology and art, reading, writing, painting, reflecting—in short, savoring the privilege of a sufficiently financed life. They bought pictures, not lavishly but with prescience and true passion, and soon their apartment was a fulcrum for the movement known as modernism; sister and brother were its advocates and promoters, collaborating in a profound intellectual and aesthetic venture. "There had never been a closer tie than theirs—in their years of early devotion," Alice Toklas commented a few weeks after Leo's death.

But for three decades she and Gertrude Stein lived at 27 rue de Fleurus without Leo and without, they said, any mention of him. He was persona non grata, the "one we don't see!" Gertrude Stein was given to dismissing things—and people. Eventually she severed relations with more than one sibling and most of her family, banishing old and some new friends with a peremptoriness both startling and bold. (Composer Virgil Thomson, later reinstated, once received one of Stein's calling cards, on which she'd written under her engraved name that she "declines further acquaintance with Mr. Thomson.") But nothing was as complete, unremitting, or profound as her separation from a once beloved Leo.

Complementary and devoted, brilliant, voluble, and deeply insecure, Gertrude and Leo Stein had been inseparable for virtually forty years, during which they each spent much of their time shoring up their images. Leo took himself as the subject and object of his inquiry; so, in a sense, did Gertrude. For both were as puzzled by their identities as they were by the personalities they cultivated: formalist and innovator, critic and artist, recluse and celebrity. With a personality that drew people toward her—regardless of what they thought of her unusual prose—Gertrude Stein dazzled and perplexed. Intense, intelligent, self-absorbed, Leo Stein also dazzled, but in his own way; he won few friends and no real fame. She pursued her objectives with methodical, relentless power; he hung back, afraid to touch the things he truly loved. Yet both of them, together and apart, knew they stood at the threshold of a new idiom, a new art, a new age; and both were determined to leave something of themselves behind.

Whether Gertrude and Leo Stein met on the street in 1920 or later or even on two separate occasions, it wasn't until sometime in 1930 that Gertrude wrote the threnody "How She Bowed to Her Brother," her literary version of their silent exchange of glances. "The story of how she bowed to her brother," it begins in its published form. "Who has whom as his." (Alice Toklas once remarked that Leo was a "whom" person—an object—not a "who" person— a subject.) "Did she bow to her brother. When she saw him. Any long story. Of how she bowed to her brother. Sometimes not."

Protected by the automobile in which she sat poised and unapproachable in 1930, Gertrude Stein by then was doubtless more self-assured, at least in public, than she had been ten years earlier. Pleased by the success she had enjoyed since she and Leo had separated, she was a literary "lioness" on the "crest of the wave," as she told friends. So perhaps she now could acknowledge her brother without stooping, or thinking she had. And that's how Alice Toklas, ever vigilant about Stein's public image, crafted her own account of their meeting.

But as part defense, part narrative, and part analysis of a disturbing encounter, "How She Bowed to Her Brother" is the story of their relationship from Gertrude's point of view. She bowed to her brother, or did she? On purpose? Or was it an accident, a reflexive nod of the head? And with what intention did she bow, if indeed she did? Dense, paradoxical, tinged with loss and anger and remorse, the short piece hesitates, stops, begins again. "If she were walking along. She would be. She would not. Bow to her brother. If she were riding. Along. She would. Be. She would. Be. Not as bowing. To her. Brother." Syncopated, faltering, and emphatic nonetheless, "How She Bowed to Her Brother" scans the myriad forms of ambivalence.

In public, however, Gertrude Stein treated the break with studied nonchalance; after all, it was Leo's paternalistic domination that had kept her from herself, or so Stein's autobiographical prose—and its many interpreters— would have it. But if she could not bear to meet him face to face, to encounter or greet him, then something deeply disturbing lay unresolved at the center of their relationship. And whenever that last, brief meeting took place, their relationship echoed in her writing, pressing it, tensing it, and shadowing forth long after Leo was to all intents and purposes excised.

If he was truly the failure many thought he was, Gertrude Stein also worried that "what makes American success is American failure." But it is interesting, as she earlier commented, "the success and failure, that one has in living."

·ONE·

DISORDER

AND

EARLY

SORROW

I

Bes Almon

The Steins in California

The founders of a new colony, whatever Utopia of human virtue and happiness they might originally project, have invariably recognized it among their earliest practical necessities to allot a portion of the virgin soil as a cemetery.

NATHANIEL HAWTHORNE,
THE SCARLET LETTER

Death starts history and fears.

GERTRUDE STEIN, *WARS I HAVE SEEN*

ON THE WARM SUNNY MORNING of June 16, 1884, Amelia Keyser Stein and her friend Bertha Benswanger hired a buggy and driver to take them north of Pittsburgh, north even of the bordering town of Allegheny, and uphill through the desolately curved roads of Reserve Township. Their destination was Troy Village and the small plot of land that twelve Jewish men had purchased there in 1847. The men were a burial society, their land a graveyard. They called it Bes Almon, or House of the Dead.

Milly, as Amelia Stein was familiarly known, had left two small children buried in that cemetery, a boy named Harry and a stillborn girl, now identified in marble simply as "Daughter of Daniel and Amelia." But Milly's other children had survived, all five born after she'd first arrived in Pittsburgh in 1864, a young bride of twenty-one. Now as she stood in the dappled light that June morning, she noticed that the footstone at one of the little graves had toppled. She handed five dollars to the caretaker to put it to rights, before climbing back aboard the buggy with Bertha.

They rode down to Pittsburgh and passed by the place on Fifth Avenue where Milly and her husband, Daniel, had first lived. Nearby was the old site of his store, Stein Brothers' Clothing and Cloths, at the corner of Fourth and Wood. "It is now a bank," Milly observed factually and without apparent emotion. She did not then, or later, commit feelings to paper.

A Baltimore native, for ten years Milly had lived in and around Pittsburgh, rearing her children as the family's fortunes swelled. But apart from those graves, little made her nostalgic for Pennsylvania. She was a visitor, glad to come and now glad to go, for she lived content and prosperous in the golden state of California, where flowers bloomed in the yard year-round and her children rowed all winter on the lake nearby.

Yet the dead daughter and son at Bes Almon cast a long shadow, falling, as it happened, across two other children, also a sister and a brother. These two believed themselves the living replacements for babies buried far away on a snowy hill in a city in the East. These two, Milly's youngest, had overheard that their parents wanted five children, no more, no fewer. "If two little ones had not died there would be no Gertrude Stein, of course not. . . . Two died in babyhood or else I would not have come nor my brother just two years older and we never talked about this after we had heard of it that they never intended to have more than five children it made us feel funny."

But if Gertrude and Leo Stein shared a guilty secret or a private victory, if they believed that theirs were contingent lives, born of accident, substitution, and repetition, they also learned early on that their parents, once a course was set, were very seldom deterred.

PERHAPS IT WAS in the spring of 1884, when Gertrude was ten and Leo twelve, that they thought they heard something about their conception, as they listened to Milly plan her journey east. Certainly Gertrude well remembered the preparations for that trip. First in her largely autobiographical family saga *The Making of Americans* and then in her memoir *Everybody's Autobiography*, she recalled her and Leo's jubilation at thinking they would naturally accompany their mother. "We bought as many books as we could to take along. We bought Jules Verne lots of them and then we did not go my mother went but we did not go but we had already bought the books to read in traveling." When their sixteen-year-old brother, Simon, hitched the family buggy on the rainy morning of June 8, Gertrude and Leo were driven through the mud to a train bound for Marysville, California, not Pittsburgh. They were going with their sister, Bertha, to stay with their governess's relatives on a dairy farm, where they would milk cows, battle mosquitoes in the heat, and sleep in feather beds. The highlight, for Gertrude at least, was Daniel's taking them home by ferry.

In retrospect, that summer was crucial. For at ten, Gertrude had been living, according to her glowing summation of it, a perfectly happy childhood. By the following year, the idyll was over; the days turned long and lonesome. "Anyway we came home in the autumn," she later reminisced, "and when my mother came back she was never well again." And that was the end of Gertrude's girlhood.

Sickness seemed to hover about the Steins. The next November, 1885, when Gertrude first menstruated, Milly called her daughter "unwell." Such a euphemism was typical, but what was not was Milly's own complaint. A short, formerly stout woman, she dwindled to 108 pounds, compared with Gertrude's robust 135, and murmured about mysterious symptoms. Three years later she was dead from cancer, at the age of forty-five.

LEO STEIN fashioned a story of early youth somewhat different from his sister's, insisting that his childhood was punctuated by those small, miserable tragedies she knew nothing about. Gertrude, for her part, would have none of it. "What's the use of having an unhappy anything," she later liked to ask. Unhappy childhoods were the pipe dream of liberal intellectuals, "the kind of people that believe in progress and understanding. . . . They always feel that they have had an unhappy childhood."

Whether he was liberal or not, Leo's memories were filled with stories of humiliation and failure. He was self-critical to a fault, and he suspected the motives behind his memories, knowing full well that his unhappy recollections might have been as fabled as his sister's happier ones. Like Gertrude, however, Leo Stein seldom spoke of his mother or her early death. "I remember my mother chiefly as a pervasive solicitude which became specific at moments of discomfort or pain," he wrote dismissively. In another context, he discharged her with a word—"insignificant." Yet she haunts his journals. "Grief," he once wrote there, "can become so intense as to be passionless." So could anger.

GERTRUDE AND LEO'S paternal grandparents, Michael and Hannah Stein, had disembarked from the *Pioneer* at the port of Baltimore, Maryland, on September 11, 1841. With them were their four youngest—Samuel, Daniel, Levi, and Solomon; behind them, in Weigergruben, Germany, were the graves of the children left far behind. But their oldest, Meyer, awaited them. It was he who apparently had induced his parents—or at least his mother—to come to America.

"It is hard to leave the place where one is born and raised," Rabbi Benjamin Szold later said at Hannah Stein's grave. "This fact made her husband irresolute in the attempt. But, she was filled with strength and confidence, as though she had been called by the voice of the Lord to give her children a new life and a new home in a new world; and to give them happiness and freedom."

"The old woman was a great mountain," seconded her granddaughter Gertrude, who used her as a model in *The Making of Americans*. "Yes it was she who lead [sic] them all out of the old world into the new one." Stein portrayed her grandfather, on the other hand, as regretting every mile of the trip; at one point he abandoned their battered wagon and started to walk home.

Hannah Stein ran back and convinced him all over again that their destiny lay in America, beyond the familiar round of poverty and persecution. Five years later, in Baltimore, as if the ordeal had been too much after all, Michael Stein was dead.

But Michael and Hannah and their children were among the tens of thousands of German Jews who had walked out of an impoverished Central Europe in the early 1840s to find in America political freedom, economic opportunity, and such mobility as dreams were made of. For the Steins, originally from Bavaria, where no real rights or privileges existed for Jews, the future lay in America. Articles pensively discussed in reading clubs, and brochures issued by the German societies of New York and Baltimore, as well as letters from those who had already taken the journey, inspired many to see for themselves—so many, in fact, that they constituted a lucrative market for miniature traveling prayer books printed on their behalf.

Baltimore was a convenient port of entry. German shipping lines ferried tobacco in one direction and Jews in the other. And after an eight- or nine-week ocean voyage, families like the Steins were relieved to find that more than a hundred Jewish families, many from villages near the one they had left, had established themselves in timber houses at the easternmost reach of the city. The Steins didn't move there, however, not at first. The oldest son, Meyer, was in Cumberland, Maryland, on the Potomac River near the Pennsylvania border. There he continued in his father's business, merchant trading, one of the few professions permitted German Jews in their homeland. Literate, well versed in buying and selling, he was successful, peddling old clothes perhaps on his back but more likely with a two-horse team. He would become a "store-prince," a man prosperous enough to have a little shop of his own.

By 1852 the ambitious Meyer moved to Baltimore to establish Stein & Brother, Manufacturers and Dealers in Clothing. Within the next several years, as they came of age, each Stein brother was invited to enter the expanding firm. Such an enterprise was common for German Jewish immigrants; kinship offered instant community while minimizing the risk of individual failure. And the system worked well for the Steins. The Baltimore Street location of Stein Brothers', as the store came to be called, quartered six floors of enterprise: on the fifth, thirty employees cut the material; on the fourth, the material was distributed to other employees, who sewed mostly at home; on the lower three floors, ready-to-wear merchandise was displayed; and in the basement, bolts of woolens were stored. Considered one of "the prominent Jewish wholesale houses on Baltimore Street, where everything was conducted in an orderly and business-like manner," Stein Brothers' flourished. And the Civil War was a boon. Union contracts in military uniforms

invariably expanded the ready-to-wear clothing market, and if collecting payment from their southern distributors was a problem, the youngest Stein
brother, Solomon, galloped southward, ignored the armies, collected the accounts, and then converted Confederate currency into hogs, which he drove
through the lines himself. So the story went.

But the war that brought large contracts to clothing houses also divided
the Baltimore community, Jewish and Gentile alike. At the Orthodox Baltimore Hebrew Congregation, where both the Steins and the Keysers (Milly's
family) worshipped, Rabbi Bernard Illoway's defense of secession secured him
a new post—in Louisiana. Rabbi David Einhorn of Baltimore's Reform synagogue, Har Sinai, preached abolition so vehemently that when rioting between
Unionist and Confederate sympathizers broke out, he had to flee to Philadelphia, his life threatened and his printing press destroyed. On April 19, 1861,
shortly after the firing on Fort Sumter, the Sixth Massachusetts Infantry was
attacked by a mob while changing trains in Baltimore. Bricks, cobblestones,
and bullets flew through the air in what quickly became a riot. Four soldiers
and twelve civilians were killed, one soldier was beaten to death, dozens on
both sides were wounded, and a southern sympathizer who shouted a cheer
for Jefferson Davis was shot dead from the train as it pulled out of the station, a dazed Massachusetts regiment aboard.

"My mother used to tell stories of Baltimore and the Northern soldiers
being stoned as they passed from one station to the other you always had to
change in Baltimore," recalled Gertrude Stein. "She remembered it and we
remembered it." It is likely the young Milly Keyser watched fearfully from a
window of her family's five-story house on Pratt Street as soldiers scurried by
in overcrowded horse-drawn trolleys.

She had grown up on peaceful Pratt Street in the large home of her parents, German Jews who had immigrated decades earlier than the Steins. Her
father, Moses Keyser, had landed in Baltimore in 1821, a young man from Fritz-
lar bei Kassel, Germany, who eventually opened a dry goods store at 72
Hanover Street. Milly's mother was Betty Preiss, a Baltimore native and
daughter of one of the city's most well-known Jewish families, one that claimed
a Dutch pedigree.

Betty and Moses had nine children and fared reasonably well—but not
to the extent the Steins did. Spurning business, according to Gertrude Stein,
the Keysers "did not consider my father's family as quite equal to them, my
father's family all were rich men my mother's family were not not any of them
but that is the way they felt about everything. . . . The Keysers my mother's
people and the Steins my father's people had different ways of counting
money."

And everything else. Baltimore Jewish society was highly stratified. "Our family was among the old bourgeois Jews of Baltimore, well below the Sephardim who are the Jewish aristocrats but equally above the newcomers from Russia," explained Leo Stein. And the "old bourgeois Jews" had their own pecking order, firmly rooted in a person's date of arrival in the States. Of course it wasn't time alone that produced gentility, it was attitude as well. The Keysers appeared self-sufficient, religious, genteel, and without strong ambition. They virtually prided themselves on not having "talent for money making, a talent which does not run in our family," observed Rachel, Milly's sister. And although Gertrude associated the Keysers with creativity and aesthetic sensibility, she felt they lacked "originality of personality," a quality presumably in abundance among the more aggressive, putatively masculine, and arriviste Steins.

Evidently sympathetic to the views of the German Jewish elite, the "gentle" Keysers (Gertrude's consistent adjective for them) were socially and financially linked to the South. They were secessionist, and despite Gertrude's assumption that the Keysers eschewed business, they had mercantile interests in Virginia, where at least one of Milly's sisters, Rachel, worked in a family millinery establishment. Milly's brother Solomon enlisted in the Confederate army and fought nobly for the cause.

Most of the Steins were sympathetic to the southern cause; notable exceptions were the irascible Daniel and his younger brother Solomon. "The war broke out, one partner was a Rebel, the other a Union man; they broke up the business," recalled a local citizen. According to his son Leo, Daniel Stein "was Northern in sentiment, though all the rest of the family were Southern, and was exceedingly disputatious." So in 1862, when Daniel and Solomon moved to Pittsburgh to establish a western arm of Stein Brothers', it was as much for political as for commercial reasons. And Pittsburgh, unlike Baltimore, was a decidedly northern town.

But Daniel did not give up Baltimore, his family, or his business and social connections. A marriage between the Steins and the Keysers, members of the same synagogue, well known to one another, would be socially acceptable and certainly to the advantage of both families. (In *The Making of Americans*, Gertrude suggests her parents' marriage had actually been arranged by one of Daniel Stein's sisters.) Daniel was not an attractive man, with his small alert eyes, stocky build, and thinning dark hair. But he was going places. And he appealed to the short, large-boned, serious Amelia Keyser, with her plain open face, never quite pretty but not without character—and, apparently, ambitions of her own.

The couple was married on March 23, 1864, in Baltimore and shortly after moved to the house in Pittsburgh that Solomon Stein and his wife, Pauline Bernard, would also occupy. The adjustment was difficult, at least initially. Daniel was volatile and opinionated, and his brother, a milder man, had married a prickly woman whose firmly held ideas of comportment irritated Milly, herself prone to recalcitrance. Moreover, the well-insulated Milly had moved from a city smelling of magnolias to a grimy, industrializing place where soot smeared clean clothes in a matter of hours. At night, said an observer, Pittsburgh looked like hell with the lid off.

But the economy was good. Although neither Daniel nor Solomon may have been able to predict as much, Pittsburgh soon became a vast arsenal for the Union's war supplies; its manufacturing and its wholesale clothing market boomed. Situated at the juncture of major rail lines and three rivers, it offered exceptional transportation as well as rich deposits of bituminous coal and iron, a growing manufacturing base, and 150 Jewish families.

Daniel purchased property just north of the Iron City, across the Allegheny River in the town of Allegheny (incorporated into Pittsburgh in 1907), where many German Jewish families lived. The streets were broad. A large park boasted pastures, ball grounds, and streams of fresh, clear water. In 1866

Amelia and Daniel Stein

the two families of Steins moved to these more pastoral surroundings, and for the next six years they lived there in the same or adjoining wooden houses.

Milly made new friends among the young aspiring Jewish mothers at their sewing circles and musicales. And she and Daniel had started their family, almost right away: she gave birth in 1865 to a son, Michael, on whom she doted; after the death of a second son, Harry, Simon was born in 1868; and after the death of an infant daughter, Bertha arrived in 1870. As the family increased in size, it also grew more affluent. Daniel and Milly moved to one of a pair of connecting houses at one of Allegheny's best addresses, Western Avenue, with Solomon and Pauline and their children next door, and employed two live-in servants, a young man and a teenage girl. Daniel purchased more property, and by 1870 could determine his personal and real estate assets to total at least $60,000. A generous man influenced, it was said, "by motives of friendship and humanity," he was able to assist those less prosperous; he loaned Meyer Hanauer, a founder of the local B'nai B'rith and also a clothier, $5,000 to educate his children.

Leo, Milly and Daniel Stein's last son, was born at about four in the morning on May 11, 1872, at the Western Avenue home. He wouldn't remember his father's store, Western Avenue, or Pittsburgh; neither would his baby sister, Gertrude, who came into the world almost two years later, on February 3, just after the family had moved yet again, this time to a spanking-new eleven-room red-brick house at 71 Beech Street. But she seldom tired of claiming her birthright. "I was born and raised a Republican in Pennsylvania," she frequently declared. Or less enthusiastically: "I was born in Allegheny Penn, a fact Alice [Toklas] always wants me to keep dark but you have to be born somewhere and I was born there."

EACH MORNING Daniel and Solomon Stein crossed the suspension bridge joining Allegheny and Pittsburgh to arrive at their store on Fourth and Wood. But their partnership was nearing its end.

Shortly after Leo was born, Daniel sold to Solomon his share of the Western Avenue property for one dollar, "to correct a mistake" and "convey to the said Solomon Stein the whole of the lot." Daniel's great-grandson was later told that the brothers argued, possibly about the property. As far as Gertrude was concerned, however, "the two sisters-in-law who had never gotten along any too well were no longer on speaking terms"; their quarreling augured the end of the business. (According to Gertrude, before her death Milly "forgave Aunt Pauline not sincerely.") Whatever the reasons, the Stein brothers dissolved the partnership and quit Pittsburgh. Solomon and his family moved to New York City, and Daniel and Milly returned briefly to Baltimore, where they prepared for an extended sojourn abroad.

They were bound for Vienna; the Steins, their five children, and Milly's sister Rachel sailed on June 27, 1875. It is not clear how long they intended to stay. Perhaps they thought they would decide only after Daniel consulted the Viennese otologist he hoped could restore his poor hearing, a family affliction that worsened with time. (Fifty-three years later, his son Leo went to the same city on the same quest. "To the psychoanalyst this seems clear enough," Leo Stein quipped.)

But Daniel Stein was a man of broad ideas and vast ambition, who set a great store by education; when Gertrude claimed he took the family to Austria to educate the older children properly, she was right. That was how Leo too understood the trip abroad; his father didn't think one could receive a true education in America. And certainly there must have been business prospects he hoped to turn to his advantage: for instance, Solomon Stein, who had opened a mercantile business in New York, bought his goods in Europe; maybe Daniel could act as intermediary, or he could work abroad for Meyer and Samuel and Levi Stein, who had left the cloth trade for banking. The future looked bright.

Having settled into a large apartment in the heart of the city, the Steins immersed themselves in Vienna's cultural life, which for them included traffic with local Jewish activities. They attended shul and enjoyed the singing of the cantor, although Milly and Rachel felt imprisoned by the high iron railings in the gallery where the women sat. Intrigued that very few shops closed for the Sabbath—those same shops were, however, quite particular about what was kosher—they observed how much finer the Passover matzohs in Vienna were than those at home ("You can almost see through them," gasped Rachel). The children pursued interests more secular. They visited the city's various public parks, flew kites in the Prater, and skated in wintertime; even their parents, Rachel reported to relatives back home, were "getting along bravely" on the ice. Milly and Rachel outfitted themselves with new hats and dresses, and in the spring Milly looked smart in a new black shirtwaist with the modish yellow overskirt everyone wore that season. Her three sons sported canes, Michael wore a derby, Bertha was given a parasol, and altogether the five children felt "as big and as gay as a big sunflower."

Rachel Keyser enjoyed her nieces and nephews, "our little dumplings" as she called them, and seemed especially fond of baby Gertrude; "*such* a darling, so plump, and round, she walks around a great deal, but not much as yet alone," she reported shortly after Gertrude's first birthday. "She can say something to [sic], and imitates everything! the lamb!" Ranking each child, Rachel reported to Baltimore that "Mikey['s] whole time is occupied with his studies, and the very little spare time he has, he devotes to skating; he skates very nicely: he is learning French also, twice a week. Symey [Simon] hasn't as much

desire for learning, he likes comfort and ease too much: he likes to play all
the time. Leo will also learn well, I think, he and the baby can sing and repeat some nice songs and verses. Bertha will be more like Symey as respects
learning." And Rachel was herself held to the same standard, especially by
paterfamilias Daniel, who advised her pointedly to "learn something useful,
in the way of handiwork; something that will always be handy and profitable
to go at and be master of."

Learning, learning something useful, the desire for learning were at the
hub of the Steins' small world. The children were duly rewarded for their accomplishments: they received books for passing examinations, books for birthdays, and they gathered, rigorously posed, around a large book in the inevitable
family photo. Before they left Europe, said Gertrude, the family went on a
shopping spree, buying not only coats and caps and muffs but "a microscope
and a whole set of the famous french history of zoology."

And with learning came feats of language. The children spoke English
and German and soon learned French; Michael showed off his skill in letters
to his maternal grandfather, and, one suspects, received ample praise. Just a
toddler, Gertrude too seemed eager to perform, or at least that was how she
was perceived. Just after her second birthday, Rachel recounted, the "baby . . .
tries to speak english, her attempts at it set us all laughing, at which she gets
indignant & says 'No *lafer* me!' " Poor Leo, himself becoming proficient in German, was horrified when his kindergarten teacher pasted a strip of paper over
a garrulous little classmate's mouth to put a stop to all that chatter.

Books and language, speech and articulation, learning and education:
such was the creed of Daniel Stein, an impetuous self-made man from America intent on establishing his, and his children's, cultural credentials. He was
an exacting and critical taskmaster. On hearing that he had taken her parents
to the opera during one of his visits to Baltimore, Rachel Keyser wrote them
she was "delighted that you had the pleasure of seeing *Aïda*," and added rogu-
ishly, "I suppose Dan let you know all the deficiencies." Proud to be discriminating—the mark of the knowledgeable elite—he was jittery about his
judgments, apprehensive about his authority. "So you are a big gun in the criticism business," he blustered to his sister-in-law Hannah Keyser in 1875, answering what must have been a difference of opinion. "Well, I am very much
worried that my letter didn't prove interesting to you, I presume some parts
of it were too much for your *native modesty*. If I had known that you possesed
[sic] such wonderful descriptive powers I certainly would have tried to persuade you to accompany me to London and Paris. This time I will not even
make an attempt for fear I [am] making a failure, ain't I getting sensitive and
nervous on the subject."

Daniel and Milly traveled often, vacationing in Italy or touring the Rhine to Switzerland. They seemed to enjoy each other and weren't above the high jinks of posing for a cabinet portrait, sticking their heads through a cardboard picture of Prussian royalty. Rachel Keyser took on the part of "mama" to their children, who were in her sole custody during their summer in Gemünden; during the winter they were cared for by a governess for the girls, a tutor for the boys, and a cook. Leo and Simon briefly attended school (Michael, at the gymnasium, was sixth in his class, his mother bragged) but received most of their lessons from the tutor, a medical student and naturalist, who took the children on collecting expeditions—butterflies and beetles and plants—in the Tyrol on the river Traun, where the family spent the summer of 1877. Milly supplied them with butterfly boxes, as well as books, flowers, and chocolate.

Rachel Keyser returned to America in the spring of 1876, presumably as planned, and Daniel himself traveled to the States for an extended period in 1877. Still in Vienna with her five children, Milly found time for lessons in cutting and fitting, lectures, the Hebrew Society, and the entertainment of visitors from America. There was nothing shy or reclusive about her, nothing that aspired beyond the compact life of the bourgeois matron, with her discreet gold earrings and her dark hair tied trimly at the back of her head. Her involvement with her family was precise, matter-of-fact, and total. She calculated the costs of daily living with practical efficiency—1,200 florins for Betty the cook, 500 for a new corset—and kept count of Bertha's piano lessons. In photographs, she and her well-appointed children appear in suitably Victorian posture. Milly looks either haughty or demure, wrapped in furs that obviously pleased her, a forceful woman, her jaw squared, her schedules fixed. She was proud of her children. And she longed for "Dear Dan," who was due to return in late summer 1878.

Perhaps it was because she missed him so that she began a small leatherbound diary on the first of the year. She narrated the events in her life in dry facts and figures: shopping lists, expenses, her children's grades, the dates she menstruated. Indulging in very few personal reflections, she began each short entry with a description of the weather and ended each with the incantatory "All's well." Occasionally she would offer something like a prayer for Dan's safe passage back to Europe.

After he returned to Vienna, the family readied for a move to Paris; by fall they were in a 150-franc-a-month apartment in the suburb of Passy. Scrupulous Milly organized everyone into a routine. On weekdays, eight-year-old Bertha and four-year-old Gertrude attended boarding school; the boys, often taken by their father for long afternoons at the Louvre, studied at home with a tutor. On weekends, the entire family shopped for toys or strolled along the regal boulevards. They visited the Grand Exposition, posed for photographers, ambled beside the Seine; they went to the theater, and occasionally

*Amelia (Milly) Stein
on horseback in Paris*

*Gertrude Stein,
about four years old*

Daniel and Milly attended the Opéra Comique. At the end of March 1879, the parents treated themselves to breakfast at the Grand Hôtel, before saying good-bye that afternoon in "real April weather," said Milly in a lyrical burst, "sunshine and rain."

Again Daniel Stein was returning to Baltimore, presumably to make the arrangements that would soon carry his entire family back to America. On arrival, he hurriedly mailed Milly the sheet music for "The Star-Spangled Banner," as if to redirect his family's interests.

But much as she missed him, Milly's tiny leather-bound diary began to reflect small, happy excursions: with the children on the avenue Trocadéro, she watched soldiers pass in review; after horseback riding breathlessly in the Bois de Boulogne, she decided to take an Arabian horse for a month. Even on days when rain sprinkled in the morning, Milly said, the sun was shining brightly by four o'clock.

Gertrude Stein retained little about Paris except a vision of her brothers on horseback, the mutton and spinach served at boarding school, the black cat that jumped on her mother's back and scared them both, the broad public gardens through which Milly loved to wander, the Proustian smell of the streets. The Steins' year in Paris was short, unexceptional, untroubled; the routine was secure, Milly's attentions to her children undivided, her health unquestioned, and their complicated, difficult-to-please father largely absent.

ALTHOUGH SHE BECAME a shadowy figure whom Leo remembered as having read in her youth "a couple of novels by a gentle Jewish writer named Grace Aguilar," and although she was virtually dismissed in public by daughter Gertrude, Milly was, according to Alice Toklas, beloved and never forgotten. "Of course Gertrude remembered her mother vividly," Toklas declared almost defensively. Certainly it was Milly who made the Steins' new American home in East Oakland, California, comfortable enough to be recalled fondly by her children.

If Milly made California their home, it was Daniel's irrepressible energy that brought them there. The impassioned man his daughter described as "big as all outdoors" required a theater wider than Baltimore or Pittsburgh or, for that matter, the entire East Coast. Small in stature, he grew large from desire, so much that his relatives engulfed him in myth, recounting how he had boldly traveled twice around Cape Horn not long after the Gold Rush, farm equipment in tow. There would be farmers in California, the aspiring capitalist reasoned, and they would need equipment.

His brother Solomon was in fact in California in 1857, when he was "hard up for money," as Solomon himself once related. Probably he had been accompanied by Daniel—two young men seeking their fortune in the promised land—and it was then, perhaps, that Dan Stein considered Los Angeles or San Jose, cities ultimately not to his liking. But it was not until 1880 that he brought his family west, in an overland journey inseparable, at least in Gertrude's recollection, from Daniel's gusty character. Her sister, Bertha, had leaned out of the train's open window, and when her handsome red felt hat trimmed with ostrich feathers blew off, their father "rang the emergency bell, stopped the train, got the hat to the awe and astonishment of the passengers and the conductor." To a child, he must have seemed a marvelous man, afraid of nothing and able to immobilize an entire locomotive to rescue a daughter's pretty hat.

The Steins stayed at the opulent Tubbs Hotel in Oakland, a stylish hostelry overlooking San Francisco Bay on one side and long stretches of rural land on another. The terminus of the transcontinental railroad, Oakland was a busy but peaceful place, full of shimmery palms and bright agapantha, luxuriant gardens and rich orchards. Situated on a plateau that rose to meet the Contra Costa mountains and named after the noble oaks surrounding it, the town was promoted as the residential alternative to San Francisco. "How far is San Francisco from Oakland?" a civic pamphlet proudly asked. "If you have business there, it is about six miles, but if you have no business there, it is about 100 miles in expense, more or less—mostly more."

With its sunny, mild climate, wide unpaved streets, and big elegant homes—turreted, curved, or gingerbreaded, according to the vogue of the day—Oakland appealed to both well-to-do San Franciscans and those who aspired to be among them. It was a frontier suburb, the "Athens of the Pacific," many locals believed, with a good library and a three-story well-respected high school that attracted pupils from as far away as Los Angeles. For excursions, the town provided double-decker horsecars that conveyed families to the sun-baked hills nearby, and the stagecoach took them, covered with dust, farther north, to the natural springs of Napa Valley. Because the streets were thick with mud during the rainy season, the local nickel streetcars had straw-lined floors so passengers could dry their dirty shoes.

East of the town's business center and its popular resort, Lake Merritt, where a mule-powered side-wheeler roamed over the water, lay picturesque East Oakland, until 1872 a separate township, advertised as "one of the most desirable suburbs of San Francisco." There the Steins rented a furnished house at 461 East Twelfth Street, at the corner of Nineteenth Avenue, for a competitive fifty-five dollars a month. Violets grew in the garden, and Milly plucked them to dry and send to her aging parents in Baltimore. Bertha, Leo, and Gertrude enrolled in Franklin Elementary, known as the school on the hill, and then attended the Swett School, while Simon went to Prescott. On weekends the younger children went fishing with their father, while Michael, of high school age, took bicycle trips to San Jose. Theirs was an outdoor life.

Daniel embraced it, as he did all his enthusiasms, to the hilt. His new passions were physical culture and American living. "Her father having taken his children to Europe so that they might have the benefit of a european education," Gertrude Stein wrote of Daniel, "[he] now insisted that they should forget their french and german so that their american english would be pure." He was a man who believed in America now, in wide open spaces, in success, and of course in hard work—even though he had not quite determined the matter of his own vocation. In the meantime, Milly began to take accounting classes at an Oakland business college.

When a house owned by the Templeton family at Thirteenth Avenue and Twenty-fifth Street became available, the Steins decided to move. Not only was the rent five dollars a month less than they were spending, but this house was set fetchingly among pepper shrubs and peach trees, eucalyptus and blue gum. There were a large barn and a hayfield on the ten acres, all surrounded by rosebushes so inviting that the neighbors tried to steal the blossoms. For Gertrude, the remembrance of life in that house remained forever unsullied.

> It was very joyous for all of them the days of the beginning of their living in the ten acre place which was for many years to be a home to them. . . . The sun was always shining for them, for years after. . . . Sunday meant sunshine and pleasant lying on the grass with a gentle wind blowing and the grass and flowers smelling, it meant good eating, and pleasant walking, it meant freedom and the joy of mere existing, it meant the pungent smell of cooking, it meant the full satisfied sense of being stuffed up with eating, it meant sunshine and joking, it meant laughing and fooling, it meant warm evenings and running, and in the winter that had its joys too of indoor living and outside the wind would be blowing and the owls in the walls scaring you with their tumbling.

A gardener tended the grounds, a seamstress did the heavy sewing, a cook helped Milly make fragrant breads and apple turnovers. Milly put up peaches from the trees, cooked sweet-and-sour fish for the Sabbath supper, and now and then tried something new, like hare. Mornings, she baked, swept the bedrooms, and mended the clothes; for a bit of adventure, she loaded her four youngest children and their governess onto the nine-thirty boat for San Francisco to have lunch in the plush dining room of the Baldwin Hotel. Afternoons, she often called on friends, whom she addressed formally, never referring to them by their first names, even in her diary. Her manners were correct and stiff, befitting one in her position. Her friendships appear to have been devoid of intimacy. The generations after her learned little personal about

Milly Stein, and certainly nothing eccentric; she was regarded as conventional and repressed.

Not so her husband. True, he was a model member of the First Hebrew Congregation, for which he served on the committee to raise funds for a new building. But by all accounts he was a peremptory man striving after something he couldn't quite name. Leo said Daniel admired Cavour and Kossuth, and Michael held that their father was a "deep thinker" with far-ranging views. Yet he was also capricious and unsettled, dabbling in mines, street railways, and cable cars, making small fortunes and losing them. There was something grand, insecure, and unsteady about him.

In 1884 he listed himself as a merchant when he registered to vote. While the San Francisco Business Directory was calling him a capitalist, in 1886 he still identified himself, somewhat modestly, as a merchant. Soon after, however, he restricted himself to selling stocks and bonds and described himself as a broker. His place of business was San Francisco's California Street, until 1889, when he became vice-president of the Omnibus Cable Company and began working on a plan to consolidate the city's streetcar lines.

At home, he made sure his children had tutors and governesses; instruction in music, drawing, and religion; plenty of outdoor exercise, including swimming, boating, and fishing; and what he deemed proper nutrition. His opinions about everything were mercurial—except, perhaps, for his belief in the salutary effect of culture. He would hustle the entire family to San Francisco for a dramatization of *Uncle Tom's Cabin*. "In Uncle Tom's Cabin I remember only the escape across the ice," Gertrude told American audiences in 1935, "I imagine because the blocks of ice moving up and down naturally would catch my eye more than the people on the stage would." At the Tivoli Opera House, there was Donizetti's *The Daughter of the Regiment*. "And then there was Lohengrin," Gertrude reminisced, "and there all that I saw was the swan being changed into a boy, our insisting on seeing that made my father with us lose the last boat home to Oakland, but my brother and I did not mind, naturally not as it was the moment."

Their lives brimmed with activities that, after western fashion, added a dollop of the renegade to a steady diet of the proper. Leo and Gertrude each had a revolver and knew how to shoot, but took their music and drawing lessons in meticulous attire. Milly made sure her daughters wore their white gloves on official errands, but Gertrude and Leo were allowed to roller-skate in the parlor. Birthdays were festive. The children covered the parlor with flowers, and for Gertrude's tenth, Milly invited her daughter's Sabbath-school friends. That same year she surprised Leo with a gaggle of spindly boys to celebrate his twelfth. "Quite a crowd for Sunday dinner," she noted.

To themselves, Gertrude and Leo were of course the center of the universe. "My brother and myself had always been together," Gertrude later recalled. Even Milly thought of her two youngest as a pair, sending them off together to Sabbath school or to their drawing lessons, to Woodward's Gardens or the great Golden Gate Park. Leo was both companion and chivalrous protector of his younger sister. When she wanted to win a prize in drawing class for copying a cup and saucer, undoubtedly it was Leo who sketched the cup so Gertrude could have the award.

The children were growing—Leo tall and thin, his wavy brown hair tinged with auburn, his solemn face lengthening; Gertrude, shorter and rounder, her baby fat tenacious, her long golden-brown hair pulled back with a ribbon—and as they grew, they were more and more inseparable. They shared, if not intimate thoughts, then interests, adventures, and outlook. Identifying themselves with country living, they loved their trekking excursions, the sunshine, the broad hills, the canyons. (A small clump of scrub oak at Dimond's Cañon was, Leo later said, the site of his first aesthetic discovery. Why, he wondered, was this bunch of scrub oak more interesting to look at than another?) One of Gertrude's most pleasant recollections was of a trip to Aetna Springs. Although they had intended to walk, from Saint Helena, some fifteen miles away, she and Leo took a ride, and when they arrived, hailed as "infant prodigies," they both conspiratorially kept the secret to safeguard the acclaim. When writing about the episode in college, Gertrude titled her story "The Birth of a Legend"—and changed Leo's name to Harry, that of her dead brother. In such ways, perhaps, the unconscious anticipates the future.

MILLY SEEMS largely absent from Gertrude's and Leo's childhood recollections, but to judge from her diary, she was enormously involved in their comings and goings; their grades and friends and parties were the center of her life. She applied the mustard plasters, she mixed together a salve for Gertrude's poison oak, she ordered white leather boots for Bertha, she fooled Simon and Leo into thinking that Fred the gardener had caught several quail, she took the children to watch the funeral procession in honor of President Garfield.

A dutiful mama, she supervised with quantifiable efficiency. "I receive $300. per month from my husband from which I pay rent and all household expenditures including my own and the children's clothing, excepting Mikey's," she chronicled. Yet after Dan, it was "Mikey," her firstborn, who captured her heart. In the fall of 1883, when he transferred from the University of California at Berkeley to Johns Hopkins, she apparently wandered through his old bedroom and peered sadly into the empty closet. A jealous younger sister later wondered if her emotionally reticent mother didn't really love Michael "the best."

"In The Making of Americans I wrote about our family," Gertrude explained. "I made it like a novel. . . . I did give a real description of how our family lived in East Oakland, and how everything looked as I had seen it then. . . . My mother had been dead a long time, there is a great deal about her in The Making of Americans." The unpublished notes for the work—notebooks, jottings, and scraps of paper compiled over years—and the finished book show how Gertrude reconceived her mother, and perhaps how she experienced her. In Mrs. Fanny Hersland, Gertrude depicted Milly as aloof from her husband and children. Fanny's detachment was a function of her "rich right American living," her well-pampered, well-wrapped upbringing: "She had a feeling of being part of the rich right being that was natural to her." Not an immigrant, not striving to make her way in the world, Fanny Hersland knew her place and in a sense relished its limits, which made her somewhat impervious to everyone around her. And her family retaliated: they ignored her.

But Gertrude also describes Mrs. Hersland's young children savoring their mother, rubbing themselves along her soft seal coat, protected by her sweet-smelling presence when she takes them to visit her city friends, who intimidate them. These children adore their mother with profound if inarticulate devotion; they resent anything and anyone who might divert her. When she tells stories about her youth to the children's governess, they feel betrayed—even amputated. "Always then, eastern living, her [Fanny Hersland's] early travelling, was a romance to her feeling, it was later a little a romance to her children. Later they had a sore feeling that their third governess shared it with them, that she owned the romance of the early living more than they owned it . . . This was not an owning of them, but a cutting off a piece from each one of them."

Gertrude may have resented sharing her mother's attentions, her stories, and her affections, but that Milly Stein was "never important to her children excepting to being them" is an exaggeration constantly modified by Stein's reiteration of it in The Making of Americans. As a statement, it did not harden into verdict until many years after Milly's death. "When my mother died she had been ill a long time and had not been able to move around and so when she died we had all already had the habit of doing without her," Gertrude wrote in 1937, adding almost coldly that the family "all soon forgot her." But although Stein insisted her mother's death was largely expected, hardly mourned, it is more likely that Milly's protracted invalidism and everything associated with being "unwell" distressed her daughter incalculably.

For strength, health, and a sound constitution were Gertrude's exuberant and compensatory values, rooted in her childhood love of the outdoors and in her fear of loss, and then transformed into a protective chant: "The exercise of ones [sic] normal functions of living, walking, talking, thinking, being,

Milly Stein

eating and drinking is an endless joy of a healthy human being." Milly's inattentiveness—her preoccupation with her own interests and then, simply and terribly, with "the pain that killed her"—culminated in a loss so intolerable, so outrageous and inexplicable, it was best forgotten. Or compensated in some way. "Oh may I join the choir invisible," Gertrude recited over and over in her girlhood. "I always wanted to be historical," she later said.

But for comfort more human and immediate, there was Leo.

AS WITH MANY FAMILIES, food among the Steins was a mode of discourse, gathering its own symbolic properties: a means for giving and withholding attention, a metaphor both for the body and for sexuality, a symbol of togetherness, an emollient, and the evocative substance which at all costs must be ingested or avoided. For their first cross-country journey, Milly kept the hamper well supplied, repacking it at every stage of the trip, Gertrude recalled. Predictably, Milly was associated with nourishment. But Daniel, preoccupied by what he consumed and by his weight—he tended to be portly—"was a very hearty eater and was subject to bilious attacks," his son Michael related, "which usually ended in a spell of Diarrhea. After such an attack he was usu-ally rather weak, but considered them beneficial as they cleared his system."

Chronically overweight, the young and handsome Simon grew painfully obese with passing years; Leo, his obverse, was long and thin and apt to fuss or push away his food. He suffered constantly from gastric problems, the source of which he indefatigably traced to his father's dinner-table despotism. Parading his authority in front of guests, Daniel ordered young Leo to eat boiled vegetables even though he knew, Leo claimed as an adult, they made him ill. That was in Vienna. When the family moved to California, Leo for-aged in the garden, nibbling on raw carrots and turnips to overcome his re-pugnance, so desperate was he to please.

For Leo's chronic stomach complaints, Milly typically prescribed cas-tor oil. If the symptoms persisted, the Steins visited a physician, usually Dr. Andrew Fine, who also lived in East Oakland, and for a short time tried a Chi-nese acupuncturist in San Francisco. Despite—or perhaps because of—Daniel Stein's recent emphasis on the importance of physical exercise for the children, Leo stayed home from school with surprising frequency, often when the nature of the illness was not quite clear. By day he walked in the garden with his mother or accompanied her in the buggy on short excursions to Pied-mont or Fruitvale. By evening, when his father returned from his office, the boy felt much better.

Leo was an inhibited child who had been an ill-tempered toddler. His sculptor uncle, Ephraim Keyser, whose European training had been financed in part by Daniel Stein, made a statuette of the boy, characterizing him as con-stantly yelling, "I kick you I slap you." But if he had once been belligerent, as he grew his mother regarded him as frail. So did the more aggressive Simon, who teased his fastidious younger brother, hiding his violin in the barn to make it smell of horses. And Leo was wont to annoy even his brother Michael, who considered himself a highly cultivated young man. Leo tagged along one day when Michael, who was studying violin, went to the house of a neighbor, a pianist, to play duets. After they had finished, Leo asked what they had played. Beethoven, Michael answered. Leo said it didn't sound like Beethoven to him. "What the hell do you know about Beethoven anyway," snapped Michael.

"Of course my feelings were hurt," recalled Leo, "and for several days the thing recurred to me resentingly but none the less in the background of my mind there was an echo, 'What the hell *do* you know about Beethoven any-way?' In fact I knew very little and knew that I knew little." It never occurred to him that he'd wounded his brother's vanity.

In fact, it was characteristic of Leo to conceal what he regarded as hu-miliating ignorance by pretending to know more than everyone else. At school, his friends taunted him admiringly, calling him "encyclopedia" in deference to the vast stores of information seemingly at his command. When the teacher asked someone to explain "this or that, I was usually the boy to answer"—as long as the teacher did not call on him by name. Pleased with himself, he also believed "I commonly made the impression on people that I knew a great deal more than I did, and was usually painfully aware of the discrepancy between what I precisely knew and what I was called on to produce."

"I once met a girl from Baltimore in London," he recounted. "She said, 'In Baltimore they used to say you knew everything so I'm going to ask you three questions. Do fringed gentians grow in swampy ground. What's the difference between iso and orthochromatic. Who was Pico da Morandola [sic].' The proper reply would have been that I knew nothing of botany or lenses and very little about Pico, but in fact I guessed closely enough about the lenses because I knew what iso and ortho meant and it had happened once when walking in the Berkshires with a cousin and her little children that they had wanted to pick some fringed gentians, but my cousin asked me to do it as the ground was too wet for the children to venture. So I knew that gentians grew in swampy ground. It is astonishing how often one is saved from a confession of ignorance by some bit of stray information." Where he had no information, he used his keen reasoning as a self-protective weapon, that and superciliousness. But he was sure that one day his friends would see the emperor had no clothes.

Leo found performances of any sort daunting. To avoid meeting the smartest girl in his class on the street, fearing perhaps that he would have to measure up to what he perceived as her standard, he would walk around the block. His dancing-school adventures, de rigueur for socially conscious Oaklanders, were disastrous. "Dancing with Sadie Hardy I stepped on everything except the floor," he remembered; "even if I knew how to dance I couldn't perform except in a state of calm indifference." His more successful performances bore for him the mark of disgrace. When large flocks of pigeons came to eat the grain the Steins had just planted, Leo threatened the pigeons' owner, saying that if they came again, he would have to shoot. They came again. Leo felt uncomfortably bound by his word, and so the former pugnacious toddler, who now feared his own aggression, explained the end of the incident as a sexual parable. "I managed by an effort to compromise, and pulled the trigger a bit early and so only scared them off."

Home was his refuge. Home was Milly. Although her diary records a greater number of Leo's friends—Hal Levy, Meyer Lissner (later a Progressive leader who served on the state legislature), and others—than any of her other children's, it also reveals that Leo spent a good deal of time with his mother, in that "pervasive solicitude" he long remembered.

But he was so self-conscious he shuddered at the word "love," never said it, and balked when he thought he might have to use it in an essay. In a school English examination, he was asked to rewrite in prose some verses that began, "Over the river they beckon to me, / Loved ones who've crossed to the other side." Unable to force himself to write the hated word or to think of a substitute, Leo skipped the question, worth fifty percent of his grade. Yet in this instance, it was certainly the content of the verse, with its images of loss and death, that paralyzed the boy, especially if the episode occurred, as it probably did, after the onset of Milly's fatal illness. By his own admission, Leo avoided talking about feelings and remembered little beyond his father's tyrannical prohibitions, prohibitions that undoubtedly made his affection for his gentle, failing mother seem all the more taboo.

Near the end of her life, Gertrude wrote to a young man on the occasion of his mother's death: "I do feel that the death of a mother is even sadder for a son than for a daughter. A daughter lives more intimately with a mother, but a son feels that his mother is all romance all tenderness and all beauty, and the loss is a complete loss, and I am so very sorry."

ON MONDAY, OCTOBER 12, 1885, after four months of not writing in her diary, Milly Stein recorded that she went to Dr. Fine to have something called "the galvanic battery" applied. It was a somewhat unorthodox treatment usually reserved for nervous complaints. Perhaps Milly was considered a hysterical female.

And after nearly seven years of journal-keeping, she concluded this and almost all subsequent entries without her ritual "All's well." All was not.

The previous April, when their lease had been up and Mrs. Templeton refused to sell, the Steins moved to a new house, at 1324 Tenth Avenue. They crated their books and bibelots, the carpets were taken up and cleaned, and the curtains were taken down; the carriage was sold, as were the horses and their hay. Although Gertrude and Leo liked the house on Tenth Avenue, they preferred to think of themselves as having grown up on the Templeton property. That was the place Gertrude Stein visited with some trepidation in 1935, only to find it dingy and overgrown, her childhood home gone, the nearby houses badly neglected. But it was on Tenth Avenue that the Steins lived for the next six years, those years Gertrude called lonesome—or more precisely, spent without the ministrations of her mother.

By October 1885, the galvanic battery and the salt baths at a nearby sanitarium were the center of Milly Stein's world. As the treatments continued over the next months, she admitted in some bewilderment that she was "not well yet." Bertha had to accompany her mother to the doctor; "I do not trust to walk alone," said Milly. She seemed to improve for a while during the winter, but most days she remained at home, walking a bit with Dan in the later afternoon or occasionally stopping by the local reading room in the evening. And she still went to see Dr. Fine.

Simon took a job at the Fulton Iron Works, Leo and Gertrude went to see *The Black Crook* with their "Pa," Bertha began riding lessons. By March 1886, when Milly was seeing Dr. Fine every day, she had effectively ceased writing in her journal; but in August she noted that a Dr. Richter joined Dr. Fine to consult on her "trouble." And in September she marked the date that Bertha enrolled in private school. She wrote the Post Street address of the Mechanics Institute Library, and that entry was her last.

The next summer the *Oakland Enquirer* announced that Mr. Leo Stein and Miss Gertrude Stein of Oakland were vacationing at Aetna Springs. Michael returned to California from the East to join his father in the stock-and-bond business. Sometime during the following year, Milly was brought from East Oakland to San Francisco, where she died on July 29, 1888. She was interred two days later in the Jewish section of Oakland's Mountain View Cemetery, handsomely landscaped by Frederick Law Olmsted. In keeping with Jewish custom, the family requested no flowers.

2

TEMPERS
WE ARE
BORN WITH

The brothers: Simon, Michael, and Leo

My father's name was Daniel he had a black beard he was not tall
not at all tall . . .

GERTRUDE STEIN,
DANIEL WEBSTER. EIGHTEEN IN AMERICA

F RIENDS CAME to see them as they us[ed] to us
governesses etc. but all stopped after death of
mother," Gertrude Stein remarked in one of her
notebooks. With Milly dead, daily routine, once so carefully maintained,
began to crumble. "The children did not have to come into meals but ate as
they pleased. Leo and Gertrude used to go off alone to theatres and concerts
in San Francisco and stay up all night talking and stay in bed all day," recollected their friend Mabel Foote Weeks, who had heard their tall tales. And
Daniel, who had never been easy, now was impossible. "Their father would
sometimes shut himself up for days on end."

Troubled, lonely, and each consumed by what Gertrude called a "rather
desperate inner life," she and Leo were now bound together even more tightly,
their pain separate but similar. As were their pleasures. "They had a great influence one upon the other—a great influence—" said Alice Toklas, "because
they were very intimate until they were no longer intimate at all, and they did
a great many things together, they discussed things together, they worked on
things together." Gertrude was fourteen, Leo sixteen; they were constant
companions. They concocted dramas and tried to imitate Marlowe, they
marched along the dusty roads carrying leftover crusts of bread; they played
word games—what is a lot, they would ask; a lot is a place surrounded by a
fence, China is a lot because it is a place surrounded by a fence—and they
were unhappy enough to later romanticize this period as the time when
they were on their own, alone, unsupervised, and free.

Early on, they had felt a marked and powerful kinship they shared only,
to a certain extent, with Michael. "It is rare to find," Leo explained, "as in our
family, a separation so complete among members as there was between
Michael, Gertrude, and myself on one side and Simon and Bertha on the
other." But mainly they regarded Michael, nine years older than Gertrude, as

of another generation. Riding horseback with his mother as the other children played in the Luxembourg Gardens, or accompanying his father on trips from Vienna to Paris, he was the first to reach adulthood and gain his father's respect. From youth, he was considered mature, composed, gentlemanly, and self-assured. In a photograph taken in Vienna, a seven-year-old Leo lounges on the floor, a dandy in the making; at fourteen, Michael looks as though he's off to a board meeting.

He was like a German Jewish burgher, responsible, unflappable, at one with his time and his world. Home from college just as the family was preparing to move to Tenth Street, Michael interrupted a party spontaneously arranged by Bertha, Gertrude, Leo, and several of their friends. There was banana cake waiting in the kitchen, and the children pooled their nickels and dimes for a gallon of ice cream. They intended a "party—sitting around on packing cases and eating and drinking with absolute careless abandon," recalled the friend who'd baked the cake, but Mike Stein "had no such Bohemian ideas as we did—No sir—Mike made us—yes he *made us*—drag out of those packing boxes, linen and dishes (I can hear Bertha protesting now) and we had to sit down, absolutely against our desires, to a set table. All the joy was gone, for me, but I remember Mikie dished up the ice cream from the freezer on [the] back porch and Leo passed it around."

That night, when the children requested second helpings of ice cream, they learned that the troublesome Simon and his friends had stolen it. Simon was the child Aunt Rachel had distinguished as without "much desire for learning," the one who hooted loudly when a Viennese comedy character "acted the drunkard." Handsome, with bright dark eyes and dark slick hair, he cared above all for his comfort. He had difficulty in school and was indifferent to the intellectual, cultural, and physical activities that absorbed Gertrude and Leo and impressed their parents. "There always was an attempt to educate him," Gertrude reminisced in *Everybody's Autobiography*, "and there was a time when I undertook to teach him that Columbus discovered America in fourteen ninety-two. I used to ask him every morning and every evening, that he could not really remember that it was Columbus was not surprising but that he could not remember fourteen ninety-two was not really a bother to any one neither to him nor to me." His parents considered sending him to a local military academy.

Daniel thought him lazy. "You may rest assured," he wrote Simon, summing up his individualistic credo,

> that unless you improve your mind by observation, reading, study-
> ing & learn to think for yourself, keep yourself tidy, be prompt in
> everything you wish to do, be temperate in eating & drinking, in

one word your mind must be educated & trained & strengthened
to control the body, otherwise a man is very little higher than the
lowest of animals, to be a common farm hand is certainly not very
desirable, in this country successful farmers are among the bright-
est & best men [we] have, many of our Presidents, Senators, Members of Congress & other noted men in all branches of life have
been raised on farms, but they were & are brainy men, it is the
mind & will-power that makes the man, I have endeavored for years
to impress this fact on your mind without success. I hope you will
change yet, you are still young, the world is before you— Your destiny is in your own hands, every person in this country has the same
& equal chances with every one else, so if you fail, you have no
one to blame but yourself, you have plenty of time & opportunities to improve yourself, you must remember, if you wish to associate with respectable & intelligent men & women, you must be
so yourself.

Since Simon, overtly casual about his father's approval, didn't compete
for it, Gertrude and Leo judged him amusing and harmless, a simpleminded
young man who liked to feed candy to children and who could swallow a whole
pot of rice pudding at one sitting. But if they merely condescended to him,
as adults they were vexed by Bertha, whom they rejected. "Simon I liked but
I did not like Bertha," Gertrude casually commented. She told Bertha's son
that his mother had always been a liar. Alice Toklas remembered that Gertrude
had liked this nephew, a geneticist, and "was glad to find she had a nephew
that was in what she considered the family tradition—which she didn't consider his mother to belong to!"

When using Bertha as one of the main sources for a fictional character
in her family novel *The Making of Americans,* Stein took an incident from their
childhood that best typified Bertha's character. Running along with her brothers, one of whom had asked her to hold an umbrella, Bertha realized she
couldn't keep up. She began to yell that she was going to throw the umbrella
in the mud. No one listened. She yelled again. Still no one listened, so she
threw the umbrella down and, frustrated, wailed that now she'd done it, she'd
thrown the umbrella in the mud. Her brothers kept on running.

But the story, which Stein used as an example of Bertha's manipulative
petulance—her "sulkiness actively expressed"—appears so frequently in
Gertrude's notebooks that one wonders if it wasn't cast partly from her own,
not Bertha's, experience. Certainly the youngest of five children, who loved
being pampered, also must have known how it felt to be left behind, unheeded,
angry, and helpless.

Leo more or less agreed with Gertrude's estimation of Bertha. According to him, both Bertha and Simon were "definitely sub-normal in intelligence." Yet we have no evidence that Bertha was as slow as later depicted. Or as sulky and disagreeable. Relatives remember her as good-looking, conventional, a bit plump, and by no means retarded—just an average woman who benefited little from comparison with her younger siblings. In fact, the swank Field's Seminary, which Bertha attended, prepared young ladies for the likes of Wellesley and Smith.

In the summer of 1890, when the two sisters vacationed together, as was customary, in the vicinity of Dutch Flat, their antagonism was not conspicuous. Years later, their former companions still associated the two sisters, pressing Gertrude for news of Bertha long after the family had left California. Probably Bertha and Simon intimidated their younger siblings, who, while asserting themselves as superior, still had to vie for the affections of their parents. "Hersland feels toward Martha as our daddy did to Bertha," Gertrude observed in the notes for her family novel, sounding pleased; she concluded that "my sister Bertha could not learn anything and that annoyed him." By implication, she, Leo, and Michael were the preferred children, motivated as well as able to excel. But because Bertha was the child closest to Milly during her protracted illness and the one who more or less took over the domestic responsibilities, her siblings' resentments may have swelled into open hostility later. In *Everybody's Autobiography,* Bertha is the unpleasant person who "grinds her teeth at night."

And as the adolescent Gertrude began to define her own sexual identity, she assigned Bertha a role that suggests complex feelings toward their mother. In her notebooks, Stein described Bertha as "pure female," with "sloppy oozy female in her," summing up her sister's character in what might have been a summation of Milly's. "The sexual character of Bertha both maternal & wifely," Stein wrote, "but diffuse all over the shop, in herself no power of concentration, sentimentalist in the sense of feeling herself the type woman, good, superior, maternal, good housekeeper, cook, seamstress, judge of propriety and right conduct, and in a sloppy, diffuse, grimy way she is all that, naturally conceives herself as all those things ideally. Incapable of carrying things out against opposition and so submissive to a man." All this was not far from her characterization of Mrs. Fanny Hersland in *The Making of Americans.*

It was also similar to the way Alice Toklas said Gertrude spoke of Milly Stein: "Gertrude said she had a very considerable personality, but she had to put it out," presumably to placate her husband. By contrast, Gertrude was not outwardly submissive and, unlike Bertha, not interested in housekeeping or cooking or sewing or propriety. But assailed by feelings she couldn't fathom,

The sisters:
Bertha and Gertrude

she wove them into her first college composition, a melodramatic account of a young woman tormented by sadomasochistic urges, nightmarish sexual visions, and incestuous longings, all of which are hinted at in the title of the composition, "In the Red Deeps," a phrase taken from George Eliot's *The Mill on the Floss*. As she lies in bed sleepless, listening to her sister breathe quietly, "fearful thoughts crowded upon me dreadful possibilities of dark deeds." Unnerved by the physical pleasure these "dark deeds" inspire, she doesn't know how to "silence that dreadful iteration of horrible thoughts." This is the nighttime, terrifying side of her personality, a secret identity, erotic and dangerous and bursting with forbidden passions. Meanwhile, the prosaic sister, a foil, sleeps undisturbed. Correct, proper, and uninspired, "my sister she is not my sister, my sister she is my sister her plan is to be represented by absolutely the same letter paper," Stein wrote many years after her college composition, when still consumed by the image of her double.

But little is known about Gertrude's primitive feelings toward Bertha or the way they connect to early sexual experiences, which can be only inferred through some of her most unguarded work, her college themes. Especially the longer ones reveal a sensual woman buffeted by the conflicting demands of desire and conscience: "Her old sense of isolation began to surge over her," Stein wrote in a story about Hortense Sanger, a character she had used in an earlier, related theme. "Again she had become one apart. Again there was something none knew beside herself, that no one else of those about her had been guilty of." Simultaneously excited and repulsed by the proximity of a man—an Italian—who presses close to her one day in church, Hortense finds she is paralyzed; she cannot budge. Her cousin will be offended by such indecency, she knows, and yet Hortense cannot change or explain such an offense against propriety and class.

As an adult, Leo too found himself netted in the tangled webs of childhood desire. He dreamed of Bertha, one time that he had mistakenly married her, she insisting they sleep together. He made her go to another bed, but the next day, when she appeared clad in a bathing suit, he pushed her away. A friend materialized, laughing, and then cousins surfaced in the form of brothers, indignant and angry as only such paternal substitutes would be in the face of so much unbridled incest.

By the age of fourteen, Leo was aware of his own sexuality. Intensely embarrassed by the presence of girls, he began to have conscious sexual fantasies about them, particularly about one May Lidell. A friend of both his and Gertrude's, she was jaunty and vivacious. Afternoons, she and Gertrude giggled together while Leo stood by abashed, too shy to make his feelings known. "I could not give expression to my admiration of May either in word or deed except in ways [so quiet] as to amount to nothing." Instead, he fantasized and masturbated, compensating for his reticence and compounding his sense of shame.

Denial and confusion, desire and prohibition: this was the stuff of adolescence. Leo later said that, as adolescents, he and Gertrude confided everything in each other except their sexual fantasies and fears. Not until adulthood did Leo learn from a female friend of Gertrude's that she, like him, was terrifically inhibited. But if she was self-conscious, in conflict, or restrained, her school companions didn't know it. Had they not liked her so much, deferring to what seemed her natural unchecked authority, they might have regarded her as a bully. Years after they had left high school and East Oakland, one former schoolmate avoided saying hello to Gertrude on a Paris street because she had been afraid Gertrude would not like her clothes and would, as in the old days, order her to change them.

Together, Gertrude and Leo were able to sublimate the burgeoning sexual sensations discomfiting to both. She liked to recall they mostly stayed at home "eating fruit and reading books." And their feelings toward each other were as emphatic as any they experienced for others. She admired him; she felt as protective of him as he did of her; she identified with him. His failures mortified her. During their second year at Oakland High School, they happened to be in the same English class. Every Friday the students were asked to recite a passage of poetry or prose. Leo climbed to the platform in front of the class one Friday and stood there stammering. The lines he had memorized deserted him. "It was no longer your brother but some one who certainly could not remember," wrote Gertrude, vividly recollecting her own embarrassment. "And anyway what he had to say was so far away and more and more what you heard had no reality. What you say yes that was a picture but what you heard really did not matter."

Leo himself regarded Gertrude as "definitely a brighter pupil than I was," although their schoolmates considered Leo gifted. "Did Leo write the 'Merry Widow'?" a former neighbor in Oakland asked Gertrude several years after the Steins had left California. "We noticed that one of the names connected with it was 'Leo Stein' so of course, thought it must be your brother." Yet both Gertrude and Leo were self-conscious and competitive, aware that they came from an upper-middle-class Jewish home and that they felt different from others in ways neither completely understood or articulated.

Some of this Leo attributed to his being Jewish. "The jew stuff had its importance because of its sex foundation and got mixed up with it because I lived in a non-Jewish community and all the little girls about whom I had feelings were goyim," he later mused. Only a few anti-Semitic incidents were recorded in Oakland, but they did occur. In 1886, for instance, Frank Collins was arrested for calling a Jewish peddler "sheeney." And Leo, when trying to show off to his friends, was stung when a classmate said, "Oh, those damned Jews always get ahead of us. . . . Excuse me, Stein, I didn't know you were there."

Gertrude described East Oakland as a place where her friends were different from the "rich right living" of the Steins. But the Steins were different, as Leo suggested, primarily because very few Jewish families lived there. Sensitive and vulnerable, Gertrude and Leo would cling to each other, taking refuge from their mother's pretentiousness and their father's irascibility, from their anxiety and their desires. They became as follower and leader, child and parent, mother and father, in roles that lurched and varied. They were confederates, they were friends; they presumed sexual neutrality.

They also shared a debunking sense of humor, protective and profound. In high school, Gertrude sat through a friend's Friday recitation. "If safe on the billows you fain would ride— / Cast over for ever thy burden of pride / Lighten thy heart of its fatal weight / Ere voices shall whisper, 'too late, too late' / For the heavily laden shall never see / The blessed port of Eternity," the girl chanted. Pleased with herself, she sat down, only to find a note on her desk, passed to her from Gertrude. "Luna, lunae, feminus, Who do you think you are, a preacher?"

GERTRUDE AND LEO browsed the bookshops of San Francisco, buying with their allowance as much as they could afford, including an illustrated set of Thackeray, personalized bookplates, and *The Rubáiyát of Omar Khayyám.* Books, inevitably, were a major preoccupation, books by Smollett and Carlyle and Trollope and Emerson and Scott, books of history, minor novels, Swift, and Lecky; she and Leo devoured almost anything they could find, claimed Gertrude. Since Daniel, according to his son Michael, "acquired a great degree of culture by his own efforts," and since Milly's family prided itself on its learning—her brother Solomon, the former Confederate, gave lectures on George Eliot at Baltimore's Young Men's Hebrew Association—the family owned a serviceable library: bound volumes of Wordsworth and other poets, a complete set of Shakespeare, Bunyan's *The Pilgrim's Progress,* and a volume of large-scale line drawings of historical incidents. Gertrude later wrote that Leo "found a good many books that I would not have found and I read a great many books that did not interest him but I did read a great many of the books that he found that I would not have found."

In the fall of 1887, Leo left Oakland High School for the private Oakland Academy. No longer listed as a resident of the Steins' home in the city directory, he evidently roomed at the school, at least until Milly's death. By the next fall, he had moved back home, where Michael, returned from Johns Hopkins and ready to follow his father into business, also joined the family. Leo continued to study, cramming "three years' high school work in seven months," he said, to prepare himself for his college entrance examinations.

Like Michael before him, Leo headed for the University of California at Berkeley, in the fall of 1889. It was a relatively young institution, built on the old Byrne ranch among large oaks, brush, and muddy paths, and overlooking San Francisco Bay and, just beyond, the Golden Gate. Leo could easily have lived at home. The trip to Berkeley from Oakland took only twenty minutes on the electric cars that ran every five minutes and cost six cents, but that first year he too packed his clothes and books and moved into a boardinghouse near campus, on Channing Way.

He was called "student at large" in the College of Letters and Political Science, which meant he didn't have to declare a major or progress in any typical fashion toward a degree. Perhaps he was already thinking ahead, as Michael had done, hoping to go east. But in the meantime he could take those courses that interested him, mainly English literature and history, and consider himself something of an outsider if he liked. And that is how he felt. In later years he recalled bursting out laughing one afternoon in the library. A student nearby, curious as to what Stein was reading, was disappointed to find it was De Quincey. The word got around that Stein was "queer." Not only did he read such heady stuff, he actually found it funny.

During Leo's first year at Berkeley, it seems, Gertrude dropped out of Oakland High School, perhaps after a fire destroyed most of it in the spring. But it is unlikely that she didn't then attend, as her siblings had, one of the area's several preparatory schools. In 1890 her name disappeared from the Oakland directory, much as Leo's had, as if she was rooming away from home. But whatever her whereabouts or activities after leaving the high school—and she herself was always vague—she invariably filled her accounts of those days with such words as "dark and dreadful."

A few years later, in college, she suggested what "dark and dreadful" meant: inchoate sexual desires, a preoccupation with death, abiding isolation, and moods so wild she said she feared for her own reason. Using an autobiographical incident to characterize her young heroine, Stein placed Hortense Sanger in a high-ceilinged, well-lit library, listening as a military band outside played Chopin's funeral march to accompany "some local celebrity, on his last journey." Motherless and at liberty to come and go as she wishes, Hortense goes mostly to the library, but this afternoon she is unable to concentrate. The music disturbs her. One cannot live on books alone, she decides. " 'Books, books,' she muttered, 'is there no end to it. Nothing but myself to feed my own eager nature. Nothing given me but musty books.' " Hortense leaves the library, her head ringing, and decides to "walk it down." She quickly climbs the steep hills outside, moving faster and faster, hoping she might "escape from myself," then pauses at the peak of the highest hill. The blue ocean stretches out below, the sea breeze soothes her hot face. Calmer, she realizes something must happen. She simply cannot struggle much longer with those terrible, violent feelings.

Just at this critical time, Stein tells us, Hortense Sanger's father dies.

DANIEL STEIN'S choleric temperament had always been hard on his children. A complicated, unpredictable man given to fads and theories about everything from food to medicine to education, he lived utterly in the present, at least from his family's point of view. He was certain of something only until he lost interest in it, and then his loss of interest was complete. "Our daddy's way of playing sixty-six symptomatic," remarked Gertrude. The character based on him in *The Making of Americans* demanded his children play cards with him, but then abruptly left the table, saying he didn't have time for the game, the children had better play with the governess since it was they who had wanted to play in the first place. Or after paying little attention to his daughter, he suddenly declared she shouldn't go out in the evening, "that was no way a daughter of his in his position should be acting." "My father whenever I had anything the matter with me always reproached me by telling me that I had been born a perfect baby," Gertrude recollected. "Fathers," she concluded, "are depressing."

With Milly dead, only Michael could moderate Daniel's fulminating: "Mike stands up against father's irritability about eating and things when business goes bad You have no right to lose your temper and act peevish like a baby, Not eating your dinner and saying it was because of not being fit to be eaten," Gertrude recorded in her notebooks. Daniel came home evenings cross and nervous, his temper sour. "Daddie [was] lending money," Gertrude recalled, and investing it, wisely for the most part, but not without anxiety or risk. That anxiety and the fact of his wife's miserable death induced him to take an interest in the spiritualists camping at the shores of Lake Merritt, who promised contact with the beyond. When a friend of Gertrude's, Cora Moore, began to conduct séances, Daniel Stein was amenable.

Tyrannical and withdrawn, Daniel Stein nonetheless wanted to remarry, or so Gertrude's notebooks suggest. They suggest also that Daniel's brother Solomon encouraged the eloquent, intelligent Meyer Sol Levy, rabbi at the First Hebrew Congregation and a friend of Daniel's, to help him find a wife. It was primarily Michael who kept his father from another marriage—a bad one, his children thought—arguing, according to Gertrude, that he had no right to bring them all up into a good position and then disgrace them.

Angry with Gertrude, annoyed with the way Bertha made coffee, complaining about Leo, exasperated by Simon, Daniel Stein was almost willfully alienating them all. Gertrude and Leo turned to Michael. They would spend the day in San Francisco and in the evening call on their older brother, who had been living there since 1890 and working under his father as assistant superintendent of the Omnibus Cable Company. Michael indulged his youngest siblings, taking them to dinner, reading the books they recommended, and dutifully admiring their prized photograph of Millet's *Man with a Hoe*. ("A hell of a hoe," he reportedly commented.)

A quiet man who liked a good cigar, did not drink, cropped his pointed beard neatly about his face, Michael Stein loved music, was patient, orderly, and persistent, and was gifted with that prosaic common sense Gertrude and Leo admired. He made a lasting impression on Leo the day Leo used a shoe to drive a nail. Michael gave him a hammer. "For hammering," he said, "there's nothing like a hammer."

For the entire family, Michael provided a tranquil alternative to Daniel Stein. But Michael loved his father and regarded him as a good friend. His sudden death, then, was for Michael all the more stunning.

Daniel Stein

ONE SATURDAY in January 1891, during Leo's second year at Berkeley, when he, Bertha, and Simon were living at home, Daniel Stein failed to appear at breakfast. The children were worried.

Leo went upstairs and discovered his father still in bed, unwakable. The coroner, a Mr. Evers, was called. He examined Stein and announced that an inquest was unnecessary, Mr. Stein had apparently died of apoplexy in his sleep, to judge from his position and the unpained expression on his face. He probably hadn't suffered or known what was happening. Michael later assumed his father's overeating had caused the fatal attack. ("Problem of nutrition is the problem of death," observed Gertrude in her notebooks, "normal death more depressing than pathological death.")

It was a blow to them all, Michael wrote to his uncle Meyer in Baltimore two days after the funeral, which was held in the Stein home on Monday. Rabbi Levy conducted the service, which was attended by "many prominent men of San Francisco." Barely able to collect himself, Michael knew several important matters needed his immediate attention. His father had left a short holographic will, and when he and Daniel's friend Meyer

Leo Stein,
Berkeley student

Ehrman petitioned for probate the next week, they were unable to give the value of the estate because the will merely provided the names of the executors, authorized them to sell without bonds, and located Daniel's real and personal property in California and in Maryland. It was determined that Stein might just as well have died intestate. Everything would be divided equally among his heirs, so that each of Stein's five children would receive approximately $60,000 dollars in land, stocks, bonds, and cash. There was also a pair of diamond earrings, eventually claimed by Bertha.

Never forgotten by his children—never forgiven by Leo—in death Daniel Stein became a different kind of adversary. To Leo, this meant his belittling father, never satisfied, would remain forever disappointed in his son. Yet if Leo remembered their father as an unmitigated despot, Gertrude's version was less unequivocal, more ambivalent. To her he was original—in him, originality "takes a practical form"—hearty and excitable, profoundly interested in everything he saw, a splendid, singular man, "a man who frightened any one because he was too impatient to finish what was not yet begun." "Slowly his children learned endurance of him," Stein wrote of the brown-eyed man she described as big as all creation. "Later in their life they were queer too like him."

Although Gertrude claimed that life became pleasant after their father's death—perhaps because she and Leo easily accepted Michael as surrogate—she started to see her father's aggressive force, his rages, his deep and curious idiosyncrasies in herself. Undoubtedly, she was thinking of both him and herself when several years after his death she began writing a long novel about her family. This is the epigraph:

"Once an angry man dragged his father along the ground through his own orchard. 'Stop!' cried the groaning man at last, 'Stop! I did not drag my father beyond this tree.' "

It's hard, she said, living down the tempers we are born with.

IN THE FALL OF 1891, Leo returned to Berkeley for his third year, taking up residence on Dana Street, not far from campus. Simon, working as a gripman on San Francisco cable cars, became known about town as the millionaire motorman; he rode the cars until he was too fat to stand on legs painfully swollen with varicose veins. Bertha kept house, and Gertrude, not in school, was taking private music lessons.

According to Gertrude's later account, Michael considered his siblings careless; they left the front parlor window open at night and slept undisturbed while fire trucks and horses screeched by. In despair, Michael would finally declare he'd have to "throw up the whole damn business." For in addition to administering his father's estate, which took almost three years, Michael had assumed legal guardianship of Leo and Gertrude, still under age, and had moved the family to a house at 834 Turk Street in San Francisco. Before they left Oakland, friends stopped by, including one who recalled with amusement that when Michael learned their "rich" uncle from New York was coming to California, he ordered the family to unpack all the household treasures, buy new carpets and curtains, and hire a cook. (The uncle stayed only one night before defecting to the grand Palace Hotel, where, he said, there were more bathrooms.)

Fond of his young siblings, Michael was by and large complacent and obliging. At twenty-six, he was determined, practical, and reliable, and in this seemed never to change. For years the nominal, if not fiscal, head of the Stein household, even after it extended from California to the East Coast and then to Europe, Michael offered his siblings security, efficiency in the administration of their affairs, responsibility, and most important, money. It was his skill with the Omnibus Cable Company, real estate holdings, and various other investments that provided Gertrude and Leo with their financial independence; they never had to work for a living.

The arrangement on Turk Street was temporary and awkward, and everyone had to know it. Leo thought of transferring from Berkeley—to Harvard, he hoped, perhaps once it was ascertained that the claims against the estate made few inroads into their inheritance. Gertrude, however, felt isolated, wandering through San Francisco alone, knowing almost no one there, reading in the Mechanics Institute Library, and pursued by complex feelings toward the parents who had abandoned her to gloomy thoughts of death. Filled with the self-importance of college life, Leo was studying the nuances of English prose style and eighteenth-century history, then Chaucer, English rhetoric, United States history, philosophy, and Latin. And so Gertrude was by herself, reflecting at night that every star in the sky "hangs down out of the blue behind it and you for the first time realize that each is a world apart."

She was on California Street, near Michael's office, on her way to a music lesson, when she saw a man hitting a woman. It was that incident, incorporated into *The Making of Americans,* which she gave as the reason behind her female character's decision to continue her schooling: "She would go to college, she knew it then and understand everything and know the meaning of the living and the feeling in men and women." But for Gertrude, there were no concrete prospects immediately in view.

Late that fall, Leo began to complain of symptoms commonly associated with the grippe. Soon diagnosed with typhoid fever, by January 1892 he had withdrawn from Berkeley and in April was granted an "honorable dismissal" from the Office of the Recorder of the Faculties. But as he explained in his application to Harvard, he had never intended to stay at Berkeley more than three years. All along, he explained, he had been headed east.

He completed his application to Harvard as a special student in May, seven days after his twentieth birthday. His objective, he said, was the study of history and preparation for law, both of which he believed he could accomplish in two years, and he was fully prepared to meet the expenses of tuition and residence (there being no funds available for special students). Two former professors could vouch for his moral character (a prerequisite) and intellectual abilities. Alexis Lange of Berkeley's English department called Leo "an excellent student, a manly straightforward boy," whom he was sorry to lose; Thomas Bacon of the history and political science department called Leo "one of the best historical students that I ever had under my instruction." Harvard was impressed enough that, in accepting Leo, Professor William Morris Davis suggested he consider entering the school as a member of a specific class. Leo declined; he repeated that he planned to stay at the university for only two years.

While Leo was preparing his application, Michael was disassembling the Turk Street home and readying his sisters and brothers for their inevitable departures. Simon took a flat at 804 Baker Street, Bertha and

Gertrude accepted an invitation to live in Baltimore with their mother's sister Fanny Bachrach. Leo looked forward to Harvard. By the middle of June, Michael himself had moved to Tenth and Howard in San Francisco, having discarded some of the family's possessions and sold others. As Gertrude would put it, the tie that bound them to their home was snapped.

In an extravagant gesture of farewell, Leo severed his connection to the West by donating more than 250 books to the University of California at Berkeley. It was an act of largesse, and a foreshadowing of grimmer renunciations to come. In any event, these 250 volumes constituted a major portion of the family's precious library.

BERTHA STEIN said she traveled east that summer by stagecoach, and arrived in Baltimore in July. The city was little changed since Milly had visited in 1884, for even by then most of the successful German Jewish population had moved to the wide landscaped thoroughfares northwest of the city, to the large homes of Eutaw Place and Linden Boulevard. The Bachrachs lived on Linden, in a spacious house that at one time or another lodged, in addition to their three children, Ephraim Keyser, several unmarried Keyser sisters, visiting grandchildren, and Bertha and Gertrude and Leo Stein.

In 1877, Fanny Keyser, known for her warmth and graciousness, had married German-born David Bachrach, who during the Civil War photographed prisoners at Andersonville. He had invented the self-toning process in photography and after the war opened a portrait studio in Baltimore that would become well known for its portraits of all American presidents after Lincoln. An avid supporter of Henry George and an admirer of John Stuart Mill, Bachrach was, according to his niece, the "ugliest man in Baltimore but a pleasant one." Less equivocally, Gertrude was fond of Fanny and her other maternal aunts, all of whom welcomed the orphans with genuine affection.

"Baltimore, sunny Baltimore," Gertrude Stein opined almost three years after arriving at her relatives', "where no one is in a hurry and the voices of the negroes singing as their carts go lazily by, lull you into drowsy reveries. It is a strangely silent city, even its busiest thoroughfares seem still and the clanging car-bells only blend with the peaceful silence and do but increase it." If at first the Steins were uncomfortable in their new home, their aunts—and in particular, Fanny—quickly put them at ease. Fanny, a bit surprised at the unconventional ways of Milly's children, fretted when she discovered they slept without pajamas. Gertrude and Leo, more than Bertha, seemed peculiar to their aunts, who expected genteel civilities but got the Wild West. Gertrude "was very Californian, you know," Alice Toklas later explained. "She was so Californian that when she went East she found it very strange. And the people she met found her strange. She was almost a foreigner."

Gertrude uncovered in her aunts a maternal connection she thought her governess had robbed her of. And she could now almost literally inhabit her mother's past, with its large cast of characters and the internecine family squabbles that had gone on for generations. Her aunts confided in her, and she no doubt confided in them. But her main impulse toward them over the years became solicitous and slightly condescending; consistently she called them her little gentle aunts, diminishing their stature as she diminished the stature, at least publicly, of her mother. When these little aunts were startled one night, shuddering at the thought that someone might be lurking in the dark behind the trees, Gertrude protectively told them to go on home, even though she herself was frightened. But in their defense, she turned back to confront the man who stood there, who meant no harm.

Daniel Stein's Baltimore relatives, a large extended family with several cousins around the same age as Bertha and Leo and Gertrude, also welcomed the three, who were automatically provided with entrée into the social life of the tight-knit German Jewish community. On the whole, however, the community intimidated Leo and Gertrude, at least initially. Again they felt like outsiders—Gertrude later compared herself to David Copperfield—not just because they came from a different, mythologized part of the country but also because they suddenly saw themselves judged by a standard they did not recognize, respect, or much understand, not at first. This community worshipped conventions of behavior and deportment that seemed even more arcane than those of Milly's San Francisco friends.

Ambivalent about the standard measuring them, Leo and Gertrude experienced a conflict between what Leo defined as his irreverence in principle, his reverence in fact. But then Leo had more options than Gertrude or Bertha. After all, Baltimore was but a way station for him, and by September he was gone.

3
TOO DARN
ANXIOUS
TO BE SAFE

Sister and brother, Cambridge, Massachusetts

After God had carried us safe to New England and we had builded our houses provided necessaries for our livelihood reard convenient places for God's worship and setled the civill government one of the next things we longed for and looked after was to advance learning and perpetuate it to posterity dreading to leave an illiterate ministery to the churches when our present ministers shall lie in the dust.

TABLET ON JOHNSTON GATE,

HARVARD UNIVERSITY

Eastern colleges too darn anxious to be safe. . . . They needn't be so scared of any of us got any chance of real stuff in us just because we are made different.

GERTRUDE STEIN, UNPUBLISHED NOTEBOOK

ERTRUDE AND LEO weren't apart for long. In the late summer of 1892, they went to Cambridge together to find lodging for him. Having rented rooms at 23 Irving Street, northeast of the center of the Harvard campus, the leafy quadrangle of Harvard Yard, Leo wrote Michael, the family banker, for an advance on his monthly allowance so he could buy bookshelves. And, he hinted, he'd also like to hang on his bare walls some of those etchings Michael had been buying for himself.

Now auditor for the Omnibus Cable Company, Michael was also working toward its consolidation with several other cable car lines as the Market Street Railway Company, a merger that had been his father's unfulfilled ambition. When the arrangements were concluded, on January 14, 1893, it was a coup for Michael—and a good investment, one of the many he would make. "Yesterday I saw a New York Tribune extra which gave the names of American Millionaires," Leo teased his brother. "We were by some oversight left out of the category." Like a man of his times and its tastes, Michael had begun buying objects of art, primarily Chinese porcelain and Japanese prints. "Can't you please send me something . . . out of your bountiful stores?" Leo cajoled.

Leo's rooms set, his trunks unpacked, he and Gertrude decided to take the Providence steamer (the Fall River boat was full) to New York to spend a few days with their aunt Pauline and uncle Solomon Stein, the relatives who had been part of the Pittsburgh clothing venture. Pauline and Solomon's son Fred would also be at Harvard that year, but Leo did not meet him until early autumn, when he called on his cousin at Hastings Hall. Fred swept away the cards and poker chips, his friends excused themselves, and he and his cousin sat and talked for hours. "Our relationship became so intimate," Fred Stein related more than forty years later, "that he acted like an older Brother or a very close friend might have acted, in trying to direct my awakening intellectual interest and my psychological difficulties, as at that time I was taking the world very seriously and was going through a sort of Sturm and Drang period." The mild, thoughtful Fred was studying social ethics with Professor Francis Peabody and may by this time have already been wrestling with his eventual decision to leave college for his father's very successful textile business.

On his own—Gertrude returned to Baltimore—Leo adjusted to Harvard with visible ease. Reciting his Omar Khayyám and delighting in Mark Twain, he flourished in the hothouse atmosphere of Cambridge, from the clatter of meals in the cavernous Memorial Hall, where he usually ate at long noisy tables ("The wisdom that is spilt there & overflows the hall is calculated to [make] the Royal Society & the French Academy hide their respective heads for shame"), to the solemn lectures at the nearby Lowell Institute on such subjects as the genealogy of music. He met a few local celebrities, among them the elderly abolitionist Thomas Wentworth Higginson, a charming raconteur who, Leo noted, liked to answer his own questions himself; he rode the clanging horsecar that stopped just south of the Yard to visit the Museum of Fine Arts in Boston—he later remembered that "nothing special happened" there— or to see the plays on Tremont Street rehearsing for their Broadway debuts; he browsed the bookshops, leaving behind a good deal of his pocket money; and for the first time in memory this young man from California heard sleigh bells jingle when Irving Street filled with snow.

He enjoyed his classwork, especially since every Harvard student at the time was at liberty to select his courses as he pleased from the university's abundant offerings. "Groups are like ready-made clothing, cut in regular sizes; they never fit any concrete individual," the innovative Charles Eliot, Harvard's president since 1869, had insisted, and accordingly, each student's curriculum should be custom-made. Eliot instituted the controversial elective system as early as 1886, enabling the young Harvard man to fashion his course of study after his own taste, so long as his taste was cultural, nonvocational, and properly liberal arts and sciences. Some students fell apart under the burden of free choice. Leo, however, regulated himself with a fairly standard diet of introductory courses, focusing on history and still targeting law school as his goal.

That fall, he walked through the red and yellow leaves scattered in the Yard to George Lyman Kittredge's Shakespeare class, as well as to an introductory philosophy course team-taught by George Herbert Palmer and George Santayana (William James was on sabbatical), a political economics class, two half-courses in the principles of constitutional law, and Albert Bushnell Hart's constitutional history of the United States. It was an ambitious, stimulating array. Fond of Hart, who aimed toward documentation, precise methodology, and formality, Leo did well, earning A's in his history, law, and political economics courses, a B-plus in philosophy, and a B-minus in Kittredge's electrifying Shakespeare, already something of a legend.

Gregarious, sociable, and considerate, Leo made several long-lasting friendships during this first year in Cambridge. Through his San Francisco or Baltimore relatives, he had been introduced to the widow Laura Oppenheimer, who lived on lilac-scented Brattle Street and provided virtually an open house, especially on Thanksgiving and other holidays, to the friends of her children. Her son Ben was preparing for Harvard, her daughter Adele for its female counterpart, the Society for the Collegiate Instruction of Women (familiarly called the Harvard Annex), as was Mrs. Oppenheimer's youngest sister, Miriam Sutro. A special student at the Annex, she provided the romantic interest for the young men meeting at the Oppenheimers', even though she was engaged to a man none of them knew and, given the men's "various degrees of affection for Miriam," all of them disliked. But she, and later her husband, Joseph Price, became and remained Leo's close friends; every May for fifty years, Miriam sent him a birthday card.

Then of course there was cousin Fred. Together, he and Leo wandered through the stacks of the Harvard library—Fred claimed Leo taught him how to use them—and toured the secondhand bookshops near Boston's Old South Church, where sometimes Fred disappeared "for days," scouring the musty shelves. Evenings in the late fall, they often walked down the winding streets east of Harvard Yard, noting the bare branches of the apple trees, weird and beautiful in the full moonlight, and discussing books or the problems of the world or the college and their courses; so intense were their conversations, Fred recalled, that one night they reached Concord, more than ten miles away, before they realized where they were. Near Fred's room in Hastings Hall was that of the languid Howard Gans, Fred's cousin by marriage. A senior preparing for law school, Gans was said to look the part of a Spanish cavalier. He spoke in a slow drawl, finished his sentences with ironic epigrams, didn't take himself seriously, and was also a loyal friend.

This core group of friends was German Jewish; Gans was one of the three identified as Jewish among the 249 members of the class of 1893. By and large, the few Jewish students came from wealthy, assimilated families and did not suffer from the more overt anti-Semitism confronted by Russian Jews in the first decades of the century. Nonetheless, anti-Semitism was a fact of life. When President Eliot proudly asserted that "Jews are better off at Harvard than at any other American college," he also confessed, with some resignation, that as a consequence, Jews were "likely to resort to it." But there was consolation to be found, because at least the Jews were "reasonably distributed through our buildings, Hastings being the only hall where there is an undesirable proportion of them."

Snobbery too was pandemic. Although William James insisted that Harvard sheltered plenty of young men who "seldom or never darken the doors of the Pudding or the Porcellian," the student aspiring to such elite social clubs carefully avoided anyone who studied too much, had gone to a public high school, came from the West, or was Jewish. A later friend of Leo's and Gertrude's who came to Harvard and immediately felt out of place was Alfred Hodder, a Gentile from Cincinnati and Denver. "Of course I'm only a cowboy," he self-mockingly told James. "You're not a cowboy," James retorted, "you're a distinguished scholar and a finished gentleman, and how you came to be so is the miracle that none of us can understand."

Hodder was shocked; this from the man whose broad tolerance he so admired. "The bad manners of New England, and the narrowmindedness, are all condensed in those last words," Hodder protested, "and through them sings the gossip of the college world."

However assimilated they considered themselves, then, Jewish students—and certainly Jewish students from the West—knew they were a group apart. And yet they were not completely isolated. Harvard was not just a bastion of wistful New England erudition, where, said Santayana, a "slight smell of brimstone lingered in the air," or where the melancholy Anglophile Barrett Wendell held weary court to the barbarians and Charles Eliot Norton's mournful art history lectures provoked the undergraduate joke that, on entering heaven, Norton would exclaim, "Oh, oh! So overdone! So Renaissance!" Harvard was also the temporary home of eager young men, students such as the African-American W. E. B. Du Bois, or Oswald Garrison Villard, Edwin Arlington Robinson, and Frank Norris, all stiff with self-importance, and idealistic, impatient, and passionate.

IN SUBSEQUENT YEARS Leo was circumspect, at best, about his intellectual debt to Harvard. "I went to college," he told a lecture audience almost three decades later, "but never learned anything there." To his cousin Fred he once said there was "not much to tell about Harvard," only a "party in your rooms on my 21st birthday."

Gertrude Stein, college days

Gertrude was one of the guests. She visited Cambridge often that year and by the spring could be seen strolling with Leo in the strong April winds or rambling around Fresh Pond with several of their new friends.

Reasonably comfortable with her aunts in Baltimore, and feeling less lonely among them, Gertrude nonetheless found herself surrounded by more surrogate mothers than she had expected: there were her aunts Rachel, who insisted with backhand precision that Gertrude was "prettiest" at the age of five, and Sarah, and of course good-natured Fanny, with whom Gertrude and Bertha continued to live. Aunt Fanny still appreciated her younger niece's western ways but tried to make Gertrude act the part of the tidy young lady, corseted, well brushed, and well mannered. Friends in Baltimore would remember that Gertrude's shirtwaist was apt to be disheveled and her face covered with perspiration; but photographs of her, generally posed by her uncle David Bachrach, tell something different. In 1893, with dignified solemnity, the nineteen-year-old arranged herself in an understated and absolutely correct outfit: smart white collar, simple pin, and what seems a dark wool dress. Her face is broad, her expression calm. But Gertrude recalled incidents that suggest she did not blend as imperceptibly with her relatives as she or they may have liked. One cousin, she related, "once loaned me five cents because I asked him to pay my car fare and I forgot to pay him back and he never said anything about it but he never forgave me for having forgotten. How did I know that, I do not know but probably somebody told me."

And in New York the formidable Aunt Pauline sternly withheld approval. Dubbed "the Dowager" by a friend of Gertrude's, Pauline Stein was an aggressive woman whose conversation stalled on money: how much it cost her to live, computed by the day, or the amount she paid her maid, or the current price of cultured pearls. Another friend of Gertrude's described a typical encounter: "In swished Aunt Pauline with a maid and after lunch coffee for me. . . . Later she surveyed me from my shoes (pale tan pumps & tan silk stockings) to my beflowered hat—and seeming satisfied but not edified by my appearance she said 'What, don't that woman wear a corset?' "

Aunt Pauline beheld greatness, said Gertrude, and threw mud at it. But she was good in emergencies and, if flattered properly, behaved rather well.

During her first years in the East, Gertrude was the recipient of Pauline's beneficence and her censure. Like Leo, and in spite of Pauline, Gertrude grew close to the New York Steins, particularly Fred's oldest sister, Bird Sternberger, the amiable, vigorous mother of two small children, who was exuberant, engaging, and acquisitive about anything nonmaterial, from philosophy to literature to law. Wed in 1888 to Louis Sternberger, then a member of the New York Stock Exchange, Bird had concluded after a year of marriage that she had made a terrible mistake. Her husband did not understand her, she claimed, and even though he was devoted to music and the arts, he was such a boor she generally forbade him the marriage bed.

When Sternberger's business began to fail, the animosity between the couple spiraled. He alleged that she had tried to miscarry their second child by riding horseback in Central Park. She threatened to hide the children in Europe. He said he was being harassed by detectives, whom she had hired to follow him, hoping to find grounds for a legal separation. But he wouldn't give her the satisfaction, he sneered, of sleeping with anyone else.

Posing for a photograph in Capon Springs, West Virginia, during the summer of 1893, Bird Sternberger stands tall and proud in a rich white linen dress cinched at the waist and finished in embroidery and lace. She hugs her two children but is strikingly tight-lipped. Her younger cousin Gertrude, who was visiting at the time, admired Bird's tenacity, her unwillingness to submit or give up what she believed. Indeed, Bird would soon defy Pauline, good breeding, and society. To Gertrude, she was simply the "bravest and strongest woman I have ever known."

Bird's misery notwithstanding, Pauline firmly believed a prosperous marriage was the measure of a young woman's success. She therefore must have

*Bird Stein Sternberger
and her children, 1893*

looked at Gertrude's prospects with some dismay. Bertha could be comfortably married off—but that arrogant Gertrude insisted on going to college in the fall, and not even one of the residential, more expensive colleges such as Wellesley, Vassar, or Smith. Rather, by the spring of 1893, she had applied for admission to the Harvard Annex as a special student and, reportedly on the strength of an application letter full of bluff, was admitted to the class of '97.

Unfortunately, the letter itself has been lost, but friends maintained that behind it lay a clear choice. Gertrude wanted to be near Leo, and to have what he had.

WHEN GERTRUDE STEIN moved to Cambridge in the fall of 1893, the Harvard Annex was in its fourteenth year of operation. The Annex, founded in 1879, when President Eliot made his Harvard faculty available to those women who could pass the school's entrance examinations, by Stein's first year enrolled about 250 students, a hundred of whom were taking a full undergraduate load. (A great many young women came and went as special students.) In 1894, the Annex was chartered as Radcliffe College, a bona fide institution of higher learning, still affiliated with Harvard—its students could graduate only with the approval of Harvard's president—but with its own student body, its own express mission, and a very independent outlook.

Located in the crisscross of shaded streets to the north and east of Harvard Square, the Annex was virtually synonymous with the seventeenth-century Fay House on Garden Street, purchased in 1885. With a warren of recitation rooms and offices, it also held an auditorium, a lunchroom, and a library famous for its high windows and tall light fixtures that descended from the ceiling on long wires. Downstairs in the reception room, returning students, tanned from the summer, gathered each September to embrace one another, their ankle-length skirts twirling and their shirtwaists starched. The tables were decorated with autumn leaves, and the class before the one entering introduced the new arrivals to the college drink, called Warren's orange frappe.

Clusters of young women carrying books, tennis rackets, and golf clubs struck a patronizing reporter as "not uniformly beautiful, according to the strict canons of art," but "about their fresh faces, frank eyes and effective though not conspicuous attire [there was] much that would be extremely attractive." Quickly each learned the unwritten rules. The Annex woman wore no makeup, did not smoke in public, and piled her hair atop her head in a pompadour or bun. She did not by custom walk in Harvard Yard, although she could socialize with Harvard students. The *Lampoon* poked fun at her but she more or less ignored it; she was, after all, taught by Harvard's best faculty and considered her education in no way inferior to that which the men received. But unlike the men, she had no dormitory or common dining hall; instead she had been furnished with the names of nearby boardinghouses where she could live with Cambridge families and eat home-cooked meals with at least six or seven other students.

Gertrude's boardinghouse was a commodious white clapboard structure at 64 Buckingham Street, between Concord Avenue and Craigie, not a long walk from Fay House. Supported by Michael and the family funds, she lived there for four years. The atmosphere was friendly, new students mingled with seasoned boarders, and "living in a boarding house was interesting," Stein reminisced afterward, for she met "a whole new lot whom I had never seen before." But when she added in an apparently breezy way that "everybody was New England there," she implicitly underlined that she was not. However much she liked her new companions, she was a foreigner in their midst.

For one thing, she found their manners perplexing. Heartily condemning the New Englanders' dour rectitude, she bristled in a composition the autumn of her sophomore year, rebuking their "intolerance . . . You New Englanders say that you have more sympathy because you conceal it. palpable falsehood. . . . You have feelings to be sure but always feelings of supreme egoism. Egoism so all-embracing that you fail to recognize it." By contrast, she wrote, the West represented "freedom, imagination, and unconventionality," terms with which she was to associate herself and her brother, converting what may have been perceived as liability into advantage.

The same seems true of her Jewish identity. Although her closest female friend, Mabel Earle, a housemate at Buckingham Street, was not Jewish, outside the boardinghouse almost all her friends were. Several she had met through Leo. Gertrude joined Adele and Ben Oppenheimer at their mother's on weekends or holidays. (Adele and Ben, like Gertrude and Leo, were a twosome, in their case both bent on careers in science.) Another friend, also a science student, was Leo Victor Friedman, who like Ben was preparing for a career in medicine. Friedman regarded Gertrude as his *"strong good friend"*; on Valentine's Day 1896, when they exchanged poems of humor and affection, he described her as "Ruddy, glowing, hearty face / Ne'er to be touched by Sorrow's pall." Author of his own set of Valentine verses was another close friend, Francis Pollak. Preparing for a career in law, he frequently joined Leo for dinner at Memorial Hall. Leo thought Pollak "the most brilliant man . . . in argument"; Gertrude later characterized Pollak, who graduated summa cum laude, as a man of "rational subtle intellect."

Although none of these Jewish students was religious, all shared a bond that Gertrude immediately recognized. The fact that one did not observe Jewish holidays and dietary laws, keep the Sabbath, or believe in what Gertrude called a personal God did not diminish her or their sense of themselves as Jewish, or oblige them, she said, "to identify themselves entirely with the Christians and turn . . . their backs on their own people." ("Even here in Harvard," she commented derisively, "we have had at least three such instances.")

While she insisted that at Harvard "to be a Jew is the least burden on the individual of any spot on earth," Gertrude also noted that in general, Jews were an express minority, frequently unwelcome. A Radcliffe student close to Stein in the years just after graduation recalled that "before I had become liberated in regard to racial questions I had never known a Jew; thought they were something different. I remember her saying, 'I'm the top of the heap,' and I said, 'The top of your heap.' She was much offended."

"A Jew admitted into the society of Gentiles is admitted on sufferance only," Stein wrote in a junior-year essay arguing against intermarriage. "As long as they like him personally all is well, but the instant he does aught that is blame-worthy, swiftly comes opposition, not only to the man but to his race. People say of him, what can you expect he is only a Jew." Not religious but firmly Jewish, then, Stein defined herself as "modern": that is, a nonbeliever who regards religious ceremonies as symbolic and reads the Old Testament for its "poetical description," as she put it, of the "rise" of a race. But what she called the poetry of the Old Testament spurred her own rhetorical flight; she described the Jews as "strong in a hereditary clan feeling, standing by each other as brothers and thus by the strength of their union, remaining un-crushed in the clash of nations round about them and having thus truly a covenant with God which has made them endure." A rallying cry, a marching song of jingoistic idealism, this was also the exhortation of one who de-manded—and expected—undiluted family loyalty, which was, Stein implied, the only protection from a hostile world.

> Wherever a Jew goes no matter into what strange lands and he meets another Jew, he has found a friend. Appeal to a Jew in be-half of another Jew and he will never say you nay. Ask any Israelite no matter how liberal, no matter how numerous and intimate are his Christian friends; ask him to tell you to whom he would rather appeal if he were in any need either spiritual or material, whether he would rather go to a perfect stranger a Jew or to his most inti-mate Christian friend and without hesitation he will reply, "To the Jew every time."

It followed that assimilation would deliver a "death-blow" to all Jews, be they modern or traditional. And of all forms of assimilation, intermarriage was the most pernicious. Jews might attend Christian schools or have Christian friends, said Stein, but they had to draw the line at mixed marriages. She was adamant. And it was a position she long maintained, despite increasingly complicated responses to her own identity.

For she always considered herself—indeed, characterized herself—as a Jew. And she never repudiated her sense of the Jew as ethical standard-bearer. In college, she explained this as originating with an "inborn . . . ethi-cal and a spiritual nature ever fostered and increased among themselves [Jews]," making them "a Chosen People chosen for high purposes." These "high purposes" became, in a secular world, the "noble aims and great deeds" to which the Jew, honoring a heritage, should aspire.

This was Gertrude Stein's college faith, one that tingled with pride, ide-alism, and purpose, as if to avert despair. Later she would associate both ge-nius and depression with Jews. And, said the writer Carl Van Vechten in 1914, "Miss Stein spoke of an excellent theory that Lincoln's parentage had a Jew-ish strain, which she said would explain many things in his career."

Stein's modern Judaism did not dispute anti-Semitic stereotypes; quite the opposite. Without irony or modesty, she argued that Jews were intellectually superior, clannish, charitable, and capable of amassing great wealth. Moreover, these characteristics were innate; Jews were basically better, smarter, kinder. In fact, considering such superiority unassailable, she simply assumed persecution was inevitable.

But writing from the heart, rationalizing her own sense of isolation, of what it meant to be different, and not least of all, confronting her own very powerful ambitions and her own very powerful fears, she knew she shared these qualities with her family, from whom she also demanded and to whom she gave loyalty; and that family was personified for a long time in the single person of brother Leo.

THE URBANE PHILOSOPHER George Santayana recalled that as a rule, teaching at Harvard "was given by professors in the form of lectures, excessive in number and too often repeated"; most of the students listened absentmindedly, he recollected, with the notable exception of a few graduates and occasionally the young Annex women, usually "more attentive and anxious not to miss anything." Despite their initial condescension, most instructors at the Annex came to regard teaching less as a necessary evil that brought in extra pay and more as a pleasure.

Hugo Münsterberg ranked teaching at Radcliffe among his finest experiences during his first years in the United States and hailed the American college woman as a mixture of beauty, brains, and virtue: "Clever and ingenious and witty; she is brilliant and lively and strong; she is charming and beautiful and noble; she is generous and amiable and resolute; she is energetic and practical, and yet idealistic and enthusiastic—indeed what is she not?" His attitude toward his female students was alternately empathetic, respectful, and patronizing—and it was based on Gertrude Stein, his model student.

Stein's housemates on Buckingham Street were also impressed. The likable, open-faced Californian brought with her a library of English classics, poetry, and history, which covered one entire wall of a sizable room. She explained such quantity by saying that when she was eleven or so, and her family thought it was headed for financial disaster, she and Leo took all their money and bought books as a hedge against the future. If they believed such a story, these same friends were also willing to believe that Gertrude was admitted to the Annex on the basis of a single letter. She invited such belief; sometimes she compelled it.

Admission to the Harvard Annex required all students, even Gertrude, to submit to a battery of "entrance" examinations identical with those required for Harvard College, which had to be completed before graduation, but preferably as early as possible. And so Gertrude spent the fall of 1893 taking several of these tests—in German, English, and history. The next spring and in the fall of her sophomore year, she had more exams, in elementary algebra, geometry, and advanced English, and during her four years at the Annex, she completed all of her tests, except the one in Latin.

Despite the exams, the elective system obliged Annex students to only two courses in composition, one taken during their first or second year, and the other, "forensics," taken as juniors. Left more or less on their own, Annex students typically enrolled in language and literature courses; history, science, and philosophy followed in popularity. During her first year, Gertrude matched courses to her first exams, taking for instance German literature and colonial American history, and sampled introductory economics and George Santayana's introduction to philosophy, which she later recalled as representing "the part of English literature I did not know."

But it was the Radcliffe psychology course Philosophy 7, taught by the immensely popular Hugo Münsterberg, that more than anything else helped shape Stein's subsequent college career. Recently arrived from the University of Freiburg, Münsterberg had been William James's first choice to replace him at the Harvard psychology laboratory in 1892. He was, according to James, "an extraordinarily engaging fellow, not of the heroic type, but of the sensitive and refined type, inclined to softness and fatness, poor voice, vain, loquacious, personally rather formal and fastidious I think, desiring to please and to shine, liberal of money, quick to forgive . . . a man to whom I should suppose one might easily become attached." Many did. Bald, bespectacled, direct, and self-important, Münsterberg wrote poetry, played the cello in a local string quartet, read philosophy, published continuously, and in time considered himself something of an authority on the American scene.

His courses on psychology reflected his scientific training and, more important, his commitment to the physiological bases of psychology. As a medical student in Leipzig, he had worked with Wilhelm Wundt, one of the principal founders of experimental psychology, and by 1889, when he first met William James, Münsterberg was preoccupied with experimental research. Conducting some of it in a laboratory installed in his Freiburg home, he was also lecturing in philosophy, adapting Goethe's *Faust* for the theater, and reading the work of Jean-Martin Charcot and Pierre Janet. But he felt that his being Jewish stymied his career.

So James's offer was well timed. The laboratory at Harvard afforded Münsterberg just the opportunity he needed to carry on his investigations into psychophysical parallelism, the belief that every psychical fact has a physiological complement but that each operates independently. Such a credo did not make Münsterberg a materialist; psychology, he said, "degenerates into an unphilosophical psychologism, just as natural science degenerates into materialism, if it does not understand that it works only from one side, and that the other side, the reality which is not existence, and therefore no possible object of psychological and natural science, is the primary reality." His purpose in the laboratory, then, was to synthesize ethical idealism with physiological psychology. James thought Münsterberg a neo-Kantian—and the "Rudyard Kipling of psychology."

Eventually Gertrude Stein became one of the most active members of his remodeled psychology laboratory, a place more exotic than any she had yet encountered in Cambridge. There, quartered in the upper floors of Dane Hall, near a noisy corner of Harvard Square, Münsterberg introduced eager young students to a new world of well-equipped workrooms stocked with rows on rows of glass cases containing models of brains, eyes, ears—all with detachable parts—as well as microscopes, preparations in wax, and various dissected specimens suspended in alcohol. Students sat at tables placed in the middle of the room and, ignoring the sounds of hand organs and streetcar bells from below, concentrated on the acoustical experiments they tackled with tuning forks, resonators, pipes, or the organ supplied specially for their purposes; others studied optics with prisms or color mixers and had access to a special darkroom. The husky Münsterberg wandered among them, often wearing his velveteen coat and bending with paternal interest over the students at their work. They remembered him as "affable, entertaining, delightful"; "a man of deep learning, high originality, and astounding versatility, interested alike in systematic psychology, in the setting and solution of experimental problems, and, years later, in the applications of psychology."

Though few in number, women had been laboratory students since Münsterberg's first year at Harvard, when he admitted Mary Whiton Calkins, a fledgling psychologist, to the lab. According to Calkins, women in the laboratory were treated in a "friendly, comradely, and refreshingly matter-of-fact way." Highly regarded by Münsterberg and her other professors, Calkins was nevertheless denied her degree even though she had finished all the doctoral requirements. "The Corporation are not prepared to give any Harvard degree to any woman no matter how exceptional the circumstances," so Eliot chided Münsterberg, her sponsor.

Gertrude had been exposed to modern psychology, at least indirectly, as early as 1887, when Michael, first a biology major and then a graduate student at Johns Hopkins, had studied physiological psychology with Granville Stanley Hall, himself a former student of William James's and the first Harvard Ph.D. to concentrate on psychology. (Hall's thesis was entitled "The Muscular Perception of Space." Later, as a preeminent psychologist and the president of Clark University, he invited Sigmund Freud to the United States to lecture.) And even if Michael hadn't brought his interest in psychology directly home, Gertrude long remembered that science, and especially Darwin, loomed large over her childhood. "I do still think Darwin the great man of the period that [framed] my youth," she wrote Robert Bartlett Haas in 1938. Certainly Darwin's theories, popularized, meshed neatly with Daniel Stein's bootstrap mentality. And certainly theories of medicine—which Stein in *The Making of Americans* called "doctoring"—were of some moment in the Stein household. Beyond Milly's unexceptional deployment of castor oil, there were those frequent trips to the galvanic battery: journeys into the unknown and somewhat heretical practices of modern science to relieve, one hoped, a mother's vague but deteriorating condition.

As a "natural believer in science," Stein remembered that in her undergraduate days "science meant everything and any one who had an active mind could complete mechanics and evolution, philosophy was not interesting, it like religion was satisfaction in a solution but science meant that a solution was a way to a problem." Yet she was intrigued by the new psychology also because she was fascinated by personality—her own, above all. "Then I went to college and there for a little while I was tremendously occupied with finding out what was inside myself to make what I was," she reminisced decades later. Friends corroborated: "She had an enormous interest in herself and her own reactions." What better venue for an Annex girl, described by Stein as "neither flesh nor fish and to be always wanting to be the other."

COLLEGE FRIENDS recalled that Gertrude "was absolutely indifferent to conventions. . . . She enjoyed being different." If she generally looked the part of the typical Radcliffe undergraduate, her waist tight and her collars high, she also wore a battered sailor hat, remembered a former schoolmate, "until it became so disreputable that a friend placed it deep in an ash barrel." But it wasn't the occasional flash of iconoclasm that drew others to her so much as the force of her convictions and the depth of her understanding. "What set her apart from all the others was her personal quality," said one of her boardinghouse companions. "Knowing her intimately enhanced every interest one had."

For his part, Leo was remembered as "wise and discriminating" by one classmate; Howard Gans admired his "habit of taking nothing on faith and subjecting all ideas to critical scrutiny uninfluenced by traditional prejudices." He honed the habit his sophomore year in the Wendell Phillips Club, a newly formed Harvard debating society intended to combat the elitism of its rival, the Harvard Union. It advertised its members as "rich and poor, athletes and fine speakers"; they were elected on the basis of performance, not privilege. Weekly subjects for discussion included suffrage, the Chinese exclusion bill, the annexation of Hawaii, and tariff regulation—issues of a topical nature implicitly designed for the future public servant. Leo spoke often at the heated

Friday-night meetings, arguing that municipalities should provide employment to the unemployed or that the speaker of the House of Representatives should not be able to compel the voting of its members to obtain a necessary quorum. (Leo's side lost the latter debate.)

But the Wendell Phillips seems the extent of Leo's club life. "I've got lots of work on hand," he figured at the beginning of his second year. "Eng 12 Phil 3 Govt 5 & 11 Pol Econ 2. And I'm at it too with both feet. I've got 4 theses agoing all at once. 2 of them to last all year." He had returned to Irving Street after the summer holiday, and now that Gertrude was nearby, he shared many activities with her. They sat together in Sanders Theater and heard the Boston Symphony, visited the Museum of Fine Arts, and on chilly weekends bundled up for the skating parties intended to lighten wintry gloom. Leo also learned tennis, which he played before dinner with Ben Oppenheimer—"I very rarely castigate the upper levels of the air and I not infrequently stop a ball which is of course all that is to be expected of such an extremely unfledged tenniser as I"—and "with tolerable regularity" disappeared into the gymnasium. Several evenings he experimented with pool.

And although he disparaged his attractiveness to women, he had become rather charming. "As a young man," recalled a friend, "Leo was very playful, very personal, something of a flirt." After a musical evening at the Oppenheimers', Leo reported wistfully to his cousin Fred of "a new Annex girl there & a mighty pretty one she is too. She is one of [Frederick] Slee's admirations. He is the only fellow in our whole crowd who has both the taste & the gumption to hunt up & become enamored of pretty girls."

Despite the bustle, in January 1894 he boasted that "midyears don't trouble me in the least. They are very much scattered and there are only a couple of them, Roman Law, History 9 & Eco 2. . . . I have kept up with my work *this* year & don't need to do any cramming to speak of."

But Leo dropped William James's Philosophy 3, or Cosmology, and was marked "absent" in both political economy and Roman law. Extracurriculars, the presence of his sister, perhaps a nagging sense he didn't belong, after all— these took their toll. But if he had kept up with his work, as he had assured Fred, maybe he had dropped courses only when confident he would be admitted, without a bachelor's degree, to Harvard Law.

In June 1894 he received his formal letter of acceptance. Distracted or not, he had, as it turned out, hardly swerved from his initial goal. And to anyone casually peering into his Irving Street abode, the fire warm and Leo idly swaying in his rocker, a huge book open in his lap, the young man looked studious, purposeful, determined. But by the end of the next year, Leo would have completely and precipitately abandoned this snug New England image and the safe harbor it most certainly implied.

·TWO·
BOTH ONES
THAT
QUITE
ENOUGH
ARE KNOWING

4
TO
KNOW
THYSELF

The Radcliffe/Harvard Crowd (Gertrude third from left)

As through the cracks and crannies of caverns those waters exude from the earth's bosom which then form the fountain-heads of springs, so in these crepuscular depths of personality the sources of all our outer deeds and decisions take their rise. Here is our deepest organ of communication with the nature of things; and compared with these concrete movements of our soul all abstract statements and scientific arguments—the veto, for example, which the strict positivist pronounces on our faith—sound to us like mere chatterings of the teeth.

WILLIAM JAMES, "IS LIFE WORTH LIVING?"

N SAN FRANCISCO a fortune-teller told a young woman that she was about to meet a man from Baltimore who would be very important in her life. He moved among wheels, the fortune-teller said, and wheels, and wheels. A month later, blue-eyed Sarah Samuels met that man. He was uniting the cable car franchises in San Francisco, and his name was Michael Stein.

By the spring of 1893, during Leo's first year at Harvard, Sarah Samuels and Michael Stein could be seen in a large horse-drawn carriage clambering over the streets of San Francisco, past the bay windows and narrow gardens of her neighborhood. He was the trim new vice-president and manager of the Market Street Railway. She was an exuberant young woman from the Jewish side of O'Farrell Street.

Eight years before, Sarah Samuels had emerged from one of those re-spectable O'Farrell Street houses as the fifteen-year-old valedictorian of her high school class, decked out for the occasion in a high-collared light brocade dress and holding a small bouquet. She wound her wavy walnut hair up in a bun and put on her spectacles for a picture so studied it now looks comic. (Soon she would take off the spectacles for photographs, tilting her head co-quettishly to one side.) Now, driving along San Francisco's planked streets with Michael Stein, Sarah wore a large hat with a plume, hoping no doubt to attract the attention she both coveted and generously bestowed on others. She was a social woman, ardent and strong-willed as well as warm and willfully broad-minded. "She would be very thoughtless one moment and would do more mischief the next by an overly conscientious effort to make it good," Gertrude wrote in a college composition, obviously basing a character called Sally—Sarah's nickname among family—on her future sister-in-law. "She jumped to conclusions rapidly and changed them rapidly. She had always been accustomed to rule and her family had been afraid of her and all men bowed before her."

Gertrude and Leo first met Sarah during the summer of 1893 when they visited Michael in San Francisco. A picnic was arranged. Gertrude produced a volume of Browning from her pocket and commanded Sally to read. Sally did so, and Gertrude decided it was all right for her to marry Mike. Apocryphal as the story may be, Sally seems to have been delighted with Gertrude, finding a friend in whom she could entrust, among other things, the anxieties of courtship. And with whom she could indulge in the analysis of character that would, in later years, beguile both women. "You & I came to the conclusion not so long ago," Sally confided after their summer holiday, "that Mike was entirely negative, certainly negatively good. Well, I've changed my mind once and for all. Mike is strong, much stronger than I am in every virtue, and in his relation to me is very near heroic." Leo had impressed Sarah in a different way. Six years later, when taking classes in literature and art, she thought back on that first summer of their acquaintance. "He certainly did a great deal for me . . ." she observed, "and when the class marvels at my poetical insight, I grin and charge it up to *his* credit account."

But Leo, the lanky Harvard man visiting San Francisco after his full year in the East, had also intimidated his future sister-in-law, who responded to him in tones both defensive and maternal. "Tell Leo that I was really glad to hear from him . . ." Sally wrote Gertrude. "I shall answer him as soon as I can think up anything to write." If she could redress the imbalance with a little romantic advice, she didn't hesitate. After he told her that a young woman had misconstrued his attentions, Sally advised him through Gertrude that he "must not forget that he is a very attractive youth, and . . . in this heathenish age, girls are not accustomed to such devotion, certainly not when the male animal is not on a mating bent."

Two years older than Leo and four years older than Gertrude, Sarah was eager for the friendship of both, although she was careful not to impose. She generally agreed with their valuation of their brother Simon, whom she found "difficult," and apologized for her "temerity in judging of your treatment of him." Bertha, however, was trickier. When she hinted that she'd like to go to San Francisco to meet Sarah, and Michael objected, Sarah was in a fix. Conscience-stricken, she asked Gertrude to intervene and persuade Bertha to stay in Baltimore, yet was nervous lest she offend Gertrude with such a request. Sarah excused herself by saying, "I know it will seem much harsher on paper than if I were telling you and hugging you between whiles." Leo was called upon to make some explanation to Bertha; he apparently did, and so the visit was avoided.

Michael resented Bertha for undisclosed reasons. When she demanded her share of the family estate, which she solicited through her attorney, he turned downright angry. "Mike is exceedingly put out at the way in which the thing was done," Sally told Gertrude, "and while he does not blame her, considers it an excellent excuse for washing his hands of her altogether." Regarding her as something of a burden, the family was relieved when in 1897 she married Jacob Raffel. Gertrude attended the wedding, the only sibling to do so, and afterward sporadically wrote her sister perfunctory letters. Eventually these stopped, much to Aunt Rachel's disappointment. "Why don't you sometime send a line to Bertha?" she remonstrated in 1912. "She feels the neglect so keenly!"

Sarah and Michael's own wedding took place in March 1894. A photograph taken around this time—perhaps a wedding picture—shows the large Samuels clan with Michael, already bald, his countenance stern and handsome, and Gertrude festively clothed in an elaborate white dress trimmed with stripes on the bodice, neck, and sleeves; its shoulders puff out with requisite flair. She seems quite satisfied.

"Her elder brother's wife has always meant a great deal in her life," wrote Gertrude Stein some forty years later of her relationship with Sally, content to ignore the almost predictable rivalry that scarred, and damaged, their relationship.

"GERTRUDE IS DEEP IN PSYCHOLOGY," Leo told their cousin Fred in 1894, just before the December holiday. In this, her sophomore year, two of her five classes were in psychology. And she loved them. Taught under the aegis of the philosophy department, the complementary Philosophy 13 and Philosophy 20a were the specialties of Hugo Münsterberg: one, a seminar in experimental psychology focusing on modern psychological literature, was physiological and empirical in orientation, and the other took Gertrude to the laboratory.

But that wasn't all. Her courses would bring her closer to that folk hero who also taught psychology at Harvard and Radcliffe, the maverick who dared speak of emotions unmeasurable by laboratory instruments. "Hardly a law has been established in science, hardly a fact ascertained, which was not first sought after, often with sweat and blood, to gratify an inner need," William James told a rapt audience at the Harvard Young Men's Christian Association. It was their right, it was in fact their duty, to believe life worth living—

William James

regardless of religious doubt, scientific skepticism, or pessimistic naturalism. "If you surrender to the nightmare view and crown the evil edifice by your own suicide, you have indeed made a picture totally black," he boomed. Instead of such surrender, James counseled what amounted to a leap of faith: why not assume life worth living, even if the assumption is unscientific; after all, "the inner need of believing that this world of nature is a sign of something more spiritual and eternal than itself is just as strong and authoritative in those who feel it, as the inner need of uniform laws of causation ever can be in a professionally scientific head."

The exhortation roused the audience. Inspired by the sage, sensitive professor, Gertrude answered his question with her own "Is life worth living? Yes, a thousand times yes when the world still holds such spirits as Prof. James." Here was someone whose faith was "not that of a cringing coward before an all-powerful master, but of a strong man willing to fight, to suffer and endure."

James's ability to bridge the world of empirical science and the world of faith, using the claims of one to correct the claims of the other, comforted the many who occasionally faced what he called the melancholy "bass-note of life."

Gertrude too had sounded this note, which found expression her sophomore year in the stories she wrote for English 22, the popular course in which Frank Norris had written his first novel.

Students of English 22 were sent from the classroom to look and think and write something, anything, even a line or two, something seen or thought or truly felt, as long as it was original. Then, every two weeks, they wrote longer compositions, until the spring, when they completed the course with a more developed piece. And so notebooks filled with collegiate angst and ambition. Stein's themes were the predictable material of a twenty-year-old fond of Poe, Wagner, and the psychology lab. But they spoke also of depression and doubt, especially when she took up the autobiographical tale of Hortense Sanger. Rewriting an early story, the one about Sanger's discomfiture in church when a man rubs too close to her, she recast Hortense's dilemma as a conflict between science and belief.

A modern woman schooled in materialism and evolution, skeptical about religion and contemptuous of those who numbly bow to established creeds, Hortense nonetheless wonders, "Are we really only the victims of blind force." In a crowded church, awaiting the sermon of a new, powerful young preacher and surrounded by heads lowered in prayer, she wishes for some kind of spiritual communion; the wish is so strong even she is surprised. " 'A longing and for what,' she muttered, 'I would not be as they.' " As if in answer to her question, Hortense then becomes conscious of the offending man. "At first she was only half-aware of it, but soon she became conscious of his presence. The sensuous impressions had done their work only too well. The magic charm of a human touch was on her and she could not stir."

With all its erotic overtones, the story is Stein's unwitting testimony to a lost connection: an enlightened woman, Hortense yearns for something she hopes the church can provide within its maternal embrace. Yet her longing shames her, related as it is to ignorance and, no doubt, an earlier, even infantile, state of satisfaction. Ignorant of the sexual component of her desire, source of both secret pleasure and intense guilt, she is thoroughly unnerved. She feels she has been inhabited by another, separate being, one impervious to her scruples and her intelligence. And like Gertrude herself, Hortense Sanger little suspects her yearning may be a coded wish for the maternal satisfactions renounced, at least consciously, after her mother's death.

But Gertrude had found in her new sister-in-law a presence maternal enough, at least superficially, for intimacies. In California the summer before her sophomore year, Gertrude had talked with Sarah about a range of private topics, including masturbation, which prompted the vigilant Sarah to take up the subject with her gynecologist. "Somehow we drifted to the question of self-abuse," she wrote Gertrude that fall, "and he let forth. How you two would

Sarah Samuels, 1885

agree! He feels just as you do towards girls and old maids and says he has every bit as much respect for the unmarried women *he knows* have intercourse and maintain appearances as for the married. He did not speak at all cynically but with great feeling."

Sarah assumed, or hoped, that Gertrude agreed with her: better to have intercourse than masturbate. Or at least premarital sex was the preferred if socially taboo alternative to autoeroticism, unacceptable in any and all cases, particularly because it was linked to homosexuality. Was this the topic Gertrude had attempted to explore? If so, Sarah responded with the prevailing medical orthodoxy:

> It seems that he [the gynecologist] has two young girls now under treatment, one of whom he feels convinced he can cure [of masturbation]; the other he knows to be hopeless. Both are of fine family. He gives them moral? lectures and *very* strong medicine to dissipate the sensations, and finds the medicine effective in most cases. When even the lectures fail, but when it gets to certain cases

where the habit is particularly abnormal in its method and of very long practice, there follows an aversion to the opposite sex, and marriage itself is of no avail. Then there is but one resource left, and to that neither male nor female will submit—the removal of either ovaries or testicles.

He has made a particular study of these physiological phenomena. I wish we had spoken to him more freely when you were here, for I am sure he could have told you of many interesting cases that might have helped you in time to come, for, my dear girl, I feel more and more every day that it is the *duty* of such women as you to fortify the weak [men] even before the necessity actually arises.

Masturbation was an antisocial menace, Sarah affirmed; indeed, even the medical community would combat its assault on heterosexuality with cruelly punitive methods.

It is not clear that Gertrude shared Sarah's views. Gertrude's very broaching of the topic suggests she was seeking answers beyond whatever she claimed as her own opinions. For she had discussed sex also with her Baltimore aunts, who, like Sarah, were unable to offer much more than commonplace pieties. Gertrude told Leo that their "simple honest old fashioned aunts" found sexual intercourse "not satisfying, and they don't want it."

But sex was on Gertrude's mind. In just a few years, after graduating from college, she would reflect that "in our modern system of education the heaviest mental strain is put upon the girl when her genitalia is making its heaviest physical demand and when her sexual desires are being constantly stimulated without adequate physiological relief, a condition that obtains to a very considerable extent in our average American college life." Dropping the Olympian affectation, she continued: such stress and strain are dreadful burdens to the "modern woman endeavoring to know all things, do all things and enjoy all things."

Gertrude Stein was this quintessentially modern woman who faced a dilemma. Hungry for experience and in need of "adequate physiological relief," she already prided herself on her modernity, which, in 1894, meant that she would be educated, trained, even unfettered—at least in intellectual terms. But the modern woman did not yet know how to integrate the demands of the flesh and the spirit, and it was in these dueling terms that Gertrude conceived the problem. So desire struggled with conscience, and self battled against self.

Nowhere is this clearer than in her English compositions, where she explored these feelings in heated semiautobiographical prose. "I know perfectly well that I will hold some time in the future the same opinions I have just been combating. . . . I know I will believe, but as I don't believe there is no help in that. Sometimes I fiercely and defiantly declare that I won't believe neither now nor in the future. 'Be still you fool' then says my mocking other self, 'why struggle, you must submit sooner or later to be ground in the same mill with your fellows.' "

The pattern of this turmoil reached a climax in the Hortense Sanger stories. Struggling with sensations she can neither understand nor control, Hortense yields to them. But submission cuts her off from all that she has believed—and from her family. Baffled and frightened, she begins to wonder who she is; it almost seems she is possessed by a second self, unknown to her before save for its irrepressible urges.

Sensuality, guilt, desire, defiance, and the matter of a second self—these were the subjects not only of English composition; they would figure prominently in Stein's experiments in the psychology laboratory.

FROM THE VIEWPOINT, however, of her coterie of friends, a group of seven or eight students, mostly Jewish and mostly interested in science, Gertrude Stein was the best example of "Cambridge atmosphere and spirit," full of "jolly spunk" and good commonsense humor. These friends—the Oppenheimers, Leo Friedman, Francis Pollak, a newcomer named Inez Cohen, and Mabel Earle—frequently vacationed together, traveled together, took psychology and chemistry and botany courses together, wrote group letters, and in some cases lived together. So comfortable were they in one another's presence, so natural and genuine was their rapport, that they designated themselves with proud self-consciousness "the Crowd." From California, Sarah, who doubtless heard of them often, entreated Gertrude, "Do send me a picture of yourself, the crowd, and any others you can spare."

The Crowd often met for such events as candy-pullings or theatricals, and all of them loved a good argument. A peripheral member, Arthur Lachman, recalled that "one of our chief stimuli came from regular attendance every Sunday at the lectures held at Harvard Chapel. Our Sunday night review of what we had listened too [sic] often [went] far into Monday's wee small hours." And to this discussion Gertrude "brought an intelligence that even at this stage of her career was remarkably keen." Other friends agreed—even when they found Gertrude obstreperous and bossy. "She loved discussion and not infrequently was as willing to talk on one side of a subject as the other," wrote Mabel Earle. "She was sometimes rather overpowering in argument and so asserted her opinions as to leave her opponent feeling somewhat futile and flattened out, though usually of the same opinion still."

After her brother Leo's example, Gertrude committed Omar Khayyám to memory, and in the spring of 1895 the two of them saturated themselves in opera, going to Boston nightly and returning to Cambridge after two in the morning. Mesmerized, Leo thought that *Die Walküre* "seemed to charge the atmosphere of the Boston theatre with an electrical life that most took off the roof," and Gertrude, as enthusiastic, excused herself from her English assignments by explaining that "the German opera threw me back in my work." For the time being, everything and everyone else took a backseat—all the more so since Leo was leaving.

While Gertrude had been writing her English 22 themes or was banging on the pipes of the psychology lab, Leo had been taking the standard courses of a first-year Harvard Law student: torts and contracts, criminal and common law, and civil procedure. They went well at first, and he said he enjoyed everything—"as well as it is conceivable I should ever enjoy steady work"—because it was "just the kind that I should in all reasonableness like as it is argumentative logical and goeth unto the 'sources.' " Although he had stocked up on law books, he also drifted into Charles Norton's famous Dante lectures and was reading an eclectic collection of Wordsworth, Robertson Smith's *Old Testament in the Jewish Church,* De Quincey's *Literary Reminiscences,* and John Charles Van Dyke's *History of Painting*—all calculated, he said, "to produce literary indigestion."

It wasn't long, then, before Leo confessed he was "kind of tired of law." He didn't say why; nor did he say what he planned, if he himself knew, but he hinted that, in addition to his earlier interest in history, "I've got a glimmering consciousness of having found something in the afar way off distance that kind of sort of really interests me but quien sabe?" Whatever it was, it wasn't contracts or civil procedure.

On March 25, 1895, Leo officially withdrew from Harvard Law School. He hung around Cambridge for the remainder of the opera season and then left for Baltimore and New York City. Although he kept his rooms on Irving Street, he did not intend to return until at least fall. So Gertrude Stein was now alone in Cambridge without a relative nearby.

"I HOPE TO HEAR about you still often and expect the best from you," Hugo Münsterberg wrote to Gertrude as he sailed to Europe in June 1895, the end of her sophomore year. He emphatically informed Mary Coes, the secretary of Radcliffe College, that Gertrude had completed the work of two courses, and rewarded her with double credit and a B; for the seminar he gave her an A.

"With best regards to your friends, Miss Oppenheimer and Mr. Solomons," Münsterberg concluded his farewell. He was referring to Adele Oppenheimer and to another in Gertrude's circle, a young man newly arrived at Harvard that autumn, who would leave, as Gertrude later put it, "a definite mark on her life."

He was a fellow Californian, born and bred in San Francisco, with a flair for psychology and a soft spot for spiritualism. The youngest in a family of five children, like Gertrude, Leon Mendez Solomons was known as something of a prodigy. He had graduated in 1893 with honors from the University of California at Berkeley and stayed on for another year as the prestigious Joseph Le Conte scholar. Then he left California for Harvard with a fellowship from San Francisco's Harvard Club. The following year Harvard awarded him the Edward Russell Scholarship, and two years later the Gorham Thomas Scholarship. He was reflective, gently persuasive, and considerate, and what he lacked in rugged physical health he made up for in intellectual acumen. "The lad was tender and delicate. A slight organic trouble that developed in his early childhood led his mother to bestow special care on his physical condition," Jacob Voorsanger, rabbi of San Francisco's Congregation Emanu-El, explained at Solomons's funeral.

The dark-haired, dark-eyed Solomons could trace his paternal lineage to a Sephardic great-great-great-grandfather, a Spanish-born merchant who immigrated to the United States in the early eighteenth century. Leon's great-grandfather Gershom Mendez Seixas was the first American-born leader of New York City's Congregation Shearith Israel, an eyewitness to the inauguration ceremonies of General George Washington, and for twenty-eight years, from 1787 to 1815, a trustee—the first Jewish one—of Columbia College. Leon's mother was a schoolteacher, and his father, an accountant who served as business manager of the Jewish paper *The Weekly Gleaner* and San Francisco correspondent for Philadelphia's well-known Jewish periodical *The Occident,* had purchased *The Voice of Israel,* another San Francisco Jewish weekly, which he coedited. But he also had a problem with alcohol.

When Solomons applied for a graduate fellowship at Harvard, he demurred, "I do not need anything more than a university scholarship. Anything extra would probably go only for books I could get along without." A friend considered him "a man of unusual mental powers who strongly impressed his ability on all who were fortunate enough to know him, even to more or less casual acquaintances." Hugo Münsterberg agreed: "I regard him as the most brilliant psychologist of the younger generation." Joseph Jastrow, a noted psychologist at the University of Wisconsin, was so awed by Solomons's early work that in 1898, when taking a year's leave of absence, he selected Solomons, Ph.D. newly in hand, to replace him. The following year Solomons was hired by the University of Nebraska. Full of promise, "one of the five or six most original men," said William James, "whom we have ever had in the philosophical department at Harvard," and one from whom much was expected, Leon Solomons died, however, in February 1900, his twenty-seventh year.

The circumstances of his death are difficult to reconstruct. At the beginning of his second semester in Nebraska, Solomons underwent minor surgery—unexpectedly, it seems, probably an appendectomy. No one antici-pated complications. Ill for five days after the operation, the young teacher suffered a fatal heart attack on the sixth, or so it was reported. However, his friend Arthur Lachman later claimed the procedure had been bungled: Solomons had been infected by an unclean catheter and died in considerable agony.

Stunned, the faculty senate at the University of Nebraska passed a spe-cial resolution to express its bereavement. The news dazed everyone, includ-ing William James, who wrote Gertrude later in the year: "Ever since Solomons's untimely and never too much to be regretted death, I have had an impulse to write you to express my sorrow to a sympathetic friend. . . . I never was more startled by anything, and never was anything outwardly at least more irrational and ascribable to mere chance than such an event. Exactly what he would have done had he lived, it is impossible to say, but it would have been absolutely original and remarkable, absolutely clear, and it might have been very important. . . . We shall never look upon his like, and seldom his equal."

Although Gertrude later remarked that Leon, like her, was another David Copperfield "when he gets East with civilized ones," Solomons was soon in the company of the Steins. He may have first heard of them from his older sister, a homeopathic physician who happened to be Sarah Stein's closest friend in San Francisco. But it was Leo's departure, above all, that brought Gertrude and Leon Solomons together in a powerful, professional intimacy.

For in August 1895, before Gertrude's junior year, Leo decided not to return to Cambridge. In Europe with Ben Oppenheimer, he received an un-usual proposition from his uncle Solomon. Cousin Fred—Solomon's son—wanted to see Egypt, and Solomon was agreeable, as long as Leo went too. He offered his nephew a trip, all expenses paid, if Leo would consent to stay in Europe, meet Fred there, and then accompany him. It was an offer Leo couldn't—didn't want to—refuse, although Gertrude thought he should come back to Cambridge instead of gallivanting about the world. But Leo was firm.

Mrs. Oppenheimer rushed to console Gertrude: "Even if Leo goes to Egypt with Fred (as I wish for Fred's sake—though I don't know how Cam-bridge will be quite the same old Cambridge without him, even though Leo goes, I do hope you and he will go off on a happy Bohemia jaunt in the Low-lands next Summer." That would be Gertrude's recompense. But if she felt excluded or abandoned, she kept it to herself. So in the fall of 1895, the other "Leos" stepped in. Leo Friedman took over the rooms at Irving Street; Leon Solomons seemed to take over the rest.

IT WOULD BE a busy, productive year. Gertrude had become secretary of the Radcliffe Philosophy Club, fascinating fellow students, one of whom retained a vivid image of her: "I can *see* Gertrude Stein sitting monumentally

Leon Mendez Solomons

in one corner, her eye fixed on a slot on the floor at the opposite corner, at which she talked, exclusively—but *very* ably—quite the cleverest person there."

As secretary, Gertrude had the task of making arrangements with the series of speakers the club invited. When not listening to these lectures, the members of the club discussed such works as Arthur Balfour's *Foundations of Belief* and James's recently published lecture "Is Life Worth Living?" or heard reports on the work of the psychology laboratory and talks on the philosophy of Richard Wagner and German idealism.

Relishing Wagner and familiar with Royce, Harvard's resident idealist, Gertrude nonetheless shared the view of the new breed of psychologists, Münsterberg among them, who wanted to keep their field, both at Harvard and professionally, separate from metaphysics. Theirs was an experimental world, one that literally could take the physiological measure of mind. "And what is thought?" inquired fellow student Boris Sidis, later an eminent psychopathologist, who earned his Ph.D. in psychology from Harvard's philosophy department in 1897. "Metaphysics! Cells and stains, that is real science." Psychology was a matter of neurophysiology. Years later, when Stein caricatured Sidis and the work that went on in the laboratory, she satirized not so much her faith in scientific materialism as she did the students' credulity: "Sidis was interested in studying sub-conscious reactions, but being a Russian he naturally expected us to do things and we did not do them. He would have a table covered with a cloth and one of us sat in front of it and then when he pulled off the cover there was a pistol underneath it. I remember I naturally did nothing after all why should any one do anything when they see a pistol around and there is no danger of anybody shooting. We all of us were somewhat discouraging to all of us," she concluded.

But she took part in many of the experiments in the psychology lab and found many of them compelling. Under Münsterberg's direction, for example, during her sophomore year, she and Solomons had set up an experiment to determine perceptible differences in intensity of color (which they called saturation) and intensity of light. They devised a color wheel to compare various mixtures of reds and whites and blacks by way of testing Weber's "psycho-physic" law: "That in order that differences of sensory experience should have, in two different cases of comparison, the same value for our reacting consciousness, or should appear to be of equal differences, the stimuli compared in the two different cases must differ from one another, not by the same absolute physical difference in their magnitude, but by the same relative difference." In other words, if somebody turns on a light in a darkened room, one will notice the effect. But if somebody turns on a light in a room filled with sunlight, the effect is negligible. Our interpretations of such differences, then, are to a certain extent relative.

Stein and Solomons decided that color saturation was independent of light—Weber's law held up. They were pleased because they could affirm the so-called teleological significance of the law: that we can identify objects in varying light. But they devised several more experiments to test the relation of light intensity to color saturation. With two color wheels placed in a window divided by a vertical board, Stein and Solomons took turns gazing at the wheels, sometimes using a black tube that shut out everything else, while several adjustments were made to both wheels; then they would report their findings. Having decided that intensity of light did not affect color quality, they concluded that representations of colored objects can vary in terms of tone, saturation, intensity, and blackness, and that any one of these could be made to change while the others stayed the same. "This is a purely psychological classification of course," they acknowledged in the published version of their results, "The Saturation of Colors," which Solomons wrote.

While he himself acknowledged there was not much more he could say—and indeed, the experiment seems almost antiquated in its narrowness and naiveté—the importance of the work lies not so much in the results as in what prompted them. Stein and Solomons were looking to understand the relation between subjective and objective experiences; and by providing a vocabulary, clumsy and mechanistic as it was, psychology was the means by which they navigated the inner and outer worlds.

Also the notion that they were doing good, important work relieved the tedium of their painstaking if not terribly rigorous experimentation. Often, as in the case of "The Saturation of Colors," results were printed in the *Psychological Review,* the new publication of the American Psychological Association. And even though Solomons later complained about the way the Harvard laboratory took advantage of its students—"To call a piece of research work done by a student who pays for the privilege of working in a particular laboratory a contribution from that laboratory as though the *lab* had *hired* the man to do the work is misleading to say the least"—he no doubt appreciated the prestige and exposure the laboratory conferred. For her part, Stein proudly sent reprints of the saturation article to friends.

At various intervals, Solomons continued experimenting along the lines indicated by the article, but Stein herself seems to have been more motivated by their next major project, on automatism. Suggesting a consciousness "beyond the margin," as James called it in his 1896 Lowell Lectures, automatism interested Stein and Solomons as much as it did William James, their new teacher, in the seminar and lab during Gertrude's junior year.

"Hypnotism & automatic writing the means of approach," James jotted in his lecture notes, referring to that netherworld of consciousness beyond the reach of direct apprehension. And whether this "alternate personality, the tendency for the Self to break up," was the work of spirits, of pathology, of a subliminal consciousness, or of demonology was, James argued, a matter for science to decide—and of crucial importance to the study of psychology. "Who shall absolutely say that the morbid has no revelations about the meaning of life? that the healthy-minded view so called is *all*?" For James, as honorary president of the English Society for Psychical Research and the founder of the American Society, "post-hypnotic suggestion, crystal-gazing, automatic writing and trance-speech, the willing-game, etc., are now . . . instruments of research, reagents like litmus paper or the galvanometer, for revealing what would otherwise be hidden."

Psychologists abroad, especially in France, considered automatic writing a pathway into the hidden, or submerged, self, that part of the personality whose functions are unknown to consciousness. Pierre Janet, professor of philosophy and neurologist at Le Havre, found that when completely engaged by conversation or some other activity, several hysterical subjects, pencil in hand, might "automatically" write messages over which they had no conscious control. It was surmised that these scrawls, something like doodles, might offer insight into the workings of another, concealed self. Similarly, Alfred Binet, another influential French psychologist, considered automatic writing a connecting link between the conscious and unconscious personalities: "The phenomena of automatic handwriting can be demonstrated with people who are not hysterical; it is the exaggeration of the phenomenon that is peculiar to hysteria." Or as William James explained, "What the upper self knows, the under self is ignorant of, and *vice versa.*" Some automatic writers were also mediums claiming access to the spiritual world. Not as intrigued by spiritualism as James or Leon Solomons, Stein nonetheless believed along with them that by disproving such claims one could learn a great deal about the mysterious ways of the mind. "Never reject anything," she would quote James as saying. "Nothing has been proved. If you reject anything, that is the beginning of the end as an intellectual."

Given to bouts of depression, insomnia, backaches, and eye strain, William James had as a young man suffered from a protracted anxiety about his vocation, succumbing to the gentle, persistent prodding of his powerful father and abandoning a career in painting for science. Though successful, prolific, and esteemed far beyond the academic community, he was in later life never wholly free from melancholy and various psychosomatic symptoms. "I am a victim of neurasthenia," he wrote privately in the summer of 1895, "and of the sense of hollowness and unreality that goes with it." His students regarded him as brilliant and kind, the epitome of tolerant good sense, yet he was subject to morbid self-preoccupation and doubt. Acknowledging this obliquely in his writing and in his public lectures, he thrilled audiences with the confidence and vigor they suspected were hard-won. His frame was slight, his eyes clear blue and benign; he was beloved by students, who affectionately parodied his occasional abstruseness. "Professor James put his hands in his trousers' pockets, leaned back in his chair, & remarked in his offhand way: 'There is no primal teleological reagibility in a protoplasm.'"

Under James's tutelage, Stein and Solomons conducted the series of experiments in automatic writing that, almost forty years later, following the lead of B. F. Skinner's 1934 article in *The Atlantic Monthly,* many used to explain what lay behind Stein's more hermetic literature. She denied the influence, attributing the impetus for the experiments to James and the results to Solomons. As she told the story of her first experiment with automatic writing:

> It was suggested that we should experiment in fatigue, and William
> James added a planchette, he liked a planchette, we made one of
> a piece of wood and strings and then we were to try each other, I
> think it was I who preferred trying somebody else, after the months

in the laboratory I had lost confidence in ourselves as subjects for
experimentation, however Solomons tried me and I tried him one
sat with the hand on the planchette and the other did not exactly
guide it but started it, anyway he had us produce writing.

They came to this conclusion after repeated attempts at inducing in one
another automatic acts. Their method was distraction. In one instance, they
mounted a glass plate on metal balls; attached was a metal arm that held a
pencil. One of them placed a hand on the arm and proceeded to read a novel.
The arm didn't move until set in motion, and then moved of its own accord,
or so it seemed. The person reading, if absorbed in the novel, couldn't say
whether the operator was moving the arm or not. In another experiment, one
of them read a novel and scribbled at the same time. And in yet another experiment, each of them read something. The operator read an interesting story
out loud while the subject read something uninteresting in a low voice. "If he
[the subject] does not go insane during the first few trials," they wrote, "he
will quickly learn to concentrate his attention fully on what is being read
to him, yet go on reading just the same." Such was their foray into automatic
reading.
     But in refuting Skinner, Stein contended that neither she nor Solomons
had ever produced any automatic acts: "I did not think it was automatic I do
not think so now, I do not think any university student is likely certainly not
under observation is likely to be able to do genuinely automatic writing, I do
not think so, that is under normal conditions, where there is no hypnotism or
anything of that kind." However correct, with the hindsight of age and the incentive of self-defense, Stein somewhat misrepresented her younger, more
credulous self. For her and Solomons, automatic writing was but a means to
an end, and in linking their experiments in automatic writing to her later writing style, specifically in *Tender Buttons,* Skinner ignored their interest in hysteria and, in particular, its manifestation in the phenomenon of the double
personality.
     This, not automatic writing, lay at the heart of Stein and Solomons's ex-
periment, written up and published as "Normal Motor Automatism," in which
they intended "to reproduce rather the essential *elements* of the 'second personality,' if possible, in so far as they consist of definite motor reactions unaccompanied by consciousness—or shall we say, out of deference to the
subliminal consciousness theory, unaccompanied by 'conscious consciousness.' " Stein and Solomons wished to determine how and in what cases the
behavior of the hysteric's second self differed from the "merely automatic
movements of ordinary people," those everyday acts undertaken, like the tying
of one's shoelaces, without much thought. These automatic activities, they
decided, were similar to the dissociated acts of a hysteric.

Assuming "we may both as far as we know stand as representatives of the perfectly normal—or perfectly ordinary—being, so far as hysteria is concerned," Stein and Solomons used each other over and over as operator and subject, trying the best they could to induce states similar to those found in the second personality. Performed without controls or published notes but with a simple trust in each other's stated responses, these pleasantly naive experiments allowed Stein and Solomons to propose a definition of hysteria. "It will be remembered," they summarized soberly, "that these phenomena occurred in us whenever the *attention* was removed from certain classes of sensations. Our problem was to get sufficient control of the attention to effect this removal of attention. In hysteria this removal of attention is effected by the anaesthesias of the subject. We *would* not, the histerique *can* not, attend to these sensations. Whatever else hysteria may be then, this, at least, seems most probable. It is a *disease* of the *attention*."

In seeking—and finding—an analogy between the acts of the second personality, typically manifested in hysterics, and what is ordinarily called automatism, Stein and Solomons were of course also investigating the mystery of themselves. Knowing oneself and the other was part of the Crowd's ethos, summarized by Francis Pollak: "If the object of life be 'to live and learn' and most particularly if the aim is to 'know thyself' (and thy neighbor better than thyself), that very '95–'96 year was the best spent of them all."

And doubtless the physical aspect of automatic writing—the movement of the pencil, the formation of peculiar semantic clusters—furnished Stein with a visceral awareness of the graphic power of writing, of iteration, and of words themselves. But their impact on her later work seems not as linear as Skinner supposed—or as simple. For these were, after all, collaborative exercises, and collaboration was a powerful incentive to Stein. In fact, the collaborative nature of the experiments was so important that many years later, when denying Skinner's theory, Stein cast Solomons in the role she would assign her brother Leo: dominant. She was subservient, Solomons prevailed. "Solomons reported what he called his and my automatic writing but I did not think that we either of us had been doing automatic writing . . ." she explained in *Everybody's Autobiography*. "But as he wrote the article after all I was an undergraduate and not a professional and as I am always very docile, and all the ideas had been his."

Characterizing herself as tractable, Stein was a bit disingenuous. Though Solomons may have been responsible for writing most of "Normal Motor Automatism," the experiment it described became the product of both participants, or so their correspondence of the time indicates. And it laid the groundwork for the experiments Stein would undertake by herself in the psychology laboratory during her senior year. She thrived in the lab, designing experiments, wholeheartedly involved with their results, and pleased enough with her accomplishments to help publicize them. She sent Sarah offprints of the article she and Solomons had written. ("Much obliged for the paper," Sarah responded tactfully. "I enjoyed it as much as the laity can, I suppose.") And Gertrude was proud when an old high school friend wrote how a former teacher "told me that she had been informed regarding your whereabouts and the wondrous fame you were earning as an all round literary-scientific critic and genius, the embodiment of wisdom etc. etc."

Stein would later depict Solomons as her superior, at least in professional standing and authority (he was older than she by only a matter of months), yet she identified with him: "Leon like me in ideas and revolt," she scrawled in a notebook a few years after their collaboration. Elsewhere in her notebooks she remarked on Solomons's influence: "Likes imitate and hypnotise each other, they have little tenderness and no love for each other but they can have sympathy and friendship." She admired the intellectual bohemianism he shared with her brother—even to the point of annoyance with the "characteristically unpleasant rapid utterance and self contemplative end of a triumphant argument . . . often in Leo & Leon." But she was sensitive to Solomons, as she revealed when sketching the hero, based partly on him, of *The Making of Americans*: "His not thin but sharpened features and clear rims to his eyes like Leon and the twitch and the movement of the hand all the fingers together, with the delicacy of feeling in them."

Leon Solomons was preoccupied with restorative diets (in his case, of graham bread); he loved tramping among the caramel-colored hills just north of Berkeley; he was diffident around women but could be responsive and kind; and classmates and teachers found him—like Leo—brilliant. So while Leo Stein traveled afar, Leon Solomons unwittingly offered himself as surrogate.

IN *THE AUTOBIOGRAPHY OF ALICE B. TOKLAS*, Gertrude Stein told of how one spring when it came time for Professor James's final examination, she sat down briefly and scrawled a note. "Dear Professor James, she wrote at the top of her paper. I am so sorry but really I do not feel a bit like an examination paper in philosophy to-day, and left." Saying he often felt the same way, James gave her the highest mark in the course, or so Stein claimed. But as might be expected, there is little evidence to corroborate the story. Indeed one friend recalled Stein's remarking that when she was a student, "women were always considered inferior. William James was gentler with me than he was with the men."

James did give Stein an A for her work in the laboratory, but in the yearlong seminar, which she took as two separate courses, he gave her an A at midyear and a C at year's end—during the opera season. When asked about these two grades, James informed Mary Coes, the Radcliffe secretary, that they could be divided or "lumped"; Coes registered a B for Stein. Whether this was preferential treatment or condescension or neither is less important than what lay behind Stein's story: she wanted the man whose empathy and iconoclasm she respected to admire her.

Stein also credited William James for steering her to medical school. As she tells the story in *The Autobiography of Alice B. Toklas,* she had no idea what to do after college; James, during her last year at Radcliffe, recommended philosophy or psychology. "Now for philosophy you have to have higher mathematics and I don't gather that that has ever interested you. Now for psychology you must have a medical education, a medical education opens all doors, as Oliver Wendell Holmes told me and as I tell you." ("Imagine William James telling any one that if she wants to go into Philosophy she'd have to study mathematics," Leo sneered when he read *The Autobiography* in 1934. "I think the real *fons et origo* of this is that [Josiah] Royce once told her that one couldn't take Phil. seriously without taking logic seriously.") But James represented an ideal father figure, wise, kind, eminently nonjudgmental, and he implicitly provided her with the lineage—from Holmes to James to Stein—she patently desired. Münsterberg, James, the psychology laboratory, and Solomons were a second family, bearing an illustrious past, promising a glorious future.

Actually, Stein was intent on medical school at least as early as her junior year at Radcliffe. That spring, as she began arranging to meet Leo in Europe for the summer, she announced her plans to friends. "How happy for you to be with a brother of whom you are so fond and proud," wrote Margaret Sterling Snyder in reply. But Snyder wasn't as enthusiastic about Gertrude's "J. Hopkins" idea.

Stein, however, was undeterred. She had no intention of following Snyder's advice to embrace "the sheltered life" of domesticity. She was headed elsewhere. Leon Solomons wrote this to his sister, who told Sarah Stein. Although Sarah was miffed to hear such important news secondhand, she didn't seem too surprised. Nor was she startled to learn that Gertrude had already picked her medical school and her specialty. Gertrude Stein would go to the Johns Hopkins School of Medicine to study the nervous diseases of women.

5
THE
FEMININE
HALF

Leo in Egypt

One can understand Titian or Rubens even Michelangelo or
Leonardo as the products of energy & imagination but not Sesshu
or Nobuzane. It is this that places all the really finest Eastern art
on a different and if not finer at least more esoteric plane than almost anything in Europe.

LEO STEIN TO MABEL FOOTE WEEKS

Japan is the feminine half of the world.

PERCIVAL LOWELL

IS FOUNTAIN PENS were in the top drawer
of his desk, his rooms at Irving Street stood waiting. When Leo dropped out of Harvard Law in the
spring of 1895, he assumed he would be back in Cambridge sometime in the
fall. Instead, he was going to Japan.

It had all begun, unobtrusively enough, that summer, after Leo and Ben
Oppenheimer set sail in late June on the SS *Waesland,* bound for the bustling
port of Antwerp. Leo was impatient throughout the ocean journey. "Three
days!" he wailed by letter to his cousin Bird, referring to the time left aboard
ship. "Alas eternity is not much more."

This was his first trip to Europe since childhood and he was eager to see
the places, dimly recalled, that had thrilled his adult imagination. Antwerp
more than satisfied all his romantic expectations. Leo pronounced it wonderfully ancient—"in spite of its commercial importance"—and exclaimed in
a letter to Gertrude that "you really are in a different world, you feel it & see
it all about you." After sightseeing in Belgium, Holland, and Germany, by the
end of July he and Ben came to the long-awaited climax of the trip, the splendid City of Light.

Surprisingly, it was something of a disappointment. "No more interesting than New York," Leo wrote Gertrude. "Its streets look the same, its life is
largely the same except that its wickedness parades itself more freely."
Parisians were so rude and ill-tempered that he couldn't help but think squea-

mishly of "the history of Paris with its Revolutionary mobs & its communes"
as soon as he took a cab from the railway station. At Versailles he and Ben
"trotted through miles of galleries lined with the most colossal aggregation of
pot boilers I ever saw," and although at the Invalides they saw some "bully
swords," the armor was "no more picturesque than a kitchen range." At least
there was the Louvre.

Before leaving America, Leo had been spending much of his time in the
museums of Boston, Baltimore, and New York. "My interest in pictures began
early," he recalled. While neither took their drawing classes long past childhood, he and Gertrude each remembered cutting out of *Century* magazine the
illustrations they liked and mounting them on white paper. Struck by a few
paintings he saw while in California, mainly Toby Rosenthal's *Trial of the Escaped Nun, Constance de Beverly* and Millet's *Man with a Hoe* (the first picture he ever saw by a Famous Painter), Leo had been enamored at about age
fourteen by an etching Michael brought home from college. "There were
plenty of apple trees all about," Leo remembered. Curious as to what made
the picture special, he said, he carried it to the orchard. "I saw that the artist
had simplified and made more evident certain characteristics of the trees
themselves—once more a matter of composition—and I improvised a definition of art: that it is nature seen in the light of its significance."

But in Paris that summer, Leo seemed to have put aside his personal
definition of art, adamant as he was about seeing and absorbing all he could.
Spending most mornings in the Louvre, especially in the Salon Carré, and "trying to get on to the inwardness of various people," he reported to his
psychology-minded sister that he was "still as fervent a Rembrandtite as ever"
and that "for color and composition I swear by Rubens." Stirred by Leonardo,
he confessed he wasn't especially enthusiastic, at least not yet, about the rest
of the Italians; still, he was determined to "find things more intelligible."

His patience bore fruit. A few weeks later Leo reported from Dresden
to his cousin Bird that he was never disappointed in Raphael—even though
"you've got to know Raphael a heap before you really know him so I'll live with
hope." He sent his impressions of the *Sistine Madonna*: "The Virgin looks to
me like a very beautiful young Italian mother just a little bit frightened at being
stood up all alone with only a baby for company while a whole lot of humans
not to mention saints & angels are looking at her and discovering her merits."
Touched by the Madonna's self-consciousness, he was nonetheless disturbed
by the painting's formal elements, which, for him, detracted from the whole.
"There are those very dinkey curtains. Little thin things without any definition and 2nd the drapery over the left leg is so clumsily managed that the poor
thing (the virgin) almost looks as though she were lame. All the same," he concluded, switching into vernacular as if embarrassed by his own audacity,
"there ain't no flies on the picture."

Assisting him with Raphael and other Italian artists was the small copy of Giovanni Morelli's "level-headed" *Kunstkritische Studien* Leo carried as guide. Written under the nom de plume Ivan Lermolieff, the book had created something of a sensation when it was first published in German in 1880, because Morelli, trained as a doctor and eventually dubbed the Darwin of art criticism, developed a purportedly scientific method to dispute many of the standard attributions of Italian paintings. (Bernhard Berenson, a Morelli disciple, claimed that his "services to the science of pictures are greater than Wincklemann's [*sic*] to antique sculpture or Darwin's to biology.") With the assistance of such modern devices as photographs, Morelli challenged traditional connoisseurship.

His volume was more stimulating to Leo than any other book on art he read at the time. He was elated whenever he found in it some confirmation of his own perceptions and was delighted with Morelli's praise of Giorgione's languorous *Sleeping Venus*. (Notice the color of her hair, Leo later counseled his cousin Fred.) Of all the paintings in Dresden, this sensually reclining goddess affected Leo most. "It is one of the most poetically beautiful paintings if not the m. p. b. that I have ever seen," he wrote breathlessly of the work's massive richness. Five decades later his opinion of the painting would have changed little; Giorgione, he claimed, was "perhaps the greatest of all lyric painters."

Dresden was more comfortable to Leo than was Paris, perhaps because his German was better than his French. He began to dream of a life there, away from the United States. "I'd rather like to live here if I had to live abroad rather than any place I've seen yet," he told Bird Sternberger. Evenings he enjoyed the opera, and days when the Gemäldegalerie was closed he lingered in a park, drinking local beer and reading Heine's poems or Max Nordau's recently published *Degeneration* ("a durn fool book"). Yet as much as he liked Dresden, he remained committed to the Louvre; if he ever wanted to buy a museum, he remarked to Bird, that would be his first choice.

Sometime in September, Leo was back in Paris, meandering through the Louvre each morning. His favorite painting was Andrea Mantegna's *Crucifixion*, the most important in the museum, he thought, and "made of color, as no other picture, even by the great Venetians or Rubens, was"; it was this picture that prepared him, he claimed, for Cézanne. But many of the paintings looked different to him—a pleasing fact—now that he was back from Dresden and Berlin, where he had soaked up as much art as possible. When he revisited the Salon Carré, for example, he said he saw as if for the first time Paolo Veronese's huge *Marriage at Cana*. Two months earlier, the painting had seemed too elaborately big and without real feeling. Now when Leo walked into the room and looked at the crowded canvas covering the better part of one wall, "I saw it as it had never been before—one and indivisible, as a pic-

ture ought to be. It was one, and I was one in the face of it. We were altogether one."

This was an experience he never forgot and one that indisputably
launched his career—after a fashion.

LEO   WROTE   GERTRUDE little of his new obsession, noting only, and
somewhat condescendingly, that "I spend most of my time . . . looking at pictures & there's not much use in writing about them to you when you haven't
seen them." This was something he would say about art for the rest of his life.

But to Bird Sternberger, he inventoried his discoveries: the Giorgione
in Dresden, the Puvis de Chavannes frescoes at the Panthéon in Paris, an exhibit of modern art in Berlin. To his sister he offered confidences of another
sort: the annoyance of a week spent in Germany with Sarah's brother, Harry
Samuels, who prevented him from getting very much out of the paintings; or
his anxiety about bills that might have arrived after he left, one for board and
another for lost library books, which he wanted Gertrude to take care of.

Michael Stein, holding the family purse strings in San Francisco, thought
Gertrude generally careless "in business matters" but kept both her and Leo
apprised of their earnings from stocks and bonds and of their family expenditures (upkeep of their parents' graves, donations for a widowed aunt's children). Each month he doled out their income, explaining why it was up or
down. He performed the task so well—reinvesting their money, distributing
it, and paying their share of taxes on the family's property in northern California—that Gertrude admitted she took her income for granted. She was,
however, called up short when a young woman she hired to tutor her in Latin
complained about not being paid for a month. Gertrude had spent all her
money on the opera, or so she remembered, and would not be receiving another check from Michael for another month. She told the tutor she had no
money. The tutor answered that of course Gertrude did; she may have spent
her month's allowance, but only those who earn their living "when they have
not got it . . . have not got it." Gertrude long remembered the reproach.

If Michael considered Gertrude indifferent to financial affairs and her
tutor thought her myopic, Leo entrusted to her his belongings and the odds
and ends left in Cambridge—some papers in the left-hand drawer of his desk
on Irving Street, a few more bills. This was even more important now that he
received the magnificent offer from his uncle Solomon that was to extend his
summer trip.

"He wants Fred to come to the Mediterranean this winter," Leo explained to his sister, "& as he doesn't want him to travel alone he proposed
that I should go with him—that I should use from my own funds only so much
as I would use otherwise and that he would pay the difference & judging from

the way Fred is accustomed to travel there will be a good deal of difference."
Excited, he relied on Gertrude to rent his rooms and above all safeguard his
books. "For goodness sakes, see that they are all there after my return or I shan't
rest easy in my grave until I've haunted the malefactors a few centuries."

Most have assumed the motive behind the trip, and Solomon's offer, was
Fred's health. True, Fred had left Harvard after two years ostensibly because
of poor health. But there were other reasons Solomon Stein wanted his only
son out of New York. Solomon's daughter Bird was going to court, and her
brother might prove an embarrassment because he had gotten into a "scrape"
with a young woman, a scrape serious enough, it was said, to be reported in
a Manhattan paper.

And Bird was desperate. Her detectives having come up empty-handed
in their effort to incriminate her husband, she felt she had no recourse but to
abduct her own children and install them in her parents' Manhattan brownstone, where she was living. Her husband went immediately to his attorney,
and a trial date was set for the fall. Solomon Stein wanted Fred gone by then.

He wanted Fred not only as far away from New York as possible but in
the constant company of someone he trusted. Leo Stein was just the man:
upright and responsible and too afraid of women to get into much trouble.
Thus when Leo consented to accompany his cousin, it was decided that he
should return to New York to meet Fred there. The cousins would journey
overland to California and then would continue around the world, bound not
just for Egypt but also for Japan, where Fred had longed to go.

All this was Leo's good fortune. Jubilant, he promised his sister photographs galore. "Do you remember," he asked almost dreamily, "when we used
to talk about the Taj Mahal . . . ?"

IT TOOK just over five days to travel from New York to San Francisco by
train. Generally the trip was grimy and dusty, even for such affluent passengers as the Steins, but in November 1895 the weather was good and the crossing unusually clean; the Mojave Desert was cool, and there was even a little
rain.

Writing chipper letters to his aunt and uncle, assuring them he was in
complete command, Leo recounted the cross-country adventures with nonchalant confidence. One Sunday, outside Chicago, he and Fred had struck
up a conversation with a drummer offering small wares to passengers; the man
complained he hadn't made much money that day because it was mostly just
Jews who traveled on Sundays. "Them Jews won't buy anything on a train,"
the man had said. "When a Jew wants to buy anything he hunts up some friend
of hisn that's in the wholesale business where he can get a discount on what
he buys."

There was "the inevitable Chicagoan who had been there when there wasn't nothin' but a village there," and the equally inevitable New Yorker who told his Bret Harte–like story about a train wreck in which passengers starved to death on the outskirts of town. This naturally wouldn't happen to him or his cousin Fred, he added hastily. He did not report misadventures, like the one that happened near Kansas City. The pair stepped off the train in their bedroom slippers to get some air; after a few minutes they realized the cars were pulling out of the station. They started to run. Fred caught the train and hoisted himself on board, but Leo, who tripped over a railroad tie, fell behind. When the train pulled into the next station, Fred telegraphed Leo to wait; he would come back and they could start over, as they did.

But overall the trip was uneventful. Fred liked the taste of California wine, which he tried in Mojave for the first time, and Leo, a veteran voyager, wasn't too jaded to press his nose to the sooty window to scan the landscape, "the one universally distributed beauty that there is." Best of all was the day they arrived: "perfect, warm and balmy, and the brown hills lay in range after range all about us, soft yet infinitely impressive." He was home.

He did not have much time to prepare for Japan, however. On the train he read Percival Lowell's *The Soul of the Far East,* whose thesis was the "topsy-turviness and general wrongendforemostness of that strange land." Fred Stein remembered that most of their early enthusiasm for Japan came not from books but from Henry Gilbert Frost, an eccentric Harvard graduate student almost ten years older than they. During Leo's first year in Cambridge, he and Fred frequented Frost's rooms atop College House, the least expensive residence for students at Harvard. "I always felt I had some mysterious experience when we went to visit him," Fred later recalled. The smell of incense floated through rooms hung with Japanese *kakemono* of indeterminate value, and a curtain of tinkling glass beads separated Frost's sitting room from the bedchamber. Fred and Leo, greenhorns in such company, listened attentively as Frost fed them tales of the exotic Far East.

Fred wanted to go. Leo worried about the expense; he had spent all his money on books. But he was interested nonetheless, and he availed himself of the exceptional Japanese collection at the Boston Museum of Fine Arts, which its curator, Ernest Francisco Fenollosa, publicized often. Fenollosa himself was a celebrated figure about town. Former Japanese imperial commissioner of fine arts, he was born the year Commodore Matthew Perry's four "black ships" (as the Japanese called them) stubbornly anchored themselves in the Bay of Yedo, prying open Japanese ports to American trade. In 1878, invited to fill Japan's first chair of philosophy at Tokyo University, the twenty-five-year-old Harvard graduate began his study of Japan's art and culture, an inquiry that would last the rest of his life and ultimately revive the nation's interest in its own artistic heritage as well as bring to the West a broader, more informed, and trendy understanding of Japanese art.

Americans had known something of color prints, Hokusai ("the Dickens of Japan"), Hiroshige, and Japanese knickknacks—that was all. Japonisme developed later in the United States than it had in France, where it had attracted the attention of the Goncourt brothers, Ernest Renan, Joris Karl Huysmans, and Théophile Gautier in the 1860s. At about the same time, the controversial American painter James Whistler was collecting Japanese prints and displaying their influence in his own work. But Leo, despite Fenollosa's attempts to educate, clung to a very traditional view of art—à la Charles Eliot Norton. As he admitted later, he was a stiff-necked purist: "I had at this time the conviction of the young and serious student, that art should be pure and noble, that what isn't, isn't really art, and so on. I questioned *genre* and illustration." American cognoscenti likewise regarded Japanese art as ornamental and not terribly serious. "From a purely decorative point of view, it is splendid," Leo echoed the popular, condescending view, "perhaps the best there is and this is what makes Japanese art so potent an influence. . . ."

His idea of Japanese culture followed suit. "There is no philosophy in Japan," Leo explained to his aunt and uncle. "This entire lack of ideas makes their art comparatively uninteresting to me." Yet despite such patronizing notions—always at their pretentious worst when he tried to woo his benefactors—Leo was curious and receptive. And in several years he would come to regard this same art "on a different and if not finer at least more esoteric plane than almost anything in Europe."

LEO AND FRED steamed out of San Francisco on the *Coptic* in late November. Fred remembered there were only about twenty first-class passengers on board, mainly missionaries. The rest, mostly Japanese and Chinese, squeezed into steerage while above them the more mobile played cricket on deck with balls made of twine. A typhoon interrupted their game, and for three days the small steamer pitched and rolled, the sky was sodden, the sea turned black. Cockroaches crawled into the sleeping quarters, and the walls stank from the smell of vomit and excrement wafting from the lower holds. When at last they reached calm waters, the doctor on board found many of the steerage passengers dead—"the more the merrier," Leo observed sardonically, "as he got paid for fixing them up to keep."

On better days, the American purser organized some of the more privileged passengers, including Leo and Fred, into a cocktail club. It held its meetings twice daily, before lunch and dinner, and membership included someone named Bardens, an English exporter, and a Mrs. Dimond, on her way to Honolulu to meet her husband. Leo remembered the rest as a motley bunch: "the Poor Foreigner, the Cuban tobacco drummer who always won at poker, and the Englishman who drank all the champagne and told the nastiest stories, and Oliver Optic who was always drunk and the purser introduced us all to him everyday and he gave us his card and insisted we make him a long visit at his home in Massachusetts."

The ship stopped briefly in Honolulu, long enough for Leo and Fred to have dinner with the reunited Dimonds, and when they boarded the steamer again, Leo noticed a new passenger, a stocky, grim-faced young man with his hat pulled low over his brow. He was an American, Hutchins Hapgood, who stopped scowling a few days later when he joined the cocktail club. "So we became a triumvirate," said Leo. "The fellows I am with are cultivated chaps and one of them is quite interesting to me, but both are very young," Hapgood wrote pompously to his friend Mary Costelloe. A Yankee from the Midwest, idealistic and Harvard-educated, Hapgood would later shed much of his arrogance, most of it in New York as a reporter under Lincoln Steffens at the *Commercial Advertiser.* He became, according to one friend, a warm, sensitive hound who "pursued God, looking into every dust bin for him." Aboard the *Coptic,* he too was without vocation, and although he had taken a master of arts degree and spent a year studying in Germany, he wandered the world in an almost indeterminate fashion, impudent, pugnacious, and bent on his freedom.

Recalling their meeting many years later, Hapgood said that "Leo at that time had the same definitely overpowering mental interests that he has shown since. . . . He and I argued the livelong days. One day I remember the subject was whether a gentle snowstorm looked natural, or whether it represented a theatrical stunt. I don't remember which side I took; but the dispute recurred frequently, not merely in Japan, but later, in Egypt, in Italy, Heidelberg, and New York." The incident Hapgood remembered occurred on one of their Japanese excursions. He lost his temper when Leo, the inveterate Californian, insisted that the first big flakes of winter snow did not seem real. That was illogical, fumed Hapgood, and the two men quarreled, staking out extreme positions on the inconsequential. "But," said Hapgood in retrospect, Leo "genuinely desired the well-being of everybody, and cared only for the highest."

Aboard the steamer early one morning in the middle of December, Hapgood opened his porthole to the vision of Fujiyama. Leo could hardly believe what he saw. From then on, nothing did seem real. "Every time I go into the street there is something of a shock," he told his aunt and uncle. To his sister he wrote that "everything is [curious] everything picturesque much is beautiful." In the evening the base of Mount Fuji was covered with clouds, its snow-capped peak "aerially majestically poised." One then felt " 'über allen [*sic*] ist Ruh.' " Leo, Fred, and Hapgood arrived in Yokohama, rode aghast in rickshaws through streets lit with paper lanterns, stayed in a long narrow room with big copper hibachis, and spent the first few mornings trotting on ponyback. Then they ventured into Tokyo, where they called on the United States consul general, visited various palaces, and bought trinkets at a bazaar—boxes and chopsticks and "mittens" for their feet. But of all their excursions, what most inspired them were visits to Shinto shrines and the Daibutsuden, or Hall of Buddha, at Kamakura, with its richly colored sculptures, furniture of red lacquer ornamented with gold arabesques, and black lacquer floor "so thick and perfect a hammer would make no impression."

In Kamakura the three men hired a rickshaw to take them to a fishing village on the sea. They watched the sunset flame red, then took a train south. In Nagasaki, by torchlight, they saw coal being loaded by women who for hours toted little buckets. Feeling awkward and clumsy but armed with the prejudices of a young and imperialist America, and echoing Percival Lowell, Leo noted the incongruous aspect of everything before him: "A gallant soldier comically fierce with black beard & mustachios comes prancing along on a comical rat of a steed. A big drunken sailor rides in a Kurirura drawn by an absurdly undersized driver. If you bump up against a house too hard you knock it down for all the walls are made of screens, light wooden trellis work covered with paper." Japan was a country in miniature, an idealized playland both seductive and sedative. Yet it also held instructions for the West, and like many who traveled there, Leo was in search of counsel.

In Japanese architecture and the Japanese home he found a tranquillity and composure he had not experienced in the houses he'd known. (Sensitive to home decoration and the deportment of rooms, he would later link the typical New England parlor to a castration complex, commenting that it was "a product of *don'ts*.") This new world nibbled at his prejudices. "A European room be it ever so tasteful in its fittings and furnishings," he wrote his aunt and uncle, "is a painful abomination of huddled incongruities after the exquisite simplicity of a Japanese interior. Tables are stiff, chairs are gawky, carpets are painful to the eye. . . . It is indeed unfortunate that our conditions make it impossible that we should not learn very much from the appointments of the Japanese."

Wearied from daily excursions, as well as from the effort of arranging for food and accommodations, and from feeling lost, Leo and his two companions tried to immerse themselves more completely in Eastern ways. They decided to rent a house in the south, still regarded as "old," or romantic, Japan. An acquaintance from the steamer with an export business in Kobe had connections in Kyoto, so there they went, and by the end of December had hired furniture, including a stove, and an interpreter, a rickshaw driver, and a cook. The last, Leo assured his brother Michael, who was always concerned about expenses, provided everything they wanted for twenty yen (ten dollars) a month; the rickshaw driver received ten.

The three young Americans had moved to an out-of-the-way section of town—"as pretty as you could imagine," Hapgood described their seven rooms, "with a beautiful tree climbing and twisting over the portal." They slept on futons, sat cross-legged on the floor in their kimonos, and ate from small stands three inches high. "The only Japanese thing we draw the line at is 'chow' or food," Leo told Gertrude. Although they consumed boxes and boxes of mandarins and drank Nagasaki beer, to them the sake tasted like sour cherry, the green tea was bitter, and the raw fish and bird broiled in its own feathers combined to produce "the vilest lot of tastes & smells imaginable."

They were not queasy, though, about their cook's procuring them Japanese "wives." "Tanaguchi herded them in but none would do till one day he brought O Haru San, and Tsuru San and O Ito San," Leo remembered. Such was customary among visiting Western men, and these young men probably had heard of it even before their arrival and it probably seemed natural to them: their stereotype of Japan included a stereotype of Japanese women, or at least some of them, as libertine. Thus they could indulge themselves in ways unthinkable at home. But they solemnly performed "marriage" rites, which, although they considered them meaningless, may have allayed residual qualms or, as was more likely, placated the young women and their families. "We went through some sort of ceremony involving signed documents," recalled Hapgood, "which were filed away in the proper bureau. We settled a certain amount of money on the parents of the girls, and then we lived a life which seems to me like a dream, as far as remoteness from reality is concerned." In his 1939 autobiography, Hapgood rationalized that when he abandoned his Japanese wife he missed her a long time afterward; but "of course, the girl and I both knew that we were to separate."

If they considered it at all, the young men did not regard their behavior as racist or exploitative; to them it was a logical corollary of their so-called cultural values, steeped with the spurious superiority of a Western male. Yet such values were also inseparable from intricate psychic systems that permitted—and craved—a margin of error. Sexually naive, Leo affected the vocabulary of the well-bred gentleman who would not stoop to desire; he dismissed sexual feelings as banal. "I always tended toward the attitude that sex-interest was not real and important but a kind of trifle or a perversity," he observed years later. He avoided intimate relationships of almost any kind, except with those few women who to him were sexually off-limits: Miriam Sutro Price, engaged when Leo met her, and married soon after; his cousin Bird Sternberger; his sister Gertrude. Instead, he turned to prostitutes—or his Japanese "wife." Puzzling over why, he eventually concluded that "the answer was fairly obvious. Fear."

And guilt. Since the age of fourteen, autoeroticism had filled him with shame, so much so that as an adult he assumed it had frustrated his sexual development. "If the development of the genital consciousness is arrested at the stage of autoerotism," Leo speculated, "then the knowledge of the positive genital function which is mature only at puberty becomes a mere knowledge about & not a tendency of behavior. The consequent behavior is therefore an application of knowledge & not the expression of an instinct since the instinct tendency has been arrested in its development." Sex was a cerebral exercise, not a felt one, and Leo preferred to avoid the whole issue, or at least to avoid it when at home and with women he considered his equals, or his intellectual superiors.

But Japan was something else. If it represented a "feminine" refuge to the harried Western man, weary of the strenuous in American life, it also offered him a fantasy of male sexual power. Yet it was burlesque. With seven geishas, ranging from thirteen to eighteen years old, in attendance at their Kyoto lodgings, Fred and Hapgood danced, and Hapgood tried to teach them a Harvard cheer. The handmaidens, as Hapgood called them, looked on with disapproving dignity. "It was the only time in my life when I felt like a feudal baron," he wrote.

Drawn to Japan because it seemed remote, exotic, and inferior, the three young men indulged both their prejudices and their longings. Summing up the monthlong stay, Leo told his aunt and uncle that "it was a time of such restfulness, such comfort such entire absence of anything disturbing, in an environment so novel and so picturesque, and it is withal so unified so entirely separate from what went before and what came after, that it forms a complete epoch in my experience."

AT THE END OF JANUARY, the triumvirate separated. Hapgood was bound for India, the Steins for Egypt by way of China, Singapore, and Ceylon.

Leo didn't like Canton or Hong Kong; "when it comes to things that delight the eye and satisfy the aesthetic sensibilities Japan is easily the superior," he observed after a few days. Hong Kong was superbly situated, its harbor colorfully dotted with steamers, junks, and sampans on one side and sea and clouds on the other. But he and Fred did not stay long enough for more than a fleeting impression; they seemed in a hurry to get to Egypt, though they stopped in Colombo, with its "kiplingesque streets" and wild elephants striding up mountain roads, and dallied at the botanical gardens of Kandy. At the coast a German steamer carried them across the Indian Ocean to the Red Sea.

By the time they arrived in Cairo, in March, Leo was exhausted. "I've reached a stage of momentary mental collapse," he wrote Gertrude. "Never in my life I believe have I felt so completely dulled so intolerably stupid so inanely played out." Their hotel, the Mena House, sat almost at the foot of the Pyramids, which interested Leo little, for they required more historical imagination than he could muster. Nor did a reunion with Hapgood help. It was only when the three travelers sailed from Ismailia to Port Said and then on to Brindisi that Leo began to feel more relaxed. The morning after he glimpsed a lighthouse on the Italian shore, fatigued as he was, he was the first to stand on deck, shivering and eager for land.

A countryside speckled with silver olive trees and deep green vineyards drew his praise, not Naples or the weather. It rained constantly, even during a day's excursion to Pompeii, but at least the rain accentuated the ruins' pathos. "In Egypt one sees the mighty tombs of the Kings of old and is impressed by the power with which they waged their war against the all-destroyer time," Leo wrote his aunt and uncle. "Those old fellows do not demand pity or sympathy but command awe. In Pompey all is different. It reminds one in its lightness, its daintiness, its triviality, of the times of Louis XV. Its weakness in the face of the great smoking mountain behind it seems so pitiful one almost regrets that its nakedness should ever have been uncovered." Leo preferred the less emotional, grand simplicity of the Doric temples in Paestum.

After a series of trips to Sorrento, Amalfi, and Capri, Leo and Fred left for Rome and then Florence, where they took rooms on the via Curtatone, near the Cascine, on the north bank of the Arno. Although Florence would draw Leo back four years later, it was then but a stopover. The cousins were moving north: to Venice and then on to Vienna and Karlsbad, where they had arranged a rendezvous with Fred's family. From there, Leo went on to Dresden and Cologne, sending Fred tips on the best places to get ham sandwiches and pipes, as well as on the paintings in the Dresden picture gallery. (This time, Leo said, he "can't go" the *Sistine Madonna* but enjoyed the Correggios, the Rembrandts, and the "handsome Holbein madonna with the incipient double chin, the rakish crown and the sleepy youngster . . . as deliciously humorous as ever.")

Having graduated from tourist to instructor, Leo was relieved to be finally on his own. Watching over Fred had become a strain, especially because Fred, who felt vulnerable, depended on what he admired as Leo's mature sagacity. By his own admission, Fred was the kind of man who couldn't own a thermometer without assuming he had a fever. From Leo's point of view, Fred required neither his medical nor his gastronomic advice; he simply needed to be more self-reliant, less tentative about what he ate, and more indifferent to everyday aches and pains. "He is so infernally dependent that it is hard to instill into him so simple a thing as common sense in regard to his own living," an exasperated Leo told Gertrude. If Leo had relished the role of mentor, it had also made him nervous.

"But this was after all not what I took pen in hand etc for," Leo ended his complaint to his sister. He was writing about their summer plans, for it was she who was the perfect companion, willing to share and learn but self-reliant in ways that cheered an older brother wary of too much responsibility. She might not be as interested as he in combing museums, Morelli in hand, but neither was she helpless. So, exhausted as he was, Leo suggested an itinerary for the two of them, excitedly recommending Antwerp as the best port of entry and then perhaps a steamer up the Rhine before going to Rheims and Paris. The possibilities, he declared, were infinite. He wanted her to see and to experience and to participate in what he himself had seen and experienced the summer before. He trusted her with what he loved.

"I AM TAKING KINDLY to my introduction to foreign parts," Gertrude calmly observed in July 1896, writing from her room in Antwerp's Hôtel du Grand Miroir. But she had been tense when the *Red Star* sailed into the harbor on a Sunday morning, as she waited for a glimpse of the brother she had not seen in more than a year. "After all one never can remember at least I never can remember how anybody anybody really knows looks like and so perhaps when you see them you wont know them," she later rationalized. She and Leo had never been separated for so long, and although—or perhaps because—her junior year at Radcliffe had been a good one, full of friends, the psychology laboratory, and Leon Solomons, Gertrude apparently worried whether this summer she and Leo could easily renew the intimacy both assumed.

Quickly she was reassured. "Well when I saw my brother it was a surprise to me but I knew quite certainly that it was my brother." There was no one quite like him. He was almost a foot taller than she, and leaner, but they shared a family resemblance, especially in the eyes, a deep cordovan brown. He wore glasses, she did not, and his chestnut hair had begun to recede from his craggy forehead while hers luxuriously coiled atop her head; but they laughed at the same jokes, liked the same people, and spoke the same unpretentious slang. They picked their way through the streets, returning to their hotel, chattering happily. "Gertrude & I talk so much tommyrot one to tother that I don't get any chance to read any more just sit round and twaddle about 20 hours of the 24," Leo joked.

One of their subjects was Bird. The acrimonious custody trial between her and her husband had dragged on for most of a year, entertaining New York newspaper readers with its dramatic disclosures. Bird herself had testified point-blank that her husband nauseated her. And yes, she kept a diary, she admitted, in which she listed his flaws and recorded his outbursts; she claimed he hissed, stuck out his tongue, and beat his fists on the floor—but she would not repeat aloud the vulgar things he'd said. Instead, she wrote them down and demurely handed them to her attorney to recite in court.

Louis Sternberger blamed his father-in-law for his wife's estrangement (he would later sue Solomon Stein for alienating his wife's affections), but Bird countered that she'd long been disappointed with him and, besides, his insolvency was notorious. Then Sternberger's attorney responded, saying Bird lost interest in her husband only during hard times—and as it turned out, after he lost a hefty sum of her father's money. Having invested with his son-in-law, Solomon Stein became suspicious about the transaction and devised a plan for restitution. But when Sternberger vehemently refused to go along, they fought, and the mild-mannered Stein went for Sternberger's throat.

Gertrude was thoroughly sympathetic. Bird shouldn't have to stay married to a man who repulsed her, nor should she have to give up her children if she wanted to leave him. But on July 1, 1896, the New York State Supreme Court ruled against Bird Sternberger, primarily on the basis of privilege. In a stunning and unusual decision, the presiding judge, evidently disgusted with the proceedings, insisted "the Court will not deprive a poor man of his children because a rich man wants them." Louis Sternberger was given custody of the children. (The ruling was later overturned on appeal.) And Bird was not granted grounds for a divorce. She was told a wife had to stay with her husband unless the court deemed it demonstrably unsafe for her to do so; and it did not.

The night Bird received the news, Gertrude had not yet sailed; she stayed close by her cousin. "Its useless to tell you she bore it very bravely for so she does everything," Gertrude comforted Fred. Although her feelings for Bird would change markedly, she later observed that to her "young eyes," Bird possessed "a quality of brilliant courage . . . the courage of resolution." Intense and energetic, with an idealism bordering on self-righteousness, Bird refused to yield to her husband and, according to Gertrude, capitulated to no one but her own father, whom she adored.

As interesting as were Bird's affairs, there were other compelling diversions that summer. Touring with Leo in Antwerp, the Hague, and Amsterdam, Gertrude wanted to do everything: ride in canal boats and play with Dutch children and wear wooden shoes. Despite her "youthful and untraveled mind," Leo allowed that she was a quick study. And with Leo she gladly consented to apprenticeship, unabashed by her excitement, safe within his intellectual embrace. "As Leo has already told you we are enjoying the delights of canal boats that don't move and head-gears that to put it mildly are singular," she scribbled to Fred. "I am also being educated up to a feel for art under Leo's able tuition and in time will be a connoiseur [sic] myself."

They visited two synagogues in Amsterdam on the Sabbath. "I am at present engaged in giving thanks that I was not born a female Israelite in ye older time or even in Amsterdam to-day," Gertrude reflected. "I don't like to sit behind galleries with a fence around it even if they are considerate enough to leave peep holes in it." They studied Dutch paintings, went to the zoo, spoke the same language: "They've got a chimpanzee & ourang there, wat as Gertrude whould express it, I don't lubs; they're too damnably self-satisfiedly human," reported Leo, in the dialect he and Gertrude used; then they drove through the countryside ("The meadows are the juiciest I ever saw") before going to Cologne and Heidelberg. In Heidelberg, they saw Hutchins Hapgood, who later remembered sitting with them "one night by the romantic castle, which was all the more romantic because of the full moon. Gertrude Stein, at that time, seemed to me an extraordinary person: powerful, a beautiful head, a sense of something granite." Won over by her "deep temperamental life-quality, which was also inspiring," he did not mind what he found in her as well as in Leo: ego. Both Steins, he felt, took their incomparability for granted.

Hapgood was not able to appreciate the anxious insecurity underlying Leo's brashest assertions; nor would he have understood his implicit competition with his friend. And evidently he responded more openly to Gertrude because the younger sister then seemed less threatening. In her he detected nothing but handsome vitality and an uncommon devotion to Leo: "She admired him and loved him in a way a man is seldom admired and loved," observed Hapgood. "It was part of her profound temperament."

After visiting Paris, Gertrude and Leo installed themselves in London for a month. Gertrude had gone to Europe with a letter of credit that her summer income of more than a thousand dollars covered, and travel was generally cheap. In September they still had enough money to rent three large rooms—a sitting room and two bedrooms—near Russell Square in Bloomsbury, not far from the British Museum, and hire a serviceable cook to prepare most of their meals. But they both found London dingy and dismal; Leo lost his enthusiasm for art and confessed that he didn't care much for the Turners at the National Gallery, which were affecting but did "not seem to prove anything." He and Gertrude consoled themselves with the purchase of a few old books and a shopping spree on Regent Street, where they loaded up with everything from underwear to hats in preparation for wintry days ahead.

Leo was anxious to return to America; his anxiety, more than the overcast London skies, may have accounted for his malaise. He had been away almost a year and a half now. Whether he had specific plans about what he would do back home, he didn't say, and he alluded to his state of mind only indirectly, mentioning that he was looking forward to a period of meditative withdrawal. If he could have his meals served at Irving Street, he said, "I don't believe I'll budge for a month."

6
EVOLUTION

Embryology class, Marine Biological Laboratory, Woods Hole
(Gertrude, second from left, front row)

We almost all feel that we are our brothers keeper and if we do not feel it we are dead to the deepest and most significant note of the times in which we live.

GERTRUDE STEIN,
"THE VALUE OF COLLEGE EDUCATION FOR WOMEN"

T'S TOO BAD about Leo. I hope he's on his feet again. I did not know that he had been miserable ever since his return."

Sarah Stein may not have been completely surprised when Gertrude told her Leo was depressed. Here was a man, twenty-four, with a fine intelligence and plenty of material advantages but without, it seemed, much ambition or any future prospects. Comparing him with her youngest brother, who had just dropped out of college, Sarah complained to Gertrude that her father was supporting a son "who did not even compensate him by doing a fair amount of studying, and when he has such ability at that. . . . In certain respects, he is a Leo on a very small scale." Pointedly she added, "But the Samuels cannot afford that luxury."

Gertrude was deeply offended. Yet it was true that Leo, back in Cambridge after his grand tour, did not know what to do. He'd abandoned the study of history; it was nothing more than a "mare's nest of illusory knowledge," he later claimed. "Until some one comes along . . . who can scientifically study the motives behind the statement, history in so far as it deals with other things than institutions & economic trends is merely guessing." While crossing the Pacific with Hutchins Hapgood he had realized that "most historical documents were intentionally falsified, and that even the few who wanted to tell the truth couldn't." Leo's disenchantment left him with no sense of purpose, no career plans, and no sense of the future.

But as long as Gertrude remained in Cambridge—she was now a college senior—Leo was content to stay. He did, after all, regard Cambridge as home; Irving Street was his permanent address and home to all his possessions. And to many it must have seemed ideally suited to Leo's temperament;

one friend would express disbelief on learning that Leo planned to forsake Cambridge and follow his sister to Johns Hopkins, where he would study history. "Don't you think when it comes to actually moving out bag and baggage— including books—that he will repent," Leon Solomons asked Gertrude.

Whatever the plan, Leo was not happy. He visited Fred Stein in New York around Christmas, caught cold, and took to the guest bed. Gertrude rifled through Leo's trunk and sent him three pairs of pajamas; he might stay in New York a bit, for it appeared to matter little to him where he was. In an era that demanded hard work, concrete achievement, and aggressive self-assertion of its men, Leo was curiously indolent.

Much has been made of Gertrude's dependence on Leo: typically, her biographers emphasize her following him to Harvard and, later, to Europe; they suggest she deferred to his opinions and his way of life, content to be second fiddle until she could stand his dominance no longer. Much less is made of his dependence on her. Basking in his sister's grand personal charm, Leo took shelter in the single-mindedness with which she got things done. More, her terrific energy, her gusto, and the ease with which she made or kept friends contrasted with his more reclusive, critical and self-critical style. If he was jealous of all this, he did not yet know it; nor would anyone have guessed the resentments she may have harbored against him. She admired and indulged him, and reportedly said of Leo many times that " 'he is my ideal of a man.' "

There was something pure about his passions and noble about his principles; he was intellectual, upright, sensitive—and truly vulnerable. Less indulgent than Gertrude, Sarah Stein considered her brother-in-law more child than man. But Gertrude obliged him easily, offered him protection of sorts, and at the level of daily chores would look after his bills and his property or run interference, if need be, with Michael and Sarah, who, in charge of the family purse, could not resist giving unsolicited advice on its expenditure.

In matters of art, however, Leo had become the family expert. He had brought Michael and Sarah bric-à-brac from the Far East and enough reproductions of Madonnas and other photographs for Sarah to start her own collection. (She showed her portfolio to her brother-in-law Simon one evening when he came to call, but Simon, who didn't understand why Jews should want so many pictures of the Madonna, shot from the room at the sight of an undressed Della Robbia.) In a desultory and small way, Sarah and Michael had begun collecting, buying from the San Francisco art dealers Vickery and Atkins; they shared the fascination with Far Eastern art, especially bronzes, sweeping San Francisco. But their taste was largely conventional. Sarah not only treasured a tiny reproduction she owned of the Venus de Milo but chuckled condescendingly at the consternation of her cook, who hated it so much she hoped she'd break it, accidentally of course.

If Sarah wanted advice, it was to Leo she turned. "Do you know Bates' bas-relief of 'Homer'?" she inquired. "It is a platinum print, and the one I speak of is about 3 feet long and 1 1/2 feet high. . . . Will you hunt it up in Boston and let me know their price. Perhaps it will be mine after all. I already see it in a deep grey-green frame, and my head swims!"

Leo enjoyed his status as art critic for the family. He liked to tell the story about one of his Baltimore uncles who had commissioned portraits of himself and his wife but, when the work was finished, refused to see the pictures or pay for them. Leo had to intervene. "I spoke to my uncle about it and said that an artist was a workman like a plumber or a carpenter and should be paid for his work accordingly & not be treated as an importunate beggar. My uncle said that seemed reasonable enough he really never had thought about it & told me to look at the pictures & if they were alright he'd send a check. I looked at them, the pictures were very bad, but the painter was not an artist in the higher sense but a likeness-maker, the pictures were very like and my uncle had never owned or looked at a painting in his life. So I told him the pictures were very good and he sent to get them & penciled a check."

If art was Leo's domain, the laboratory was Gertrude's. In the autumn of 1896, her senior year at Radcliffe, she went back to the Harvard psychology lab. Hugo Münsterberg was still in Germany, and William James, who had taken over for him the year before, entrusted the laboratory to Edmund B. Delabarre of Brown University. And there was another change. Leon Solomons had gone home to California, partly for his health; he would study on his own as a Harvard nonresident. From afar, he urged Gertrude to continue some of what they had begun together. "I hope you have not given up the work on fatigue. It's a big enough subject but you might as well try it as anyone else," he encouraged petulantly, feeling the pang of distance. "As soon as you let me know what plan you and the powers that be have decided upon, I will send on my suggestions."

Previously, Gertrude and Leon had used no subjects other than themselves, supposing their results could be generalized to a larger population. If she was to continue that work, she would need a statistically meaningful pool of subjects. Moreover, she intended to enlarge the scope of their study beyond automatic writing and its resemblance to hysteria to an analysis of predisposed character traits. Assuming that "habits of attention are reflexes of the complete character of the individual," she wanted to align various habits of attention with various character types. Whether her subjects were suggestible, easily distracted, whether they concentrated well or resisted her guidance would tell her something significant, she must have hoped, for she intended to study the various "types" of people who demonstrated a "greater or less tendency to automatic action." She gathered a group of Radcliffe and Harvard students, most of them the so-called New England types, she noted, in whom "the habit of self-repression, the intense self-consciousness, the morbid fear of 'letting one's self go' . . . is so prominent."

To coax the subjects to write automatically, she used methods similar to those of her experiment the year before, except that now Delabarre helpfully suggested she work with a planchette suspended from the ceiling. Each subject held a pencil, rested an arm on the planchette, draped a hand over its edge, then listened while Gertrude talked or read. When she determined that the subject was sufficiently distracted, she unobtrusively guided the planchette into the movement she desired, a figure eight or a long curve or an M shape. If the subject's hand began to move, following her pattern, she might then vary the action to see whether she could teach the subject a new movement.

She carefully observed the subjects, systematically collected her data, and then divided the subjects into two distinct groups. "Type I" she described as consisting "mostly of girls who are found naturally in literature courses and men who are going in for law." They were nervous, imaginative, and able to concentrate when something held their attention. "This type, although in some cases suggestible," Stein wrote, "is on the whole auto-suggestible rather than responsive to influences from without, unless the appeal is directed completely to the automatic personality." "Type II" subjects were blonder, paler, more phlegmatic, and if "emotional, decidedly of a weakish sentimental order." These students had weaker powers of concentration; they were also more fatalistic and listless.

Having published her results in the *Psychological Review* and reminded readers of her work with Leon Solomons—they had determined hysteria to be a disease of the attention—she could now go a step further. She characterized the Type II subjects as "hopelessly self-conscious," and concluded they were more like the people described in the literature on hysteria she had read. "In Type II we have the cases of subjects very much nearer the true hysterique," she explained, "where powers of attention, or rather lack of powers of attention, induced an extreme suggestibility and a great tendency to automatic movement." She was vague about what more could be said or why she considered her findings conclusive, probably because she went into her experiment predisposed, grouping her subjects according to her own prejudices, which were bolstered by many in the psychological community, particularly those who, like Stein, coveted an authoritative, scientific base for their questions about identity. It didn't help that Solomons, whom she asked to help edit the article, inexplicably crossed out the one sentence that clarified the overarching purpose of the experiment.

The year after the findings were published, Stein told a group of Baltimore women that her purpose had been to study "the nervous conditions of

The Harvard psychology laboratory

men and girls at college." And she of course had been planning to specialize at medical school in the nervous diseases of women. In fact, Stein's preoccupation with psychology dovetailed nicely with the long hours she was spending in the upper-floor laboratories of the Museum of Comparative Zoology, above the dank halls and mounted birds. Since her junior year she had been walking to the dark red conclave of buildings north of Harvard Yard, taking introductory zoology with Charles B. Davenport, then a Harvard instructor and later the eugenicist who directed the Station for Experimental Evolution at Cold Spring Harbor, New York; she was also studying the morphology of animals (Zoology 2) with George H. Parker, a young man influenced, like Gertrude and so many others, by William James. James apparently had advised the aspiring zoologist to concentrate his work on the nervous and sensory systems of certain animals—a subject intriguing to Stein—and Parker obliged; he eventually became one of the country's first neurobiologists.

Parker recommended Zoology 2 for those who planned a career in medicine; it was a prerequisite for his course on the comparative anatomy of vertebrates, which Stein took her senior year. Her courses in zoology were neither a requirement, however, nor the result of Parker's charisma as a teacher. They were taken with genuine interest. In her senior year Stein not only signed up for another course with Parker, on the nervous system and its terminal organs, but undertook the study of vertebrate embryology with Edward L. Mark, Harvard's well-respected Hersey Professor of Anatomy, and a course in cryptogamic botany, which was highly recommended for much of the zoology curriculum. Thus, if Gertrude left Radcliffe with anything like a major, it would be zoology.

In fact, toward the end of her senior year her friend Francis Pollak, now a law student at Columbia, pleaded mournfully, "Please don't be all scientist when I come up. . . . I can imagine what a society made up with people with five laboratory classes is like."

Although Stein admitted later in life that she "began specializing in science" and "was awfully interested in biology," she was usually quick to add that she soon "turned into philosophy and psychology." But her involvement with biology and zoology was profound—and was compatible with her interest in psychology; indeed, the fields were not far apart, and many in the scientific community felt that psychology—specifically the study of the brain—was a branch of biology, governed by it and equally subject to research and experiment. Modern zoology, according to Alexander Agassiz, son of the renowned naturalist Louis Agassiz and a wealthy patron of the Museum of Comparative Zoology, depended on research, that is, laboratories and not collections.

One could expect that zoology and psychology, as fields increasingly interested in experimentation, would each in its own way help answer the riddle of how living things function. More important, they were also likely to inquire, from an evolutionary viewpoint, about differences in nature: what caused these differences, how they were handed down generation after generation, how they were altered. "Evolution was as exciting as the discovery of America by Columbus quite as exciting, and quite as much an opening up and a limiting, quite as much," Stein reminisced in her memoir *Wars I Have Seen*. "By that I mean that discovering America, by reasoning and then finding, opened up a new world and at the same time closed the circle, there was no longer any beyond. Evolution did the same thing, it opened up the history of all animals vegetables and minerals, and man, and at the same time it made them all confined, confined within a circle, no excitement of creation any more."

Evolution to Gertrude also implied progress, and progress implied permanence. For her there was no contradiction; that which is permanent is stable and dependable. "Permanence and progress were synonymous," she wrote. "If things are permanent you can believe in progress if things are not permanent progress is not possible and so the nineteenth century believed in progress and permanence, permanence and progress." Her belief was that science could uncover the plan by which things change and that change, therefore, is ultimately predictable. Such a belief redressed the anguish of loss, emotional pain, and sudden death—all of which Stein experienced as an adolescent, all of which had been unpredictable, all of which she preferred to forget. "Naturally if you were born in the nineteenth century when evolution first began to be known, and everything was being understood, really understood everybody knew that if everything was really being and going to be understood, and if there was going to be progress there would not be any wars, and if there were not any wars then everything could be and would be understood, and even if death and life were not understood and eternity and beginning was not understood well that is to say if they were not understood more than science understood them better after all except in the unhappiness of adolescence better not think about that."

The theory of evolution, as Stein used it, linked her study of zoology to the taxonomy of character she had been developing in the psychology laboratory. By grafting the methods of the psychology lab to the rough-and-ready classification of character according to type or race—a classification essentially zoological in its study of biological difference but all too often spliced with pseudoscientific stereotypes—it was hoped one might better understand human development and personality. Stein speculated, for instance, that the mental depression of some Jews might be a function of race. She tested her theory on Solomons, who rejected it. "I do not think there is any special tendency toward melancholia among our people," he answered her, "but there is a much higher percentage of all kinds of abnormality, due in all probability to the close intermarriage which necessarily prevails among a people scattered widely in small groups."

While working in the psychology laboratory, and long afterward, Stein enlarged her taxonomy of character and racial types. Often, as in the case of her study of Harvard and Radcliffe undergraduates, her classification of character was binary and essentially adversarial, as it would be in her magnum opus *The Making of Americans.* There she divided character into categories of resisting and attacking, or dependent/independent and independent/dependent. But the heuristic divisions of character into dueling types could not have sprung from laboratory conditions alone; there had to be sources of a more personal nature. One need look no further than Stein's sense of herself with respect to Leo: she and her brother were complementary and competing, the same yet different.

From this point of view, it is possible that Gertrude was inquiring after herself and her brother when she asked Solomons about the incidence of melancholy among Jews. Leo's protracted slump, his inability to concentrate for long on a single project, his lethargy, and his virtual paralysis of will looked like the classic symptoms of neurasthenia. A malady of indeterminate cause and cure, it was a diagnostic grab bag of psychosomatic ills and melancholia that affected countless upper-middle-class men and women. In any event,

Gertrude's recital of Leo's symptoms no doubt prompted Sarah Stein to send condolences about his depression. But Sarah was amazed by Gertrude's proposed cure. "What do you mean," she asked, when she heard of Gertrude's Baltimore plans. "What do you mean by 'going to keep house and nurse him according to all the latest medical school theories'?"

GERTRUDE LOOKED FORWARD to commencement and class day. She hoped Francis Pollak would come to Cambridge to help celebrate along with other members of the Crowd. Unable to attend, Pollak wrote in apology. "Wherefore," he concluded stentoriously, "now that the preparatory stages of existence are over for good, may you always be happy and useful in the ways in which you most want to be useful in all that there is yet to do, and may the memory of that preparatory stage be always for both of us as fresh as it is now."

Before Gertrude could officially leave the preparatory stage, she had one more examination to complete. And if not for that exam, she would have been awarded her degree magna cum laude in the spring, having finished all her other course work in a great burst. "I have heard from various sources that you are working so hard as to endanger your health and reputation," Leon Solomons teased from California. "First thing you know you will have to put in a year out here before setting up shop in Baltimore. And you won't enjoy that I warn you." But hard as she worked, she had put off "the real study of Latin until the last moment, carrying a Latin grammar under her arm and apparently hoping she might absorb it through her pores," remembered several friends. One showed her that *isieme esiumibus* were the endings of the third declension but wondered if she knew where the dividing lines were. "She wrote a *Caesar* examination that she said was very consistent, either all right or all wrong. Then in fun she used the Bible as oracle to see if she had passed, and found her finger on a passage in *Lamentations*. The prophecy was true."

She flunked. And despite the retrospective accounts of friends who recalled Gertrude's nonchalance, she herself was surprised. "Thinking that I had passed that examination this June," she explained to Dean William Welch at Johns Hopkins Medical School, "I began this summer a course in embryology at Woods Hole. As [I have done] already some work in this course it would be a very great favor to me if I might be allowed to finish & so defer my latin examination till the following June. I will of course pledge myself to have my work completed for the degree before my second year at the medical school. If however this cannot be granted me, I will then endeavor to complete the work this summer. For further testimonial as to the quality of my work, I can refer to Drs. Mark & Parker in the Zoological Dept. of Harvard College, and Professors Munsterberg, Royce, James, and Delabarre of the Psychological department under whom I have done all my advanced work. If necessary, I can also get references from the other departments."

Welch answered in July with disappointing news. Gertrude could be granted admission to the medical school for the coming October—but only if she produced a certificate proving "she has completed *all* of the work required for the degree at Radcliffe . . . even if the degree is not conferred until the following June. If however (as is now the case) her failure to have the degree is due to any deficiency no matter how small, in the work required for the degree, she will not be permitted to enter." Although Gertrude had to pass a Latin exam before October, she refused to give up her course at the Woods Hole Marine Biological Laboratory, where both she and Leo planned to spend the summer.

In the spring of 1897, as Gertrude was finishing her senior year, Leo had written to Johns Hopkins requesting a catalogue and any "circular or announcement giving more detailed information about the courses in science." It was his intention, he said, to "pursue studies in Biology." And to ready himself for his new departure, he too had applied to the Woods Hole laboratory; he was accepted, and he was eager.

Woods Hole was, after all, the premier place for summer study in biology. Founded with the support of the Women's Education Association and the Boston Society of Natural History, the Marine Biological Laboratory was not affiliated with any one institution; nor did it draw on any one faculty for its instructors. Rather, as its first director, the zoology professor Charles Otis Whitman, declared, "the whole policy is national in spirit and scope. The laboratory exists in the interest of biology at large, and not to nurse the prestige of any university or the pride of individual pretension."

Surrounded by the cold blue waters of Buzzards Bay and the Nantucket and Vineyard sounds, the biological station was set in a former whaling center where battered vessels bound for Cape Horn had been stocked with rope and hogsheads and sea biscuits. Many of its buildings had long been standing idle when taken over by the station in 1888. Host at the time to seven investigators and eight students, the laboratory expanded quickly, and just nine years later, director Whitman proudly claimed that he had "not a station devoted exclusively to zoology, or exclusively to botany, or exclusively to physiology . . . but a genuine biological station, embracing all these important divisions, absolutely free of every artificial restriction."

Investigators—specialist and student alike—came together in this small village two hours by train from Boston, now the summer watering place for the country's top biologists. Researchers such as Franklin Paine Mall, professor of anatomy at Johns Hopkins Medical School, visited for a few weeks or more; Charles Davenport might drop by; George Parker was a regular. Facilities were good. Two sections had been added to the main laboratory, a plain gray timber building, and other buildings were going up. Researchers and students often ate together in a common dining area at the corner of Water and

Collecting expedition, Quisset Harbor, the Steins at center

West streets, called, in friendly military fashion, the Mess. The small community occasionally danced at the town hall or listened to music in the evening—usually someone played a piano, and possibly Gertrude was urged into a duet or two. Then the group would head off to the various boarding-houses where they stayed. At Mrs. Coombs's, Gertrude sometimes entertained friends after work by "reading" their handwriting.

Swirling tidal currents kept the bay fresh and clean, and for far-flung expeditions, a steam launch carried the biologists to Quisset and other nearby harbors to collect ctenophores. The men rolled up their pants as they waded in the water; the women held their long skirts aside while passing their long-handled collecting nets to and fro. Once or twice a week an investigator in residence presented a paper to the public, perhaps on the study of genetic variation or parthenogenesis. The neurological seminar, organized the year before Gertrude and Leo arrived, gave investigators an opportunity to present unpublished research on nerve tissues. It was a challenging environment. But it was summertime. As the president of the laboratory's trustees explained, "The ardor of biological research has driven individuals and even small parties to the dangerous and often fatal waters of tropical America and Africa, but no missionary spirit drives us to Woods Holl [*sic*]. Cool and invigorating breezes stimulate the work of the day and the evening, the long collecting excursions, and the application of mind in the general and private laboratories."

Among the sixty-three successful applicants to one of the three courses at the station that summer, Gertrude and Leo arrived in the rocky Cape Cod village in early July. Leo had applied to study elementary invertebrate zoology, which emphasized firsthand experience in its introduction to the anatomy, classification, and ecological relations of marine animal life. Why he made this choice is not known. But obviously his sister's commitment and enthusiasm were factors, as was his desire to get to sources and away from the soft suppositions of history. If evolution and science could provide answers, knowable or predictable, or at least promise to solve the conundrum of human development, their powerful promise also stirred his imagination.

In science, as Leo once put it, "the relations of the simplest elements to the complicated wholes would be traceable & calculable. Such a complete statement might throw no light at all upon the meaning or destiny in a metaphysical sense of the word but it would clarify the processes in time & space & supply to a greater or less extent a power of controlling them." The study of structure and form contained its own elegance, and while it could not provide him with metaphysical or, more to the point, psychological self-assurance, biology offered him a direction and the rationale for pursuing it.

Rewarding patience, discrimination, and artistic ability, the study of biology also was an occupation offering some degree of refuge for men who shrank from professions considered more aggressively male. And Leo had been a longtime collector: from beetles and butterflies as a boy in Vienna to the old books and Japanese prints he now delighted in owning. Taxonomy was a familiar subject, and one satisfying to Leo, who, like his sister, took pleasure in discriminating among similar things each of which was different.

Collecting expeditions took place on Wednesdays and Saturdays, in marshes and mud flats; the students dredged and skimmed, and Leo's work so impressed the biologist Charles Wilson Green that when he ran into Michael Stein at a Johns Hopkins alumni dinner, according to Sarah, he "spoke very highly of Leo as taking hold so well although it was his first scientific work." Leo's course was introductory; Gertrude's course, in embryology, was advanced. She studied the often transparent eggs of fish, the best type, it was said, for elucidating vertebrate embryology. She attended the nine-o'clock morning lecture and in the afternoon went to the laboratory. Hair parted in the middle and tied back, she walked about the salty village in typical female attire: ankle-length dark skirt, long-sleeved white blouse, neatly arranged bow tie. But her size— she had grown stouter—prompted Winterton C. Curtis, an independent investigator later used by Clarence Darrow during the Scopes trial, to write scornfully: "For us that summer she was just a big, fat girl waddling around the laboratory and hoisting herself in and out of the row boats on collecting trips."

Overall, the courses Gertrude and Leo took were directed more to the rules and mechanisms of classification than to experimental procedure. But in 1896, when the neurological seminar was organized (including among its members Stewart Paton, with whom Gertrude would work at Hopkins), its focus extended to the study of animal behavior, and one might imagine it intrigued those who were anxious to discover more about psychology through physiology.

But there was still Latin to learn. Gertrude hired as tutor Margaret Lewis, a longtime investigator at Woods Hole, a graduate student at Radcliffe, and the person who first acquainted Gertrude with what she subsequently called "property values." More successful with a tutor than she had been alone, on September 27, 1897, from the Bachrach home in Baltimore, Gertrude informed Dean Welch at Hopkins that, having passed her Latin examination, she would now like to apply for admission to medical school. Four days later, Leo submitted his application to Hopkins to finish his bachelor's degree and then move on, he hoped, toward a doctorate in zoology.

"HUMAN KIND might be divided into three groups—" jested the debonair William Osler, Johns Hopkins's first professor of medicine, "men, women and women physicians."

In 1898, of the 171 graduates of Radcliffe who were living—the number included Gertrude Stein and her friends—only six-tenths of a percent were studying medicine. (Almost fifty percent, by comparison, were teaching.) And although college-educated women married in greater numbers than did their counterparts of the 1880s, to the wider public they appeared unfeminine and unmarriageable—strange, deviant, unnatural. A woman doctor was almost unthinkable. "To be addressed in public as a doctor," the physician Marie Zakrewska told the pediatrician and neurologist Mary Putnam Jacobi, "was painful, for all heads would turn to look at the woman thus stigmatized."

At the end of the century, more doors were opening to the female medical student formerly admitted only to women's medical colleges. Yet she continued to meet resistance at every level of her career. William Welch, professor of pathology at Johns Hopkins and generally open-minded on other subjects, dreaded the idea of women in medicine. One of the Big Four—the men indispensable to the new medical school at Hopkins—Welch argued that women in the classrooms would prevent the faculty from talking about those matters too indelicate for a lady to hear. (Later he did admit that the "embarrassments which one can conjure up have not materialized at all.") But Dr. Jacobi explained the matter differently. Men didn't want women in medical schools because they feared the competition. "Opposition to women physicians has rarely been based upon any sincere conviction that women could not be instructed in medicine, but on an intense dislike of the idea that they should be so capable," she insisted. "Failure could be pardoned them, but— at least so it was felt in anticipation—success could not."

The founding of the medical school at Johns Hopkins had been a victory for women generally and, in particular, for the bold group of Baltimore women who, because they financed the school, stipulated its conditions. These women demanded that females must be admitted on the same—not equal—basis as males. The trustees, who had already accepted the women's $100,000, then recoiled; they now said one hundred thousand was fine but nothing could be done without another four. Recalled one of the women, M. Carey Thomas, then dean of Bryn Mawr College and later its president, "Mr. Gilman [president of Johns Hopkins], although he had approved of our attempting to raise the money when we consulted him beforehand, used every unfair device—and he had many in his bag of tricks—to persuade the trustees to refuse this $100,000 and would finally have defeated us had it not been that two of our fathers, mine and Mamie Gwinn's, were on the board and another father, Francis T. King, was president of the hospital board."

Under the auspices of the Women's Fund for the Higher Medical Education of Women, committees up and down the eastern seaboard then raised the funds necessary for the medical school—and their vision of it. "Pres. Gilman and some of the trustees really do not want (sub rosa) the women to succeed," Dr. Welch confided to his colleague Franklin Mall, "for they do not like the idea of co-sexual medical education. I do not myself hanker after it," he conceded, "but I do not see how they can refuse such a large sum of money." Contributions had come in from Alice Longfellow, Sarah Orne Jewett, First Lady Caroline Harrison, and Julia Ward Howe, as well as the physicians Emily Blackwell and Mary Putnam Jacobi, but it was Mary Garrett's contribution that was decisive. Daughter of a former president of the Baltimore & Ohio Railroad, she donated more than $300,000 toward the founding of the medical school—strings attached. A placard was to be placed on one of the buildings to commemorate the Women's Fund, and not only were women to be admitted on the same basis as men, they were to be eligible for all prizes, positions, and awards on the same—again, the same, not equal—terms.

And Garrett also specified the standards for admission. All successful medical school applicants must hold a bachelor's degree or its equivalent; they must be prepared in biology, physics, and chemistry; and they had to demonstrate a reading knowledge of French and German. Thus the school was founded "under the inspiration of two ideas," as Francis King told members of the fund-raising committee at a luncheon in their honor. "There is, in the first place, the idea that medical education properly belongs to a university; that it is an intellectual matter, and not a mere trade, to be practiced for pecuniary profit, and then there is the further idea, and which more especially concerns us, that women are to participate in the full in this intellectual as-

Gertrude at her microscope, with skull

pect of medicine, and to follow it to the highest plane of intellectual development to which it can be carried."

On October 2, finally satisfied with her Latin, the admissions committee of Johns Hopkins Medical School welcomed Gertrude Stein as a first-year student. Days later, Leo Stein was admitted to Hopkins to finish his undergraduate program and carry out his plans. All that remained was housing.

THE TURRETED red-brick buildings of Johns Hopkins Hospital and Medical School, including the newly erected Women's Fund Memorial Building, stood on a hill on the eastern outskirts of Baltimore. Not far away, and easily accessible by horsecar or electric trolley, were the rowhouses of East Biddle Street, their well-scrubbed white marble stoops lined neatly up and down the street. Gertrude and Leo rented the two stories of 215 East Biddle. To take care of the more mundane part of living, they hired a German housekeeper, Lena Lebender, who fretted over Leo's diet and babied Miss Gertrude, whom she loved. Upstairs, Leo read, sitting among the strewn cushions of his book-lined study. It was directly over Gertrude's bright office, cluttered with heavy volumes, papers, a skull, and a microscope; only "a pipe and a bull-dog, the time-honored paraphernalia of a medic," were lacking, joked Ben Oppenheimer, imagining the "Bohemian life" of the Steins.

Michael had disapproved of the housekeeping scheme initially. Sarah wrote Gertrude that he wished "you could make up your minds to board with the Bachrachs or some other congenial people, while in Baltimore, as he can't quite see who will run the house when you are at college and Leo reading, and he particularly wonders at your investing in house-furnishings before you are sure that you will like house-keeping." In a postscript to his wife's letter, Michael came to the point: "I should not think you folks would want to make any inroads into your capital and you certainly have not enough money on hand or coming in to decently furnish a house." Gertrude was annoyed, especially since Mike and Sarah seemed to think she could not afford both to visit them as she had planned and to furnish a flat in Baltimore. Irritated, she precipitately canceled her California trip.

Sarah was disappointed. She wanted Gertrude to see baby Allan, born in November 1895. "There is certainly nothing in the line of happiness to compare with that which a mother derives from the contemplation of her first-born and even the agony which she endures from the moment of its birth does not seem to mar it," sighed Sarah on paper shortly before Gertrude entered Johns Hopkins. "Therefore my dear and beloved sister-in-law go and get married—for there is nothing in this whole wide world like babies—" she exulted, adding somewhat testily, "Leo to the contrary, notwithstanding."

7

RESPECTABILITY

Gertrude at Johns Hopkins, about twenty-eight years old

As my father used to say to us when we were children and were
to make up our own minds, "You're the doctor."

LEO STEIN, *APPRECIATION*

BALTIMORE JEWISH SOCIETY... would in
a short time stunt anything from a sensitive plant to
a Sequoia," Leo Stein told a friend. Yet whether he
liked it or not, he and his sister were again taken up in its band. Proud and
somewhat self-satisfied, this cluster of affluent German Jewish families observed itself and all those related to it, publishing the comings and goings of
its members in the social column of its newspaper, *The Jewish Comment,*
which prided itself on acquaintanceship with the important, if anxiety-
provoking, issues of the day: assimilation, the fate of Captain Dreyfus, intermarriage, the role of the Jewish patriot during wartime, Russian Jews, and
Jewish literature (Israel Zangwill's 1900 American tour was a matter of excitement). Even the progress of Gertrude and Leo's cousin Ernest Keyser, a
"rising young sculptor, in the Latin quarter" of Paris, was of local significance.

Quickly Gertrude and Leo rubbed up against the limits of this world.
Its values were cloying. Its ranks were closed. And sister and brother were sensitive to the condescension of people they regarded as conventional; soulless
and inane, Leo called them. With slightly more tact, Gertrude told a Baltimore women's group, "There is nothing more striking to a person who has
come from a town like Cambridge to a place like Baltimore than the complete
difference in the ideals and occupations of the two places." To her, Cambridge
was by far superior, and she was not shy about saying so.

Bursting with Charlotte Perkins Stetson's *Women and Economics* that
night, she tried to convince her audience "you people are in the wrong" about
higher education for women, and delivered a strong apologia for her own
choices. "If a girl goes into society [instead of attending college] she is spending some five or six years in doing what? Nothing in the wide world except the
task of a peacock, the spreading of his tail before an admiring audience." And
such a woman didn't know much, if anything, of the future awaiting her. She

was ignorant of "the facts concerning health and education that she should have been learning . . . to prepare herself for maternity."

As far as Stein was concerned, then, a college education didn't "unsex" the female, as had been argued repeatedly, or make her "unfeminine"; instead it tended to "rightly sex women" and thus more truly prepare them for whatever lay ahead. That meant that the college-educated woman, albeit ready for motherhood, need not cling to marriage for her livelihood or, for that matter, feel incompetent in the face of any task. College trained the intellect, Gertrude explained, and so there was nothing a college-educated woman couldn't do.

"Mind you," she also admonished, "it is not only in the things studied that this is valuable but in the four years away from home with no one to protect you or be fond of you unless you earn it." Speaking from firsthand experience, Stein was proud of what she regarded as her own intellectual, and personal, achievement. An ingenue from the West had come to the East, aimed high, and accomplished what she had set out to do. Her words fell quickly, passionately. "The life of college is on a small scale the life of the world, as ye sow so shall you also reap and it is here that for the first time that you are thrown wholly on yourself, without any aid of family or heretary [*sic*] friends and if there is anything worthy in you it must come out for here you must earn whatever you get and through that discipline you become a self respecting human being."

The women in the audience could not help but hear the personal note, and as their speaker gathered her papers, they perhaps cheered, roused out of their routine by the individualism they loved. Or more likely, they bristled, clapping tepidly at the intense young medical student—a woman, no less— who had challenged their most cherished domestic assumptions. But Gertrude knew what she faced. After Leo berated Baltimore society, delivering in *The Jewish Comment* "an amiable and tender discourse on Philistinism, Provincialism, and Pharisaism," he told Fred that Gertrude had laughingly said "the people here will probably think I'm referring to Cincinnati or Podunk or such."

"Respectability likes to see nothing except in terms of respectability," Leo had observed. And to him the Baltimore Jewish community was nothing if not respectable. "Any rift in the costume that answers the purpose of the real body, and that permits the latter in its actuality to be glimpsed, outrages respectability," he wrote in the *Comment* article, castigating his audience's smug prudishness. "The notion that anybody persists in seeing things that it has shut its eyes to irritates it exceedingly. Not that it is always or even most of the time a fool. It knows the things are there, it even gives them a kind of recognition, but the claim to equality is what it repudiates. They can exist, but in a world apart—a world that may be visited, a world that may be instructed, a world that may perhaps—happy fate!—be elevated by progressive development to be equally exalted heights of respectability."

Yet Gertrude and Leo did find one or two friends in Baltimore, among them Hortense Guggenheimer, on whom they lavished their spare time and broader views. "Well we have contributed materially to keep at least one person from the pit or rather indeed we have snatched her out of it," Leo jested, only by half, to Gertrude, "now our places are assured in the kingdom of heaven." Leo lectured Hortense on subjects as varied as trees and art history, and she responded so well that her older, more sophisticated cousin, Dr. Claribel Cone, observed, "Hortense never shows to better advantage than when with the Steins."

Claribel Cone did not at all conform to the Steins' Baltimore stereotype. An 1891 graduate of the Women's Medical College of Baltimore (the only medical school in Maryland that admitted women at the time) and a Jew, she was first in her class and one of five to win an internship at Philadelphia Hospital for the Insane (Blockley Hospital), which, it was said, would have been glad to disqualify her on two counts: because she hadn't been trained in Pennsylvania and because she was a woman. But no one and nothing deterred Claribel Cone. When Gertrude and Leo settled on East Biddle Street in 1897, she was professor of pathology at the Women's Medical College and soon to be its president; she was also pathologist at Good Samaritan Hospital and a postgraduate research member of the Johns Hopkins pathology department, working with Dr. William Welch. But she never opened a private practice or worked with patients. She was interested only in the laboratory and reputedly told friends that she'd seen a private patient once in Philadelphia, and once was enough.

Cone loved research, almost to the exclusion of everything else. A deeply solitary woman, she awed her relatives, one of whom remembered her as fascinating but difficult, visiting family and peremptorily taking long walks at mealtimes. "Do you know that every now and then it dawns on me," she herself remarked, "that people do like to be thought of—I am so busy and free—occupied all the time in my work—that I do not stop to think of this enough—I believe some of the unhappiest as well as the happiest moments of my life have been due to my preoccupation in work."

Elegant, large, and forthright, "Dr. Claribel," commented one of the young women studying medicine with Stein, was "as magnificent as ever, and as unmovable." Her habits were not only legend but true: she did carry an open umbrella to ward off the bats in Ely Cathedral; she always traveled first-class, and when attending the theater bought one seat for herself and one for her packages; she wore high-necked, ankle-length black even after hemlines rose and colors lightened, but she draped dazzling lace shawls so elegantly about herself that once, when she was standing in the lobby of the Munich opera house, the Kaiser mistook her for royalty, offered her his arm, and escorted her to her seat. Claribel wound her long flat plaits on her head and ornamented the bun with a silver skewer; Alice Toklas called it a silver dagger. She bought two of everything—except of course paintings, which she would have, had it been possible. By the time of her death, she and Etta, her younger sister, had enough Manets, Renoirs, Degas, Bonnards, Cézannes, and Matisses to be considered among the foremost collectors of modern art in America.

Dr. Claribel often entertained in the family brownstone at 1602 Eutaw Place on Saturday nights; she offered Gertrude and Leo hospitality as well as a model for their future life in Paris. Management of the family home had fallen to Etta—Sister Carrie had married and moved to North Carolina, and Dr. Claribel was too busy. (In the family, younger siblings addressed older ones deferentially, with a "Brother" or "Sister" before their name. To Etta, Claribel and Moses were Sister Claribel, Brother Moses; to Claribel and Moses, however, Etta was simply Etta.) Etta apparently oversaw the Saturday-night refreshments and the decoration of the home. With $300 given her by her oldest brother, Moses, she went to New York in 1898 and bought five paintings by the American impressionist Theodore Robinson. But she took up her housekeeping duties with some ambivalence. "I hate, I despise Baltimore," Etta would tell her new friend Gertrude. The "hateful old clothes & teas & dinners & sich [sic] like" of the city's matrons depressed her, although she, unlike Gertrude, never completely renounced them.

Leo, who was spending more and more time among the Barbizons at the Walters Art Gallery, proudly showed off his collection of Japanese prints to the Cones and entertained Etta with his artistic discoveries. She credited him with teaching her everything she knew about art. She was a renegade in her own way, capable of deep and passionate friendships, seemingly modest but deliberate and headstrong. Like Claribel, she was of medium height, broad, and thin-lipped; she was once described as resembling Gilbert Stuart's portrait of George Washington. Less regal than the handsome, severe Claribel, Etta had no formal education beyond high school, and appeared content to command less attention; but she was devoted to the piano.

Only Henry James could do justice to the Cone sisters' complex connections, said Alice Toklas. Though intimate and affectionate, Claribel and Etta could annoy each other profoundly, as Hortense Guggenheimer reported to Gertrude; "Etta seems scarcely able to tolerate Claribel: everything she says, does, or looks, however innocent, irritates Etta so that she can hardly contain herself, and they are continually jumping at each other's throats." But each appreciated and needed the other. Imperious and often aloof, Claribel was capable of admitting to Etta, "You have a kind of penetrating instinct into the natures of people owing to a kind of sympathy & the feeling you have—I get at people with thorough judgement—hence I often never get there at all! You may interpret that as you like." While Etta craved companionship, Claribel

Dr. Claribel Cone

preferred solitude. "Throughout life—that is what I do—and have been doing—there is something subtle—and indefinable—that impels me to be alone—it interests me—to send people whom I might like away from me."

The sisters' relationship fascinated Gertrude. "Go on with how one of them is more something than the other one, and how each one of them thinks it of themselves and the other one," she reminded herself in notes to the dual portrait she penned of them in 1910. "Tell about the others connected with them their duties and how they did them, what effort they had when they were traveling, how they quarreled, how they spent money, how they each had what they wanted," and "how they were afraid of heart complaint," which had killed their father. "Aunt Etta was strong as an ox," recalled a nephew, "but a terrible hypochondriac."

Like the Steins, the Cone sisters were the children of German Jews. Their father was a dry goods merchant, born Herman Kahn, who came to America in 1846 and settled in Jonesboro, Tennessee. He and Helen Guggenheimer, who had emigrated to Natural Bridge, Virginia, in 1838, were married in 1857; they had thirteen children, ten boys and three girls. Born in 1864, Claribel was

Etta Cone

their fifth child; Etta, their ninth, was born in 1870, just after the family moved
to Baltimore, where Herman ran a wholesale cigar and grocery business eventually called H. Cone & Sons. After the establishment was dissolved in 1884
and Herman, with his heart trouble, was retired on a guaranteed yearly income
of $10,000 (twice as much as he needed for his family's comfortable living), his
two oldest sons, Moses and Ceasar, acquired several small southern textile
mills. By 1893 these were headquartered in Greensboro, North Carolina, and
were leading manufacturers of denim, corduroy, and flannelette.

　　Always generous, Moses and Ceasar provided handsomely for their family. When their sisters met Gertrude and Leo, they were already well situated
and more or less set in their ways. Dr. Claribel would pick up the trolley at its
stop near Eutaw Street, and sit alone until it clambered to the East Biddle Street
stop, where Gertrude Stein would board. Then the two determined women
would sit together until the end of the run, on Broadway, near Johns Hopkins
Hospital, and walk east on Monument Street. Dr. Claribel, generally quite talk-
ative, would complete whatever tale she had begun the day before. She liked
her new young friend, perhaps admiring the Californian's lack of pretension or

her seriousness about her work. It was Claribel who had invited Gertrude in 1899 to speak to Baltimore women about the value of a college education.

AFTER THE TWO WOMEN PARTED, Gertrude usually entered the three-story red-brick Women's Fund Memorial Building on Wolfe Street or the physiology building nearby for her routine first- and second-year medical school courses. For the first year the standard fare was anatomy, which she studied with Franklin P. Mall; physiology, with William Howell; and physiological chemistry, with John Abel and Thomas Aldrich. She especially liked anatomy, and had immediately warmed to its teacher, a slight, acerbic man recruited by William Welch in 1893 from the University of Chicago, whose anatomy department he had founded. At thirty-one, Mall, a former student of embryologist Wilhelm His, had earned such a brilliant reputation that Welch considered his luring him to Hopkins a personal triumph.

Mall was a man of few words. Committed to science and scientific research, he intimidated many students, who shrank from his clipped comments and satiric quips, and found in his inductive teaching methods too little encouragement, too much reserve. He did not lecture. He believed the student learned best who learned by experience, and he turned his first-year students loose in the laboratory, giving no special instructions when they had to perform a dissection, no description of what to observe, no indication of how long to take. Once when Mall noticed a student standing idle in the laboratory, he asked him whether he had a problem. The young man replied he didn't know what to do. Mall walked out to the hall, found a broom, and on reentering silently handed it to the student. "Doctor Mall believed in everybody developing their own technique," remembered Stein. "He also remarked, nobody teaches anybody anything, at first every student's scalpel is dull and then later every student's scalpel is sharp, and nobody has taught anybody anything."

From the very first, Stein demanded that she be judged on the basis of performance, not gender, and this was easiest in Mall's laboratory, for she performed well and Mall singled out good students. Yet the recollections of other students give a sense of the prejudice young female medical students had to confront. "Hen medics" or "damned co-eds" were tolerated as long as they were modest and pliable. Said Emma Lootz Erving, one of Stein's closest friends at Hopkins, "Do you think I'd have got a degree myself if I hadn't worn my best hat? It had roses on it." A former classmate, a male, told Stein's first biographer that Gertrude was hardly retiring or docile at the medical school. "Miss Stein took the provision of the foundation absolutely literally, and very embarrassing it was for us." Miss Stein, he elaborated, said she was fully entitled to examine men with venereal disease.

The women knew they were the objects of some contempt. Another classmate, Dorothy Reed Mendenhall, remembered that a visiting nose-and-throat specialist tried to embarrass the women by dragging in "the dirtiest stories I ever heard, read or imagined, and when he couldn't say it in English, he quoted Latin from sources not usually open to the public." That memory, she noted fifty years later, "still comes up like a decomposing body from the bottom of a pool that is disturbed." She also recalled unpleasant practical jokes. Leo said that the men in Gertrude's anatomy class wouldn't waste their time making brain tract models, a sideline of Franklin Mall's, which one German anatomist disparaged as an "excellent occupation for women and Chinamen." Leo claimed Gertrude made fun of this kind of " 'research' work . . . saying that the women who were at Johns Hopkins for the first time fell in with Mall's hobby for making models of the brain tracts, to show how interested they were." But, Leo continued, Gertrude said she didn't mind; the task was so mechanical it was actually relaxing.

And there was anti-Semitism. A male student, applying for an internship in obstetrics, reminded the illustrious Dr. John Whitridge Williams that he, the student, was Jewish. "I want to know whether or not it will interfere with my advancement in your department." Williams paused before answering. "If a Jew and a Gentile have equal merit, I prefer the Gentile; but if the Jew is the better man, I'll take him any time." Years later, the student observed without rancor that "we are all aware that the racial prejudice which exists in the academic field rarely gives the Jew even that square a deal." Williams, Dorothy Reed Mendenhall claimed emphatically, "couldn't stand [Gertrude's] marked Hebrew looks, her sloppy work and her intolerance." But recalling that most of Stein's classmates disliked her, one of them paradoxically insisted, "This was not a question of race or religion, most of the class paid little attention to this and there were Jewish students who were well liked. I do not recall that *they* liked her. She had the arrogant manner of many of her race, the disagreeable features, and was also very conceited."

Several male students were offended by her looks: "Fat, awkward with frowsy black hair, a rather waddling gait and hands usually covered with stains," one described her. "I have often wondered whether she did not care about her personal appearance or whether she exaggerated what really amounted to ugliness in order to accentuate her individuality." Said another: "She was stout, clumsy and heavy-footed, and sloppy in her dress and appearance; she was sloppy in her work." Neither did this young Jewish woman conform to conventions of femininity in deportment. Like Franklin Mall's, Stein's intolerance was a kind of intellectual arrogance, according to Mendenhall. "As a thinker, she was tops but she could do nothing with her hands, was very untidy and careless in her technique and very irritating in her attitude of intellectual superiority, which was marked even in her youth." Another classmate related that "her technique in all things was sloppy, her interest in clinical subjects nil, consideration for other people entirely lacking and her conceit unbounded." And another observed: "I can truthfully say that she never impressed me as a brilliant woman—the rumor went the rounds early that she had been a favorite pupil of James at Harvard. Maybe we had our doubts—or doubts about James or Harvard. But after all we may have been unappreciative."

Gertrude herself remembered that she had a difficult time with the drawings she was supposed to make in anatomy, and never figured out the difference between concave and convex. She disdained learning by rote, valuing only the "self-inspired," as she called it, the creative and original work that, as she would come to find, was not necessarily rewarded outside Mall's laboratory. As another classmate, a woman, explained, Gertrude was always her "own vigorous self, tramping across town or into the country swinging down the corridors full of life and sanity and humour."

Opinionated and direct, she did not mince words, and while many resented her candor, others loved her for it. "I am sure she always wished to be very friendly," said one, "but this attitude might be considered intrusive by some." Gertrude habitually spread her materials all over the laboratory table on which she worked. One day the student working next to her pushed her bottles of stain and her papers aside to make more room for himself. " 'Have you ever heard the expression "Place aux Dames"?' she asked. 'Oh yes,' said the man, 'it means "women have their place." ' At which Miss Stein was hugely amused."

Gertrude liked to argue. Some years after they left Hopkins, another medical student, Marian Walker Williams, told her, "I should like to see you and be sand-bagged on the head when I didn't agree with you and sandbag you back again." Another student thought her "extremely interesting to talk to, particularly if the subject was not . . . medicine. She had all sorts of . . . ideas about people, was very fond of discussing music and its influence on people, and . . . she told me she frequently went . . . to New York for the opera." Although fellow students had misgivings about her interest in medicine, friends and relatives never questioned Gertrude's commitment or enthusiasm, even if they were apt to tease her. Disappointed when Gertrude and Leo decided to spend the Christmas holidays in Cambridge, Fred Stein tried to entice Gertrude to New York by appealing to her new preoccupation. "Bring down your carving knives, fetch along your microscopes, & include bandages. . . . Come then to our Tuesday evening rough riding club . . . there will I furnish you with the medical *person's* delight, 'stiffs,' after every ride there are swarms of them." Gertrude must have found this letter amusing. It was one of the few from Fred she was to save.

BALTIMORE SOCIETY may have been narrow, but Gertrude and Leo were delivered from at least some of its prejudices by their scientific training, or so Gertrude humorously pointed out when describing a student picnic. A dozen female medical students rented several boats—eleven of them could row—from a man so dubious about their skills he tried to come along. The young women convinced him they were perfectly competent. They rowed, docked, landed, made a fire, and prepared the crabs they had bought to eat. "Although medical students we objected to roasting them alive, and so we neatly severed their brains from their spinal cords not that we had ever heard of that performance perlimienary [sic] to crabcooking and then we roasted and ate our crabs."

Science was a conscientious passion that transcended the petty prejudices of the bourgeoisie by aspiring to the neutral, objective—and ideally genderless—domain of knowledge. That, at least, was the rhetoric.

Still intrigued by studies of the brain, Gertrude in the Hopkins laboratory took particular interest in the neurological work of Lewellys F. Barker, then an associate professor under Franklin Mall. She sent Leon Solomons one of Barker's papers—probably on the skin's sensations of pain, pressure, and temperature, a subject Solomons had also investigated. She was drawn to the overlapping fields of neurology and psychology and evidently planned to continue her experimental work in that direction. She alerted Solomons to some projects involving hypnotism. Solomons answered that "I suppose you have found out by this time that it is very doubtful whether dogs can be hypnotised."

There is no record of Stein's proposal, but Solomons's enthusiasm is grimly tantalizing. "The experiment that you suppose would be interesting in itself," he told her, "if you could easily kill the animal instantly without changing his condition, if it gave positive results, but I doubt very much whether it would throw any light on hypnosis." Meantime, Gertrude had sent him a draft of her article "Cultivated Motor Automatism," asking him to rewrite certain sections. Obliging, he also inserted punctuation marks—"things of which you may have heard even though you so obviously disapprove"—and handed the finished product to Hugo Münsterberg for publication in the *Psychological Review*.

Despite her later disclaimers, Gertrude considered herself a good subject for her own psychological observations. Attentive to them, during her first year of medical school, she began to discern slight changes in her behavior, especially in her automatic habits. She confided worriedly to Leon Solomons, who assured her that "it is a natural reaction and a perfectly healthy one. Your general view of things that you had before, was the generality and breadth of superficiality," he consoled, "as it always is in the case of the philosopher—don't breathe this heresy to anyone." He reminded her that the philosopher ignores details but the true scientist systematizes them. And since she was becoming a true scientist, "a change in your automatic habits is not surpris-

ing to me." In fact, he said, improvement in her visual sense and in her powers of observation meant only that her attention was more focused, and that
in turn implied an inevitable decrease in her automatic habits.

Her attention had been focused specifically on the serial sections of a
human brain stem that Lewellys Barker had brought back from Leipzig. Using
them in teaching the histology of the central nervous system, he had interested Stein in studying the part of the brain called the nucleus of Darkschewitsch. ("I have often wondered," Barker later wrote, "whether my attempts
to teach her the intricacies of the medulla oblongata had anything to do with
the development of the strange literary forms with which she was later to per-
plex the world.") Both she and Florence Sabin, in the class two years ahead
of her, went to work.

Not long after she left medical school, Gertrude disparaged Sabin, who
was also one of Mall's protégées, and some of whose results were incorporated
into her first book, *An Atlas of the Medulla and Midbrain,* published the year
after she finished her medical training. Stein in her notebooks used Sabin to
represent a "college girl type of faithful studentship." To Stein, Sabin was the
pedestrian student, dogged, faithful, and without much imagination—which
is the way some of Sabin's male colleagues, somewhat jealously, regarded her.
(Sabin graduated near the top of her class and was one of the first women,
along with Dorothy Reed Mendenhall, offered an internship at Johns Hopkins Hospital.) Rivalry was a common fact of medical student life, as Stein
herself admitted in *The Autobiography of Alice B. Toklas;* there was a "good
deal of intrigue and struggle among the students." And she was not exempt
from it.

But the surface of life seemed untroubled. "And the moon was shining
bright upon the Wabash," the men in the laboratory crooned as they poured
and measured. Gertrude's hands and arms, recalled a classmate, were covered
to the elbow with dye. Arthur Lachman's New Year's greetings to her included
wishes that "all your slides will be clear as crystal, that each test tube will solve
its mystery, and each stiff prove a treasure trove." At home on East Biddle,
she and Leo entertained some students, among them Florence Sabin, who recalled, with admiration, Leo's unusual collection of Japanese prints, and when
Gertrude invited her to a performance of *Tannhäuser,* she regretted that exams
kept her from going twice in one week.

Often Gertrude would play the piano with her friend Etta Cone.
Gertrude's dedication to music was passionate, agreed her friends, until she
gave it up. (In this she was like her father: when she was finished with something, she was finished.) And then there were the melodramas at the Holli-
day Street Theater, excursions to the bank of the Catonsville stream, or long
and lazy weekend afternoons at the Bachrachs'. Friends later remembered

these soft green spring days when Gertrude, who loved to lounge, reclined among the flowers in the backyard, feet propped up, reciting poetry. According to a neighbor, she recited Wordsworth most often, and Gertrude herself recalled a fondness for his longer, more boring poems, which she delivered without hesitation or self-consciousness in her deep-pitched, melodious voice.

The more reserved Leo plunged so completely into his new course of study that a friend entreated Gertrude to "tell Leo to stop working for a degree long enough to write a letter once in a while." After visiting him in Baltimore his first year, Adele Oppenheimer said she "felt sure once again that you will certainly write an epoch-making book in the room right over Gertrude's sunny crowded office." Perhaps he thought so too. No doubt, like his sister, he more and more had been considering himself a scientist. "In a biological laboratory," he reflected many years later, "one does not learn to criticize animals but to see them. One does not learn to characterize them in critical but in descriptive terms."

He did not seem depressed anymore, and as long as he was actively involved in his studies, he was reasonably immune to the constrictions of Baltimore society. "Your letter seems almost to 'bubble' with enthusiasm for your work," wrote a friend. "I am glad you are taking the chemistry this early for a solid foundation . . . in biology." Leo told his cousin Fred that, in addition to chemistry, he was taking courses in geometry, general biology, freehand drawing, and cryptogamic biology. He was also doing independent research on the anatomy of tadpoles. "The latter popped up very recently," he explained, "and involves agreeable incidents like getting up at five o'clock in the morning and going to the country to find frogs' eggs and frogs and getting back in time for a nine o'clock lecture." In May he went to a geological camp near Cumberland, Maryland, and had "an excellent time climbing round on the hills"; by the end of the academic year he had earned his highest grades in his science courses. Florence Sabin remembered him representing "a type then rare in America—of a very mature individual who went to a University not to follow any curriculum but to take a course here and there, either to study with a certain professor or to pursue a certain subject."

Leo decided that in June, upon receiving his bachelor's degree, he would return to Woods Hole to prepare for graduate work by taking a course in embryology. Although he was still concentrating on zoology, he looked forward to physiology and physics as well. All in all, it had been a good year.

WHEN LEO RETURNED to Woods Hole during the summer of 1898, after classes were finished at Hopkins, Gertrude boarded a train bound for California. But since the timing wasn't right, as she had hoped it would be, for a summer course at Toland Medical College or at Berkeley, the trip was pure diversion.

Sarah, Allan, Michael, and Simon Stein, 1897

Sarah Stein eagerly anticipated her sister-in-law's visit; she was "inexpressibly glad." Generally masking her wariness of Gertrude and Leo, whom she regarded as privileged and indulged, Sarah often measured her life against theirs, barely concealing the conflicts her in-laws stirred. "By comparison with you workers," she wrote them, "what an empty life I lead, but somehow these days, I am perfectly happy if I do not detect a wheeze in Allan's chest. . . . Such is life." But she tensed when Gertrude brazenly criticized her handling of her son. "I must sit me down to write you a few lines to ask you what you mean by constantly alluding to our spoiling the kid," declared Sarah. "Your last letter no longer implies, it boldly states that you are ashamed of me, a former advanced woman."

Whatever she thought of Sarah, or however she upbraided her, Gertrude considered herself an advanced young woman and in California was eager to demonstrate as much, partly by brandishing her new medical school skills. Leon Solomons's young nephew, born with webbed fingers, provided an opportunity. Adele Jaffa, Solomons's sister, one of Sarah's closest friends and herself a homeopathic doctor, was grateful for Gertrude's offer to take the case to a Baltimore surgeon. Reporting on her son's progress, Adele confided self-deprecatingly that "if you will pardon the unscientific description . . . *Nature* seems to be an intelligent, invisible person, handling the child. I hope you will have the good fortune to have your first case a rather rapid *normal* one—after that only abnormal ones are interesting." Years later, long after she had left medical school, Stein echoed Jaffa's sentiment in reverse, stating she disliked

the abnormal: "The normal is so much more simply complicated and interesting."

Gertrude's brother Simon had bought a new horse, for which he rented
an entire stable, but was otherwise much the same, slightly more overweight,
eating almost eleven meals a day, according to Sarah, and much less pre-
sentable. Sarah hoped Gertrude might straighten him out. For the last several years she and Michael had been living in a large Victorian house on
Pierce Street, where Simon often visited and played with his curly-headed
nephew Allan, who took quickly to his aunt Gertrude. She, Sarah, and Allan
walked hand in hand by the sea while Michael took pictures of the excursion.
Gertrude's visit was a success.

Gertrude's recollections of that summer included the doughy-faced
boys, mostly from the Middle West, who milled about the streets of San
Francisco, wandering through Chinatown and down to the wharves before sailing for the Philippines. "The Spanish-American war made us Americans conscious of being a world power," she wrote with the hindsight of four decades,
"conscious of the school of realism, conscious of England being nineteenth
century, with Kipling and the white man's burden." The war was for her the
"beginning of killing the nineteenth century": that which had once seemed
certain would no longer be so, not just globally but personally.

Within two years, she would have enlarged her circle of friends to include women unlike any she had known before; Leon Solomons would be
dead; and Leo, never certain himself for very long, would abandon Hopkins
and zoology—and America. This too would spell the end of the nineteenth
century, and the beginning of a new life.

GERTRUDE STEIN said she enjoyed the first two years of medical school,
when her work was geared toward research and laboratory experiment. Only
toward the end of the second year did she begin her instruction in the clinical application of what she had learned: how to listen to a healthy heart, for
example, or attend to rasps of breath.

Third-year medical students donned white coats to work under the vigilant eye of Dr. William Osler, the professor of medicine whose epitaph would
read, all joked, "Here lies the man who admitted students to the wards."
Known for his own sartorial style (frock coat, striped trousers, top hat, rose in
his buttonhole), the precise and discerning Osler went to the hospital's clinical amphitheater every Wednesday to consult with third- and fourth-year students about such scourges as typhoid and pneumonia. For those interested,
nothing compared with working under Osler, considered an artist by Claribel
Cone, who thought his genius for sympathy and perception such that his clinical cases became masterpieces "as rich in suggestion, as universal in appeal
as a Giotto, a Rembrandt or a Giorgione."

At twelve o'clock on Tuesdays, Thursdays, and Saturdays, Dr. Osler punctually met the third-year students, Stein among them, in the dispensary to examine select cases—the unwashed maladies, as he termed them. "The whole art of medicine lies in observation," Osler told his students over and over, watching them use their eyes and ears, instructing them on how to touch a patient and where. He demanded each student follow the progress of a case, whether the patient went into the wards or home to recuperate. But Gertrude didn't like disease. She grew alarmed about her health, reported a friend from medical school: "She thought something was the matter with her blood—so she hired a welterweight to box with her." "I did not like anything abnormal or frightening," Stein later claimed, repeating her allegiance—ambivalent as it was—to the so-called normal.

In this year, her grades began to slip. More or less the equivalent of C's, they weren't poor enough to warrant "conditions," a probationary tag conferred by the medical faculty each spring on students faltering in examinations and clinical work. Gertrude's work was still adequate—although classmates later described her laboratory work as weak, her clinical approach as "crude and superficial." In retrospect it can be said that her grades pointed to a growing disaffection with medical school, exacerbated, no doubt, by the prejudice she confronted. One incident reveals what she had to endure. The students, studying urine, were told to use their own as a matter of convenience. In the laboratory one morning, Gertrude placed a large bottleful on her desk. At noon someone put glucose in the bottle. That afternoon a few smirking classmates watched her confusedly test the urine, unnerved, no doubt, at the result.

If she was discovering her forte was not the bedside, Gertrude's commitment to research seemed unwavering and consistently rewarded. She was pleased to see her work on the brain in Lewellys Barker's comprehensive study, *The Nervous System and Its Constituent Neurones,* published in 1899. Actually, it wasn't Gertrude but Leo who decided to abandon his scientific studies during her third year in medical school.

He quit the doctoral program at Hopkins, to which he had been admitted in December 1898, having completed the requisite undergraduate science courses with ease. Disposed to the quiet seclusion of university life, he had found no true home within its borders. And though he did well in his classes, zoology had lost its charm and, with it, the evolutionary system back of it. "The gross fact of heredity with change was acceptable," Leo said, "but what influenced the atoms & molecules in one case to continue to form the same kind of beast & in another to change it was never plausibly made out. When I was young I was an ardent Darwinian but though I believed it ought to be plausible, I in fact never felt that it was."

For the remainder of 1899, Leo stayed in Baltimore, which, without classes at Hopkins, was more stultifying than ever. In the spring of 1900, in an article on the Jew in fiction for *The Jewish Comment,* he could hardly disguise his contempt. Excoriating readers who preferred sentimental tripe over the work of the Russian immigrant Abraham Cahan, he observed that those who thought Cahan degraded Jews by depicting "sordid types" did not "recognize the advantages they derive in having the literary treatment of the Jew confined largely to the ghetto world." These comfortably bourgeois Jews, suspicious of everything but money and anxious lest they be linked to the new Russian immigrants, were but a ghetto "with a shirt on." Leo had no use for Jews who had turned their backs on what amounted to their own origins, retreating behind a complacent, assimilated gentility. Gertrude agreed.

The vehemence of his attack suggests, however, that Leo was not free of the society he scorned. For in that plumed community, he smelled his own failure. He didn't fit the image of an eligible young man on the make; he had spurned business, didn't fix on a professional career, and genuinely preferred a museum to that "ghastly dining club" he had frequented with some of his peers. He enjoyed a few people, such as Hortense Guggenheimer, but when that friendship was misconstrued, at least by those who circulated the rumor that she had fallen in love with him, he raged at the cramped values such gossip implied. He felt pinned and wriggling.

But he liked having female friends, and he sought out a new acquaintance of his and Gertrude's, the spirited Mabel Foote Weeks, a graduate from the Harvard Annex's first class and now on the staff at Dr. Sachs's preparatory school in New York City. The round-faced Weeks, who knew Bird Sternberger and was good friends with Gertrude's classmate Emma Lootz, was perceptive, loyal, and intent; she was interested in eighteenth-century literature, and flashed the irreverent wit Gertrude and Leo admired. She would be associated with Barnard College for thirty-two years, first as teacher, then as assistant dean. This woman of clarity and firmness, beloved by friends, colleagues, and students, was sure enough of herself, she once said, to take everything into account.

Shortly after they met, Leo was often in New York, staying with Fred Stein and hanging about the lively offices of the *Commercial Advertiser,* where Hutchins Hapgood worked. Leo called on Weeks and sometimes went with her to the Yiddish theater. She thought him shy, but, she remembered, "he wanted to talk. . . . His manner was personal; he always used to say the best conversation was between you and me. I always felt that there was a touching of minds." When she came to know both Leo and Gertrude better, she couldn't resist comparisons, even though she said she considered them "as two quite independent people whom I have come to know in different ways and for whom I have different feelings." She outlived both Steins, and over the years she reflected on the contrast between them. "Gertrude's personality was magnetic; she had a laugh from the middle of her and a sort of warmth and zest and enjoyment which gave her a tremendous appeal, particularly to young people. Leo didn't win people, but was much more withdrawn. She insisted that everyone meet her on her terms. Leo in a way couldn't meet anyone on any but his own terms, but he wasn't a bully. Gertrude bullied everyone."

The romance between Mabel Weeks and Leo Stein—if indeed that's what it was—was never to blossom, though Weeks hinted that something special had occurred between them, so special it had momentarily threatened their friendship. She wrote that she had reconciled herself to occupying but a tiny place in his life. "And you Leo," she asked, "can you feel as I do and can you have associations with me as easily & [naturally] as I feel I can with you. Can you continue to give me what is mine with perfect freedom." If he could, she said, their friendship would "take its place with the profound & lasting things in both our lives." It did.

In the spring of 1900, after Leo had spent a desultory year shuttling back and forth between Baltimore and New York, meandering, writing sometimes, unsure of what he wanted to do, Mabel Weeks decided to spend a year at Cambridge University. Her decision may have helped crystallize his plans. "I'm all too easily distracted and variously stimulated," he explained to Gertrude. Unable to act, unable to sit still, he said that in the past, "when I couldn't break through in one direction instead of letting her rip and waiting the event I tried to break through somewhere else." But now, he hoped, things would be different. For he too would go abroad, for perhaps a year, perhaps more.

"Only one week from today and Baltimore . . . will be of the past." He counted the days, tasting his freedom. In the summer he and Gertrude and Mamie (as Mabel was affectionately called) would visit the Paris Exposition and tramp through Italy, and then, after Mamie left for England and Gertrude sailed back to her fourth and final year of medical school, he would study Renaissance art and make Florence his home. Andrea Mantegna's *Crucifixion* haunted him still; perhaps he would write about it one day.

To that end and without much planning or, it seems, much forethought, Leo Stein sailed from Baltimore on Wednesday, June 6, 1900, aboard the steamer *H. H. Meier.* With him were Mabel Weeks, his sister Gertrude, and his uncle Ephraim Keyser. *The Jewish Comment* conveyed the news.

8
NEW
AMERICANS

First-generation New Women: clockwise from left,
M. Carey Thomas, Bessie King, Mamie Gwinn (center),
Julia Rogers, Mary E. Garrett

I have seen college women years after graduation still embodying the type and accepting the standard of college girls—who were protected all their days from the struggles of the larger world and lived and died with the intellectual furniture obtained at their college—persisting to the end in their belief that their power was as a man's—and divested of superficial latin and cricket what was their standard but that of an ancient finishing school with courses in classics and liberty replacing the accomplishments of a lady. Much the same as a man's work if you like before he becomes a man but how much different from a man's work when manhood has once been attained.

I wonder will the new woman ever relearn the fundamental facts of sex. Will she not see that college standards are of little worth in actual labor.

GERTRUDE STEIN, "FERNHURST" MANUSCRIPT

FRIDAY, NOVEMBER 22, 1901, was an unusually mild day. Rain was forecast for the weekend, but the evening was clear and the air soft and fresh. Ten or so young people, women and men in their late twenties or early thirties, were making their various ways to a restaurant in downtown Manhattan, a small, comfortable place they called Little Hungaria, where the food was good and not too dear. Tonight there would be a party. Justice William Travers Jerome had won his bid for district attorney on the Fusion ticket, and several of the men in the group—Fred Stein, Howard Gans, Alfred Hodder—felt as if they'd single-handedly defeated Tammany Hall.

The feeling wasn't entirely unwarranted. These young men—poker buddies, confidants, and tireless campaigners—had indeed helped elect Jerome to office, and to celebrate, Deputy Assistant District Attorney Howard Gans, the treasurer of Jerome's campaign committee, had organized the dinner. He was the droll member of the group, the one whose laconic style scarcely concealed his passions, the one who liked to gather his friends for a party, though usually this meant only a small dinner after a poker victory. He was also the one who had accompanied Jerome on several of his spectacular and well-publicized raids of illegal gambling houses. (Jerome, frequently seen at the gaming tables himself, had nothing against gambling per se, just illegal gambling and the police corruption that customarily went with it.) On these occasions, Jerome stood aloof while his assistants broke down doors, and then, when the ruckus was over, he called court to session right on the premises, taking a Bible from his hip pocket for the swearing in of witnesses. At the signal, Gans swiftly drew up the papers and pushed for prosecutions, but his main job was to clench his fist in his pocket and wield it like a gun. He loved his work.

Howard Gans had kept his more retiring friend Leo Stein abreast of such derring-do. Buddies since Harvard, he and Stein were related through Fred Stein, another major player in Jerome's campaign. And all were part of the politics of reform sweeping the city—and the nation—although Leo was mostly a bystander, and no longer that once he had withdrawn to Florence in 1900, more than a year earlier. Gans had urged otherwise. You ought to come back and help improve the country, not fool with pictures and fans, he'd said. Leo laughed. I ought to reform myself, he rejoined, before taking on anyone else.

Forty years later, Leo reconsidered, with some surprise: "It was a longer job than I expected."

Jerome's progressive confederates were amateurs in politics, as one of them, Alfred Hodder, fondly observed. Fred Stein was one of the hardest-working and most self-effacing of the crew, recalled Hutchins Hapgood, a peripheral member: "I have never seen his ego obscure his personality or take from his essential wisdom or his usefulness as a simple citizen." Committed to fighting New York City's political machine and, at the same time, to weaning the immigrant Jewish population from more radical measures, such as socialism, he would hammer out strategy at the two-room Jerome campaign headquarters, perched atop a brightly lit saloon—that is, when he wasn't downtown working for his father in the more lucrative woolen trade. (He had spent years, commented Hodder, living down the reproach of being a rich father's son.) His largest contribution to the campaign came after he heard that several Yiddish newspapers wanted to be paid for their support. He was furious. " 'Take it; take all you can get,' Mr. Stein advised them; 'we like to see Tammany waste its money. We've got not a cent to bribe you with. But we've any amount to fight you with; and we will just establish a paper of our own and put you out of business.' " Immediately, though he didn't know a word of Yiddish, Fred Stein put together an eight-page newspaper, partly in Yiddish and partly in English, which for eleven days he distributed free.

Alfred Hodder was the literary member of Jerome's band. He too was going to Little Hungaria that night, on his way from a bachelor suite at the Benedick, near Washington Square Park. Handsome and courtly, with a pugnacious chin and trailing a scent of romance, Hodder seldom failed to charm. "He had the laughing insolence of the conscious intellect," recalled Hutchins Hapgood, "something like Bertrand Russell in the quick-coming flashes of his mental life." Concurring, Russell himself lamented Hodder's complicated private affairs. "He had a very brilliant mind, and in the absence of women could talk very interestingly," noted Russell, with some derision.

A former protégé of William James, Hodder was that wild westerner James had insulted by calling him a natural-born aristocrat. Born in Ohio and already admitted to the Colorado bar before arriving at Harvard in 1890 as a graduate student (and already a widower), Hodder was a gifted student of philosophy, psychology, and political economy. In the middle of his second year, however, he suddenly resigned a prestigious fellowship and left for Germany—to study philosophy, it was then believed. The real reason was that the woman who later claimed to be his second wife was pregnant.

But on that November night in 1901, his friends at the table understood that Hodder was now divorced and his ex-wife had returned to Europe. (Eventually, after their child died, Hodder insisted he wasn't divorced because he had never officially married.) He also needed money. He had been teaching literature at Bryn Mawr College—he had left in 1898 under somewhat dubious circumstances—and since then had been working in a vague way for Lincoln Steffens at the *Commercial Advertiser,* volunteering articles on topics that caught his fancy. Although he had written a series with a friend, collected as *The Powers That Prey,* about the New York underworld, and published a grim novel, *The New Americans,* about the battle between the sexes, he earned no steady income. So it was a relief when Fred Stein, ever the considerate friend, proposed Hodder as Jerome's private secretary. This would enable Hodder, as Jerome's Boswell, to write a portrait of the campaign, perhaps one of Jerome himself, and to save his pride.

Hodder and his friends not only intended to reform government, as Gans said, but eagerly sought, or thought they did, to modernize the relations between women and men. As the title of Hodder's novel suggested, they aspired to be New Americans: New Men and New Women, who enjoyed a more honest, less encumbered rapport, one based on respect, autonomy, sexual candor, and equality. They had no specific program, though some would later work for suffrage, but they had a vision. The feminist Neith Boyce, recently married to Hutchins Hapgood, was one of them; so, in a way, was Bird Sternberger, who had organized a women's discussion group; and then there was another who joined the New Americans that mild November night: Gertrude Stein.

Alfred Hodder enjoyed talking with Miss Stein. He had known her before, but until that night only through Leo. He hadn't thought much about her. The same seems to have been true for Gertrude, who admitted over dinner that when she'd first met him, "she had hated me at sight," Hodder said afterward, "because I showed her a politeness and a deference that she knew I could not feel, and did not feel."

Intrigued by such bluntness, Hodder patiently listened to Gertrude's criticism of his novel *The New Americans*—the women were well drawn, if superficial—but then sat flabbergasted as she launched into a frank discussion of the relations between the sexes. While at Radcliffe, she reportedly said, she and her friends believed women and men were alike in all things; it had been a religion with them. At medical school she'd learned otherwise. Women and men were different. Women matured more quickly—"like negroes," she put it—but then mistakenly assumed their early development a sign of ultimate ability. Not true. Reevaluating her experience at Radcliffe from the perspective of Hopkins, she realized how insulated she'd been at college, how oblivious to the paternalism she now suspected was largely responsible for a woman's success. And all this was quite discouraging. "We hate the courtesy, but when it is not given to us we don't succeed," Hodder recalled Stein saying, "and then we hate the failure, and hate the men who have treated us as they treat men."

It was not three years since she had argued, fresh from Cambridge and full of confidence, just the opposite. The college-educated woman, she had told her Baltimore audience, was adequate to any task. Now she, Gertrude Stein, seemed to be saying the New Woman should do herself a favor and embrace her lot. Matrimony and maternity were her destiny, and only through these could she lead a happy life.

What had happened?

IN THE SUMMER OF 1900, the Paris Exposition drew unprecedented and exhausted crowds through its 270 acres of pavilions, rolling sidewalks, and palaces. Henry Adams stopped, fatefully, at the Gallery of Machines on the Champs de Mars, where he comprehended at once the coming century's major symbol. A young writer, Logan Pearsall Smith, decided the whole thing was monstrous. Mass civilization, groaned his sister, Mary Costelloe, without even a trace of beauty. But Alfred Hodder maneuvered well among the dynamos and flashing lights, even arranging a surreptitious meeting with his lover, Mary Mackall Gwinn, a Bryn Mawr teacher who was herself involved with the college's austere president, M. Carey Thomas.

Although Gertrude and Leo and Mabel Weeks were also at the exhibition, they were not as thunderstruck as Adams, Smith, Hodder, or Gwinn. For they had spent a companionable summer, during which they had walked

Alfred Hodder,
the Byron of Bryn Mawr

nearly eighty miles of Italian countryside in a matter of four days, as they bragged before Leo returned to Italy. Weeks said it was the best summer of her young life, and Gertrude agreed it had been satisfying for her too.

Many years later Weeks recalled Gertrude that summer as already un-self-conscious and direct about her goals. In Venice, crossing the Grand Canal on her way to the Accademia, she declared repeatedly how much she wanted glory from life, said Weeks, "for it was evidently her central ambition." Despite such passionate longing, back at Hopkins that fall Gertrude had to formulate plans more prosaic. She would graduate from medical school in the spring; then what?

In December, she broached to Leo the idea of their living together in New York and asked a sculptress friend, Estelle Rumbold, if she could help land Leo a job with one of the city's museums. Leo wasn't enthusiastic. For one thing, he dreaded Manhattan's many diversions and the "sort of irregular aesthetic study that I was doing last year." And while he was sure he could write occasional reviews, or even free-lance for the *Commercial Advertiser* or some other paper, piecework would not suffice; "that is too trivial a course to depend on now or for the future," he claimed. "I'm all too easily distracted and variously stimulated." He preferred Florence, he had decided after several months there; it offered a "limited field," essential to one as scattered as he.

In this at least he was not at all like his sister, whom he admiringly regarded as the only member of the family to have "gone so far as to get the adequate preparation for anything." And New York, he knew, wasn't Gertrude's only option after Hopkins. She had written the noted psychiatrist Adolf Meyer, chief neuropathologist at the Massachusetts State Hospital for the Insane in Worcester. The hospital, in conjunction with Clark University, was a training school for the study of nervous diseases, and she wanted to consult Meyer about possibly working under him there.

Aware of his research—Meyer's article on hereditary ataxia in the journal *Brain* had motivated her mentor Lewellys Barker to study inherited disease—Stein was doubtless intrigued by his vaunted willingness to alter the treatment of mental disorder. Pursuing the character of the whole person, Meyer added biography to physiology and relied on narration as much as theory and research. "True medical study," he stated, "must begin before the patient is dead." Observation, induction, and living testimony: all these had their place in Meyer's study of nervous disease, and accordingly he stressed the importance of accurate case histories. This would be a novel approach, one attractive to the woman whose objective long remained the study of character.

Stewart Paton, a clinical neurologist on the faculty at Hopkins and himself an attending physician at the Baltimore city asylum, had originally suggested that Gertrude, given her own interests, approach Meyer. But little did she know that a few days after she'd mailed her letter to him, Paton dashed off one of his own. "My dear Meyer," Paton warned, "for heaven's sake don't take Miss Stein in the Hospital. I simply thought she might do P.G. [postgraduate] work under your direction."

If Paton trembled to think of Gertrude's working in the hospital, it may have been because he, like others, would have had ample occasion to observe her at bedside. At Hopkins, fourth-year medical students devoted themselves—as they still do today—almost entirely to clinical experience and exposure. In addition to witnessing and assisting surgery, these students, divided into four groups, served two months in rotation in the surgical, gynecological, and obstetrical departments of the hospital, each morning visiting the well-scrubbed wards to familiarize themselves with various cases and presumably develop a rapport with the patients. They prepared surgical dressings and performed minor operations, and for obstetrical duty visited patients throughout the city and assisted at childbirth. During their stint in the lying-in wards, they were on call day and night until they filled a quota of nine deliveries. "Don't you think you are 'borning' too many babies in Baltimore now," Mabel Weeks asked Gertrude in December.

It was also in December that Stein must have visited Meyer in Worcester. There is no record of the interview or its aftermath, but Alice Toklas once alluded to Gertrude's almost becoming "an intern, in a mental hospital." Toklas referred to the "abnormal" Gertrude so disliked and noted that "that was what decided her, really as much as—" She broke off, as if she'd said too much, then hesitated and soon added that Gertrude "could never bear it, the insane women around her."

The insane women at Worcester may have provoked her to reconsider her future, but it was obstetrics that was her nemesis.

The course was taught by John Whitridge Williams, nicknamed "the Bull" by his students, the large, gruff doctor about whom anti-Semitism was alleged; it was he, said Gertrude's fellow student Dorothy Reed Mendenhall, who could not bear Stein's "Hebrew" look or manner, all the more so, evidently, when she protested his needless vulgarity. A thick-necked man more than six feet tall, whose pipe continuously dangled under a nicotine-stained mustache, Williams was known for an attitude both crude and cavalier toward his subject. One of his students recalled that the Bull's "justly celebrated course in anecdotal midwifery" featured stories told "in a rare Rabelaisian vein completely unmindful that a half a dozen women medical students were present." Gertrude Stein, it was said, complained. Dr. Williams was so pointlessly blunt, so tactless in his classes that unless he modified his tone, she would boycott. Unperturbed, Williams answered that his classes were part of the curriculum, "and since he was free to teach them as he wished, he was forced to require [Stein's] presence or ask her to withdraw from the school."

She did not withdraw, of course. Nor did she earn the respect of many male students, some of whom were shocked at her—not Williams's—temerity; they retaliated by calling her "the Battle-Axe." But Gertrude would have been able to cope with Williams, the likes of whom she had already encountered, though perhaps in milder form, throughout Hopkins. Neither his coarseness nor his anti-Semitism nor the lack of support she received from her male colleagues would derail her, even though all of that inevitably took its toll over four years. Rather, it seems more plausible that she rejected medicine when whatever brought her to its study also drove her away, and that, symbolized by the insane at Worcester, was played out in the obstetrical arena.

Medical orthodoxy and the public at large defined women and their sexuality solely in terms of reproduction, and the nervous condition of women, Stein's subject, was frequently associated with some failure of the reproductive system. A champion of the maternal ideal, perhaps all the more vehemently in light of some misgiving, Stein was unquestionably in conflict about maternity, its relation to herself, its connection to illness—a trio of mingled strands that included Milly Stein and those awful days of her protracted death as well as Gertrude's own knotty feelings about sex and sexuality. But she had sorted out much of this, at least overtly; she characterized herself as an unusual woman not just because she was one of the few who studied medicine, but also because her sexuality would not be defined in—or confined by—simple reproductive terms.

Yet skepticism now stalked her. Medical school had eroded her naive confidence, so much so that she would soon demand that the New Woman "relearn the fundamental facts of sex," and would understand that the world of equality she had banked on was only a college-bred illusion. But if gender divided everything from biology to opportunity, what about those insane women at Worcester; were they the outgrowth of a secret sexual malfunction, the female's screaming second self ascendant at last? If so, perhaps the alternative was maternity and motherhood after all.

But not for her.

Confronted with such alternatives, Gertrude Stein would—understandably—engineer an eleventh-hour failure at medical school, and thereby help ensure success.

"WHAT IS all this non-medicated rumble that issues from your quarter," Leo wanted to know in February 1901, sensing disquiet in Baltimore. "Is it representative of a phase or a general condition." Whatever it was, Gertrude continued to charge ahead, making her plans with Adolf Meyer, who now expected her at the Worcester hospital sometime after commencement, in June. Her feelings about medicine notwithstanding, she did not expect to give it up or forgo her degree.

On the day of her exams, when it was clear she faced failure, Stein took ill in the Hopkins hospital gardens. She was terrified. Long afterward, a friend remembered her saying she had failed by the name of two eye nerves; yet in *The Autobiography of Alice B. Toklas,* Stein told of her departure from medical school with the relief and bravado of thirty years. "As the graduation examinations drew near some of her professors were getting angry," she wrote.

> The big men like Halstead [*sic*], Osler etcetera knowing her reputation for original scientific work made the medical examinations merely a matter of form and passed her. But there were others who were not so amiable. Gertrude Stein always laughed, and this was difficult. They would ask her questions although as she said to her friends, it was foolish of them to ask her, when there were so many eager and anxious to answer. However they did question her from time to time and as she said, what could she do, she did not know the answers and they did not believe that she did not know them,

they thought that she did not answer because she did not consider the professors worth answering. It was a difficult situation, as she said, it was impossible to apologize and explain to them that she was so bored she could not remember the things that of course the dullest medical student could not forget. One of the professors said that although all the big men were ready to pass her he intended that she should be given a lesson and he refused to give her a pass mark and so she was not able to take her degree. There was great excitement in the medical school. Her very close friend Marian Walker pleaded with her, she said, but Gertrude Gertrude remember the cause of women, and Gertrude Stein said, you don't know what it is to be bored.

Reading this account, Leo was surprised. "It is all false, though the incidents are partially true."

Edith Hamilton, then headmistress at the Bryn Mawr preparatory school in Baltimore, remembered that Gertrude sharply minded not getting her degree. Most friends had no inkling of trouble underfoot; they took her graduation for granted and wondered whether afterward Gertrude would stay in Baltimore or go elsewhere for postgraduate work. Her failure to receive her degree baffled those closest to her; one friend had bought her a graduation present in sure anticipation of her success. And to a great extent, it surprised her too. When the medical school class of 1901 gathered outdoors one gentle spring afternoon for a graduation photograph, Gertrude quite naturally joined them. Forty-three men and seven women, all neatly dressed, arrayed themselves in several rows around Dr. William Osler, who sat, hands folded, in their center. Clad in a dark skirt and white full blouse, Gertrude stands with her female classmates at the rear of the group as if to say they know their place. She looks almost demure.

When the photograph was printed some six weeks later and a number was attached to each student for purposes of identification, Gertrude received no identifying mark. The key for the photograph bears the note: "Shown in the picture but did not graduate—G. Stein."

Late in the afternoon of June 5, 1901, a faculty committee consisting of "the big men"—Drs. Abel, Halsted, Howell, Mall, Osler, Welch, and Williams—had convened in the dean's office. On the motion of Dr. Osler, it was voted that Miss Gertrude Stein not be recommended for her degree.

TEN DAYS LATER, Gertrude tactfully extricated herself from her obligation to Adolf Meyer. "My dear Dr. Meyer," she wrote, "I was not able to complete the work I had begun under Dr. Mall so I will have to remain in Bal-

"Shown in the picture but did not graduate—G. Stein"
(top row, third from right)

timore another year. This will defer the work that I meant to do with you until the following year when I hope to be able to come to Worcester." The implication was clear: in due course she would have her degree.

Mall himself thought so. On August 14, Mall wrote Lewellys Barker, now at the University of Chicago, that "Miss Stein failed to graduate with us last June. She comes up again next Feb. After that I will do all in my power to make her round out her work started with you. She is you know difficult to manage as she has the [weakness] to [bite] off continually more than she can [swallow]." In October, he again reassured Barker that "Miss Stein will be back and devote the whole year to the brain. I will tell her what you said regarding her work & will urge her to go to Chicago. I know you would like to finish it!!"

By October, however, it seems Gertrude had moved even further away from medicine and her degree.

It seems also that whatever prompted her to abandon medicine helped her, paradoxically, to confront her sexuality and thus ready her for some of the most confounding, painful, and exhilarating experiences she had ever endured, experiences that would permanently alter the direction of her life. Chronicling them in an autobiographical novella, she initially depicted herself as a character in flight; but she was not one seeking escape. Flight represented for her a passage from the failed consolations of science and toward a new definition of her career, her sexuality, indeed her entire life.

The first section of this novella, originally titled "Quod Erat Demonstrandum" and later changed to "Q.E.D.," takes place in the late spring of 1901, the year Gertrude sailed from America during the summer, her failure at Hopkins raw. And like Stein, the fictional protagonist leaves Baltimore for Europe physically tired from "a succession of wearing experiences" and the "disillusionment of recent failures." On board ship she encounters two young women, completely unlike her, whose patrician outlook, sexual experience, and gift for innuendo waken her "long emotional apathy."

Modeled on Mabel Haynes and May Bookstaver, two Bryn Mawr College graduates, these characters were almost literal transcriptions of their counterparts and conformed, more or less, to the brainy bluestocking stereotype Stein associated with their alma mater. They also bore the unmistakable imprint of M. Carey Thomas herself, Bryn Mawr's magisterial and evangelical second president, who ran the college with determination, courage, and a steely grip. A complicated woman, she annoyed many, for instance William James; Bertrand Russell found her easily shocked, and Alfred Hodder, employed by her in 1895, thought she was "in all ways of thought about the conduct of daily life, exceedingly conservative." Doctrinal and dogmatic though she may have been, she was farsighted and intrepid on matters of women's education. Sometimes derided as a "men's college for women" and occasionally called "Jane Hopkins" because its curriculum resembled that of the Baltimore university, Bryn Mawr had been founded in 1885 by Pennsylvania and Baltimore Quakers, but its character was stamped by Thomas herself, first as dean and since 1894 as president.

"So long as men and women are to compete together, and associate together, in their professional life," she said, "women's preparation for the same profession cannot safely differ from men's." The Bryn Mawr woman was welcome to spend four years amid the college's solemn gray Gothic only after passing the Harvard entrance examination or a comparably rigorous Bryn Mawr one. No special students were admitted on contingency: rather, applicants had to be well versed in Greek, Latin, and mathematics. Once enrolled, students lived in a self-enclosed, self-governing community that brooked no instruction in drawing, domestic science, instrumental music, or painting; these subjects reeked of women's seminaries, according to Thomas, and neither inculcated the intellectual ideal nor provided professional training. She encouraged the Bryn Mawr woman to embrace "intellectual renunciation"—her term for scholarship idealized and unencumbered by marriage, family, or secondary pursuits—and to enjoy the fruits of such a life knowing that other women, on whom she could depend, shared these aims.

At Hopkins, Stein had met some of the women inspired by Thomas and influenced by her companion, Mary Mackall Gwinn, head of Bryn Mawr's English department and clandestine lover of Alfred Hodder. Different in temperament from Thomas—and languorous, lovely, tall, and refined—the ethereal Mamie Gwinn was held in awe by the students. She had lived with Thomas for many years at the Deanery, the latter's residence on the Bryn Mawr campus. Their lives were the subject of gossip both at Bryn Mawr and in Baltimore, where Mamie paid a visit to her mother every fortnight, an event that neatly coincided with Mary Garrett's arrival at the Deanery. The Bryn Mawr students were unfazed by all this; gender solidarity invariably meant sexual experimentation as well as shared intellectual experience. And while the students may have speculated about Thomas's two friendships, they doubtless found the existence of sapphic intimacies less remarkable than the rumor that the Byronic Alfred Hodder, a married man with a child, had fallen in love with Gwinn.

In public, Leo Stein said he never heard Hodder speak of a woman, but when Bertrand Russell lectured at Bryn Mawr in 1896 (and his wife, Alys Smith Russell, Carey Thomas's cousin, gave private talks in favor of free love), he found the campus buzzing with Hodder–Gwinn gossip. Unquestionably, Gertrude also heard the rumors from the Bryn Mawr graduates she met at Hopkins Medical School, women including her friends Grace Lounsbery, Mabel Haynes, and Edith Hooker. All had known Gwinn at Bryn Mawr, and whatever they thought of her private life, they shared her staunch confidence in the New Woman: an affluent, unconventional creature of perception and ability, a successful Isabel Archer, who lived life as she saw fit, freewheeling, superior, asserting her rights as a woman and a human being.

And these New Women—Lounsbery, and Bookstaver, and Haynes—would help change Gertrude Stein's life.

Stein was invited to socialize with them in Baltimore, and attend their afternoon teas. Not of their circle, with its secure grace and tony arrogance—Lounsbery, for example, could claim she was related to the Adamses—the uncouth Stein amused them nonetheless. "I found both her and her brother very rough," Grace Lounsbery told Stein's biographer Elizabeth Sprigge. "Not at all well brought up, coming from a pretty rough sort of background. They rather exaggerated their roughness too—as people do if they have any kind of inferiority complex. I remember people coming to pay an informal call on me in Baltimore, and Leo had his dirty shoes up on a couch and didn't get up."

Another of the Bryn Mawr group was May Bookstaver, the special friend of Mabel Haynes. Daughter of a former New York State Supreme Court justice, Henry Bookstaver, the intelligent and appealing Bookstaver was a steadfast advocate of women's suffrage, an active member of the National Woman Suffrage Association who in the first decade of the twentieth century served on the executive board of New York's Women's Political Union. It was to Book-staver that Stein was attracted, even though she knew, or suspected, the liaison between her and Haynes.

Bookstaver was the "American version of the English handsome girl," according to a description in "Q.E.D." A woman of "passions but not of emotions, capable of long-sustained action, incapable of regrets," she seemed self-assured and urbane in matters of the heart; her deceptions were intricate, her intentions obscure, her conversation suave. And she, unlike the cousins in Baltimore, perceived that Gertrude's sense of self was as yet untested, her sense of the unconventional—and of her own sexuality—largely theoretical.

"Q.E.D." begins as a shipboard romance between two dissimilar women whose "pulses were differently timed." Stein cast herself as Adele (perhaps after Adele Oppenheimer), a young Jewish woman—or so her manuscript suggests—"distinctly oriental in type," who possesses "the failing" of her "tribe" (she likes to talk). Adele is also proudly "middle-class," which means affectionate, honest, reasonable, and moderate in all things: "in short, the ideal of affectionate family life, of honorable business methods." But she is not at all middle-class in intellect. As Adele merrily puts it, "I probably have the experience of all apostles, I am rejected by the class whose cause I preach."

But the middle class, Adele concedes, tends to sidestep experience, intellectualizing passion rather than indulging it. Having refrained from physical contact and the wisdom of its secrets, she turns to her provocative shipmate. "I could undertake to be an efficient pupil," she seductively admits, "if it were possible to find an efficient teacher."

During the seafaring days that follow, the intimacy between the two women deepens until Adele begins, in Jamesian fashion, "to see . . . to catch a glimpse" of emotions heretofore unexplored, desires long suppressed. When the ship finally docks in Europe and Adele is reunited with her brother, she sinks almost with relief into the cozy world of "family friendship." But something has been irrevocably roused within her, and it begins to waken more fully once Adele arrives in Spain to be with her brother. Sitting in the courtyard of the Alhambra, "watching the swallows fly in and out of the crevices of the walls, bathing in the soft air filled with the fragrance of oleander and letting the hot sun burn her face and the palms of her hands, losing herself thus in sensuous delight she would murmur again and again 'No it isn't just this, it's something more, something different. I haven't really felt it but I have caught a glimpse.' "

A few days later, on a hilltop above Granada, the rippling palms of the city stretched out below, Adele watches a young Spanish woman climb toward her. Silently the woman sits beside Adele; then wordlessly they part.

Adele knows that they have communicated that which passes beyond understanding. The glimpse into this uncharted female world is now an epiphany, Adele realizes, stretching luxuriously on the hard ground and reading, with dawning comprehension, of Beatrice in Dante's *Vita Nuova*.

"OH WHY AREN'T YOU... with us it was so foolish of you to stay in that awful American place when you could be here," Gertrude wrote Mabel Weeks rapturously in July 1901.

Since January, Gertrude and Leo had been planning a summer together in Spain and North Africa; letters had gone back and forth about the renting of bicycles and whether or not to visit Seville. Weeks had been invited, but she had regretfully declined, so it was only Gertrude and Leo, contented and comfortable in each other's presence. So Gertrude portrayed her fictional sister and brother in "Q.E.D.," placing them on a hillside in Tangier, "agreeing and disagreeing in endless discussion with an intensity of interest that long familiarity had in no way diminished, varied by indulgence in elaborate foolishness and reminiscent jokes."

"There is no doubt the South . . . is the land of me," Gertrude wrote Mabel. "I love the Moors so much it is almost a pain. . . . The Alhambra, and the sunshine and the brown legs and the smells are all mine all mine."

The sun-burned landscape reminded both her and Leo of California. "It really does most wonderfully. And it is beautiful. Such glorious brown hillsides, such splendid jagged [mountains] that do *not* look like picture books," Leo wrote. They left their commodious hotel in Granada for Madrid, where the pictures in the Prado were being moved and the El Grecos had not yet been rehung. They went to the outdoor opera and heard Puccini. Sleepless and tired, they canceled their visit to Toledo and pressed on toward France. They slept an entire day in Bordeaux and arrived at their Paris hotel on August 29.

Etta Cone had come to the city only an hour before, accompanied by her cousin Hortense Guggenheimer and another woman, Harriet Clark. They had been touring Europe since May, when Leo met their ship in the port of Naples, surprising them as they disembarked. Now reunited in Paris, the friends on holiday walked along the rue de la Victoire and looked in the little shops for Japanese prints, took in Molière at the Théâtre Français, and ate with relish at the Boeuf à la Mode. If Gertrude's thoughts were elsewhere, Etta Cone didn't notice. To her, Gertrude seemed lively as ever. Neither the recent debacle at Hopkins nor Gertrude's feelings about Bookstaver were mentioned in Etta's diary of her trip.

Indeed, although she revered Leo—his talk, she said, was "far more interesting & full[y] as exhaustive as Baedeker"—Etta was buoyed by Gertrude's swinging confidence and easy dominance. Gertrude thought nothing of rout-ing her from bed when she decided Etta had lounged long enough, or of charging into Etta's room whenever she pleased to talk about French literature. Ebullient, she was at home wherever she went, at the dressmaker's or the Panthéon. She and Etta strolled along the rue de la Paix, peeking into the jewelry shops before scouring the city for more Japanese prints—Etta admitted she too "got the fever"—and ambled on the rue Lafitte before taking a carriage and riding through the Bois de Boulogne. At night after dinner they amused themselves with something Etta called a "writing bee" in her hotel room; then they would sit and chat past midnight.

"Talked with Gertrude on her pet subject of human intercourse of the sexes," Etta recorded in her travel diary. "She is truly interesting." When Etta and Hortense left Paris for London at the end of September, Etta wrote at length of Gertrude and Leo; to her, each was—and would remain—exceptional.

Gertrude stayed on in Paris to bid Leo farewell before he returned to Florence, and then she joined Etta's party in Southampton for the voyage home. Aboard ship once again, with nothing but the vast blue waters extending in all directions and the long days ahead, she may well have recalled the shipboard experience of three months before. And perhaps she initiated Etta into some of what she had glimpsed, for Etta's last entry in her travel diary suggests that new sensations crowned these final days of her first European tour. On October 8, 1901, somewhere mid-ocean, on a dazzlingly clear day, Etta remarked that she spent most of it below in a *"beautiful state of mind* but one which brought out the most exquisite qualities of Gertrude." In a different ink—and, it seems, at a later time—she added a sad afterthought: "My vanity." She wrote nothing more.

AFTER LEO HAD LEFT Baltimore in the spring of 1900, Gertrude gave up their apartment on East Biddle and moved to East Eager, another street of identical red-brick houses with spotless white stoops and doors. She and her new roommate, Emma Lootz, were tended by the faithful Lena Lebender, who, even in Leo's absence, continued to supply both advice and food. Leo had been master on East Biddle, said Emma Lootz, but now Gertrude exercised complete control; "everything was arranged to her liking."

Generally, the women medical students at Hopkins had been disappointed by Gertrude's recent failure. "We women felt pretty badly but Gertrude did not seem to care a rap," recalled Florence Sabin. "She said she would have had more respect for those who had passed her if they too had given her failing marks for she didn't know any more about those subjects than the ones in which she had actually failed. Also she said that she didn't care a rap about the degree."

When Gertrude returned from Europe in the fall of 1901, she listed herself as a nurse, not a student, in the Baltimore city directory. She planned to resume research work on the brain, just as Franklin Mall supposed. Dorothy Reed Mendenhall observed that because of his interest in Gertrude's work, the faculty had been persuaded to give Stein another chance. "Dr. Mall set her a problem similar to one Dr. [Florence] Sabin had completed successfully in her fourth year. This was the sectioning of [a] . . . human brain and its reconstruction, and a study of the development of the centers in the brain and the tracts leading from them. She worked on it for weeks and finally handed her reconstruction to Dr. Mall in the hope that it would be credited to her instead of obstetrics and allow her to graduate."

In November, Stein was working on the project originally begun with Lewellys Barker. Franklin Mall assured him that "Miss Stein is diligent[ly] at work with her model. She must have the brain of a child 6 months old in order to connect her work with Miss Sabins! Can you not supply it? I told her that I would write to you asking for material." Had Mall's disappointment with Stein's work occurred in the way some of Gertrude's colleagues remembered, the disappointment was short-lived. Or premature.

Florence Sabin, in fact, remembered that "Dr. Mall, who liked independence, and thought [Stein's] attitude of not caring for the degree showed a good spirit, welcomed her back." Yet disillusioned in profound ways and obviously distracted, her personal life demanding more concentrated attention than she could share with brain anatomy, she began to lose interest in her research. By this time she probably had realized she would not take her medical degree after all, and perhaps she rationalized she hadn't wanted it for some time, which was no doubt true. As Mabel Weeks presciently observed, "Gertrude successfully integrated her character around her limitations." For as faulty and self-serving as her memory of events may frequently have been, in retrospect she knew how liberating her failure was.

She didn't finish her work until the following spring. In January 1902 she mailed the second part of her neurology paper to Barker in Chicago, and although he approved of the work, he advised that when the paper was finally ready, "you might go over it once with special reference to the literary form." Tactfully, he added that she might enlist some help: "When we are so close to our own work as we necessarily are, points of form will elude us and a second head is an aid."

But when Barker received Stein's completed manuscript, it was accompanied by a letter, presumably from a colleague of Barker's, that emphatically opposed its publication. "I do not believe she has yet measured up to your hopes," the unnamed colleague told Barker. "Such a paper . . . is worthy of serious reflection before acceptance. . . . It seems to me unfinished, & lacking in constructive thought. The materials for building are corrected &

BOTH ONES THAT QUITE ENOUGH ARE KNOWING *151*

ready for use but only here & there can one see a bit of the new structure. I am disappointed to find the author's effort discontinued just at the point where she seems to have completed preparation to begin the serious work of construction from the data before us." After some technical points, the writer of the letter concluded that "Professor Mall, Dr. Sabin, and myself are unfavorably impressed with the paper as I have here explained; but after all your opinion will be of most value."

The paper was not published. According to Florence Sabin, the baby's brain Gertrude had been using was so badly bent one could make nothing of the model, and Dr. Mall chucked the whole thing into the wastebasket. By that time, Gertrude really couldn't have cared less.

IN THE FALL OF 1901, when Gertrude treated Alfred Hodder to her views of the New Woman, she was spending less time at Hopkins and more in New York City, where May Bookstaver was then living. But the romance was foundering. Forced to recognize May's ongoing relationship with Mabel Haynes, Gertrude faced a moral dilemma that, at least in terms of her fictional account, disturbed her as much as having fallen in love with a woman. Struggling between "revulsion and respect," and attempting to relinquish her "established convictions," the protagonist in "Q.E.D." confronts her own sexuality while embroiled in a complicated triangle that upsets her scruples but doesn't inhibit her actions. As she says, "The game was worth the candle."

When in New York, Gertrude usually stayed at Solomon Stein's residence, where both Fred and Bird were living. The family was still close; the differences that would devastate their relationship were unforeseen. And her New York cousins were hospitable, welcoming not only Gertrude but William Jerome and his cronies at their brownstone. It was at one dinner, shortly after New Year's 1902, that Gertrude again saw Alfred Hodder.

Once more, their conversation turned to *The New Americans* and, with it, the relation between the sexes. Women were generally more intelligent than men, Stein had decided, even though she admitted, according to Hodder, that the average man had a practical "faculty," which women lacked, for knowing what to do and doing it. Indeed, she said, she preferred to depend on the average man in the event of an emergency than on the cleverest woman. Hodder countered that perhaps Miss Stein's experience at Hopkins suggested such a conclusion, as the best class of men may not have gone in for medicine. Gertrude vehemently disagreed. And then, to his horror, she drew conclusions he neither expected nor much liked.

A woman paid so heavily for being born female, Hodder heard Stein say, that no man could ever compensate her for the injustices she inevitably endured. Woman therefore had the right, Stein continued, to take whatever she could and hold tight. "This was not an epigram," Hodder exclaimed in amazement; "it was a confession of faith. Seemingly whether a girl is born 'superior' or 'inferior' "—he repeated Stein's argument—"she is born with a moral 'pull.' "

Astounded by such audacity, Hodder relayed the argument to Mamie Gwinn. "I suggested that the same logic would apply, and is applied, by socialists, to the case of men born weakly or stupid or incompetent: nothing can ever make it up to them; and to the case of men born of an inferior race. But this she thought outrageous. Of course the interesting point is her testimony both deliberate and inadvertent that the girls feel [beaten] and unhappier than if they had not tried, and are resolved with a brutal explicitness to exploit any one they can."

The next time they met, Gertrude gave Hodder a copy of an essay she had written that would illustrate her views. Evidently it was "Degeneration in American Women," composed sometime after October 1901 and possibly intended as a lecture for one of Bird's women's groups, now focused on child-rearing; the passion, however, was personal.

Stein was responding to a recent article, "The Increasing Sterility of American Women," published in the *Journal of the American Medical Association*. Its author, Dr. George H. Engelmann, upbraided those women who had in one way or another avoided childbearing; particularly reprehensible were educated women who practiced "voluntary sterility," or birth control. (Low birthrate was a matter of some concern for the Anglo-Saxon nativists worried about survival amid an increasingly immigrant population.) Having determined that more than twenty percent of American women were childless, Engelmann was none too happy.

Neither, it seems, was Gertrude Stein.

The subject of her rejoinder was essentially obstetrics in another form. Inveighing against so-called voluntary sterility, which, as Stein put it, "is of course all due to moral causes," she launched a pro-maternity platform. She agreed with Engelmann: women simply weren't having enough babies, and the worst offenders were those college-educated women who either delayed childbearing or ignored it altogether.

Implicitly referring to her own experience at medical school, from which she evidently still reeled, Stein argued that the modern American woman confuses "her education her cleverness and intelligence for effective capacity for the work of the world." Little aware that she is, however, really powerless, this woman "also finds herself the superior because on account of the characteristic chivalry of the American man the code of morality which her sheltered life has developed seems adequate for the real business of life and it is only rarely that she learns that she never actually comes in contact with the real business and that when she does the male code is the only possible one." She had said as much to Hodder.

But if the modern woman was excluded from the real business of life, Stein's solution—unlike Carey Thomas's or Mamie Gwinn's—was not to support advanced educational opportunities or demand equal treatment. Rather, Stein sent women home. Women would never be happy, she argued, until they learned that childbearing was their best and only business. But this was not the male medical orthodoxy it appeared, even if its echo was clearly heard. For Stein, maternity was the one area where women could not be outclassed by men. And so they should embrace it.

"Don't talk to me about wife & mother & whole end of woman!" exclaimed Marian Walker Williams, a Hopkins classmate of Stein's, recently married and still studying medicine. "I wouldn't have believed you capable of it except that you are the victim of moods which at times resemble fixed ideas."

But maternity is a matter of the "normal," Stein insisted, something like eating or drinking, and "the exercise of ones normal functions of living, walking, talking, thinking, being, eating and drinking is an endless joy of a healthy human being." (Mamie Gwinn, on reading Gertrude's article, said Stein's mother must have been a nervous invalid.)

Was Stein, as Gwinn surmised, trying to neutralize the image of Milly with a paean to the healthy, normal woman, sexually unremarkable and beyond society's reproach? Had the inmates of the Worcester hospital unleashed terrible memories and haunting fears? Or was this an affirmation of her mother and of her feelings toward her?

And what of Gertrude herself? Did she see herself as part of the natural order she extolled, or as a special kind of "degenerate," which, in literal context, was the word she used to refer to those unreproductive women responsible for a declining birthrate? Surely another meaning of the word hovered near, for the righteous sexologists of the day had termed homosexuality "degenerate." Was Stein then, paradoxically, exempting herself from the domestic virtues she prescribed by proclaiming, however implicitly, her difference? Was she then redefining "degeneracy" to suit her ends, shifting the word's meaning in this, an early verbal slide?

Obviously, her paper didn't answer these questions directly, but in its shrewd circumventions it helps reveal her thinking. "Of course it is not meant that there are not a few women in every generation who are exceptions to this rule," Stein wrote with bravura, "but these exceptions are too rare to make it necessary to subvert the order of things in their behalf and besides if their need for some other method of expression is a real need there is very little doubt but that the opportunity of expression will be open to them."

It almost seemed as if the exceptional woman—the lesbian, in fact— proved the rule. And so it was the unprocreative heterosexual female who, socially and morally remiss, failed in her duty. Stein, then, straddled two worlds: she was a champion of the "normal" who could afford to ignore its conventions. A stopgap solution, it sufficed temporarily and, if rickety, was sturdy enough psychologically to traverse the contradictions she experienced. For she was changing her life.

When giving the essay to Hodder, Stein explained that she had hated to have to write as she had, but felt forced—so Hodder told Mamie Gwinn— "sentence by sentence to believe what is practically committing mental suicide so far as her whole natural pose is concerned." Stein wanted him to read the paper anyway. Perhaps she even supposed—or hoped—he would pass it on to Gwinn. He did. Gwinn was appalled.

Her response didn't surprise Hodder, but Leo's perplexed him. He took no active part in his sister's conversion, Hodder said of the absent brother; "he has backed her up from start to finish in her wish to be like a man; only he has told her frankly what a man is like, has told her his own life as he has lived it."

·THREE·

SPEECH
IS THE TWIN
OF MY VISION

9
GILDED CAGES

Bernhard Berenson at I Tatti

We shall go on to consider how you may become a perfect man. . . . To this end you must read books. . . . Whatever book you read remember you are only to grasp the idea, accurate analytical knowledge will not be necessary. Aim to surround yourself with an atmosphere of leisure, strive to make home happy. . . . You must be able to sympathize with your noble wife and to this end all your knowledge should be acquired. Ah, me, you are a grand creature! Free as the wind, born to become woman's helpmate. So you must be noble. Remember, as I before said, you are free, but my dears, freedom consists in your being protected. . . . See how happy is the little canary bird in its gilded cage! I *defy* anyone to say it is not free. Were the door opened, some ravenous cat would eat it, or it would starve to death, or the cold would freeze it, while now it is fed and loved. . . . Let its life be an example to you.

MAY BOOKSTAVER AND GRACE LOUNSBERY, "KING'S PASTURES"

Of all the great Italian cities, I have happiest memories of Florence.

HECTOR BERLIOZ, *MEMOIRS*

LCOHOL AND STRYCHNIA: working men lived on them and had breakdowns; men not living on them were not working—"not at least so as to keep up with the procession." Thus Alfred Hodder, dead in 1907 at age forty, had characterized his male friends.

Leo Stein took no stimulants. His goad—or balm—would lie in Tuscany. He had headed to Italy alone upon leaving Paris in late September 1900, shortly after parting from Gertrude, then bound for home and her fourth year as a medical student. Envisioning his own year of study, he admitted his interests were varied and a bit undisciplined. But art, poetry, and aesthetics excited him most, and as far as these went, he wanted to concentrate on Mantegna and, after he left Italy, maybe a series of aesthetic essays on Dürer.

As for literary theories, he had nothing much in mind; someday, though, he would like to write an interpretation of *Hamlet*. It was an ironic foreshadowing.

Leo arrived in Florence the first week of October and settled in two rooms on the north bank of the Arno, in a house owned by a half-paralyzed expatriate Englishwoman who had lived in Italy for thirty years. His rooms at 20 Lungarno Acciaioli were big enough for pacing, despite the clutter of majolica, porcelains, pampas grass, peacock feathers, chairs, tables (seven), mirrors, and a couch. Hanging on the walls and scattered on the tables and mantels were reproductions: Rubens, Van Dyck, Raphael, Correggio, Ghirlandaio; portraits, landscapes, interiors, still lifes, religious images; nothing neglected, and so excessive that he immediately got rid of twenty or so and then, whenever the landlady wasn't looking, gently eased out the rest. But there was that view. From his windows he could see to the southeast, beyond the Ponte Vecchio, the crisp green-and-white façade of the Church of San Miniato al Monte, perched in Romanesque splendor above the city. And the location was perfect: only steps from the magnificent Uffizi galleries and not far, in the opposite direction, from the Brancacci Chapel at Santa Maria del Carmine, where he would look at Masaccio's powerful frescoes for hours. These were always his favorite among Florentine treasures.

Down the street was a fencing academy, where he took lessons for exercise, and in the neighborhood were more than half a dozen places for afternoon chocolate or ice. Yet Florence had none of the "confiding charm" Leo associated with Venice. "Florence is so eminently serious minded so erect in carriage and severe in temper that I feel it to be almost distant," he wrote Gertrude. Quickly, however, he established a routine. At eight each morning the housemaid, Assunta, brought water for his bath, and half an hour later she served dark Italian coffee with warm bread and butter. He spent mornings in galleries or churches when they weren't too cold, and took Italian lessons and fenced in the late afternoons. He was pleased and calm and soon confident enough to report to Gertrude that his dreams churned less; he felt more patient, quieter. "The mere fact that I can quietly sit down and write a letter now is symptomatic and I find the same thing reading and thinking. Of course it merely means a relative change but the periods of restless impatient ineffectiveness are it seems to me growing proportionately less." He was reading *Tom Jones* and Gibbon again. "How I envy those eighteenth century chaps their quiet progression with plenty of time to walk around the block even when there's a short cut across lots," he said. "Well I shall take my time now and if nothing comes out of it well and good."

And he wasn't lonely. Hutchins Hapgood had given him a letter of introduction to the art critic and connoisseur Bernhard Berenson, describing Leo as one of those friends with whom he "exchanged the quick-coming impressions of daily life in New York." Stein had been eager for the introduction. By age thirty-five, Berenson had established himself as a critic of considerable stature, publishing in rapid succession, along with his contributions to *The Nation,* five books on the art of the Italian Renaissance. In Europe almost without break since the spring of 1887, the Harvard graduate had initially been backed by a group of Boston patrons, most notably Isabella Stewart Gardner, who, thinking it would last only a year, sponsored his trip in Europe. But he did not return to the United States for seven years, and when he did, he reveled not in the fiction he had been sent to write but in his *Venetian Painters of the Renaissance.*

The book was essential to BB's transformation. Known familiarly only by his initials (and as Bernard, not Bernhard, after World War I), the Lithuanian-born Jew reared in Boston's North End had rapidly become an expatriate of exquisite taste and burning ambition, a dapper young art critic with precise manners, witty, authoritative, and taken with himself. Diminutive, well-dressed, his beard always cropped to a point, Berenson had been influenced, like Leo Stein, by Giovanni Morelli's so-called scientific approach to attribution, which combined disciplined observation, scrupulous comparison of works of art, systematic study of form—especially anatomy—and the avoidance of abstract theory, philosophy, and mysticism. This purportedly objective study of painting appealed to Berenson, who called on the master in 1890. Shortly after their meeting he announced he would dedicate his "entire activity, his entire life, to connoisseurship," and thereupon made a pact with himself, he later liked to believe, to devote himself "to learning, to distinguish between the authentic works of an Italian painter of the fifteenth or sixteenth century, and those ascribed to them [*sic*]."

With painstaking attention to detail, Berenson's plan, as Mary Smith Costelloe explained, was to "classify Italian paintings with the accuracy of a botanist in classifying plants." Costelloe was Berenson's sharp-tongued champion, his collaborator, and his lover. American-born, friend to Walt Whitman, cousin to M. Carey Thomas, and daughter of Quaker feminist Hannah Smith, Mary Costelloe possessed a "kind of vital force," said a cousin; she was like Goethe in temperament, and needed men to fall in love with her. Tall and radiant, she had mesmerized the women of Baltimore when she delivered a risqué talk, "The Duty of Self-Development," to friends and relatives. Speaking with a slight lisp and wearing a dress of emerald-green velvet, the young Mary Smith unabashedly asserted that one's highest duties were liberty and self-fulfillment. Then she took her own advice. When she met the Anglo-Irish barrister Frank Costelloe in the United States, she fell immediately in love, dropped out of the Harvard Annex, became a Catholic, and moved to England to marry him.

She met Berenson in England, where her parents had resettled to keep an eye on their impetuous daughter—to no avail. It wasn't long before Mary Costelloe left her husband and two children to take up with the charismatic aesthete, traveling with him to inspect various works of art and in 1894 publishing a revised catalogue of the Italian paintings at Hampton Court. This was two years after she had legally separated from Frank Costelloe, who meantime won custody of their children. By then she and Berenson were renting adjacent villas on the steep road from Florence to Fiesole, ostensibly so they could work together on the books that made his reputation. They married in December 1900, a year after Costelloe unexpectedly died; Mary's mother kept her children.

Mary's affairs were of great concern to her family, especially to her sister Alys and Alys's husband, Bertrand Russell, as well as to the many friends who discussed her at length; even Leo Stein, almost as soon as he'd settled in Florence, sent back to America his opinion of Mary. He wasn't particularly impressed, he wrote Alfred Hodder, and he told Gertrude that at first blush Mary seemed but Berenson's intellectual parrot. For her part, she considered Leo a bore who at least didn't try to pick her and BB's brains and steal their work, but slowly she grew accustomed to her husband's gangling new friend and admitted to her anti-Semitic mother that at times she rather liked him.

Leo was cool at first also toward Berenson, whose egotism—what Leo called that "colossal I sticking in him"—swelled to a veritable "persecution mania." "He says that almost all recent writers of Italian art were not only fools but thieves as well, for they take everything that they have from him and almost never acknowledge their indebtedness." And this was Berenson on most subjects. Speaking of Yiddish literature, he noted that many old Lithuanian myths ought to be saved. "But there's no one can do it except myself and I'm forgetting them," he reportedly told Leo. "Why he should suppose that the preservation of the myths of a large community should be dependent on his sole activity rather puzzles me," Leo observed afterward, "but I didn't ask for an explanation."

Berenson and Stein did warm to each other, and after a few meetings, Stein conceded that BB grated less. "It's like a cold bath," he explained to Mabel Weeks. "After the first plunge you don't mind it." In fact, Berenson intrigued precisely because he was intent on pushing beyond Morelli toward a psychological criticism of art informed, as Mary Costelloe put it, by "the laws which govern the development of an artist, *the laws of habit and attention.*" His *Florentine Painters of the Renaissance* (1896), influenced by William James's *Principles of Psychology,* was after a theory of aesthetic pleasure, which Berenson sought to link to the perception of art. The visual enjoyment of art, he claimed, is actually derived through the sense of touch. Because "sight alone gives us no accurate sense of the third dimension," it must be "helped

Mary Smith Costelloe
Berenson

on by muscular sensations of movement, [which] teaches us to appreciate depth, the third dimension, both in objects and in space." Since painting is confined to two dimensions, Berenson further reasoned,

> the painter must . . . do consciously what we all do consciously—construct his third dimension . . . by giving tactile values to retinal impressions. His first business, therefore, is to rouse the tactile sense, for I must have the illusion of being able to touch a figure . . . before I shall take it for granted as real, and let it affect me lastingly.

It is, Berenson concluded, these "tactile values" that link the art of painting and the pleasure it affords.

Such an amalgam of psychology, empiricism, and audacity helped him achieve the recognition he craved, allying him with the realistic school of art criticism, which also interested Leo, although he felt that Berenson's scheme depended too much on psychological theories, about whose validity Leo had "serious doubts." And he may have surmised over time that Berenson's tactile values offered no insight into abstract art. Nonetheless, from evening to the wee hours of the morning, the new friends discussed Berenson's theory, and BB, who basked in such attention, decided Leo was good for what ailed him. "I got a violent neuralgia . . ." he told Mary, "which left late in the evening in an exciting discussion with Stein. It was about tactile values & . . . it was such a pleasure to discuss with a man who thinks so clearly & knows what I mean."

They saw each other at least once a week, when Leo visited I Tatti, the spectacular rural villa the Berensons were renovating, nestled below the tiny village of Settignano, northeast of Florence. Commanding magnificent views of the nearby valley—glistening olive trees and golden fields speckled, in the summer, with scarlet poppies—the house stood three stories high, its buff-colored exterior ringed by dark feathery cypresses, and was surrounded by a walled garden boasting lilies of the valley, anemones, tulips, roses, heliotropes, and marvelous carnations, pink, red, yellow, white, all set among fiercely manicured lemon trees that grew in pots. Within, the Berensons painted each huge room in a single color: the dining room blue-green, the drawing room yellow, the huge library blue. Aubusson rugs of deep hue spread over the red-and-straw-colored tiles, the walls were hung with Italian Renaissance art, and affluent comfort radiated from every well-appointed object.

But it wasn't stuffy. Members of the Anglo-American colony in Florence congregated there, especially on Saturdays, to gossip while a young pianist, Miss Cracoft, played Bach. That winter, a typical group included, along with Stein, the red-faced Maud Cruttwell, an Englishwoman who "wrote the book on Signorelli & is doing the orthodox thing with Mantegna"; Alfred Benn, "a middle aged man who has written a Greek philosophy & is now writing on Rationalism in the XIX century"; and Mary E. Lowndes, who, Leo told Gertrude, appeared "intelligent and very decent. She translated Höffding's psychology and writes reviews for *Mind* and philosophical literary things." Although Leo enjoyed the musicales, overall the " 'gang' as much as I have seen of them doesn't rouse my enthusiasm." The women, he said, were the kind one read about: distinctly outré, a kind of female advance guard of culture, what Mary Berenson called "Virgins of the Hills." Mainly, they were lesbians.

With its indifference to the private lives of its foreign residents, Florence was a congenial place for those who did not conform to stereotypes about gender or sex. Similarly, the Berensons were largely open-minded about sexual practices—although Bernhard balked at the subject of free love, at least when Mary exercised it. Entertained, however, by the affairs of others, Mary and Bernhard shrugged at homosexuality. "Indeed," Mary once reflected, "I sometimes wish I had encouraged my own tendencies that way."

Taking pride in their enlightened unconventionality, the Berensons and their circle condescended to those unworldly individuals ignorant of the wide range of sexual behavior. One night when a guest announced she would write a novel with no male characters in it, "only she was afraid it would resuscitate Mrs. Grundy from her grave to protest," another meekly responded, "Why you can't have anything very shocking in a novel that has only women in it. There is nothing they can do." The rest of the company, Mary noted with satisfaction, "dissolved into uncontrollable laughter."

The Berensons demanded from their friends that they share their intellectual or aesthetic preoccupations and, especially, be *simpatici.* Sex was a private matter, though good material for gossip. After meeting Alfred Hodder, the Byron of Bryn Mawr, Mary granted him her highest praise: "He seemed to us 'our kind.' "

Liberal within, this circle was regarded by some as precious, complacent, snobbish—criticisms Leo Stein would himself make in time. But during his first year in Florence he was so animated by Berenson's friendship and so comfortable with this group that he joked to Mabel Weeks that "there will be no good books on art till Berenson and I shall have written them."

IN DECEMBER, with an inky rain slicking the narrow streets, Florence turned clammy and chill. Stores were stocked with fur-lined cloaks and gloves, ulsters, and heavy woolen underwear. On Fridays, said Leo, the piazza della Signoria looked like market day in Moscow, and weather was the premier topic of conversation. Leo practiced Italian by conjugating the cold with friends.

When the iron stoves placed in the long galleries of the Uffizi spewed so little heat he couldn't stay more than an hour at a time, he began to dream of Greece and, back in his warm rooms, burrowed into Murger, Zola, and Richardson's *Clarissa.* He continued to hike up to I Tatti to see Berenson, who, early the next spring, insisted Leo stay for a week while Mary went to visit her family in England. But despite Berenson's company—or perhaps because of it—Leo grew claustrophobic in Florence. In April he escaped to Rome to meet Mabel Weeks (Greece was apparently out of the question) and then in May rushed off to Naples to introduce Etta Cone and her friends Hortense Guggenheimer and Harriet Clark to the wonders of Europe.

Hortense Guggenheimer, it was said, had come to Italy partly in his pursuit, but Leo's gallantry didn't extend beyond occasional games of jackstraws or expert direction through crowded Roman streets and the Vatican. He accompanied the women to Florence, where he guided them through gallery after resplendent gallery, pointing out his favorite paintings and calling their attention to matters of composition and style. "It is marvelous to me to find him absolutely well groomed in every possible field of thought," exclaimed Etta, now irrecoverably launched onto her own career of studying and collecting art. Yet the accommodating young intellectual who expertly introduced his friends to the riches of Florence nursed a secret so humiliating he thought of himself as a "Hyde unacknowledged by the impotent Jekyll."

He had felt this way since boyhood. When attracted to female classmates, especially one with a brightly arched instep, he had been too afraid to approach them or to express his emotions in any but the most roundabout, unreadable way. Mostly, he subsided into autoerotic daydream, where, as he put it, "the full tide of desired contact was made by fantasy." But it was not masturbation that shamed him in adulthood; instead, it was a fetish he neither understood nor condoned that harnessed this shy, appealing man to a mortifying sense of his own private deformity.

Later, when psychoanalytic and Freudian terms entered his world, Stein spent many years combing through the childhood feelings that may have accounted for his fetish. As a youth he had been confused by sexual urges he couldn't control, linking them to the fear of castration gleaned from early childhood memories. These, in conjunction with his attraction for—and repulsion from—his mother's body constructed the conditions of a fetish, or what Freud called a "permanent memorial" to the horror of castration. Leo recalled, moreover, being both intrigued and repulsed by his mother's physicality: she "had very little feet, she was of course a very little person." So in this almost classic case, to allay his fears he developed a talisman in the foot or shoe, which became the fetishized object.

Milly Stein's last pregnancy and her prolonged invalidism must have confounded young Leo further with a throng of puzzling questions about why his mother's body was subject to such demonstrable, frightful change. And then there was the inchoate anger of a boy always on the verge of losing his mother to a domineering father, a man seldom pleased, at least in Leo's recollection, with his delicate young son.

Did an adult fetish provide symbolic protection for an anxious son threatened by the fear of castration, and grant him the symbolic power he felt he lacked? Perhaps. As Leo reflected, "The shoe or foot could not have the sexual value that it has as a fetish if it were taken for what it really is. There must in the case of every fetish be carried over to it values which an impartial acquaintance with the object would not give to it. The same is true of symbols of all kinds. These also have that kind of residual value." But the causes for his inventing something—virtually a substitute penis—are of course a matter of speculation. During an intense period of self-analysis, however, Leo himself entertained a similar notion, suggesting that "an exaggerated identification of the other sex" led him to endow it "with the potency—Fetishism."

Apprehensive about his masculine identity and troubled by the female body (more desirable, to him, when clothed), Leo associated women with power. "For me sex meant female as though males were not really sex objects and it had for me always an element of menace," he observed. He was petrified by women, as he realized when analyzing his own problems:

> I defended myself so completely against women that I could not even pay them conventional compliments, nor admit their virtues except in the most matter of fact way. I could not flirt nor flatter. I preferred except when some interesting woman forced the pace the company of men. On the other hand the fantasy sexual experiences were always directed toward women—there were none homosexual though at moments during the analysis I would find myself having intense homosexual feelings in the presence of men—once almost disconcertingly when I happened to look down & noticed the shoes of a young man with whom I was talking who had small feet & rather feminine shoes—and others were habitually and extravagantly masochistic and for many years concentrated on the shoe fetishism. This was true even in actual fact with prostitutes but even this has the quality of fantasy since it doesn't need to be accepted as a real relation. I noticed that I would revolt as soon as there was any assumption on her part that my attitude of submission was real.

Superiority was masculine; Leo feared the opposite, that he was not masculine enough, authoritative enough, powerful enough, and that his wishes and inclinations were in fact feminine. "Sexual identification with woman so strong," he jotted in one of his notebooks, "that there would have been complete loss in her if the self defense had not been so strong." Leo eventually would recognize that identifying sex with the feminine meant "terrific sex masochism in fantasy." Publicly, however, he belittled the significance of sex, regarding it as "not real. . . . Therefore women were, in an imaginative sense, not felt as *people*."

However persuasive or provocative, the insights of psychoanalysis took Leo only so far in the unraveling of a complicated fantasy life. And as invaluable as he found these insights and as much as he respected Freud, he also regarded both the terminology of psychoanalysis and its practice insufficient in many ways. His own attempts at analysis proved unsuccessful: "I must confess that when on several occasions I tried to be analyzed, I found the absurdity of accepting the analyst's assumed role (when he was obviously as full of prejudices and self-importance as over-ripe cheese is full of maggots) to be utterly incompatible with the all-necessary transference."

Likewise, he found some of the bases of Freudian thought problematic.

"I have never been content to accept the Freudian *normality*," he observed to a friend. In 1927, calling its "interpretation of homo and heterosexuality . . . too impossibly naive," he said that "the psychoanalyst's norm is like that of the economist who accepts the current capitalist society as a normal society. This society takes as its rule of life the *Sermon on the Mount* and the *Preamble to the Declaration of Independence,* and it imprisons and persecutes whosoever tries to live in accord with its own declared doctrines. So the psychoanalyst would make the patient accept a healthy view of sex and personal relations, but practically tries to force him to accept as normal the compromises that are current in the society in which the analyst lives."

A narrowly focused psychoanalysis did not necessarily grasp what such friends as Alfred Hodder almost understood: the social world they inhabited cast men into rigid and often inappropriate roles that, ironically, reinforced the doubts they harbored about themselves and their heterosexual identity. Some men took drugs; others were violent; some—Leo Stein—lapsed into neurasthenia, taking refuge in a fetish that enabled sexual performance.

But whatever his fetish temporarily granted him—assurance of his masculinity even as he unconsciously wished to be something else—it also robbed him of his self-respect, compounding his sense that he was, indeed, inferior in all ways. He anguished for many years, humiliated, disgusted, certain he was playing double. "I must simply recognize that fear of what others thought of me & inability to buck up against this had reduced me to finding more satisfaction in masturbating with a woman's shoe than in all the social, intellectual activities which I pretended were my real interests."

LEO AND GERTRUDE wrote each other regularly, sometimes once a week, generally twice a month. Neither assumed they would be apart for very long, perhaps not more than a year; the length of the separation depended on what Gertrude decided to do after medical school and whether Leo would accompany her or stay where he was.

Gertrude once boasted that Leo told her everything, even about those ships in the night, as she called his brief amorous affairs. He later denied this, saying they never exchanged intimate confidences. But such a denial was probably an exaggeration born of years of bitterness. Their discussions that summer probably included Gertrude's revelation about her own sexuality and her feelings for May Bookstaver. And certainly Leo's year in Florence may have disabused him of many of his earlier assumptions that the "Virgins of the Hills" were a bunch of "freaks." That, his own sexuality, and the fact he and Gertrude agreed that relations between women and men were too often founded on loveless inequality would have made him a responsive listener, one perhaps even envious of his sister's ability to explore avenues closed to him.

As soon as he and Gertrude parted in Paris in the fall of 1901, after their trip to Spain and North Africa, Leo longed for the camaraderie of the past months. So he swaggered. "I had a perfect devil of a time the night you left," he boasted. "It cost me a hundred and fifty francs for champagne cabs and the lady between 12 midnight and six o'clock but it was more than worth the price of admission."

Once back in Italy, Leo hastened to I Tatti, where he and the Berensons sat through a silver twilight speaking of love. Leo admitted he'd never been in love himself but adamantly maintained, in spite of Mary's protest, that "the world has outgrown chivalry along with feudalism & all that rot." He was looking for a "modern" partnership: the "equality-life-as-it-is idea," Mary Berenson said. She accepted this yet couldn't understand why her friend Gladys Deacon, then being courted by an Italian count, preferred the distant attentions, for the moment, of a Leo Stein. The count had sent a huge bouquet, and Leo but a postcard of flowers.

Italy, however, did not bring Leo back to his desk. Still hoping that Florence would focus his attention and curtail his physical restlessness, he inevitably found its diversions irresistible. "When in Florence, I used to pick around in the junk shops as everyone does," he later reminisced. He had begun buying: an old copy of a Titian drawing, authenticated by Berenson, which he purchased during his first few weeks in Florence; and in Paris, with Gertrude, he'd looked for Japanese prints, "to have them round continually & see what happened."

Since his youth, when his Hungarian tutor had introduced him to the joys of collecting, Leo had relished its satisfactions. But in later life he couched this, as he did so many things, in the language of failure. "Once my brother Simon and I were chasing a green lizard across a meadow, which, when apprehended, left its quivering tail with us and vanished. . . . Despite all this," he reflected, "I must have taken much pleasure in these collections." With its silent assertion of mastery, collecting also implied detachment and objectivity: a captor, even a neophyte biologist, posed as a dispassionate intellectual, his covetousness and longing safely poured into the collected object, itself a kind of fetish. And this object, this fetish, was what the collector exhibited, not his greedy desire. He revealed nothing personal—except of course his collection. And thus the collection mediated between him and others. This was something the reticent, inhibited Leo well understood. Observing once that the great Renoir collectors were "men who were lonely, who were socially isolated, who felt the dearth of warm human companionship," he hinted that in his case too, collecting interceded between him and other people.

That fall and winter a lonely Stein browsed the shops. In December, especially proud of his purchase of a Latin translation of Xenophon printed in

Bologna in 1502, he could reel off to Mabel Weeks a list of what he called wild and venturesome extravagance: cabinets, tables, chairs, brass lamps, iron boxes, satin hangings, Venetian glass, wooden saints, terra-cotta saints, and ivory-handled daggers. By March, he had added seven swords and a half-dozen pommels, a sixteenth-century Horace, fifteenth-century editions of Virgil, Boccaccio, Valerius Maximus, and Petrarch, and a fine folio Cicero, in four volumes, printed in Paris circa 1555. Most of the books were in good shape, he told Weeks, except for the accidents that made them available to "poor people like us since it knocks out the collectors [sic] value."

But Stein decided he couldn't stand the sodden gray of another Florentine winter. He saw a good deal of the Berensons, taking shelter from the tomblike cold in front of the fires at I Tatti, and looked forward to spring, when he could take bicycle trips to Siena. "Spring & summer in Italy and winter in the larger cities of the north that is now my program," he declared. Even if the weather was just as bad in London, he reasoned, at least one could find more to do. Quietly, he gave up his book on Mantegna.

That Easter, 1902, he went sightseeing with the Berensons, looking at art from Pisa to Siena and driving through the fragrant countryside. He started to feel homesick. Each morning he walked to the Vieusseux library to read American newspapers, and he confessed that, away from the States, he felt more patriotic than ever. "I blow the American trumpet as though it was the whole of Sousa's band," he said, although he contemplated never setting foot on the continent again. One flexed one's nationalism in absentia.

American expatriates relished a good argument about their homeland. Mary Berenson was dismayed to learn from Leo that Alfred Hodder considered Florence acceptable for "bloodless aesthetes" but *"Life"* should be a matter of marching music. She was also amazed by Leo's boosterism, which she thought self-deluded. Nonetheless, he too was poised between two worlds, each oddly saturated with the rhetoric of gender: the civilized female world of Europe, with its aesthetic values and refined pleasures, and the upstart and virile America, stepping to a democratic drumbeat.

Talk of this sort persisted deep into the spring and summer, long after reinforcement for the American side arrived in the form of Gertrude Stein.

MEDICINE, NEUROLOGY, JOHNS HOPKINS: all were relegated to the past. Gertrude dispatched the final version of her article on the brain to Lewellys Barker that spring and didn't look back. What lay ahead was another summer with Leo, first in Tuscany and then in Umbria until the weather turned cold. After that they would settle somewhere in London, probably with the help of the Berensons.

Invited to I Tatti with Leo one Tuesday evening in May, shortly after her arrival in Florence, Gertrude struck Mary Berenson forcibly. "A fat, unwieldy person, the color of mahogany," Mary described her, "but with a grand, monumental head, plenty of brains & immense geniality—a really splendid woman." The Berensons invited Gertrude and Leo to join them in the summer at Mary's mother's home, Friday's Hill, in the hamlet of Fernhurst, about forty miles southwest of London, where there were a pond for swimming, hundreds of acres of woods, a private tennis court, a cricket field, a hockey ground, and a meadow "so brilliant in its deep sunwashed color and so beautiful in its contours and compositions," said Leo, that he and Gertrude could not resist renting three rooms in a cottage nearby for September.

Located on a small knoll, their cottage, Green Hill, was surrounded by red cows, white ducks, "lamby sheep," and lordly roosters, as well as an occasional pheasant diving into view from the thickets. It was a sylvan scene when a group of young people crowded on the veranda at Friday's Hill, although Mary Berenson's brother Logan Pearsall Smith described "a black contingent of Steins [that] would occasionally darken our drive, led by the great Gertrude herself. All these would settle like a flock of birds on our terrace, where tea was provided and talk was free."

BB was there, ailing and enervated. Gertrude sized up his condition, medical-student fashion, and diagnosed neurasthenia, for which she prescribed a diet of raw eggs and milk. Berenson began to flourish, said Leo. "The more I see of him the better I like him," he told Mabel Weeks. For all his complaints, Berenson had been able, at least for the present, to span the worlds of Europe and America. "There is something robust about his delicate sensitive organization that gives his thought and conversation a vitality that is rare," Leo observed with admiration. "He has the great advantage over most people of being able to dig his stuff out of himself without turning it up crude."

When he sprained his ankle trying to do handsprings, Leo had to skip the latest installment of the ongoing American debate. Bertrand Russell was insisting that educated Americans were oblivious to fresh political ideas, especially compared with the cultivated English. Gertrude heartily objected. So had Leo. "On the whole I remain constant," he confessed, "for after all there is something tonic even overtonic about America that I miss here and would not like to miss permanently. If America only were not so far away and if the climate in the possible parts were not so chilly."

But there was a reverie that promised the best of both worlds. "Some day I'll make up my mind that I can stand them and then Gertrude and I will retire to Connecticut or Duxbury or somewhere and live happily ever after."

For now, though, they settled for rooms at 20 Bloomsbury Square, which they had rented for five or six months. The future—and America—would take care of themselves. Meantime, Gertrude and Leo had evaded the strenuous life and, it seemed, its gilded cage. Or, as she would later say of her native country, "Your parent's home is never a place to work."

10
BROTHER
SINGULAR

Brother Singular

There is art from day to day, as well as art from century to century. One recalls a rare meal at the Tour d'Argent or Voisin's, but one eats bread day in day out. And bread is also food.

LEO STEIN, *APPRECIATION*

Man hopes, genius creates.

RALPH WALDO EMERSON,
"THE AMERICAN SCHOLAR"

You fat talk so much.

GERTRUDE STEIN, UNPUBLISHED NOTEBOOK

D ON'T FORGET the importance of the Haig diet in connection with affections of the brain and the nervous system," Michael Stein advised his sister in the winter of 1901, just as she was beginning to talk of leaving Hopkins. Whether he was responding to Gertrude's agitation or simply expressing enthusiasm for the regime his wife had recently tried, he was conversing in familiar terms; the Steins still used food, its ingestion and exchange, to communicate love, affection, power, anger, desire, rejection—all the constituents of family life.

Leo approached foods fearfully, and he avoided some altogether, those he invested with magically destructive powers. (This is not to say his dietary concerns weren't well founded, both physiologically and psychologically.) As an adult, he sometimes refused to eat anything but raw vegetables, believing they cleansed and purified the system. Unlike Gertrude, he was perpetually thin; for many years he regarded his size as a function of temperament, and until he read Freud, he assumed that his gastric problems lay behind his unfocused ambition. Nutrition, as necessary to human development as sexuality, was on a par with aesthetic experience, he said, insisting that aesthetic experience was itself "something as essentially practical as food."

Gertrude suffered from stomach pains every time she and Leo fought. Although she tended to be overweight, among the siblings Simon was the most distinguished by size, growing so obese the varicose veins on his ankles ulcerated and he could not stand. Gertrude's weight was trivial in comparison. Yet if descriptions—by and about her—suggest her size made others and not her self-conscious, it is doubtful she regarded her weight with complete equanimity. No one did, except perhaps Leo. Even Simon expressed surprise when he heard how much she had gained during her first years abroad, though he was quick to console her. All good-natured people were fat, he said.

One medical school classmate, remembering that "both mentally and physically she was unusual, and unconventional, and therefore attracted attention," wondered unhelpfully whether she "took advantage of her cumbersome figure to give it a certain dignity." True, while sitting at a friend's villa

Gertrude Stein at the Villa Curonia

in Italy, Gertrude posed cross-legged, ample and self-assured, a veritable Buddha, but an unpublished notebook contains lines from Chaucer's "Merciles Beaute," intended as an epigraph to an early work: "Since I from love escaped / am so fat / I never think to be in his prison lean."

Whatever the travails of being heavy in a world that valued thin, Gertrude over the years came to regard food not just as conveying love and security but also as affording sexual pleasure. (Not surprisingly, Alice Toklas initially proffered herself as both secretary and cook.) "Toasted susie is my ice-cream," Gertrude wrote in 1913 at the conclusion of "Preciosilla," her celebration of physical love; "I am clad in sweet syrup and odors," she declared the same year in "Miguel (Collusion). Guimpe. Candle." And in the more famous "Lifting Belly," she writes a comic hymn to erotic love: "Lifting belly is so kind. / Lifting belly fattily. / Doesn't that astonish you. / You did want me. / Say it again. / Strawberry. / Lifting beside belly. / Lifting kindly belly. / Sing to me I say."

Although Gertrude Stein had her appetites, her own acceptance of their full reach did not come quickly or easily. Often she liked to assert her middle-class birthright, even though much of her taste, her sexual orientation, and eventually her writing put her beyond the pale of the typical bourgeois and certainly beyond the bourgeoisie of Baltimore. Her attraction to temperance, balance, and the golden mean—the nub of middle-class decorum—evidently lay at first in their ability to curb the passions. Quivering, eager, distracted, morbid, violent: so she characterized the autobiographical persona of her college compositions. Should this wild young woman not forbear, she asked. And if the solaces of the middle class were the leitmotif of her Radcliffe compositions, they definitely were a theme in those conservative exhortations "The Value of College Education for Women" and "Degeneration in American Women." But especially in the latter, Stein revealed ambivalence toward her own prescription, exempting herself from the ranks of women she ushered toward motherhood. She was the exception about whom she spoke, the woman who would find her own form of expression.

Exceptional and middle-class; unique but normal; singular not solitary: she also straddled two worlds. In England in the fall of 1902, however, she felt stretched too far. For the first time in many years, the future lacked the clearly defined yardsticks—Latin exams, baccalaureates, medical degrees—of progress and achievement. Exhausted from the strain of her final separation from Hopkins and distressed by a rocky relationship with May Bookstaver, Gertrude was depleted and depressed. Only her enormous physical strength and health, she later told a friend, pulled her through.

So when Logan Smith asked the guests at Friday's Hill whether they'd be willing to live their lives over, Gertrude's answer probably came as no surprise. Bernhard Berenson, Bertrand Russell, and the novelist Israel Zangwill all shook their heads emphatically, but in true American fashion, both Gertrude and Leo Stein said they'd like to have a second chance.

BY EARLY NOVEMBER 1902, Gertrude and Leo had settled into Bloomsbury Square, in the residential neighborhood that would give its name to the unconventional writers and artists gathered behind conventional Georgian façades. The Steins knew few people there. They accepted a dinner invitation from Israel Zangwill, who to Leo's regret would not be in London for the winter, but generally they declined the overtures of what Leo called the "socialisticy gang," presumably friends of Mary Berenson's, such as Beatrice and Sidney Webb.

Most of the people Gertrude and Leo met, they met through the Berensons: Zangwill and the British writer Robert Trevelyan, a tall, unworldly young man suffused with poetry, and the Shakespeare scholar J. M. Robertson—"anti everything," Leo described him. "We had a long and violent argument about genius and social conditions," Leo recounted to Mabel Weeks. "[Robertson] has a conviction that geniuses is lying round 'most as thick as blackberries and only need decent social conditions to make them sprout." Positive that the rarity of genius had little to do with social conditions one way or another, Gertrude and Leo both held a different view. "A discoverer, an inventor, an original . . . no training or culture can make him nothing can be offered him except opportunity," Leo later stated in a notebook. A genius, he speculated, was one who met every situation freshly, unconcerned with what was generally acknowledged as true, caring only for *"what must be."*

Besides this romantic conception of genius, Gertrude and Leo shared a personal stake in its definition, which, over the years, both used to bolster their sense of self. Was genius to madness near allied, ruminated Leo, a different limb of the same tree, stronger than the branch that grew eccentrics or cranks, straighter than the one for hysterics? Then, perhaps, he could have reasoned, his own sufferings suggested a form of genius. He did believe that most kinds of education killed genius by thwarting instinct and then, beyond that, that "most men of genius are more or less throttled by their unconventional knowledge." But how did one define genius, he asked. Perhaps it was something like "significant originality," he ventured, adding glumly that whatever is significant is always socially defined and determined. Perhaps not; after all, can't genius be useless and still be genius? Or must genius be defined only by its products? The question was pertinent to a man who feared he might never produce.

Gertrude posed similarly revealing questions: "If you stop writing if you are a genius and you have stopped writing are you still one if you have stopped writing," she asked in 1936 in *Everybody's Autobiography,* a book rife with anxiety, not the least of which had to do with her difficulty writing at the time. And like Leo, she had been seeking a personal definition of genius. How did one know one was a genius—this question plagued Gertrude. "Lots of people are convinced they are one sometime in the course of their living but they are not one and what is the difference between being not one and being one," she wondered in the same book. Deeply competitive, both Gertrude and Leo gauged excellence in comparative terms; and because they competed with each other, they each tried to distinguish themselves as separate from and superior to the other. By the time *Everybody's Autobiography* was published, Gertrude had decided—and was willing to say publicly—she was the only genius in the Stein family, which had room, evidently, for only one. "It was I who was the genius," she asserted, "there was no reason for it but I was, and he was not."

Some twenty-five years earlier, however, when less compelled to separate herself from Leo or exaggerate her successes—and rationalize his failure—she meditated differently on the subject of genius. "A man of genius is what," Gertrude wrote in an early manuscript, probably in 1910. "Is he an artist, is he not." Struck by Leo's observation that an effective genius requires courage and egotism, she puzzled over the question of genius until she came up with a formula of "maleness" to help explain it. Maleness might very well be a quality belonging to genius, she speculated, something true of Matisse and Picasso—and "moi aussi, perhaps."

But would the absence of maleness foil genius? The question inevitably brought Leo to mind. "So often they say the most brilliant brother if he had written or what not would have been greater but the chances are that he though more brilliant lacked just that," she mused in an early notebook. "The genius is not different from other men excepting that he has that. He is of his kind and he is great only by virtue of that."

But what of her? Genius was no genius without action; and whether action was a function of courage or ego or even aggression, it was for Gertrude Stein synonymous with maleness. Without the virility of action, there would be no productivity, no product, no genius. Such was the culture of production that she and Leo inherited and which, as a woman, Gertrude strategically adapted, claiming a degree of its "maleness" for herself. In such a system, Leo had then to be the passive, feminine member of the family. And he suspected as much.

IN THE LATE FALL OF 1902, Leo frequently saw Josiah Willard, coauthor with Alfred Hodder of *The Powers That Prey.* That book, an exposé of criminals, police, and white-collar crime in New York, was suited to Willard, who had done much of his fieldwork in bars and back rooms. A hard-living, well-educated vagabond with, as Hodder said, a habit for courtesans, liquor, and the underworld, Willard was anything but effete. Yet there was a gentleness in his manner and a goodness in his heart that led Hutchins Hapgood to declare the fierce Willard his best friend. Hodder admired him, as did Leo, and both coveted Willard's experience as the stuff of pure romance: he had gone from a year in reform school to ten days in the company of Leo Tolstoy, writing of his various experiences all the while. Josiah Willard predeceased Alfred Hodder by a matter of weeks in 1907; he was thirty-eight.

Willard was in London that fall ostensibly to study the police for a magazine article. He had not " 'reformed' in the conventional sense of the word," Leo told Mabel Weeks, but remained "what he was, with added personal dignity, centrality, and grace. Altogether an eminently satisfying person." He squired Leo into a world more ribald than the world of art and aesthetics, and it was a male world that excluded Gertrude. She grew lonely. She frequented the bookshops near Bloomsbury Square, and spent most of her time in the cavernous British Museum, where she read and jotted down names of authors and titles of books into the tiny gray copybooks that reminded her, she said, of childhood and resembled the tablets used by medical students at patients' bedsides.

Malory, Brian Melbancke, Roger Boyle's *Parthenissa*, William Congreve's *Incognita*, *The Female Quixote* by Charlotte Lennox, Aphra Behn's *Oroonoko*: names and titles followed more names and titles; Bunyan, Sara Fielding, Henry Brooke (whose *The Fool of Quality* Stein called "hard reading," and whose three novels and diary Gertrude also listed in her copybook). Piloting herself through English literature in rough chronological order, as if she were methodically preparing an idiosyncratic survey of significant titles and long-forgotten authors, she was bent on supplying a literary background. No doubt influenced by Weeks's devotion to the eighteenth century, she added satires, letters, and diaries to her lists of eighteenth- and early-nineteenth-century novels. And seventeenth-century drama, as well as Elizabethan prose, which she later claimed had caught her fancy during those long dark days in the reading room.

Interspersed with the lists, addresses, and occasional reminders to herself was a homemade course on Japanese art. The notebook jottings inventory mostly major names in Japanese art, like the literary titles in rough chronological order. After ten or so printmakers of the eighteenth and nineteenth centuries, Stein listed several secular painters of the Heian period; she noted such figures as Kose no Kanaoka, commented that "twelfth century beginning of Jap. individual genius," registered the work of Toba Sojo as "strong in action," and called Nobuzane Japan's "greatest colorist."

But nowhere does Stein reveal the nature of the appeal: whether, for example, she was drawn to the female figures of Torii Kiyonaga (whose name she underlined), or whether it was the expressive realism of Kitagawa Utamaro that so compelled her attention (it would emerge in altered form in her writing). The intense, flat colors of the Japanese print, and the clarity of line; the subject matter of the Ukiyo-e school, with its emphasis on ordinary people and simple pleasures; the repetition of images and the patterned richness found particularly in the Heian period and in Utagawa Kunisada's satirical portraits of "types" of women—all of these bear comparison with Stein's later writing, for she and Leo must have discussed Japanese prints at length. And of course surveying the history of Japanese art yielded immediate, practical applications, for she and Leo—or at least Leo—were still buying.

Only a reminder to buy more copybooks, in one of her oldest notebooks, suggests Gertrude had deliberately embarked on the course of study from which she hoped to emerge a writer—although clearly she was working toward some as yet unannounced goal. Increasingly, she was surrounded by writers, artists, and aesthetes—those Bryn Mawr women, Hodder, the Berenson circle—whom she admired. But she who had spent years studying the midsection of the human brain knew less about literature than they, and her program of study in the British Museum was calculated in some degree to redress the imbalance.

Whatever her perceived deficiencies, Gertrude knew she possessed exceptional verbal gifts, believed she had something of interest to say, and was still committed to the study of human character. Perhaps she now felt that literature, rather than science, would give wider berth to her talents, interests, and ambition, especially since the life of a writer did not require the kind of brutal conformity demanded by the medical profession. That had not proved the estate of true inquiry where women and men met on equal, dispassionate grounds to pursue questions of mind. And what Stein had sought there she would find elsewhere, in the realm of self-expression that medical discourse had discouraged.

In spite of these plans—and conceivably because of them—she grew more and more unhappy. Her time was unstructured, the skies were leaden, her mood darkened. "The dead weight of that fog and smoke laden air . . ." she would soon describe that winter in London, "the soggy, damp miserable streets, and the women with bedraggled, frayed-out skirts, their faces swollen and pimply with sordid dirt ground into them." London sagged. When at last her depression began to lift, she admitted "it was very bad while it lasted"; many years later she recalled that "the dismalness of London and the drunken women and children and the gloom and the lonesomeness brought back all the melancholy of her adolescence."

She told friends she would last until January, and then would take "a little vacation from England and Englishers cause though the country is most lovely and the galleries and book stores all that one could ask I am not yet enamored of those institutions that have made Englishmen what they are." She was going back to America. Leo said he would soon follow—after a little detour in France that, as it happened, went on until 1914.

DURING THE WINTER OF 1903, as she floundered between careers, fearing failure both in love and in work, Gertrude Stein reflected on the career of Alfred Hodder.

On February 3, she turned twenty-nine. "It happens often in the twenty-ninth year of a life," she would soon write, "that all the forces that have been engaged through the years of childhood, adolescence and youth in confused and ferocious combat range themselves in ordered ranks—one is uncertain of one's aims, meaning and power during these years of tumultuous growth when aspiration has no relation to fulfillment and one plunges here and there with energy and misdirection during the storm and stress of the making of a personality until at last we reach the twenty-ninth year the straight and narrow gate-way of maturity and life which was all uproar and confusion narrows down to form and purpose and we exchange a great dim possibility for a small hard reality."

"One smiles as one thinks back over one's varied career," Stein rationalized, not long after returning to the United States. Inserting her life and a smattering of Leo's into a story about Alfred Hodder, she continued her meditation on the problem of vocation and its relation to love:

> First it was scholarship, then law, then medicine then business then an attempt at art or literature, all begun with enthusiasm pursued a little while with industry, found wanting in meaning and value, abandoned with joy and the next profession ardently adopted only to be dropped in its turn when found unsuited to the vital need of one's true self. And it must be owned that while much labor is lost to the world in these efforts to secure one's true vocation, nevertheless it makes more completeness in individual life and perhaps in the end will prove as useful to the world—and if we believe that there is more meaning in the choice of love than plain propinquity so we may well believe that there is more meaning in vocation than that it is the thing we first can learn about and earn an income with.

At twenty-nine, Gertrude Stein had abandoned medicine, confronted her sexuality, and embarked on a new career. She was in New York, living in a large wooden structure, the White House, on 100th Street and Riverside Drive. In early spring, with her roommates Mabel Weeks and Harriet Clark, Etta Cone's former traveling companion, and the sculptress Estelle Rumbold, she could watch the ice floes slide down the blue Hudson before the locust trees began to flower. She could read and write. And just a few minutes away by streetcar lived May Bookstaver.

Although there exists a seventy-three-page manuscript fragment entitled "The Making of Americans Being the History of a Family's Progress," dated from this period and usually considered the first of Stein's postcollegiate literary works, it seems she composed another story—about Hodder, vocation, and Bookstaver—at the same time or earlier. No doubt hearing the Alfred Hodder–Mamie Gwinn gossip at Fernhurst during her visit the previous fall, Stein used their romance as the basis for the story she called "Fernhurst: The History of Philip Redfern A Student of the Nature of Woman." But the tale of Hodder's illicit relationship with Gwinn was also the tale of her own affair with May Bookstaver, in which yet another narrative was embedded: Stein's polemic about women and women's rights.

"I am for having women learn what they can but not to mistake learning for action nor to believe that a man's work is suited to them because they have mastered a boy's education," Stein wrote in "Fernhurst," as if in answer to Bookstaver, an ardent champion of equal rights and women's suffrage. "In short I would have the few women who must do a piece of the man's work but think that the great mass of the world's women should content themselves with attaining to womanhood." Such was the argument Stein had made to a startled Alfred Hodder the year before, when they had dinner at Fred Stein's. And the feminist Bookstaver must have been just as astonished. The two women clearly disagreed, especially since Stein suspected that for all their talk about equality, her Bryn Mawr friends considered women superior to men.

Nowhere was this more true than in Stein's depiction of M. Carey Thomas. "We the generation of women who have rights to refuse should I suppose be silent and not bring the world to observe the contradiction in her doctrine and the danger of her method," Stein wrote, refusing silence. She disagreed fundamentally with Thomas about the inalienable rights of *all* women. Thomas's views were understandable, for Thomas's generation—but not for Stein's.

> Had I been bred in the last generation full of hope and unattainable desires I too would have declared that men and women are born equal of this generation with the college and professions open to me and able to learn that the other man is really stronger I say I will have none of it. And you shall have none of it says my

reader tired of this posing, I don't say no I can only hope that I am
one of those rare women that should since I find in my heart that
I needs must.

Thus, women should not be duped into thinking they were stronger or
more successful than men; not all were. But there were those rare ones—those
geniuses—who were the exception, the exceptional, the true successes.
Gertrude needs be one of them.

THE COURSE of Stein's relationship with Bookstaver had not been smooth.
The three strong-minded women—Bookstaver, Mabel Haynes, Stein—were
as motivated by the erotic power they exerted over one another as they were
by their passion. Or, to a large degree, power and sexuality became the same
thing, at least in Stein's view.

And this is how she regarded Hodder's complicated affairs, in which she
saw a parallel with her own. Hodder too was enmeshed in a triangle of love
and power. As Philip Redfern in "Fernhurst," Hodder considered himself, like
Stein, "a student of the nature of woman"—but so naive, said their friend
Josiah Willard, he would not have known a dramatic experience if it was
stripped naked and put into bed with him. He was also a romantic cursed with
a sense of chivalry desiccated enough to be positively immoral; he was an intellectual westerner from Ohio displaced among eastern niceties; he was a student of philosophy who "preferred the criticism of life in fiction to the analysis
of the mind in philosophy"; he was a man whose instincts were "decadent"
but whose ideals were pure; and he was desperately in love with someone beholden to another. In him, Stein recognized herself, and feared for herself.

In the story, Redfern, a clever young teacher of philosophy full of himself and his theory of "naive realism" (a comic variation of Hodder's own
philosophic treatise on "crude realism"), falls in love with the ethereal Janet
Bruce, an English teacher at Fernhurst College and a favorite of its imperious dean, Helen Thornton. Modeled on M. Carey Thomas, Thornton was a
complex figure, devoted and single-minded in her pursuit of women's rights
but with an "instinct for domination" that made her "unmoral." But to Stein,
Janet Bruce was, in her own way, as "unmoral" as the dean. "Miss Bruce's unmoral quality consisted in her lack of recognition of expedience, her utter indifference to worldly matters. She could lose herself in a relation without any
consciousness that other lives and natures were at work and a recognition of
such responsibility would come to her no more than to Miss Thornton."

If "Fernhurst" echoed the story of Stein's relationship with Bookstaver
and Haynes, with Bookstaver as Bruce and Haynes as the dean, Stein played
the part of Redfern, student of women. But she identified also with the posi-

tion of Nancy Redfern, the plainspoken, clumsy, abandoned wife, possessed of "straight Western morality and . . . narrow new world humanity." When Dean Thornton subtly insinuates her husband's infidelity, Nancy Redfern, utterly inadequate to the crisis facing her, looks for and finds proof in one of her husband's letters. She "had her evidence," Stein wrote ominously. And here the story abruptly ends.

In a coda, Stein summarized the fate of her characters. For a while, rumors persist about the lovers; students see them engrossed in one another at train stations. ("Naive realism is most absorbing," the students jest.) But Dean Thornton eventually resumes control over Bruce, quashing all rumors about her and Redfern—which seemed to outsiders what happened with Thomas and Gwinn, at least in 1903. Such was also the stalemate Stein confronted with Haynes and Bookstaver. Despite Stein's presence in New York, she apparently had not supplanted Haynes in Bookstaver's affections. Nor was she sure of what she herself wanted from the affair. Mabel Weeks reminisced years later that at the time Stein was having affairs with various women (not, however, with her).

As for Redfern, he (like Hodder) leaves teaching, lunges into politics, and flounders without anything or anyone to moor him. The prognosis was gloomy, inspirational after a fashion but forbidding: "He never ceased to struggle and he never ceased to fail." No doubt it was a warning.

ALFRED HODDER AND GERTRUDE STEIN were not the only ones preoccupied that winter with their love affairs. Gertrude's cousin Bird Sternberger was still in court. Flanked by brother Fred and by Howard Gans, she had not stopped fighting for sole custody of her two children. The previous spring, determined as ever, she had returned to the Appellate Division of the New York State Supreme Court to try to revoke Sternberger's visitation rights. Although the children lived with her, their final fate was undecided; for seven years, in fact, the case had dragged on through a number of decrees and reversals, each judge overruling the decision of the last. Furious, both Bird and her estranged husband continued to file acrimonious motions and appeals. The case was filling volumes.

Sternberger, meantime, tried to forestall Bird, insisting he wanted both his wife and his children back—perhaps now that Solomon Stein was dead he felt he could reunite his family. His finances were sound enough, he argued; members of the Jewish business community as eminent as Joseph Seligman had signed an affidavit on his behalf. Bird was unmoved. She said her husband slept through his children's visits, that he was indolent, crude, and temperamental. Attack met counterattack—hostile, pitiful, demeaning— through a bitter autumn. Sternberger alleged Bird wanted to get rid of him to marry Howard Gans. Bird's attorney answered that Sternberger had had a tryst upstate. Sternberger angrily insisted he'd been framed. When Alfred Hodder, who had gone with Fred Stein to rout Sternberger from a Utica hotel, did not testify or provide a statement, Sternberger seemed vindicated. Bird was miserable and relentless.

Everyone who knew her was involved in the case, including Gertrude, who probably sometime during the winter of 1903 began to compose a work of fiction based loosely on it. It was "The Making of Americans Being the History of a Family's Progress," an early version of the later, more monumental *The Making of Americans*. Now, turning to Bird's ill-begotten marriage, Stein cast her cousin as Julia Dehning, a well-intentioned Daisy Miller thirsty for the best in life: "a very vigorous specimen of self-satisfied domineering American girlhood." Henry Hersland was her cultured suitor, a man who "brought with him the world of art and things, a world to her but vaguely known." But the heroine's solid middle-class family—especially her father—disapprove. "He was not their kind and they did not trust him and men and bourgeois as they were they found his mystery no attraction." The heroine does not yield, the couple marry—and the marriage fails, for the heroine loves her father above all others, even above her new husband.

As narrator, Stein took it upon herself to caution the doomed suitor:

> Be doubly warned attractive and weak brother, be sharply on your guard for it is a woman from such a family life who is so often taken by the glitter and the lightness of your thin and eager nature, your temper selfish and demanding, but when the close life of the marriage comes, she looks to find in you weak creature that you are the power and support, the honesty and steady courage she has always known and hence will spring your woe and loathsome sadness that begins and never has an end. Brother weak pleasant selfish brother, beware.

Sensitive to the psychological triangle of father, daughter, and prospective husband, Stein made it the centerpiece of her story. But who was the weak and attractive brother she warned? Henry Hersland—the name indirectly evoked her dead sibling Harry—was not based on Louis Sternberger alone, even though Stein, for all her commiseration with Bird, empathized with him. Rather, this "weak pleasant selfish brother" seems to stand for all those not strong enough—not yet, anyway—to be truly original. "Brother Singulars," Stein wrote in an oft-quoted and oddly prophetic passage,

> we are misplaced into a generation that knows not Joseph. We flee before the disapproval of our cousins, the courageous condescen-

sion of our friends who gallantly agree to sometimes walk the streets with us, we fly to the kindly comfort of an older world accustomed to take all manner of strange forms into its bosom and we leave our noble order to be known under such forms as that of Henry Hersland, a poor thing and hardly even then our own.

Later incorporated into the full-blown *Making of Americans,* this passage suggests that Stein's "brother singular" is a combination of herself and her own brother Leo. Although she had not yet settled in France, she did suffer the condescending forbearance of relatives who never quite accepted or understood her. And Leo had indeed fled a provincial America for the comfort of an older world.

The passage also contains grim advice. Gertrude's eccentric, demanding, and attractive brother singular is cautioned against disappointing the one who loves him. Such disappointment will be repaid, she says, in loathsome sadness without end.

QUITE MANNERED, this early "Making of Americans" reflected some of Stein's recent reading, and demonstrated, even more than "Fernhurst," a deliberate attempt at style. The result, however, is self-conscious in the extreme—a concoction of eighteenth-century prose and biblical rhetoric, replete with bows to the reader ("Bear it in mind my reader if indeed there be any such"), stilted cadence ("When the twelve months were passed away no gravest cause had come"), and stiff structure ("variety and richness of trimming"; "jewel ornaments" rather than "jewelry"). But Stein is aspiring toward nothing less than an American Jewish Genesis, an undertaking much bolder and ambitious than "Fernhurst."

Early on, for instance, Stein announces she intends the book not as "a simple novel with plot and conversations" but as "a record of a family progress respectably lived and to be carefully set down and so arm yourself with patience." The five extant chapters of the book (the others were later sliced out of the notebook in which they were written) suggest Stein's intention was again the study of character, this time by means of a comparison between two sisters and their two unhappy marriages. Such a comparison purported to reveal the character of both women and, by extension, the family whose so-called progress they represented: "The old people in a new world, the new people made out of the old that is the story that I mean to tell for that is what really is and what I really know."

What Stein really knew was the story of first- and second-generation German Jewish immigrants in America. Thus, to understand a family's "progress," or development over time, Stein must consider its Americanization. "It has always seemed to me a rare privilege this of being an American, a real American and yet one whose tradition has taken scarcely sixty years to create. We need only realize our parents, remember our grandparents and know ourselves and our history is complete." But for Stein "progress" is an equivocal term and Americanization—or assimilation—an equivocal process, one she calls the "fever to be an Anglo Saxon" and sardonically characterizes through the naming of the four Dehning children. Julia, the oldest, is named for her maternal grandmother, "in unperverted transmission" from old world to new; her younger sister is named Bertha, "as a modern version" of the paternal grandmother; the next child, born after "the first distant mutter of the breaking Anglo Saxon wave had come to them," is named George, with a "complete neglect of ancestry"; and the youngest child's name invokes not tradition but the "call of elegance as well as foreignness and so this child like many of her generation was named Hortense."

This was, then, the story of an upwardly mobile family seeking assimilation, social acceptance, and culture, a story in which the congratulatory pride of the self-made chafes a younger generation born to unearned privileges. Abraham Dehning, based directly on Gertrude's uncle Solomon and indirectly on her father, is afraid that modern conveniences, too much education, and "literary effects" will make his four children—and especially the brilliant Julia—soft. "Well it won't be long now before you will all have a chance to show me what you can do for yourselves and whether all these modern improvements and all this education business will teach you as much as peddling through the country did to us," he chides them. Anxiously his children answer again and again, just wait, "I guess we will be good for something."

Living up to expectations, exceeding those expectations, choosing a vocation that will ensure productive achievement: such are the preoccupations Stein transferred onto her protagonist, deciding not to dramatize the protracted denouement of Bird's marriage but rather to examine the conditions making her disastrous choice of husband inevitable. In crude terms, these conditions are character and environment, which by determining Julia Dehning's fate give Stein the opportunity to meditate on a "family's progress" and to synthesize her longtime interests in the so-called given, inherited traits of character, modulated by environment, all working together in the development of species.

It is a dreary business this living down the tempers we are born with. We always begin well for in our youth there is nothing we are more tolerant of than our own sins writ large in others and so we fight them lustily in ourselves but we grow old and we begin to see that these our sins are of all known sins the really harmless ones to own nay that they add a charm to any character and so our struggle with them soon dies away.

Stein insists that psychological features, modified by individual temperament and environment, are passed down through generations. Part of Julia Dehning's young history is her "struggle to live down her mother in her"—and so we might suspect that part of Stein's history, as she perceived it, was her own struggle with the temper she was born with, and then her acceptance of it. Interestingly enough, friends perceived her as positive and dominant—the same terms Leo used to describe his father. But in a story about physical attraction and marital failure, Gertrude was writing also about regeneration—and sexuality.

CHARACTER, according to Gertrude, determines fate. But the matter is not simple. If temperament is as much an inherited quality as eye or hair color, she nonetheless intended to observe the variation in given hereditary qualities—"the new people made out of the old"—as well as the qualities themselves. As she points out, in a passage later deleted from the text:

> In the eighteenth century that age of manners and of formal morals, it was believed that the temper of a woman was determined by the turn of her features; later, in the beginning nineteenth, the period of inner spiritual illumination it was accepted that the features were moulded by the temper of the soul within; still later in the nineteenth century when the science of heredity had decided that everything proves something different, it was discovered that generalizations must be as complicated as the facts and the problem of interrelation was not to be so simply solved. You reader may subscribe to whichever doctrine pleases you best while I picture for you the opposition in resemblance in the Dehning sisters.

"Opposition in resemblance" helps the former student of heredity understand the way given qualities blend and separate among the siblings in whom they are incarnated. Passionate women such as Julia Dehning "afflict their world with agitation, excitement and unrest," and quieter women such as Julia's sister Bertha "dread the loss of all themselves and every second go on losing more. . . . The restless ones know as keen sorrow as those who make no stir; but emptiness is more sickening long kept up than overfulness. The stomach overloaded is always very sick but then it can discharge itself upon the world. The empty starving stomach can only weaken sadden grow more helpless."

Empty and full, famished and gorged—oppositions described in images of hunger and satiety provide a psychological matrix for Stein onto which she maps the psychological features of family. The brilliant older sister Julia purges herself so she can eat again; Bertha, submissive, hungry, and forever unfulfilled, passively submits to the will of her family.

We are reminded that the entire clan of Steins represents "opposition in resemblance": gentle Keysers and aggressive Steins; homebound Bertha Stein and clever Gertrude, brilliant Leo and his slower siblings. Where Daniel Stein was quick to anger, his brother Solomon seemed patient and judicious. (Much later, in *The Autobiography of Alice B. Toklas,* Stein implicitly contrasts her mother with Pauline, Solomon's wife, saying the two "had never gotten along any too well.") But all these parental figures, especially the dogmatic patriarchs, were anxious for the success of their children, those second-generation Jews who preserve their "middle class tradition"—here a euphemism for their Jewish identity—while they seek acceptance and success as Americans.

In Stein, the influence of America on the bourgeois family is paradoxical. It may be a privilege to be an American, but America also implies a poverty of imagination—a shallowness, a deracination, a repressed sexuality—which Julia Dehning, as the oldest child, is partly spared: "Perhaps she was born too near the old world to attain quite the completeness of crude virginity for underneath her very American face body and clothes were seen now and then flashes of passionate insight that lit up an older and hidden tradition." America is physically and emotionally barren, "like a large and splendid canvas completely painted over but painted full of empty space." And the middle class in this American landscape, the second-generation German Jews, still unsure of themselves, cling to respectability, convention, and ignorance. Derivative in their tastes, anxious to please, they are a gullible, insecure group, suggests Stein, suspecting contamination in all things carnal.

And so when the Dehnings learn that the sister and the aunt of Bertha's fiancé died of consumption, they close ranks and call off the engagement. Bertha defers to her family's wishes, for even Julia opposes her, melodramatically portraying her cut down in her prime, her future children dead. Unlike the skilled doctor who is delivered from such prejudice by scientific training—a theme Stein sounded as early as her first days in Baltimore—the bourgeois family uncritically worships "all the respectable wisdom that you can obtain. All those facts and theories that their creators keep as abstract truths are for you so real so carefully to be obeyed. A little knowledge is a dangerous thing for them that have this little."

A few years earlier, when he left Baltimore for good, Leo had asserted that the deviant, the singular, the truly noble, the genius would not be tolerated unless, as Gertrude wrote in her early "Making of Americans," they were "well dressed and well set up. This is the nearest approach the middle class young woman can hope to find to the indifference and distinction of the really noble. . . . Singularity that is neither crazy, faddist or low class is as yet an unknown product with ourselves. It takes time to make queer people time and certainty of place and means. Custom, passion and a feel for mother earth are needed to breed vital singularity in any man and alas how poor we are in all these three."

THE GERTRUDE STEIN who months before had administered eggs and milk to Bernhard Berenson in the English countryside as she adamantly argued in favor of American life now sat in a timber house near the Hudson River trying to write a book about an American family. But her ambivalence about both family and America belied her impassioned flag-waving. Returning to New York had not solved her problems. And Leo had never arrived. He had gone to Paris to paint at about the time his sister embarked on her new career.

His letters must have been full of his new adventures. Were hers? Neither survive. Yet whatever she said, whatever she felt, she had begun a career that, though tentatively at first, would allow her to assert the superiority, the singularity, and even the sexuality she claimed as her own. She could flout, as she increasingly did in "The Making of Americans," the high-toned conventions that Bird Sternberger, for all her modern airs, nonetheless represented. And the bogus progressivism represented by the Bryn Mawr women, despite their more imaginative sexuality. But this meant she stood alone.

Stein later excised from her "Making of Americans" notebook the chapters dealing with Julia's younger sister. In these chapters, perhaps Stein was more sympathetic to the younger, duller sister, just as she was sympathetic to the insensate Nancy Redfern. Perhaps Stein understood the emptiness, the hollowness and unfulfilled desire, that the quiet sister suffered and feared. For although Stein, who banished doubt through posture, appeared neither passive nor quiet to those who knew her, she often perceived herself this way—probably never as strongly as when surrounded by cousins and, ironically, by her own brilliant, older, and restless brother Leo.

11
QUOD
ERAT
DEMONSTRANDUM

Gertrude and the Cone sisters, Italy, 1903

In the literary anarchy which marks the exit of the nineteenth century aesthetic emotion is often confounded with interest in plot and incident. The same human nature which is thrilled by the clever disentanglement of an ingeniously entangled set of events may also take keen delight in a picture of simple life; but there is no more reason why we should confuse these two sources of enjoyment than there is to put the pleasure of the mathematician unravelling a complex problem side by side with that of a schoolboy watching a fight. . . . However difficult the definition of art, one thing is clear: It is a source of aesthetic enjoyment and has as little to do with what may be called a plot interest as it has with sportsmanship.

ABRAHAM CAHAN, ON ISRAEL ZANGWILL'S
THE CHILDREN OF THE GHETTO

LEO STEIN'S ACCOUNT of how he came to settle in Paris makes a good story. Sometime in the fall of 1902, Laurence Binyon at London's Japan Society had introduced Leo to a writer on architecture, an older man who took a paternal interest in the youthful American. They spoke several times afterward, and at their last meeting, the man asked Leo his plans for Christmas Eve. Leo hadn't made any, and he wasn't particularly bothered, but his new friend, distressed, insisted Leo spend the holiday with his family. Leo tried to excuse himself; he would feel embarrassed and clumsy, he said. His friend would not hear of such foolishness. Relenting, Leo promised to come, if he was still in London; then, on the afternoon of December 24, he crossed the Channel.

Leo's retrospective account of events, whether literally accurate or not, suggests yet again that whenever too much was expected of him, he vanished.

Before he left for Paris, he spent a comfortable few months in London, sometimes with Josiah Willard and sometimes with Gertrude, at bookshops or at the British Museum, where they would read beneath the dome of the reading room. And he continued to buy, though more moderately than before: a lovely edition of Samuel Johnson's work, an anthology of poetry, odds and ends mostly, and a painting by the British postimpressionist Philip Wilson Steer, which purchase—Leo's first oil—made him feel like a desperado. "One could actually own paintings even if one were not a millionaire," he marveled. His book on Mantegna a thing of the past, Leo intended to write more broadly on aesthetics. He had been stimulated by Berenson's theories of aesthetic pleasure, and also aroused by Alfred Hodder's *The Adversaries of the Skeptic*. He read and reread Hodder's book, which he incorporated into his own thinking—as Gertrude also seems to have done. And she couldn't escape Leo's enthusiastic commentary on it. No one else had.

Both as his Harvard dissertation and now in book form, revised and expanded with the assistance of Mamie Gwinn, Hodder's treatise, obviously influenced by William James, rebutted the idealist philosophy of Josiah Royce and F. H. Bradley with what Hodder called a commonsense skepticism. Nothing can be known beyond the outer limits of the "specious present," he wrote, defining it with James as the moment of experience: that which is immediately apprehended, that which is "now existing." As an intuited duration containing both past and future, the specious present is a "saddle-back of time," James explained, "with a certain length of its own, on which we sit perched, and from which we look in two directions into time."

Hodder argued that knowledge of the specious present prevents knowledge neither of other moments nor of other selves; nor is it separable, finally, from the lived world. We live in a fluid multiverse, he contended, something like the pluralistic universe James defined as a "republican banquet . . . where all the qualities of being respect one another's personal sacredness, yet sit at the common table of space and time." Within that world, we mind our manners—such are the ethics of the specious present—but regardless, within its countervailing currents we can be certain only of the moment itself. And to any "metaphysician who looks patiently and steadily," Hodder insisted, "there is revealed a world not in essentials different from the world revealed to the plain man." Such is the Crude Real.

Although Gertrude parodied Hodder's concept of the crude real in her manuscript "Fernhurst," her later definitions of the "prolonged" or "continuous present"—as literary devices—unquestionably had their source in James's and Hodder's work. The specious present, a world lived in and for the moment, implicitly assaulted the conventions of a narrative line, with its lockstep of past, present, and future, and offered in their stead a rationale for "including everything and a beginning again and again." Or, as she more clearly defined it in the lecture "The Gradual Making of *The Making of Americans*," the continuous present is the way we perceive time from within, "a sense of space of time that is filled always filled with moving."

Reinvigorating the language of Hodder and James from the vantage point of her own literary experiments, Stein was speaking with the knowledge, and forgetfulness, of a backward view. For Leo too had used Hodder's work, even earlier, as a basis for his first speculations on aesthetics. He had been initially wary, but when Leo read Hodder's thesis in 1900, he confessed to Gertrude that it "suggested the only path in which I can walk in comfort. If I find that it breaks down I think I shall be able to drop metaphysics for good." Hodder was delighted. "The argument for the Crude Real is taking possession of [Leo] step by step," he bragged to Mamie Gwinn. A victory over Leo was a victory indeed.

In London in the fall of 1902, when Leo was trying to formulate his own theories about aesthetics and appreciation, he turned back to Hodder. He had picked up Benedetto Croce's recently published *Aesthetic* but had found little there to inspire him directly, he later claimed, although the volume obviously helped focus his questions: How do we understand a work of art? What do we see when we look at it? Is the aesthetic experience relative, or will it succumb to some sort of general principle? Reading William James's *The Varieties of Religious Experience* for a breath of fresh air, he began to compare aesthetic and religious experience. But it was Hodder's book and their talks together that Stein seemed to savor most. "A letter from Leo Stein announces that after reading and re-reading the Specious Present he has become convinced," said Hodder, pleased.

The idea of the specious present helped Stein distinguish, in the first place, between aesthetic and emotional experience. "For example once at a concert I kept my attention on the music & appreciated keenly & directly and at the same time I was interested in watching a stream of emotional accompaniment following along," he explained a few years later to a friend. "Now to have confused the two, the objective musical existence and the accompanying emotional suggestion would have been *sentimentality*." Sentimentality was the belief that attention was focused on one thing when in fact it was fixed on something else. "In the crudest cases you depart entirely from your real theme as where you think a chromo beautiful because your Grandmother owned it or something, but the subtler cases are generally such as results from an inadequate analysis where the essential thing is overlaid with separable parts but is treated as single & indivisible. Such for example was the musical illustration above."

Leo had started translating his idea of the specious present into aesthetic terms. Aesthetic vision, he would write in 1906,

is essentially a perception of "existence" and the vitality of your aesthetic experience will depend upon the amount of "existence" which you can realize. For example the "daffodils that come be-

fore the swallows" etc is not a description of Spring it *is* Spring.
There is much descriptive verse there is no "descriptive poetry" because poetry realizes it does not describe. Expression is translation
into communicable form of the experience of actual existences.
Leaving out happy accidents the thing rendered is [not] the thing
seen but the thing complete. That is not the theme [that] is translated but the subject, not any abstractable part but the whole. So
the Daffodils etc are not part of an experience but for aesthetics
they are that experience complete. Therefore there is an element
of error implied in saying that is the Spring. It would be better to
turn it round & say the Spring is that.

Forty years later, he summarized his position succinctly: Art "is not what we
say *about* anything. It is what we say."

To demonstrate, he had been developing a physical corollary to his aesthetic, one he never abandoned. It was a visual game of sorts, devised (he
later said) when he asked himself what a painter sees while painting. To find
out, he placed a plate on a table and looked at it. Nothing happened. But
one day, after looking at the plate every day for a month or so, he saw it differently. It was now divorced from everything previously associated with it—
food, for instance—"it became something every part of which implicated
every other part. One could not see any square inch without every square inch
being involved," he recalled. "It was, one might say, no longer a composite
object, but . . . a projection of my own organic sense, and that organization
was experienced not as in myself, but as in the object. This was creative seeing . . . definitely a form of expression."

"The point [of the game] is to see the plate not as an object of recognition not as a plate but as spatial existence," Stein clarified in early 1906, in the
first written evidence of his game. "Note the difference," he suggested, "between things as seen ordinarily, that is the common kind of mere recognition
seeing and this existential seeing." In terms anticipating Gertrude's more radical experiments, especially in *Tender Buttons*, he instructed his friend to take
a simple object:

A good thing to begin on is a common china plate preferably not
too white and look at it. It is not necessary to look at it as though
one were trying to hypnotise oneself rather to use a favorite phrase
of mine look at it steadily and let your ideas play about.

Spurred on by his results, he also suspected that further discoveries were
for him largely a matter of luck. His enthusiasm was neither dependable nor

sustained. As quickly as he announced his findings he rejected them, unable to take a first, decisive step. Anything, everything, kept him from having to commit himself to paper; the present was specious indeed. "I am slowly blazing my way through the aesthetic wilderness and if certain things will only be good enough to explain themselves I shall proceed apace," he told Mabel Weeks in September 1902. "Only things are often so contrary (and so am I) that I am not very confident in this speedy prospect."

A perfectionist, Leo could not write about his ideas unless he believed them insuperable. He didn't want merely to prove himself equal to those he read; he wanted to best them. "It doesn't seem to me that there's any use," he confided to Mabel Weeks, "unless I succeed in getting a more radical analysis and simplification of elements than anything which so far as I know has yet been attempted." Yet perfectionism was but another name for terror; he feared he'd be revealed an intellectual lightweight.

The more excited he became, the more anxious. Envying those laborers whose work forced them to produce something concrete—those "who could not merely in the silence of their inner selves attempt a construction to equal impossible ideals"—he recognized his perpetual state of preparation. "Not that I hankered after production as such but rather desired the unburdening which comes from production," he told Weeks in a strangely retrospective tone, revealing more than he knew. He didn't covet achievement per se; rather, he desired relief from the demands of his desperate ambition.

But there was no unburdening, except perhaps in the aesthetic game he devised, which allowed him to live fully—and see fully—in the specious present. This, as a consequence, renewed his interest in painting. In fact, he began to wonder whether he too should take up the brush.

WHEN GERTRUDE LEFT LONDON in the fall of 1902, Leo intended to join her in New York. That was the plan, but as usual his route was roundabout. In no hurry to return to America—Gertrude notwithstanding—he quit London precipitately, according to his memory of events, and went to Paris for another look at the Louvre and the street life. There were several people he could visit, his cousin Ernest Keyser for instance, an artist, as well as a young cellist and family friend, Pablo Casals.

In Paris after Christmas, Leo arranged some dinners with Casals, and it was after one of these, he later recalled, that he first began to paint.

And then he knew he was staying.

He said he told Casals that if he'd been born thirty years earlier, he might well have been an artist. Casals perhaps asked, quite reasonably, why not now? Whatever conversation took place between the two that evening, Leo remembered that afterward, he returned to his hotel room, lit a fire in the fire-

place, and took off all his clothes. Staring into the mirror on the wardrobe, he
began to draw.

In the following days, Leo went to the Louvre to sketch statues, and resolved to take lessons at the Académie Julian. Established in 1860 as a more
democratic alternative to the École des Beaux-Arts, where admission requirements were stiff, the Académie was located conveniently on the rue de
Dragon and admitted anyone, including foreigners, who paid the fees and provided a name (even a landlord's) as a reference. Once admitted, students
worked on their technique more or less as they saw fit; when professors came
twice a week to criticize, the students who wanted to avoid their comments
simply covered their easels.

The tolerant atmosphere at the Académie Julian was generally regarded
as supporting both individual talent and the official salons. Some, however,
thought the Académie stuffy, its American students traditional, its teachers
mediocrities. When Leo arrived, its alumni included his cousin Ernest Keyser,
the American artists Robert Henri and Edward Steichen, the Irish novelist
George Moore, the British art critic Roger Fry, the British painter Wilson Steer
(whose landscape Stein had recently purchased), and Henri Matisse, whom
Stein would soon know personally.

All students were provided with instruction in the discipline of drawing, first from plaster casts and then from the life model; the Académie also
supplied, if one desired, a social life. Leo's was scant. Gertrude told the Hapgoods he painted ten hours a day. "I don't see how you have stood your long
seclusion—" an American friend wrote him, "but then you never were in the
fight." But in Paris, even more than in Florence, Leo could ignore the nip of
such a remark. Here he was surrounded by men who had found an alternative to America in the established and respected role of Paris art student.

He would need a place to live and work. Ernest Keyser suggested rooms
at 27, rue de Fleurus, a small street near the Luxembourg Gardens, not far
from Montparnasse and easily approached from the boulevard Raspail. Rents
in the district, with its gardens, courtyards, and former convents, were as low
as five hundred francs a year, about one hundred dollars, for a one-bedroom
apartment. Studio space was available for artists, and many artists lived in the
neighborhood—among them the painter Jean-Paul Laurens, a longtime
teacher at the Académie Julian. But the neighborhood was hardly fashionable
and had a comfortable, provincial feel. The lamplighter in his blue smock still
appeared on the streets every evening, torch slung over his shoulder.

The building at 27, rue de Fleurus was of a newer sort, a light, faceless
stone. One entered through an archway into a small courtyard, where to the
right was a two-story pavilion adjoining a high-ceilinged studio with northern
light. It was perfect for Stein. The apartment consisted of four rooms, a

kitchen, and a bath. Some speculated it was practically the only bath on the street; most neighbors rented tin tubs from traveling carts that hoisted water pipes from the street to their apartments. Leo was content. He hung his Japanese prints, the landscape by Steer, and before long another purchase, a small painting by Du Gardier of a woman in white with a white dog on a green lawn. "Now everything with me seems so changed that there are hardly more than points of resemblance between the conduct of life as it is now and [as] it was before," Leo informed Mabel Weeks shortly after moving in.

He felt free. Nothing mattered but painting. "Imagine for two months I haven't read a book except a couple of novels of Flaubert . . ." he exulted. "I read the reviews in the Nation without the slightest impulse to order the book & without any yearning to be abreast of modern scholarship on any subject. . . . It's almost the same to me whether logic is merely symbolic or not in fact I believe I could listen to a man maintaining that art is in its essence, in some way shape or form a reproduction of nature without wanting to punch his head, but about this last I'm not quite sure."

Everything but painting went to pot, he told Weeks, and he was having the time of his life. He worked on a portrait six and a half by four and a half feet: "I only started it yesterday & I [see] it was an awful shock to me when all that canvas got up on the easel and stared me blankly in the face. After a few minutes however I began to feel more comfortable in its presence and now I don't care shucks." Every morning he walked to the Académie, where the walls were covered with palette scrapings, and students chattered in several languages in airless rooms. He worked from the life model until lunchtime, when he returned home, ate, and sketched until evening. Then he went back to the Académie. He rented his apartment and studio through the summer, and signed up for fencing lessons; he planned to stay for a while.

Evidently he was studying with Adolphe-William Bouguereau, a very successful French artist who also taught at the École des Beaux-Arts. Amply honored and eminently conventional, Bouguereau devoted himself to mythological subjects rendered in expert academic style: polished satyrs and candy-box nymphs cavorting in healthful landscapes. Leo studied sculpture briefly with Raoul Verlet, known for his admiration of the Greeks and Michelangelo. On the whole Leo said little about his teachers; he noted, noncommittally, that the academicians were "often as marked personalities as the radicals. They simply belong to different crowds. Bonnat and J. P. Laurens were as definite and individual as Manet or Renoir."

Stein's sketches and oils of the period were elementary exercises in rendering, not without promise. He had a certain technical ability and an increasing sense of form. By and large, however, they were placid and safe. A new friend, the American sculptor Mahonri Young, remembered Stein well from these days: "Leo was a true art person, and he was interested in art and he liked to talk about it and he liked to theorize and philosophize about it. Then after a while he thought he knew so much about it he could do it. So I met him in Julian's Academy, where he was trying to do it. Well, nobody has less talent." But the grandson of Brigham Young nonetheless thought Leo's insight, appreciation, and offhand generosity unusual.

Stein one day invited Young, who was in the same sculpture class, home to his atelier. "I have a book that will interest you," he told Young. At the rue de Fleurus, he handed Young a large green-covered volume, a portfolio, of twenty exquisite sketches by Degas: folds of drapery minutely rendered, charcoal studies of a jockey, a woman ironing, ballerinas with limbs extended, sculptural nudes. Young was breathless. The marvelous book must have cost two hundred dollars. "In those days," he said later, "that was a lot of money." But Stein had it, and with it, he opened Young's eyes to Degas.

Later in life, Stein dismissed his art student days, belittling both his work and his commitment to it: "I couldn't acquire any craft because as soon as the initial spontaneity was gone I was done for. I never could acquire habits. . . . The fact that I did something three hundred and sixty-four days in the year would not influence me to do it automatically the three hundred and sixty-fifth. In consequence, there were no accumulated skills, and so even after starting to do something well I usually continued to do it worse and worse."

This was partly true. But it was also true that his devotion to painting continued unabated for the next several years. In 1906 he told a friend that painting still consumed most of his time: "It is what I should have begun to do much sooner, but one is not born again in the spirit till the time is ripe and since it was necessary that I wait it is I suppose well that I waited." When discouraged, though, he did stop painting for short intervals. Then, he reported with relief, he would be at it again. "I don't any longer spoil things the second day because I don't know what to do with them. Even the third has been safely passed." That was in 1908. Two years later, after telling Gertrude he was through, that same night, after midnight, he began to work on a giant canvas.

In 1910 he did indeed quit, and for a very long time. Recalled Stanton Macdonald-Wright, an artist friend, "He had sat in front of a plate of fruit for days, hoping to be able to express something in paint & had finally given it up." By this time, Leo had become completely infatuated with a young Parisian model. And she with him.

TO THE END of her life Etta Cone affected innocence. But she was a clever and passionate woman, perfectly capable of subterfuge, especially if she thought propriety was at stake. Perturbed by rumors after Gertrude Stein's death that "there was something *between* Gertrude and Alice," she insisted to

Leo Stein,
Seated Nude
(*oil on canvas*)

her niece, "I never believed it." Then she added the conventional coup de grâce. "After all, what can two women *do*?"

The question had the agreeable result of deflecting attention from herself. Etta Cone would have her niece believe she was a genteel maiden aunt, whose knowledge of sexual matters was bashful and limited. But partly as a consequence of such coyness, the exact nature of her early intimacy with Gertrude remains unclear. One thing is certain, however: theirs was an intimacy—Etta called it "one of the real inspirations in my life"—that both women prized.

When Gertrude arrived in Europe on June 21, 1903, Leo was in Paris, where Gertrude would return after a visit to Italy. Etta had been there a month, guiding her sister Claribel and a cousin, Aimee Guggenheimer, through Florentine streets like a veteran, Berenson's *Florentine Painters* firmly in hand. That day, a Sunday, the group walked to the railroad station to meet Gertrude's train and help her settle in their hotel. Personal talk had to be postponed until after midnight, for Gertrude was having dinner that first evening with the Berensons. The Cones must have been impressed.

Etta was delighted by Gertrude's arrival. "It's great having Gertrude here," she exclaimed in her travel diary. The next day, as the two friends

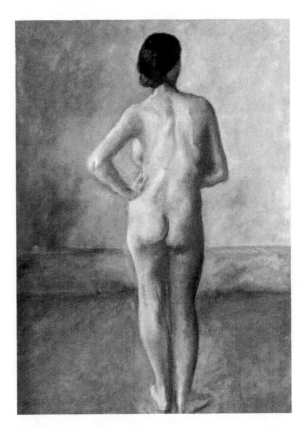

Leo Stein,
Standing Nude
(*oil on canvas*)

strolled to the piazzale Michelangelo after dinner, Gertrude talked over the subject of Etta's future. It was not so much a question of what as of where—Baltimore? North Carolina? Europe, perhaps? Both Etta's parents were now dead and Sister Claribel was on her way to the Senckenberg Pathology Institute in Frankfurt. The talk was helpful. "It was great & Gertrude was in fine humor," Etta reported to her diary, neglecting to say what, if anything, had been concluded.

Stein spent most of those warm summer mornings and early afternoons with the Cone party. They visited the Accademia, where she and her friends stood rapturously in front of a Botticelli and found "charm & humor," Etta noted, in other paintings. They headed to the Church of San Lorenzo to look at Michelangelo's tomb sculptures in the Medici chapels—Gertrude insisted on the resemblance between Michelangelo's *Night* and Etta—and Etta introduced Gertrude to the Perugino fresco at the Convent of Santa Maria Maddalena dei Pazzi. With Stein in tow, art history à la Berenson seemed less important than fantasy and fun. "Gertrude has me down . . . for a suggestion I made as to why a 'woman [was] lost in the art of sculpture—too many housekeeping fronts of the body.' " Etta nonetheless read her Berenson in the grand galleries of the Pitti Palace as Gertrude "played" with Sister Claribel and Aimee Guggenheimer. The days were almost always bright and fair, and Gertrude loved the outdoors ("The Western sun-lover feel[s] that to be in Tuscany is to be at home," she wrote); she walked the hill to Settignano with Sister Claribel while Etta rode the tram from the Duomo.

They took pictures at a café table where they stopped for something to drink. In the photographs, the three women are tired, happy, dressed almost the same, in long dark skirts and, despite the weather, high collars and long-sleeved blouses; Stein wears a panama. The friends walked to Fiesole, a hill-top town northeast of Florence, where they ate a fine dinner and got drunk. "Had a good old talk with Gertrude," Etta declared again and again. "Gertrude is great fun."

For the next few days after her arrival, Stein divided her time between the Cones' hotel and I Tatti, where the Berensons, in their elegantly hospitable style, were entertaining also Hutchins Hapgood and Neith Boyce. When the Hapgoods moved back to Florence, to the Villa Solferino, Gertrude walked with them in the nearby Cascine park many evenings, listening for nightingales. Thoughtful, attractive, and straining under the yoke of marriage, Neith Boyce was, according to Mary Berenson, waiting for her first novel to be published to assess her worth in the world. Until then, most of her days included a routine quarrel with her husband, "beginning with the fact that I won't be sociable with the green Americans at the pension table," Boyce noted dryly, "& ending up with the fact that I am a bad wife. As it was in the beginning, is now and ever shall be."

Impressed with Stein's frank intelligence, Boyce was also capable of observing Gertrude's habits with disdain. A disheveled Gertrude arrived at the villa late one afternoon, her dress mussed and "much the worse for wear," Neith observed. Yet she respected Gertrude's air of independence. Once, after coffee and ices, Stein lit a cigarette—"Not usual in public!" Neith marveled. She, Neith, smoked only in the privacy of her garden. The Cone sisters smoked too, but Neith would not have suspected as much. Invited to join them for dinner one evening, she declined; she had declined a similar invitation a few days before Stein arrived, recording in her diary that Hutchins had joined a Miss Friedenwall "& a lot of other Jews," some of whom were, mercifully, "going away tomorrow hurrah!" Gertrude Stein, however, like the more fastidious Bernhard Berenson, was acceptable—up to a point. "We enjoyed G's visit, though she rather got on my nerves at times by her habit of not bathing & wearing the same clothes all the time," Neith wrote.

She and Stein conferred about Berenson's health. He looked as drawn and weary as when Stein had seen him the year before at Friday's Hill, and

Neith Boyce Hapgood

seemed just as depressed. Having donned her most professional bedside de-
meanor, Stein diagnosed the source of the problem as the hardship of his
youth, and instead of milk and raw eggs this time prescribed a change of scene.
"America ought to be a good thing for him," she told Neith, advising the tonic
that had worked for her. In Florence this summer, she seemed much more
optimistic and happy than she had been in London. Understandably, the
thought of her next stop, Rome, where she would rendezvous with May Bookstaver and Mabel Haynes, left her anxious.

Since early June, in fact, Stein had been trying to persuade Etta to go
with her to Rome. During their long walks, she almost had her way. But Etta,
obviously aware of the subordinate role she would be assigned, managed to
resist, albeit with some regret. Besides, she was already committed to accompanying Claribel partway to Frankfurt. On July 2, along with Gertrude,
Aimee, and Claribel, she took a tram from Florence to Vallombrosa for a picnic; after lunch they smoked cigarettes and lounged under the tall dark pines.
Then Etta and Gertrude strolled together along the shady country road. Etta
was sad. She would not see Gertrude again for six months or more, Gertrude,
the person to whom she would declare "deepest love and devoted friendship."
Later that day, Gertrude boarded the train for Rome.

IN ALL, she was seven weeks in Rome. The Hapgoods did not see her again
until August 21, when she showed up at their newly rented villa in Bagni di

Lucca unexpectedly, the letter announcing her arrival having gone to the wrong address. Full of stories about the death of Pope Leo XIII, Gertrude seemed in typically good spirits.

She must have had a reasonably good time. With May Bookstaver and Mabel Haynes, she had braced for the awkwardness of a threesome; the tension of the previous year in New York was still on their minds. To judge from the sparse correspondence that still exists—fragments of letters copied into Stein's notebook—misunderstanding and suspicion had continued to wrench their affections. Bookstaver's protracted involvement with Haynes depressed Stein, who must have felt as sunken as her main character, Adele, in "Q.E.D." Though in love, she recognized the limits of her own feelings: "I have neither the inclination or the power to take Mabel's place and I feel therefore that I have no right to step in between them." But she resented the money that Haynes was able to lavish on Bookstaver, tilting the balance of power and affection in Haynes's direction. "Some day if we continue she will in spite of herself be compelled to choose between us and what have I to offer?" Stein wrote in "Q.E.D." "Nothing but an elevating influence. Bah! what is the use of an elevating influence if one hasn't bread and butter."

Moreover, if Stein in New York was having affairs with several women, as Mabel Weeks had said, this surely complicated the relations between Stein and Bookstaver. And if true, it makes sense of some of the more obscure references in "Q.E.D.," which hint at the broad scope of Adele's inconstancy: "No I am not a cad. Helen has come very near to persuading me that I am but I really am not. We both went into this with our eyes open, and Helen fully deliberately as myself." But also in "Q.E.D.," the struggle between the two antagonists, born of mistrust and pride, devolves into a battle among three women, each seeking power over the others. Theirs was a tale of passion and complex jealousy. And Mabel Haynes in real life was a vexing adversary for Gertrude Stein: she was a successful lover, a successful medical student, a woman of apparently easy privilege.

That hot July in Rome, Haynes, Bookstaver, and Stein were inseparable, each trying to read between the lines of the others' behavior. Summing up the encounter in her notebook as she prepared to write "Q.E.D." barely two months later, Stein outlined the major events of those edgy, unpleasant days: "Whole Roman experience beginning with the meeting on the Via Nazionale. 1. Day, meeting [dine] on Campagna. 2. Important. Scene in my room. evening declaration of [illegible]. 3. St. Paul without the walls walk down the hill sore foot, cab, evening [illegible]. 4. Tivoli restaurant. [flees] grasp. 5. Afternoon lying on couch after two days of no chance. Observation. 6. Restaurant. 7. Last day Sistine & street car."

"I did look disapproving when you said you had been marauding with

your friends—" Emma Lootz Erving responded to news of Stein's Roman experience, "but I may as well believe when you say you were good—tho' I'm
afraid our conceptions of virtue differ." Although Stein's closest friends apparently knew of the complicated triangle, she herself said nothing when
walking with the Hapgoods in the hills near Lucca the next month. To them
Stein was unchanged: jolly, energetic, full of advice about pneumonia and food
for their baby. Over the following days, as she and Neith tramped through the
countryside, ecstatic at the scenery, Gertrude seemed to inhale deep pleasure
from the landscape. It was too beautiful to paint, she said, unlike France and
England with their picturesque low skies.

At a café they drank vermouth with syrup and stared at the bright blue
sky. They took a long walk to Corsagna, through beds of wild flowers and a
nursery of young trees, by cascades and old stone walls, all set against hills
that stretched languorously ahead. They hiked through a chestnut forest and
passed sharp green hedges covered with clean linen laid out to dry. At the next
café, they ordered bread, beer, cheese, and plums. They gossiped. Stein gave
her friends the New York news, divulging Alfred Hodder's affair with Mamie
Gwinn, a "schoolmarm," Neith understood Gertrude to say, "a shy shrinking
person of forty-odd summers," and swearing, by contrast, that Leo was not involved with any one woman. As for herself, Gertrude announced, she was
going to Paris to write a novel, something semiautobiographical and perhaps
risqué after the picaresque manner of George Borrow.

"Gertrude's visit has been fun," Neith wrote when Gertrude was preparing to leave. "She is very amusing and good-tempered, enjoys life, chuckles a
lot, I like her deep voice and laughter." Neith and Hutchins were astonished
when Gertrude sat in the sun without a hat for an hour or more, streaming
with sweat. "Can't see how she does it, even Italians fear the midday sun,"
Neith puzzled. "She doesn't like baths in the tub, perhaps that's her way of
bathing!"

In Florence again, Stein joined the recently arrived Mabel Weeks for a
walking trip to Siena. Stein was more candid with Weeks about her Roman
adventure than she had been with the Hapgoods. Many years later Weeks reportedly said that Gertrude was more anguished than she had ever seen her,
gushing "Oscar Wildean justifications" of her trying love affair, with its de-
ceits, maneuvers, and conspiracy.

These persisted. When Bookstaver and Haynes arrived in Siena, furtive
exchanges of glances, perceived slights, double entendres kept the relationship stormy. Gertrude, usually so verbal, seemed unable to make May understand her feelings. Letters written around this time, which Stein copied
into a notebook for use in "Q.E.D.," reveal the emotional turbulence. "What
a lot of nonsense," reads one, undeniably written after one of their meetings:

I can talk as soon as I cease to be intimidated by your actual presence. But what can one do. There must be some talking done, else what would become of the sacred rites of conversation and as when we are together I can't and you won't I must have at you with a pen. It may have the additional advantage of making you desire to. . . . Leo didn't turn up for a week and I spent it in a gorgeous novel of Trollope and Bulwer Lytton. . . . Incidentally I reread [Hodder's] the New Americans. There is a lot of wonderfully brilliant writing in it. At present I am going to see you next spring and instead of that I should be devoting my energy to meditating on how seven volume novels are written. Get thee behind me Satan. At present I end with that simple childlike verse of Mabel's. If you love me as I love you no knife can cut our line in two.

Another, less ebullient letter was written in all likelihood a few weeks later, after Gertrude arrived at Leo's apartment in Paris. Relations between her and Bookstaver had again soured, and Gertrude was angry:

Write to you yes that sounds simple but what [the hell] is it that I am to write. I did write you a long letter but with more than my customary discretion I suppressed it. I can't write you what I think because I am afraid you might find that an impertinence and [I am afraid] my mood toward you is a little too bitter to indulge [in description of Paris boulevards] in a letter of descriptions. What is it I want oh damn it all you know well enough. I don't want you ever again to deny that you care for me. The thought of your doing it again takes all the sunshine out of the sky for me. Oh you are wrong a thousand times wrong and you and your silences and your submissions. Well I don't know that this effusion is any more peaceable than those that have been suppressed. However I suppose something must go once it might as well be this. Do you know a phrase of Hodders concerning Isabel is very illuminating. He says of her She had indomitable pluck that is she was incapable of changing her plan of life she hadn't imagination enough. It seems to me it is something on that principle that you object to conclusions and the recognition of your motives. You hate conclusions because you may have to change them. You will stultify yourself to any extent rather than admit you too have been in the wrong. I hate to send you this because you will insult me as usual by assuming that I am meaning something that I do not mean. I don't want . . . to interfere with anyone's claims on you but I do want you to realize that you . . . ought to be strong enough to . . . come somewhere being honest. Nothing can justify such cringing, such slavish subjection, such abject lying.

Clearly proud of her letter, Gertrude preserved a draft to revise and incorporate into the first and final pages of "Q.E.D."

That work was to be her Borrowesque novel, written in Paris while Leo painted. When it was complete, she copied it in ink into a notebook, wrote "Finis" in a large hand, and dated the manuscript October 24, 1903. At the bottom of the last page, in pencil, she added, as if in a whisper, "the actual answer"—presumably May Bookstaver's response to Stein's hostile tirade: "I don't understand what you mean by my having denied that I care for you when have I ever done so. I do love you and I am sorrier than I can say that you should have ever been so bothered."

Stein knew she had not gotten through.

"HOW OFTEN do we find ourselves prostrate before the wall of lamentation beating it with our impotent hands praying to a God that will not hear. Our faith stronger and our life weaker than ever before," Gertrude Stein wrote as she sampled sentences, discarded phrases, tried again. "They say that old people do find themselves at last face to face with a solid blank wall. It sounds it seems [sic] to have something beyond it but it won't move." And then again: "At the end of our powers we are like the exiled Jews before the wall of lamentations. Our faith is stronger than it ever was but we are hopelessly stopped." These sentences, never used, were intended probably for a more personal, more dismal finale to "Q.E.D." than the bleakly resigned one Stein chose. Her heroine is frustrated but not without vision, the vision her antagonist lacks. Adele cries of her uncomprehending lover, dropping her head on her arms, "Can't she see things as they are and not as she would make them."

Stein had said much the same thing and experienced much the same frustration. Trying to take a more philosophical view of their tattered relationship, she wrote May Bookstaver from Paris (she preserved part of this letter as well):

Good God no I am not angry. I haven't anything to be angry about worse luck. No one is to blame. I couldn't once and you can't now and it is nobody's fault, it is only our common misfortune. The only thing that would ease my pain would be to know that you too are suffering but as you are not I must rest [comfortable] although I do admit that it soothes my pride to know that you too can be inadequate and that you have failed me in my need as completely as

I ever failed you. However I may be able to come over to New York
for a few months about the first of March and perhaps by that time
you can find it in your heart to be good to me. But really dear the
only thing that does anger me is the fashion in which you persist
in deluding yourself. You will never learn that things do happen
and that you are not strong enough to stave them off. You do ex-
asperate me with your willful blindness. You never realize things
as they are but always as you would make them if you were strong
enough which you are not. However these are my last remarks on
the subject. I promise you I will never bore you with it again.

Although her anger seethed between the lines, she was now more ambivalent
in her feelings toward May, and more detached. This may have been exactly
what Gertrude was hoping for when she began to turn them into fiction. "The
things that have really impressed your imagination," a friend observed a few
years later, "were the things you touched when you were hard at work."

"Keep up the good work of writing," Emma Lootz Erving encouraged in
early October. Later that month she wrote again. "Thanks for a letter from
gay Paree. I'm glad literature is entrancing." Leo's enthusiasm for his new vocation had been contagious. Snug in his apartment, Gertrude, like him, found
a niche. "I hope life in Paris is better than life in London," Emma commented.
"Your literature must be as good as Henry James's—or I shall be disappointed."

Stein's later claim (in *The Autobiography of Alice B. Toklas*) that she
did not read and was not interested in Henry James during her "formative
period" was more than a bit coy. She and her friends were devotees who
scrupulously weighed every nuance of the master, including his prefaces. In
fact, deference to William James's brother was paid directly in the pages of
"Q.E.D." when Stein compared Helen Thomas with Kate Croy. Moreover,
Stein had been making a careful study of Henry James's style, copying long
sections of *The Wings of the Dove,* for example, into her notebooks and deliberately using Morton Densher as a model for her character Adele. She
played with James's metaphor of vision and its necessary emphasis on perceptive intelligence, or the lack of it, and adopted for Adele the credo of "seeing things as they are."

Gertrude was influenced also by Leo's use of visual metaphor, for he was
grappling daily with the meaning of seeing and understanding. Such was the
impetus behind his so-called aesthetic game, his concentration on the object.
Leo remained interested in literature, continuously commenting on its structure and style. He recommended *Clarissa* (later one of her favorites) to his
sister, and said he admired its steady, relentless pace; "I don't believe there is
another such closely knit book in the language but it does take a lot of paper

to give the whole work without a single stitch dropped." He had enjoyed Fielding's *Tom Jones,* partly because it "lacks all merit of character construction," although "it has structure." Gibbon was still a favorite. Gertrude too liked the long, leisurely rambles into eighteenth-century prose, as her book lists indicate. No doubt she and Leo, who discussed much together, discussed this. And her writing.

When Gertrude finished "Q.E.D." in 1903, she gave it to Leo to read as a matter of course. Years thence, he remembered having thought "the stuff was interesting—it was the original material of [her story] Melanctha . . . [but] the writing was impossible. There was no objective situation." By then, 1934, he had been angry for a long time; yet during their days together on the rue de Fleurus, he was unquestionably and necessarily supportive about her work, as she was about his. Friends who wrote them invariably asked in the same breath about Leo's painting and Gertrude's writing, as if it was unthinkable to consider one without the other. Leo considered his sister's psychological portraits splendid, her curiosity about people vivacious and unflagging, her observations keen, her humanity hearty; even in his bitter years he maintained that in her early work she had had something to say.

But in the last sections of "Q.E.D.," the deeply felt moral dilemmas and the sensuality of the early part of the book, where the lovers meet and parry, become contrived; Stein had not yet found a way to integrate the intensely felt with her disposition toward intellectual constructs. This is of course the central irony of her subject: Stein had written a book about a taboo relationship and, given the taboo, was almost forced to take refuge in indirection, ellipsis, verbal subterfuge. Such too is the irony she directs at Adele, the character who squarely sees "things as they are," but whose geometric formulation leaves her defeated and inert. What could her next step be? It was a question that Stein, as incipient artist, had to ask herself. And it was not unlike the questions that confounded her brother.

WHEN HER MANUSCRIPT was finished, Stein claimed, she put it in the cupboard and never gave it a second thought. More likely, she considered its writing an exorcism of sorts; it was an unpublishable exercise, to be "hidden with intention," as she commented in "Here. Actualities," a short piece written in 1932, not long after the manuscript resurfaced. She could not bear to reread it, she told the writer Louis Bromfield, but she let him look at it in hopes he might be able to arrange for American publication with "anybody reliable." "There are great difficulties, but it's possible they may be overcome," he responded carefully. The novella was not published in Stein's lifetime.

IN PARIS IN OCTOBER, on their way back to the United States, the Hapgoods were anxious to see the Steins, those "very queer Americans." Tall and short, lean and thick, male and female, both attired in the costume of the day but without the customs that went with them, they were "without manners," said Neith, yet interesting nonetheless. Leo and Gertrude made a happy couple, glad to be in each other's company and ready to launch their new adventures.

Leo had fallen out of favor with Mary Berenson, whose mother had objected to his presence in Fernhurst that summer. Mary had arranged for him and Howard Gans to rent a place near Friday's Hill, but when "the Jews" came to dinner, Hannah Smith was annoyed. Her son Logan, who did not care to meet any more of them, disappeared, and although Howard Gans passed muster, Leo fell deeply out of favor. Hannah Smith said he bored Roger Fry to distraction and horrified one visitor with his "nasty sexual views." That wasn't all. Carrying a dark cloud wherever he went, he depressed everyone. Not until the second of September, when he left, did she feel the "black and threatening 'aura'" had lifted. Mary Berenson promised not to invite him back.

For his part, Leo resentfully told the Hapgoods he was disillusioned with Bernhard, whom he thought an unmitigated snob. Gertrude, perhaps taking Berenson's side, said she admired "the splendid insolence of the true aristocrat." Such was the genuine artist. And, said Neith, Gertrude "was all for the feeling of permanence, continuity."

A bohemian, yes; without manners of a conventional sort, yes; an intelligent eccentric, a budding writer, a conservative. "She was intolerant in the pride of her strength but no one could have had theoretically, a broader outlook": Stein had described herself well in a Radcliffe composition. "She was tremendously moral, riding with great vigor all those hobbies that belong to the women known in the current phrase as advanced. She was painfully self-righteous in the midst of the most violent denunciation of self-righteousness."

She was also decisive, ambitious, and eager to begin her new career. Paris and her brother's atelier, where she was certainly welcome, would serve. She would stay. That is, after she went back to America to see, among other friends, Etta Cone.

12
TOWARD A MORE QUINTESSENTIAL METHOD, 1903–1905

The Steins in Paris, circa 1904
(left to right: Leo, Allan, Gertrude, Therese Ehrman, Sarah, and Michael)

I am beginning the buying all over again—but shall stop—how these abayas wrap themselves about me! how the saris wind themselves about my very heart—"throat" would be better for they strangled out all other impulses—and the metal bowls and the beads—now that I stop to reason about it, it is silly foolishness this collecting of things!—but it must have some solid foundation— some foundation deep in the hearts of peoples—for look at the thousands who are moved by the same impulse—and look at the museums that have been founded to satisfy this impulse— It is the craving for beauty that is such a vital function of the human soul—that's it—the craving for beauty—for perfection— Some say that it is one way of finding the path to God.

CLARIBEL CONE TO ETTA CONE

I often used to wonder why I was ready to pay for a picture a sum which would buy me an estate. . . . Of course the pictures had a speculative value but I never considered that. The interest had the nature of a love affair, an irresistible desire. I have a similar feeling when I read Shakespeare and more rarely other poets; but in general the peculiar passion is of the nature of love. . . .

LEO STEIN, UNPUBLISHED NOTEBOOK

"WE IS DOING BUSINESS TOO," Gertrude cheerfully reported to Mabel Weeks in late 1903, "we are selling Jap prints to buy a Cezanne at least we are that is Leo is trying. He don't like it a bit and makes an awful fuss about asking enough money but I guess we'll get the Cezanne."

In Paris, invigorated by the world around him—a daily carnival of crowds on the boulevards, noisy painters packed into the rooms at the Académie Julian, exhibits opening and closing almost daily, each furiously debated—Leo was again seized by the urge to buy. With no great ambition to become a major collector, and lacking the means in any case, he took a profound pleasure in a variety of artifacts: the paintings of Steer and Du Gardier, Japanese prints, the swords, books, pieces of furniture he had acquired in Italy. Although they sated his hunger, at the same time they increased his appetite.

In Italy the previous summer, he had found a picture, probably a drawing initially attributed to the shadowy figure Bernhard Berenson had dubbed "Amico di Sandro," or friend of Sandro Botticelli. Leo liked the picture but doubted the attribution; he brought it to Paris in the fall to have it appraised. Gertrude proudly dispatched the results to Mabel Weeks: the Amico di Sandro wasn't an Amico "cause it's so much better. That is Leo's connoisseurship."

Still, he had been looking for something modern, something by a living artist to excite him just as much. "I wanted an adventure," he recalled of his first days in Paris in early 1903, when everything was a letdown. The official salon bored him, and as for the paintings at the Société Nouvelle, works by Henri Martin and Jacques-Émile Blanche and Charles Cottet, they were "livelier" and "showed what was trying to be the art of the then today. There was a certain freshness and vivacity in many of the pictures, and yet they were somehow not art with a big A." Stein told Berenson, who was in Paris that spring, of his disappointment. Although not particularly interested in modern art himself, Berenson asked, "Do you know Cézanne?"

Stein did not. Berenson suggested he visit Ambroise Vollard's gallery on the rue Lafitte. Leo had passed the small shop many times, peering through the doorway at the stacks of pictures banked against the walls, but as yet he hadn't ventured inside. The bulky, black-bearded Vollard, who had a reputation for being earnest, was perceptive enough to sense Leo's sincerity, and he quickly put Stein at ease. Leo began to visit the shop frequently, studying pictures at various angles and in different lights. Vollard's collection was more to his liking than what he'd seen at the salons. And since Mantegna's *Crucifixion,* "with the color running through it," along with works by Piero della Francesca and Domenico Veneziano, had prepared him for this brave new world, he soon bought Cézanne's *Landscape with Spring House.*

It was not until a few months later, in August and in Florence, that Leo plunged into the world of modern painting. Day after day he looked at the Cézannes owned by Charles Loeser, a wealthy American collector of everything from pictures to ivory-headed canes. This was nothing short, Leo later said, of a debauch. When he returned to Paris in the fall, he was eager to buy.

Gertrude was with him, and the two of them began to haunt Vollard's shop. "It was an incredible place," she wrote in *The Autobiography of Alice B. Toklas.* "It did not look like a picture gallery. Inside there were a couple of canvases turned to the wall, in one corner was a small pile of big and little canvases thrown pell mell on top of one another, in the center of the room stood a huge dark man glooming. This was Vollard cheerful." Sister and brother insisted on seeing some Cézannes like those they had seen the past summer, "one of those marvelously yellow sunny Aix landscapes of which Loeser had several examples." After looking at a great many, Leo and Gertrude settled on *The Conduit,* a small, compelling picture of deep green.

"In the years . . . 1904–1910 I was madly enthusiastic for Cézanne," Leo noted in an unpublished manuscript. "Then, especially the earlier part of this period, $1000. was a huge price for a Cézanne, except for a few favorite elaborate still life's [*sic*] and one could get excellent landscape & figure pictures and also small or less elaborate still life pictures for from 100 to 400 dollars." Over time he and Gertrude came to own more Cézannes than could be seen at the Musée du Luxembourg, including *The Man with a Pipe,* the striking *Smoker,* two medium-sized compositions of bathers, two views of Mont Sainte-Victoire and other watercolors, a number of lithographs, and a shapely, powerful still life of apples.

Cézanne was the cornerstone of the rue de Fleurus collection: curving landscapes of peculiar force, solitary figures isolated in introspective depth, modeled apples of subtle eroticism. "Great mind, a perfect concentration, and great control," Leo characterized the artist to Mabel Weeks in 1905. With unhesitating judgment, he perspicaciously defined the source of Cézanne's strength in one of the earliest appreciations of the painter's work:

> Cézanne's essential problem is mass and he has succeeded in rendering mass with a vital intensity that is unparalleled in the whole history of painting. No matter what his subject is—the figure, landscape, still life—there is always this remorseless intensity, this endless unending gripping of the form, the unceasing effort to force it to reveal its absolute self-existing quality of mass. There can scarcely be such a thing as a completed Cézanne. Every canvas is a battlefield and every victory an unattainable ideal. Cézanne rarely does more than one thing at a time and when he turns to composition he brings to bear the same intensity, keying his composition up till it sings like a harp string. His color also, though as harsh as his forms, is almost as vibrant.

Leo praised what he most admired in Cézanne, the persistent struggle "with the problem of rendering matter stable and organic form substantial." Cézanne's effectiveness, Leo wrote ten years after his letter to Mabel Weeks, lay in his fresh solutions to compositional problems, his ability to take the impressionists' idea of color and use it to build form. Cézanne, Stein said, "fixed his mind upon the solid thing itself. He tried to get, above all else, substantiality, finality, the eternal, the secure."

While Leo usually cast his appreciation of Cézanne in formal terms, he also responded deeply to the artist's reclusive temperament, his "inability to cope with men or things," for Cézanne, like Stein, had "innumerable phobias and manias. Especially he feared women and the designs on him which he imputed to them all." The painter Leo so admired was "a man oppressed, tormented, isolated, with only one real aim in life—to paint, attain to mastery, and in the end to create." Stein, who had trouble finishing anything, admired this above all else.

ON A RAW DAY in January 1904, Leo Stein was in Cherbourg. Michael and Sarah and their son, Allan, now eight years old, were arriving, bundled against the cold in heavy woolens. The small party also included eighteen-year-old Therese Ehrman, come along to study piano and take care of Allan. The Steins had pulled up stakes in San Francisco, packed their trunks, and set off for the old world. It would be a better place, they thought, to educate their son. Besides, Michael had grown uneasy. He had dabbled successfully in real estate, and retired from the cable car business because, some supposed, he hated to work on the side of management. But during a recent strike, it was also said, Michael Stein had driven the first car out of the barn. Perhaps it was the shower of hard little pebbles thrown by striking workers that changed his mind. As a rule considerate and mild-mannered, he avoided controversy when he could, and that trait contributed in no small measure to his success in business. But strikes meant inevitable friction, no matter what one's side, so Michael retired by age thirty-eight. Living on the proceeds of his rental property, he followed his younger brother to Paris, dreaming vaguely of opening an antique shop.

The change suited his wife, who may well have been the author of it. In San Francisco, Sarah had studied music, early Italian art, and literature; she was an avid theater- and concertgoer and loved to talk about drama and music, but, she told Gertrude, she had been suppressing her "Salon-lady propensities." "A woman cannot be a salon-lady in these days, I fear, without flirting a wee bit, can she?" Sarah inquired sheepishly. " Self-restraint, however, was contrary to her nature. Blessed with deep smothering sympathies as well as large, willful enthusiasms, she craved more than San Francisco could offer. She was fated, said Alice Toklas, to be a provincial Madame de Staël. But Henri Matisse, whose work she'd soon buy and revere, characterized Sarah Stein as the "really intelligently sensitive member of the family."

Escorting the excited new arrivals into Paris, Leo showed them to their rooms in the venerable Hôtel Foyot, near the Luxembourg Gardens and not far from his own apartment on rue de Fleurus. That night, no one slept. Michael and Sarah would need an apartment, furniture, utensils, everything.

And although it hardly seemed possible, within a few days they found temporary and frugal lodgings on the third floor at 1, rue de Fleurus. They chose carefully, to save money, and for a bath trooped to Gertrude and Leo's.

Almost immediately, Leo took Therese Ehrman to the Louvre, where he kept her enraptured for hours. Afterward, they stopped for a bun and a chocolate at Rumpelmeyer. Leo wore a wide, dark hat balanced rakishly on his head, and the supple corduroy of the artist; he had also grown a mustache. He loaned Michael and Sarah the art books he had in English and some in German and French. "Mike and Sarah are becoming more devotedly Parisian every day," he reported with satisfaction, "and are gradually burrowing deep into the museums."

In a matter of weeks, Sarah, Michael, Allan, and Therese Ehrman settled more permanently into a second-floor apartment at 58, rue Madame, the site of a former convent and a few minutes' walk from the rue de Fleurus. They had two large bedrooms and a huge living-dining room, forty by forty-five feet, which they decorated with odds and ends picked up for very little money. In the summer the rooms began to fill with restored furniture, heavy dark pieces bought in Florence and much like those Leo had been acquiring.

Michael still superintended family finances, including Gertrude's and Leo's, and soon after he arrived scolded Leo for an extravagant purchase. Unaffordable, said Michael the banker. Although Therese remembered the purchase as Japanese prints, it was just as likely something else, for Leo had been immersed in the art flooding Paris that spring. "The salon Champs de Mars opens this week," he wrote Mabel Weeks in 1904. Furthermore, an "exhibition of French primitives is getting under way. Durand Ruel has a big collection of Pissaros [sic] & there are a couple of centenary exhibits."

That spring, Gertrude went to America, insisting that if she stayed in Paris, she would have to visit the United States annually at least. (She returned only that once, in 1904, and then didn't go back for almost thirty years; "no one really knows what is essential," Leo wryly concluded.) She visited Mabel Weeks, her cousin Bird, Howard Gans, and Alfred Hodder in New York, and old college and medical school friends in Boston, and probably saw May Bookstaver for what may have been the last time. But the romance was over.

When Gertrude returned to Europe in June, she sailed with Etta Cone. Disembarking in Genoa on the twenty-fifth, they were met by Claribel, and then swiftly boarded a train to Florence and Leo. He had gone there for the summer to paint—or at least to try. A year of Cézanne had forced him to reconsider all he'd learned. As he worked on landscape studies, he "was so taken up with looking and appreciating that [he] could get no farther." Something was wrong; he couldn't match method to vision.

He explained his predicament: "The investment of the disembodied aesthetic real to speak somewhat cryptically the rendering of it to sensible experience is of course the [illegible] real function of art & it is therefore no wonder that the eastern artist who went at it rationally working from within outwards should have accomplished it so far more absolutely than the westerner who so rarely rightly envisaged the problem." This method—almost a form of contemplation—was the very one not taught, if it even could be, at the academies.

Indeed, the search for such a method made his studies at the Académie Julian seem futile, Leo said.

> Of course one repeats that it is necessary to learn the vocabulary etc. etc. but when oppressed by the doubt of the more essential needs that is of little comfort; or rather (for comfort is not the word) I feel that somehow one must achieve along the lines of a more quintessential method. I feel at times more like a Paracelsus seeking a philosopher's stone than like a plain prosaic nineteenth century realist studying the forms of things to sound out their nature and their characters. I envy the Buddhist his seeking for a purely disembodied ideal which needs form only to render it to sense and then the finer the sense the more reticent though yet more trumpet tongued the expression. This is something which sounds like yet is so different from the economy of means that one hears so much of in the discussion of Whistlers and other etchings. One in method is so much more the construction of essentials, the other so much more the elimination of inessentials.

To Leo, Cézanne was able to eliminate the inessential to "give stability and durability to fluctuating values." He accomplished something akin to what Leo had been seeking with his aesthetic game, his habit of closely scrutinizing objects while his ideas played around them. As he wrote in 1916, "With practice even people who are not artists can learn to see so as to become conscious of a thing's reality." And the reality of a thing was what he was after; that is what rendered the object—any object—significant. "A china plate by Chardin may be beautiful, although the same plate in itself would pass unnoticed. It did not pass unnoticed by Chardin, and there precisely is the important point. The artist did not look to see what the plate was like, but just to see it, and anything so looked at comes to have the value of existence. Man has a deep sense of his insecurity and transitoriness, and nothing appeals to him more strongly than reality. . . . In painting no one has dealt so powerfully with the rendering of some aspects of reality as Cézanne."

Leo Stein,
Head of a Peasant
(*oil on canvas*)

Shortly after the publication of *The A-B-C of Aesthetics* in 1927, Leo summarized what he—and so many others—had learned from Cézanne. "The effect of Cézanne's work was to emphasize a return to more formal composition, to open up the field of compositional experimentation in fresh ways, to break up a few academic conventions, and to make people ready to accept as possibly good, and even probably good, anything they could not understand and appreciate."

Leo's discovery of Cézanne—and his interpretation of Cézanne—would find a way as well into his sister's work, an oeuvre that was to be no less confounding, experimental, and demanding than those pictures beginning to hang on the walls of the atelier.

"I WAS A COLUMBUS setting sail for a world beyond the world." So Leo recollected himself in Paris in the autumn of 1904 when he ventured beyond the timid confines of Montparnasse, where American artists still worshipped Whistler as their patron saint.

All that was changing. Steeped in Leo's new discovery, he and Gertrude went to the Grand Palais for the second Autumn Salon. There were fourteen paintings by Matisse as well as Cézanne's *Three Bathers,* owned by Matisse, who had loaned it to the show. "I went again and again," Leo later reminisced. "I looked again and again at every picture, just as a botanist might at the flora

Leo Stein,
Standing Nude
(oil on canvas)

of an unknown land." Matisse made a strong impression, "though not the most agreeable." There also was Toulouse-Lautrec, "an imp of Satan," as Leo called him, "of great genius, a powerful designer, a sinuous and vigorous draughtsman and a keen satirical wit."

Accounts differ as to which Stein purchased what, and when. "They frequently bought in twos," recalled Gertrude, referring to herself and Leo, "because one of them usually liked one more than the other one did." Rejoined Leo: They never bought in pairs, not once, and until Gertrude bought a "cubist Picasso, she was never responsible for a single picture that was bought, and always said so." Even Alice Toklas demurred when confronted with Leo's allegations. Asked by Alfred Barr, Jr., whether it was true or not, she cagily replied that it "is for you to judge their value."

Gertrude and Leo shared their funds and therefore jointly owned all their paintings. They conferred on every purchase, although the initiative was unquestionably Leo's, and they consulted Michael about finances. "My old[er] brother was our financial manager and from time to time I'd ask him whether we were spending too much," Leo explained. "If he said no we'd spend more, if he said yes we'd spend less and so we managed."

In the fall Michael surprised Gertrude and Leo with news of unexpected extra funds in their account. They returned to Vollard. "You people . . . with all your surplus money," Emma Lootz Erving cried in November. The windfall (8,000 francs, Leo calculated years later, or about $1,600) went toward Gauguin's *Three Tahitians* and *Sunflowers,* Cézanne's small, rhythmic *Bathers* and *Group of Bathers,* and two Renoirs—possibly *Brunette* and the etching *Two Bathers.* (According to Leo, Vollard threw in Maurice Denis's *Mother in Black* for good measure.) They did not buy Manet, Degas, Vuillard, Bonnard, or van Gogh; that would remain, hoped Leo, for the future. "You must have some dandy things," Emma wrote in December. "Why don't we see some Renoirs and Cezannes over here?"

Leo was ecstatic. At the Autumn Salon, he recollected, he had decided to buy a Bonnard, a Vuillard, and something else, but over lunch he "got an idea that was thrilling: to buy a big Cézanne figure instead of a lot of little pictures." He returned home to discuss the idea with Gertrude. She herself later recalled that after they convinced Michael about the wisdom of such a hefty investment, Vollard took her and Leo into the deeper recesses of his shop, where they looked at the pictures week after week until, exhausted, they would stop for cake at Fouquet's. "Vollard," Leo said, "was enthusiastic, and wanted us to have the largest range of choice." They settled on the commanding *Madame Cézanne with a Fan,* a stunning depiction of the artist's wife in a red armchair. Vollard, who had loaned it to the Autumn Salon, thought he had seen Gertrude and Leo as well as Michael seated on a bench in front of the portrait, gazing silently upward. Now Gertrude and Leo carried it home, elated, in a taxi. Under its influence, Gertrude later declared, she wrote the stories called *Three Lives.*

Leo began to talk on "L'Art Moderne" to all who would listen. "To make the subject clear requires a discussion of the men of '70," he emphatically told Mabel Weeks, "of whom the Big Four and Puvis de Chavannes are the great men and the inspirers in the main of the vital art of today. The Big Four are Manet Renoir Degas & Cézanne." Of the four, Manet was the most painterly, less a colorist than Renoir but unmatched in his "sheer power of handling" and with a "limpid purity in his color and feeling for effect, a realization of form and vitality in rendering." His only problem lay in an inadequate "power of conception," preventing him from fusing all elements into "that perfect poise of the completely achieved." What texture and mass were to Manet, color was to Renoir; and Degas was "incomparably the greatest master probably of movement of line, with a colossal feeling for form and superb color." Cézanne, however, was "the most robust, the most intense, and in a fine sense the most ideal of the four."

Leo's formulations to Weeks in early 1905 were quick, sure, and prescient. In a few broad strokes, he was able to discern the major aesthetic aim of this new modern art. "The work of these four men is exceedingly diverse," he wrote with passion and formal clarity:

> In fact there is in general aspect no resemblance whatever. They do not constitute a school in any sense in which that word can be reasonably used and yet they have something in common. Their work is all non-dramatic. When figures are composed in a group their relations are merely spatial. At most they are relations of movement concurrent or opposite. This fact is intimately related to another, that the work is done in the main direct from life. This is in a sense not true of Degas, for though he makes elaborate studies, his compositions are not painted from life; yet even with him the model remains dominant. The consequences of this are enormous and in Cézanne we find their logical working out. They mean that the path of pictorial accomplishment lies in the reaching to the last drop the virtue which lies in the model.

He went on to provide this nondramatic school with an ancestry:

> The roots of this procedure lie far back. Holbein did it with his line, Velasquez did it with his values, but never till this recent time was the conception fundamentally worked out. Velasquez is, in fact, to me a man more of Monet's type, only ten thousand times finer—for the things that Monet does not badly, nor too well either, Velasquez did magnificently. Both of them are what might fairly be called naturalists with the addition of a sense for composition both in color and form. Renoir, Manet and Cézanne substitute for that the abstraction of the quality of color, and form from the model. Manet pushed the thing through to the bitter end, for he was continually experimenting, but Renoir succeeded with his color and Cézanne with the form or rather what is the essence of form—mass. Degas most perfectly combined both things, adding composition and movement, but losing perhaps a trifle of the pure virgin force that the other three have. Whistler lost it almost completely, substituting for it an artifice so brilliant in its accomplishment as almost to succeed in disguising the loss.

Leo wrote as he must have spoken, ideas toppling over one another rapidly, his spectacles (when he wore them) glistening. He was a defender, a champion; he had a cause. To Mabel Weeks and others, he sent pictures of his recent acquisitions. The atelier, now more of a public room than a studio, contained dark wood Renaissance chairs with leather seats and a long refectory table on which were piled books and papers and pipes. Leo posed in back of it for a photograph, looking serious, settled, and modishly Parisian in his hat and corduroys. The sideboard behind him in the picture grew cluttered with art objects and curios.

Across from the refectory table, which served as a desk, was a couch covered with a heavy rug. Near it was a small claw-footed chest, and over that the portrait of Madame Cézanne hung for a while. Near another wall, which began to fill with pictures, was a large cast-iron stove. It was a good room for working and entertaining, and large enough, it seemed, to contain the whole of modern art.

WHEN MABEL WEEKS passed Leo's letters and photographs around in New York, she managed to enrage their artist friends. "They take the attitude that the minute the subject is handled intellectually the subject of art is desecrated," Weeks told Leo. Exasperated, Leo answered that "from the point of view of a formal analysis the 'masters' are representatives [in] that the interest of Michelangelo is in form[;] of Piero [della Francesca,] likewise of Leonardo in form & movement etc etc." But some of his artist friends in Paris were equally intractable. "At the beginning," he reminisced later with satisfaction, "some of my friends who thought a strayed sheep like myself ought to be brought back to the flock, decided that one of them should speak seriously to me about my blunders, but Bancel La Farge told me that no one would take on the role of bell-the-cat."

Many of his new acquaintances, American artists studying or working in Paris, were influenced by what they saw at 27, rue de Fleurus. The romantic Russian-American Maurice Sterne met Leo shortly after arriving in Paris in 1904, and soon Leo, who loved to share his discoveries, brought this former student of Robert Henri to Vollard's to see the Cézannes. Sterne recalled that Stein was "interested in my art education." It wasn't long before Sterne spoke respectfully of how "Cézanne's 'style' is intricately a part of his rendering of form and movement."

Across the street from Sterne on the boulevard Arago lived another of Henri's students, Patrick Henry Bruce, a redheaded artist from Virginia with an acerbic tongue who reputedly thought Dreyfus guilty; he too profited from Leo's abiding interest in Mantegna and Cézanne. The artist Max Weber, a newcomer to Paris in 1905, said the first Cézanne he saw "was at the home of Leo Stein." The same was true for the American painter Andrew Dasburg, who came to Paris several years later. He and another American artist, Morgan Rus-

*Leo in the atelier, circa 1904. Behind him, from left to right,
hang Du Gardier's* Woman with Dog, Renoir's *Brunette,
Denis's* Mother in Black, *and Cézanne's* Bathers. Gauguin's
Still Life with Sunflowers *hangs on the wall perpendicular,
next to a Japanese print.*

sell, borrowed Cézanne's apple still life from Leo to study. "Yesterday and the
day before I have been making a copy of a small Cézanne that belongs to Mr.
Stein," a thrilled Dasburg wrote in 1910. "I wish that Stein would let me copy
another one which he has, a figure composition that is a beauty." Paying
homage to Cézanne and, by implication, to Leo, Russell in the summer of 1910
sent Stein a postcard depicting Mont Sainte-Victoire: "This is to compare with
your water-colors."

And then of course there was Gertrude, who in later life didn't credit
Leo at all, remembering only Cézanne and then Flaubert as early stimuli. But
the atelier where Leo revealed so much of his taste was also Gertrude's work-
place; although Leo did not paint there, his presence was surely felt, his talk
surely heard. Sister and brother were collaborators, and when they posed for
a picture, Gertrude stood close, her hand companionably tucked in Leo's arm.
Without irony, Maurice Sterne remembered those two as the happiest cou-

ple on the Left Bank. Mabel Weeks, who understood each of them individually, saw them the same way. "So you don't have any more discretion than to show my last weather report to Leo," she complained to Gertrude in 1905. "That's the trouble with you devoted brothers and sisters and husbands and wives— Everything goes circulating around."

Leo of course knew of Gertrude's work and of her struggles with it. Since finishing "Q.E.D.," she had been casting about for a new subject. She had transcribed sentences from the letters of her friends—not just May Bookstaver's—and formulated projects and abandoned them. Leo recommended she try translating Flaubert's *Three Tales*. This suggestion and the Cézanne portrait in front of her desk eventually led to the small volume *Three Lives*.

Like Leo—or because of him—Gertrude considered Cézanne "the great master of the realization of the object itself." She wrote this in a notebook after the purchase of the portrait of Madame Cézanne and continued throughout her life to link her writing with what she had learned from that picture. Despite protestations to the contrary, her interpretations of her own work rang with Leo's early formulations; indeed, her brother must have lurked somewhere behind her references to Flaubert and Cézanne. "Everything I have done has been influenced by Flaubert and Cezanne," Stein told her friend Robert Bartlett Haas the year she died, "and this gave me a new feeling about composition. . . . Cezanne conceived the idea that in composition one thing was as important as another thing. Each part is as important as the whole and that impressed me so much that I began to write *Three Lives* under this influence and this idea of composition."

Gertrude's interest in both Flaubert and Cézanne, like her brother's, was formal. "Flaubert has no emotion about his material but complete emotion about his expression," she observed. Reflecting similarly almost forty years later, she noted that the "realism of the people who did realism before was a realism of trying to make people real. I was not interested in making the people real but in the essence or as the painter would call it value." Gertrude would, like Cézanne, take ordinary subjects and grant them the full value of their existence. By rendering them in an unusual and almost lyrical nondramatic prose, she wished to eliminate what Leo called "the inessential" in order to grip those disembodied and vitally felt presences, "bodiless and featureless and footless," as William James had described them in *The Varieties of Religious Experience,* the book that had so deeply impressed her brother. These were what Leo termed the "disembodied aesthetic real" and James hailed as "as real in the realm which they inhabit as the changing things of sense are in the realm of space."

"Cézanne wanted a complex whole to satisfy an indefinable demand," Leo wrote late in life. So in a sense did his sister, who would construct an idiom by which she too could express those vitally felt presences that her brother perceived—and which eluded him.

THREE LIVES evolved slowly during the first half of 1905. In its initial, expanded phases, it was called "The Progress of Jane Sands being the history of one woman and many others" and was to include a story about "Maggie . . . a gentle soul"—evidently an early version of one of the *Three Lives*, "The Gentle Lena." The proposed book would consist also of the story of a woman painter and "The Tragedy of the Wirkin sisters," probably based on the Cone sisters and their "tragedy." (Gertrude used this melodramatic term in her early notebooks.) The last story title listed is the most intriguing of all: "The busted twins."

Originally named George Sand(s), Jane Sands represented Gertrude Stein; the story of her "progress" was to be the story, noted Gertrude, of "The Making of an Author." An early copybook contains the faded plans for this fictional autobiography as well as trial sentences and phrases, most of which were discarded, and faint suggestions as to how "The Making of an Author" would develop into "Three histories by Jane Sands." A few sentences remain, probably an early introduction to the "Three histories": "There is always a lodge in every Paris house. There are many masters of these lodges in Paris. They are called concierges. Our story is the history of one of them and of the many servant girls that he in his place came to know." Stein excised the rest of the introduction from her notebook and dropped the device of the concierge, apparently desiring to tackle her subject matter directly.

She retitled her proposed book "Three Serious Stories" and recorded on a scrap of paper its description: "A German woman, a German American woman and a negro woman, three serious stories and in each story one of them." She had given up the idea of an author's "progress" and was concentrating on the creation of character through a narrative that did not, in any formal sense, move forward linearly. Perhaps still reeling from Hodder's specious present and Leo's explanation of Cézanne, she constructed her first story, "The Good Anna," out of a series of echoing rhythms and phrases, building up a portrait of this German-born servant as if each repeated phrase ("Anna led an arduous and troubled life," "If we live till then") were part of a geometrical structure on canvas, one that resembles a certain woman but, on closer inspection, reveals itself to be composed of dabs of color and reiterating shapes. Assembled from these simple phrases, the completed portrait is perceptive, psychologically convincing, and in a curious way static, even though the phrases, through repetition, do modulate their meaning. But the "Good Anna" is always good; Anna's employers vex or please her in predictable ways; dominating, and herself dominated, Anna lives and dies within the small compass of a regulated life. Yet within this small compass, she is rendered in a sober, often ironic, and frequently flat manner, which, paradoxically, brings her life to expression.

Although "The Good Anna" bears the closest relation to Flaubert's tale "Un Coeur Simple," the model for Anna was Gertrude and Leo's Baltimore housekeeper, Lena Lebender, a woman so devoted to them she was inconsolable when they remained in Europe. Hortense Moses (formerly Guggenheimer) reported Lena's dolor to Gertrude in the spring of 1905, around the time she was beginning *Three Lives*. "She needs you and Leo more than anything else," Hortense wrote. "She seems to be looking forward only to your return,—everything else seems to be a makeshift until that happy time arrives." Lena blamed Leo for keeping Miss Gertrude away. "She said (I wish I could quote it just as she said it, with the tears streaming down her cheeks), 'I had a nice German letter from Mr. Leo and I'm going to answer it, but he needn't think I've got anything good to say to him. I don't want him to *die*—and I don't want him to suffer, but I would like him to be sick for a while like he was here once . . . then he will come home and that's *all* Miss Gertrude needs to make her come too!' "

In "The Good Anna," Gertrude excluded Leo and characterized herself as Miss Mathilda, Anna's last and favorite mistress, a "large, cheerful, but faint hearted woman," somewhat lazy, wont to come home "with a bit of porcelain, a new etching, and sometimes even an oil painting on her arm"—much to the frugal Anna's horror. However, it is not the relationship between Mathilda and Anna that is the heart of the story so much as Anna's attachment to her friend Mrs. Lehntman, the widow who was, one is repeatedly told, "the romance in Anna's life." A midwife who took care of unwed mothers before her involvement with a "mysterious and evil" doctor who "got into trouble doing things that were not right to do," Mrs. Lehntman embraces the sexuality Anna quite comically tries to regulate, even in the lives of her pet dogs. Mrs. Lehntman, the wise, amiable kind of "woman other women loved," encompasses sexuality defined in its broadest terms: in this case, premarital sex, abortion, lesbianism. And it is she who helps women regain control over their own bodies.

Anna must renounce this figure, reminiscent of the May Bookstaver character in "Q.E.D.," and the one who anticipates Melanctha in the third of Stein's *Three Lives*. Again pulses are differently timed, as in "Q.E.D.," except that now, writing in what sounds like her own voice, Stein ominously warns:

> In friendship, power always has its downward curve. . . . It is only in a close tie such as marriage, that influence can mount and grow always stronger with the years and never meet with a decline. It can only happen so when there is no way to escape.

Without formal commitments, "friendship goes by favor. There is always danger of a break or of a stronger power coming in between. Influence can only be a steady march when one can surely never break away."

Oddly, one of the most vulnerable relationships would prove to be that of sister and brother. But in 1905 neither would have guessed as much.

BESIDES COPYING favorite passages from letters or books, Gertrude saved the titles of books she read or planned to read: Sir Thomas Browne's *Religio Medici, The Spectator,* Samuel Richardson's *Sir Charles Grandison,* Urquhart's translation of Rabelais, Bacon's essays, Disraeli's *Vivian Grey,* the letters of Walpole and Byron, Ben Jonson's plays, *Gulliver's Travels,* and several of Herbert Giles's translations of Chinese literature. There was no American literature on the list, and there is, as a result, no way to know if she planned her character Maggie after a character in George Eliot's *The Mill on the Floss,* using this novel again, as she had in her Radcliffe themes, or whether she had in mind Stephen Crane's *Maggie: A Girl of the Streets.* In later years, Stein remembered reading Crane, and Leo seemed to exempt him from the condemnation of American literature he dashed off to Mabel Weeks.

American literature, he argued, contained none of the wit or wisdom or art one might better find in the comic strip *The Katzenjammer Kids.* His views, as he explained them to Weeks, reveal literary taste similar to Gertrude's.

> Jack London presents you with a juvenile eternally elemental. Edith Wharton so far as I have been able to read her books, which is to be sure not very far, plumbs the infinite depths of human nature with the down of a nestling. The painters that I meet here are of the same stamp. At thirty and forty they seem immature beside Frenchmen and spaniards that I know of twenty and twenty five. And then the joylessness. Hardy, Dickens & Thackery [sic] at their dismalest Balzac & Guy de Maupassant . . . in their work the miseries the terror, the horror is the result of contact, fatal contact often, with the real grisly fate with the black actualities of experience. In these on the other hand there is almost never such a contact there is not enough understanding of real passion, the characters & the authors alike are only up against their own immaturity & there they stand and twist in impotent warfare against themselves. But the joylessness has no limits.

Leo preferred Aristophanes, Rabelais, Cervantes, Jonson, Laurence Sterne, Molière, Swift, Fielding, and any other "whole hearted indecency." Gertrude, in a postscript to the letter, agreed, although she was quick to add that Leo should have included her. "Leo he said there wasn't no art in [Robert Morss] Lovett's book and then he was bad and wouldn't tell me that there was in mine so I went to bed very miserable but I don't care there ain't any Tchakowsky Pathetique or Omar Kayam or Wagner or Whistler or White Man's Burden or green burlap in mine at least not in the present ones. Dey is werry simple and werry wulgar and I don't think they will interest the great American public. I am werry sad, Mamie."

Her joking aside, whether hostile or not, Gertrude basked in her brother's good opinion and praised his taste, especially in matters of art. Her own penchant for Alexander Schilling, a landscape of whose she'd bought in New York—a picture, Mabel Weeks commented, that "any housewife might buy"— had been replaced with one for Manet. She abandoned Wagner and claimed emphatically in one of her later autobiographies that she'd cared for music only during adolescence and, in another, that she'd never liked it at all. Khayyám, Kipling, even Whistler—these were dismissed as embarrassments. "I suppose it will always be a hard task to follow your advances," admitted her college chum Leo Friedman, "for no sooner have I come to regard Whistler as more or less simple after all and not wholly beyond my comprehension than you turn to a new altar. Probably you have forgotten the talks you gave me on Whistler when I saw you last." Mabel Weeks understood. "I'd hate to be confronted by all my past enthusiasms, and I fancy Paris makes one grow very fast."

THE "COLLECTION OF WORTHIES," as Gertrude called them, on the walls at 27, rue de Fleurus had been expanding. Sometime after the Autumn Salon of 1904, Leo had bought *Au Salon: Le Divan,* Toulouse-Lautrec's painting of prostitutes at a brothel. It hung prominently in the studio, the large blocklike shapes of the lesser figures effacing the identity of the main one; intriguing and repelling, she created a disturbing effect, as did the painting's hallucinatory greens, so different from its generally warm tones. Other purchases at this time appear to have included Degas's drawing *After the Bath* and Delacroix's *Perseus and Andromeda.* The latter had caught Leo's eye at an auction, where it was offered for an absurdly low price. When Leo's bid was doubled by someone else, Leo bid again, was outbid, and then gave up. But a short time later, he happened to see the small painting in a shop window and went in. The dealer told him the painting was not in his line, it had been acquired only because the price was so low, and he offered to sell it to Leo at the price of Leo's last bid, plus commission. Leo took the deal gladly and never lost interest in the painting. "It is a long time since Delacroix has been the fashion," he wrote in the late 1940s, "but I consider him to be by all odds the greatest French painter of his century."

In the spring of 1905, after scouring the Salon des Indépendants ("I went through the Independents' as thoroughly as I had gone through the Autumn Salon," Leo reflected decades later), he purchased Félix Vallotton's sensuous *Nude Reclining on a Yellow Cushion,* a painting which was obviously inspired by Manet's *Olympia* and because of which Gertrude, who did not like it, dubbed Vallotton a "Manet for the impecunious." It was a controversial picture. Vallotton's "naked woman, lying with one hand resting where she draws her living, is the result of a skillful and honest draftsman," wrote the critic Louis Vauxcelles. "Her head is true and curious, expressing all the passivity of prostitutes." But she also seems awkward and dislocated, her passivity reinforced by the large, empty green space behind her.

The Vallotton nude eventually left the Steins' studio, but for a while it hung prominently over the claw-footed chest, near the portrait of Cézanne's wife and across from the writing desk. Images of women were packing the high-ceilinged room. In the flare of the gaslight was a display of color and image quite fantastic: pictures of provocative nudes luxuriously displayed, pictures whose bright splashes of color jarred, pictures of prostitutes and mothers and artists' models. Both subject matter and style distressed visitors. The American artists Alfred Maurer and Mahonri Young enjoyed startling their more conservative compatriots, grandly conducting tours of the atelier when Gertrude and Leo were in Italy. "Young and I shocked some American the other day with [the paintings]," Maurer wrote Leo during the summer of 1905. "The lady wanted to know if I was in earnest."

Aware of the subtle relation between painting and what he called "sex interest," Leo speculated that it was this quality "that makes English portraits of women far more valuable than portraits of men." Gertrude vaguely alluded to the same thing when, in *The Autobiography of Alice B. Toklas,* she observed, "Vollard said of course ordinarily a portrait of a woman always is more expensive than a portrait of a man." Surely the portraits of women at 27, rue de Fleurus did not lack for "sex interest," each in its own way, nor did the portraits in *Three Lives,* which grew in their midst. Sex interest was to be had in every painting, on every Saturday night, in every formal discussion.

Such was true of Henri Manguin's large *L'Atelier, Le Modèle Nu,* which Leo purchased in April. But this picture was important also, as Leo later said, because it braced him for "the nastiest smear of paint I had ever seen": Henri Matisse's raucous, insolent, and rather grand *The Woman with the Hat.*

IN THE
THICK
OF IT

The atelier circa 1905–1906. On the right, Cézanne's
Madame Cézanne with a Fan *is flanked by a Japanese print
and a Leo Stein painting; on the left, it seems, is Gauguin's*
Three Tahitians, *between another Gauguin and the Amico
di Sandro and above a Renoir nude. On the perpendicular
wall is Picasso's* Young Girl with a Basket of Flowers, *and
on the wall opposite is Matisse's* The Woman with the Hat.

This I mention because I am very well acquainted with the present relish of courteous readers and have often observed with singular pleasure that a fly driven from a honey pot will immediately
with very good appetite alight and finish his meal on excrement.

JONATHAN SWIFT, "A TALE OF A TUB"

(INCLUDED WITH A DRAFT

OF GERTRUDE STEIN'S "MELANCTHA")

"You ain't never ashamed to be with queer folks Dr. Campbell."

GERTRUDE STEIN,

"MELANCTHA: EACH ONE AS SHE MAY"

PLEASE IF YOU NEED more money, say so, for both Sister C. & I are fortified beyond our needs & you know how welcome you are," Etta Cone wrote generously to Gertrude Stein in April 1906. "By the way, if you need some more cash, don't hesitate," she offered the next month. "You needn't lux-uriate in the feeling of poverty, for it's no use to."

But for all her magnanimity, Etta was also capable of refusing Gertrude, and she had done just that during the winter of 1904–1905, while she was in Germany. "It seems to me a little foolish to spend the whole winter in Deutsch-land," Gertrude had peevishly chided, urging Etta to come to Paris. "It isn't more a trip than going to Blowing Rock [North Carolina] and you do that for a few weeks." Etta was firm, however, and Gertrude knew that, of all people, Etta could resist her.

For even though she regarded Gertrude as a leader, a comet, a force in-spiring devotion and a bit of awe, Etta Cone was very much her own woman. She also had something to offer Gertrude beyond admiration; she responded to the more haltering, anxious part of her friend, the side that solicited and gratefully accepted advice and support. In the matter of clothes, for instance, Etta took charge. "Have just bought myself material for three pongee waists," Gertrude wrote, anticipating their reunion in Florence that summer. "Shall I have them made at once or shall I wait for your over seeing eye."

Leo recommended his former residence at 20, Lungarno Acciaioli, to Michael and Sarah Stein as well as to Etta for that summer. He and his sister were retiring to cooler, greener Fiesole, where they could escape the city's heated congestion and enjoy long walks on the fragrant roads of the Tuscan countryside—that is, when not jaunting by rail to points farther afield in pursuit of art and stray friends. In Venice, for example, they met up with Mahonri Young, whom Leo urged to return with them to Fiesole. "I can't afford it," Young glumly replied. Leo considered. "Do you know that little figure of yours of the workman? . . . I'll give you $30. for it. That'll pay for your trip."

In Fiesole, Young was enlisted in the Steins' frequent hiking trips, which he hugely enjoyed, and was introduced to Etta Cone. According to legend, he soon proposed marriage but Etta declined. ("Gee, don't tell me Young is married," she later joked at the news of his wedding. "My last hope.") When asked about the incident, she shrugged and said she had never met a man to equal Brother Moses. Indeed, Etta was devoted to her family, especially to Moses, the de facto paterfamilias, whose early death in 1908 deflated her for years. And she was devoted also to the imperious Claribel, whose demands maddened beyond all measure.

Claribel herself had regally entered Florence that summer, eventually to accompany Etta to Paris, where the latter would be spending the fall and winter ensconced near Gertrude—in an apartment in Michael and Sarah's building, at 58, rue Madame. Claribel also wanted to go to the vernissage of the Autumn Salon on October 18. But little could she—or the Steins—know what they would see, or what it would come to mean to them all.

The Steins and the Cone sisters were walking through the large exhibit halls of the second Autumn Salon when suddenly they came upon a room where, as Claribel recalled some twenty years later, "the walls were covered with canvases—presenting what seemed to me then a riot of color—sharp and startling, drawing crude and uneven, distortions and exaggerations—compositions primitive and simple as though done by a child. We asked ourselves, are these things to be taken seriously?"

They weren't the only ones asking the question. *"Donatello chez les fauves,"* cried Louis Vauxcelles when he saw a mannerly quattrocento-style bust sitting incongruously among hot-colored canvases by Derain, Manguin, Matisse, and Vlaminck. So these wild beasts of painting—the Fauves—were named in reproach. "The visitors howled and jeered," recalled Leo. And of all the painted offenses, Matisse's *The Woman with the Hat* was the most stupendous. A woman ablaze in electric greens and purples and reds so febrile they seemed applied in a fury of seething brushstrokes peered, coquettish and defiant, from under a huge, outlandish hat. "People were roaring with laugh-

ter at the picture and scratching at it," Gertrude recounted. The Steins were
mesmerized.

Although Gertrude in *The Autobiography of Alice B. Toklas* insisted it
was she who wanted the picture—Leo was not as interested, preferring something lesser—Sarah and Leo each told a different story. Sarah remembered
that Leo had called the painting to her attention. Moved not just by its wild
colors but also by the figure's odd resemblance to her mother, she too wanted
to own it. She and Leo decided the four Steins should buy it jointly, and—so
Matisse understood—Leo requested it go first to 27, rue de Fleurus in order
that he could figure out why he liked it. Therese Ehrman later said that Leo,
the least strapped financially, put down the money for the picture. But in 1908,
Sarah Stein lamented to an American acquaintance that to her undying regret she had consented to letting Leo buy *The Woman with the Hat* instead
of acquiring it herself. Not until 1915 were she and Michael able to purchase
the painting, which Leo left behind when he moved from the rue de Fleurus;
Gertrude sold it to them for $4,000.

In 1905, the price was 500 francs. Told that no one paid the catalogue
price, Leo bid 400. Matisse refused. Leo recalled that Matisse sent word that
he did not think his price excessive, and Leo had to agree. Things had not been
going well for the painter. Gertrude heard he had been so discouraged by the
response to his work at the Autumn Salon, he went only once; Madame Matisse did not go at all. Nonetheless, he held to his price because, according to
Gertrude, Madame Matisse insisted. "Oh no, said Madame Matisse, if those
people (ces gens) are interested enough to make an offer they are interested
enough to pay the price you asked," Gertrude wrote, "and, she added, the difference would make winter clothes for [the Matisses' daughter] Margot."

At thirty-six, Henri Matisse was hard-pressed. Son of a grain merchant
in Picardy, he had gone to Paris originally to study law, but during an attack
of appendicitis, when a neighbor happened to bring him a box of colors, his
vocation was changed forever. With the grudging approval of his parents and
a small stipend, he enrolled at the Académie Julian to study with the conservative Bouguereau (as had Leo). Matisse found the atelier of the symbolist
painter Gustave Moreau more to his taste, however. Under Moreau's tutelage,
he studied at the Louvre and entered the École des Arts Decoratifs; in 1895
he was accepted by the École des Beaux-Arts. The president of the venerable Société Nationale, Puvis de Chavannes, nominated Matisse for associate
membership, and a safe, undistinguished career was assured. But in 1897 not
only did his impressionistic *Dinner Table* offend much of the Société's membership, his own father cut off his allowance.

Matisse pushed on. Influenced by both Chardin and Cézanne, he experimented with color and surface, bought art, and grew poorer as his family

waxed larger; Matisse was father of three. To augment their meager income, Amélie Matisse, whose unconscious beauty, said Alice Toklas, was almost tragic, made and sold hats until her health collapsed; the Matisses' two sons were sent to live with grandparents. In the spring of 1904 the inestimable Ambroise Vollard gave Matisse his first one-artist show, and that fall the artist had fourteen paintings and two sculptures in the Autumn Salon. Leo saw the work, which he said made a strong if disagreeable impression with its splotchy pointillism ("the ugliest technique—to my thinking—ever invented"). Not until the next summer, painting with André Derain in the heat of Collioure, a Mediterranean seaport, did Matisse make his first so-called Fauve paintings. "Decisive," said Leo Stein.

Soon after Leo purchased *The Woman with the Hat,* Henri Manguin introduced him to Matisse, hardly a swashbuckler. The somber, bespectacled painter, who resembled a country doctor, had taken a studio at the Couvent des Oiseaux on the rue de Sèvres to work on his next major project, *Le Bonheur de Vivre.* Stein bought a drawing from him; the two men talked. "Matisse was really intelligent," recollected Stein. "He was also witty, and capable of saying exactly what he meant when talking about art." Stein considered Matisse's use of color extraordinary, his talent rich, his integrity admirable: "He showed me a picture which had been ordered. The people had just been in to see it and were very much pleased and wanted to carry it off at once. It was a time when Matisse was poor but he said no, the picture is not yet finished. The people were just leaving and when they were gone Matisse said to me sadly, I'm sure they won't want the picture when it is done and a few weeks later he told me that was what happened."

Leo continued to praise Matisse long after he grew disenchanted with almost all of the artist's contemporaries: "Matisse has great maturity." He knew exactly what he wanted and worked relentlessly until he saw it realized. Stein remembered being shown a large interior (probably *Harmony in Red*), which the artist said "he couldn't make come off. We talked of it for a bit & then I went away. The next time I came it was finished but very different from what it had just been. It was like many pictures of that time mostly green and red, but now all the greens that had been were reds and the reds green. He had got his effect by reversing the colors."

Stein admired Matisse for what he himself lacked: discipline, the "discipline that came hard." He watched his new friend struggle with *Le Bonheur de Vivre,* a large and complex arcadian landscape in which nudes embrace, recline, and play pipes about a central ring of joyous dancers. When it was finished, in early 1906, the two men were friendly enough for Matisse to ask Leo if he would hang it at the rue de Fleurus, Matisse's own apartment on the quai Saint-Michel being too small. Initially dubious about the ambitious

Blue Nude: Memory of Biskra (*oil on canvas, 1907*),
one of the last Matisses purchased by Gertrude and Leo

frescolike painting, Leo soon decided to buy it, paying a reported 1,200 francs, a paltry sum by today's standards but more than twice the amount paid for *The Woman with the Hat*. It was synthetic, bold, and rhythmic (a special word of approbation for Stein), and Leo deemed it the most important painting done in our time.

Then began a flurry of buying: in addition to *The Woman with the Hat* and *Le Bonheur de Vivre* and the sculpture *The Serf*, Gertrude and Leo acquired such oils as *The Invalid, Small Door of the Old Mill, Olive Trees, Yellow Pottery from Provence,* and *Margot (Marguerite in a Veiled Hat)*, about which Leo found the hat the most interesting thing, "painted with colors so curiously related that I never was able to discover how they came to be effective as they were." In 1907, *Blue Nude: Memory of Biskra* and the oil sketch *Music* went to the rue de Fleurus. Then no more.

Forty years later, Leo explained that while he continually admired Matisse's work and was consistently interested in what he was doing, "because he always kept moving and generally moved forward," he, Leo, bought no more pictures, "for they were rhythmically insufficient." ("Rhythm is movement, and where there is no movement it has to be as though there were movement," Stein insisted. "Rhythm is my element, rhythm and space.") He did not like Matisse's flat, decorative work: "The static quality of Matisse left me more and more stranded," he commented, revealing not an aesthetic judgment as much as buried frustration with his own painting. Stein's work would not find nourishment in Matisse's, except intellectually; and a few years thence, it would find neither intellectual nor aesthetic stimulation in cubism.

But in 1924 he observed that he "always believed that Matisse was on the main highway of modern painting." And he explained ten years later to the collector Dr. Albert C. Barnes, "The Matisse that I knew was not yet sure of his road. He still had velleities (velleity—a very low degree of desire or volition, not leading to action) of creating a deeper rhythm, of expressing something, etc., and his earlier work from 1905 on (that is, commencing with *Le Bonheur de Vivre*), on which he was working when I first went to see him—tended to split into the decorative and 'interpretive' series. The successful synthesis came considerably later."

Gertrude maintained that from the first she found *The Woman with the Hat* "perfectly natural," even more natural than the Cézanne portrait of his wife. Although in later years she acknowledged no debt to him, Gertrude, like Leo, was affected by Matisse's work. "Matisse not a storm-tossed soul," she noted in the first years of their acquaintance. "His emotion is clear, and is pressed through obstacles, but his emotion always remains a clear thing, his emotion is not muggy or earthy or quivering. . . . Matisse is clear in his emotional power, that has a clarity and pushed through all obstacles and the more the resistance the difficulties the more vivid the expression." In addition, her appraisal of his work paralleled Leo's: she disliked "flat painting," and Matisse's "in between decorative period was and is a failure, it is only carried by his beautiful colors and his power in drawing but they have no real existence."

The Woman with the Hat and *Bonheur* and other paintings of this period appealed to Gertrude so much that her own work began to echo with Matisse. As Leo recalled, her "critical interest in art and literature was awakened by her personal problems in writing. The Cézanne, Matisse, Picasso pictures that I bought were of great importance to her in respect to her work." Moreover, she must have often heard Matisse speak about his work, whether to her or Leo or Sarah Stein or even Guillaume Apollinaire, who published an interview in 1907 in which the artist explained that he had discovered in his early paintings a "recurring element, which I first took to be a repetition that made my paintings monotonous. In fact, it was the manifestation of my personality, remaining the same regardless of the varied states of mind that I experienced." This formulation seems almost to underpin the stylistic logic of *Three Lives,* and it decidedly anticipates Gertrude's description of her novel *The Making of Americans.*

About the time Matisse exhibited *Le Bonheur de Vivre* at the Independents' Salon in March 1906, Gertrude completed *Three Lives,* then called "Three Histories." She informed Mabel Weeks she had written a book that "will certainly make your hair curl with the complications and tintinabulations [*sic*] of its style," and then added with pride, "I think it a noble combination of Swift and Matisse."

ETTA, NOW MINUTES AWAY from Gertrude and Leo, took piano lessons once or twice a week. Leo was painting, and Gertrude had been working constantly on her three stories. Originally titled "The Story of a Gentle Soul," the tale now called "The Gentle Lena" followed "The Good Anna" and was, like its predecessor, a portrait of a woman, here the German-born Lena Mainz, a compliant soul imported to the United States by an overly solicitous and selfish American relative. Lena is a gullible, guileless creature without much will who submits to her fate, which includes an arranged marriage to a reluctant groom. He fails to show up for the ceremony the first time around; Lena is somehow to blame. After the marriage takes place, with Lena as submissive as ever, her passivity and gentleness dissolve into spiritual torpor. She sinks deeper and deeper into lifelessness after the birth of each of her three children, and shortly after her fourth child is stillborn, she too dies.

A doleful story of diminished expectations, "The Gentle Lena" is another portrait rendered, even more than "The Good Anna," through recurrent phrases, repeating rhythms, and a simplified, almost ungrammatical language. The unusual style dramatizes the awkward yet often lyrical sensibility of one whose inner life consists mostly of an occasional "gentle stir within her": "This place Lena had found very good," and "Lena had good hard work all morning." Lena's colloquial "german voice" soothes the family she first works for, but otherwise it is barely heard. Similarly, Lena is constructed from without, mainly through her relations to others, who cajole and push and cheer and scold the gentle, inarticulate, and tractable woman. She barely talks; she cannot resist; she is spoken for.

Several thematic motifs connect this story with both "The Good Anna" and "Melanctha: Each One As She May," the last in the series. All the main characters, Anna, Lena, and Melanctha, are or become motherless; all three are separated from the sustenance of beloved women friends; the desires of all three are unfulfilled, repressed, or unrealized; and in all three stories, childbirth is the fatal subtext. ("Melanctha" begins with the birth of a child and its subsequent death, which augurs Melanctha's death at the end of the story.) Unlike Anna and Lena, however, Melanctha is an active seeker, keen for "real experience" and desiring power, "the power she had so often felt stirring within her and which she now knew she could use to make her stronger."

As in "Q.E.D.," the major autobiographical source of "Melanctha" is Stein's affair with May Bookstaver, here rewritten as the love affair between the young mulatto Melanctha Herbert and an African-American doctor, Jefferson Campbell. Stein in fact appropriated so much of her relationship with

May Bookstaver that Mabel Weeks was surprised to learn May hardly recognized herself in Melanctha—although she did acknowledge that the dialogue between Melanctha and Jeff Campbell had been taken almost verbatim from actual conversations. Leo also recognized the source of the story; in the 1930s he laughed at the then prevailing notion that "Melanctha" had anything to do with African-Americans. It was, he averred, "Q.E.D." rewritten.

Although Leo was literally right, Gertrude did have an interest in the black community, dating to her first years in Baltimore and reflected in early college compositions that include sensuous paeans to that deliciously slow-paced city, "where no one is in a hurry and the voices of the negroes singing as their carts go lazily by, lull you into drowsy reveries." Her attitude was patronizing and her racism complicated, for it included her own identification with the African-American, as a woman, a Jew, a westerner: she too was an outsider. In a college theme, Stein had noted that "a little negress, (delicate with beautifully cut features) and her brother" were the only friendly children she met when she first came to Cambridge.

During her medical rounds at Johns Hopkins, especially when on obstetrical call, Stein paid special attention to blacks, whose "philosophy of life," Leo had teased her, differed in some respects from that of Richardson's Clarissa Harlowe. These forays into another culture may have been reassuring to those whose bearing and sexuality fell outside prevailing norms. Indeed, both Gertrude and Leo accepted the common, racist notion linking the African-American with illicit sexuality, a connection assumed and promoted by the medical and scientific texts they read, to say nothing of the white community. And Gertrude, the medical student whose specialty had been the nervous diseases of women, was probably aware that much of the medical and scientific world linked the black female's sexuality with that of the lesbian. When Leo sketched a picture of her in the winter of 1904–1905, Gertrude told Etta Cone that he said "it looks like me, I think it looks like a nigger, he says that certainly comes to the same thing."

The name Melanctha harks back to those medical school days when, as a daydreaming student, Stein had doodled while listing the symptoms of a tubercular larynx. Amid tic-tac-toe games, arrows, and names—Tristan, Isolde, Stein Brothers—she had scribbled "Melancthon," her own spelling of "Melanchthon," the name of the sixteenth-century German humanist whose original name was Schwartzerd, or black earth. Melanctha is thus an amalgam of the sexuality and primitivism Stein associated with blacks, and of the passion and angst she associated with medical school, medical discourse, and May Bookstaver. A woman so melancholy—filled with dark bile—that she considers killing herself, she also epitomizes desire and intelligence in their rawest human form: "complex, desiring Melanctha," Stein calls her. And yet she is conceived as a stereotype: a passionate mulatto woman, earthy and erotic, excluded from the white world and dispossessed of what Stein shallowly describes as "the earth-born, boundless joy of negroes"—a "good warm nigger time."

Stein's racism is a romantic primitivism that suggests, in addition to com-

"Melanctha" in manuscript

plex and not especially pleasant social attitudes, her early attempt to forge a
new style and, in so doing, condemn an abstemious status quo. Her choice
of subject matter, in this case a black woman and her lovers, must have
in some way helped her do this; it is no accident that of the stories in *Three
Lives*, "Melanctha" is the most resolutely experimental. Nor are its experimental qualities—its challenge to prevailing notions about language and expression or even appropriate subject matter—incompatible with Stein's rather
conventional social stereotypes. Stein intended to develop an alternate mode
of expression, one consistent no doubt with what she regarded as a more authentic aesthetic idiom. And ironically, in this story she is much less condescending toward her characters than in "The Good Anna" or "The Gentle
Lena." Stein's attitude toward the characters of "Melanctha," however racist,
is an ambivalent but deliberate Swiftian protest against bourgeois values written, as it happens, at the time when Belgian king Leopold II's horrific abuses
in the Congo were being widely publicized and discussed.

The uniqueness of "Melanctha" resides less in its overtly social content
than in what Stein had called the "tintinabulations of its style": the story's cadence and sound. The joy of the two lovers, Melanctha and Jeff, is a matter
of rhythms and pacing, of subtle dialect and connectives; two individuals are
brought together by a series of parallel structures, all punctuated with the word
"and," until the two become part of each other and part of a larger, erotic world:

> And Jeff took it straight now, and he loved it, and he felt, strong,
> the joy of all this being, and it swelled out full inside him, and he
> poured it all out back to her in freedom, in tender kindness, and
> in joy, and in gentle brother fondling. And Melanctha loved him
> for it always, her Jeff Campbell now, who never did things ugly,
> for her, like all the men she always knew before always had been
> doing to her. And they loved it always, more and more, together,
> with this new feeling they had now, in these long summer days so
> warm; they, always together now, just these two so dear, more and
> more to each other always, and the summer evenings when they
> wandered, and the noises in the full streets, and the music of the
> organs, and the dancing, and the warm smell of the people, and
> of dogs and of the horses, and all the joy of the strong, sweet pun-
> gent, dirty, moist, warm negro southern summer.

Yet lyrical moments like these do not last; indeed, they cannot, Stein
suggests. This story subtitled "Each One As She May" is also a tale, like
"Fernhurst" and "Q.E.D.," of lovers irrevocably out of step. "It was a struggle
that was as surely always to be going on between them, as their minds and

hearts always were to have different ways of working." In Jefferson Campbell and Melanctha Herbert, Stein embodies the conflict, as she perceived it, between the responsible, conventionally moral, and upstanding physician who needs to understand and articulate his feelings (after the fact) and the young substitute teacher, a woman who lives so completely in the present she "never can remember right."

Representing the virtues of middle-class values and a conventional life, Jeff Campbell speaks for Stein's conflict-ridden adherence to "just living regular": "Dr. Campbell said he wanted to work so that he could understand what troubled people, and not to just have excitements, and he believed you ought to love your father and your mother and to be regular in all your life, and not to be always wanting new things and excitements, and to always know where you were and what you wanted, and to always tell everything just as you meant it." But Jeff Campbell is also a doubter who projects his divided feelings onto Melanctha. Campbell tells Melanctha, "Sometimes you seem like one kind of a girl to me, and sometimes you are like a girl that is all different to me, and the two kinds of girls is certainly very different to each other, and I can't see any way they seem to have much to do, to be together in you." His words hurt, and his self-doubt finally drives Melanctha away.

Jefferson Campbell's wish to tell "everything just as you meant it" is inadequate in the face of real, deep, passionate feeling. He is a letter-writer; he is addicted to words. As Melanctha says, "You always wanting to have it all clear out in words always, what everybody is always feeling." But he cannot do this, for he does not know himself what he feels, so transient are his emotions. If the presumptively transparent language he approves of fails in the face of deep, conflicted, or difficult feelings, so too does Melanctha's inarticulate, endless search for bodily wisdom.

In a very real sense, Melanctha as well is without an effective language; she clings to others—the selfish, decent Rose Johnson, the dashing Jem Richards—to give her solidity and strength. She too covets a "regular" life: "Always she wanted to be regular, and to have peace and quiet in her, and always Melanctha could only find new ways to be in trouble." Without Jem or Rose, she fades away, feverish, aimless, an emblem of illness as well as sexuality. "Melanctha was lost, and all the world went whirling in a mad weary dance around her." She dies in a home for poor consumptives.

Melanctha is Stein's artist manqué; Stein does not condemn her. She can find no place for her as yet; Melanctha is unable to live within the limits of ordinary discourse, unable to move beyond them. The same is true of Jefferson Campbell, who learns love and sorrow and will be, one suspects, never again the same. He cannot "doctor" Melanctha; he cannot fix her. It is he who needs help, not she. And when he and Melanctha separate, he must disappear from her story, even though his point of view was the most elaborately articulated, and his painful experience the most passionately rendered. Having learned to love and to suffer, he is no longer part of the tale. It is as if Gertrude Stein were not yet able to imagine where a Jefferson Campbell could go.

Stein must have sensed that she herself could move beyond the impasse of Jefferson Campbell and Melanctha Herbert; she would not be an artist manqué, lost in a mad weary dance, heartsick or silenced, contaminated and condemned. The stereotypes she had used had stereotyped her, and she would now work to refuse a number of them. She had finally completed the Bookstaver story, and irrevocably entered a new world, perhaps best symbolized by the unkempt ateliers of Paris, including the one she and Leo occupied.

FOND OF SHARING their discoveries, Gertrude and Leo took Maurice Sterne and Etta Cone to Pablo Picasso's Montmartre studio, an untidy and dimly lit den of paints, easel, box spring, wounded table, oil lamp, and canvas. It was on the top floor of an oddly shaped building that Picasso's friend Max Jacob called the Bateau-Lavoir, after the laundry barges of the Seine. The visitors trudged up the three flights of stairs. No one was there, but a note had been tacked on the door. Picasso had drawn a picture of himself in a crouching position, pants down. Leo frowned, Gertrude chortled, and Miss Cone looked embarrassed, recalled Sterne, but when he suggested the Steins add this picture to their collection, Gertrude stopped smiling to glare at such silliness. Their collection was no laughing matter; neither was Picasso.

And their collection now included work by this young Spaniard, which Leo had happened on in the fall of 1905, shortly after purchasing Matisse's *The Woman with the Hat*. Pablo Picasso was then twenty-four, poor and undiscovered. And unusual. There was a contemptuousness about him, an unassailable certainty that kept him from showing his work, as a rule, to the public. He did not exhibit at the Autumn Salon or with the Independents. (Leo recalled that once when they attended a salon together, Picasso turned to him and said, "I don't see how these fellows can exhibit this stuff; of course my work is bad too, but then I know it," and added, "Perhaps they know it too, but they show because it's the best they can do.") Sardonic, impetuous, jealous, and intense, he lived with green-eyed Fernande Olivier and was devoted, above all, to his work. He was also proud and shy, said Leo, and though not pretentious felt himself very much "a man apart."

Picasso was born in Málaga in 1881. His father, José Ruiz Blasco, was an artist of modest talent who became a passable drawing teacher at the Barcelona Academy of Fine Art, where Picasso studied briefly before a stint at the Madrid Academy. He returned to Barcelona in 1899, then soon left

Spain (and dropped his father's patronymic) for the allure and penury of Paris. A man allergic to fathers of any sort, he resisted, insofar as possible, discipleship and yet absorbed everything—and sometimes everyone—he saw.

Picasso had settled into the Bateau-Lavoir in 1904, preferring to paint undistracted at night when the din at the ramshackle building began to calm. During the day, however, he reveled in noise and color, particularly the spinning array at the Médrano circus, where he watched clowns, acrobats, and saltimbanques. It was at the urging of a former clown, the crafty art dealer Clovis Sagot, that Leo Stein first saw a smattering of this work. He had been browsing at Sagot's shop on the rue Lafitte, a few steps from Vollard's. Leo was amazed. "This was the real thing," he exclaimed, and according to his reminiscences, he bought the gouache *Acrobat's Family with a Monkey* a few days later.

Gertrude remembered that their first Picasso purchase had been a blue-toned painting of a nude girl carrying a basket of red flowers, which she hated. For hours she argued with Leo at Sagot's shop. She thought the girl looked flatfooted. Guillotine the feet, suggested Sagot. Leo bought it anyway, for 150 francs (the equivalent of thirty dollars). He came home and told Gertrude, who was eating her dinner. She threw down her fork. "Now you've spoiled my appetite," she cried.

Eager to meet the artist, Stein asked his tall, square-headed friend Henri-Pierre Roché to do the honors. The future author of the novel *Jules et Jim* was known as a good introducer, "a born liaison officer," said Leo. Roché arranged a meeting.

Picasso hardly spoke. He "seemed neither remote nor intimate—just quite completely there." He was solid, lithe, sexual, talented, and his concentration was extraordinary. When he looked at a drawing with those patent-leather eyes, he seemed to bore a hole through the paper. Leo was captivated. The man's gift was enormous; his figures had a Raphaelesque grace; he already drew better than Rubens. Gertrude had to see this.

"Gertrude loved Picasso," a friend recalled years later. "His spirit was akin to her own, and engaged her affection even up to her death. . . . He delighted her. The pleasure he gave her went beyond his work, it lay in his personality."

"Something had been coming out of him," Gertrude wrote in her portrait of Picasso from around 1909, "certainly it had been coming out of him, certainly it was something, certainly it had been coming out of him and it had a meaning, a charming meaning, a solid meaning, a struggling meaning, a clear meaning." She and Leo reportedly spent 800 francs when they first visited Picasso's studio in 1905. By the next year, his planar *Two Women at a Bar,* the El Greco–like *Absinthe Drinker,* the self-possessed classic portrait *Woman with a Fan,* an intense *Woman with Bangs,* and the masterpiece of the period, *Boy Leading a Horse,* were hanging at the rue de Fleurus, along with *Young*

Girl with a Basket of Flowers. These were included in a collection now boasting the work of Renoir, Matisse, Toulouse-Lautrec, Degas, Vallotton, Manguin, Bonnard, Gauguin, assorted quattrocento art, Japanese prints, artifacts, and of course Cézanne. Picasso was on his way.

And if his mordant wit, iconoclasm, and talented vitality appealed to the Steins, he was in turn fascinated by them. The Steins "made a real pair," Fernande Olivier remembered. "He, with a professorial air, bald, wearing gold-rimmed glasses. A long beard with reddish highlights, a shrewd eye, a large, stiff body given to strange positions and unfinished gestures. The exact type for a German-American Jew." Gertrude was "stout, short, solid, with noble features, emphatic and regular, and intelligent, clairvoyant, lively eyes. Her voice and her whole behavior were masculine." Both of them, as far as Fernande was concerned, didn't much care what others thought, and didn't much mind the ridicule they, according to Fernande, encountered. They were too intelligent, too rich, and "he wanted to paint."

Leo and Gertrude were eager to introduce Matisse and Picasso to each other. The meeting took place sometime in March 1906. "There was no fusion," Leo recalled with gentle diplomacy some forty years after. "As different as the North Pole is from the South," said Fernande Olivier. Leo elaborated: "The homes, persons and minds of Picasso and Matisse were extreme contrasts. Matisse—bearded, but with propriety; spectacled neatly; intelligent; freely spoken, but a little shy—in an immaculate room, a place for everything and everything in its place, both within his head and without. Picasso—with nothing to say except an occasional sparkle, his work developing with no plan, but with the immediate outpourings of an intuition which kept on to exhaustion, after which there was nothing till another came." Neither Gertrude nor Leo preferred one painter over the other—at least not yet.

But Gertrude was evidently pleased when Picasso, who had begun portraits of Leo and her nephew Allan, suggested he do one of her. (Matisse had never asked.) So Gertrude patiently seated herself in the chilly clutter of the studio while Fernande Olivier read La Fontaine's *Fables* in a silky voice. "Picasso sat very tight on his chair and very close to his canvas and on a very small palette which was of a uniform brown grey color, mixed some more brown grey and the painting began," Stein related in *The Autobiography of Alice B. Toklas.* It took more than eighty sittings, Stein later claimed, but slowly that spring, an Ingresque portrait of a massive figure draped in folds of brown emerged on the canvas. Then Picasso, dissatisfied, rubbed out the head. Gertrude left for Italy, and he finished the face in the autumn without her.

WHEN GERTRUDE STEPPED off the omnibus to begin her trek up the hill to the Bateau-Lavoir, she thought about her stories, perhaps considering the sensual, intelligent Fernande Olivier for her portrait of Melanctha. Occasionally, Etta Cone accompanied her, visiting Picasso's studio and becoming, like Gertrude, intrigued with the young unmarried couple Etta formally called Picasso and Madame Picasso. Cone was interested in the artist's work and farsighted enough to purchase eleven drawings and seven etchings that March, not long before her job as Gertrude's "lazy typewriter" ended.

It was to Etta that the task of typing Gertrude's "Three Histories" had fallen, and she was more than happy to perform the service. But when she visited Claribel in Frankfurt, she complained of stomach pains (probably from ulcers), which, along with the demands of her family, would occupy her most in the coming months. She didn't return to Paris; she simply couldn't, she said. Gertrude was duly annoyed.

Two years later, Gertrude decided that the splendid and rich Etta was emotionally parsimonious as well as self-deceived: Etta imagined herself special but was nothing more than a protagonist of her own shadow play. Gertrude sounded bitter. Systematically categorizing all her friends, Stein lumped Etta and even Fernande Olivier with the "spinster women": "Completely self-centered and completely vain, they hold the world as a mirror up to themselves and that mirror always completely flatters which is the true mark of the spinster, of all the people in the world they are the only ones to whom one cannot tell the truth, they would never forget or forgive that."

It seems Etta's reserve—and her implicit rejection of Gertrude—were exactly what Stein herself never forgot, never forgave.

PICASSO CANVASES were packing the atelier. So were people. There was no other place where one could see art by Cézanne, Gauguin, Toulouse-Lautrec, Renoir, Manet, Manguin, Matisse, and now the young Spaniard. The story circulated that William James, visiting the Steins briefly during one of his trips to Paris, humbly surveyed the walls of the studio and said, "Another world of which I know nothing."

So many people clamored after a look that Gertrude and Leo concluded they had better organize one night a week—they chose Saturday—when they would be at home to open their doors to just about anyone who could claim to have been sent by someone else.

"Our collection became in time one of the sights of Paris," Leo cheerfully remembered. And he and his sister were proud. At the home of an American neighbor, a millionaire living in Paris, to look at his Rembrandt and Dürer etchings, Leo despaired. "The walls were grey the paintings were low toned [as] the conversation was. He showed us some wall paper which his successor had put over his grey walls at Mt. Kisco. It has very red parrots on it & very green foliage. We loved it but didn't let on."

At the rue de Fleurus nothing was gray or moderate, not even the host and hostess. Cultivating the slightly outrageous, they were nonetheless warm, unpretentious, and gracious, receiving "art students, students of philosophy and languages at the Sorbonne, writers, young poets, musicians, and scientists who came to study the painting by Cézanne and those of other rising artists," Max Weber recalled. "For hours they stood around the large table in the center of the spacious and well-lighted room, examining portfolios full of drawings by Matisse, Picasso, and others, and folios well-stocked with superb Japanese prints. This salon was a sort of international clearing-house of ideas and matters of art for the young and aspiring artists from all over the world. Lengthy and involved discussions on the most recent developments and trends in art took place, with Leo Stein as moderator and pontiff."

The savvy Ambroise Vollard noted that "outsiders might easily have imagined themselves in a public gallery; no one paid any attention to them. People came in and out, and Leo Stein never moved from his favorite position: half-reclining in an armchair, with his feet high upon a shelf of his bookcase." Part of the attraction was the Steins themselves, Leo typically swathed in a silk Japanese robe, Gertrude in velveteen, both of them comfortably unconventional. "Lo and behold your image accosts me . . . with disheveled hair & a kimono, with never the shadow of a pair of stays to make you more shapely," wrote their friend from Cambridge days, Mrs. Oppenheimer, when she saw a photograph of Gertrude in the studio. The Steins, said the famed art dealer Daniel-Henry Kahnweiler, created a stir at exhibitions, where their footwear startled academic devotees, and presumably because they wore sandals they were refused service at the Café de la Paix. "But they could not care less about the ways of waiters," observed Apollinaire, "and calmly [they would] pursue their aesthetic experiments." And enjoy a ruckus. "Gertrude had a laugh 'like a beefsteak,'" a friend would write; and even if Leo looked like "an old ram," he had, and scented, wit.

Their almost theatrical presence inevitably inspired anti-Semitism, as did their growing collection. Mary Cassatt, who denied having visited the Steins' collection, sniffed, "They are not Jews for nothing." Presuming Gertrude and Leo to be husband and wife, she reported that "Stein received in sandals and his wife in one garment fastened by a brooch which if it gave way might disclose the costume of Eve. Of course the curiosity was aroused and the anxiety as to whether it *would* give way; and the pose was, if you don't admire these daubs I am sorry for you; you are not of the chosen few." More suavely but with no less venom, the painter Jacques-Émile Blanche repeated Raymond Duncan's California gossip about the Steins. "They, immigrants from Austria, had first collected copper objects in everyday use and then sold things so as to collect things of greater value. Buying and making collections of ob-

The atelier, circa 1905–1906. Among the works hanging are
Picasso's Young Girl with a Basket of Flowers, *Bonnard's*
The Siesta, Manguin's L'Atelier, Le Modèle Nu,
Cézanne's The Smoker, *Picasso's* Head of a Young Man,
and Denis's Mother in Black.

jects which catch people's fancy is a quality that the Jewish race has brought
to the pitch of genius. . . . Indeed, works of art become a banker's security."

"Our collection was not a collection of specimens," Leo firmly stated,
as if in response to years of insinuation. And in truth it was not. Collecting
had become a collaborative enterprise that all four Steins in Paris—Gertrude,
Leo, Michael, and Sarah—shared, and during the height of their collaboration, it had an unmatched brilliance for which it justly earned renown. But
skeptics were legion, then and later. The collection of Matisses at the rue
Madame was compared with the wider-ranging one at the rue de Fleurus, especially after Picasso began to dominate; even the style of hospitality was contrasted, one to the other. It was a divisive world, and after Gertrude and Leo
split their collection, it became even more so.

People inevitably remembered Gertrude and Leo in combative terms.
"Of course Gertrude knew nothing about painting," Gabrielle Picabia is re-

ported to have said. Others agreed. "Neither, so far as I could make out," intoned Clive Bell, "had a genuine feeling for visual art." He accused the two of arid intellectuality: "The truth seems to be that they were a pair of theorists—Leo possessing the better brain and Gertrude the stronger character, and that for them pictures were pegs on which to hang hypotheses." Daniel-Henry Kahnweiler, appreciating Gertrude's "calm certitude" more than Leo's "trenchant affirmations," explained that Gertrude's taste was personal and came from the heart, not the head.

Many of the artists who visited the studio regarded Leo, not Gertrude, as the Stein who best understood them and their work. Maurice Sterne, who accompanied Leo and Gertrude to Vollard's when they were deciding whether to buy Cézanne's portrait of his wife, said Gertrude played no real part, except to give consent for the large expenditure. "Never in those early years of the century did she take the initiative herself in the purchase of a painting," Sterne claimed. "It was always Leo." Stanton Macdonald-Wright, who with Morgan Russell conceived the color experiments known as synchromism, also maintained it was Leo who was "totally sincere & honest & dedicated to his studies in the art field—I'm quite sure that all the pictures—with the possible exception of a few Picassos . . . were chosen by Leo for their joint collection." He was "appalled years later to read that Gertrude had achieved repute as a collector." Vividly recalling one night at the studio shortly after Leo purchased some Cézanne watercolors, Macdonald-Wright caricatured Gertrude as standing before the watercolors "dressed in a long, brown corduroy kimono, swaying gently from right to left pontificating as usual— Her summation of their artistic value was 'they seem to float' whereupon, suddenly, she levitated, cigarette & all & alighted in the pose of Ingres' 'Odalisque' on a couch with a beatific smile. The whole episode struck Morgan & me as highly ludicrous as Gertrude was no sylph & as I had myself bought 4 of those watercolors . . . in which we had found something vastly more than their 'lighter than air' qualities."

Most visitors remembered how much Leo liked to talk. "People came," he later wrote, "and so I explained, because it was my nature to explain." He would then pace the studio briskly, fiercely animated as he referred to the paintings hung up and down the walls. "I was in the thick of it." Those offended by the display of relaxed nudes and rich colors often became angry with what they deemed Leo's presumption. But many responded gratefully. "The center of attraction was Leo's brilliant conversation on modern French art and the remarkable collection mostly of contemporary paintings which he made at little cost with the aid of his independent and exacting judgment," recalled the American journalist Agnes Meyer many years after visiting the rue de Fleurus as a student at the Sorbonne. And Leo himself proudly remembered that

Matisse once asked him to give a short talk to a group of young people at Matisse's studio. Leo nervously declined, noting with satisfaction that Matisse asked no one else.

For Leo, the collection was the concrete articulation of convictions he wished to express but otherwise could not. And as a result, the collection was remarkably fluid. His mind changed; his taste shifted. Paintings were then sold or traded. In 1907, the two Gauguins left the collection to accommodate another Renoir, and in 1908 the Toulouse-Lautrec was sold for the same reason; the Delacroix *Perseus and Andromeda* was never given up, and one of the last Picasso sketches Leo owned reportedly financed the cancer operation that ended his life.

Despite the fluidity, Gertrude and Leo were in 1906 a stable center within a large family of pictures, artists, naysayers, admirers, critics, and friends. They were happy. They felt very much part of something important. And they could display or conceal themselves, as they wished, behind their remarkable collection. Some remembered both of them silent; others remembered one or the other voluble on those crowded Saturday nights. And when the door to the pavilion was closed behind their last guest and locked with a final click, how they must have smiled at each other, and laughed over the evening until they climbed the stairs and bade each other good night.

·FOUR·

AN

ALARM

HAS NO

BUTTON

14
QUARRELING

Leo, Gertrude, and Michael, circa 1906

Mostly every one does some quarrelling.

GERTRUDE STEIN,

THE MAKING OF AMERICANS

HAT WAS IT. The Steins had decided. Sarah and Leo would paint, Gertrude would write, Michael would manage to finance the entire operation. And they would make Paris their permanent home. Gertrude asked Hortense Moses in Baltimore to send her and Leo's etchings to Mabel Weeks so Weeks could sell them, and Leo had a Baltimore cousin ship his warehoused books to Paris. When these arrived, he spent his days excitedly arranging them on the dining room shelves, dipping into a few here and there. But painting, he said, was his first love.

And his main reason for staying. Working nonstop, he had amassed a number of canvases, two of which hung in the studio. Next to *Madame Cézanne with a Fan* was Leo's back view of a seated woman, a broad and stolid composition, its masses resembling those of the Cézanne portrait more than the Renoir bathers on the adjoining wall. On that wall, not far from Matisse's *The Woman with the Hat* and Toulouse-Lautrec's *Au Salon: Le Divan* was another of Leo's accomplishments. This was a portrait of Michael Stein, direct and frontal and rendered in simple, bold strokes; in some ways it almost anticipates the portrait Matisse himself would paint of Michael. Both of Leo's pictures were respectable, unpretentious, uninspired—and obviously influenced by Matisse and Picasso.

The Steins and the Matisses often met on Sundays, when Matisse would show them, and particularly Sarah, his week's work. "I think she was the one who fascinated him in her sense of appreciation," Therese Ehrman said many years later. She recalled how, in her callow youth, she had resented the interminable Sunday afternoons that had separated her from her piano. "Well, sometimes Matisse came to us. He'd come with bundles of pictures under each arm, and Sarah would tell him what she thought of things, sometimes rather bluntly. He'd seem to always listen and always argue about it."

Gertrude liked to argue, but writing was her métier. And once she made her vocation known, even the most skeptical of her Baltimore acquaintances clucked tepid approval, conceding, "You will most likely make a success of it." Yet she guessed the typical American audience wouldn't like her stories. "I am afraid that I can never write the great American novel," she admitted in mock regret. "I don't know how to sell on a margin or do anything with shorts and longs, so I have to content myself with niggers and servant girls and the foreign population generally."

She well knew that Hutchins Hapgood's *The Spirit of the Ghetto,* about Jews living in Manhattan's Lower East Side, had been a critical success, and sweet-natured Hutchins had promised to read her work himself, although he warned that publishers customarily refused to read short stories, assuming novels more profitable. Upon hearing this, Gertrude dispatched her manuscript to the Hapgoods in Florence and began a novel.

"I am now just starting on a new one, now that the other has been sent to Hutch," she reported to Mabel Weeks in May 1906. "It does not seem to matter much to me whether it gets published or not," she added defensively.

As a matter of fact, Mabel Weeks had detected quite a lot of defensiveness in Gertrude of late. Why did she repeat her decision to stay in France, this time in terms of what Weeks called "the emigrant theory"? "I was particularly amused at you abandoning your wholly [unanswerable] argument of doing as you liked," observed Weeks, "for such questionable ground as the emigrant theory, which identifies you with the class of emigrants that particularly infuriates the American who feels his oats. Why the Congressional records, I hear, are just full of denunciations of the one-and-two generation citizens. As for me, I think we ought to be thankful for that if we can't get any more."

If Stein had defended her choice to stay in France with something like the emigrant theory, arguing that Jews—and therefore she—were kept outside the mainstream of American life, she no doubt was responding to the tides of Anglo-Saxonism sweeping through her homeland. Although she rarely mentioned current events in her letters, she was aware of the Russian pogroms— "The Russians is very bad people and the Czar a very bad man," she had written Etta Cone—and the increased number of Eastern European and Russian Jews landing on American shores. Nonetheless, Weeks was perplexed as to why Stein now seized on this as her reason for staying in France; she did not, it seems, mention Dreyfus or French anti-Semitism. But perhaps Weeks could not imagine that her friend felt a misfit, and in more ways than one.

Gertrude was definitely edgy that spring and in no mood to celebrate her cousin's final victory over Louis Sternberger and the New York State courts. Finally granted a decree of divorce, with Sternberger given only limited access to the children, Bird began in April 1906 to plan a European hol-

The atelier, circa 1906–1907. On one wall are Picasso's
Boy Leading a Horse, Absinthe Drinker, Young Acrobat on
a Ball, *an unidentified painting, and* Woman with Bangs,
*and perhaps a Leo Stein painting; and on the adjacent wall
are Vallotton's* Nude Reclining on a Yellow Cushion, *under
which is a Matisse (possibly* Yellow Pottery from Provence),
Denis's Mother in Black, *and* Cézanne's The Smoker.

iday for herself and the children. She wrote Gertrude right away. Could they
stay at the rue de Fleurus while Gertrude and Leo were in Italy? If so, could
Gertrude let her know how to arrange for meals? For a tutor for her son?

It so happened that Bird's request, dated April 9, crossed with a letter
of Gertrude's, dated April 8. Recently vexed with Bird, Gertrude evidently
treated her cousin to a harsh and surprising inventory of her faults. Plainly offended, Bird assumed this was Gertrude's rather crude refusal of her request,
and she answered with her own litany of complaints.

On receiving it, both Gertrude and Leo called Bird's letter an "absolutely
insulting *misinterpretation*," implausibly based on Gertrude's initial letter,
sent *before* Bird's request had reached France, which Bird hadn't stopped to
consider, Leo snarled. Gertrude was even angrier. She dashed off yet another
letter, so startling in its ferocity that even she referred to it as "terrible."

Bird was stunned. She then tried to defend herself, but as far as Gertrude was concerned, self-defense merely proved her cousin more wrong. Gertrude responded by severing all relations. "Since you apparently do not understand the fundamental wrong of which I accuse you, there is indeed nothing further for me to say. Sincerely yours, Gertrude Stein."

Now truly distraught, Bird appealed to Howard Gans, who in turn approached Leo. Leo, loyal as ever, defended his sister, denounced Bird, and rebuked Howard for having patronized Gertrude by daring to try to smooth things over. When Gertrude said she wanted nothing to do with Bird, she meant it, he said. Howard's unctuous diplomacy was self-serving and dishonest. And Leo was finished with polite society and its equivocal courtesies. He had entered a new world. "I am done I hope for all time with mere surface understandings & relations," he told Gans. "I want nothing less than rock bottom. Your letter to me had for me so little trace of rock bottom that it drove me to a fury of disgust."

But since there was no real quarrel between Howard and Leo, and because neither desired one, they continued to write each other, even though Howard, in love with Bird and soon to be her second husband, would not acquiesce to Gertrude's depiction of his fiancée as a lying, selfish ingrate. He preferred the role of intermediary, Leo's disgust notwithstanding. Howard could understand Gertrude's refusing Bird the apartment, he said, "but that she should couple that refusal with such a tirade seemed to me so unnecessarily harsh, as to be shocking. . . . Now just because it wasn't on a plane with Gertrude as I knew her I ascribed it to a fit of irritation which I could understand."

But the Gertrude her friends once knew, Gans thought, was disappearing. On the contrary, she responded. She was perfectly entitled to have "pounded" her cousin as she had, for Bird, feigning innocence, practiced the most intolerable kind of deception. Her never mentioning the quarrel to Michael and Sarah when she invited them to stay with her during their upcoming visit to America was a case in point. Bird got what she deserved: "I pounded and I meant to pound it in."

In an exculpatory letter to Gans, of which she preserved parts, Stein justified herself almost obsessively. "[If] Bird doesn't lie then she has certainly a very intricate way of telling the truth," she fumed. "You are a pack of stupid fools you see nothing except what's got a label attached—nothing nothing." But as Gans soon observed, although Gertrude still had her sense of humor, she'd lost her sense of proportion.

By saying he didn't understand the basis for the whole quarrel—a petty misunderstanding, easily the by-product of long-distance communication, which had passed too quickly into something irrevocable and cruel—Gans was saying what no one else dared. There was something else going on. And he was right. The quarrel was symptomatic. From afar, Bird had become the world Gertrude and Leo had left behind, that world of smug and quantifiable culture, of secondhand taste, and as Leo put it, of mere surface understanding.

Even more: Gertrude unquestionably demanded something Bird was incapable of giving—solicitude, perhaps, or the appreciation and recognition increasingly important to Gertrude while she had been writing her stories. For it was when she was packing them off to send to Hapgood that she grew most severe. Bird's asking for the use of the apartment and studio—the most important and obvious symbol of the new life Gertrude and Leo had created—must have seemed crude, insensitive, even deprecating. Did Bird not understand what the studio meant, who came there, what hung on its walls? Bird's inability to esteem Gertrude at the time she most needed admiration had to have contributed to an unremitting sense of injury. After all, Gertrude well knew the Baltimore gossip, enclosed in a letter from Hortense Moses that had arrived a few weeks before she mailed "Three Histories" to Hapgood: " 'Gertrude Stein.' 'What has *she done* anyhow?' 'What is *she*?' 'Why talk about *her* so much?' 'What has *she* ever accomplished?' "

"The deep joy of understanding something is what you people can never know anything about," Gertrude stormed in her notebook. "I don't envy your thick skinned stupidity." So the aspirations and mettle that once made Bird brilliant and courageous now rendered her boorish; "responsive to immediate stimulus of every sort," Stein commented, "she needs everything for anything can feed her." Gertrude herself was the one who wanted nourishment.

The end of the friendship was neither easy nor painless. For at least another year the two cousins danced around each other, until Bird admitted that the relationship, as they had known it, was over. With angry resignation, she fired off the last communication of any depth. It gives some sense of Gertrude's position.

I did not realize your present contempt and fierce conviction of my duplicity & other contemptible qualities. I did not then know that "my colossal selfishness," "my inability to understand you, your ideals, & what you stand for," "my avarice for culture," "my refusal to bring up my children according to your ideals," to be false to my own honest convictions, all made you feel a contempt & disgust for me, such as would make it seem hardly possible for us to "resume relations" of any kind and impossible to be friends as in the past. . . .

For it seems to me that finding me in the wrong in one par-

Howard Gans

ticular, you seized the occasion to heap on my head all sorts of irrelevant abuse. You say your object was my reformation, but for
that you certainly went too far, for what you said seemed so exaggerated and the tone in which you said it showed so much temper
that it was impossible to consider it as serious criticism, however
serious it proved to be in its effect on our relations.

Gertrude didn't flinch. Bird "admired and depended on me," she remarked in one of her notebooks, "she has a passional affection for me, it would
have been nicer in me to have been friends but I really don't care and it would
not have been so instructive." Although she did care, she never forgave her
once beloved cousin. "She has not enough charm to be magnetic and she has
no sensibility, she is not passionate enough to be magnetic and she is absolutely without a trace of sensuousness and so she never has really had any
women friends, she could only be important to a man like Howard who as Sally
puts it pastures on her. She understands nothing—nothing, not because she
is stupid but because she is so insensitive."

Bird lacked moral courage, said Gertrude, who was soon to write in *The*

Making of Americans, "It takes very much courage to do anything connected with your being unless it is a very serious thing."

"REMEMBER I want you not to [submit] to me because of your fear of me but to submit yourself to me because of your appreciation of me," Gertrude wrote in a draft of a letter, probably to Bird. As if answering it herself, on another piece of paper she scribbled, "Begin Americans with fear." The break with Bird, the condescension of her family, the anxiety about her stories, and the craving for recognition—all flowed through the first outlines of a new book, which had been stimulated by the recent quarrel.

With her three stories launched, Stein picked up her "Making of Americans" manuscript, the one about Bird and her family, and began enlarging its scope. She would contrast the Dehnings, based on the New York Steins, with a family closely modeled on her own. Opposition, difference, and resemblance still appealed to her. The Herslands, another German family—German Jewish—came to America rich in hope, like the Dehnings. They settled first in Bridgepoint (Baltimore), but then discovered the golden West, a splendid place where the tyrannically grand patriarch David Hersland dreamed of a great fortune and where his three children, Alfred, Martha, and David, were born.

In addition, Stein wrapped Leon Solomons and his family into her depiction of the Herslands, making them—and Leon in particular—central to the book. In the early notebooks, David Hersland was a blend of Solomons and Stein herself; his sister Martha combined the characteristics Gertrude attributed to her own sister Bertha, those she associated with Leon Solomons's sister Selina, and those she imagined about Jessie Donaldson Hodder, Alfred Hodder's common-law wife. Similarly, the oldest of the Hersland children, Alfred, would be based on Michael Stein, Leon Solomons's brother Lucius, and Louis Sternberger.

The New York Steins—cousins Bird and Fred and their youngest sister, Amy—remained the source for the main Dehning characters, Julia, George, and Hortense. The marriage of Julia Dehning and Alfred Hersland would now be just one strand in a larger tapestry of family life. As Gertrude observed in an early notebook, "The real drama is David Hersland and Julia Dehning, Dave's final split like mine with Bird because of her not realizing him and her dishonesty when in a hole. Dave saying on one occasion What right have you to talk like God almighty you never succeeded in doing anything. Perhaps not but I have a fighting chance to do a big thing sometimes and that makes it right for me to feel just like I talk it big to you."

While the Herslands and the Dehnings are successful in worldly terms—assimilated, prosperous, well educated, and "taken to ideas and to culture"—

they meet with failure elsewhere. As Stein reconceived the book, it would end after Martha Hersland, her marriage a shambles, returns to take care of her elderly father, after Alfred Hersland and Julia Dehning marry and divorce, and after David Hersland dies prematurely. In fact, as Stein imagined it, the epilogue of the story would be "yes I say it is hard living down the tempers we are born with." And then the symphonic book would conclude like Beethoven: "Clang repeated clang."

Death and not marriage would define the novel's trajectory: the Hersland matriarch, Fanny, fades away so quietly and completely her children hardly notice her absence; Jenny Dehning (based on Pauline Stein) would die after an appendectomy (perhaps like Leon Solomons); and David Hersland dies before his time. His death, mirroring Solomons's, inspires the lyrical last segment of the finished book. But it becomes something more than an occasion for elegy; it is a metaphor for those ends and beginnings, and through it Stein will wrest a new style, a new voice, and a new form of self-reliance. "To be dead is then really to be living," Stein observed in a notebook entry titled "Introduction to David Hersland." And "Complete disillusionment is when you realize that no one can [agree with you] for they can't change," she writes in the final version of *The Making of Americans*.

> The amount they agree is important to you until the amount they do not agree with you is completely realized by you. Then you say you will write for yourself and strangers, you will be for yourself and strangers and this then makes an old man or an old woman of you.

Although the writing of *The Making of Americans* began with Stein's anger with and disappointment in Bird, with that disappointment came the recognition that "after failing again and again in changing some one . . . you must join on with new ones or go on all alone then or be a disillusioned one who is not any longer then a young one."

The decision to stay in Paris was, in a sense, a decision to move on all alone. With Leo, of course.

IN THE SPRING OF 1906, a crowd of family and friends gathered at the port of New York to greet Michael, Sarah, and Allan Stein as they arrived from France. Among the well-wishers at the dock was Bird Sternberger, thin-lipped, heartbroken, contrite.

Michael and Sarah, eager to introduce Matisse's work to America, had accelerated their plans after the San Francisco earthquake. Simon Stein was safe, as were other family members and friends, but all the chimneys on all the Steins' income property had crumbled, leaving huge holes in the roofs. Michael and Sarah needed to reach California as soon as possible to assess the damage.

Gertrude and Leo soon left Paris themselves, en route once again to Fiesole, where they settled not too far from the Berensons in Settignano. They rented a small stucco house, the Casa Ricci, whose rear opened into an arched patio covered with clay pots and a profusion of flowers and that overlooked the valley. The house was on a quiet street just above the town's central piazza, where tourists ambled through the straw market on their way to the nearby ruins. Below stretched Florence, looking small enough, said one of Gertrude's friends, to take in one's arms.

The Steins could go into the city by tram or on foot or could stay nearer to home and traipse through the green and gold countryside. Mary Berenson, driving back to I Tatti from a neighbor's, spotted the new arrivals. "A most fearful apparition—" she sneered, "a round waddling mass, & a tall blaze of bright brown beside it. These queer things turned out to be Gertrude Stein & her brother, she fatter than ever (but fairly clean), and he with an enormous bright brown beard & corduroy clothes to match, made with wide trousers & fly-away jacket, like the typical Parisian 'art student.' They simply hurt one's eyes."

The Steins had more or less fallen out of favor with Mary, an increasingly unhappy woman who was gaining too much weight, doing too little, and harboring such vigorous prejudices her husband called her an "Angry Saxon." The habits of her friends annoyed her: the Hapgoods' untidiness and Neith's silences, Israel Zangwill's heavy boots kicked near the sofa, to say nothing of the way he ate or his Zionism. But she appreciated them all: Zangwill, witty and large-minded; the Hapgoods, frank and easy; and the Steins, who could be entertaining and perceptive. "They are people who are above all interested in character," Mary Berenson noted, "& as they have good minds they arrive at a closeness of observation—especially Gertrude—that we know nothing of." But after his failed last visit to Friday's Hill, she had drawn a neat line through Leo's name in her diary where it appeared under the heading "Friends."

Everyone fell in and out of favor among the expatriates in and around Florence, everyone was an object of gossip or speculation. After a short visit, Gertrude and Leo's uncle Ephraim Keyser returned to America saying he had heard more about Baltimore in Fiesole than he would have at home in ten years. When Gertrude and Leo, known sardonically in Florence as "the Stein frères," joined the Hapgoods at I Tatti for dinner, they gossiped about the recent twist in the travails of Alfred Hodder, now being sued for bigamy by his spurned common-law wife. Another friend had one on the Stein frères themselves. "There is a lovely story about Gertrude Stein . . ." a friend of the Berensons wrote, virtually smacking his lips. "It is very 'improper'— Shall I send it you in my next?"

The Steins walked to the Hapgoods', at the Villa Linda, Gertrude wearing only a flapping kimono held by a blue pin. "Her figure is something," Neith gasped. Gertrude half joked to Mabel Weeks that Hutchins Hapgood was one of the world's great moral lights—as she herself was, of course. Hapgood had liked her stories. "Full of reality, truth, unconventionality," he had called them, citing "Melanctha" in particular as "a powerful picture of the relations between a man and a woman and the inevitable causes of their separation." He was, however, hesitant about Stein's technique, which made for hard reading. The stories irritated with their "innumerable and often . . . unnecessary repetitions," their "painstaking but often clumsy phraseology," and "what seems sometimes almost an affectation of style." But he shrugged that off. "The gist of my criticism is: au fond, they are excellent—superficially irritating and difficult and I fear to most people unattractive."

He recommended she mail the stories to his friend the publisher Pitts Duffield, but Duffield didn't respond for three months. When he did, he said her book was too unconventional for him, and much too "literary": "Where one person would be interested in your application of French methods to American low life, a hundred, ignorant of any sense of literary values, would see only another piece of realism; and realism nowadays doesn't go." He would, however, forward the stories to Neith Boyce's agent, a Miss Holly, in New York.

Defeat and anxiety seeped into the new project, perhaps delaying Stein's progress. Over the next five years she amassed voluminous notes, planning scenes and outlining character, recasting and expanding her design, and finally constructing an immense number of notes in the pocket-sized copybooks she carried with her everywhere. But at least one visitor to the Casa Ricci that summer heard Gertrude call herself the lazy novelist. She worked slowly, methodically, and deliberately amid a steady stream of visitors: Uncle Eph, Maurice Sterne, the artist Paul Chalfin.

And then there was a riveting newcomer in their midst. David Edstrom was a tall, blond, self-dramatizing Swedish sculptor who had come to Florence, he said, to weep and to die. He had an intelligent face, according to Mary Berenson, but basically looked like a slugger. Hutchins Hapgood thought him a genius. He told tales that rivaled Boccaccio's. Spellbound, Hapgood decided to ghostwrite Edstrom's autobiography, so day after day, Edstrom dictated and Hapgood transcribed. The two men were inseparable, a pregnant Neith skeptically glum in the background.

Leo declined to join the all-night parties with Hapgood, Edstrom, and Sterne, the three of them, as Hapgood later recalled, "in an ecstatic heaven of mutual admiration." But both Leo and his sister were watching. Gertrude used the threesome as the basis for an early word portrait, "Men," about the short-lived but flushed feelings that often exploded into violent brawls. "Sometimes men are kissing," she wrote. "Men are sometimes kissing and sometimes drinking." And sometimes one knocked another down. Edstrom grabbed Sterne by the throat. Hapgood separated them, and the next day an abject Edstrom apologized in Sterne's room on the Lungarno Acciaioli. They were passionate about art, one another, women, men.

The histrionic and volatile Edstrom had a reputation of turning on people—spitting out insults, for example, about Gertrude and Leo—and then embracing them as friends. Regardless, Edstrom astounded Hapgood when, in December, months after the Steins had returned to Paris, he took off with all Hapgood's manuscript. He landed on the doorstep of 27, rue de Fleurus to pour out his grievance. Hapgood had used him, abused him, sucked him dry.

Anticipating Edstrom's bid for the Steins' sympathy, Hapgood wrote them in hopes of heading Edstrom off. Although he too turned to the Steins, he had already grown disenchanted with them, preferring Edstrom's torrential style to their cooler cerebration. As he confessed to Mary Berenson during the summer, more and more he was "feeling the drawbacks of the Stein frères." He was annoyed especially with Leo, whose intelligent intuition in no way compensated for his pedantic rudeness, his intransigence, and an unresponsiveness as physical as it was emotional. Attractive to both men and women, Leo probably recoiled from Hapgood's large affections. Hapgood later commented that Leo would not even consent to a harmless affectionate embrace from either sex. There seemed to be no personal affection coming from him, and without that, insisted Hapgood, there was little on which they could base friendship.

Nonetheless Hapgood wanted to enlist Leo's support. Saying he refused to take sides, Leo confessed he thought Hapgood's manuscript should not be published. Gertrude agreed, reportedly declaring that a gentleman simply did not divulge information about his intimate relationships. Hapgood should know better, even if Edstrom didn't. Hapgood, feeling betrayed, was livid.

They could never understand each other, he raged at Leo, condemning him for his frigid pursuit of the so-called truth. Mary Berenson tried to calm Hapgood: Leo wasn't a harsh or cruel man, nor did he abandon his friends, she said. And Leo did try to assuage Hapgood's feelings, to some extent successfully. But when Hapgood saw the Berensons again, Mary nailed the situation: Hapgood and Leo's relationship, she said, was founded in mutual insult. So it remained.

Early in 1907, Hapgood went to Paris, without his family, to hunt for Edstrom and the manuscript. Stein went to Hapgood's hotel on the rue de Beaune and the two men sat down for a long talk. Stein was "sweeter and less aggressive than I have known him," Hapgood wrote his wife. The men parted friends, neither trusting the other fully, and for the rest of their lives they continued to hurt each other, disagree, and care. "He has neglected the Instinctive and the Emotional to the point that his brain is now without juice of creative force," Hapgood soon exclaimed to Mary Berenson. "I deem him an impressive intellectual Failure." (Then Hapgood reconsidered: "If he is a Failure—what am I?") As late as 1939, he still craved from Leo the very contact Leo most feared. "I can't remember even once, your ever saying anything pleasant or agreeable about me," Hapgood complained. "Or at least, your ever attaching any value to me."

When he stopped by the rue de Fleurus that winter, Hapgood was handled summarily by Gertrude. She couldn't understand his attitude, especially toward Leo. As staunchly supportive of her brother as he'd been of her, she said Hapgood was a disappointment. He had always been insightful and sympathetic, but his recent narrow-mindedness and intolerance were perplexing. The Edstrom affair then revealed his problem: lack of self-consciousness. "He fools everybody and fools them long and no wonder he is fooled himself," she noted.

While Gertrude analyzed, Hapgood listened, by turns entertained, flattered, and appalled. A few months after his visit, Gertrude and Leo treated Bernhard Berenson to a similarly devastating analysis of *his* character. "It was very valuable but somewhat depressing," commented Mary Berenson. Briefly humbled, Berenson said Sarah Stein assured him that Leo's part in all this was due entirely to Gertrude. But after more than three decades, Hapgood well remembered how he felt when dissected by the Steins. Both of them were "capable of absolute esthetic and moral condemnation of human beings, and . . . incapable of close human association. Coming in contact with only a few elements of personality, which fit in with their *a priori* ideas, they never get the full personality of anyone."

GERTRUDE CONSIDERED HERSELF an expert on character. It was her forte, her object of study, her passion, and had remained so since college. Moreover, she continued to believe character was knowable, traceable, even audible. Recently she had begun trying to sound its depths by attending carefully to its various modes of expression, studying not just collections of letters and epistolary novels but the very real letters sent by friends and acquaintances. All was grist for the new novel.

"I shall save you some of my letters," Sarah Stein had promised from America. In fact, she handed over something even better suited to Gertrude's purpose. As they finished their business in California—and showed off the Cézanne and Matisse canvases they had toted across the Atlantic, jarring even the most devoted art lovers—Sarah and Michael decided to bring a young San Francisco woman back with them to Paris.

They had met Annette Rosenshine in a roundabout way, through Harriet Lane Levy, a girlhood friend of Sarah's and now a journalist and drama critic for the San Francisco *Wave,* an up-and-coming art weekly. Levy had first introduced Sarah and Michael to a woman named Alice Toklas, whom Sarah liked immediately. Dark-haired and sultry, Toklas hankered after more than what California offered young devotees of Henry James. The Steins, thinking Toklas would adore Paris, asked if they could accompany her there, but Toklas declined, offering her friend Annette Rosenshine in her stead. Years later, Rosenshine cynically wondered whether Toklas hadn't subtly engineered the whole business just to be rid of her.

Sarah reluctantly agreed to the substitution. True, Annette Rosenshine had immediately "seen" the Matisses, but she was a withdrawn, unattractive, and sometimes obstinate young woman, whose cleft palate had badly damaged her self-esteem. A diligent art student at San Francisco's Mark Hopkins Institute (the Steins' odd paintings had in fact been quite a blow), Rosenshine knew enough, however, to recognize the Steins' proposal as the chance of a lifetime. So arrangements were made, Rosenshine crossed the Atlantic with the Steins, and she took up residence at the rue Madame in the lodgings where until recently Etta Cone had lived.

Sarah remained dubious about her new charge and, according to Rosenshine, was nervous about the impression Annette might make on Gertrude and Leo. But Gertrude and Leo were courteous from the first, providing a light supper to the new arrivals; Leo, as was his custom, offered to navigate Rosenshine through the labyrinthine Louvre. As she later recalled, Leo was far from overbearing; he strode softly through the corridors, pointing out very little, and then only as if gallantly providing her the opportunity to look on her own, allowing her attention to alight where it would. Everything was going well. She was therefore stunned when Sarah bluntly suggested she move to the suburb of Neuilly. No, Rosenshine replied, with equal candor, she preferred to stay.

Clearly the arrangement wasn't working. Sarah asked Gertrude to intervene. Rosenshine later remembered that Gertrude was delighted: "A human guinea pig had fallen into her lap that she could control, instead of my being a disturbing element in their midst."

The Bird fiasco hadn't disheartened Gertrude; she was still bent on reforming friends. ("I was very full of convictions," she once said, and she liked to help people "change themselves to become what they should become. The changing should of course be dependent upon my ideas and theirs.") She began her work on Rosenshine that winter by listing her faults. "I was crushed and startled by her crude attack," Rosenshine recalled. And more than forty

years later, she still quaked with resentment. But she had freely revealed herself to Gertrude as one might confide in an analyst.

The pouting, talented, and willful Rosenshine alternately despised and
enjoyed these sessions. Gertrude was warm and charismatic, full of worldly
wisdom. She also respected her new charge; Annette was intelligent, vain, and
aggressive, she thought, and more self-reliant than she knew. So Stein assigned
Rosenshine tasks, and the young woman became part of the daily ménage at
the rue de Fleurus, running errands, typing, and otherwise helping out, taking up where Etta Cone had left off. After hearing of Gertrude's new secretary, Etta wistfully asked whether her "successor [has] done her duty by my
place what she usurped & does she [do] your type writing."

Like Gertrude's relationship with Etta Cone, this had erotic under-
tones. In subsequent years, unfortunately, Rosenshine destroyed Gertrude's
letters to her; she discussed their liaison in a memoir in expurgated terms, although she hinted, once in a while, of something more—as when Alice Toklas advised her to set her cap for Leo, and Gertrude was amused, "knowing
that she had that situation well in hand." That "situation" was something,
Rosenshine acknowledged, that changed her life.

She did, however, say also that when Gertrude was asked for advice
about sex, she replied curtly that "sex was an individual problem that each one
had to solve for herself or himself." Nonetheless, Stein pressed Otto
Weininger's curious *Sex and Character* on many of her friends, almost as if it
were a handbook of her own views.

Shortly after his book was published in 1903, Otto Weininger, a tormented twenty-three-year-old Viennese Jew, killed himself in the house where
Beethoven died. Such was his last, tragic bid for greatness, successful after a
fashion and hailed by many, especially anti-Semites and homophobes, as the
necessary and logical conclusion to his book. It was said that Weininger, a
Jew and a homosexual, merely had killed the Jew and the "woman" inside him.

Whether one pitied or admired Weininger, his book was another matter: bigoted, self-hating, and largely contemptible. With this diatribe against
women and Jews, couched in pseudo-scientific jargon that, paradoxically, denounced scientific jargon, Weininger intended to construct a science of character based not on psychology's recent preoccupation with weights and
measures but on "a permanent morphological form, so that in characterology
we must seek the permanent, existing something through the fleeting
changes." For Weininger, this permanent something is sex, or the maleness
and femaleness present in all humans.

The most interesting and even progressive aspect of his theory was his
insistence that sexual types—pure male or pure female—are fictions existing
only in absolute conditions. For Weininger, all life and certainly each part of

the body—even cells—are sexual. Moreover, all life is bisexual. Maleness and femaleness are distributed in the world in every possible proportion. Weininger argued that contrary to popular belief and medical orthodoxy, homosexuality was not an acquired habit, not inherited, not atavistic, and not a symptom of degeneration; sexual inversion, he said, was a constitutional product of intrinsic development. Perfectly healthy in all respects, homosexuals had no wish to be other than what they were. And since according to Weininger there was no ethical difference between homosexuals and heterosexuals, the "ridiculous" statutes outlawing homosexuality should be repealed. In this, Weininger's book was a plea for social tolerance.

His task, though, was to study the individual proportions of the male and female principles in human character, and in the second half of his book, where he listed the traits he associated with maleness and femaleness, Weininger revealed his fanatical loathing of women and Jews. Femaleness, he contends, is a psychological characteristic unquestionably inferior to maleness. Women are unconscious; men are conscious. Women are untruthful, and lack standards for right and wrong; they are at bottom matchmakers, for when they are not preoccupied with their own sexual life, they want to control that of others; they have no individuality and no ego; they are nothing. Weininger condemned (and feared) the emancipated woman. And what women are to men, Jews are to Aryans: inferior, immoral, soulless.

He did make a few concessions. A small number of women at least did deserve emancipation; those were the biological females who were psychologically male. "A woman's demand for emancipation and her qualification for it," reasoned Weininger, "are in direct proportion to the maleness in her." Thus most women need not apply. In the United States, the feminist writer Charlotte Perkins (Stetson) Gilman shook her head. "Never before in all our literature," she wrote, "has the ultra-masculine view of woman been so logically carried out, so unsparingly forced to its conclusion."

Yet despite the terrible ranting of Weininger's book, both Gertrude and Leo liked it. Gertrude thought Weininger might well be a genius, for the acuity of his psychological observations and his moral enthusiasm reminded her of Leon Solomons. And probably she recognized some of her own sentiments, those that had shocked Alfred Hodder in 1902 when she told him most women should content themselves with conventional lives, submit cheerfully, and perpetuate the race. But of course she still believed, as Weininger did, that there were exceptions—herself for one.

Leo too fell under Weininger's spell. Shortly after *Sex and Character* appeared in English in the spring of 1906, Leo urged his friend Andrew Green to buy a copy, and sometime later he pressed the book on Henri-Pierre Roché. Soon Leo and Roché were locked into discussions that lasted until early the

next year. Apparently Leo, like Gertrude, found in Weininger some explanation for his own complicated feelings, his own sense that he was not like other
men. Perhaps he was a biological male with a high proportion of femaleness
in him. He never said so directly; but as self-loathing as Weininger's schema
was, it may have offered a private relief to one who, self-hating as he was, suffered anxiety about his maleness in relative silence.

Leo's preoccupation with Weininger was relatively short-lived, replaced
in 1909 by a growing respect for the work of Sigmund Freud. But for three
years, neither Gertrude's nor Leo's enthusiasm for Weininger flagged. In fact,
Weininger's classification of character began to saturate Gertrude's *Making
of Americans* notebooks, spreading among the careful documentation of character she had been compiling for the novel. It helped release her from the experimental psychology that had previously given form to her observations and
provided the rationale for the experiments she had conducted by herself at
Radcliffe. This book was the positivistic and simultaneously intuitive model
she had been seeking. "Everybody looks like somebody to someone," she
wrote. And she reminded herself: Use Weininger.

FOLLOWING WEININGER'S LEAD somewhat literally at first, Stein
divided all the women she knew into two general classes: the mother and the
prostitute, one consumed by the object of sex, the other with the sex act itself. She adopted another Weininger category, that of the servant, then added
several of her own, such as the lady and the spinster, as well as an array of
subcategories, among them mistress prostitute,.pure prostitute, lady masculine and pseudo-masculine. She classified Etta Cone as a perfect spinster; Fernande Olivier as a variation of the maternal; and she relegated her sister
Bertha to the order of servant. She devised similar categories for men: Anglo-
Saxon, successful, masculine prostitute (or passionate adolescent), lurid,
Bazarofian (after Turgenev), old tabby, idealist. There was yet another category for both men and women: the earthy. She figured she was an earthy boy,
masculine in general outline.

Her taxonomy was complex and mechanical. In a notebook she labeled
"The Diagram Book" she outlined the major categories, cordoning all the people she knew into various groups. Character was defined not only by type but
also by the "flavors" that modified each type. These flavors could be "cultural,"
or "napoleonic," or "ethical," or "tolerant." In addition, everybody contained
"two depths," one above and one below. These also defined the contours of
personality. For instance, her nephew Allan Stein combined his mother Sarah
on top and his father Michael below; and while Michael combined "Daddy
on top—Keyser below," Stein listed herself as containing the inverse ratio of
paternal and maternal: "Keyser on top—daddy below." Later in the notebook,

she referred to these two "depths" as temperament and sexual nature, which, she surmised, needed to be fused together if an individual was to function creatively. Hutchins Hapgood provided a good example of a person in whom they did not fuse.

Stein's notebooks swelled with classifications, modifications, speculations. Picasso was a Bazarov with a dirty sexual bottom. Alfred Hodder was an idealist. So too was Leo, sometimes. And then there was the tripartite structure of sex, mind, and character. "The conception of the sexual character determining the type of intellect and the temperament being either the background or to the detriment of the whole being the controlling force is constantly showing itself more clearly," she theorized in recondite fashion as she continued to ponder the personalities of friends and acquaintances. Of Leo she wrote: "Impulsive, impatient, proud, original, non-temperamental, lyrical, intellectual, mature, serious, sexually masculine, and aggressive, sensitive and tender hearted and influenceable by much patience and independence." And he was integral to her system, not only as object of study but also as advisor, counselor, guide. "Ask Leo" or "As Leo said" or "Leo explained it," she told herself over and over.

She pushed Weininger's book on her friends, especially Americans, who were unpersuaded. "By the way," wrote Marian Walker Williams, "in an idle moment I read that book on sex which you said exactly embodied your views—the one by the Vienese [sic] lunatic. It struck me that you made a mistake in your statements—it was evidently before not after he wrote the book that he went insane. We had a considerable amount of fun, however, in calculating the percentage of male and female in our various friends according to his classification. But he was really a very half-baked individual."

If Gertrude's fascination with the misogyny of an avowed anti-Semite perplexed her friends, particularly her women friends, it may be that they overlooked one unquestionable, if unconscious, reason why she had sent them the book. She was sending them a message, much as she'd been sending Bird a message. She had chosen a new home, she had chosen an occupation, and she had chosen much, much more. "I stays in Europe, think-you, where the beauty and harmony of reposefull adjunctcy is properly estimated," she wrote. After all, Weininger had not only argued for the acceptance of homosexuality as a normal biological condition but suggested as well that the lesbian—the woman with a surplus of maleness—was the exceptional woman, much more than the sum of her parts. It was she who was worthy of emancipation, she who might be the true genius.

15
BANQUETS

Alice B. Toklas, by Arnold Genthe

An alarm has no button.

GERTRUDE STEIN, *G.M.P.*

ER FATHER TOLD HER she had been born
a day too late and never could catch up. Fond of
neither him nor the comment, Alice Toklas, well-
bred enough not to flaunt her displeasure, bolted as soon as she could.

One saw her hovering in the background, near the tea table at the gath-
erings at the rue de Fleurus, and remembered her making conversation with
the wives of the male artists come to call on Gertrude Stein. That was in the
1920s, when she seemed a shadowy figure, richly arrayed in bright print
dresses, large hats, and dangling earrings. She sat quiet, thin, and absorbed
by the fingernails she pared with a concentration offensive to anyone needing something more of her. What she gave, she gave to Gertrude.

In her youth, however, she was neither thin nor hunched nor Roman
Catholic (the religion she took up after Stein died). She had gray-green eyes
and shiny black hair, she was Jewish, musical, and a bit stocky though not too
happy about that; all the high-minded, she thought, were thin. She wore tai-
lored suits, mostly pearl gray, which came to be known for the panache with
which she decorated them. She had a taste for adventure and, although she
didn't have much money, a taste for wealth, displayed perhaps most prominently in her sense of style. In San Francisco, Annette Rosenshine read in the
morning paper about the white sailor hat Alice had worn to the opera the night
before. This was a woman with presence, said to stop traffic in the Latin Quarter with her high heels and gold-topped cane. A potential impresario with a
flair for the theatrical, she volunteered to prepare all the food for a literary luncheon given by her friend Harriet Levy and then dressed herself in a maid's
uniform to serve the guests with a deft and quiet irony.

Alice Babette Toklas was born in San Francisco on April 30, 1877, to
Emma and Ferdinand Toklas. She was the older of two children; her brother,
Clarence, ten years her junior, was in many ways, at least in later life, treated
by her as negligible. Her small-framed, violet-eyed mother was, said Toklas,

a serious person who had no serious interests. She had taste, though, dressed well, and loved to arrange cut flowers. Toklas's father, on the other hand, gave the impression of great indifference to most things except, she noted, her mother and her brother. The Toklases lived with Alice's maternal grandparents. Alice adored her somewhat cultivated grandmother, who assumed she was better educated, or at least more refined, than her O'Farrell Street neighbors—it was said she had studied music with Clara Schumann's father—and intended that her granddaughter follow her example. She insisted on the French theater, Saturday-morning piano lessons, and frequent visits to the Tivoli opera house.

When Alice was thirteen and her grandmother died, the Toklases moved to Seattle, the original site of her father's prosperous mercantile business. They lived there in a fashionable neighborhood, joined fashionable clubs, and educated their daughter at the Mt. Rainier Seminary, a few blocks from their home. In 1893, Alice entered the music conservatory at the University of Washington. But her college career was cut short: Emma Toklas had cancer. In 1895, the Toklases returned to San Francisco so Emma could be nearer the surgeons there. When she died two years later, Alice took over her maternal grandfather's all-male household on O'Farrell Street, to which Ferdinand Toklas had insisted the family move. Unprotesting, Alice submitted; she arranged the menus, contacted the grocers, and generally took over the other domestic chores, but in a house steeped in the stale cigar smoke of uncles and cousins, said Annette Rosenshine, Alice's light was dimmed.

Ferdinand Toklas began spending most of his time with his son, or so Toklas later alleged. She kept more and more to herself, and her male relatives, ignoring her, took no notice when after dinner they drank their brandy and she fled to her room. She continued her piano lessons with Otto Bendix, himself a former student of Liszt's, but stopped after he died and, she said, she realized she had no talent. But on her own, imaginative, and with social aspirations, she knew how to amuse herself. Each spring, for example, she punctually spent a week or two in Monterey at Sherman's Rose, Señorita Bonifacio's adobe inn, sitting in the romantic old garden and meditating on the legend of General Sherman, who, as a young lieutenant, had planted a rosebush and promised to marry Señorita Bonifacio when the roses bloomed. Before the holiday ended, Toklas would treat herself to lunch at a stylish hotel nearby, engage a carriage for a drive, and, the ride over, tip the groom handsomely, descend from the carriage, and return to Sherman's Rose on foot. By her spree's end, she was ready to face another year of cigar fumes.

The San Francisco earthquake of 1906 brought an end to all that. Alice, her brother, and their father emerged unscathed, and Ferdinand Toklas even recovered after a time from his conviction that the disaster would give San

Franciscans a black eye in the East. But Sarah and Michael Stein had come to town, and they whetted Alice's appetite for Paris. It might be more diverting after all, she told Harriet Levy, to watch life go by in Paris than to observe it from the bay window at home.

But Alice needed money. She was carousing with friends such as Ada Joseph and her sister Eleanor, nicknamed California Nell, two women swankier and more sophisticated than her old friend Annette Rosenshine, whose charms had palled, and she was in debt from the purchase of a silver fox cape she could ill afford. After Nellie married and Ada decided to go to London, Harriet Levy loaned Alice a thousand dollars against the settlement of her grandfather's estate. Harriet Levy wrote Michael and Sarah Stein. She and Miss Toklas would be in Paris early in the fall of 1907.

MABEL WEEKS had approved of Gertrude's "Three Histories." Big, earthy, and rich, she called it, admiring Stein's ability to isolate her subject, "stripping yourself of all your knowledge of other conditions as thoroughly as you strip your style of all the terms of convention." With a style so underived, Stein surely was forging an individual medium.

But Weeks doubted that the manuscript, as it stood, would be published very easily. "I know you do not think the things [important] that you have neglected, but to a publisher a slip in syntax is as excruciatingly painful as a false note in a familiar tune, and indeed I do not see what is gained by it." Weeks found the style at times overworked, the repetition cant, and the dispassion a thinly veiled didacticism, especially in "Melanctha." Reservations aside, she arranged to send the manuscript of "Three Histories" on to Macmillan through Georgiana King, a friend on the Bryn Mawr faculty. King's enthusiasm for "Melanctha" was unalloyed. "She considers that it is written on the level of poetry rather than prose," Weeks told Stein, "and finds in that an explanation of the repetition and refrain and conscious cadence which I occasionally found a little annoying."

Georgiana King read the stories in April 1907 and dispatched them in turn to a reader for Macmillan, who quickly rejected them. By September, Gertrude, though disappointed, had another plan. Refusing to alter her work in the slightest, she decided to try a midwestern publisher, perhaps hoping that the houses in that part of the country were less stuffy than the literary citadels of the East. She directed Mabel Weeks to send "Three Histories" to Bobbs-Merrill in Indianapolis, but the results were again disappointing. Although the Bobbs-Merrill readers considered the portraits original and literary—"despite the foreignisms of the style," they said—ultimately they found them too intense and "overcomplete." A discouraged Mabel sent the verdict to Gertrude, hinting none too softly that a revision might be in order.

Ruffled, Gertrude accused Mabel of having little faith in her work. That was nonsense, Mabel shot back. If Gertrude distrusted her, someone else should take over, someone Gertrude trusted more. Gertrude retreated, and Mabel resubmitted the manuscript. Again it was rejected.

Yet the small copybooks for *The Making of Americans* were steadily being filled. Stein was intent on untangling the knotty subject of character, her own and that of everyone she knew. Studying autobiography (in particular, Herbert Spencer's) and eighteenth-century biography, she instructed Emily Dawson, Mary Berenson's cousin, to send from London the English translations of the diary and letters of Madame D'Arblay (Fanny Burney), as well as the letters of Lady Mary Wortley Montagu and Hugh Walpole, and the memoirs, if such existed, of William Tecumseh Sherman, Abraham Lincoln, and John Adams. In the meantime, she continued to study letters, and not just those that had been published. She ordered Annette Rosenshine to give her all her mail, and, cowed, Annette complied.

Gertrude was especially pleased by Alice Toklas's letters, full of advice and what seemed to be manipulation from afar, of Rosenshine. Of course, Toklas was understandably horrified when, soon after she arrived in Paris, a guilt-ridden Annette confessed that for months she had been handing her letters over to Stein. With withering hauteur, Toklas did not reply but thenceforward referred to Rosenshine, behind her back, as "Stinker."

The revelation of Annette's perfidy took place sometime in the fall of 1907, shortly after Toklas and Levy had come to France. They had landed on September 8, rested in Caen, and reached Paris the next day. After settling at the Hôtel Magellan, they notified Sarah and Michael, and dined that very night at the large loft on the rue Madame. Gertrude was there waiting.

Alice later embellished her first impressions of Gertrude, transforming her into a shimmering golden presence in a comfortable corduroy caftan, a coral brooch that Leo had given her brightly centered on her chemise. "I thought her voice came from this brooch," Toklas remembered. "It was unlike anyone else's voice—deep, full, velvety like a great contralto's, like two voices." Toklas was stirred, and Stein knew it. She surmised almost at once that Toklas wanted to make her into an idol, much as she apparently had done with Sarah in San Francisco. This kind of worship made Gertrude self-conscious; adulation, she noted, "make[s] your clay feet stick out." What's more, it was a form of control: "she is docile, stupid," Gertrude wrote, "but she owns you, you are then hers."

Nonetheless, Stein asked Toklas to call. They set the time for four o'-clock one afternoon. Alice and Harriet went to a gallery the day of the appointment, and when Alice realized she would be late, she sent a *petit bleu* to apologize in advance. Arriving finally at the rue de Fleurus, she discovered a furious Gertrude stomping up and down. How dared Alice Toklas be late for an appointment. "No one has ever treated me so inconsiderately—" Gertrude thundered, ". . . and I am not accepting it." Alice was speechless, tears welling in her eyes. Gertrude calmed herself and decided they could begin again the day after the next.

Both Toklas and Levy at different times described this astonishing fury, which they didn't know had been staged largely for effect. Stein wanted to terrify Toklas, to shake her out of the submissiveness and impersonal quality at the source, Stein thought, of her subtle power. "I impressed the first day I was made into an idol," Gertrude remarked in her notebooks. "Then she got on top out of relation as always, then I impressed with an axe, and she has never quite lost that." When they did meet again, Stein and Toklas walked to the Luxembourg Gardens and had praline ice. Satisfied that her brutal treatment had stimulated Toklas to a "moral perception," Stein lectured her as they strolled through the park. Toklas responded in a way that pleased Stein. "In people like Alice and Bird," she observed, "the apology is necessary for them to recognize that they have made reparation." Alice succeeded where Bird had failed.

Yet Gertrude remained suspicious. Attracted, she also feared her new friend, sensing in her a capacity for subtle deceit and stratagem, qualities she articulated to herself as "crookedness." In her notebooks, where she often worked through her feelings, Gertrude decided Alice was "not without intention sensation and relation in the beginning, but they all get lost through evasion, crookedness, pride, cowardice and stupidity and all these together make a crookedness that is extraordinary but never evil, it does nothing except preserve her sense of superiority." Furthermore:

> The whole of her . . . is made up of every conceivable kind of weakness, crookedness, lazyness, stupidity, everything induce[s] crookedness, the concentrated Bertha evasive female, the charlatanism, the practical sense, the melodramatic imagination, the passion for vulgar beauty, and then finally the pride [and sensitiveness] of her finest quality and so she is undoubtedly a creature made to be crooked but never evil.

Having vented her spleen, Stein felt better. Crookedness was but the custodian of frailty, she decided. "I don't [think] she would be evil even in self-defence," Stein concluded. "That is where she is different from her daddy."

Whatever Stein's misgivings, Toklas's complicated love affairs provided Gertrude with a new field for her psychological observations. "It is interesting to be really behind the scenes in the rise and fall of her favorites among women," Stein wrote. She categorized Alice's sexual nature, Weininger's pure prostitute, and watched her variously satisfy her emotional needs. With feigned indifference she noted, "Alice and Harriet and Nelly [Joseph] a bunch of sentimentalists . . . No real emotions for any [one] not even pay attention to them and you are wiped out unless they need you." Smitten first with Nellie, then with Harriet, and now with her, Toklas was one of those modern Madame Maintenons: "Glorieuse, they learn all things well, thoroughly, quickly, and intelligently, they want to influence but are not impatient if they cannot, indeed they don't insist if they meet genius. They hold themselves to be inscrutable, they are fearless, but never genuinely tolerant or charitable."

Stein was satisfied. Alice Toklas, aged thirty, brandishing a long ivory cigarette holder and wearing dainty gray silk slippers to match her skirt, was an old-maid mermaid who dressed like a whore.

ALICE TOKLAS AND HARRIET LEVY raised their social standing by telling stories of the San Francisco earthquake. "Now Leo and Gertrude looked upon us with approval," Levy recalled. "We had established ourselves as objects of interest worthy to be presented at their table." For weeks they told earthquake stories, until Levy thought these should be freshened a bit. She approached Alice. "We may even have to be burned with the house," Toklas tartly replied.

But the Steins readily took their new friends in tow, arranging for Fernande Olivier, temporarily separated from Picasso and in need of money, to give them French lessons at two francs per lesson. And according to Toklas, when she and Harriet moved from the Magellan to an apartment on the rue de la Faisanderie, Gertrude was not pleased. It was unsuitable, she presumably declared, and suggested a more appropriate residential hotel at 107, boulevard Saint-Michel. She also took the matter of Harriet's mental health seriously. Sarah Stein referred Levy to Gertrude for analysis of some of her psychosomatic complaints, so together she and Leo listened to Harriet recite her dreams (jokingly they suggested she go to Sigmund Freud to have them interpreted) until Gertrude dismissed her as a hopeless neurasthenic wrapped in the cotton wool of her vanity. But by this time, Gertrude was even more infatuated with Alice.

Gertrude also took Alice and Harriet to Picasso's studio. Her and Leo's relationship to Picasso had not at all cooled: quite the reverse. Levy recalled that Leo's "feelings for Matisse paled before his growing appreciation of Picasso," and that "with Gertrude there was no question of choice."

In 1907, Leo and Gertrude rented him another studio in the Bateau-Lavoir so he could work in a large space without distractions. They continued to purchase his work and apparently advanced him money, acquiring *Boy with a Milk Can,* a large *Standing Female Nude, Head of a Young Man,* and

Harriet Levy and Alice Toklas, Fiesole

several drawings and sketches. When Picasso needed money, he went to Leo, sending in return, for instance, a preparatory sketch for his composition *The Peasants.* Although Leo and Gertrude frequented Picasso's studio, neither, it seems, had seen his huge new canvas, first called *The Bordello,* until returning from Fiesole that fall.

It was a radical work, a crucible of Cézanne, El Greco, African sculpture, Iberian mask, and Matisse's *Le Bonheur de Vivre,* all reconstituted in a painting of grotesque imagery and compelling innovation. "Monstrous, monolithic women, creatures like Alaskan totem poles, hacked out of solid, brutal colors, frightening, appalling!" gasped the writer Gelett Burgess when he was conducted to Picasso's studio to see *Les Demoiselles d'Avignon.* And although nothing else had so loudly sounded the death knell of nineteenth-century painting, the Steins did not buy.

Gertrude and Leo must have seen the violence and savage eroticism with which Picasso had reconstructed the female image. Leo probably noted the way in which Picasso's canvas confronted spatial problems and created depth—the very elements that had intrigued him in Cézanne's work. But nothing he or Gertrude said of the painting when they first saw it has been preserved, and when Leo commented on the painting in 1947, he was so thoroughly disenchanted with Picasso that he rejected *Les Demoiselles* out of hand as a "horrible mess." He did, however, call Picasso "a man of talent"— but that, Leo said, was no reason to worship everything he painted.

Similarly, Gertrude recalled in her small volume *Picasso*, published in 1938, that "little by little there came the picture Les Demoiselles d'Avignon and when there was that it was too awful. I remember, Tschoukine who had so much admired the painting of Picasso was at my house and he said almost in tears, what a loss for French art."

"Picasso said once that he who created a thing is forced to make it ugly," she explained. "In the effort to create the intensity and the struggle to create this intensity, the result always produces a certain ugliness." But, she added, "a picture may seem extraordinarily strange to you and after some time not only it does not seem strange but it is impossible to find what there was in it that was strange." One was an outlaw, she observed wittily, until one was a classic. In later years, Gertrude cited herself, not Leo, as the one who was receptive to Picasso; Leo, she suggested, was not as discerning as she.

Yet even though they had rejected *Les Demoiselles,* Leo and Gertrude purchased Picasso's provocative *Nude with Drapery* in the fall of 1907 and—moreover—acquired the related sketchbook. They mounted each leaf on canvas and hung those too on the wall; it was characteristic of the Steins to appreciate the process through which such major paintings as the *Nude* emerged.

Retrospectively stated, then, Gertrude's and Leo's assessments of Picasso were inevitably freighted with the acrimony sister and brother bore each other over time. Their assessments became disagreements, which hardened into denial.

HARRIET LEVY recorded her first visit to 27, rue de Fleurus thus: "Leo turned to me and asked 'Are you a monist?' I had no idea what a monist was." She answered she was not. Alice Toklas said nothing, looking blankly into space. Perhaps, Levy later guessed, Leo was teasing. But she never knew for sure.

Many found Leo's brusqueness appalling, although he usually interrogated quite sincerely, as if querulous abrasion was the only mode through which he could speak. Sheathed in his long dark kimono and reaching occasionally to a small brazier for a handful of heated nuts, Leo "looked at his paintings with a fresh and sensitive eye," recalled the set designer Lee Simonson. Like so many others, Simonson was intimidated by Stein until he warmed to his quiet generosity and intelligent, frank, and commonsensical talk. Leo showed off his paintings, said Simonson, with a rapture positively thrilling for those who would listen.

But he could also be a strain. He carried himself like a never satisfied question mark, said David Edstrom, and could be enthusiastic to the point of utter exasperation. When the Matisses visited Florence in the summer of 1907,

Pablo Picasso,
Montmartre, circa 1904

Leo guided Henri through various churches and galleries, but like an impatient child, was unable to restrain himself from asking every few minutes what Matisse thought. The pressure was exhausting.

Yet Leo was kind, and he took deep pleasure in the work of his friends. If there was something evangelical about him, there was also unaffected delight. After Maurice Sterne brought the young German painter Hans Purrmann to the rue de Fleurus, Leo rushed to Purrmann's studio early the next morning to see his drawings. Impressed, Leo then showed them to Matisse, who would soon advise Purrmann on an informal basis. The incident wasn't unique. Leo was a facilitator, and a good one.

His own painting did not, however, dramatically improve, although every afternoon he studied the nude model at the Académie Colarossi on the rue de la Grande-Chaumière, where such friends as Max Weber and Hans Purrmann painted. Afterward they might adjourn to a nearby café to talk art, or Leo would wander off to meet a model named Jane Cheron, a real beauty, according to Leo's friend Andrew Green; looking over a batch of photographs from Leo, Green wondered with raised eyebrow whether Leo had been "doing 'Rodin' sketches" of her. Leo seemed more comfortable sexually in the company of those models who did not threaten him too much.

Then there were the salons and exhibits. The Cézanne retrospective at the 1907 Autumn Salon was accompanied by the publication of the artist's letters in the *Mercure de France,* and both stimulated Leo all over again. That

December, he bought an exquisite small still life with apples by Cézanne, having raised money for the purchase by selling his Japanese art books. This was the picture many young American artists, notably Morgan Russell and Andrew Dasburg, saw at the rue de Fleurus and never forgot. Unsurpassed, said Leo, in sheer expression of form, this was the one painting he insisted on keeping when he and Gertrude separated their belongings. "The Cézanne apples have a unique importance to me," he explained, "that nothing can replace."

Along with a new Manguin, *Study of a Reclining Woman,* and a new Renoir, Leo had added several new Matisses, including the lyrical *Music (Sketch)* to the collection; sometime after the Independents' Salon in the spring of 1907, he acquired the aggressively exotic, dark, and scandalous *Blue Nude.* Although not as vehement as that of his sister-in-law Sarah, Leo's appreciation of Matisse persisted; he admired the "forced deformations," as he later termed them, of the painting *Young Sailor II,* which Matisse had shown him the previous fall. And both Matisse and Picasso inspired his own work, especially the open and closed curves he'd been playing with on his canvases as he tested various shapes for heft and volume, also as a result of reading Cézanne's letters.

So it was probably with enthusiasm that Leo became a charter member of Matisse's new class, which opened its doors in early January 1908. For some time, the painter had been instructing Sarah Stein; she invited Hans Purrmann to join her, and they entreated Matisse to teach more regularly. When he finally consented, she and Purrmann took care of the organization and Michael Stein arranged the finances.

Classes were held in the Couvent des Oiseaux, in the building where Matisse kept his own studio. Huge windows afforded plenty of light and opened onto a pretty interior courtyard. Besides Purrmann and another German, Rudolf Levy, Sarah encouraged Annette Rosenshine to join, as well as Max Weber, Greta and Oskar Moll, Patrick Henry Bruce, the Swedish painter Karl Palme, and two Hungarian painters, Joseph Brummer and Bela Czobel. Occasionally Maurice Sterne and other artists dropped by. Most of the students were connected to Matisse through the Steins, and as a result, many outsiders assumed everyone there was American. "Where did these people come from," Gertrude poked fun years later, ". . . from Massachusetts."

But the group was polyglot; and they were serious and scared. When Matisse appeared each week, they followed him from easel to easel and listened with sinking hearts to his criticism. The stocky Purrmann fretted so much over his work he began to lose weight. Annette Rosenshine reminded herself she didn't care, she'd be leaving Paris soon. Matisse insisted on discipline, discipline in drawing, in color, in the unity of form. "This manner of yours is a system, a thing of the hand, not of the spirit," Matisse reproached one student.

Henri Matisse,
a wild man of Paris

"Your figure seems bounded by wires." Max Weber was thrilled when Gertrude took him aside one evening to tell him Matisse had said he was the most interesting youth in Paris.

"The antique, above all, will help you to realize the fullness of form," Matisse told his class. His standards rigorous, even academic, he nonetheless insisted the students develop their own style and was disappointed when they seemed only to imitate him. "You must be able to walk firmly on the ground before you start walking on a tightrope," he said. "True, I believe I could tell you whether you are on the tightrope or are lying underneath, but I don't see how that would be of any use to you. You must do your own criticizing."

Leo Stein also received Matisse's tart instruction, no doubt beneficial but demoralizing as well, and probably the reason Leo dropped out of the class early; he returned occasionally, but only as a visitor. He did not, however, stop painting. Or talking. But he preferred to discuss specific works before him; never, in these years, did he like to talk in the abstract. A young American woman, Inez Haynes, who visited the Steins' atelier in the spring of 1908, remembered Leo challenging the idea of expertise, insisting almost anyone "could pick out a better picture for the Albany State House than he." And anyone, he insisted, with some degree of instinct could tell just by looking carefully at the pictures on the wall which came first, or who influenced whom. He didn't claim to know what this artistic instinct was; nor would he try to define it through formulations that bore no relation to individual paintings. Rather, he liked to talk about what was happening right before one's eyes. This was his forte, said Gertrude: when discussing individual paintings he was truly imaginative, genuinely inspiring.

As for the inevitable generalities, Haynes remembered Leo's saying only that "Matisse and his crowd were trying to get that impalpable something which constituted the difference between a work of art and a photograph of an engraving of it." Would this new school of art succeed at capturing that impalpable something? Leo was not yet sure. "He had only known these pictures for four years," Haynes wrote in her diary, clearly impressed with this unpretentious, unusual man.

What Leo desired was a method for looking, not a rubric under which works of art could be catalogued. And most recently he'd received an indirect boon from William James. (This may in fact explain Stein's frustrating question to Harriet Levy about monism.) The publication of James's controversial *Pragmatism* was pivotal for Stein, especially since he found James's tonic agnosticism compatible with his own thinking—and his own insecurities about it. "It is the distinction of William James," he said in 1926, "that he not only didn't know precisely what he meant but knew that he didn't know."

Because James's pragmatism could embrace uncertainty while providing a ground for action and belief, it reinforced Leo's own relativism. Suggesting that truth was multiple and a matter therefore of function, James argued that, other things being equal, emotional satisfactions count for truth. As he said in *The New York Times* in 1907, "What we here call theoretic truth . . . will be . . . irrelevant unless it fits the . . . purpose in hand."

In pragmatism, Leo discovered a method agreeable to his own developing sense of art criticism: in that field, as in everything else, there were no absolutes. Instead, there was only method: "The pragmatic power required for valid critical work is very great," he explained to Mabel Weeks in 1909. "In order to criticize a work you have to see all that the insider—whether it be author or advocate—does, and then see beyond."

Despite the excitement with which he read James and talked about painting, when friends suggested he write down his ideas, Leo demurred. He was in no hurry, he said. He was not ready. His health was not good. Behind such protestations may well have been the nagging fear that, having rejected abstractions and generalizations, he had boxed himself into a corner. He was uncertain about his own convictions, or made anxious by them, and so James's criterion for truth—emotional satisfaction—was for Leo an impossible standard. His emotions were too turbulent. This was of course a psychological dilemma more than a philosophical one. Leo was unable to commit himself on paper to a single idea or a single painting; nor could he pledge himself emotionally to a single person—except Gertrude. Yet this would also change.

Or appear to.

ALTHOUGH THE ATMOSPHERE at 27, rue de Fleurus seemed dizzying at first, neither Levy nor Toklas felt particularly uneasy. "No consequence hung upon what you told, what you said," observed Levy. Others, however, thought of Leo and the whole Stein clan as insufferable proselytizers. "Pills for the artistic liver," the American artist Morton Schamberg described his visits at the Steins' to the artist and writer Walter Pach. While working on an article about Matisse for *Scribner's* magazine, Pach told a friend that "since Matisse has been teaching, the bunch is worse than ever."

Ever eager to promote Matisse, Sarah Stein had introduced him to the photographer Edward Steichen. Steichen arranged the artist's first exhibit in the United States, held in New York in April 1908 at Alfred Stieglitz's Little Galleries of the Photo-Secession, called "291" after its Fifth Avenue address. And now that the Russian collector Sergei Shchukin was buying more of his paintings, Matisse had reached a plateau of undeniable success: he was able to raise his prices—even those he charged the Steins.

Sensitive to these circumstances, Inez Haynes speculated that Matisse "must have wanted to enlarge his clientele, to sell to other countries, to museums. Yet here were beloved, beseeching friends to whom he was bound by every possible tie of gratitude, who wanted to buy, at his own price, almost everything he painted."

Haynes was equally sensitive to the difference between the acquisitions of the rue de Fleurus and those of the rue Madame. "I wonder if the family rivalry entered into it," she wrote in her diary. "It is a very interesting and complicated situation surely; the two hungry families pouncing on everything the master produces."

But as it happened, *Music (Sketch)* and *Blue Nude* were the last Matisse purchases made for the rue de Fleurus. Part of the reason was that neither Gertrude nor Leo was enticed by Matisse's recent work. And by the time Harriet Levy acquired his *Girl with Green Eyes* in 1909, Gertrude lampooned the artist as "Cher Maître," privately deriding him for this picture and the earlier *Red Madras Headdress*, which she considered too theoretical and facile and as "worldly chic" as the work of Manet or Delacroix.

But there were other, less canonical reasons for the Steins' disaffection. Gertrude resented Matisse's intransigence over prices. When she and Leo wanted to purchase one of his new pictures, perhaps his *Bathers with Turtle*, Matisse gave them an ordinary buyer's price and wouldn't budge. "There was

a mutual friendship, that is true," Leo remarked in 1914, "but that never mixed
with business in the case of Matisse." And Alice Toklas, who later bore a
grudge against Matisse, claimed that when he subsequently signed a contract
with the Bernheim-Jeune gallery in September 1909, he again refused to
change his prices to accommodate Gertrude and Leo's budget. Gertrude
thought him mulish.

All right, she agreed, if Matisse refused to make any concessions for
them, he would no longer be able to ask them for money whenever he needed
it. During the past year, they had advanced him a total of between 2,000 and
2,500 francs, and as far as she was concerned, that entitled them to buy "le
grand tableau." Now he changed the rules. "Brutal egotism of Matisse shown
in his not changing his prices," she confided angrily to one of her copybooks.

If she was obdurate, she may have felt she had to be. Inez Haynes
sensed as much the day she and Gertrude left Matisse's studio at the same
time. Gertrude appeared distracted and cold, breaking the awkward silences
only occasionally with a perfunctory question that made further talk impossible.

There was also the matter of Sarah, Haynes guessed, who had become
more of a rival. Her almost religious devotion to Matisse could be irritating.
And on Saturday nights, she and Michael held their own salon in their spacious cheerful loft for those interested in their growing collection. Many people, whether or not they liked Matisse's pictures, preferred the atmosphere
of the rue Madame, which they felt was less intimidating. Reclining on the
couch in a long gown, her antique jewelry aglow, Sarah was breathless with
ecstatic but ingratiating praise.

Harriet Levy herself noticed that the Steins had slowly divided into two
camps. "I lived between the passions of the Steins," she recalled. She so
feared Sarah's wrath that she dared not, at the time, buy any of Picasso's work;
nor would she expose her cowardice to Gertrude's inevitable scorn.

LEO STEIN flirted with Toklas's friend Nellie Joseph, who had come to
France with her husband, Frank Jacot. Such behavior offended Toklas, who
harbored her own feelings about Nellie. Worse, Leo tried to analyze the young
woman. Toklas recalled severely that "I had known her [Nellie] for years and
resented his appropriation of her. I said some harsh things, but Leo merely
laughed at me." Evidently he did not take Toklas's sense of proprietorship seriously.

Gertrude enjoyed the volatile intricacies of Toklas's amours. "Stinker"
Rosenshine was in deep disfavor, and by the spring of 1908, Nellie Jacot also
was losing her ability to charm. Observing that Toklas was "both indifferent
& frank about Nellie, whom she found 'looking old,' " Sarah reported to

Gertrude that there was no longer "much doing in that quarter." As for Harriet Levy, Sarah continued, spiritual interests seemed to have supplanted romantic ones. Infatuated for a while with David Edstrom, Levy was now wholly captivated by the Church of Christian Science. In fact, that winter all the Steins had read a series of articles in *McClure's* magazine about Mary Baker Eddy and her science of divine metaphysical healing. Gertrude began to analyze Mrs. Eddy's character, and Leo laughed, but Sarah Stein, long interested in palmistry, was so enthralled that she soon gave up painting and declared herself a practitioner.

The affairs of Toklas and Levy bored Leo; even Sarah eventually tired of them. The two women were fixtures; they moved into an apartment on the rue Notre-Dame-des-Champs, wanting to stay near the Steins. But both Gertrude and Michael confessed to a certain "faiblesse" toward them and looked forward to their appearance in the summer in Fiesole. Sarah and Michael had arranged for them to rent the Casa Ricci; the four adult Steins and Allan would take the Villa Bardi, a more spacious house with a huge stone terrace, perfect for entertaining guests, perfect for a family idyll—the last, it would turn out, before the fissures became unbridgeable rifts among them.

After Annette Rosenshine returned to the United States in July, Sarah and Michael left for Florence. They were followed by the Cone sisters, who were also making their summer pilgrimage. Despite Etta's less and less frequent visits to Paris, her friendship with Gertrude was still close. But while her relationship to Baltimore had remained ambivalent, her friends must have suspected that, denounce it as she might, Etta refused to give the city up. Nor was she willing to loosen her connection to a Baltimore friend, Mrs. Ida Gutman ("my pet adoration," Etta called her). So Etta continued to evade Gertrude's demands while at the same time she looked to her for guidance and advice.

That summer Alice Toklas met the Cones. Predictably, the air was charged, as if the Cones sensed radical changes to come. Toklas herself recalled little of the event, except to note meaningfully that after lunch she and Etta disagreed over the bill. Nor were the Cones enamored of her. Claribel later maintained that she did *"like"* Alice; she just thought her uninteresting. With Etta, she mischievously persisted in mispronouncing Alice's surname, making it sound like *taktlos,* the German word for "tactless."

Gertrude didn't introduce Toklas or Levy to the Berensons but instead went off by herself to swim with Mary's friends, shocking them with her size ("Oh, how fat!" the stout Mary Berenson exclaimed). Or she and Leo spent their afternoons together in the Berensons' library, stretched out on the floor smoking cigars and drinking lemonade. (The books "showed evidence," Berenson shuddered decades afterward.) In the moonlight, after dinner, the Stein frères sat on the Berensons' terrace recounting the love affairs of Parisian models. Leo had become, he suggested, something of an expert. And although Mary feigned indifference, she was partly intrigued. It was a pleasant summer.

Gertrude recommended Otto Weininger to all her friends. Leo, Michael, and Allan shaved their heads to prepare for the Tuscan heat and from the Fiesole hill looked into the purple twilight. Then it rained for two weeks in July, so much that the cypresses seemed to ooze. Alice, now enthralled by Gertrude, began to weep. Harriet was so bored she decided to "Fletcherize."

Fletcherizing was a craze inspired by a self-taught student of nutrition, Horace Fletcher, who had become world-famous for his theories not of food but of mastication. Food, he argued, must be chewed thoroughly, preferably until it reached such a tasteless liquid mass that it virtually swallowed itself. And the more one chewed, the less one ate, naturally; less was much better, said Fletcher, at least in matters of oral consumption. His unexceptional advice—don't eat unless hungry; never eat when distraught—had been elevated into something called Fletcherism, a cash cow for its founder, who had himself, he admitted, been overweight, depressed, and prone to illness before developing the method by which he shed both sixty pounds and his malaise. On his fiftieth birthday, he bicycled nearly two hundred miles just to test his mettle, prove his point, and harvest some publicity. It worked. William James Fletcherized; so did his brother Henry. And Leo and Michael Stein, unaffected by Christian Science and palmistry, were receptive to Fletcher's injunctions to chew.

Prey to chronic digestive problems, Leo stepped gingerly up to the program. "He spared us no detail of the effect on stomach & intestines," Mary Berenson remarked in her diary. The day after hearing Leo's description, however, she wrote her mother that she too had tried the technique: it took her half an hour to eat a piece of toast—much too long. Leo was more patient. He was willing, Edward Steichen recalled, to chew his soup by the spoonful.

OF THE SUMMER RESIDENTS Fletcherizing in and around Florence in 1908, all were returnees. Missing were the Hapgoods, who were in the United States. They hadn't forgotten Gertrude or her "Three Histories," which seemed to preoccupy her that summer much more than chewing or even the Toklas ménage. Neith had promised to find out whether any publishing houses would let Gertrude underwrite "Three Histories" herself; it seemed a court of last resort. In July, Neith reported that her agent, Miss Holly, would look at the manuscript and offer guidance for five dollars. Meantime, Mabel Weeks had turned the manuscript over to May Bookstaver Knoblauch, recently married, and now on good terms with Stein despite their rocky past. She would shortly become Stein's unofficial agent.

Miss Holly recommended "Three Histories" to Grafton Press in New York City and May Knoblauch negotiated for its publication. The publisher refused to undertake the book at its own expense but offered to print a thousand copies, list the title in its catalogue, and distribute the book for $660. Grafton advised that the title be changed to "Three Lives" to suggest more precisely the book's subject. Stein was thrilled enough to comply with a change of title, and by November, after she and Leo had returned to Paris, the contracts were ready. Soon she would be a published writer. No doubt this, not Fletcher, temporarily settled her stomach—to say nothing of the flirtations of Alice Toklas.

THE SPECTACLE of the fall of 1908, at least in retrospect, was a dinner given in honor of the genial, gentle, and grave Henri Rousseau. There was a spirit abroad in Montmartre that night, many later insisted, which endowed the riotous dinner with an aura as potent as that at one of Gatsby's parties. And perhaps as ephemeral. Presumably, the banquet symbolized the ingenious whimsy of Montmartre; much less romantically, it may have been that last gasp before dissension, time, and ambition sundered the group of creative people gathered ostensibly to pay homage to the Douanier.

In *The Autobiography of Alice B. Toklas,* Gertrude Stein recalled that the dinner had been arranged to celebrate Picasso's purchase of Rousseau's *Portrait de Mlle M.* for five francs. That seems possible, even though Leo's retrospective account of the affair roundly dismissed other "post-fabricated explanations"; he maintained *he* had been the unwitting cause of the evening. Visiting Picasso, who was not at home, Leo paused to talk with Fernande, who had recently moved back to the Bateau-Lavoir. Rousseau dropped by; he had just been giving a violin lesson. When Leo asked him to play, Rousseau declined, saying he was tired. Fernande suggested he come to dinner later and play for a few friends. A time was arranged, and before long so many others clamored for an invitation that the event seemed destined for myth.

Harriet Levy and Alice Toklas, Fernande's French students, were also invited. Levy remembered that the dinner had been planned in honor of the Douanier, whom everyone loved. It was arranged that the thirty or so dinner guests, including Levy and Toklas, Gertrude and Leo, the poet Max Jacob, Apollinaire, Georges Braque, the painter Marie Laurencin, the critic Maurice Raynal, and the poets André Salmon and Maurice Cremnitz, would meet for an aperitif before climbing the hill to the Bateau-Lavoir. Apollinaire would bring Rousseau at eight, everyone else would bring musical instruments, poetry, or songs. Fernande Olivier would do most of the cooking, and prepared dishes would come from the catering grocer Félix Potin, who, as it turned out, never supplied a mouthful. Potential disaster was avoided when several guests foraged for food in the neighborhood and returned with bread, sliced meats, cheese, butter, and wine.

Both the food and the decor of the Bateau-Lavoir became part of the legend. The studio was hung with Chinese lanterns, one of which was said to drip hot wax all night on Rousseau, who sat in a chair raised on a packing-case platform at the head of the table. After he finally arrived—the festivities were well under way—and took his seat of honor, Leo drew out his violin and Braque his accordion. Cremnitz sang, Rousseau played, people danced, and Apollinaire sat at one end of the table writing letters. There were toasts, songs, and in some versions of the event, fights either real or staged by Salmon and Cremnitz. Neighborhood revelers wandered in and out. Apollinaire demanded that Harriet Levy and Alice Toklas sing a hymn of the "Indian Territory," and Levy answered with a rousing rendition of the University of California fight song. Meanwhile someone, evidently Salmon, was chewing the flowers off Levy's or Toklas's hat (both claimed the distinction). And then, sometime before dawn, at party's end, Gertrude and Leo and Harriet and Alice put the sleepy Douanier into a cab.

Matisse, however, was not part of the festivities. As far as Gertrude was concerned, he and Picasso inhabited separate spheres. "The feeling between the Picassoites and the Matisseites had become bitter," she would write in *The Autobiography of Alice B. Toklas*. Gelett Burgess, the California writer who with the Steins' help had interviewed artists of Paris, offered a thumbnail sketch of both the cross-fertilization and the downright rivalry circulating in their studios. He placed Matisse at the center of a hubbub in which younger artists were trying to wrest from him his leadership:

> Poor, patient Matisse, breaking his way through this jungle of art, sees his followers go whooping off in vagrom paths to right and left. . . . Whereas, little madcap Picasso, keen as a whip, spirited as a devil, mad as a hatter, runs to his studio and contrives a huge nude woman composed entirely of triangles, and presents it in triumph. What wonder Matisse shakes his head and does not smile! He chats thoughtfully of the "harmony of volume" and "architectural values," and wild Braque climbs to his attic and builds an architectural monster which he names Woman, with balanced masses and parts, with openings and columnar legs and cornices.

Stein's fascination with this widening breach between the so-called Picassoites and the so-called Matisseites was a measure both of her own disenchantment, first and foremost with Matisse, and of her devotion to Picasso. In *The Making of Americans,* she named the idyllic western American hometown of the Herslands after Gosols, where Fernande Olivier and Picasso had spent the summer of 1906. She began to refer to Matisse as if his creative work lay behind him, but in Picasso's case she forecast the future. "I sometimes think that Matisse has done what Van Gogh tried to do and Pablo will do what Gaugin [*sic*] dreamed of."

Here were two different men, two different artistic points of view, two different temperaments. Labeling Matisse an "emotional practical realist," Stein studied his hands—heavy, she decided—to better understand his character. His methodical self-assurance derived from "the tenacity with which he holds to his central idea [of] himself and his art . . . the dogged persistence of the thing that for the time he knows." Less critical of Picasso, she and Leo worried about his boundless and uncontrolled facility; they thought that his magnificent work might tend, if he was not careful, toward the insubstantial. But if she fretted lest he dissipate his talent, Gertrude also said he was one who "walks in the light and a little ahead of himself like Raphael."

She was also understandably quick to sense a rivalry between him and Matisse. "When Mat & Pablo met they both said how the other had grown old," she observed. And by that fall, the tacit conflict between them and their supporters had grown more overt. As one of the jurors for the 1908 Autumn Salon, Matisse dismissed several of Braque's submissions, painted the summer before at L'Estaque. Reportedly calling them "little cubes," Matisse, in signaling his disapproval of the new tendency not just in Braque's work but in Picasso's as well, inadvertently named the movement with which these two artists would be associated. That movement was cubism.

And it became, among many other things, the prism through which Gertrude and Leo Stein would refract their profound disappointment with each other.

16
I Could Be
So Happy

Le Café du Dôme: Leo and Nina at left, Max Weber in rear

It is not so easy to know what one wants as people commonly suppose.

LEO STEIN, LECTURE ON EDUCATION

N INA OF MONTPARNASSE, as she was known to the neighborhood, was short and solidly built, unaffected and spontaneous, her face beguilingly innocent, her hair an unruly fuzz of chestnut curls. *"Méchante,"* respectable concierges said, frowning and shaking their heads when she sang near their doors, literally for her supper. Adoring young men called her the soul of the quarter.

Her headquarters was the Café du Dôme. There, in the blue smoke-filled room, amid heated argument and the clacking of billiards, Nina sat surrounded by admirers, most of whom were artists and for many of whom she'd posed. Her real name was Eugénie Auzias. The daughter of a provincial professor of mathematics, she had come to Paris in 1901 at the age of eighteen to study singing; she never entered the Conservatoire, having flunked her qualifying examination because she preferred the company of a young man to the rigors of practice. The affair over and her allowance from her father cut off, she sang in the streets, extending her beret to catch whatever coins might come her way. When the street singing began to damage her voice, she alternated it with a little posing, then a little prostitution and more posing. "What a salty thing Nina was!" exclaimed Hutchins Hapgood, who remembered her well. Maurice Sterne recalled tossing a few sous from his window and listening while she cursed at whoever had thrown a rotten apple. When her imprecations drew nothing but laughter, the infuriated Nina further damaged her voice with a round of Rabelaisian oaths so raunchy that her accompanist quickly hurried her away. "Don't you recognize her?" Sterne's concierge asked. "I thought all Americans knew her. Nina is crazy about music and Americans."

Nina said she first saw Leo Stein in the spring of 1905. He was striding tall, a lilt in his gait, through the Luxembourg Gardens, his arms swinging, his wavy red beard glistening in the sunshine. She pointed him out to friends, who told her this was the amazing American Maecenas. Nina was unfazed. The man with the elastic step and the ecclesiastic grace would be her husband one day, she determined. Her friends laughed. But in the end she was proved right. On February 28, 1921, after a long and lurching romance, Eugénie Auzias and Leo Stein were wed.

In 1905, however, Leo Stein rarely visited the Café du Dôme, and Nina had little opportunity to catch his eye until a friend, the American sculptor Arthur Lee, took her to 27, rue de Fleurus one Saturday night. Nina was terrified. She had nothing to wear but a plain blue jacket and a tired old skirt. Arriving at the Steins', she was relieved that at least the crowd was as poorly dressed as she; yet despite the couture and a cordial Gertrude, who hospitably unfolded a volume of sketches, Nina was too frightened to understand what was being said and much too shy to approach Leo. She merely registered surprise that, on leaving the rue de Fleurus, many of the guests, who had just praised the paintings, once out of earshot began to poke fun at them.

A few years passed before Nina again saw Leo, this time on the rue Notre-Dame-des-Champs, where Alice Toklas and Harriet Levy were living. Recognizing her and mistakenly assuming her gestures were intended for him, he started to approach. (As he later explained to Mabel Weeks, "Her looking is more active than most people's acting.") Nina ran away, anxious lest the man she worshipped from afar actually confront her. But she was sure he had followed her to the Dôme, even though when he came in, he only stared for a moment, then turned on his heel and left. The following day he came for a game of billiards. He caught Nina's eye and smiled. She made a face. He smiled again. That was the fall of 1908.

The next time they saw each other at the Dôme, Nina walked to Leo's table and asked him whether *bacchante* was spelled with two cs. It was the right opening. They laughed, their nervousness eased, and from then on Leo was a regular. Meanwhile, he pressed Neith Boyce Hapgood, before she returned to America, to help him with the art of flirting. Despite the lessons, he remained unsure of himself and uncertain of Nina, so he just asked her to pose for him.

Trembling, she went to the studio he had rented, disrobed, and scrambled onto the model's platform. Silently Leo began to sketch. He looked up, contemptuous. "Yes, you are right," she remembered him saying, "you are badly built and not at all inspiring." He must have been petrified, confronted by both his desire and hers, but he hurt and humiliated Nina, who made matters worse for herself by trying to seduce him. Leo didn't respond; she was mortified. He offered to pay for the session, but she proudly refused the money and walked out of the studio shaking. That was in the spring of 1909, shortly before Leo and Gertrude left Paris for the summer. Leo said he thought nothing more

Nina of Montparnasse

about the matter, and told a friend he couldn't be bothered about women, but in a matter of months he and Nina of Montparnasse were lovers.

AT ABOUT THE TIME Leo's flirtations with Nina began in 1908, Gertrude hired Alice Toklas to replace Annette Rosenshine. The unofficial position was secretary. Toklas could help her read the proof sheets for *Three Lives,* which were on their way from Grafton Press, and perhaps type sections of *The Making of Americans,* which, though by no means finished, had grown huge; it would eventually swell to more than a thousand pages.

The book had changed considerably over the past few years. The story of the Herslands and the Dehnings was now subordinate to a series of insights on character, inspired partly by Otto Weininger and amplified continuously by Stein as she filled notebook after notebook with comments analyzing her friends' personalities and foibles. As she incorporated these character studies into her book, they reshaped her endeavor, altering the scope and style of her novel.

Stein's long novel began as a family saga linking human history to the

cycles of nature. In the opening pages, among the earliest written, Stein celebrated her childhood home in a Whitmanesque passage stylistically reminiscent of "Melanctha": "In the summer it was good for generous sweating,"
she wrote,

> to help the men make the hay into bails for its preserving and it
> was well for ones growing to eat radishes pulled with the black
> earth sticking to them and to chew the mustard and find roots with
> all kinds of funny flavors in them, and to fill one's hat with fruit
> and sit on the dry ploughed ground and eat and think and sleep
> and read and dream and never hear them when they would all be
> calling; and then when the quail came it was fun to go shooting,
> and then when the wind and the rain and the ground were ready
> to help seedlings in their growing, it was good fun to help plant
> them, and the wind would be so strong it would blow the leaves
> and branches of the trees down around them and you could shout
> and work and get wet and be all soaking and run out full into the
> strong wind and let it dry you, in between the gusts of rain that
> left you soaking.

Set amid this landscape were characters whose different ways of loving, eating, sleeping, and feeling absorbed Stein more and more, especially when her
faith in the concept of progress started to wane. In fact, her interest in families—their marrying, reproducing, and perpetuating themselves over time—
had become less compelling than the idea of character itself and in particular
the way certain traits manifested themselves in different people. Character
was no longer a category subject to the vagaries of time and change; it would,
as it did in Weininger's system, exist outside of time—in the specious present.

With her interest slowly shifting, she turned away from her fascination
with Spencerian evolution—she even said that Spencer "had no imagination
for facts or people"—to replace science with art in an attempt to solve, as she
later put it, "the enigma of the universe." Explaining her departure from
Spencerian evolution, she said she had passed through "three stages" in her
development: "Early just being of the earth, then ethical questioning that May
[Bookstaver] laughed at asking to find out—then experience in Spain when
got the awful depression of repetition in history, then realisation much later
that I did not believe in progress, that I was in that sense not an optimist." In
a way, *The Making of Americans* records this development, for what had begun
as a treatise on the importance of family "progress" was developing into a treatise also on the meaning of art, its author repeatedly commenting on the very
process of its making.

Stein intended to have her main character, David Hersland, still modeled on Leon Solomons, "discourse on immortality through work or the family." Hersland, unmarried, childless, and dead in his prime, would come to represent Stein's belief in the importance of creation; creation was that which resisted mortality. Through work, especially artistic creation, or through family, one escaped (to an extent) nonbeing. Leo himself explained to Mabel Weeks when Gertrude was bringing her novel to its conclusion that "without religious or ethical interests of a vital kind the notion of the absolute extinction of life & intelligence . . . was unacceptable."

This was not a new theme for Gertrude, for it had underwritten her medical career, as well as her earlier essays with their censure of women who chose not to bear children. Now for Stein—accepting herself as a Jew who did not for a moment believe in an afterlife and, increasingly, as a lesbian who probably would not have children—a "history of every one" somehow promised to release her from the terrifying cycles of nonexistence, which is what she meant by "repetition in history." (Repetition as a stylistic device was, however, something else.)

"I want sometime to write a history of every one, of every kind there is in men and women," she said in *The Making of Americans*. "It would be such a satisfaction always to be right about everyone, such a certain, active feeling in me." This "being completely right" was the only way it could "come to be in me that to be dead is not to be a dead one. . . . To be completely right, completely certain is to be in me universal in my feeling, to be like the earth complete and fructifying."

She seems to be saying that to know everything—to encompass everyone—is to be like nature, which, always dying and being reborn, counterbalances the chilling repetition that had so horrified her as a young woman. Stein initially set as her goal the describing, defining, and comprehending of individual character not by means of each individual's inner perception of the world—such, as she readily admitted, was "never really present to us as present, to our feeling"—but by an elaborate classification system that promised "a history of every kind of men and every kind of women and every way one can think about them."

This pseudo-scientific system promised to chart all character types so as to account, ironically, for individuality. "There are many ways of being a man," Stein observed early in her novel, "and some sometime one gets to know almost all of them . . . There are many millions made of each kind of them, each one of them is different from all the others . . . this makes of him an individual."

To Stein, the individual was simultaneously unique and representative; each person resembled someone else—"everybody too is like somebody else always to me"—but was also distinct: a concoction of varied qualities mixed together, "as when things are cooked to make a whole dish that is together then." The central ingredient of character was something she called a "bottom nature." Other personality traits were still called "flavors," a kind of seasoning; but by the time Stein wrote the second large section of the novel, the Martha Hersland section, she devised another system, whereby she also classified character in a series of oppositions like those she had used when experimenting at Radcliffe.

Her new categories, called "resisting" and "attacking," suggested character was best understood in images of combat. "[Series] of human struggles," she jotted when preparing her novel: "The struggle between people I watch so often between the clouds and the sun burning them away." And true to her Spencerian heritage, Stein believed struggle to be a principle of growth.

Those who had "resisting being in them" included most of Stein's maternal relatives the Keysers, her brother Michael, Nina Auzias, Pablo Picasso, Ulysses S. Grant, Julius Caesar, and herself. But all of these differed from one another in terms of how resistance combined with other elements in their character, so that while the average type was generally slow-minded, Julius Caesar was "transformed by nervous energy into rapidity of conception." Similarly, although her category of "attacking" included Sarah Stein, Alice Toklas, Bird Sternberger Gans, William James, and Leo, each could be further placed into one of two ambiguous complementary and distinctive sets: independent dependent and dependent independent.

Effectively systematizing the conflicts at the center of *Three Lives,* all of which had to do with power and power relations, these categories suggest that Stein understood aggression and dependency to be mainsprings of human behavior. And although she did not associate aggression, on the one hand, or dependency, on the other, with male or female, her definitions intimate a criterion of gender:

> To begin then with one general kind of them, this is a resisting earthy slow kind of them, anything entering into them as a sensation must emerge again from through the slow resisting bottom of them to be an emotion in them. This bottom in them then in some can be solid, in some frozen, in some dried and cracked, in some muddy and engulfing, in some thicker, in some thinner, slimier, drier very dry and not so dry and in some a stimulation entering into the surface of the mass that is them to make an emotion does not get into it, the mass then that is them, to be swallowed up in it to be emerging, in some it is swallowed up and never then is emerging. . . . There are another kind of men and women that have attacking as their way of winning fighting, these have poignant and

quick reaction, emotion in such of them has the quickness and intensity of a sensation, that is one kind of men and women. . . . Generally speaking then resisting being is a kind of being where, taking bottom nature to be a substance like earth to some one's feeling, this needs time for penetrating to get reaction. . . .

Attacking being as I was saying has it to be that emotion can be as quick, as poignant, as profound in meaning as a sensation. This is my meaning. I am thinking of attacking being not as an earthy kind of substance but as a pulpy not dust not dirt but a more mixed up substance, it can be slimy, gelatinous, gluey, white opaquy kind of thing and it can be white and vibrant, and clear and heated and this is all not very clear to me and I will now tell more about it.

As convenient as it may be to read stereotypes into the categories of resisting and attacking—and stereotypes do shape much of Stein's thinking—she nonetheless appears to be aiming at something more polymorphous in her erotic imagery, something about the power of sex that often escaped articulation, especially in her own case. By temperament and intellect, for example, she defined herself as "masculine" and said she thought her "erotic emotion" masculine as well. But she determined her "actual sexual nature" was "pure servant female." Thus it was easy to misconstrue a woman like her, she observed, and logically, anyone else. Flavors and types could intermix so radically that they were emptied of their meaning. And so Stein, despite her taxonomic obsessions, was also willing to ignore them.

Nowhere did she evade them more than in the areas of love and power. Her complex schema bordered on the absurd. But its importance was in the underlying impulse. Conventions of gender, like conventions of language, were heuristic, provisional, shifting. And therefore the act of loving was diverse, open to interpretation and all manner of people. "A great many have very many prejudices concerning loving, perhaps even more than about eating and drinking. This is very common," Stein observed. "Not very many are very well pleased with other people's ways in having loving in them." The aim of her massive system was discovery and naming; and in naming, there was celebration. "I like loving."

A "HISTORY OF EVERY ONE," if accomplished, could provide an explanatory model of human psychology, one that theoretically could link all people, including Stein, through and beyond time. As a primer of psychological types and responses, then, *The Making of Americans* was Stein's attempt at an all-embracing theory, which she clearly recognized as a way of leapfrog-

A History of Every One

ging time and what it meant to be dead. She would penetrate nothing short of the mystery of the universe; this was to be the enacting of her credo, her work of art, her grand synthesis, and as such, the book would be her bid for immortality, the work she always identified as her major achievement.

This was a tall order. And she knew it. Yet her theory made more sense to her than William James's pragmatism, for her classifications provided aesthetic satisfactions, not predictive or pragmatic ones. "Realising that I was not a pragmatist just recently [I realize I] do not believe all classification is teleological, then realise, that aesthetic has become the whole of me." Leo's explanation of pragmatism had interested Gertrude only insofar as it helped her articulate her exception to it. "When Leo said that all classification is teleological I knew I was not a pragmatist I do not believe that, I believe in reality as Cézanne or Caliban believe in it. I believe in repetition. Yes. Always and always. Must write the hymn of repetition."

As she became more conscious that the basic presumption of her novel—that of progress—no longer worked for her, Gertrude evidently seized on the stylistic device of repetition, so important to *Three Lives,* as a means of bridging the gap between her and others, between her individual life and human history, between the vulnerable self bound to time and something everlasting. "Loving repeating is then in a way earth feeling," she rejoiced. "In some it is repeating that gives to them always a solid feeling of being." Alfred Hodder had once explained that repetition was the only way of asserting permanence for those who doubted the existence of anything outside their field of perception. Repetition was thus a cause for celebration, springing Stein from the prison of solipsistic isolation, offering the consolation of deep, abiding, sensually powerful rhythms. "They are all of them repeating and I hear it, see it, feel it. More and more I understand it. I love it, I tell it. I love it, I live it and I tell it. Always I will tell it."

With repetition creating semantic units of nuance and sonority, Stein insisted her work be understood on aesthetic terms, the terms on which she constructed it. Her classification system was therefore an end in itself; her aesthetic was one of character complete and self-sustaining. Regardless, the insights motivating her work were demonstrably psychological and decidedly personal. In fact, when she failed to detect such "repeating," she despaired, incorporating even her dejection into her narrative.

> I could be so happy knowing everything. . . . I get an awful sink-
> ing feeling when I find out by an accidental hearing, feeling, see-
> ing repeating in this one and then I am saying if it had not been
> for this little accidental thing I would not have known this re-
> peating in this one and it is so easy not to have such an acciden-
> tal happening. Alas, I say then, alas, I will perhaps not ever really
> ever be knowing all the repeating coming out of each one. . . . I
> am desolate because I am certainly not hearing all repeating.

She too was the subject of her book, and the book was about her making of it.

STEIN WAVERED, apprehensive and uncertain. Over and over, she started her analysis from yet another angle when the previous did not satisfy her, when she failed to attain her goal or capture the elusive nature of this or that. "Always I am having a confusion inside me about that one and always I am beginning again and again and again. . . . I am puzzling, I am in a confu-sion, always then I am coming back again and again and seeing, feeling, think-ing all the ways any one can see that one."

Resemblances multiplied, baffled, perplexed. Sometimes they fell into an ordered system, sometimes not. "I am all unhappy in this writing," she con-fessed. "I know very much of the meaning of the being in men and women. I know it and feel it and I am always learning more of it and now I am telling it and I am nervous and driving and unhappy in it. Sometimes I will be all happy in it." When Stein integrated the "Fernhurst" manuscript into her novel, copying it verbatim into the second section, she noted that "categories that once to some one had real meaning can later to that same one be all empty." Still later she regretted, "Perhaps no one ever will know the complete history of every one. This is a sad thing. . . . Sometimes I am almost despairing."

But Mabel Weeks, who was soon to read the first three installments of *The Making of Americans,* found the material "the most wonderful and illuminating, the most candid and objective confessions of the growth of an individual genius that I've ever read." Stein's ambition had been the description of all women and all men; her novel was the poignant record of its failed and valiant unfolding.

GERTRUDE STEIN was a woman who could not stand solitude. She was alone infrequently and then, it seems, only by accident. So in the winter of 1909, while Leo painted in his rented studio or flirted with Nina at the Café du Dôme, Alice Toklas spent a large part of her day at the rue de Fleurus. Each morning she walked to the Steins' from the sunny apartment she and Harriet Levy shared. But she did more than keep Gertrude company or type sections of *The Making of Americans,* whose rhythms, she said, were technically suited to her fingers, trained as they were on Bach and Chopin. More than fifty years later Toklas tenderly remembered those days. "By the time the buttercups were in bloom, the old maid mermaid had gone into oblivion and I had been gathering wild violets."

Although Gertrude liked to consider herself the aggressor in the relationship, Annette Rosenshine and others suspected that Alice engineered its first stages, that she was in fact more willful and manipulative than she let on, and that she decided very soon after meeting Gertrude that this was a woman worthy of such skills as she possessed: wit, tact, and a considerable talent for cultivating the gifts of others. "Alice was capable of creating a background of competent showmanship that she had never been able to do for herself, and sorely needed this outlet for her thirst for fame." Even Gertrude observed that Alice enhanced herself by "giving people what they wanted." Other friends who knew Toklas and Stein later in life declared that contrary to popular opinion, there was nothing subservient or quiescent about Toklas; rather, she was a consummate opportunist who wielded silence with razorsharp precision, a shrewd observer who meticulously arranged all the details of Gertrude's life and kept her circle of friends closed. But theirs was a collaboration, as many recognized, that served both women well.

In 1920, Leo Stein provided his own assessment of Alice Toklas to Mabel Weeks:

> She's a sort of all-important second fiddle. She did play first fiddle to Annette but I reckon she did it rather badly. Playing second

to Nelly & Harriet, and above all to Gertrude has been her star role. She is generous with things because after all she doesn't care for them herself. A few fripperies to enhance her own sexuality is all that she wants. She gets, beyond that, more satisfaction in being responsible for other people's satisfactions. She's a kind of creative parasite on other people's pleasures. She's too introverted to get them through herself. . . . Gertrude & Nelly & Harriet & others direct her energy which is great through channels where her talents get their play before they come back to rest as eventual satisfactions. They are real channels where otherwise she would have nothing except abortive fantasies. She's a kind of abnormal vampire who gives more than she takes . . . She's capable of great kindliness & great cruelty—because she's really indifferent to everything except her own satisfactions. Within her sphere & limits being nice is far more effective & gives more scope than not being so. There's something of Becky Sharp if you can imagine, an introverted Becky, ie Becky no longer ambitious or keen.

Of course, he added characteristically, there might not be a word of truth in all this. But he meant no insult and believed what he wrote. Many agreed with him. At one time, even Gertrude had.

Gertrude had indeed grown fonder of Toklas and revised some of her earlier opinions. Toklas might be a liar—as well as ungenerous, without conscience, mean-spirited, and crooked—but she also possessed a keen moral temperament, an intuitive sense of beauty, a creative sensibility. True, her sense of people was formulaic; true, she admired academic learning a bit much and dressed in those "whore clothes." But there was something lyrical, seductive, irresistible about this lithe woman, who stood so firmly behind Stein's long novel.

Still, there were complications. One was Harriet Levy, to whom Toklas felt obliged. Again Gertrude had to confront a love triangle and a rival. Like Mabel Haynes, Harriet Levy was successful in Stein's professional field; and she had preceded Stein in Toklas's affections. Acutely conscious of the repeating patterns in her own life, moreover, Stein admitted that Toklas reminded her of May Bookstaver. Invoking Weininger, she said that Toklas's "sexual base is May, the elusive, finer purer flame of the prostitute." Harriet, on the other hand, was a prude whose aggressive vanity could compare with Mabel Haynes's.

Levy had been annoying Gertrude. "Shuts Alice's friends out while feeling virtuous about Alice," Stein observed. "Shuts me out because of my association feels very virtuous toward me but don't consider me. Always chooses the way she will show her virtue and for the rest is naturally nasty." Stein's annoyance grew fiercer. "Harriet arms herself, she has put herself in a triple lined double back action automatic safe, has put the key away in another and hired 16 policemen to guard them day and night. She has no principle of growth for she has no power to struggle except to self-defense no power to suffer except from being scared." Worse, Levy did not appreciate Gertrude. She measured success only in worldly terms. "Harriet is more stupid than Aunt Pauline," Stein seethed. "Aunt Pauline recognizes greatness and throws mud at it. Harriet is too stupid too insensible to recognize that there is anything intrinsically greater or better than herself in existence." Stein declared war. But not on Harriet, at least not directly. Her objective became Toklas. Thus Stein assumed she, not Toklas, was the aggressor in the relationship, and her assault, she said, was like Grant's on Lee: "Always a forward pressure, often suffering fearful loss (Wilderness campaign) perfect discouragement and then takes to drink for amusement but always a forward pressure till the final achievement."

Despite Stein's victory, the early days of her and Toklas's relationship were stormy. And Harriet was not the only reason. Toklas was jealous of Stein's earlier attachments, especially to Annette Rosenshine. "From the way Alice acts about the Annette business I may come gradually to think that she cares more about loving than about me," Gertrude commented, "that is she cares more about having completely possession of loving me than of loving me, in short the perfect emotion is more to her than the object of it and if I get to think so her tears won't touch me, not so very much." Stein, wary of Alice's knack for melodrama, resented "being owned" and, cherishing her autonomy, wanted parity in her relationships because, she said, she wanted freedom.

Less unnerved than attracted by Alice's idealization, Stein carefully plotted the course of her affair. Alice's other friends—Nellie and Ada and Harriet—had once given her what she needed, or so Stein noted in the early days of their relationship: "the vulgar, worldly, successful, ignorant, insolent, rich, made-up kind of beauty." Stein was contemptuous of these rivals and convinced she could supplant them to provide Alice with something less meretricious to worship. As Annette Rosenshine put it, "Alice at last in Paris had found the brilliant personality worthy of her talents." In return, Alice would love Gertrude with an adoration absolute and uncompromising.

YOU'VE WRITTEN an odd little book, commented the head of Grafton Press, and most people won't take it very seriously. Frederick Hitchcock was referring to *Three Lives*. Skeptical about its reception, he had wanted Stein to include a preface, possibly written by someone else, to help explain her intentions. She refused. Well, said Hitchcock, "I shall do all I can under the circumstances." *Three Lives* was published in August 1909, while Gertrude and Leo were in Fiesole. By the fall Gertrude told Hutchins Hapgood that Hitchcock and his Grafton Press had robbed her, and the next year, on hearing that Gertrude was working on another novel, Hitchcock himself groaned, "Tell her I'm dead!"

When *Three Lives* first appeared, its cover dark blue and its lettering bright gold, it was well wrapped, small, and fat—like its author, quipped Michael, who was spending the summer with Sarah and Allan in Le Trayas, near Saint-Tropez. Sarah immediately sat down to read the stories; they held up nicely in print, she informed Gertrude. Friends to whom Gertrude sent the book were more directly flattering. It stirred up a sleepy Baltimore, said Etta Cone; most of course pronounced "Melanctha" indecent, but Hortense Moses was as usual the exception: " 'Melanctha' is stunning! All the time I was reading it I felt as if I were looking at one of those Matisse drawings that Mike and Sally showed us—so simple and so powerful." In Italy, the usually acerbic Mary Berenson seemed almost genuine when she declared that the hills rang with discussions of the book. "The theme of your 'Melanctha' is one of the most interesting pieces of psychology that I know, the inevitable *tempo* each person has for doing & feeling, & the misery of caring about a person with a different *tempo* from one's own."

Gertrude sent the book to William James, who, after just thirty or forty pages—all he ever read of it—unabashedly judged it "a fine new kind of realism." Leo said that Henri-Pierre Roché had suggested she send a copy to André Gide. She was not shy about pushing *Three Lives* into the hands of anyone who might help promote it; she eagerly awaited responses from H. G. Wells, George Bernard Shaw, and John Galsworthy, as well as both Booker T. Washington and W. E. B. Du Bois. (Of these, only Wells seems to have responded, although not until 1913, when he overcame his aversion to Stein's style and decided he liked the book.)

Mabel Weeks also overcame her reservations about "Melanctha," calling the story poignant and profound. That summer she visited Gertrude and Leo in Italy. The friendship had by no means grown musty with distance or time. Instead, hunched over long dinners of eggs cooked in tomato, prepared by the Steins' cook, she thoroughly answered Gertrude's questions about her life in New York—she was now a dean at Barnard—and scooping sweet cheese with a spoon at twilight, she listened just as carefully while Gertrude talked about Alice Toklas and Harriet Levy. "I was a New Englander, and Leo made fun of my twenty-six cast iron principles," Weeks wrote later, "but people told me everything."

Leo was aware of the relation between Gertrude and Alice, Mabel

Weeks now knew, but as yet Sarah and Michael Stein seemed unaware. Nor do they seem to have acknowledged her sexuality. As a result, Gertrude was apprehensive, even more so since Sarah was again applying Christian Science to Harriet's ailments, not suspecting their real cause lay in Toklas's desertion. So Mabel Weeks went to the south of France as a kind of emissary.

"You can imagine," Weeks told Gertrude, "that to me it must have been rather grisly to hear that the whole fabric of Harriet's painfully acquired faith is resting at present in Sally's repeated assurances that there is nothing in the relation between you and Alice." But Sarah was uneasy and wanted to talk about homosexuality with Mabel, who worried lest Sarah misconstrue her views. She appeared to be looking for moral pronouncements, Weeks told Gertrude, but Mabel adamantly offered her none, explaining tactfully that since her own experience had never included an attraction for other women, as far as she was aware, she was incompetent to judge. Weeks reported all this to Gertrude, who was obviously anxious to hear what her sister-in-law thought.

Gertrude and Sarah, both fancying themselves perceptive interpreters of character, had been vying for preeminence with each other and among their friends. Gertrude fretted that Sarah's native warmth made her seem more approachable, giving her the advantage. But Weeks's report on Sarah's analytic skills was reassuring: Sarah might have more "cases," numerically speaking, but Gertrude's talent for "simplifying, emphasizing, and clarifying character" unequivocally made her the superior interpreter. Mabel concluded that it was an imperial Gertrude who had the "personality for domination."

After two weeks with Sarah and Michael, Mabel headed to Paris to meet at last the renowned Alice Toklas. Alice took over the role of cicerone, greeting Weeks at the noisy train station and promptly conveying her to the atelier at 27, rue de Fleurus. Mabel was deeply impressed. Alice's conversation was arch, her gaiety natural, her brilliance constant and gentle, she reported back to Gertrude. Toklas ministered to her for two entirely pleasant weeks, so successfully that Mabel decided she didn't like Harriet much either. Alice Toklas was winsome, witty, and gracious. Harriet Levy, though nice, had a rubbery mind.

ALICE WASN'T the only one eager for Gertrude and Leo to return to Paris that fall. Nina also was waiting. Leo asked her to pose again. She protested. He admitted he wanted her to come to his studio merely to talk. He wanted to learn more about her, he said. And this was evidently as far as he could then go.

Perhaps sensing that his former brutality was the result of a dread greater than hers, Nina agreed. Sitting on his sofa, she recounted the story of her life. There had been many affairs. At present there were at least three men in love with her. One of them was the American painter Morgan Russell, a former student of Matisse's and a transvestite. When Nina tried to break off with him, he became so desperate she felt she could not leave. But it was Stein (or Steiney, as she came to call Leo), she confessed, whom she really adored. Listening to her stories and participating vicariously—the only way he could initially take or give pleasure—Leo began to care for Nina more deeply than he had expected. As he later said, she was the one person in front of whom he did not have to pretend.

When they became lovers, Leo could not spontaneously tell Nina he loved her, and throughout that fall, whenever the two met, he remained both distrustful and intrigued. And yet he was happy. "Your love is for me an unhoped for and unexpected richness," he told her, "and my gratitude is and will be profound and lasting." But he also held back.

Though loving and tenacious and firm in her feelings toward Leo, Nina would not give up the delicate and handsome Russell. That left Leo caught "in a perfect whirlpool of tragicomic romance." Yet he played the avuncular part well, respectful of both Russell's feelings and Nina's sense of responsibility. Having himself broken off with Jane Cheron, he did not demand the same of Nina, claiming he wanted only her love, given freely and without obligation. He professed he could not be as passionate as Russell and confided the deeper reason: he feared the power of his own feelings and that, once unleashed, they would smother her. That was why he now preferred to meet her at her place rather than his.

Her freedom ensured his own; but more than that, her freedom protected him from the overpowering emotions he obviously feared. He therefore appeared the most liberated of lovers. "Nina I love you greatly . . ." he wrote her when she left Paris to visit her family during the winter of 1910. "I wish you to be happy, but above all happy in your own being." He wrote her almost every day; he hoped they could spend at least a month together during the summer. This was, he proudly claimed, his first real romance. He reveled in it. "You are for me something completely delicious, your freshness, your frankness, your joi de vivre all give me the feeling of fullness in life. You are perhaps the first who has succeeded in awakening in me the little tenderness I do have," he confessed. "I have always had sympathy enough but it was very difficult to make it worthwhile. I have long known how to comfort people by reasoning etc . . . but with you I feel myself capable of caresses, whether of hand or word." He was inspired. He wanted to learn to write French better, he wanted to paint and to sculpt, and above all else, he was now prepared to do what he had never thought possible: write a book.

LEO STEIN craved solitude, at least in small doses. Sociability exhausted and often disappointed him. But he was completely at ease in his sister's com-

pany, and as he once told Nina, although he really didn't care whether anyone else understood him, it was essential that Gertrude did.

She felt the same way. Her notebooks and letters were still full of Leo's
observations; the two analyzed their friends' characters, relying on each other's
judgment and insight. And she must have been pleased with the way Leo
seemed to need her approval, even showing her Nina's letters during the early
days of their affair. He waited for Gertrude's verdict as if it would justify or
confirm his own feelings, and insisting the letters had genuine quality, he was
thrilled when Gertrude corroborated with an emphatic "decidedly."

They knew of each other's romances. Most of their friends, however, had
been told nothing of Gertrude's affection for Alice, their summer companions
in Tuscany least of all. In fact, the rumors spreading over the Florentine hills
in the fall of 1909 had nothing to do with Alice Toklas; just when Gertrude
and Leo were becoming less dependent on each other, albeit neither yet recognized what was happening, the gossips were prattling. Were the Stein frères
lovers, some wondered. Talk wafted to the United States, where Isabella
Stewart Gardner, now BB's wealthy client, heard tales of incest. Berenson
quickly dismissed this as the kind of nonsense that usually originated in a playful remark from the likes of the Florentine journalist Carlo Placci. Nonetheless, allegations slowly multiplied over the years, significant perhaps only in
gauging how Gertrude and Leo stirred others to conjecture.

But even Mabel Weeks, late in life, was subject to such surmise, speaking of incest when she spoke of Gertrude and Leo. She was, of course, like
others, implicitly acknowledging their special intimacy. But she recalled something more. It was a conversation about incest with Gertrude that, if it took
place, had occurred probably when Weeks spent a month in Fiesole with the
Steins in 1909. According to her, Gertrude said she had suggested to Leo that
she and he become lovers. "There is no doubt in my mind about it," Weeks
said with force. Leo, Weeks added, had dismissed the proposal as caprice.

The Steins invited ceaseless speculation perhaps because they were
iconoclasts—nonchalant, odd, often candid to the point of being rude. Financially independent, they were also American expatriates and Jews who bore
each other a singular, almost determined affection. But it was that affection
that may have struck Leo's psychoanalysts, Abraham Brill and Smith Ely Jelliffe, both of whom (said Leo in 1919) were inclined to find the "incest bug"
wherever they looked. Perhaps they regarded his feelings toward Gertrude as
a palimpsest in which they could still see traces of Milly Stein. Leo, who began
to consult one and then the other in 1915, thought their interpretations pro-
crustean and found Brill in particular remarkably primitive. He dismissed the
notion of incestuous feelings.

As years passed, Leo was inclined to reconsider their views. He had an

odd dream: he was having sexual intercourse with Gertrude and was interrupted twice, first by Alice Toklas and then by a maid or neighbor. Leo grew
angry, realizing the door had been unlocked, and said he was too upset to continue. Gertrude told him not to worry. But we are brother and sister, he
protested. That's true, answered Gertrude, and someone spoke to me about
us just the other day. Yes, Leo conceded, but that was just rumor; now everyone will know. Then he left the room and went into the kitchen, where several maids and a cook were eating from a huge plate of honeycombs. Upon
waking, Leo concluded that Brill and Jelliffe may not have been as mistaken
as he had supposed. But then again, he noted, dreams are never what they
seem.

Leo did not say how he interpreted his dream, but he must have been
aware that if he desired Gertrude—or more to the point, whatever she represented—he also wished to have that desire frustrated. Alice Toklas and the
neighbor were welcome intruders, devised in this case by Leo himself, who'd
left the door open, and when they failed to restrain Gertrude, whom he perceived as uninhibited and voracious, he could not continue. So he frustrated
himself, tamping both his appetite and his aggression. That took him to the
kitchen, where maternal women feast. The image suggests genitalia: were
these women able to love one another in ways denied the dreamer?

A year after Leo Stein died, his editor, Hiram Haydn, encouraged Nina
to write her memoirs. If she could, she told Haydn, she would pour into his
ear "many things which bother me much having to do with Gertrude's and
Leo's affection for one another, things I realized too late. I don't know how to
expose them in my memoirs." She did not say what they were. Only a Gide
could do Gertrude and Leo justice, she sighed, and delicately pluck such gos-
samer chords.

17
A FINE FRENZY

Toklas and Stein in Venice, 1910:
"I'm having the time of my young life," said Toklas.

Writing books is like washing hair you got to soap it a lot of times before you start to rinse it.

PAINFUL, BEAUTIFUL, IMPRISONED: so Gertrude Stein described the monumental painting, nearly seven feet tall, of muffled reds and greens in Picasso's studio. It was the historic *Three Women,* which early in 1909 hung at the rue de Fleurus.

Although in later years Leo Stein took pleasure in scorning Picasso, his relations with the artist were now still good. For his part, Picasso seemed eager to show Leo work in progress. The rue de Fleurus was a major, if amateur, gallery, and the Steins were enthusiasts ready to buy. Moreover, Leo with his canny eye was quick to make connections, even aggravating ones, that linked Picasso to the history of Western painting. Such was Leo's gift—and his limitation.

Often perceptive, Leo's opinions were a source of rancor, friendly at first, then not so. A story long remembered about Leo and Picasso was of the night Leo said Pablo drew as well as Rubens; nettled, Picasso answered, "Why shouldn't I draw like me?" Ignoring the painter's need to be prodigious, Leo was also quick to suggest that Picasso labored in the grip of Cézanne. Eight years after buying *Three Women,* he said Picasso "aimed to rival Cézanne's massive form and held lightly his own endless and intelligent capacity for illustration." But according to Leo, Picasso, as a Spaniard, couldn't accept Cézanne as "the father of us all" (the phrase was Matisse's). A jealous, precocious son, he had no choice but to handle Cézanne as an adversary—and perhaps, in a lesser way, Leo as well. "At last his distortion led him away entirely from representation," Stein commented in 1917, "and only when the comparison with Cézanne was evaded by the reduction of volumes to formal symbols was he satisfied."

There were nonformal aspects of Picasso's painting that Stein didn't recognize, at least not publicly: the self-contained sexuality, for example, with its haunting and ferocious androgyny. Avoiding it, Stein inversely revealed how sensitive he was to Picasso's power, and how anxious he was in the face of sexual desire or its configurations. And these were precisely the feelings he could not put into words.

Regardless, Leo readily disparaged what he did not like. When he and Matisse visited Picasso's studio sometime in 1908, apparently to look at his painting *Bust of a Woman*, "they made no bones about laughing straight out in front of me," Picasso told his dealer, Daniel-Henry Kahnweiler. "Stein said to me (I was telling him something in order to try to give an explanation): 'But that's the fourth dimension!' and he started laughing right there and then." In his retrospective telling of the story, Picasso may have been trying to set one man against another. Kahnweiler, who replaced Stein as patron and promoter, must have known Picasso was not as yet indifferent to Stein's opinion. However, the tantalizing implication was that Kahnweiler always understood, even if Leo didn't. Without question, the dealer got the message. Stein retaliated by dismissing Kahnweiler as nothing but a "faithful disciple," which Leo decidedly was not. But Kahnweiler fired the last shot: "Leo's trenchant affirmations often changed, bearing witness to a basic instability."

Stein was still buying Picasso's work, avidly it seems, despite his aversion to *Les Demoiselles*. Recently he had acquired a series of protocubist works: *Green Bowl and Black Bottle;* two landscapes from La Rue des Bois, with angular trees set amid geometric shapes of green, brown, and dun; *Still Life with Glasses and Fruit;* and *Vase, Gourd, and Fruit on a Table.* As usual, Picasso kept Gertrude and Leo up-to-date. During the summer of 1909, when he and Fernande were in Horta de Ebro, he announced "two landscapes and two figures," and sent photographs of the pictures Gertrude later designated the first cubist paintings. Once back in Paris, he invited the Steins to a private show of them at his studio. That day, both Steins probably saw the new idiom. But only one of them would thoroughly embrace it.

"Picasso and Braque invented, contrived, excogitated, or educed cubism," Leo wrote years later. Volumes suspended in space, interlocking planes, stylized geometric reductions, a palette abruptly reduced to shades of gray: these were the hallmarks of analytic cubist painting, which implied, above all else, a searching quality, a quest for the essence of form, and which, according to Daniel-Henry Kahnweiler, represented the position of objects in space instead of imitating them by illusionistic means. "Cubism differs from the old schools of painting in that it is not an art of imitation but an art of conception which tends towards creation," rallied Apollinaire. It was a new language, one that presumed to liberate the object from verisimilitude. Leo eventually would call it pretentious and silly.

Marvelous tilting rooftops melded into sand-colored angular buildings and cubes of sky. Two of Picasso's paintings, *Houses on the Hill, Horta de Ebro* and *The Reservoir, Horta,* went to the rue de Fleurus. Although Gertrude is often credited with the purchase of these landscapes—it was she who in a sense claimed them—at the time of the purchase she and Leo were still buying jointly, that is, if Leo wasn't adding to the collection himself, especially when he hankered after a Renoir that caught his eye.

Gertrude had not yet bought anything on her own, and although she was unequivocal in her support of Picasso, Leo had hardly spurned him. Later he would say that the paintings he bought after 1909 were purchased only because Picasso owed him money, "and this cleared the account," but Picasso still seemed comfortable with Leo's response to his work and still assumed he would continue to buy. He promised, for instance, in the spring of 1910 to send a photograph of his *Portrait of Vollard* as soon as it was finished. And that summer he said he thought Leo would find Gelett Burgess's recently published article about the "wild men" artists of Paris as hilarious as he had.

It was probably when Picasso and Fernande Olivier returned to Paris in the fall of 1910 that the relationship between the two men began to curdle. Leo was not impressed by Picasso's latest work, culminating in the highly abstract and stylized *Portrait of Kahnweiler.* "As long as he was not committed, but only experimenting," Leo recalled, "all went well enough between us, but when he had finally made the turning point there was nothing to go on." The two argued. Leo remembered Picasso standing in front of a Cézanne or a Renoir, asking scornfully, "Is that a nose? No, this is a nose." He would then draw a pyramid. "Is this a glass?" He would then draw two circles and two crossed lines. "I would explain to him," Leo related, "that what Plato and other philosophers meant by 'real thing' were not diagrams, that diagrams were abstract simplifications and not a whit more real than things with all their complexities. . . ."

Picasso himself was irked. Leo could be a pompous bore, and his condescension was galling. Finally Picasso exploded. "You have no right to judge. I'm an artist, and you are not."

Indeed. But Leo was refusing to admit Picasso into his, Leo's, domain. He, not Pablo, studied aesthetics; he, not Pablo, knew something about art and art history—to say nothing of philosophy and ideas. Picasso was no fool, with his inventive genius; Leo conceded his powerful imagination and talent. But Picasso lacked intellect. As a result, late in life and still of the same opinion, Stein declared that although Picasso was indisputably a phenomenon, he could have been a better painter. "Breathing life and charm into things is what made me take to Picasso in the first place," Stein reminisced, "and if he had gone on doing this with increase of passion and of power as he matured, my interest would have continued and doubtless grown. But when he became an intellectual at a contemptible level of degradation I couldn't accept it. Of course his talent didn't die, it became in fact more mature. There is more power of expression and design in the later work than in the earlier. It is not the lack of ability that puts me off, but the silliness."

Leo would say almost the same thing about his sister.

PICASSO'S so-called intellectual pretensions coincided with Leo's return to aesthetics. He had been casting about, looking for some way to articulate his inchoate discoveries about the art of seeing. In the fall of 1909, Bernhard Berenson had found Leo again quite keen on metaphysics, so keen that he asked Mabel Weeks to send him back issues of *The Journal of Philosophy*. He was getting ready to write his book.

During that fall and winter he read and reread William James and occasionally dipped into aesthetic theory—Croce, for example, whom he mentioned in later years. James was scintillating, but most everyone else, particularly art critics, left him cold. Surely he knew the work of Julius Meier-Graefe and read Maurice Denis's articles in *The Burlington Magazine*, but even Robert Dell, who had been acting as the magazine's Paris correspondent, was slow to embrace the modern painters. And none of the various critics' understanding of aesthetics—not to mention of modern art—satisfied Stein.

Roger Fry's recent essay on aesthetics, for one, struck Leo as inadequate, although he didn't say so in print until 1926, when he castigated both Fry and Clive Bell as being members of a "tiny minority" whose "esoteric ecstasies" the world at large didn't share. According to Leo, these men did not bother themselves with "the global concern that is art" or with what and how people see. "If art meant really only a rapture-in-contact-with-isolated-abstract-form, there would be no good reason for bothering the general run of people with it." Leo was interested in something else: the process of seeing, or more loosely, the psychology of vision—that is, what people perceived and how these perceptions translated into aesthetic values.

But to speak of aesthetics "objectively," and not in sentimental terms, one had to begin with the rudiments. It was necessary to translate words such as "beauty," "sublimity," and "grace" (the terms used, for instance, by the philosopher F. H. Bradley in his Oxford lectures) into a more precise vocabulary, or at least one that had for Leo an almost tangible heft: "form," "volume," and "movement." "I believe that every authentic artist has some quality that is dominant and that will be found in his every aesthetic expression ie every expression which attains to actual realization."

"For me . . ." he explained to Mabel Weeks, "the thing that Matisse has as his dominant character is clarity, ie clarity to me is an objective something.

Picasso, Leo Stein
(*1905–1906*)

I can't speak of the clarity of his color or form properly but rather for me his color and form result in a total expression for which clarity is the best term." Michelangelo and Cézanne were the masters of volume, and insofar as Leo had been able to study Rembrandt, it seemed that his métier was "fullness."

These qualities were so real to Leo that he could imagine them "like samples cut into little squares and stood in rows and preserving definitely their character," even though they had "no particular shape any more than 'cheerfulness' or 'perspicacity.' . . . However they go a long way for me toward giving definiteness to my aesthetic appreciations. For, I believe that these special qualities are the whole of aesthetic values." In other words, the thing represented (subject matter) had no inherent aesthetic value. Rather, subject matter provided merely "the organization of the elements used in expression." The difference between an apple of Cézanne and a nude of Michelangelo lay "mainly in the complexity of organization."

All this was just a beginning. He hoped eventually to bring pragmatism to bear on the psychology of attention and to find a way to talk about what we perceive when we look at art, but was unclear as to how to bring it off. "If I don't . . . it will be because because because in sum I don't," he declared. "But all the same I must do it. That is to say that it is very important to me."

For years Leo had avoided committing himself to paper. Each time he tried to write seriously, he fell ill. He considered his debilitating ailments (mainly gastric) the primary cause of his problem, making him feel lifeless and despondent; yet he knew there was more to it than mere indigestion. "It might seem peculiar that I'm so occupied with my health because in the ordinary meaning of the word I am never sick," he confided to Nina in 1910, "and I'm the farthest thing from a hypochondriac."

He sought out a variety of remedies to cure himself, mostly dietary fads. To date, Fletcherism had been the most successful, virtually eliminating his insomnia, colds, and the sweeping inertia that dulled his perceptions, but during the past winter his symptoms had outwitted the Fletcher prescription. Proper chewing was irrelevant to one who didn't eat, and Leo had completely lost his appetite. He grimaced when he sat down at the table and was exhausted after only a few strained mouthfuls. When the cook had her day off and Alice Toklas stayed to fix dinner, Leo sometimes swallowed her French toast, but by the late spring of 1910 he was desperate. He decided to put his condition to good use, fasting for twelve days. It had worked for Upton Sinclair's neurasthenia; but for Leo, no results.

Gertrude had hoped that he would accompany her to London to help promote *Three Lives,* but Leo felt too poorly. It is easy to suppose that his symptoms were triggered at least partly by the mounting and sturdy praise she had been receiving for her book. Even Frederick Hitchcock at Grafton Press had granted that, although sales were disappointing, the book was receiving more favorable notice than he'd thought possible. *The Nation* complimented the stories' "quite extraordinary vitality" and suggested that if Miss Stein would "consent to clarify her method, much may be expected." Similarly, Boston's *Morning Herald* noted that "the characters themselves stand out clearly in spite of the strange halting sentences, the groping for expression," and the *Kansas City Star* went even further: "At first one fancies the author using repetition as the refrain is used in poetry. But it is something more subtle still; something involved, something turning back, for a new beginning, for a lost strand in the spinning. It makes of the book a very masterpiece of realism." In Paris, young American painters now heard that Miss Stein was not only an art collector but—to the cognoscenti—a writer "with a novel style," as the artist Manierre Dawson wrote in his journal shortly after arriving in France.

Surely Leo envied such attention and success, which must have made his own hesitating attempts to write *his* book all the more difficult. But if publication of *Three Lives* prompted a renewed attempt at writing on his part, its reception doesn't entirely explain his recent paralysis. Already prone to impasse and despair, for the past few years he had become even more adept in avoiding the activity—writing—that was for him most fearsome. His intention had always been to write, painting aside; yet whenever friends asked why he wasn't committing his art criticism to paper, he provided some excuse or other; he talked too much, he once claimed, as if talking dissipated his ideas or his will. Later, however, he hinted at reasons more profound. In 1924 he admitted that if he published the book so many had urged for so long, "they would say, surprised like: Is that all?"

As he contemplated the task before him, he grew restive, complained, could not eat. But his ailment was also a plea. Subtle shifts were taking place in his relationships with both Gertrude and Nina, and Leo needed reassurance of some sort. In the spring, Alice Toklas was going with him and Gertrude to Italy; this decision seemed not to bother him, at least not consciously. Indeed, before they all left Paris, Leo actually began to eat again, finding relief in a new diet consisting mostly of pasta and oatmeal, green vegetables, fruit, and plenty of fluid. Merely the thought of Italy calmed him; no place was more beautiful than the country that reminded him, as it did Gertrude, of a pastoral California. Roses in Tuscany grew large as teacups, strawberries there were tender and fresh, plums and cherries offered sweet solace. By May, Leo reported to Nina that in Fiesole he was feeling better, eating well, and even making progress on his book. It wasn't so much Gertrude's success that had made him anxious; it was Paris and Nina.

In fact, distance from Nina soothed his troubled stomach. Sexual desire and his own aggression had alarmed him the past year. He had felt obliged to suppress much of his jealousy toward his rivals, generally artists like (until recently) him, perhaps in the same way he suppressed his resentment of Gertrude. For Nina, who, ironically, resembled his sister in her determination, wouldn't give anything up.

Leo had meantime become friendly with Morgan Russell, whom he regarded as both his foe and a neophyte. He loaned Russell the Cézanne apples, welcomed him to the rue de Fleurus, and in the coming years advanced both money and advice. Privately, he told Nina he thought Russell's talent limited; Russell made good pictures, not great ones. Yet it was Leo who urged Russell, in the United States after the outbreak of World War I, to reclaim his Paris studio before the Germans got there; it was Leo who urged Bird and Howard Gans to buy one of Russell's pictures; and it was Leo to whom Russell felt grateful for years of steadfast moral support.

Nina's loyalty to this rival may have been in part a matter of self-protection. Her Steiney was mercurial; he refused to take her to Italy that summer, and when she made plans to visit him in Fiesole, he lamely suggested she stay in France to assuage Russell's feelings.

Then, as soon as Leo left Paris without her, Nina began an affair with yet another man. Leo learned of it from Nina herself, insisted he wasn't angry, and cloaked in the icy mantle of his superiority, scathingly analyzed her character—as if alienating her would distance him from his pain. Having few interests but aspiring to knowledge, he told her patronizingly, she used love as her means to explore life. Of course, she could change her ways, perhaps by concentrating on one man—him?—from whom she could learn all she needed to know. But naturally Leo wouldn't want her to change too much, and after all, she was free to live and love as she wished. There was not much either of them could do. Their affair was at a stalemate.

Gertrude disapproved of Nina, a shallow opportunist who adapted her loving to anyone she happened to fancy, a maternal woman, in Weininger's terms, attracted mainly to men she could control, usually younger than she. Nina would continue this way, Gertrude predicted, until she found someone to dominate her. When she subsequently cast Nina of Montparnasse as "Elise Surville" (Elise on the Town) in a word portrait, Gertrude acidly noted "this one is one helping every one to be one not succeeding in living." Elise Surville sang, laughed, knew a great many men and a number of women; though "interesting" to some people, she also helped at least one of them "be a dead one." Was Nina killing Leo—or just his relationship with his sister?

Despite such animadversion, Gertrude was sympathetic, at least during the early days of Leo's romance. She probably thought his infatuation would pass; it had before. But shrewd observer that she was, Gertrude must have seen also that Leo responded to Nina differently, even if he was more than willing to leave her behind.

He planned a summer of research, work, and celibacy. At the Casa Ricci, he and Gertrude and Alice seemed to get on well; the arrangement was apparently working. They visited Perugia together in early June, after which Gertrude and Alice went to Assisi and Leo to Rome. Leo faced the future with renewed zest, arriving in Rome on June 8, laden with notebooks and great expectations. After checking into the Hotel Central on the piazza Colonna, he dashed off notes to the people preoccupying him most, his sister and Nina. Throughout his stay, he would report to them on his intellectual progress and his health.

He rented a small room conducive, he thought, to work. In a few days, he said, he was making discoveries of utmost importance, not the least of which was that he could write moderately well, or at least well enough to get his ideas across. He felt fit. His appetite was good. He ate comfortably in a nearby restaurant at lunchtime and in the evenings brought fruit and vegetables to Maurice Sterne's atelier, where the two of them simmered tomato sauces on Sterne's boilerette. Leo excitedly told Sterne about his affair with

Nina and each day impatiently looked for a letter from her. "I am more happy to know love and to be loved by you," he effused, "than—than—than—than if I found a beautiful Cézanne for nothing." It was the highest of compliments. But he also dissembled, feigning indifference when he wrote Gertrude, as if uncomfortable with her judgment—or perhaps his sense of betrayal. "Nina's letters are very good," he observed condescendingly, "but there is almost no news in them." They were love letters—but this fact went unspoken.

Mornings, Leo walked to the Vatican in the early sunshine; during the hot afternoons he wrote in his notebook at the hotel. "I hope this time to succeed in finishing my work." Mindful of his own propensity for self-sabotage, he put his fingers to his forehead for assurance. It felt cool, which he took to mean he was sound and calm. The weather was beautiful, he enjoyed eating, he was brimming with ideas. But when he returned to Fiesole on June 26, he collapsed.

THE TWO FUNDAMENTAL IMPULSES of all animals are those toward nutrition and sexuality," Leo wrote, "& man has *perverted* both." Obviously referring to himself, he suspected that herein lay the secret of his malaise.

After a desultory month entertaining visitors from the United States and trying his hand at sculpture, at the end of July he had recovered sufficiently to continue his research in Venice and points north. His first night on the canals reminded him of his first experience there, in the summer of 1896. But a cubbyhole for a room—the city was reeking with tourists—and a deluge of mosquitoes quickly chafed his nostalgia.

At the Accademia and the Scuola di San Rocco, Leo was happy. Uninhibited and relaxed, he wrote to Morgan Russell. "This much is certain," he said of Titian, "his imagination is the real thing, as real as M.A.'s [Michelangelo's] or Rubens's, if not as important." Of Tintoretto, he commented, "Great energy, great invention, great facility . . . when a subject is offered to him he at once began to interpret it as a dramatic situation, he was full of ideas & suffered probably from an embarras de choix." The result was "something stupendous," yet "not even second rate." The forms, Leo concluded, "show they were never *seen* together but only put together to render an invention."

Titian and Tintoretto notwithstanding, Leo wasn't sorry to press on after just a few days. ("I don't much like Venice, where I feel confined," he later confessed, "and annoyed by the ever-recurrent perspectives down the canals.") He traveled by train to Munich, where it was raining, and checked into the Hotel Drei Raben. The city was clean, Leo reported to Gertrude, "and if you're satisfied with their definition of sweetness & light you couldn't find anything more perfect." He had come for an exhibition of Islamic art, and he soon ran into friends who remarked on his serene contentment—the kind that, said one, "comes only to those who can exist on one meal a day, and can beat almost anybody at argument." Stein talked and talked, perhaps glad for the company, and although his friends listened intently, as soon as he ambled off they forgot most of what he had to say.

He was percolating with ideas about aesthetics. The main thesis, a friend told Morgan Russell, appeared to be that "the quality of beauty resided in the resolution (just as in music for example) of seeming disharmonies into ultimate harmonies." Conflicts weren't erased in the synthesis, just held in an equipoise. "Stein's word 'friction' I remember now as the other term to suggest the conflicting elements," the friend continued. But this friend and others, willing to learn from Stein, were inevitably put off by his manner. He "perched himself aloft," according to one. "Why the devil does he do it?"

Ostensibly ignoring modern art and the Blaue Reiter group, Stein stayed less than a week in Munich, a decision he regretted after arriving in Berlin, which he found even uglier than Chicago. The Kaiser's taste in art was predictably awful, especially that grotesque marble parade of Prussian history lining the Sieges Allee. Nor did he cotton to beer drinking. And Berlin was no place for a vegetarian. At least the sweets were tasty, especially the fruitcake, and of course there were the museums. "The collections are good but they're of little particular importance to me," Leo wrote Gertrude, "except the bronzes of the Renaissance, some Holbeins and Durers a little Masaccio & a few other things at the Kaiser Friedrich Museum." He would stay a little while at the Hotel Milano, he said, in a pleasant room with a terrace from which he could watch the people strolling below. Oddly, he seems not to have availed himself of modern art in Berlin either, or at least did not mention any; he merely said his work was going so well that he could imagine his book as finished—after many years, of course—and he was looking forward to the future. He even dreamed of a new studio in Paris. Michael had been helping him negotiate an atelier, which he planned to furnish with the items he had been picking up in Florence, tables and other small items of furniture, and this too must have represented a break, a stab at sovereignty, and incipiently a life independent of his sister's.

For they had been drifting imperceptibly apart. There was the subject of Picasso, whom Gertrude adored and in whose work she found confirmation of her own. But there was more. She had been gathering about her a circle of women friends, expatriates mainly, among them the American painter Grace Gassette and her mother, Mary Berenson's cousin Emily Dawson, and the writer Alice Woods Ullman. These women formed primary relationships—sometimes sexual, sometimes not—with other women; they supported one another emotionally or financially, and unstintingly promoted Gertrude's work.

The most important of them was Mildred Aldrich, who had come to Paris in 1898, recuperating from a venture in theatrical journalism that had included her own publishing gambit, the magazine *The Mahogany Tree*, which lasted only a year. Aldrich then worked as a theatrical impresario and agent, something like New York's well-known Elizabeth Marbury, and now peddled French plays to the American market. Stein's senior by twenty-one years, called Mick by her many friends, Aldrich had a grandeur about her that neither prosperity nor poverty altered. The lone, unknown mourner at Oscar Wilde's burial who'd tossed a bouquet of violets into his grave, she had plenty of stories about Rodin and Maeterlinck, and "writes plays, smokes cigarettes . . ." Gertrude admiringly told Etta Cone, "a very interesting woman."

Aldrich liked Gertrude and, for the most part, Alice Toklas, although she was dismayed by what she considered the latter's anti-Semitism. About Gertrude, however, she was always unequivocal: "I had known Miss Stein when she first arrived in Paris, fresh from Johns Hopkins—a brilliant mind, delightfully tolerant—a clean straight thinker and an amusing talker." Seated before the startling canvases at the rue de Fleurus, Aldrich never considered herself more than a rank outsider; she happily admitted she thought the posture of Matisse's *Blue Nude* distorted and the feet ugly. She was equally dubious about some of Gertrude's writing. But she was thoroughly convinced Stein was up to great things, and was so loyal that when she wrote her autobiography in 1925 she made no mention of Leo.

Leo was, everyone knew, often tiring. He could be churlish and cruel, kind and insightful, and massively self-deceived. Howard Gans, Hutchins Hapgood, and other men were alternately infuriated by and forgiving of him. He had integrity, Bernhard Berenson grudgingly admitted toward the end of his life, and Stanton Macdonald-Wright remembered Leo as lovable, quiet, and shy; "even after all these years," he commented in 1971, "whenever I think of him, it is with a feeling of affection." A Baltimore friend related that while she and Leo were walking in Florence one day, they came across a group of children stepping on the lip of a well that overlooked a deep drop. She moved uneasily away, but in a typical reaction, Leo gently lifted them down. The children would inevitably clamber up again, but his friend noted that "you *did lift them down*." "Perhaps he was a stuffed shirt," concluded the writer Ettie Stettheimer, but socially "he had a good deal of charm, was easily amused and seemed warmly aware of the person he was communicating with."

Although he valued honesty above all else, Leo was compulsively given to rationalization; he assured himself and others repeatedly that *this* time things would be different, *this* time he would lick his stomach trouble, his sexual fears, his writing block. And during the summer of 1910, he tried to convince himself that he was standing on the threshold of change, that even though he had not, since the age of fourteen, spent more than a hundred days in "concentrated thought," soon he would be free. He had scanned the bookshops in Berlin and bought more volumes, chiefly the works of Sigmund Freud, which he sent on to Paris. But the few of them he kept to read quickly enhanced his sense of promise. Here was an explanatory model, offered without judgment, of the human psyche.

Annette Rosenshine said both Gertrude and Leo were acquainted with Freud's *Interpretation of Dreams* when she met them, and Leo later recalled that he first came across Freud's name in 1909 while reading a book of Hugo Münsterberg's. By the summer of the next year, both Gertrude and Leo had heard of the work of the Viennese analyst, and both were interested—"the richest & deepest that I know on the subject of sex," Leo affirmed. Even Gertrude appeared enthusiastic, or at least curious, although eventually she would dismiss all Freudian theory with the declaration that "Gertrude Stein never had subconscious reactions." Nonetheless, privately she acknowledged, perhaps speaking of her own past, that Freud was a stage one must go through.

For Leo, however, Freud had an immediate and, over time, a lasting impact. "Suppressed instincts make a misshapen nature," he agreed, hoping that here was the key to the secrets of his troubled mind and doomed digestion. Leo would criticize Freud for explaining far too much, but he was always grateful for the radical propositions intended to understand, and to free, the mind. "At present man knows too much to live by his instincts and not enough to live by his reason," Leo wrote Mabel Weeks after he began to read Freud seriously in 1910.

Leo believed reason a precondition of freedom, both personal and social. And in personal matters, if reason could work for him, allowing full play of his instincts, then perhaps he could actually write the book he wanted, a book that would begin, he said, "with discussion of what knowledge is possible, and end with a Hosannah to man in the highest when he shall have become completely rational as well as completely instinctive and shall have as much use for God as for a doctor." Such a book was in the most profound sense to be about himself, unconstrained and renewed, and it remained the one goal he ceaselessly sought.

LEO TRAVELED directly from Berlin to London, the last stop of his research trip. In his room on Torrington Square, not far from the British Museum, he began to fidget. He hadn't heard from Nina in a while. It was mid-August, and although his and Gertrude's old college friends the Oppenheimers were in town and he was thrilled with a Japanese exhibit at Shepherd's Bush, he noted nervously that only a few, cryptic postcards from Nina had arrived. Perhaps he should have gone to Paris, he thought; perhaps those vague references in her earlier letters implied a new amour. Agitated, he told his sister of his suspicion, then withdrew: "I had never taken any interest in the matter from the start I did not propose to take any now."

Soon Leo learned from Nina that she had in fact gone to Seville with someone else. Insisting that she still loved Leo, she was, however, concealing a good deal about what she was doing and with whom, stroking her beloved Steiney like a wizened confidant. She would tell him the whole story as soon as he returned to Paris, but Leo read between the lines. "I'm quite sure that it's finished," he commented to Gertrude. And he was hurt. "If she had wanted to keep things up she should have adopted radically different tactics. Instead of making a mystery of it she should simply have told me the story in the course of her letters & I would have taken it as an episode. But with all this monkey business on her part she produced a definite break in the current & I don't believe it will be possible to make it flow again."

He felt he had no choice but to end the affair from London. He composed a letter, purposeful and nonchalant. "I am beginning to break out of my intellectual chrysalis and this winter will be for me a period of work," he wrote Nina, hiding his anger not only from her but from himself as well. "For my work, I need my health. For that, I need my diet, and all that would have annoyed and aggravated you infinitely. It is best, then, if you have come to have a little adventure, to close the first volume in a satisfactory way. I'll look forward to having many talks and walks with you, and we shall be in all ways possible the best of friends."

Evidently feeling he had betrayed a trust, he justified his action in a letter to Gertrude. "I didn't see how I could fit Nina into the scheme of things & I feel quite certain that a continuance would soon have proved irksome to her & led to a breaking off. I'd rather a good deal have it come this way. . . . I think that on the whole considering what I am & what Nina is the course has been quite ideally run." Leo probably expected—and received—his sister's approval.

He decided to stay in London a little longer than he had originally planned. His work was going well, and he enjoyed the Japanese exhibition enough to toy with the idea of visiting Japan again. But when he was about to return to Paris and the rue de Fleurus, he asked Gertrude not to tell anyone exactly when he would arrive, "as I don't want any one waiting for me so to speak."

If Gertrude assumed Leo's affair with Nina over, she was wrong. He was working hard on his book, true to his word, and trying to keep his distance from Nina, but he wasn't successful in the latter except perhaps during his fasts. He chose not to eat for days at a time, purifying his vision—or so he must have hoped—to scale new heights of consciousness. When Berenson came for dinner at the rue de Fleurus in October, Leo took only hot water and honey. Walking Berenson back to the Ritz, Leo exulted. He was in the throes of a wonderfully creative, lucid period. "At last he has settled his *universe*," Berenson cynically observed.

MARY BERENSON'S guests gathered about the cool leafy terraces at I Tatti. "Miss Stein came, fat beyond the limits of imagination," Berenson reported to her mother, "& brought an awful Jewess, dressed in a window-curtain, with her hair completely hiding her forehead & even her eyebrows. She was called Taklas."

That was in the middle of June 1910. The relationship between the Berensons and the Steins creaked and strained. Whenever it seemed prudent, Bernhard dissociated himself from the Steins, caricaturing the entire family to Isabella Stewart Gardner as a "tribe of queer, conceited, unworldly, bookish, rude, touchy, brutal hyper-sensitive people." But his feelings were mixed, especially regarding Leo. He had been Leo's friend and admirer, Berenson lamented edgily, but the now deaf prophet of Montparnasse had fallen "under the influence of his sister—a sort of Semitic primeval female straight from the desert," and his friendship had cooled to "friendliness, and not unmixed with contempt."

Berenson had spoken to Leo about their relationship during a visit to Paris, after the two of them met to authenticate a possible Velásquez and then walked together through the Louvre. Berenson understood Leo to say Gertrude was angry, believing Bernhard had tried to rob the family of the "glory" associated with their discovery of Matisse. Failing to do so, he "turned tail became frightened & studiously avoided mentioning his [Leo's] Matisse's or Sally's name."

There was some truth to the charge, at least insofar as it involved dominion, ambition, and hurt feelings. Balking at the Steins' devotion to modern art—he himself wasn't much of a fan—Berenson had exempted Matisse, whom he met through Sarah Stein in 1908. Not only did he like the artist, he was impressed enough to buy a canvas, *Trees near Melun,* and to defend Matisse in print. This, apparently, was what Gertrude meant about his stealing the Steins' thunder. But the rumor that he was in collusion with the Steins to promote Matisse reached him only, it seems, when Gertrude's charge did. "Where & when by the way did you hear that I was supposed to be in league with the Steins to boost Matisse for our profit?" he queried Mary heatedly, as if this was news to him. According to Gertrude, however, he'd already turned tail.

"I do not know how one stands it, & yet I do & even like them," a frustrated Bernhard confessed to Mary. Genuinely fond of the family, Berenson felt he couldn't afford to be identified with them—but not just because he thought them unreliable. They also remained for him the stereotypical Jews he had sought to avoid; perhaps they represented Berenson himself and, in later years, the promises he'd never fulfilled. Publicly he despised and secretly he envied Gertrude's career. "Could not tolerate the late Joyce, not to speak of Gertrude Stein," Berenson confided to his diary in 1950, "because in my own mental churning I anticipated & discarded what in me might have led to them."

Mary Berenson's feelings, and her anti-Semitism, were closer to the surface. The Steins had once again "infested" the area, she complained after they took up residence in Fiesole in 1910. Their "pretended omniscience as to character!" was maddening. She too was eager to keep a distance, or at least pretend to those more hostile than she that she would. She paid little attention to the Steins, she assured her mother, who had never forgotten their horrid presence at Fernhurst. They dropped by only occasionally, and then only at teatime for a free meal, which was of course inexpensive because Leo ate nothing but a furtive brioche.

Neither Gertrude nor Leo had ever cared much for Mary; she had the sexuality of a jellyfish and the brains of a pincushion, Gertrude declared. Gertrude preferred BB. And he made an excellent specimen. She studied his character, measuring his ambitions against his gifts, and compared him with other friends and acquaintances; she likened him, curiously enough, to Alice Toklas. Both were assimilated Jews who shared a trait Stein regarded as Jewish: they "mostly run themselves by their minds."

Charged by her own paradoxical feelings about being Jewish, Stein's typology of character was not without its prejudices. The notion that Jews ran themselves by their minds—whatever that ultimately meant—was but one of them. Related to this was the arid intellectuality of Jews, who "have good minds but not great minds and if you have a good mind but not a great mind your mind ought to be no more than a purveyor to you, because inevitably you are greater habitually than your mind. That is the secret of the inevitable mediocrity."

There were exceptions to the generally anti-Semitic rule. She was one; she recognized "the danger." Leo too was an exception, for the time being. Although he ran himself by his mind, he and men like William James, a Gentile, had "pretty great minds." Berenson, however, did not. Neither did Alice Toklas. "Alice runs herself by her intellect," Stein had said early on, "[but] there is not enough intellect in her to go around and so she fails in every way."

Berenson and Toklas did have other, compelling qualities. They were passionate, lonesome, and proud. "I think Alice is nearer BB than anybody else only she is crooked her being a lady." Both were vain; both worshipped success, decorating themselves with its accoutrements and surrounding themselves with tokens—and people—who represented achievement. BB and Alice "feel passionate affection for success for things," observed Gertrude, "for scents and clothes, and good form." Simultaneously fascinated and repelled by their ambition, she respected their hunger for it. In fact, she shared it.

And she loved Alice.

"YOUR NEWS was surprising. When did Harriet go?" Mildred Aldrich asked Gertrude.

When Sarah and Michael Stein rushed back to San Francisco to be at the bedside of Sarah's dying father, Harriet Levy had unexpectedly decided to go with them. News of her decision reached Gertrude and Alice in Italy in early July. It was quite a relief.

Now with Harriet out of the way, Gertrude asked Alice whether she wanted to stay on alone at the rue Notre-Dame-des-Champs in the fall; she already knew the answer. "I am a person acted upon not a person who acts," Alice told Gertrude's first biographer; she preferred to live with Gertrude. And so their life together officially began in the late summer of 1910.

To celebrate, they departed Fiesole for Venice, where like newlyweds they had photographs of themselves taken among the plump pigeons in the piazza San Marco. In one of these pictures, Gertrude sports a large, lavishly trimmed hat, and Alice, an elegant small purse draped from her shoulder, wears a slim paisley dress, long beads, and a compact turban. She does not smile, and while she seems to stand slightly behind Gertrude, she is unmistakably a force in her own right. Pleased with the photographs, they made one into postcards, which they sent to friends. The first public signature of their relationship, it anticipated the way they would, in their long future together, enjoy constructing a double persona, one that hinted at their intimacy only in the most predictable terms: Alice was the submissive, elegant, shadowy junior; Gertrude was wider, larger, greater. They were married, they said, half parodying the form and half taking it seriously; and in a sense, they were.

Leo was immediately apprised of Alice's imminent arrival at the rue de Fleurus. He had no objections but was cordial and welcoming, sending Alice postcards during his travels; he seemed to regard her amiably. He was no longer painting, the plan for a new atelier having fallen through, so he helped rearrange the apartment on the rue de Fleurus to accommodate his writing and to make Alice more comfortable on his return from London; when she encountered difficulty storing Levy's furniture, he tactfully intervened with the landlady. As far as he was concerned, Alice's presence meant he was more or less free to conduct his experiments in eating without disturbing Gertrude's meals. His sister and Alice should fend for themselves, he advised, until he

settled on a diet that worked, and could join them for meals. "I am still experimenting with diets as there is more for less of measuring, weighing, preparing it will be better for all parties if I do it separately."

So he fasted and wrote. His visit to London had been inspirational, he
reflected. On entering the main hall at the Japanese exhibit, he remembered
seeing a large screen of the Kan school. "It suddenly broke upon me what Plato
and the Greeks attached so much importance to, the civilizing significance of
esthetic expression." It was this fundamentally humanist belief in the salutary effect of art that Leo wanted to convey without recourse to anything as
fatuous as subject matter. "Appreciation leads to art and art to further appreciation": this became his credo.

But the world he envisioned was not the one he inhabited. So he fasted
and read, hoping to deflect the past—"a bad bringing up"—with a measure of
self-control and purification. Freud could wait.

ON OR ABOUT December 1910, said Virginia Woolf, human character
changed. She was alluding to its depiction in the novel but probably was referring also, more topically, to the tremendous jolt caused by an exhibit at London's Grafton Galleries. The exhibit, *Manet and the Post-Impressionists,* had
shocked the British public into a confrontation with character the likes of
which they had never seen: Matisse's boldly decorative *Girl with Green Eyes,*
for instance, and Cézanne's massive and portentous portrait of his wife. For
this, his first "Post-Impressionist" display, Woolf's friend the artist and art critic
Roger Fry brought the moderns Cézanne, Matisse, van Gogh, Seurat, Gauguin, and Picasso to England, borrowing two paintings from Leo—Picasso's
Young Girl with a Basket of Flowers and a landscape by Matisse. But Leo was
relatively unconcerned with the show, although he was making his own in-
vestigation into human character.

On Christmas Eve 1910, he made a thrilling discovery. He had spent the
evening reading biology, then had taken a hot bath and gone to bed, but instead of sleeping, he began to imagine various animals and their behavior. "To
use my old formula," he later wrote, "I kept my eye on the object and let my
ideas play about." As he observed these animals and considered the development of the nervous system, it became clear to him that binocular vision played
a significant role—perhaps the most crucial—in the development of consciousness. "It seemed to me that the progressive development of the nervous
system meant the progressive concentration of energy at a given point. With
hearing & vision the distant was brought near, with vision it became more definite & finally with binocular vision the object was separated from the ground
and similarly could be grouped and differences distinguished. Consciousness
was essentially the recognition of kinds."

Leo lay in bed until nine the next morning, when he jumped up, took out his notebook, and began to write. Freud was irrelevant. This was the breakthrough. This was consciousness, and Leo could define it. He scribbled furiously. "Earliest sense organs immobile the eyes the only sense organs that can be directly [moved] in higher vertebrates contrasted with the fixed eyes of *instinctive* animals like the insects. Consciousness depends on conditions where sense stimulus leads to local muscular response without general organic response. The mobility of the human eye compared to animals. The poet's eye in a fine frenzy rolling becomes a singularly literal fact."

Ecstatic, Leo believed he was on the threshold of something marvelous, "a metaphysics without 'the one and the many,' a sociology without ethics, a psychology without 'consciousness' and an esthetics without 'emotion.' " It was not a materialist or mechanical conception of the universe, he told Mabel Weeks, to believe that consciousness was "nothing more or less than binocular vision." But as far as he was concerned—and he admitted that he was still working out his ideas—binocular vision implied that "everything that can be known is spacial [*sic*]. Ideas are in space pain is in space emotions are spacial." And space could be recognized quantitatively and qualitatively; "hence science & aesthetics." This was his silent rejoinder to the experiments of the cubists, whom he obviously had taken more seriously than he ever acknowledged.

Some two years later, as he looked back at that night, Leo said he felt as if he had lighted a lamp at one end of a great avenue. And even late in his life, he held fast to his belief in the importance of binocular vision. "It separates things from their backgrounds," he wrote in *Appreciation*, "and so gives them individual existence. In this way a composite visual field and a consequent auditory one were made distinctly available. Then by rhythmic movements dependent on man's bipedal balance, in walk, developing into march and dance (perhaps the earliest art expressions) this massive whole came to be articulated, and the world of appreciations became the world of art."

That cold night in December 1910, Leo Stein discovered the cornerstone of his aesthetic. One can well imagine him the morning after his epiphany earnestly describing his insight to his sister. She would listen carefully. And soon she would emphatically, irrevocably pronounce judgment.

18

MYSELF AND STRANGERS, OR THE INEVITABLE CHARACTER OF MY ART

Just before the flowers of friendship faded

What's the use of portraiture, to tranquilise your mind.
GERTRUDE STEIN, "POSSESSIVE CASE"

. . . there was some connection between loving and listening.
GERTRUDE STEIN, "TWO WOMEN"

WHILE IN CALIFORNIA, Michael and Sarah Stein were in touch with Alice Toklas's father, who, plying them with extravagant boxes of fruit, invited them on every imaginable kind of spree. Doubtless he associated them with his daughter's good fortune—and his own loss; it must have been clear to the taciturn gentleman that with Harriet Levy back in San Francisco, his daughter was loath to return. He said little. Only now and then did he muster a "Doesn't Alice ever say anything about coming back?" Of Alice herself, he diffidently asked nothing.

She meanwhile had settled into a routine at the rue de Fleurus, gathering the results of Gertrude's late-night writing each morning and dutifully typing them into neat sheets. Bent on making life comfortable and happy for Gertrude, she now and then prepared meals or ran errands, and always offered encouragement as Gertrude, day after day, went on writing.

The reception of *Three Lives* had undeniably spurred Gertrude, much as it had Leo. She was intent on finishing her long novel, and alternately pleased and uneasy with the results. She sent an installment on to the redoubtable Mabel Weeks, who was circumspect: "I do not think it will ever have many readers because of the repetition," Weeks warned. Perhaps in response, Stein opened the second section of her book with the defiant pronouncement, "I am writing for myself and strangers." Weeks protested. "I don't like you saying you write for yourself and strangers. I think you ought to say you write for yourself, strangers, and Mamie Weeks."

Stein continued to interpolate lengthy character analyses into the novel, especially in the third section, where she introduced a host of figures modeled on friends and the intensive studies she'd been making of them. Probably as a result of this, she experimented more and more with word portraits of friends, acquaintances, family—anyone who struck her fancy—portraits not to be included in the big book but to take on a life, and eventually a style and stature, of their own.

She claimed that the first of these was her portrait of Alice Toklas, written one Sunday evening when the cook had the night off. Toklas had prepared dinner, which she liked to serve hot, but when she called Gertrude into the dining room, Gertrude refused to sit, insisting instead that Alice listen to her read the piece she'd just written. It would be called "Ada."

This was definitely one of Stein's earliest portrait sketches, though probably not the first. Completed presumably in December 1910, "Ada" tells of an unhappy young woman who, after her mother's death, keeps house for her father and brother. Once she and her mother told each other "charming stories"; now bereft, Ada is "one needing charming stories and happy telling of them and not having that thing she was always trembling." With the money left her by her grandfather, Ada leaves her father and brother, never to return, and soon becomes "happier than anybody else who was living then"; she finds that special someone who listens to her stories and who, like her mother, "was loving every story that was charming." Telling stories, making stories, listening to stories—these were metaphors for the act of love. "Trembling was all living, living was all loving, some one was then the other one." And loving was intimately connected to writing. No longer did Gertrude write for herself and strangers; now she wrote for, and with, Alice Toklas.

Other manuscripts from around this time suggest how closely Toklas was involved with Stein's work. "Dearest," Stein scrawled at the end of "Rue de Rennes," obviously left for Toklas to read, "This is a trial, I have no idea what its like and very much doubt if it tells the story. If not I will try it again." On the manuscript of "Bon Marche Weather," she wrote, "Dearest, I wish I had been good and not written this, first place because I would have liked to obey you, second place cause its *rotten.*"

Toklas sent Harriet Levy a copy of "Ada," for despite all that had happened, Levy was willing to help promote Gertrude's work. But Alice sensitively thought to spare Levy's feelings. She hadn't read the manuscript, she reassured her old friend, although Harriet must have guessed who had typed it. The preposterous claim suited Gertrude; this was the same gibe she later levied at Etta Cone in *The Autobiography of Alice B. Toklas:* the genteel Etta had faithfully typed *Three Lives,* wrote Stein, without committing the indiscretion of reading it.

Stein had used Alice's name in an early version of "Ada"; the name Ada, on the other hand, had been used for Etta Cone in a portrait of the Cone sisters, "Two Women," written around the same time. Perhaps Alice insisted she be given Etta's pen name, or perhaps Gertrude took seriously Harriet Levy's concern that, if published, the piece would devastate Alice's father. In any case, the early version did not use a pseudonym for Alice, who was clearly identified. And whatever her reason for changing the name, Gertrude liked the sound "Ada" and she would use the name again and again in her work. ("To aid, to aid to aid and an aid. She is an aid to all whom she aids," Stein would write in "Didn't Nelly and Lilly Love You," which ostensibly refers to the early days of her romance with Alice.)

Stein appeared not to care when the Cones complained that she had "bared their souls to the public gaze" in her portrait of them. Indeed, she blithely took for her subject matter all forms of sexual alliance, heterosexual and homosexual, from "men . . . kissing" to women being "quite regularly gay." Still, she made concessions to Toklas and to privacy, not only by masking Alice's identity but also by replacing a reference to Toklas as "an old maid mermaid" with the more innocuous and ambiguous "that one."

If an aspect of Stein's style—her penchant for indefinite pronouns—was a form of subterfuge, she considered it also a strategy, one she associated, in retrospect, with Picasso's Horta landscapes: "The line of the houses not following the landscape but cutting across and into the landscape, becoming undistinguishable in the landscape by cutting across the landscape. It was the principle of camouflage." For her, then, camouflage moved her portraits beyond a mere surface likeness to something more general, abstract, perhaps universal. Her goal was not to reveal character by means of dramatic situation or gesture but rather to create a life in the present ("being living") through an arrangement of participles, repetitions, and nonlinear semantic units, all intended to have, as she said of Picasso's work, "completely a real meaning."

The portraits did not accumulate detail—the color of an eye, the length of a hem—but attempted to reproduce what Stein later called each personality's rhythm in a language to her mind no more opaque, not theoretically at least, than the language we use every day. It was simply more spare, more intimate, in a way more precise. How was saying, for instance, "never hardly" really different from saying "always sometimes"? And wasn't such a question, in the final analysis, an inquiry into both language and character?

Encouraged by Toklas's enthusiasm, Stein kept writing. Her gallery of portraits filled with individuals, such as "Elise Surville" (Nina Auzias), "Julia Marlowe" (the Shakespearean actress as Bird Sternberger Gans), "A Man" (David Edstrom), "Orta, or One Dancing" (Isadora Duncan). And there were group portraits. In addition to "Two Women," there were "Men" (David Edstrom, Hutchins Hapgood, Maurice Sterne); "A Family of Perhaps Three" (Mildred Aldrich, her mother, and her sister); "Miss Furr and Miss Skeene" (Ethel Mars and Maud Hunt Squire, two American painters who became lovers).

With the exception of "Ada," "Miss Furr and Miss Skeene," and an anecdote about the Matisses titled "Storyette: H.M.," the portraits were non-narrative and employed techniques being perfected both in *The Making of Americans* and in portraits then being painted by Picasso such as those of Vollard, Kahnweiler, the dealer and critic Wilhelm Uhde. And not only did Stein substitute depersonalized indefinite pronouns for proper nouns, she used a spare vocabulary like a palette and modulated tone, aim, and angle with the repetition of gerunds and participial phrases. "Sometimes I like it that different ways of emphasizing can make very different meanings in a phrase or sentence I have made and am rereading," she explained.

These were not linguistic exercises divorced from meaning. "Being living," in the fullest sense, implied success. "Making for success," Stein headed a page in her notebooks. There were many different types of success and all manner of response to it. There was practical success, conventional success, man-of-the-world success, and the type enjoyed by the "earthy successful," in which group she included herself. A compulsive systematizer, she crowded her notebooks with varieties of success. And so too her portraits parsed its meaning. Julia Marlowe "was not liking any one who was not succeeding in being living." Hans Purrmann "certainly was one succeeding in living," and as for Morgan Russell, "some were not certain whether he would or whether he would not be succeeding in living."

Success also implied succession—one coming after another—and dominance. Possession and power remained integral parts of Stein's conscious life; domineering and achingly vulnerable, she registered the slightest shift in any relationship. And this too was the subject of "being living," much as it had been in "Fernhurst," "Q.E.D.," and *Three Lives*—and much as it whirled through her relation with Leo.

EARLY IN THE WINTER OF 1911, Alice Woods Ullman put Gertrude in touch with the magazine publisher H. H. McClure, to whom Stein immediately sent two portraits. McClure was completely baffled.

Having finished the third section of *The Making of Americans*, Stein was again circulating her manuscript among friends, who were in turn trying to snag a publisher. McClure had been polite enough to say he might consider a story, and Stein sent "the nearest thing to a magazine short story that I am likely to write." Whatever she mailed—perhaps "Ada"—he rejected it. Harriet Levy promised to contact John O'Hara Cosgrave, her former employer at the San Francisco *Wave* and since 1900 editor at *Everybody's* magazine, about the "big" novel, which would soon be more than a thousand pages long.

Stein was writing steadily. It was no accident that her increased output coincided with Toklas's presence at the rue de Fleurus—and with the mounting hubbub about cubism. She virtually oozed portraits, one after another, and by the spring contacted the publisher George Doran, saying she would soon have enough for a book. At the same time, she suffered extreme self-doubt. The long novel, with its aim of knowing and understanding everyone, seemed impossible. "It is not such a very joyous feeling," she grieved, "having the motion of having everyone as a piece to one, it does make of everything a thing without ending and all the time then there is not any use of anything keeping on going." Then—perhaps primed by Toklas—she cheered herself on. "I am a rare one. I have very much wisdom."

Leo meanwhile told friends that his own book wouldn't appear until at least 1920. He was fasting for weeks at a stretch now and had a thin, ascetic, almost ethereal air; he was also alone much of the time. Nina, whom he saw infrequently, accused him of loving her less. "The basic change is not in my relationship with you," he explained, "but rather with myself . . . I have become more and more isolated." He had grown hard of hearing, although he was not, as Berenson had characterized him, thoroughly deaf. Nonetheless, this too isolated Leo. On Saturday nights, when the crowds came to the rue de Fleurus, he usually absented himself; he would stop by the atelier for only a little while before retiring to his room. He was weary—particularly of all that talk about cubism and Bergson and realism and cubism. "Elan vital & duree reel are merely verbal makeshifts like the rest." Grand theories were pretentious nonsense. Truth was individual. He wasn't interested in problems of being, the absolute, and "all that kind of intellectual rubbish."

He still visited the Louvre, and when he went there with Henri-Pierre Roché in the spring, Leo spoke animatedly of evolution, imagination, and Kant on the principle of identity—that and his increasing estrangement from Gertrude. The central issue, or the most demonstrable one, had become Picasso. Leo thought Picasso was going in the wrong direction; over Leo's objections, Gertrude admired Picasso's new work. She was a champion of abstraction. Leo was contemptuous. Theirs was a naive furor filled with simplistic divisions between representational and abstract art. "There is a group of modern artists who have consciously developed an abstract art," he wrote in 1927. "But in fact, there never was an art that was not abstract. There is no expression that is not abstract except what is actual duplication." Moreover, the abstractions of cubism, he decided, were trivial; that is, they were abstractions of subject matter, not form. In June he told Gertrude that he'd had dinner with Picasso. He was up to the "same stunt," scoffed Leo, who "didn't look at the pictures except casually."

Leo believed that despite the ingenuity of its practitioners, cubism represented a dead end for painting. "Cubism may have some results," he conceded in 1913, "but I can not imagine that it can remain long as an integral thing." To Leo the best art brought together subject and object; cubism failed because it lost touch with both the object and the onlooker. It was a descent into artistic solipsism, navigated solely by the artist's psyche and virtually impermeable to the spectator, who, for Stein, was an indispensable part of the artistic process. Cubism might be an authentic experiment, but it was also an aesthetic mistake; ultimately vapid, it was influential, he continued to argue in 1924, "because metaphysical novices tend to take the abstract for the real."

He did eventually admit that "the genuine novelty that cubism has introduced into art is analysis in a sense that was never found [in it] before." Cubism attempted

> to analyze a solid into its simultaneous aspects & to then imagine that by presenting the side & top view of a cup at once, or the front and back view of a box, some progress had been made in getting at the essentials. . . . It did not like the old painters imitate natural objects, but it tried to express certain values that natural objects had. . . . "Cubism" in so far as it is something really distinctive always sought an analytic basis more elemental, more fundamental than the apparent objects. Analyzing was supposed to have made manifest the deeper meanings of things.

Yet it was doubtful whether there had ever been "the slightest real value in all this analytic art. . . . The analyses that painters of the cubistic type make discover nothing. It is really only a pseudo analysis & amounts to nothing more than [impressions]. The rational processes are nothing but delusion. . . . It is likely to have certain permanent stylistic consequences but in principle it is absurd & in practice it is utterly ineffectual so far as its intrinsic objects are concerned."

However, Leo seasoned his criticism with so much invective that he could not have been inveighing against cubism or Picasso on purely intellectual grounds, as he later maintained. What annoyed him most of all seems to have been his sister's defection to the prolific, sexually attractive, and persistent Picasso. And that was far more devastating than he ever could acknowledge.

The perceptive Gertrude must have known this. Thus, when she commended herself as the only one who had understood what Picasso was doing, she doubtless relished the idea that she had bettered Leo in appreciating Picasso. Moreover, she relished the idea that she too "was expressing the same thing in literature." Like the cubists, she would invent a means for breaking with the past—and with her brother.

Gertrude Stein and Pablo Picasso "became as brother and sister," so

"Our collection was not a collection of specimens." By 1912–1913, the walls of the atelier were arrayed with (left to right) Matisse's Le Bonheur de Vivre; *Vallotton's* Nude Reclining on a Yellow Cushion; *Picasso's* Seated Nude *and* Woman with a Fan; *Matisse's* Music (Sketch); *and (next row) Matisse's* Olive Trees; *Picasso's* The Reservoir, Horta; *an unidentified work; his* Houses on the Hill, Horta; Landscape, La Rue des Bois; *and* Young Girl with a Basket of Flowers; *and Manguin's* L'Atelier, Le Modèle Nu. *Below the last are Daumier's* Head of an Old Woman; *Picasso's* Still Life with Glasses and Fruit (?); *Renoir's* Brunette; *Manet's* Ball Scene; *and an unidentified work.*

Gertrude and Alice would soon claim. They had to be aware of the implications of the remark.

COMPLETELY CHARMING, was how Gertrude characterized Picasso in her portrait of him. Like its companion "Matisse," this portrait represents in summary her own responses to the artist over the years. Matisse was characterized simultaneously by his ability to be "clearly expressing something"— what Leo had called his clarity—and by his "not greatly expressing something being struggling." Stein hinted that the absence of conflict in Matisse's work weakened it. ("Matisse not a storm-tossed soul," she observed in her notebooks, "his emotion is clear, and is pressed through obstacles, but his emotion always remains a clear thing, his emotion is not muggy or earthy or quivering.")

This view of the atelier shows, among other works, Picasso's
Two Women at a Bar *and* Portrait of Gertrude Stein; *Cézanne*
drawings; Picasso's Young Acrobat on a Ball, *under which are*
three more Picassos, including Violin; *and Cézanne's* Madame
Cézanne with a Fan. *Two other Cézannes,* Landscape with
Spring House *and* Bathers, *can be glimpsed at the far right.*

Picasso was another matter altogether: "This one was always having something that was coming out of the one that was a solid thing, a charming thing, a lovely thing, a perplexing thing, a disconcerting thing, a simple thing, a clear thing, a complicated thing, an interesting thing, a disturbing thing, a repellant thing, a very pretty thing." His work was, in other words, multiple, paradoxical, dynamic—qualities Stein admired and was trying to effect in her own work. "I have the eye," she later wrote, "but not the hand of the artist."

By the summer of 1911, writing portrait after portrait, Stein was moving more deliberately away from the storytelling she celebrated in "Ada," stories with "a beginning and a middle and an ending," almost as the cubists were moving away from traditional constructions of space. Narrative—beginnings and middles and endings—was an emblem of the terrifying aspect of history that she wanted to escape.

Reflecting later in life on her career, she observed that "when one first begins writing one feels that one would not have been one emerging from adolescence if there had not been a beginning and a middle and an ending to anything. . . . But then gradually well if you are an American gradually you find that really it is not necessary." (Americans were given particularly to lyric form, she intimated; they weren't too involved with history.) She surmised that the entire writing of *The Making of Americans* represented her attempt to "escape from inevitably feeling that anything that everything had meaning as beginning and middle and ending." She wanted to exist without the "necessary feeling of one thing succeeding another thing."

Hindsight though it is, her account seems fairly reliable. The simultaneity she saw in Picasso's recent work, for instance, offered liberation and confirmation, and they melded well with her ongoing investigations into the underlying structure of personality. Absorbed in the immediacy of character, not in its past or future, she was using it as the medium through which she expressed the rhythms she said she heard. And these rhythms inevitably directed her attention to the texture of language itself.

And yet as her texts became more slippery—more remote from naturalistic reference points—they referred in an oblique way to their creator, who reveled in sound. She was, after all, the artist who heard and created and was driven by the same inner urgency motivating Picasso. This had nothing to do with conscious intention. "Pablo and I . . . refuse to run ourselves by our minds . . ." she declared. "Our initiative comes from within a propulsion [that] we don't control, or create." She was an artist, not an intellectualizing Jew, and as such, did what she had to do. And so she articulated her vision of the artist she wanted to be: romantic, self-created, unique.

Stein was not interested in emotions—what her brother had termed sentimental responses to the object. She wanted to grasp the object—in her case, the nature of character—as a thing-in-itself. Ironically, this was a task Leo had defined recently for Morgan Russell as "a certain immediacy of intellectual contact which makes things intelligible almost without conscious powers, simply as the result of dwelling on them or where there is thinking, there is a thinking around, about, over and under, which envelops the object and sucks its substance, its central spirit." This, said Leo, was precisely what Cézanne was able to accomplish.

"Does the reality of the object count," Gertrude asked herself, "what I might call the actual earthyness of the object the object for the object's sake." For her and for Picasso and for Braque and for Cézanne, the answer was yes. They responded to the "actuality" of the object, she said, unlike Matisse, who responded only to his emotion about it. "He truly said he painted his emotion but in order to paint it he had to have it attached to the crudely materialistic object when he gets away from this he is lost. He still makes lovely but not significant painting. Now Cezanne is the great master of the realization of the object itself. . . . This is what Pablo probably meant when he said that Matisse always gave the crude feeling of the object but he never really paints the object."

For her to accomplish as much, she had to rely on her own sense of what constituted a portrait: not just the subject but the artist's response to the subject. The completed portrait did not depend on its literal likeness to the subject for its artistic value. Rather, as Leo had said as early as 1906, "Keep your eye on the object and let your ideas play about it."

And in this, she and Leo agreed—in theory.

STEIN'S FICTIONAL MISS SKEENE abandons her lover. She visits her brother and never comes back. Brothers were a problem.

Etta Cone, who revered her Brother Moses, had not recovered from his death, which, she still believed, had snuffed out all the good in life. By contrast, Alice Toklas dissociated herself from her younger brother, Clarence, and seems to have had little to do with him, outside of a property dispute. In 1937, Clarence Toklas committed suicide.

After just two days in Fiesole with Alice and Gertrude, Leo was at his wits' end. "It's probable that this is the last time I'm coming here . . . with my sister and Miss Toklas," he wrote Nina at the end of March, "even though the presence of the latter greatly ameliorates the situation by giving my sister the society which she needs and thus leaving me completely free. But even that isn't enough for me." True, Toklas performed many of the emotional tasks that formerly fell to him, but what he hadn't reckoned on was how alienating such liberation might be. He reacted by reinforcing his seclusion, cutting himself off from almost everyone. Often his behavior seemed intentionally provocative. Mary and Bernhard Berenson had commissioned the French artist René Piot to cover their huge library with frescoes, but the results were disastrous. Everyone agreed—except, of course, Leo. Tactlessly, he buttonholed Mary Berenson, his tall frame leaning over as he yelled in her ear: at least the frescoes were better than those futile drawings and watercolors the Berensons usually liked.

Gertrude was torn. When Baltimore gossips whispered that Leo was ill, she stiffly reprimanded Etta, whom she held responsible for the rumor. She didn't want anyone in Baltimore to suspect something was wrong. "Tell the worried ladies that if I grew fat from eating nothing I should be worried," Leo counseled. "I prefer to be physiologically normal and get thin from fasting." But Gertrude recognized that her brother had become a man obsessed, swept forward by a mania that both worried and rankled, and reminded her no doubt of their mother's withdrawal into a consuming illness.

She resented the way eating absorbed all of Leo's attention. When she and Alice called on Mary Berenson—weird Miss Toklas still wrapping herself in a window curtain, noted Berenson, and now wearing a basket on her head—Gertrude said that since Leo began his "starving experiments," going twelve, twenty, even thirty days without eating, he'd been in fine health and good temper. But Gertrude added that Leo "lost every bit of mental energy he ever possessed, that he never reads or talks seriously, never paints or looks at painting, that he seems like an old man in his second childhood." She was of course exaggerating; or Mary was. But Mary perceived Gertrude's frustration. How could anyone be so absurd as to think he could make a perfect physique, Gertrude reportedly cried. After the age of forty, we must assume we have to live in increasingly cumbersome bodies. Gertrude was thirty-seven. Leo would be forty in but a year.

Back and forth Leo scuttled that summer, in Fiesole and then in Paris to be with Nina. He told Henri-Pierre Roché that he was about to begin "the definitive fast"; he longed for the self-control he believed fasting might bring. If Gertrude couldn't abide the fasts, neither could she possibly approve of Leo's romantic arrangement, which even he called peculiar. Nina and Leo continued to protest their love to each other but neither remained constant; Leo disappeared into himself, and Nina into the arms of other lovers.

But Gertrude evidently felt jealous as well—and threatened. Awaiting Michael and Sarah's return from America, where they had been for more than a year, she wondered whether Sarah and Leo would now find in each other what they no longer sought from her. She confided her fears to Mabel Weeks; Sarah might become one of Leo's disciples, she said. Weeks laughed. What would Sally care about diet, philosophy, or Nina, she asked. But Gertrude was referring to something else, something she didn't mention: Sarah might agree with Leo about Gertrude's work.

No publisher had shown the slightest interest in her portraits.

THAT SUMMER, three more of Gertrude's pieces had been refused by a publisher. Worse yet, the fate of *Three Lives* was not secure. Grafton Press was folding and in the spring had turned the copyright of *Three Lives* over to "Miss Gertrude M. Stein" for the payment of one dollar. Alice Ullman, Harriet Levy, and even Hortense Moses and May Knoblauch, the latter acting as Stein's agent, tried to help, and Knoblauch vigorously tried to place Gertrude's portrait sketches as well—to no avail.

Gertrude did not stop writing or circulating her work. Dismayed though she was, she redoubled her efforts; she was determined to vindicate herself with a passion proportionate to her dismay. She packaged five pieces and sent them to Harper & Company, asking the publisher to forward the parcel to Henry James. She sent Henri-Pierre Roché's translation of her "Picasso" to Jean Cocteau, and gave Roché more manuscripts to read and, possibly, translate.

His response, however, was no longer enthusiastic. These damned repetitions, he complained, "have a sea of sisters which I think, have perceivable meaning for nobody but you." And as for rhythm, "that sort of rhythm is intoxicating you—it is something like masturbation."

"Quantity, quantity, thy name is woman," Roché continued. "Of course it is very enjoyable to let oneself go & write heaps—but . . . Why don't you finish, don't you correct, don't you re-write ten times the same thing till it has its very shape worthy of itself?" Her faith in what she was doing, he suggested, and the strength of her personality shook away most people's doubts—at least in her presence—but without knowing her or the models on which she based her portraits, it was impossible to understand them. "More and more your style gets solitary": Roché sounded a complaint of Leo's.

Gertrude responded immediately and to the point. Roché's letter was unimportant and stupid, the product of male bias and male ignorance.

> I made an epigram the other night, I said that women take their impression to be an intuition, men take their impression to be a construction. Now it is perfectly true that more men construct than women and so one might say that construction is a man's business. Being beautiful is a woman's business but there are a great many women who are not beautiful and they act stupidly the ones that are not beautiful if they act as if they were beautiful and xpect to achieve the results of one being beautiful. Now to take the instance of yourself and myself. You are a man and I am a woman but I have a much more constructive mind than you have. I am a genuinely creative artist and being such my personality determines my art just as Matisse's or Picasso's or Wagner's or any one else. Now you if I were a man would not write me such a letter because you would respect the *inevitable* character of my art. It would be very much (if I were a man) as if [Patrick Henry] Bruce were to advise Matisse. You would not do it however you might wish my art other than it is. But being a man and believing that a man's business is to be constructive you forget that the much greater constructive power of my mind and the absolute nature of my art which if I were a man you would respect.

Roché was contrite. He answered meekly that he had written such letters to men and certainly hadn't meant to advise her, but rather just speak to her as he would to a man friend. Gertrude was satisfied. The two remained friendly. She provided him with a letter of introduction to May Knoblauch and instructed Knoblauch to give him any of her manuscripts, should he ask for them. "He also may want to do something with some of my things."

THE ARTIST Stanton Macdonald-Wright remembered hearing Gertrude read her Matisse and Picasso portraits at the rue de Fleurus. Leo was encouraging, he recalled: "I know that Leo felt that she had a definite talent for verbally visualizing events and people."

But after Alice and Gertrude returned to Paris in the autumn, the siblings were edgy. Gertrude was consumed by work, Leo by his fasts. He was as dismissive as Picasso toward the Autumn Salon and the flap over the cubist room; for Leo it was his fast that soaked up most of his attention. This was, he hoped, the royal road to salvation: "What *I* need is not religion but digestion." Fanatical and desperate, he diminished himself physically, even as his sister grew more visible—in ambition, ego, presence.

To Leo, however, just the opposite seemed true: his light never shone more brightly than when he converted himself into something like pure essence. He apologized to Nina that he couldn't sustain the passionate and corporeal relationship she required. Perhaps she evoked in him the feelings stirred by his own mother, emotions that carried such unresolved conflict that he temporarily decided, in the coming years, that his problem was a "mother complex." Yet he promised Nina he loved her deeply while he crouched behind his health, withdrawing from her ostensibly to control the desires he could not otherwise suppress. Fasting provided escape and granted him the terrible, paradoxical freedom of an illness.

Yet he believed the fasts helped his work. In October 1911, he wrote Mabel Weeks a forty-page letter crammed with his discoveries. Then he wrote another, almost as long, confiding that he had induced a religious experience of sorts in which he "enjoyed an enlightenment and saw nirvana as one who was of it." Although the experience had passed, in its wake he was assured of the bankruptcy of both metaphysics and religion.

> I believe that God is as much a superstition as witches if not more so, that questions of determinism & freedom of the will, monism and pluralism, idealism and realism etc. are utter nonsense, that is meaningless questions, the product of bad science bad logic and superstition. . . . The attempts to formulate the universe metaphysically seem to me foolish because they all proceed on the assumption that concrete terms can be purified of their contents and as abstractions still retain their old meaning.

Implicitly—if not explicitly—he seemed to be debating Gertrude. And she decided to respond. But not in person, not yet. In prose.

·FIVE·

RIPENESS

IS

ALL

19

Two

Mabel Dodge at the Villa Curonia

Which is then the important one, certainly one of the two of them. One of the two of them is certainly in a way the important one.

GERTRUDE STEIN,

THE MAKING OF AMERICANS

They are both ones that quite enough are knowing. Quite enough are knowing each one of them.

GERTRUDE STEIN, *TWO*

S O   D E V O T E D   in their early years were Gertrude and Leo Stein that later in life, when contemplating the past, each thought of the other. In 1947, although they had not spoken for thirty-three years, having either denied or rationalized their relationship, Leo planned to write a book about the sister he'd loved and lost. It was to be about Gertrude and himself, "a study in opposites," he called it: "Gertrude the person who takes herself entirely for granted and I who do not take myself at all for granted."

The year 1912 was a peripatetic one. Leo left Paris that winter in his quest for isolation—"not," as he explained to his sister, "that I am habitually overrun with society but I wanted for a short while to get away even from familiar streets, museums, everything." And from her.

Yet even the streets of London, where he now found himself, had changed. From his customary location on Torrington Square near the British Museum, he saw, instead of hansom cabs and sandwich men, autobuses and Boy Scouts. And for art, the futurists, many of whom he knew. He informed Alice that Umberto Boccioni and Filippo Tommaso Marinetti were having dinner with him just after their show opened at the Sackville Gallery.

Both Leo and Gertrude later disclaimed interest in this group. "Everybody found the futurists very dull," Gertrude wrote in *The Autobiography of Alice B. Toklas,* where she allied herself with the conservatism of the portrait painter Jacques-Émile Blanche; she insisted that the futurists thronged around Picasso, imitating the master. Leo too linked the futurists with the cubists but with less derogation: "There was no end to their experiments," he recalled blandly. "The futurists were specially interested in interpenetration—ie in the notion that simultaneity of experience should find its expression in simultaneity of presentation." But he remembered their first experiments as inexpert and clumsy.

Disclaimers aside, however, both Steins showed some interest in the antics of the Italian art incendiaries. Gertrude told a friend that when their show opened at the Bernheim-Jeune gallery, on February 5, 1912, Marinetti "brought a bunch of painters who paint houses and people and streets and wagons and scaffoldings and bottles and fruits all moving and where they are not moving there are cubes to fill in." Although she was not attracted to the futurist cult of violence and speed, she rallied to its trumpeting of the subversive and the unpredictable, and even to its machismo. Marinetti denounced classical Greek sculpture, and when the Polish sculptor Elie Nadelman swore angrily, Marinetti turned and hit him. Gertrude was tickled.

Nadelman had been the Steins' discovery, according to Berenson, who was introduced to his work by them in 1909 and then sent "influential" people to see it. So handsome he was nicknamed "Le Beau," Nadelman impressed Gertrude, who at first credited him with the passionate insight and poetic sensibility she associated with her brother, among others. "Nadelman exalted," she wrote, "the light would be glad to bathe itself in his statues, kin in a way to Hodder but not of the same family. Hodder a split idealist, Nadelman a complete thing. An artist an exalted sensitive scientist like Goethe." And like Leo, he was reclusive, rarely leaving his studio during the day.

It had been Leo who brought Picasso to Nadelman's studio and purchased several drawings as well as Nadelman's small plaster *Venus of Knidos*. But while Leo remained loyal to the artist, Gertrude wavered. The analytic Nadelman lacked "profundity of emotion"—perhaps in this too she thought he resembled her brother. And when she compared him with Leonardo, she did not entirely intend a compliment: "When he is a scientist he is not an artist," she decided, but "Pablo and Michael Angelo are artists every moment of their being." No one rivaled Picasso.

Gertrude now linked Nadelman to Leo through their "worship of intelligence." That phrase, Nadelman's name, and a brief analysis of Leo were entered together on the same notebook page: "Repetition in Leo," she observed, "fierceness of arrangement in his head and no relativity and no recognition of error because he has done it so well." She who categorized and classified, however, was exempt from her own charge.

Leo struggled alone with his book. Nothing satisfied. In London, a friend took him to meet the director of the Tate Gallery, "one of those humble-minded five-cents-a-pint lunkheads," as Leo described him, "who never can

carry away from a statement any thing more than the lightest weight." He withdrew again into seclusion.

Gertrude followed a different course. Sustained by a fundamental and
unshakable sense of her mission, despite all qualms she continued to write.
By the end of November 1911, at long last she was finished with *The Making
of Americans,* having transformed David Hersland's unexpected death into a
lyrical tribute to the precariousness of perception, memory, feeling, thinking—
of all that which is "being living." And this was preceded by a poignant meditation on the significance of "two knowing each other . . . two having known
each other very well." It was a fitting monument, humane and deeply felt, motivated not just by the death of Leon Solomons but by the sorrow of loss.

The remembrance of those guileless feelings toward Solomons chimed
with the recollection of another college friend, Francis Pollak, whose early
marriage had affected Gertrude so profoundly that she had broken off all relations. He too seems to enter the last pages of the novel, where the narrator
admits feeling betrayed. "It was a thing like something having been a lost thing
that never had been a thing any one had found before it was lost." Loss, remembrance, death, and the murderous rage they induce swirl through the finale of *The Making of Americans,* all part of that throbbing desire to make sense
of one's life. And it is clear that by these last pages, David Hersland has become Stein herself, "one clearly telling something and not telling it again and
again," speaking against the backdrop of unpredictable departures.

And so the highly autobiographical family novel ended as she wished, a
kind of exorcism culminating with the repeated clang of a requiem. "Any one
has come to be a dead one," she wrote. And as she observed in her notes for
her novel, "Much Leo in writing about David."

THE MAKING OF AMERICANS spawned a host of new projects, and
not just the portraits Stein continued to write. By the time she sent her hefty
manuscript to the United States, again enlisting friends to help her place it,
she was already working on several more volumes: a collective portrait of several women; a study of a family of five; and 120 pages of "a long gay book."

"They were regular in being gay, they learned little things that are things
in being gay, they learned many little things that are things in being gay, they
were gay every day, they were regular, they were gay, they were gay the same
length every day, they were gay, they were quite regularly gay." Here, in the
early portrait "Miss Furr and Miss Skeene," Stein conjugated the word "gay";
in the new book, the word reappeared, resonant with a sexuality to be explored
in the many affinities shared by both friends and lovers. "In this book there
will be discussion of pairs of people and their relation," Stein commented as
she planned the new work, "short sketches of innumerable ones, Alice Pablo,

Pablo Fernande, Leo and I, Sally and I, Harriet & Alice, Annette & Laurie [Strauss], Matisse & Mrs., Manguin & Matisse, Mike & Sally, Miriam & Joe [Price] everybody I know [Michael] Brenner & Nina, Leo and Nina, Leo & Jeanne [Jane Cheron], Jeanne Boiffard & me . . . everybody I can think of ever, narrative after narrative of pairs of people, that will be the long book."

This new book, though derived from her word portraits and *The Making of Americans*, differed from them in intention. "I began to wonder if it was possible to describe the way every possible kind of human being acted and felt in relation with any other kind of human being," Stein later explained. "It is naturally gayer describing what any one feels acts and does in relation to any other one than to describe that they just are what they are inside them." Urged into the consideration of relationships, she ventured warily into the external world. But she would not—indeed could not—give up her subjective impression of it.

And then perhaps responding to Freud—or to Leo's reading of Freud— Stein decided she wanted to open her book with "the aspect of nature as beginning in a baby and in children." She was less interested in infantile sexuality than in childhood loss, the loss of that "everlasting feeling" which connected child to mother: "Some, and we can know them, have a curious uncertain kind of feeling when they think of themselves as they were then and some so lose the feeling of continuous life inside them." Each individual dealt differently with loss, wrote Stein; some tried to replace their sense of childhood by having children. Others denied they had ever experienced it. But for those who could not compensate their loss, the world was broken,

> more broken for them than death breaks it for them, ending is less of a breaking to such kind of them than beginning, they have then when they think it inside them that they were a baby then and knowing nothing they have then inside a loss of the everlasting feeling, to such a one such a beginning, being a baby and knowing nothing, breaks the everlasting feeling breaks it as dying as ending never can break it for them.

In a subliminal way, Stein was still confronting the agony of loss and the imminence of departure, both of which anticipated—and probably prepared for—her rupture with Leo. For in his own needy, crusty, and famished way, he had been a nurturer.

LIKE HER BROTHER-IN-LAW, Sarah Stein declared she would no longer paint. The suddenness of the decision, after all her enthusiasm and dedication, bewildered her friends. Yet she was insistent. Christian Science restoked her ambition. She might never be a first-rate painter, but she could

be a fine practitioner; of this she was certain. And there was something de-
vout about Sarah, friends observed. Surely she could fill the place left by Mary
Baker Eddy's death, they conjectured, and hang out her shingle: happiness
guaranteed; Jewish victims particularly welcome.

When Sarah returned to the rue Madame, she and Gertrude did not get
along. Gertrude had predicted as much. Competitiveness drained their affection; Gertrude increasingly perceived Sarah's devotion to Matisse and then
to Christian Science as encroachments on her terrain. Gertrude's evaluation
grew harsh: Sally, self-deceived and self-righteous, was a mere commentator
without deep convictions of her own. Her passions were a function of enthusiasm, not imagination; she was a lobbyist who lived for and through the
work of others, affixing herself to causes, whether Matisse or Christian Science, and siphoning from them the sustenance she otherwise lacked. She was
a medium, "transform[ing] all the material that is given her she gives it forth
personally, she is rather empty in between."

No discernible incident accounts for Gertrude's increased hostility, although Sarah's response to both Gertrude's work and Picasso's had probably
been deficient—to say nothing of Gertrude's new life with Alice. Gertrude was
convinced Sarah didn't take Alice seriously enough: "Alice is the only person
that Sally has ever met who has not impulse to be good nor any impulse to be
sentimental nor any impulse to be endeavoring so she is for Sally completely
intangible."

"I can fancy her as not on the best of terms with you . . ." a perplexed
Mabel Weeks wrote Gertrude in 1912. "The indifference, the detachment seem
inexplicable in Sally whose human genius requires, one would think, materials and material on a large scale." Gertrude had suspected drugs.

She was intrigued, however, by the similarities between Leo and Sarah—
or perhaps more to the point, by her own growing disillusionment with both
as they renewed their friendship with each other. She suggested this to Weeks,
who begged her to reveal more. "I have always had a curious feeling about
Sally—" Weeks confessed, "that she had a certain power over Leo, a certain
skill in manipulating him, and when you both broke with her more or less, I
think she was filled with a sort of blind rage. When she felt that Leo no longer
noted her as an artist she had to stop painting. But I think at bottom she has
always felt a confidence that she could get him to be aware of her."

To understand through juxtaposition the two people who had once been
close to her, Stein began a new book. Originally titled "Two," or "Leo and
Sally," it was "a study of two," Stein said in the winter of 1912, about "a man
and a woman having the same means of expression and the same emotional
and spiritual experiences with different quality of intellect." It was also a way
to explain why her relation to each had changed.

Leo, even more than Sarah, had become a source of frustration. He was not writing his book, he was not painting, he persisted in his relationship with Nina, and he was by no means fulfilling his own or his sister's expectations. "After making him noble and her vibrating discourse on passion for distinction and victory without ambition or interest in fellow-man," noted Gertrude in the memoranda she kept for her project, "bound to turn inward and stop development. satisfy themselves become imperative need. She needs audience and takes dope. He destroys his[,] critical faculty his dope."

Gertrude began to analyze his character in her notebooks. Leo did not have a rich inner life—which she felt she possessed—and as a result he, like Sarah, could draw inspiration only from an object. He had no power of construction, and hampered by his limited experience, he exercised his "critically creative" analysis only when he had something concrete to analyze; that was why, to Gertrude, Leo was indubitably brilliant and original when talking about specific works of art but not when philosophizing in the abstract. "He has the power of thinking that Pablo has," she decided, "but much greater paucity of internal experience about everything but the art created by others."

That Leo had become interested in anatomy—binocular vision, for example—as a way of understanding attention confirmed for Gertrude his lack of inner experience. Moreover, as far as she was concerned, he misunderstood the entire creative process. "Great thinkers eyes do not turn in," Gertrude noted, "they get blank or turn out to keep themselves from being disturbed. It is only sentimentalists and unexperiencing thinkers whose eyes turn in. Those having wealth of experience turn out or are quiet in meditation [or] repose." But Leo couldn't turn outward.

Impoverished by self-absorption, Leo had lost touch with the objects of thought; he was losing touch with the world. "It is because of this that most apparently logical people are so illogical because rationality means that you have to be rational about something. Darwin the real rationalist . . ." Gertrude commented.

> Most people who [are] noted for logic are those having the clarity of the non-appeal to experience. Sometimes it is very good if well started, it can never run long. It is impossible that it should. It either becomes sentimentality, logic chopping, idealistic conceptions, mania or it don't go on long. Real thinking is conceptions aiming and aiming again and again and always getting fuller, that is the difference between creative thinking and theorising.

The difference between her and Leo, then, was her ability to aim again and again; her method was not analysis; it was, as she had told Henri-Pierre Roché, construction. She would not classify and categorize with finality or in submission to anyone else's ideas but was always willing to start over, try again, incorporate, exchange, expand. Leo was the opposite. He could not become fuller; he was wasting away, feeding on himself.

Reconstructing herself as creator, Gertrude unconstructed Leo, relegating him to the role of critic, who devours, needily, the work of others. As she would soon write in "Possessive Case": "He's not as good a genius. / Oh do you think so. / Do you esteem me." Her worshipful days were over.

If Leo's decline dispirited her, it also was a relief. Implicitly, his failure spelled Gertrude's success, or so she later suggested. And that, she concluded, was "the beginning of the ending . . . we always had been together and now we were never at all together. Little by little we never met again."

ALFRED STIEGLITZ was a man with a calling. German Jewish, born in New Jersey, ten years older than Gertrude and eight years older than Leo, he was a photographer gifted with impeccable timing. Combative and entrepreneurial, he demanded that photography be regarded as art, first in his own work, then in the journals *Camera Notes* and *Camera Work,* and finally in the restless propagandizing that led to his formation of the Photo-Secession, a band of kindred photographers who repudiated the provincial and the average.

As the nation's self-appointed stumper for the avant-garde, Stieglitz opened an art gallery at 291 Fifth Avenue in Manhattan, hoping to gather about him those sophisticated enough to disdain everyone else; "291" was rapidly transformed from a brownstone into a state of mind. "There insomnia is not a malady—it is an ideal," Djuna Barnes approved.

Stieglitz's roots were in the universe, rhapsodized another friend. "He hasn't the intelligence of a Leo Stein," thought the artist Morton Schamberg, "but he is sincerely interested and getting into a position where he can do lots of good." Mabel Weeks was skeptical. "He's a good many different kinds of fool, don't you think so?" she asked Gertrude. "I suspect him of something of a pose in the interest in the new things, because he is so pitifully eager to shock people with them." But Stieglitz was no fool; he'd engaged as collaborator on *Camera Work* the talented Edward Steichen, Milwaukee-bred, well acquainted with Paris, and largely responsible for scouting some of the journal's singular contributions. And Stieglitz's gallery soon became an important clearinghouse for modern art—including photography—one could not see elsewhere in the United States.

Through Steichen, Stieglitz had been introduced in 1909 to the marvels of the rue de Fleurus, chief of which was the loquacious Leo Stein. Enthralled by a conversation that included a reassessment of Whistler (second- or third-rate), an evaluation of Matisse's sculpture (better than Rodin's), and a disquisition on the Old Masters, Stieglitz promised he would print anything

Leo wrote, devoting one, two, three, any number of *Camera Work*s to his views. But Leo didn't write anything. Gertrude did.

In the fall of 1911, Alfred Stieglitz was again in Paris. During his three weeks there, when Steichen suggested he visit Leo Stein, Stieglitz claimed he didn't want to tamper with first impressions. Disingenuous as the reason may appear, he was busy steeping himself in Rodin, the set designer Gordon Craig, Vollard, the Bernheims, the Louvre, various salons, and finally, Matisse and Picasso. "I am sure he is the man that is counting," Stieglitz observed of the latter.

Back in his New York City gallery, the restless promoter was therefore receptive to the hand-delivered package that arrived at "291" in February. It contained Gertrude Stein's written portraits of Matisse and Picasso. "They interest me hugely," Stieglitz wrote her, "and I feel as if I would like to publish them." He proposed a special edition of *Camera Work* in which Stein's pieces would appear accompanied by several Matisse and Picasso reproductions. "You have undoubtedly succeeded in expressing Matisse and Picasso in words, for me at least," he congratulated her.

"I am genuinely pleased that you liked my things," she answered humbly. Until now, no one had shown the slightest interest in her recent writing. "I am still sending the volumes of the short and longer things but they come back, quite promptly and with very polite hand writing and sometimes regretful refusals," she wrote a friend. But pleased as she was, she admonished Stieglitz not to change her punctuation. Having worked so hard and been rejected for so long, she would compromise none of her effects.

It was with some relief, then, that Gertrude and Alice packed in the spring of 1912, planning an extended holiday in Picasso's native country, not Italy, that year. They stayed primarily in Madrid, where Gertrude wore her ecclesiastical brown corduroy with sandals, cap, and cane. Alice preferred the romance of black: black silk coat, black gloves, a black hat. From Paris, Leo and Michael supplied them with the latest gossip. Pablo had gone to Kahnweiler, settled some accounts, and left his rue Ravignan studio, decamping to Céret with Éva Gouel, formerly the mistress of the painter Louis Marcoussis. Fernande Olivier, now involved with a young futurist, was modeling—the futurist had no money—and had moved in with Picasso's friends Germaine and Ramón Pichot.

Gertrude later said she'd not been surprised. The previous winter, she and Alice had visited Picasso's studio; finding him absent, Gertrude left her calling card. A few days later, when they returned, they noticed he'd painted Gertrude's card into his canvas and also the words "ma jolie," a refrain from a popular song. Gertrude was certain that Fernande was not "ma jolie"; Picasso had a new lover. And Gertrude wanted the painting. Taking advantage of Leo's trip to London, she decided to buy *The Architect's Table* on her own.

Pablo Picasso,
The Architect's Table
(*oil on canvas, 1912*)

This was her first independent purchase, and the feeling must have been exhilarating. The price was steep, however, so she contacted Kahnweiler, who
allowed her to pay for the picture in two installments. She settled the first in
April and promised the balance in the fall, when she returned from Spain.

With Gertrude gone, fewer and fewer visitors appeared at the rue de
Fleurus on Saturday nights. Mainly stragglers still knocked, and fifteen or so
people came by one Saturday in May, but for Leo the party was over. He
showed the collection to individuals and spent most of his time with Nina;
he visited Matisse or Nadelman occasionally, stopped by the galleries, and
went horseback riding at least twice a week. In his sister's absence, he flourished. Leo hadn't had such fun since he'd had the measles, Michael reported.

When Leo wrote his sister, tactfully omitting mention of Nina, he sent
news of a sumptuous Renoir show at Durand-Ruel's gallery; this too was his
passion, for ever since his interest in Picasso had dwindled, a preoccupation
with Renoir had overwhelmingly taken its place. Infatuated with Renoir's
color, Leo also appreciated the painter's subject matter, ideal women eroti-
cized in a fashion quite different from that of Picasso's hatched and sculptural masses. Something in Renoir's forms haunted Leo; in fact, he often
yearned for them as if they were magic totems that might provide, at last, satiety or peace. Without them, he was bereft, agitated, overcome. And confused

by his own desire. He long remembered the night, sometime in 1908 or so, when he'd tossed in bed, sleepless, over Renoir's *Washerwoman and Child*. Earlier that evening, Picasso and Braque had talked of nothing else, Stein recalled, so he'd gone to the gallery where the painting hung to see it for himself. The painting was blazingly beautiful, luminous, afire from within. Standing in the cold, Leo looked through the gallery window; he walked away, went back, looked again. He went to a café and then returned once more. The picture was still, light, and lovely. Thoroughly agitated, he returned to the rue de Fleurus and told Gertrude that she and Michael should go to the dealer's the next day. Gertrude was astonished, for never before had Leo asked anyone to decide about a painting for him. The following afternoon he bought the Renoir, and he never looked back.

Soon he vowed he would buy a late Renoir when and if he could, and wouldn't hesitate to offer Picassos in exchange, as he eventually did. He would even sacrifice one Renoir for another. In August 1912, while Gertrude was still in Spain, he purchased a small Renoir head—"fine as [any] of them"—at Bernheim's by offering one of his small Renoir landscapes and cash. As for his escape from the heated intellectualism of cubism into this rich sensuality, Leo later maintained that Renoir's "pictures were made to look at, not to be talked about."

Over the years, his respect for Renoir never ebbed, even after he had given up on many other early enthusiasms. Writing of him in 1918, the usually skeptical Stein adopted a language positively theological, if none too critical. He declared that Renoir, blending self-expression with his devotion to the visible world, was as "a man once-born, one who has never trafficked with sin but who came to birth in the full light of grace." To that balm and joy Stein remained forever committed: "A greater than he may come when one with equal gifts shall plunge to deeper spiritual levels and make manifest the more inclusive drama of life, the victory of the powers of life over the powers of death. But the shadow of death has never clouded the art of Renoir and if he has a limitation, it is the very simplicity, the serene graciousness of his pure and noble joy."

This was the highest compliment Leo could bestow. And as he began to retire from the world that was once his domain and his delight, Renoir offered lush solace. Alfred Stieglitz wisely observed that Renoir's women looked a little like Nina.

SISTER AND BROTHER were rejecting each other in a protracted symbolic dance. As Gertrude drew closer first to Alice and then to Picasso, conspicuously disagreeing with her brother about cubism, Leo withdrew from the kinds of success and achievement that obsessed her. Purposefully nonchalant about her recent triumph with Stieglitz, he dismissed "that Stieglitz pamphlet" when she inquired whether the special issue of *Camera Work* had yet arrived. He refused to read her new writings, although he still acknowledged that "Gertrude by long and careful systematic study has gotten . . . an enormous knowledge of individuals and of individuals in their individual relations." He didn't know, however, that he was one of the individuals she was studying.

By the middle of June, after almost six weeks in Madrid, Gertrude had finished much of "Two." It incorporated everything she'd been thinking and feeling about Leo, even her responses to his letters. If Leo mocked May Knoblauch's "good middle class" opposition to Teddy Roosevelt's presidential bid, that too was part of the text—buried, theorized, and very much there.

"Two" is among the most personal and variable of Gertrude Stein's early work not only because of its autobiographical urgency but also because of its heralding the stylistic shifts that would culminate in the still-life portraits published as *Tender Buttons*. With its swaying rhythms, "Two" begins in the repetitive style of the early portraits. Using the idea of "sound" as a metaphor for expression, Stein explores the "sound coming out of each one of them," or the way all characters, male and female, signify themselves. "Sound is coming out of each one of them, out of each one of the two of them. Sound is in them in each one of the two of them. Each one of the two of them is having sound coming out of them." Again, Stein is interested in how two people are the same, yet different; how each can take the same terms and respond to experience individually.

To demonstrate as much, Stein modulates a limited vocabulary, subtly varying syntax and diction to contrast her two characters.

> He being one and needing being one feeling that he was creating being living was needing that sound sounding was coming out of him. She being one and needing being feeling that being living she was creating was needing that sound sounding was coming out of her.

Superficially, the difference between these two is largely predictable, even though Stein's rhythmic use of participles can be evocative. Her male and female characters—insofar as they are characters—fall into stereotypical patterns. The male is deliberate and cerebral, defined in terms of vigor and intention and determination and decision: "Thinking being existing, he was existing in being thinking." The female character is defined by emotion; for her, "thinking is feeling." For Stein, though, neither extreme is salutary: each is simply the inversion of the other.

As her working notes suggest, Stein intends a complex characterization by paralleling the two characters from youth to the present, highlighting not just their failures but also their integrity, nobility, vision. As a youth, Leo "did not talk too long." He was free then, "he felt what he said" and "he felt seeing." Yet something changed, and it seems that part of Leo's failure was his denial of what Gertrude called "repeating." She may very well have meant the repetitions in her own writing that Henri-Pierre Roché found so excruciating:

> One can be repeating, one is repeating, repeating is being existing, if repeating is being existing he is expressing that that thing is not interesting and not being interesting it has not the meaning not the meaning of being something being existing.

Although Leo had criticized "too much repetition" in *The Making of Americans,* until recently he had been involved with his sister's work, offering for instance comments in the form of notes on the novel. But Gertrude often rejected critical commentary. As she was later to say, almost defiantly, "No artist needs criticism, he only needs appreciation. If he needs criticism he is no artist."

In "Two," Stein extends her vocabulary and rhetorical range. Not only does she parody the sound of Leo's pragmatism:

> He can say that which he says in saying what he says in saying what he says as concluding what is concluded in deciding that that which is said would be what is if what is said were what is—

but her comic rendition of Sarah's ecstatic vision is a rhythmic tour de force:

> She smiling yet, she hitting the pin that is sticking and not pricking the skin that is hanging, she likely yet and not forgetting, she hardly yet and not remembering, she and the water trickling, she and with absent breathing, she and with laudation and intoning, she with appetite not returning, she with diminishing attention, she with artificial washing, she with captivating trying on that which is fitting and might not be becoming, she with elucidating self-abnegation, she with entire repudiation, she with anticipating praying, she with augmenting dispersion, she is the one having a connection that expressing is the thing that rising again has risen, and rising is rising and will be having come to rise. . . . She is the anticipating of a new one having been an old one. She is the anticipation of expression having immaculate conception. She is the

anticipation of crossing. She is the anticipation of regeneration. She is the anticipation of excelling obligation. She is the anticipation. She is the actualisation. She is the rising having been arisen. She is the convocation of anticipation and acceptance. She is the lamb and the lion.

With both concrete and abstract nouns, Stein has begun to present—not describe—a form of thinking and feeling different from that of the "two." Implicitly, she portrays her own creative artist, neither one of the two and therefore largely exempt from the stereotypical patterns of male and female, as well as the stereotypical uses of language. Thus, as her prose grows more concrete, if no less cryptic, she seems to be making an implicit statement about the artist she is and will become. "A distant noise was farther than he heard and this because he had defective hearing," she writes beguilingly. Then she adds, "He was alight and this was showing when he stood where he stood and his clothes were burning."

Increasingly bold in her use of language, Stein increasingly enjoyed its pliancy and playfulness, sometimes using it referentially, sometimes not. She charged her portraits with a suggestive, intrepid tongue, and reveled in abrupt shifts, abbreviations, ambiguity. No doubt exhilarated by Picasso's latest efforts, and particularly by her purchase of *The Architect's Table*, Stein was stimulated by the direction his work was taking, with its visual puns, its incorporation of words and letters, its apparent capriciousness, and its insistence on the materiality of the canvas itself.

"Yes I have gotten a new form," said Gertrude in "Monsieur Vollard and Cezanne," reputedly written in 1912. Alice Toklas approved. "Sweet pinky," she scribbled on a note to Gertrude. "You made lots of literature last night—didn't you. It is very good. I like this one best. You are doing most handsomely. Would you mind if I didn't think you a Post-impressionist. You aren't lovey you are not a cubiste either." Gertrude was in a class by herself.

GERTRUDE'S NEW FORM was soon to be associated with one of her most notorious portraits, that of the American heiress Mabel Dodge. Gertrude first met Dodge in the spring of 1911, introduced by Mildred Aldrich. Plump, flirtatious, with a lovely voice and pretty eyes framed by long lashes, Dodge was a woman yearning. "Do I contradict myself? Very well then I contradict myself" was embossed, in circular design, on her letter paper. Yet she was sincere about the restless enthusiasms that clutched her, including the array of men and women with whom she was occasionally but intensely involved. She was a loyal friend, a mercurial lover, and quite taken with Gertrude. When she read her, she positively shivered. "Gertrude Stein was prodigious . . ." recollected Dodge. "She used to roar with laughter, out loud." Gertrude was the first to teach her that "nothing is any more than it is to oneself." This was the very theory, commented Dodge, on which Leo too based his aesthetic.

In Paris, Dodge had accompanied Gertrude and Alice and Leo to several artists' studios before returning to her sumptuous hilltop estate, the Villa Curonia, a majestic jumble of rooms and styles north of Florence, in the green suburb of Arcetri. She lived there, a bohemian dignitary, with her architect husband, Edwin, and her son from a previous marriage. After they arrived in Italy in the spring, Dodge invited her new friends, Gertrude and Alice, for lunch; she dispatched her motorcar to fetch them. "Why are there not more real people like you in the world?" Dodge exhaled afterward.

Gertrude had given Dodge a manuscript, presumably of *The Making of Americans*. Dodge's response did not disappoint. "There are things hammered out of consciousness into black & white that have never been expressed before—so far as I know. States of being put into words the 'noumenon' captured as few have done it. To name a thing is practically to create it & this is what your work is—real creation." Gertrude was clearly encouraged by such comprehending praise. "And your palate [*sic*] is such a simple one—the primary colors in word painting & you express every shade known & unknown with them. It is as new & strange & big as the post-impressionists in their way & I am perfectly convinced it is the forerunner of a whole new epoch of new form & expression."

But the piece most readily associated with the "new epoch" was not written until the fall of 1912, when Gertrude and Alice, after a brief return to Paris, were Mabel Dodge's guests at the Villa Curonia.

Leo had been in Florence that summer, entertained by the Dodges, who drove their automobile about the Florentine hills in the moonlight. Daytime, he ambled to the Villa Curonia from Fiesole, where he rented lodgings. His feet dusty from the long walk, he would dawdle for hours, talking loudly to anyone who would listen. His deafness was worse, his isolation palpable. "All he wanted in life," observed a friend, "was an Ear!"

Then Nina joined him. Upon learning that she felt nervous and sick in Paris, Leo had immediately responded, inviting her to Italy. Together, they walked through the greens and browns of Tuscany until a sunburned Nina could go no farther. But the couple were happy. Frank, kind, and often separated by distance or Nina's other lovers, they'd been able to avoid the imbroglios that might have irreparably injured people less resilient, open-minded, or committed. "Neither makes any demand upon the other," explained Leo, "the relations are those of absolute confidence, perfect candor, complete toleration, and unlimited goodwill, affection, and mutual esteem."

Although Leo now kept Gertrude amiably apprised of his excursions with Nina, an undercurrent of anger frequently washed over his letters to his sister. Back at the rue de Fleurus, Gertrude had failed to notice that he'd had the Renoirs and Cézannes, the Manet and the Daumier cleaned. "The light yellows & the sky have become something entirely different," he wrote of the Cézanne landscape, vexed by Gertrude's inattention. Brother and sister were careful to avoid each other. So when Gertrude and Alice were shown to their rooms in the Villa Curonia in September, Leo and Nina had already departed. It was best if the four didn't meet.

As a houseguest, Gertrude wrote far into the night, working by candle-light with the house in the hush of dark. Each morning she left manuscript pages for Alice to type. "The days are wonderful and the nights are wonder-ful and the life is pleasant," begins "Portrait of Mabel Dodge at the Villa Curo-nia." As Stein composed, Mabel Dodge was in a nearby room, locked in the embrace of her son's tutor.

Gertrude knew of the affair, which fluttered at the edge of her new piece, just out of reach. But to look only for a love affair in the portrait is to assume that behind the series of images, a recognizable likeness can be found, one that releases the portrait into unclouded meaning. This was not at all Gertrude's intention, despite her use of the word "portrait" in the title. Rather, ever since "Two," she'd been playing more energetically with the unforeseen and sportive, writing sentences whose structure seemed ordinary enough but whose imagistic elements often pointed back to themselves, ostensibly to give pleasure.

> A bottle that has the time to stand open is not so clearly shown when there is green color there. This is not the only way to change it. A little raw potato and then all that softer does happen to show that there has been enough. It changes the expression.

The portrait opens to a throng of possible meanings, all of which charmed Dodge, who basked in their erotic energy. "There was not that vel-vet spread when there was a pleasant head. The color was paler. The moving regulating is not a distinction. The place is there." "What they see in *it* is what I consider they see in me. . . . My English friend . . . writes 'it is bold effron-tery to do this sort of thing' (*If* she knew me!!). Others say (as they would of me! they know *so little* they *are* saying it of me!) 'there is no beauty in it.' " Even some of the uncomprehending agreed. At a luncheon in Boston, a friend of Mabel Weeks's declared the portrait contained the rhythm and images of the "sexually emotional life." "I have read Miss Dodge's portrait but all I can say is—I don't understand!!!" a friend of Gertrude's wrote from Florence. " 'There was William' suggests all sorts of things— . . . & I felt I had been born several hundred years too soon!!"

Galvanized by the portrait bearing her name, Dodge privately printed it in Florence in a handsome watermarked edition of 300, and Gertrude distributed it to friends and acquaintances: the painter Marsden Hartley, the sculptor Arnold Rönnebeck, Alfred Stieglitz, May Knoblauch, Mabel Weeks, and her old Hopkins schoolmate Emma Lootz Erving, who confessed that "on the Portrait I flunk . . . even if you class me with the admirers of Bouguereau, I can't help it." Mary Berenson was appalled. "And many people take it seriously as a new & worthwhile 'departure,' " she wrote her sister. "It isn't even funny, only horrible." But Logan Smith, Mary's writer-aesthete brother, was intrigued. "Her Post-Impressionist prose is fantastically absurd of course but to invent anything so crazy shows a kind of originality—there has certainly never been anything like it."

Leo had had enough. His patience, already worn, could not bear this final assault. "I can't understand the Portrait of Mabel Dodge, but none the less feel that I am not exceeding my reasonable privilege in thinking it damned nonsense. A portrait of a person that I know pretty intimately which conveys absolutely nothing to me, a far from inexperienced reader with no prejudices in the matter, seems to me to have something the matter with it."

According to Gertrude, however, her subject—a person or a relationship—in no way obliged her to use mimetic conventions. She wanted her readers to derive meaning from the words she used, not from an outside referent. Indeed, her writing was subordinate to nothing outside; the subject of the completed piece lay in the piece itself—as with music. "Creating is not remembering but experiencing," she told a friend years later. "It is to look and to hear and to write—without remembering. It is the immediate feelings arranged in words as they occur to me." To the present, not the past, Gertrude was loyal.

Leo vehemently objected to all this. He said he could feel the force of lines like "There was not that velvet spread when there was a pleasant head," but when rhythm became an end in itself, "there I halt." Rhythm produced an evocative force, but without communication, literary style was a vapid dance around nothing.

> The crucial matter is, does she succeed in communicating what she means. In some of the earlier portraits like the Picasso and Matisse it may be that they mean something to those not familiar with the subject but most of the latter do not. Her attempt is the same as that of all symbolic literature which includes all poetry; in some respects even the *Iliad* is not merely a story but a kind of thing— the quality of poetry according to Aristotle that makes it more philosophic than history—but the real question is whether or not she communicates and the general verdict is that she does not . . .

Leo confided to his diary around 1943. "Those who are interested in this or that are so because they know the people. . . . Of course those who are bent on understanding can understand anything."

He wrote a parody—"Liquidation confluent with purpose by involution elaborates the elemental"—and was indignant when "Gertrude and even Alice have the cheek to pretend they understand this . . . but as Gertrude thought it very nice and I had very sarcastical intentions we evidently didn't understand it the same way."

But Gertrude did understand. She reported—doubtless with grim satisfaction—that when their friend Israel Zangwill had read "Portrait of Mabel Dodge at the Villa Curonia," he said, "And I always thought she was such a healthy minded young woman, what a terrible blow this must be for her poor dear brother."

"I loved the Zangwill story," Harriet Levy said when she heard it, "but it is not the kind of propaganda that lands the Nobel prize."

In 1938, however, Gertrude dryly summarized what had happened: Leo's response to her writing "destroyed him for me and it destroyed me for him." She had been betrayed. But that was not, as usual, the whole story.

20
THE
DISAGGREGATION

Pablo Picasso, Portrait of Leo Stein *(gouache on cardboard, 1906). Etta Cone acquired the picture from Gertrude in 1932.*

And this our life, exempt from public haunt,
Finds tongues in trees, books in the running brooks,
Sermons in stones, and good in everything.

AS YOU LIKE IT, ACT 2, SCENE 1
(THE FOREST OF ARDEN)

H E WAS AS TIMELY as a street vendor," said Alice Toklas of Leo Stein.

Seldom charitable toward the brother Gertrude had adored for almost forty years, Toklas claimed he'd wounded his sister too deeply ever to be forgiven. Instead, he was forgotten. "She really had put him and the deep unhappiness he had caused her so completely out of her mind that finally he and it no longer existed."

But interviewed about ten years after their deaths, Toklas strained to be kind. "He was a very generous person—he was very sweet, very sweet," she conceded. "He gave her the picture that he knew was important to her—the Cézanne portrait. No, he was petty in some ways but not in that sort of way. He was very generous and very chivalrous. In that respect he was an admirable brother to her. No, it was merely on intellectual grounds that he could become difficult—not only to his sister but to hundreds of others."

Toklas was corroborating Gertrude's verdict on Leo: he had become intellectually insufferable. "He continued to believe in what he was saying when he was arguing," Stein explained in *Everybody's Autobiography,* "and I began not to find it interesting."

GERTRUDE'S "Portrait of Mabel Dodge at the Villa Curonia" excited enough controversy to delight its author. Tempers blazed at the Café du Dôme, the detractors shouting their long-held complaints against the Steins. Gertrude loved the attention; it boded well for publication. And news from the strong-willed Mabel Dodge was always hopeful. Now in New York, acting as Stein's unofficial propagandist, she planned to link Stein's recent work to the Armory Show, an upcoming exhibit of modern art. "You will be the glory of America," Picasso told Gertrude.

She couldn't wait. She was hungry for publication. She decided to go to London to look in person for a publisher; that seemed the best method, despite her trepidation. Aiming to exploit Roger Fry's second postimpressionist show, recently closed, she and Alice prepared a letter of introduction. "Miss Gertrude Stein," it read, "who as you may or may not know has been so intimately connected with the so-called Post-impressionist movement is coming to London for the purpose of placing her work with a publisher best suited for such xpression."

Stein and Toklas stayed at the Knightsbridge Hotel for two weeks, enlisting all their friends in Gertrude's quest. They initially were encouraged by the response of supporters such as Logan Smith and Roger Fry himself. ("His being a Quaker gives him more penetration in his sweetness than is usual with his type," observed Gertrude of Fry, "it does not make him more interesting but it makes him purer.") Nothing happened. Stein approached John Lane of The Bodley Head (who after years of delay republished *Three Lives* in 1920), as well as Frank Palmer and Sidgwick & Jackson. All shook their heads in disbelief. "I have read through a portion of the MS which you gave me on Friday . . ." wrote Palmer. "I say I have only read a portion of it, because I found it perfectly useless to read further, as I did not understand any of it. I have to confess to being as stupid and ignorant as all the other readers to whom the book has been submitted." Befuddled, the editors at Sidgwick & Jackson, to whom she'd given the long piece "Many Many Women," were even more discouraging. "Under ordinary circumstances we should like to recommend another publisher to whom the work might appeal; but we regret to say that we do not think it probable that you will find any publisher for work of this kind."

Stein and Toklas stayed in London past Gertrude's thirty-ninth birthday, Monday, February 3, 1913. From Paris, Leo reported that a group of Hungarians, Armenians, Turks, and Jews, certain there would be a party, arrived at the doorstep on the preceding Saturday night. He informed them they had the wrong day and, besides, no one was home. Relations between him and Gertrude, already deteriorating, were worsened by her gloom about publication. "A prophet can support not being honored in his own country when other lands sufficiently acclaim him," Leo speculated, "but when the acclamation otherwise is faint the absence of support at home is painful." That he refused to see any merit in his sister's recent work drove a final cutting wedge between them. "Gertrude . . . hungers and thirsts for gloire and it was of course a serious thing for her that I can't abide her stuff and think it abominable," he told Mabel Weeks.

A few days after Gertrude's birthday, Leo wrote his old friend. "For I have come to the end of something and perhaps the beginning of something else," he said, "a moment that seems proper for a statement like what is to come." He felt good, his stomach was calm; he was living simply, still horse-back riding many an afternoon and spending his evenings with Nina. Their bond was stronger than ever. He was satisfied with the current state of his work—so satisfied, in fact, that he decided to give it up. "I don't suppose I shall ever write that book," he said, "certainly not for many years."

Convinced that he'd vaulted an important intellectual hurdle, he felt he could now express ideas that had previously eluded him. One of these, the most important, had to do with consciousness. "Consciousness for me is discontinuous . . ." he explained to Weeks.

> If you listen to yourself talking you will notice that you don't know the words except as you hear them, you can't anticipate your ideas for you can know them only when you find them. The thread on which they are strung is not experience. In fact there may be no such thread. Bergson claims to experience it in the durée réelle but I don't believe there ain't no such thing in experience & that B's élan vital & durée réelle are pure mythology.

"My formula is that we find things, our emotions[,] will[,] attitudes and all the rest, and that the simplest way of stating the matter is to say things happen." That consciousness was singular and unified was largely a fiction. If we think that our thoughts are in our heads, he observed, that's because our eyes are in our heads. Looking sharply and thinking deeply were intimately, integrally related. And of course ideas exist in space, he continued. The world is spatial, our relation to it is spatial, even consciousness is the sum of spatial relations, not a thing alone or apart. What we think is basically a function of what we see when we stand where we stand.

Profoundly influenced by William James, Leo was struggling toward an antimetaphysical, pragmatic definition of consciousness, one that would ultimately explain aesthetic perception without divorcing perceiver from objects perceived—which is what he believed cubism had done. He rejected the notion of an isolated consciousness, omnipotent and willful, and was trying to topple the artist from what he viewed as an unwarranted elevation. But his timing couldn't have been worse. He was formulating his ideas—indeed, had to formulate them—precisely at the moment Gertrude insisted—indeed, needed to insist—that the artist was just that inspired being answerable to no one.

Unfortunately, Leo's ideas are vague. He merely sketched them for Mabel Weeks, and none of his remaining papers suggests he now wrote anything more than sketches. However, he seems to have embraced a relativism compatible with his own psychic proclivities. Nothing was intrinsically mean-

ingful, not even art. No conviction was absolute; only relations were important, and as a result, he preferred to qualify all his statements. But such
qualifications served a deeper psychic end, inhibiting action and preventing
him from holding securely to his positions, his sense of self, and his desires.
So Leo deferred and procrastinated; his was, said an onlooker, a postponed
life. One thing, though, he was sure of: he and his sister agreed on practically
nothing.

For Gertrude, consciousness—and in particular the consciousness of the
author, what she later extolled as "the human mind"—was an incontrovert-
ible entity, unique and marvelous. It was at the center of her work and its
method, which she evidently gave Mabel Dodge to understand, for she heartily
endorsed Dodge's explanation of both. Stressing both passive intuition and
conscious reflection, Dodge wrote that Stein

> always works at night in the silence, and brings all her will power
> to bear upon the banishing of preconceived images. Concentrat-
> ing upon the impression she has received and which she wishes
> to transmit, she suspends her selective faculty, waiting for the word
> or group of words that will perfectly interpret her meaning, to rise
> from her sub-consciousness to the surface of her mind.
>
> Then and only then does she bring her reason to bear upon
> them, examining, weighing and gauging their ability to express her
> meaning. It is a working proof of the Bergson theory of intuition.
> She does not go after words—she waits and lets them come to her,
> and they do. . . .

If Dodge was correct, Gertrude felt the artist to be sublimely inspired. Clear-
ing the mind of convention, the artist sits and waits for inspiration. In Leo's
phrase, "things happen." But this was not all. The artist also imposes her will,
examining, weighing, and gauging. At the center of her work is the human
mind, transcendent and powerful, in the present, creating the present, and
free. "The human mind writes what it is," she once explained. It has nothing
to do "with sorrow and with disappointment and with tears." Or with time or
memory.

Mumbo jumbo, Leo later declared. "Probably the worst of all the illu-
sions is the illusion of the divinity of man." Such delusions of grandeur, he
thought, were a form of egotism that wrecked "society on the rock of the individual, and . . . the individual on the rock of his enforced self-defense."

Writing this in 1927, he may well have been considering his sister. To
her and other pseudo-intellectuals of the recent past, "science was an abstraction, but art was, at the very least, an adumbration of the real. The real,
whether it was conceived as a system of absolute ideas, or as a restless, ever-

hungering will, was most completely apprehended by contemplative passion, a mystic absorption whose character was aesthetic. Only so could man, cabined, cribbed, confined, break from the tentacular clutch of circumstance and touch what things are free from the taint of time, space, and mortality."

But according to Leo, there was no absolute real and no absolute self. Moreover, those artists professing a connection with some mystic realm had simply reverted "to lost simplicities, to primitive states of feeling which are being overlaid by the complications of invention." This kind of art, despite its radical cachet, was regressive and infantile.

His was a paradoxical position, a populist elitism that declared all things radically equal except those which were not. Reviled by Toklas as benighted—"sad and mistaken," she later said—Leo could not, however, be categorized any more easily than his sister. Perhaps sensing as much, he cultivated the terms of his withdrawal on that basis. "Everybody can see how ridiculous are tweedledum's pretensions but believes that as tweedledee he has at last solved the almost insoluble problem of art."

"I'm a rank outsider," he told Mabel Weeks in early 1913. "I am no longer a prophet in Israel or at best only a Jeremiah." As if to deliver himself of a bygone era, he shaved his beard and, with the insouciance of a Whitman, declared himself for the country and the open road. This was preparation for the greatest change of all, the divestiture of one of his former selves. He called it "the fairly definite 'disaggregation' of Gertrude and myself."

"YOU PEOPLE IN NEW YORK will soon be in the whirlpool of modern art," observed Leo of the imminent international exhibition. "I wouldn't be in New York during the coming show, not to get a Carnegie Hero pension or medal, whichever it is."

Familiarly called the Armory Show after its location, the massively advertised exhibit opened in the cavernous 69th Regiment Armory in Manhattan, with the 69th Regiment Band playing incongruously in the balcony. A dazed public strolled through makeshift rooms filled with more than 1,300 examples of modern art. For one month in the winter of 1913, it was the talk of the town. "We are going to put a mark on American thought that will be simply indelible," Walter Pach, one of the show's organizers, told Michael Stein. Spectacular crowds—totaling 100,000, Pach estimated, and most of them paying—came to gawk at Ingres and the Italian futurists or to argue in front of Marcel Duchamps's bewildering canvas *Nude Descending a Staircase* (an "explosion in a shingle factory," gasped one horrified journalist). Gibes, parodies, and apocalyptic pronouncements sprouted in all quarters. The conservative art critic Kenyon Cox intoned, "This thing is not amusing; it is heartrending and sickening."

But Hutchins Hapgood was ecstatic, and even though Alfred Stieglitz privately derided the whole affair as a "Pink tea adjunct," in print he praised the "Revitalizers" for infusing life into "an art that is long since dead, but won't believe it." Blaring one of the loudest trumpets was Mabel Dodge, who pronounced the Armory Show the most important public event since the signing of the Declaration of Independence—"& it is of the same nature."

She also considered the exhibit a perfect opportunity to showcase Gertrude Stein's work. "Well, you believe that there is too much smell of death in most of the painting you know," she told one of the exhibit's promoters. "You want the new spirit. You want fresh life. Why don't you see that you can apply that to words?" Dodge was serious and indefatigable. She handed over a copy of Stein's portrait of her to everyone who might be of use, including Hapgood, who wrote for the New York *Globe,* and Carl Van Vechten of *The New York Times.* She herself wrote for the March issue of *Arts and Decoration,* which was devoted to the Armory Show, a piece connecting the revolutionary in art with the work of her friend. The effect was explosive. "Every one in NY is saying '*Who* is Gertrude Stein?' " Dodge reported. "The name of Gertrude Stein is better known in NY today than the name of God!"

"Hurrah for gloire," Stein answered. By now, she had been elevated to an object of parody. A bemused spectator at the show offered a typical opinion in the February 8 issue of the *Chicago Tribune*:

> I called the canvas *Cow with Cud*
> And hung it on the line,
> Altho' to me 'twas vague as mud,
> 'Twas clear to Gertrude Stein.

"You *are* becoming a lion, aren't you?" asked Mabel Weeks. Gertrude's friend Mildred Aldrich was pleased but circumspect. "Stiffen your spine," she cautioned. "Don't let gloire break it."

LEO LOANED MATISSE'S *Blue Nude* to the Armory Show, as well as the two Picassos recently shown in London at Roger Fry's second post-impressionist exhibit. But he claimed to have little interest in modern art. More and more self-conscious, he shunned all that might put him in the public eye. And if anything, the furor over Gertrude only alienated him further.

Rivalry wore a professional face. Leo took refuge in studied indifference, as did his sister. The mutual idealization propping their relationship gave way to the resentment that had flowed through it, underground, for years. Gertrude would remember the past angrily: "Dear Mary," she wrote the wife of the novelist Louis Bromfield, "thanks a thousand times for being such a sweet wife of a genius . . . I once did that and I know how difficult it is for wives of geniuses to be sweet about it." In 1933, she publicly excised Leo, omitting him from her saga of the prewar period, *The Autobiography of Alice B. Toklas,* and then, as if the dismissal was too peremptory, she justified herself in its sequel, *Everybody's Autobiography*: "telling about my brother was telling about myself being a genius." There was no room for two. How she lorded it over me, Leo later exclaimed.

Leo consistently maintained that Gertrude in her precubist days did have something to say, but since she couldn't use ordinary syntax or make words in their "ordinary meanings" have any "punch," she perverted the syntax and abused the words. Like Picasso, she coveted Cézanne's power but lacked his gift. And she trafficked in a realm, the intellectual one, where, according to Leo, she knew absolutely nothing. "Gertrude and I are just the contrary," he told Albert C. Barnes. "She's basically stupid and I'm basically intelligent."

Whatever their pronouncements, at the time or after the fact, the widening gulf between sister and brother caused both untold grief, or so friends thought. One of these was Marsden Hartley, the American painter, who in 1913 was devoted to Gertrude. This quiet, "gnarled New England Spinsterman," as Mabel Dodge called him, was awed into extravagance by the rue de Fleurus. The studio was an oasis, Gertrude the salt of the earth. She bought one of his drawings for twenty dollars and then gave him the same amount as a gift. "I hardly expected such solid enthusiasm," he wrote her modestly, "for I know fairly well your critical sense and know it is not satisfied so readily."

Hartley also came to be a friend of Leo's. "There was a door leading to another adjoining studio which was always open a few inches & out of which would peer a strong face," he recalled. That was the companionable Leo. "Not to know Leo was to miss a lot." Hartley believed that the loving friendship of sister and brother had been tragically destroyed, and neither had "ever inwardly recovered—I could go deeper here because I knew them both very well—" he later reminisced, "but [courtesy] and breeding forbid."

"There was more than just a quarrel about Cubism there," remarked Virgil Thomson. "Alice didn't really want them to be as close as they had been." Etta Cone and the writer Virgil Geddes thought Leo's affair with Nina, not the arrival of Alice Toklas, was the final and irrevocable blow. Gertrude was furious, said Mabel Weeks, about Leo's liaison with a virtual woman of the streets. She felt abandoned and betrayed by the brother she'd assumed would always be there for her; his hostility to her writing was but another form of this deeper, more painful abandonment. Mabel Dodge accused a jealous Alice of taking advantage of Leo and Gertrude's estrangement, purposefully maneuvering herself between them. The painter Maurice Grosser also assumed it was Alice who provoked brother and sister to silence. Toklas was not going to share her treasure with anyone.

In the past, however, Gertrude had never been unwilling to sever relations when she felt injured, when someone she valued—or overvalued—appeared to fail her. Her pattern was to idealize a friendship and then destroy it. Surely Alice couldn't accomplish what Gertrude didn't herself desire. Leo never felt Alice caused the break; she simply facilitated it and in doing so allowed him to free himself from his sister, who was, he said, "about the only thing that was in any serious way a check on my independence." To Leo, Alice was a godsend; it was she who enabled the separation to occur without a bang.

Doubtless this was in part true. Toklas did enable the separation, but of Gertrude from Leo as much as the reverse. And there was no outburst, just the constant drumming pressure of jealousy, mistrust, betrayal. To the untrained ear, nothing was amiss. Bernhard Berenson visited the rue de Fleurus early in the summer, before the members of the household parted, and thoroughly enjoyed himself. The dinner table was crowded, the conversation lively. "Gertrude really looked handsome," Berenson reported to his wife. "Leo without beard & moustache priestlike . . . Picasso was there, a delightful *torrador-like* [sic] gamin. I chaffed him about his latest [declensions], & he protested like Luther that he could not do otherwise."

Neither, as it turned out, could Gertrude. Or Leo.

THAT PAST SPRING, 1913, Gertrude had asked Daniel-Henry Kahnweiler to appraise three paintings by Picasso that she and Leo jointly owned: *Three Women, Boy Leading a Horse,* and *Portrait of Gertrude Stein.* Kahnweiler calculated 20,000 francs for the first, 12,000 for the second, and 6,000 for the portrait. She had bought more Picassos—*The Little Glass* and a small still life—and was computing the value of the pictures she and Leo had acquired together.

There were, of course, reasons for the calculation that had nothing, at first blush, to do with Leo. Self-promotion was a costly venture. George Duckworth of Duckworth & Company in London had agreed, reluctantly, to undertake the reprinting of *Three Lives,* but he demanded that Roger Fry write an introduction and Gertrude contribute about fifty pounds to defray publication expenses. Gertrude was nervous. She admonished Mabel Dodge to make sure anyone interested in her work was willing to pay, "because I don't want to get known as giving them away." Then she decided she and Alice should stay in Paris in June, because of the "stress of poverty."

Neither her brother's indifference to her work, nor the world's, diverted Gertrude; quite the opposite, it seemed. She wrote all the time. She had been working intermittently on a portrait of Dodge's friend Constance Fletcher; she had written a number of short pieces since returning from London; and she was still involved with several longer pieces, presumably "A Long Gay Book" and a new one "about the Paris crowd," initially titled "The New Book," which would turn into *G.M.P.* (published as *Matisse Picasso and Gertrude Stein*).

These pieces were different from her previous work, experimental and even more daring. "Do all Matisse's life in the new manner, then Pablo in the old," she counseled herself in the manuscript of *G.M.P.*, aware of the new turn her writing would take. As in "A Long Gay Book," she wanted to develop a series of complex characterizations, using herself and her friends almost as points of departure for meditations on success, despair, disappointment, art, creativity. But once again, as in "Two" and "Portrait of Mabel Dodge at the Villa Curonia," Stein wanted to portray her subjects in their full immediacy. To do this, she conceived of them as inseparable from the language and vision creating them.

"A tiny violent noise is a yellow happy thing," she abruptly wrote in "A Long Gay Book," later explaining the stylistic change as her desire to immerse herself more deeply in the present. Stein continued to move away from the sonorous prose she had built out of generalizing participles and pronouns, toward the specificity of short declarative sentences. The "historical" style of *Three Lives, The Making of Americans,* and many of the portraits had exhausted itself, she confided retrospectively to her friend Robert Bartlett Haas. In *G.M.P.*, she said, "words began to be for the first time more important than the sentence structure or the paragraphs."

This, she would explain, was the result of her fascination with "looking," instead of, the assumption is, with the "listening" that undergirded her long novel. "When I was stating anything what anything was, I was also looking, and that could not be entirely left out," she recalled. But the model of pictorial art could take the writer only so far:

> The trouble with including looking, as I have already told you, was that in regard to human beings looking inevitably carried in its train realizing movements and expression and as such forced me into recognizing resemblances, and so forced remembering and in forcing remembering caused confusion of present with past and future time.

To delve into the present more deeply, to free herself of remembering and the resemblances that memory always entails, she desired nothing but words, singular and shimmering in the present tense, where, as she would insist, "there is no remembering and there is no forgetting because memory has to do with human nature and not with the human mind." Or, as she would suggest in *Tender Buttons*, words were meaningful in and for themselves: "There is no

Pablo Picasso, Portrait of Gertrude Stein *(oil on canvas, 1906):*
"The only reproduction of me which is always I, for me."

use there is no use at all in smell, in taste, in teeth, in toast, in anything, there
is no use at all and the respect is mutual."

   In her 1913 article on Stein, Mabel Dodge described the writer as manipulating "language to induce new states of consciousness and . . . so language becomes with her a creative art rather than a mirror of history." Stein's
own comment on Marsden Hartley's paintings, sent in that same year to Alfred Stieglitz, reflects a similar system of values: "It is genuinely transcendent,"

she complimented Hartley's work. "Each canvas is a thing in itself and contains within itself . . ." It was not, she asserted, anything like "poverty stricken realism," the very soul of resemblance and memory.

In her notebooks, however, Stein always kept much more than single words before her, lightly penciling topics, instructions, and proper names at various points, almost as if they were chapter headings or expressive markings in a musical score. She deleted all such references in the finished product, leaving her readers nothing but the associative power of her evocative language. But if theoretically interesting, the prose in many of the long passages of "Two," "A Long Gay Book," and *G.M.P.* labors under a glut of nonmeaning; Stein's rhythms reduce to slack monotony and her images to a commotion of woolly associations.

A text like *G.M.P.* demonstrates above all else Stein's assertion, even in the face of constant rejection, that she was an essential side of the triangle—Gertrude, Matisse, Picasso—altering the course of modern art. In its first pages, the outline of a story emerges: an artist and a group of artists are discouraged with the temper of their times; some are intent on "creating being existing"; there are leaders and followers and hints of conflict, and departures and separations. "Union is not strength and division is not disaster, separation is not unwieldy and perpetuation is not friendly." There seems to be a discussion of stylistic change. "The music of the present tense has the presentation of more accent than the best intention multiplies. . . . So then the change was spread and there was no sofa and there was no pudding. Coloring was disappearing. There was no repetition." There is also the faint aroma of an argument with Leo. "Resembling is not a suspicion. It is autocratic. There is no rebuke. A fence is not furnished. No mind is matter. This is so little that there is no minor mirror. All the tickling is tender."

And retrospectively, there is the promise of what is to come in Stein's writing. Images of color, of food, of cooking, and of physical objects swirl together in an imaginative mélange of pleasure and eroticism. "Tooth cake, teeth cake, tongue saliva and more joints all these make an earnest cooky." But these did not just express the rhythm of the external world, as Stein would later suggest. More than ever, she invoked the joy of the internal, reflected in daily routine, sensual pleasure, and domestic life, in "a chocolate supper, a roasting rabbit, and a supposition." Comic and quick, the images amaze, clash, fail, or metamorphose: "There is no gender. . . . Like the spoon and the educated banana there is no correct description. There is light and there is manner."

This was Stein's break with the past. Her new departure was also in its way a divestiture—one that, peculiarly, paralleled the disaggregation at home.

"It's such very orderly literature, much more so than Pablo's." Alice applauded when she read through Gertrude's new work. "La jolie is quite messy compared to this. You never were messy, lovie, but it's more crowded now & I like it. You can almost say anything you please, can't you. Kisses."

IN PARIS, Alice Toklas readied herself for another summer's holiday in Spain by studying Spanish at the Berlitz school. Leo rented a small villa in Italy near Settignano, just above the walled gardens of the stately Villa Gamberaia and not far from the Berensons at I Tatti. There was no overt enmity between Gertrude and Leo; likewise, there was no desire to spend the summer together.

Stein and Toklas stopped briefly in Barcelona before settling themselves comfortably at the seaside Grand Hotel in Palma de Mallorca. "We are having a beautiful time seeing a great deal of native life thanks to a man we have met down here," Stein wrote Claribel Cone. They stayed at least two weeks, during which they visited the garden, said Stein, where George Sand wrote and Chopin sat, and then they headed by steamer for Málaga and Valencia. In August they were amid the turquoise and hot tiles of Granada, where Gertrude had not been since her trip with Leo twelve years before. It was as sultry and wild as she remembered. She and Toklas lingered for almost two months, stretching languidly in the fierce sun, dawdling among the bright blues and whites of the Alhambra. This place, which on her first visit Stein had associated with sexual awakening, would now be associated with momentous changes in her work. And this association meant Alice.

Although the chronology is probably inaccurate—Stein's new experiments had begun long before the sojourn in Granada—her associations reveal that during this period she opened herself more fully to pleasure in sight, in sound, in touch, in her body and in Alice's. Her language would become as sensual as she herself, and her work would now enter a realm of playful experiment, sometimes failed but always animated by invention and fantasy and often rife with erotic imagery. The return to Granada was a homecoming of sorts, only this time, Stein fully realized the power of desire and reveled.

So it was probably in Spain that Stein wrote the delightfully lyric "Susie Asado," with its homey puns—"sweet tea" (sweetie) and "tray sure" (treasure)—and "Preciosilla," which seems almost a companion piece. "Nuts are spittoons," she declaimed in "Sacred Emily." "That is a word." This was the text that contained "Rose is a rose is a rose is a rose," not only as a statement of literary certainty, but also as an image as provocative as the less eloquent "Cow come out cow come out and out and smell a little." And it is virtually certain that during the summer of 1913 Stein began to play with the series of experiments published as *Tender Buttons*. These were, she herself said, the culmination of her recent efforts.

Begun as a series of "studies in description"—before publication she dropped that subtitle—the work was divided in three parts, "Objects," "Food," and "Rooms." The first two sections were further subdivided into categories announced in boldface. The "Objects" include such prosaic items as a box, a red stamp, a long dress, a seltzer bottle, Mildred's umbrella, and a table—all common, everyday items possibly scattered about a room—as well as objects less easily certified: glazed glitter and careless water, a piece of coffee, and something called "suppose an eyes." These, like the notion of "tender buttons" itself, do not signify directly. They are the strings of buttons bought at Bon Marché, they are the series of prose poems, they are an imperative cry to "tend her buttons," they are nipples, they are oxymorons, they are words. They are allusive, elusive, composed. They are perplexing, tantalizing, askew.

Similarly, the section "Food" proceeds, at least from one point of view, logically; it contains items for breakfast, items for dinner. But the category "Chicken" is repeated four times, and under the headline "Salad" we learn, "It is a winning cake"; as for "Dining," Stein states emphatically, "Dining is west." Strewn among the categories are word games, free associations, puns, alliteration, and onomatopoeia. "Salad Dressing and an Artichoke" seems at first a nursery rhyme; then it turns wildly: "Please pale hot, please cover rose, please acre in the red stranger, please butter all the beef-steak with regular feel faces." "Asparagus" teases with meaning: "Asparagus in a lean in a lean to hot" suggests the tender stalks cooking upright. Yet what follows—"This makes it art and it is wet wet weather wet weather wet"—makes little sense until we read the end of the last section, "Rooms": "The care with which there is incredible justice and likeness, all this makes a magnificent asparagus, and also a fountain."

Such deliberation—care—is a form of resemblance, a way of enticing meaning from objects; the finished product is art, is magnificent, is something made (the fountain), from which water gushes. Imaginary gardens, as Marianne Moore later wrote of poetry, with real toads in them; a "stouter symmetry," Stein writes, not a fearful one.

Like many who read her work over the years, Stein was not shy about glossing her text. Shortly before she died, she explicated "A White Hunter," one of the so-called objects of *Tender Buttons*: "A white hunter is nearly crazy," is an "abstraction of color," she said. "If a hunter is white he looks white, and that gives you a natural feeling that he is crazy, a complete portrait by suggestion, that is what I had in mind to write." Of course the explanation begged more questions than it answered. More useful were Stein's more general comments in which she linked the writing of *Tender Buttons* to her fascination with looking. "I began to wonder at about this time just what one saw when one looked at anything really looked at anything," she said in a lecture delivered in the United States in the mid-thirties. "Did one see sound, and what was the relation between color and sound, did it make itself by description by a word that meant it or did it make itself by a word in itself." *Tender Buttons* was Stein's attempt at an answer. In her lecture "Poetry and Grammar," she explained:

> I was making poetry but and it seriously troubled me, dimly I knew that nouns made poetry but in prose I no longer needed the help of nouns and in poetry did I need the help of nouns. Was there not a way of naming things that would not invent names, but mean names without naming them.
>
> I had always been very impressed from the time that I was very young by having had it told me and then afterwards feeling it myself that Shakespeare in the forest of Arden had created a forest without mentioning the things that make a forest."

Alice Toklas repeated the same motives to Virgil Thomson: Stein's aim was "to describe a thing without mentioning it." Her forest of Arden was a magical place of transformation, full of that which had been heretofore unmentionable.

Embracing the things of the world for their particularity and not their function, Stein wrote her own "Leaves in grass" (as she called it), loving, expansive, and self-referential. Much of *Tender Buttons* seems an erotic song dedicated not just to the things of this world but also to the world Stein and Toklas shared. "Why is a feel oyster an egg stir," Stein rhetorically—and provocatively—asks in the "Orange" section of "Food." Toward the end of the "Objects" section, the puzzling category "Peeled Pencil, Choke" (a kind of artichoke?) yields the equally piquant "Rub her coke." The last part of "Objects," entitled "This Is This Dress, Aider," appears to refer not just to Ada, or Alice, but also to a Rabelaisian gourmandizing:

> Aider, why aider why whow, whow stop touch, aider, whow, aider
>   stop the muncher, muncher munchers.
> A jack in kill her, a jack in, makes a meadowed king, makes a
>   to let.

Many of the sources for this new work are erased, speculative, unknowable. Over time Stein tended to present her work as largely self-born and self-begotten, even though she readily admitted a debt to William James and Flaubert and Cézanne. But the word in Paris, according to Edward Steichen, had been that Stein's repetitive style, à la her portraits of Matisse and Picasso, bore the mark of the poet Charles Péguy. It is true that as early as the spring of 1910 she mailed a small volume of Péguy to none other than William James, as if to clarify *Three Lives*. And by 1913, she of course knew the work of Max Jacob and Apollinaire; the latter published *Alcools* in the spring of the year as well as *The Cubist Painters,* which Stein must have read. Then there was Wassily Kandinsky, whom she included as one of the voices in her piece "IIIIIIIII," her first attempt at a play. Marsden Hartley had been influenced by Kandinsky's *Concerning the Spiritual in Art,* and although Stein preferred Hartley's work to Kandinsky's, her new friend Arnold Rönnebeck kept her apprised of the Russian artist's prose poems; he sent a few examples in 1913 that he said showed "Kandinsky's intentions in using the *word* itself as a pure interior sound (Klang)—and how, thus applied, it loses its quality as a name of a certain object." Stein was obviously stirred by analogies between painting and writing, in retrospect and at the time of composition as well.

Ironically, Leo's trenchant criticism may also have had a subliminal impact on this work, moving Gertrude away from the world of predictable objects predictably named and toward her subjective, liberated, often jarring responses to them. ("The sister was not a mister," she teases in *Tender Buttons.*) For she was not immune to Leo's opinion, as her long and deep fury indicates. "He said it was not it it was I," she remembered Leo's commenting on the portraits. "If I was not there to be there with what I did then what I did would not be what it was. In other words if no one knew me actually then the things I did would not be what they were." But in these new pieces, she often identified her objects—red roses, a feather, sugar, rhubarb—and then reconceived them.

More: if Alice was part of the subtext of *Tender Buttons,* so was Leo. Stein explains, answers, counters. Her antic voice is irritated, emphatic. "The Saturday evening which is Sunday is every week day. What choice is there when there is a difference. A regulation is not active. Thirstiness is not equal division." Along with images of looking are images of dividing, resembling, separating, mending, changing, arranging—all of which would have very real counterparts when Gertrude received the incredible news: Leo was moving out of the rue de Fleurus.

WHILE GERTRUDE AND ALICE were in Granada, Leo was trying to explain to Mabel Dodge that one could better see the Tuscan landscape, or any landscape for that matter, when one was rid of notions of right and wrong. Dodge was confused. An absolutist at heart, despite her vaunted iconoclasm, she granted that while everything may seem to be in flux, "our changeless ideal is fixity!" Not so for Leo.

In fact, for Leo everything was changing. In Settignano for most of the summer, striding to Florence in the dusty heat to take in the galleries, he was a frequent visitor at the Villa Curonia, where he talked much of the fragrant night away with an exhausted Mabel Dodge and her enthusiastic lover, the radical journalist-poet John Reed. Quietly, Leo began to formulate a plan. By the end of September he was certain: "I shall soon cease to be a Parisian," he informed his friend Lee Simonson. He would eventually remain shaded among the tall Tuscan cypresses, soothed by the curve of the distant hills and the silver web of green olive trees. There, amid such peace and exempt from public haunt, he would "grow cabbages and things in the classical style."

Having rented the Villa di Doccia from his and Gertrude's friend Florence Blood, he undertook its renovation; he was preparing to stay on, he said, for "the next few years, perhaps forever." The villa, surrounded by pear and peach trees, had more than a dozen rooms, a garden, a view of the Villa Gamberaia, and "blessed, blessed solitude." There was a huge fireplace, for reading or for dozing beside, and he planned to make his own furniture—"If people have to sit in the chairs I make it'll be another inducement to them to keep away." He wasn't a misanthrope; "I loves my fellow man but I hates to hear him talk." The Armory Show and the hoopla in its aftermath had been the last straw.

Although Leo consented to help Morgan Russell with a catalogue introduction on his and Stanton Macdonald-Wright's synchromist paintings, soon to be exhibited at Bernheim-Jeune, Leo declared himself finished with art and Paris and the various manifestos, factions, and declarations—all the "inanities that grow from the confused brains of clever young persons. . . .

> I don't believe that ever before have there been so many cliques and such little ones. Russell and Wright find virtue in each other's work and in none other, Picasso and Braque are a world apart, the six futurists form an independent system. [Robert] Delaunay stands in lonely grandeur on a mountain top. For a while he had [Patrick] Bruce in his train but Bruce has ruptured the bond that left him revolving in Delaunay's sphere of influence and he is now a system all by himself. If Russell has invented the ugliest art form Bruce has achieved [one] that is by all odds the stupidest. One could list these systems almost indefinitely. . . . Russell and Wright's manifesto in their catalogue could in its [temper] take the place of any of the others. The only man who commands a certain measure of recognition from the different hereiarchs [sic] is Picasso. Many of these wonderful self subsisting systems feel that they owe something to Picasso for emancipating them from the "object" and allowing them severally to prolong their native wood-

notes wild unrestrained by anything except their creative imagination and their program.

Leo was alternately disgusted and bored. While others began to see him as conservative and bourgeois, he felt merely disillusioned, displaced, and tired. "I don't expect to live to be a Methuselah but I do expect to survive them," he said of the competing claims for artistic ascendancy. He did edit the Russell–Macdonald-Wright essay but respectfully refused to comment on its content out of consideration for Russell's feelings. Russell was hurt anyway.

Leo wasn't alone in his frustration. Marsden Hartley voiced a similar complaint to his friend Andrew Dasburg. "One wonders when the days of affectation will be over and real artists will move forward and do the stuff as artists should. Logicians can work at anything but it takes an artist to produce a picture—no matter what the method might be."

Tidings of Leo's pronouncement, coupled with what seemed the incredible decision to move to sleepy Settignano, ripped through New York. "Stupendous, momentous, stultifying," Lee Simonson characterized Leo's letter of explanation. Mabel Dodge read it and called it "prodigious"—although she admitted she didn't agree much with Leo's point of view. "I *do* admire you for being able to live the life you plan!" she told him. "To me real fortitude consists in doing cheerfully the things one doesn't *have* to do." Stieglitz wanted Leo to proclaim himself in the next issue of *Camera Work* and intended to pit the retiring Methuselah against "some power to be." In Philadelphia, the brash collector Albert Barnes, on hearing Leo's news, offered to show him how to finance anything he might now write about art: "Things you can say better than anyone else I know." True to his word, Leo remained silent.

Gertrude would have had no inkling of her brother's decision to abandon the rue de Fleurus if she had not heard of it from other sources. ("Yes and so when they said he was divorcing I could not believe that it had been done by him," she wrote years later, in what could have been an allusion to her incredulity.) It is likely he did not put his news in writing. His letters to Gertrude that remain make no mention of his moving to Italy, for undoubtedly Leo felt he ought to deliver the blow in person.

After overseeing repairs on his new villa, he left for Paris around the first of October; Gertrude and Alice arrived from their vacation at about the same time. He was excited and nervous, and he had warned friends in Italy that Gertrude might be angry. She was evidently stunned. The breakup of their household, despite everything, was inconceivable. She and Leo had lived together virtually without interruption for forty years, certainly without admitting, despite recent animosity, that they wouldn't live together for another forty. Leo had taken his action unilaterally in what must have seemed precipitate, selfish, even underhanded haste. And if his decision satisfied in some measure Gertrude's own unspoken wish, the manner of its achievement would have been galling. Leo was not supposed to initiate action.

Of course, Leo had always been the prodigal sibling who, for all his other problems, was able to launch himself. And despite the radiating confidence that endowed her steady purpose with force, there was something sedentary about Gertrude. As she later put it, "If you are way ahead with your head you naturally are old fashioned and regular in your daily life."

Her public persona, however, was one of equanimity. Whatever fury smoldered within, she was generally noncommittal about Leo's news, or perhaps seemed relieved. So onlookers assumed, now fully aware of the friction that had scraped away at the Steins' relationship. "I was very pleased that you do not object to your brother's migrating to Italy—" Florence Blood wrote Gertrude, "& I very much hope you will sometimes come to visit him at the Villa di Doccia." But Gertrude Stein never again set foot on Italian soil.

THE BREAKUP of the household at 27 rue de Fleurus was an item worthy of the New York *Sun*. Mildred Aldrich swiftly delivered the hot news to her friend the art critic Henry McBride, intimating that the real casualty was the family gallery. "You have seen it for the last time together," she told him ruefully. "I believe Leo takes the Renoirs and the big Matisse 'Bonheur de la Vie' and many of the Cézannes although Gertrude keeps the most valuable one—the portrait of his wife and the Cubist pictures as well as Matisse's 'Femme au Chapeau.'" McBride rushed the story into the paper.

But he lost or destroyed Aldrich's account of Gertrude's feelings. And so they disappear, remaining only in a few recollected vignettes and a handful of hurriedly written notes. Sister and brother argued on paper. "So far as I can make out the situation boils down to this," Leo penciled, awkwardly trying to make peace. "You left out of consideration the effect on my mind of not only being asked my advice but of *having taken it* throughout while [I left] out the effect on your mind of it being your room & that you arranged it to suit yourself. As to whose omission is the more flagrant depends upon the question whether the act of removing that picture which produced the effect on your feelings was or was not justified by mine." Toklas recalled scuttling back and forth between brother and sister, paintings in hand, as they determined who would keep what. Gertrude and Leo were no longer speaking.

They disagreed over Cézanne's apples. Adamant about keeping them, Leo refused to give them over, even for a price. "I'm afraid you'll have to look upon the loss of the apples as an act of God," he told his sister. Toklas was bitter, Gertrude silent and seething.

The Steins' joint account and expenditures also had to be reckoned and divided; this procedure took them all the way back to Leo's first Japanese prints and Gertrude's early Schilling purchase and of course the publication of Gertrude's *Three Lives,* which had been covered by their common funds. Then there was the matter of household expenses. Leo answered one of Gertrude's written inquiries with a note of his own. "It would appear that during the second year that Alice lived with us my allowance for living expenses was based on what it actually cost me plus 50 fr. a month, and that not at first, so that I was contributing a grossly disproportionate share to the household expenses, and the year before that your expenses kept up their proportion very fully . . ." Leo calculated. "I was perfectly satisfied, however, as it offered a simple method for our individual liberation and I considered it cheap at the price."

He felt justified in taking the reproductions and many books. Gertrude apparently did not object. And except for the question of the Cézanne apples, the parting of the pictures was fairly amicable. "We are, as it seems to me on the whole," Leo wrote his sister, "both so well off now that we needn't repine. The Cézannes had to be divided. I am willing to leave you the Picasso oeuvre, as you left me the Renoir, and you can have everything except that." He wanted to keep his Picasso drawings, however, which still delighted him. He had been "anxious above all things that each should have in reason all that he wanted and just as I was glad that Renoir was sufficiently indifferent to you so that you were ready to give them up so I am glad that Pablo is sufficiently indifferent to me that I am willing to let you have all you want of it."

Never was Leo's generosity doubted, and the offer appeared more than equitable to Gertrude. "I very much prefer it that way," Leo concluded, "and I hope that we will all live happily ever after and maintain our respective and due proportions while sucking gleefully our respective oranges."

Years later, Picasso is said to have sneered that Leo probably never tasted a drop of that juice in his life.

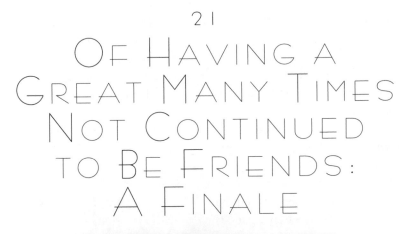

21

OF HAVING A
GREAT MANY TIMES
NOT CONTINUED
TO BE FRIENDS:
A FINALE

Gertrude Stein, by Alvin Langdon Coburn, 1913

EO HAD COMMITTED treason, the full extent of which would become clear over time. For now, his relations with Gertrude teetered between stormy silence and peevish reconciliation.

Both girded themselves for the future. Gertrude immediately sought out Daniel-Henry Kahnweiler to appraise three Picasso canvases, *Young Acrobat on a Ball, Three Women (Large Composition in Red),* and *Nude with Drapery,* which she was willing to sell. In exchange, she received from Kahnweiler 20,000 francs and Picasso's recently painted *Man with a Guitar.* She intended to keep collecting the artist's work as long as she could afford it—which wasn't long—but she also needed cash because she intended to abandon 27, rue de Fleurus almost as soon as Leo did.

She and Toklas had begun looking for another place right after she'd heard Leo was leaving, as though his departure would empty the apartment of more intangible, irreplaceable things: those early years of buying, those guests and all those nights analyzing them, all that freighted past. Picasso promised to help look, but for a time Gertrude saw nothing she liked. Then, at the end of 1913, she and Toklas discovered a lovely apartment on the balcony level of the Palais Royal. True, it wouldn't be available before mid-July 1914 and Leo was leaving at the beginning of April, but it did have four large bright windows overlooking the gardens, and Gertrude and Alice decided to take it.

Leo was also discarding parts of his former life, renouncing not just Paris and the art world but several tokens of his allegiance to them. This was good news for the collectors who learned Leo was disposing of pictures. In the United States, Albert Barnes was excited. The former research chemist who had made a fortune patenting the antiseptic Argyrol had met Leo and Gertrude in December 1912 while on a buying spree in Paris. The Steins sold him two paintings by Matisse then, *View of the Sea, Collioure,* for 900 francs, frame included (the frame cost 12 francs), and *Still Life with Melon,* for 3,100. Having sized up Barnes's temperament and his purse, Gertrude told him she would sell two Matisses but not one; she thought him a greedy American millionaire, waving his checkbook in the air. But the sometimes overbearing Barnes and Leo understood each other: both were ardent, amateur aestheticians, and both were reformers at heart.

And now, as soon as Barnes learned Leo might be disposing of more paintings, he said he would outbid any French dealer, especially for two of Leo's Renoirs, "Mother with child, & the little nude standing in water." But Leo had already sold *Standing Nude,* and was keeping the other; he sold a Cézanne landscape to Barnes for 15,000 francs in the spring of 1914 instead. Over the years Barnes was prepared to buy whenever Leo was ready to sell.

The American collector John Quinn was also a beneficiary of Leo's move to Italy; he eventually acquired Matisse's *Blue Nude* and *Music (Sketch),* much to the disappointment of the artist, who inevitably found out when Leo began to sell. Of the Picassos that did not go to Gertrude, Leo sold *Boy Leading a Horse* to Kahnweiler for 10,000 francs. He had been trying to sell that canvas for almost a year, hoping it would finance his new Renoir, *The Cup of Chocolate;* which he bought regardless. The Renoir filled him with such delight, he said, that he could imagine getting rid of all his canvases but that—at least not yet.

The cafés of Montparnasse sizzled with surprise and outrage; people wanted to know what Leo was getting rid of, to whom he was selling, and for what price. Pricked vanities took refuge in branding him a dour reactionary, especially now that he seemed interested only in Renoir's creamy visions. For the most part Leo didn't seem to care. He was concerned solely about Matisse, whose work he did admire, and Matisse's feelings. He sent the artist an explanatory note, which, unfortunately, made matters worse. "Someone told me, and it was authentic," Leo wrote Nina, "that Matisse complained not that I had sold his paintings—that wounded him naturally, because it showed that they did not have for me a value sufficient to prevent me from doing it—but because I wrote him only to excuse my action." Leo did not have the gift of tact; indeed, he was so clumsy when defensive that he seemed supercilious, nothing more.

By the end of March 1914, most of these affairs were settling themselves. Several canvases (a Cézanne, two Vallottons, another Matisse) awaited sale at Bernheim-Jeune, and Leo was packing his thousands of books into crates. Boxes spilled across the apartment. Both Gertrude and Leo were dimly aware—although neither of them would have admitted as much—they might never see each other again. And yet amid all these disruptions, or perhaps because of them, Gertrude managed to finish *Tender Buttons.*

"I HAVE BEEN DOING a lot of work," Gertrude reported to Claribel Cone, "a little stranger than the last but now that I am used to it, I think very well of it." Opaque, provocative, and mysterious, *Tender Buttons* aches with the circumstances of its creation, especially in the section titled "Rooms"—evidently the last composed—where one cannot help but hear echoes of the changes occurring at 27, rue de Fleurus. "It happened in a way that the time was perfect and there was a growth of a whole dividing time so that where formerly there was no mistake there was no mistake now," Stein wrote. "For instance before when there was a separation there was waiting, now when there is separation there is the division between intending and departing." Between Leo's announcement and his actual departure were months of haggling, discomfiture, silence. Sister and brother had not drawn closer; neither was roused to tender evenings recalling simpler times. "This made no more mixture than there would be if there had been no change." Furniture was dragged across the floor as Leo staked his possessions. The apartment began to look empty; it cried out for rearrangements. "A table was much bigger, very much bigger. Changing that made nothing bigger, it did not make anything bigger littler, it did not hinder wood from not being used as leather." And of course there remained the matter of the pictures. "There was a whole collection made," wrote Gertrude, perhaps still indignant about the Cézanne apples. Or: "This shows the disorder, it does, it shows more likeness than anything else, it shows the single mind that directs an apple." She and Leo both wanted the same thing, this she knew. "Giving it away, not giving it away, is there any difference."

On and on, Stein's prose started and stopped, halting at the threshold of meaning before disappearing altogether into personal reference. And yet her private circumstances, indeed the very rooms she and Leo had inhabited those many years and the paintings lining their walls, seem to rise to the surface. "A plain hill, one is not that which is not white and red and green, a plain hill makes no sunshine, it shows that without a disturber. So the shape is there and the color and the outline and the miserable centre, it is not very likely that there is a centre, a hill is a hill and no hill is contained in a pink tender descender."

"Act so that there is no use in a centre," she counseled herself—or her reader—at the beginning of "Rooms." These were not only real rooms but also rooms of consciousness, spreading, flowing, mobile. "If the centre has the place then there is distribution," she noted, as if speaking of Renaissance perspective. But the center did not hold, and at least in aesthetic terms, this was cause for celebration.

THE SATURDAY NIGHTS continued, but without Leo. Walter Pach recalled that if you wanted to see him, you could knock on the door of his little study, and he would let you in and talk Freud, stomachache, politics, and art. Gertrude took charge in the studio, captivating such visitors as Margaret Sanger's brother William, who came in early January and found his friendly hostess "quite interesting—has a decided Hebrew cast—a well-modeled face." When he asked her if she planned to go back to America, she laughed and said she'd been thinking of it for the past ten years, but had now given the idea up. She found the politics of the socialist magazine *The Masses* boring; she was witty and opinionated, Sanger concluded, and apt to baffle you with her constant sidestepping. She intended to give little away.

Privately, Gertrude was anxious. Leo's decision to abandon her and Paris was such a final and public condemnation that recognition—that is, publication—must have seemed crucial all over again. She nudged her friends, who rallied round her work, suggesting new venues or sending it on to prospective publishers themselves. Even relatively recent acquaintances, among them former *New York Times* writer Carl Van Vechten, joined the effort, for Gertrude was frequently able to inspire fierce loyalty and a protectiveness in the many who met and never forgot her. The sheer force of her personality was dazzling.

Henry McBride kept her name before the public in his *Sun* column, photographer Alvin Langdon Coburn tried to arrange an audience for her with Henry James. (James gently demurred, pleading "complete retirement.") Yet despite such efforts and the enormous publicity following the Armory Show, her long novel *The Making of Americans* and most of her shorter work remained unpublished. *Three Lives* had not been reprinted and "Portrait of Mabel Dodge at the Villa Curonia" had been printed only privately. American magazines with large circulations continued to send polite rejections, and she continued to submit her work to them, still hoping for the broad readership she believed she deserved. "Portrait of Mabel Dodge" was dispatched to *Century* magazine; other manuscripts went to *Everybody's;* all came back.

Mabel Dodge was irrepressible, however, and as eager as before to get Gertrude into print. But Gertrude insisted that the plays she had recently sent Dodge be produced, not published, although she knew full well they were far from conventional and not likely to be understood as dramatic in any strict or facile way. As Dodge's friend the actress Florence Bradley warned Gertrude, the American producer-manager "never applied his brain to his audience—he has only applied his audience to his brain." Stein herself compared these plays in later years to landscapes, and indeed they were static pieces which she aptly characterized as explorations into "what could be told if one did not tell anything." Works such as "IIIIIIIII," "White Wines," and "What Happened" presented a medley of voices, theatrical but hardly commercial. The characters have no names; there are no stage directions and no sense of who speaks when, or even whether the speakers are to speak consecutively or at the same time. And so Stein's plays languished unseen, exactly as Dodge had assumed would happen.

Dodge thought it wise to publish the plays first, with an introduction by her of course, which presumably could soften a recalcitrant public. Gertrude was annoyed. "I do *not* want the plays published," she snapped at Dodge. "They are to be kept to be played." Moreover, if Dodge was thinking about placing Stein's pieces in newspapers, she might as well return them. "I definitely do *not* want anything of mine published in newspapers or weeklies," she barked.

Gertrude had begun to mistrust Dodge's motives. Leo thought the reason was that Dodge skimmed off the "gloire" rightly due the creator, not the publicist, and said that Gertrude grew more irritable every time a newspaper squib linked Dodge's name with her own, as was often the case. More than once, Dodge recounted this explanation in her memoirs. When she asked Leo why Gertrude was angry, "he laughed and said because there was a doubt in her mind about who was the bear and who was leading the bear!"

Yet this was only one aspect of Stein's growing disenchantment with Dodge. "Mabel should have stuck with Edwin," Stein reportedly said when she learned Dodge was divorcing. She disapproved of Mabel's incessant amours and considered her recent lover, John Reed (who wrote for *The Masses*), a "very ordinary college type, whose brilliance lies in his weakness." Flirtatious, unreliable, self-serving, was Stein's characterization of Mabel Dodge, especially after she tried to dissuade Stein from publishing with Claire-Marie, a small New York press run by the poet Donald Evans. As soon as she heard that Evans had made an offer, she wired Gertrude, then wrote to explain: "I cabled you *not* to publish with D. Evans after having a long talk with E. A. Robinson who is our 'dark poet' here, & who knows more about things than most people. He knows Evans & believes in his ability but he thinks the Claire Marie Press which Evans runs is absolutely third rate, & in bad odor here, being called for the most part 'decadent' & Broadwayish & that sort of thing."

Gertrude was enraged. How dared Mabel—especially when all her grandiose plans to get Gertrude into print had turned to dust. Or worse. The publisher Mitchell Kennerley, for instance, had kept "Many Many Women" so long that a lawyer had to be called. Almost as soon as she received Dodge's letter, Gertrude mailed off her three intertwined pieces "Objects," "Food," and "Rooms" to Evans.

"I am sending you three of my things which could make a book as they would go well together," she informed him. Originally he had wanted to publish her plays for a ten-percent royalty on the first 500 books, and fifteen percent after that, and good publicity; she assumed the offer still held even if she substituted these pieces. It did. In fact, Evans was delighted and got to work immediately, asking her to send a title for the volume. Gertrude suggested *Tender Buttons,* dropping the subtitle "Studies in Description." Evans set the publication date for mid-May.

Stein didn't forgive Dodge. "Mabel finally wrote me that a man named

Robinson (Edwin Arlington) had said that Evans was a degenerate, a remark which I thought very funny coming from Mabel," Stein told Carl Van Vechten in July. "What Robinson meant was plainly on the face of the [Evans's] poems, but it occurred nowhere else, I felt sure." She added that Marsden Hartley had described Robinson as a Presbyterian poet. "At any rate I put all Mabel's acts up to femininity."

Apparently Hartley had also told her that Donald Evans was a friend of Van Vechten's. "Perhaps that is why Mabel did not want me to get too closely tied up with them," Stein speculated, attributing to Dodge her own rivalrous impulses. But if Dodge had been hypocritical or jealous—as was certainly possible—she had been sincere too; her suggestion that Stein send her material to Robert Coady, who with Michael Brenner had opened a gallery in New York, was not the brushoff Stein supposed. Stein assumed they had nothing to do with publishing and could be of no help, but Coady and Brenner did indeed try their hand at a small magazine, *The Soil,* which eventually published her work. Dodge probably knew of their intentions when she first suggested them to Stein. But Stein, convinced of Dodge's self-aggrandizing perfidy, was implacable.

The friendship was doomed. Correspondence between the two sputtered for a while and then failed. Although Dodge cultivated a sly ingenuousness, she was no doubt perplexed and hurt. In later years, when she occasionally broached Stein, trying to revive their former affection, she received no encouragement. But like many of Stein's other friends, she never denied the friendship she once genuinely felt toward Gertrude, and she never admitted knowing why it ended.

The end of the friendship with Dodge was part of the repeating drama Gertrude enacted throughout her life—with her cousin Bird Sternberger Gans and later with the poet Georges Hugnet, the writer Bravig Imbs, and the painters Eugene Berman and Pavel Tchelitchew. "How many cases are there of not continuing to be friends," Stein asked rhetorically in a long meditation on the subject written in the twenties. "There are a great many cases of not continuing to be friends." Gertrude frequently entered into intimacies of powerful but unexpressed eroticism—her later friendship with Ernest Hemingway is a case in point—until some perceived and unforgivable injury provoked her. Then she terminated the relationship, often abruptly and irrevocably. Sometimes she stated her reasons, sometimes she did not, but usually the less intimate friends were treated to an explanation of why they were being banished. Miriam Price, a friend of Gertrude's and Leo's from college days, was accused of clinging to the conventions of the past; evidently Price had not responded well to Gertrude's work, thus committing the most unpardonable sin.

"I agree with you that a person and her creation is 'indivisible' but I don't agree that a person is *only* her creation," Price wrote in her own defense. "A personality is a bigger thing than anything she or he creates. It would be a sad thing indeed if all personal relations depended upon the people concerned developing exactly the same." But from Stein's point of view, she'd been betrayed. Unable to take her at her own valuation, her former friends had let her down. And since it must have seemed that to remain friends was to deny all she had become—or had wanted to become—Stein declared herself finished with them. ("I'm the only person I know," Carl Van Vechten once said, "who never quarrelled with Gertrude.")

The draconian nature of her responses suggested more was at psychological stake than circumstances overtly revealed. Desperate to have her sense of self confirmed, Stein couldn't risk feeling undermined: a point which Alice Toklas well understood. But Leo, of course, could not.

THEN THE APARTMENT at 27, rue de Fleurus was quiet and empty. Leo was gone. "In short in this spring and early summer of nineteen fourteen the old life was over," Gertrude wrote almost thirty years afterward.

WEEKS AFTER LEO LEFT, Gertrude and Alice decided it was not necessary to move after all. They would renovate instead, install electricity and a fireplace, and decorate with Spanish carvings. They ordered stationery and had embossed at the top of each sheet, in circular fashion, "rose is a rose is a rose is a rose," from Gertrude's "Sacred Emily." They built a vestibule, and papered and painted, and plastered over the doorway that had led to Leo's room. "It all becomes so civilized after my departure," was Leo's acid comment.

Early in April, with the skies a watery blue and the air clear and fresh, two heavy wagons, each drawn by three large horses, clambered up a hill in Settignano. They were full of Leo's belongings, which were then duly deposited at the Villa di Doccia, where the floors were still wet and the carpenter had yet to make cupboards and shelves. Leo didn't care. He unpacked into eleven of the fifteen rooms, unloading books, sixteen Renoirs, more paintings and drawings. He outfitted the kitchen with provisions and, grateful for the kitchen knives Gertrude had sent on, was soon making dinner for his visitors from America, Miriam Price and her husband, Joe.

Although they were now neighbors, the Berensons no longer considered Leo "one of them"—they were courting a set that included both Edith Wharton and the dealer Joseph Duveen—and snubbed him socially. They did, however, allow him to use their voluminous library, and in the years to come, one often saw Leo trudging up and down the hill to I Tatti, a bulging sack of books slung over his shoulder.

He also walked into Florence that spring of 1914, and then reported to his sister about the goings-on there in cheerful, newsy letters which neither mentioned Gertrude's work nor opened any confidences. He asked her whether she could pick up a copy of Boswell's *Life of Samuel Johnson* for him, and in turn she requested that he scan the antique shops to find her and Alice a table.

Leo's letters to Nina were far more personal. The two lovers would reunite in August, when she planned to join Leo in Italy. Mabel Dodge would have returned to the Villa Curonia by that time, and Florence would be full of its usual complement of American visitors. Gertrude and Alice, however, would not be among them. They were going to London, hoping to finalize negotiations with John Lane for a reprinted *Three Lives*. The timing seemed perfect. *Tender Buttons* had appeared recently, and true to his word, Donald Evans had had the book handsomely printed and well advertised.

The reaction to *Tender Buttons* was promising, and Gertrude was receiving the publicity she wanted. And although she couldn't know, the reception to the book forecast future responses to her work in general. Many reviled it, others ridiculed it; one reviewer said he felt as if an eggbeater had been applied to his brain. But for some it was the harbinger of the future: modern, revolutionary, and bracing, a musical mix of words and sounds that refreshed the language, composed by one of the most remarkable writers of the twentieth century. It was hailed also as a farrago of nonsense that bamboozled both the public and her overzealous friends.

Her friends, however, were delighted—even those who, like Harriet Levy, were baffled. Neith Boyce Hapgood discovered a rhyme in the "Roast Beef" section of "Food," which Stein denied knowing about. Carl Van Vechten, in a piece titled "How to Read Gertrude Stein," printed the rhyming phrases in verse form:

> Lovely snipe and tender turn,
> Excellent vapor and slender butter
> All the poisonous darkening drunk,
> All the joy in weak success,
> All the joyful tenderness,
> All the section and the tea,
> All the stouter symmetry.

Stein was pleased. Whether or not she sent a copy of the new book to Leo is unknown.

ON JULY 5, 1914, the day before Gertrude and Alice left for several weeks in London, Carl Van Vechten and his future wife, Fania Marinoff, en route to Florence, stopped by the rue de Fleurus for lunch.

Gertrude, her breasts drooping low over her belt, wore a brown corduroy skirt, a nondescript shirtwaist, and carpet slippers. She laughed easily; her voice was hearty and rich, and she looked relaxed. She provided Van Vechten, who wanted to write an article about her work, some biographical information and a few comments on *Tender Buttons,* including her explanation of the title: "You see, I love buttons. I often go to the Bon Marché and buy strings of them. So, symbolically, they seemed to connect themselves with the three headings of this book." Van Vechten apparently understood. These are the things that fasten our lives together, he concluded, "and whose complications may be said to make them 'tender.'" He read aloud from the book. Then Gertrude told him: "I tried in Tender Buttons to get a combination of sound and picture that would make the effect. I worked over them awfully hard, and I think I succeeded."

Alice Toklas wore a print dress with lacy sleeves, in Van Vechten's description, and was very different from Miss Stein, in both temper and appearance. Waspish and aloof, she contributed mostly malicious remarks: George Moore was too respectable, Russian dancers used vulgar colors, she couldn't stand Yvette Guilbert or Pavlova. Both she and Miss Stein looked much as they had the previous year. Only the apartment had changed, Van Vechten observed silently, barer now that Leo was gone.

They discussed Leo that afternoon, especially his well-known love of definition. "Mr. Stein's phrase 'Define what you mean by ——' is almost famous," Van Vechten commented. Even John Reed had amiably included it in a farce he'd composed while staying at the Villa Curonia: God decides to create the Perfect Woman, only to be admonished by the Voice of Leo Stein, which booms, "First define what you mean by Woman!"

In the published version of his interview with Gertrude, Van Vechten recalled seeing Leo in Florence on the piazza Vittorio Emanuele. "I sat at lunchen [sic] time on the terrace of the *Giubbi Rossi* [sic] with Mabel Dodge when he strode into view, sandals on his feet, a bundle over his shoulder, and carrying an alpenstock. He was on his way to the mountains, and, if I remember rightly, he asked me, in response to an invitation, to define what I meant by 'cocktail,' something singularly difficult to do in Italy."

Gertrude was no longer amused by Leo's verbal tics. She told Van Vechten that no longer could she bear to argue with her brother.

"MABEL [DODGE] recounted an amusing talk with Leo about Gertrude," Neith Boyce Hapgood wrote in her journal while visiting the Villa Curonia without Hutchins in August 1914. "It seems that he is perfectly frank about her and Alice—the girl who lives with her—and separated from her partly on that account and partly because of her work." According to Dodge, Leo said

"Alice was making herself indispensable. She did everything to save Gertrude a movement—all the housekeeping, the typing, seeing people who called, and getting rid of the undesirables, answering letters—really providing the motor force of the ménage. . . . And Gertrude was growing helpless and foolish from it and less and less inclined to do anything herself, Leo said; he had seen trees strangled by vines in this same way."

Albert Barnes's memory was less poetic. He remembered asking why Leo had left Paris to live in Italy. "Gertrude is crazy," Leo said. "I can't stand her anymore."

"I believe she is crazy," wrote Gertrude Stein. "He was as he often is extremely disagreeable."

MUCH OF GERTRUDE'S writing during this year and the next suggests agitation. Images of social and domestic discord appear and disappear: curtains, plumbers, plaster, and chairs portend renovation and rearrangement, much as they did in *Tender Buttons*. "We went and looked. It was easy to do. If you measured," she wrote in a piece called "No."

> Too
> Many
> Of
> Us
> Beside
> And then
> Bother.
> Brother.
> That is a word
> Hold
> Hold him.
> I hold him.
> Not this.
> Over.

She continued to play with short declarative sentences of seeming sense, repeating and varying concrete images while experimenting with sight and sound, using puns and off-rhyme and homonym, sometimes breaking down language into its most discrete phonemic units. At its worst, such experimentation was a vast, tedious game of verbal charade; at its best, the fanciful dislocation of word, sense, and syntax was a linguistic adventure, constantly sliding toward and away from meaning. Her short portrait "Guillaume Apollinaire" opens, "Give known or pin ware," a recapitulation of Apollinaire's name

in Steinese. The portrait is not meant to be a likeness; it is a playful meditation on the meaning of words, something well suited to the subject himself.
And like Apollinaire, she experimented with format. She invented her own
puns, "eggs ample" and "nine tea," and in "Carry," she meditates on letters:
"rest less that makes a curve a curve has v, v is c that is to say rest has not t,
not in tea, not in t. Rest has in s s."

One of Stein's most sensitive interpreters has called this a period of
vacuity; but during this period, as Stein embedded autobiographical compo-
nents into the fabric of her work, she also permitted emotions to range among
the more verbal elements, thereby enriching the texture of the largely inscrutable pieces without overwhelming their rippling surfaces. Often em-
ploying the techniques she had been developing in her plays—fragments of
dialogue; abrupt shifts in mood, place, or speaker—she alternated between
revelation and concealment, and some of the fragments were demonstrably
erotic, sensual, irritated or conciliatory; they offer tiny insights into her intimacy with Alice Toklas. "Little sweet blessing," Stein wrote in "A New Happiness," "We won't go to England, Oh blessed baby, oh sour face oh lily Anne.
Oh cherished joy. That's what you are. Say it nicely. That's what I am. Oh
you cherub. Not cherub thin. Cherubim. Oh lovely cake. I incline to call you
awake. That's not teasing, that's love." "Possessive Case"—originally intended
as a study in or with possessives—contains sections written in Toklas's hand,
as if the two had entered a colloquy, sometimes argumentative and trucu-
lent, sometimes conversational and confidential. "Your brother-in-law is still
mad . . ." Stein wrote. "He is serious and last like, he went to work and he
was troubled and if he wasn't troubled he would leave town, he would stay
away, he could complain, he does complain."

Most of the recognizably autobiographical elements seem to point to Leo,
a "little lingering lion," according to *Tender Buttons*. "I innocently meant to go
away," Stein began "Painted Lace," almost taking on his persona. "I mentioned
digestion. I heard it spoken of and ears"—an allusion to Leo's fasts and his deafness; later in the piece she referred to someone named Theo. Moreover, most
of the emotional tension and psychological force in these pieces seems to
come from the recent rupture between sister and brother, adding both pressure and depth to an otherwise shimmery and even coy verbal surface. Staccato declarations and a cacophony of voices open to an interior monologue,
enigmatic but mixing fancy with bravado, insistence with self-questioning.

"To-night bore away," the piece "One Sentence" starts provocatively.
Does it help to know, however, that the work appears to have begun as variations on a phrase. "One Sent Tense" is transformed several times in Stein's
manuscript notebook, becoming "Sentence," and "One Cent Ten," and "Sentence" again—all of which were crossed out before Stein decided on the final

title. The tensions of sentences are at issue; so are talking and hearing. "A young deaf man deaf deaf too a young man deaf to hear, two hear, a young deaf, holey holey to hear." The flat, dry tone of the early part of the work gives way to a series of staccato lines, apparently unrelated and spoken at various times, perhaps by various speakers. The result is a fragmented, broken communication, a terrible disconnection between those who speak and those who listen: "He has not spoken to me since yesterday. He has not even spoken to me."

Anger supersedes vulnerability. "What is the use of Florence. I think if he comes to be thin then there is use in feathers." Confrontation alternates with withdrawal. "I have very bad headaches and I don't like to commit to paper that which makes me very unhappy."

"One Sentence" and pieces like it often remain obscure, impenetrable. Yet they are emotionally vital, revealing beneath their verbal pyrotechnics the poignant loneliness experienced with every departure.

Then Stein rallies: "We have decided to ask for another brother."

"HAVEN'T YOU HEARD? The Archduke Ferdinand assassinated . . . at Serajevo . . . Where *is* Serajevo [*sic*]? His wife was with him. What was her name? Both shot dead."

"WE CAN UNDERSTAND CIVIL WAR," wrote Gertrude Stein in "We Have Eaten Heartily and We Were Alarmed." "It is easier for families to fight than for neighbors that is in some countries. In my country it is easier for families to fight."

THE LONDON *TIMES* urges calm. There's no reason for anxiety. But a month later, on July 29, Austria–Hungary shells Belgrade. In Paris two days later, the socialist newspaper editor Jean Jaurès is assassinated. The Russians mobilize. The French mobilize. On August 3, Germany and France are at war. Italy declares itself neutral; as of midnight on August 5, Britain too is at war.

Daniel-Henry Kahnweiler chooses Switzerland over conscription in the German army. His gallery, closed for vacation, remains locked. Braque, Derain, and two of Nina Auzias's brothers go to the front. Apollinaire enlists, Matisse tries but is rejected. Michael and Sarah Stein learn that the nineteen paintings by Matisse they'd loaned to the Fritz Gurlitt gallery in Berlin have been confiscated. The Berensons are in England. Bernhard thinks they ought to go to the United States, but Mary insists they return to Florence. Gertrude Stein and Alice Toklas leave London for Salisbury Plain, where they are the weekend guests of Alfred North Whitehead and his wife, Evelyn. They remain for more than two months, not returning to Paris until mid-October. "We are nervous because we did not expect that there ever would be this war."

IN SETTIGNANO, Leo Stein and Nina Auzias discuss the future with dread and foreboding. Italy has not yet declared war, but it seems only a matter of time. Soldiers are encamped everywhere. Terrified, some of Mabel Dodge's guests at the Villa Curonia want to leave the country as soon as possible. Others delay.

Nina and Leo do nothing, not yet. She'd arrived that August, as planned, and Leo's friends were surprised at the palpable difference she made in his life. Leo was very much in love, Neith Boyce Hapgood told the Berensons; he looked ten years younger, was "quite handsome without his beard, & not at all deaf—it was really a re-birth." The happy couple kept more or less to themselves, meandering at leisure through the countryside. Nina had been taking singing lessons in Paris, which Leo encouraged and subsidized, and dreamed once again of a career. He too began to dream. Feeling stronger than he had in a long time and pushed by war's urgency, he toyed again with the idea of someday writing something—but only long after completing the psychoanalysis he'd recently started.

He confided the details of the analysis to the Prices, who carried word of it back home, but whatever Leo said or they reported is not known. It is not clear whether Leo had begun to work with an analyst in Florence, or whether he used the term "analysis" loosely and meant only his avid reading of Freud. But he was enthusiastic about his new venture; no doubt he had concluded that the fasting cure was for him no cure at all.

Yet personal happiness is dimmed by war. Both Nina's brothers are wounded. Mabel Dodge closes the Villa Curonia and anxiously waits in Naples for John Reed, en route from America, to meet her there. Neith Boyce Hapgood and Carl Van Vechten hurry back to New York. The Americans who do not flee volunteer. In October, Florence Blood and her companion Princess Ghika leave the Villa Gamberaia for France, hoping to establish a hospital in a large country house the princess owns near Biarritz. "Everyone's son or brother or husband is at the war—" says Alice Toklas shortly after reentering Paris in the fall. "They like it but not as much as the frenchies—they adore it."

Leo briefly considers joining up, "though being a human bullet," he decides, "seems to me the silliest of occupations." He vacillates between optimism and pessimism, hoping against hope that no country will be beaten too seriously; that "would be the triumphant refutation of militarism"—all "these wonderful war machines" leaving the world very much as it was. If that happened, perhaps it would "lead to a development of socialistic internation-

Nina in Settignano

ism that will sweep away the old institutions in time." But in the interim, people are losing their lives.

Again, he begins to spiral downward into depression, perhaps because he is again confronted by action he cannot or will not take. Perhaps he senses that Nina will soon leave; that he too, in fact, will be confronted by yet another move. War is never kind. But his misery has more personal and long-standing causes, and the upshot of his analysis is despair.

And perhaps it's Leo's deepening gloom that sends Nina to a pension in Florence in December. The professed reason is convenience; there she can be nearer a music teacher than at the Villa di Doccia. Within a month, she is back in Paris. The arrangement with her teacher has not worked, nor did anything else. Leo appears indifferent as to whether she stays or not; he urges her to pursue her studies and suppresses his feelings. Yet soon after her departure he starts one of his most punishing fasts, which lasts more than two weeks. He sips a little vegetable bouillon as he divests himself of all the pleasures he has recently enjoyed, denying his appetite and indulging himself in the illusion of power.

Leo Stein in America, circa 1915

But he remains devoted to Nina, writing her again and again that despite his ostensible apathy when she left, without her existence and love he will be isolated and lost, cut off from all human affection, and obliged to return to America to seek solace among old and cherished friends. Nina at a distance is still a Nina beloved, and for a time Leo is warmed by her sympathetic reassurances. All the while, and over the coming years, he subsidizes her living expenses and lessons, arranging that Michael withdraw 1,500 francs each quarter from Leo's account. As soon as she earns money from her singing, he assures Nina, he will give her less. He does not want her to feel dependent. That frightens him.

IN JANUARY 1915, Leo sent Gertrude a postcard to tell her of Nina's imminent arrival in Paris. He and Gertrude had been writing sporadically, mainly about furniture. Leo wrote now assuming that Nina would be welcome, and hoping she would be treated as a member of the family.

Instead, she was not admitted to the rue de Fleurus. No answer, no invitation, no response came from Gertrude. Leo did not know what to say. Perhaps his sister found the situation complicated, he consoled Nina; certainly she lacked savoir-faire when it came to that. Platitudes aside, he was openly furious.

And it was obvious, as it never had been before, that the thick doors that had closed behind him would remain firmly shut.

ON APRIL 27, 1915, Leo Stein sailed from Genoa to the United States.

"BROTHER BROTHER go away and stay."

GERTRUDE STEIN AND LEO STEIN never again spoke to each other.

EPILOGUE:
A FAMILY ROMANCE

Gertrude Stein in America, by Carl Van Vechten, 1934

Kipling wrote the story of the man who was; this will be the story of the man who wasn't.

LEO STEIN

The past was never past enough.

GERTRUDE STEIN

WHEN IT CAME, *la gloire* was generally good to her. Gertrude Stein was able to capture the imagination of those who also considered themselves "modern," or who were afraid not to be.

But her life consisted of battles, and if she threw herself into the fray, something like the Red Queen, she never entertained regrets. "When a thing is broken, it's finished, it's dead," she reportedly said. "You throw it away."

IT WAS NOT LONG before Leo Stein himself considered his early retirement a form of defeat. "I could only see a choice between a strenuous effort to accomplish something and throwing up the whole damn business," he told Mabel Weeks, his longtime confidante. "The second phase would mean essentially a sort of complete withdrawal from participation in the world's affairs, even in that little sphere in which hitherto I participated."

This was unacceptable, all the more so because of the Great War, but back in New York, homeless and without Nina, he sank into one of the deepest, most debilitating melancholies he had experienced. Rescued finally through the psychoanalytic ministrations of Abraham Brill and Smith Ely Jelliffe, he began at long last to write: mostly short pieces for *The New Republic,* usually on the occasion of an art exhibit. Yet as his name became more known and requests for his opinion more frequent, he relapsed into the crippling inertia that made his life intolerable.

He continued to swing from depression to hope, from planning for the future to fearing that for him there would be none. He continued to encourage Nina in her career and to support her financially—much to the horror of his brother Michael and sister Gertrude—and genuinely convinced of her talent, he wanted her to pursue her studies after joining him in New York. When she claimed she was unable to book passage, he tried to go to France, only to be denied a passport. Classified as the son of an enemy alien—though a naturalized citizen, Daniel Stein was German-born—Leo was grounded. The United States too was at war.

He grew restless. At Mabel Dodge's Fifth Avenue soirées, he was subdued. Dodge recalled him visiting in Provincetown, Massachusetts, perched on a lonely rock, spinning around himself a cocoon of thought. He stayed mostly enveloped and self-absorbed; for every foray outward there was a prolonged, concomitant retreat. After being operated on for a fistula in 1916, he recuperated among the appetite-conscious at John Kellogg's Battle Creek sanitarium until he could bear it, and himself, no longer. He returned to New York and began to write again, reimmersing himself in psychoanalysis. He visited relatives in Baltimore, had several affairs and was loved by one deeply sensitive woman safely committed to her husband. Then, in 1918, he left for Taos, New Mexico, where he bought a small house. He planned to study the Pueblo Indians, and while there he may have amassed a collection of museum-quality pre-Columbian art that included more than six dozen pieces: jars, bowls, ornaments, human figures, masks, and an astonishing votive axe. True to form, he sold the entire collection in 1928 to George Heye.

Leo did not stay long in Taos but rather returned to New York in 1919, to camp for a time at Maurice Sterne's studio on Washington Square. Sterne was amused by Leo's preference for a womblike sleeping bag over the traditional amenities of a couch. His choice seemed so fitting. His friends were devoted, sustaining him through the years to come. And many never forgot his contribution to their first glimpse of modern art. Albert Barnes summed it up perhaps best when, in 1933, he dedicated his tome on Matisse to Leo, "the first to recognize the genius of Matisse and who, more than twenty years ago, inspired the study which has culminated in this book."

Occasionally Leo sent Gertrude a card or a note. In February 1916, he wrote a longish, friendly letter from the States, half apologizing for his anger. "Long ago, about a year shortly after Nina had returned to Paris I was about to write you when I got a letter from her saying that she had written you but that you had not answered. That froze congenial currents of the soul & my intention dried up." He received no reply. "I wish you'd answer his letter," Mabel Dodge, hardly the person best situated to plead Leo's case, told Gertrude. "He's always reading your letters to other people." Still no reply.

In December 1919, the war over and his passport reissued, Leo was back in Settignano, striking his friends as kinder, more empathetic, deafer. "He speaks of nothing except what he calls 'Sikeanalsu,' " said Mary Berenson of his passion for psychoanalysis. ". . . Under its influence, or perhaps OUT of his sister's influence, he seems to have become a gentler more humane being."

Again he wrote Gertrude. "I sent you a note from New York before I left as I found that the antagonism that had grown up some years ago had gotten rather dissipated and that I felt quite amiable, rather more so even than I used to feel before that strain developed." He was as close to contrition as pride and defensiveness allowed. He continued in a confidential tone:

> It's rather curious, the change that has come over me in the last month or so. You know all those digestive troubles & most of the others that I had, I eventually found to be merely neurotic symptoms & all the time in America or at least intermittently during all that time I was trying to cure the neurosis. But they're damned hard things to cure & it was, as it was with the digestive cures always up and down, till recently I was in almost utter despair. Then, indirectly through Harriet as it happened, I got on a tack that led to better states. This has finally led to an easing up & simplifying of most of my contacts with things and people and brought about a condition where it was possible to write to you. The fact that I was coming to Europe had nothing to do with it, as I was thinking of writing anyway.

Leo was taking some responsibility for their strained relations, and obviously trying to salvage them. " 'The family romance' as it is called is almost always central in the case of a neurosis just as you used to get indigestion when we had a dispute—so, I could tell pretty well how I was getting on by the degree of possibility—I felt of writing as I am doing now." Gertrude would have none of this. Leo's self-discoveries—indeed, his self-absorption—did not stir her to action.

In the spring of 1920, Leo visited Paris. And although Gertrude and Alice would never have admitted it, he stopped by 27, rue de Fleurus. He even drafted a letter in Gertrude's study. Evidently she was not at home. Then, heading back to Italy, he realized he had forgotten the small notebook into which he jotted his observations. He wrote Gertrude, asking if she could please find and send the book. Alice quickly complied. Gertrude seems neither to have answered his inquiry nor to have acknowledged his thanks. Nothing he could say, nothing he could leave behind, would budge her. He did not write again.

GERTRUDE STEIN AND ALICE TOKLAS did not stay long in Paris after returning there in October 1914. By the next March, they left for

Mallorca, where they rented a small furnished house 260 steps above the Mediterranean, surrounded by pomegranate trees and blooming carnations. They didn't go back to Paris until the following spring, 1916, when they joined the war effort, working for the American Fund for French Wounded delivering supplies to hospitals. Since they needed their own vehicle, Gertrude applied to Howard Gans and her cousin Fred Stein, who helped raise the money to buy and ship a serviceable Ford.

After the war, they resumed their life at 27, rue de Fleurus, which before long became a watering place for the eager American expatriates rushing to Paris to cut their literary teeth. Paris in the twenties was almost synonymous with Gertrude Stein, her art, and her hospitality—"the well-sieved literary salon for those who were asked to come a second time," as one observer, not invited to return, commented. Writers of a new generation flocked around the woman, part mother, part mentor, whose writings had become a cause célèbre; these writers sought advice, encouragement, good company, and in large part found everything they'd hoped for. Of them, Sherwood Anderson was among the first to dispel the lingering notion that Stein was effete and decadent. In *The New Republic,* he simply domesticated her, suppressing her sexuality by placing her in a great literary kitchen, "standing there by the table, clean, strong, with red cheeks and sturdy legs, always quietly and smilingly at work." Such a wholesome white mama, sprung from a midwestern imagination, naturally scorned both the esoteric and the ready-made, "laying word against word, relating sound to sound, feeling for the taste, the smell, the rhythm of the individual word."

Stein diligently pursued her own career, experimenting with sentences and grammar and promoting her experiments with the same systematic, single-minded intensity that had characterized her earliest endeavors. In 1922, the collection *Geography and Plays* appeared, at her expense, and thanks to the eager young acolyte Ernest Hemingway, excerpts of *The Making of Americans* began at long last to appear in *The Transatlantic Review.* In 1925, at her urging, Robert McAlmon and his Contact Editions published the novel in its entirety.

Yet despite the continued efforts of such loyal friends and despite her well-established, if often ridiculed, literary reputation, Gertrude Stein had trouble finding publishers for her work. She showed William Carlos Williams a cabinet filled with unprinted manuscripts and asked what he would do in her place. In his *Autobiography,* the poet recalled his stringent response: "If they were mine, having so many, I should probably select what I thought were the best and throw the rest into the fire." Stein was offended, but later, when asked why she wanted all her manuscripts printed, even those written only for herself, she answered candidly: "There is the eternal vanity of the mind. . . . Anything you create you want to exist, and its means of existence is in being printed." It was up to the critics, not the creator, to separate the wheat from the chaff.

In 1930, financed by the sale of Picasso's *Woman with a Fan,* the resourceful Alice Toklas took it upon herself to publish Gertrude; she brought out five volumes of Stein's work in what they called the Plain Edition. But it was not until the 1933 publication of the ingenious *Autobiography of Alice B. Toklas*—in which she romanticized the Paris she had shared with Leo while excluding him from her memory of it—that Gertrude Stein stepped onto the platform of international celebrity, Alice Toklas right behind, with the kudos and fanfare she had coveted. That and the 1934 premiere of *Four Saints in Three Acts,* Virgil Thomson's opera based on Stein's text, clinched the case for Gertrude Stein: she was one of the most well-known literary personages people hadn't read. And now, after years of rejecting her work, Boston's venerable *Atlantic Monthly* serialized her, and Bennett Cerf opened to her the doors of his Modern Library.

She was not returning to America, she often said, "not until I am a lion." Perhaps this was an unconscious admission that she had desired to replace or become her brother; it was a phrase she repeated often and with feeling. So it was no surprise that during her 1934–1935 lecture tour in the United States, she beamed with the joy of a child, charming those who met her in person. Readers, detractors, gawkers, as well as students, reporters, detectives, hotel personnel, and garage mechanics, many of whom had expected her to mutter esoteric nonsense in a foreign accent, were pleasantly surprised by her straightforward frankness and were assured of her sanity. She was sound of mind and body and, as she put it, born legitimate of two respectable parents. To many of those who, like Scott Fitzgerald, saw her during this gala tour, she was "the same fine fire to everyone who sat upon your hearth—for it was your hearth, because you carry home with you wherever you are—a home before which we have always warmed ourselves."

There were, however, those who'd been banished from the hearth, not just Leo but also friends and family with whom she differed, quarreling with some, ignoring others, and going out of her way to injure still others, often for no apparent reason. During her American tour, she hurt and insulted what was left of the old crowd, especially those who failed to take her at her own valuation. Wounded by Gertrude's effort to fob off the manuscript of *Three Lives* on her for a thousand dollars, Etta Cone felt snubbed; so did Emma Lootz Erving. Mabel Weeks was deeply upset. In New York she finally approached Gertrude, who hadn't responded to any of her invitations; Gertrude said flatly that if Mabel wanted to see her, she'd better come to Europe.

Many of the castoffs turned to Leo, who was himself distressed by *The*

Autobiography, claiming, though, that he didn't really want recognition for his role in discovering Matisse and Picasso or for supporting their work. But of course he did. And what was worse, he was completely expunged, replaced only by (he felt) his sister's colossal vanity; that, braggadocio, and amazing self-confidence enabled her, he observed, "to build something rather effective on her foundations."

What also galled him was the public's acceptance of Gertrude as a literary phenomenon. "That her long sustained persistence, combined with her social enthusiasm, should have given her a standing is not surprising in our day," he told Mabel Weeks. "But—imagine the stupidity of anyone sixty years of age who makes that remark about learning the qualities of sentences and paragraphs from the rhythm of her dog's drinking."

Yet admiration for his sister sometimes tempered his outbursts. He always held that her forte was her fine-tuned psychological insight, a gift he thought damaged by the nefarious influence of cubism; but he granted she had integrity. She took herself quite seriously, declining to turn her American lecture tour into a sideshow when she refused to speak to a crowd larger than 500 people. "There is not enough money in the world to persuade me to stand up before a horde of curious people who are interested in my personality rather than my work," she reportedly said. And though Leo believed that despite some nice rhythms, Gertrude communicated with and to herself alone, he figured that if the public willingly submitted to such foolishness, so be it. When her short book on Picasso appeared in 1939, although he doubted whether there was an essential statement in it that was not "radically stupid," dressed up as profound insight and confounding the gullible reader, he conceded, "Ah well. Some must take that role and why not she."

He was not alone in his criticism of his sister's work. But unlike those who were not persuaded by Gertrude Stein's literary gifts, Leo Stein had become the half-noticed older brother of a famous sister, as the critic Alfred Kazin, who met Leo a few weeks before the latter's death, mused. He had been reading in Berenson's library when Kazin came to call. Kazin described him: "Like a Jewish Uncle Sam—very rustic, nervous, deaf, but full of talk and little wisecracks," showing visitors around. He was courteous, gentle, yet fidgety and somewhat uneasy, and very excitable; he stopped in Berenson's study and launched into a long monologue—after all, he couldn't hear his audience—on his latest passion, a treatise on lying. Preoccupied with lying, what it meant, why people did it, he had been studying it with the eagerness of a young man about to embark on his life's greatest adventure. "It's important! It's the big thing! No one looks these facts in the face! Animals can't lie and human beings lie all the time!"

"But God what a liar she is!" he had said of his sister some fourteen years earlier. Others had said the same thing. The difference is that by the end of his life Leo thought lying opened the gateway to human character, human complexity, the human heart. Doubtless he had a point.

LEO STEIN AND NINA AUZIAS were married in 1921, after their long and difficult courtship. When he returned to Europe in 1919, he knew he loved Nina as much as ever but he feared harnessing her to himself, a neurotic deaf man with an uncertain future. "You can have all—marriage, baby, home, but I do not pretend to offer under these conditions happiness," he warned. "That is not to say I am balking, only that I don't see the way. I wish I could. I feel almost a passion to be a father, but as I've often said, a deaf father seems to me a little like the father of a living doll." Nina nonetheless consented to join him in Settignano. They had no children.

Often he said that without his beloved Nina, he would never have been able to survive. But his temperament remained solitary and self-regarding. "I have played a lone hand," he explained to a friend, speaking essentially of his longtime devotion to another mistress, psychoanalysis. Intensely suspicious of others, he had undertaken his own analysis and developed an unorthodox method that blended the insights of mysticism and the insights of Freud, with William James's pragmatism added to the brew. His goal was to experience the self as other; by knowing oneself from the outside, one began to see what one was. The crucial question for him was "to how great an extent can situations commonly supposed to be subjective, be *experienced* as objective." This was a method, he claimed, not an epistemology, and its use lay in its success. Later, apparently without irony, he dubbed the method "Practical Solipsism."

Self-analysis granted Stein long periods of relief and, by the mid-twenties, the conviction that he'd conquered the most debilitating of his neuroses. He rarely complained about his stomach, he digested without much problem, his sexual life with Nina was fulfilling. He was writing. "It is about time to saw wood if we're really going to build habitations for our gods," he told Morgan Russell. "Posterity does not respect programs."

Bristling with ideas, Leo published a series of articles in *The New Republic* on art and education; he also completed, at long last, his book, published in 1927 by Boni & Liveright as *The A-B-C of Aesthetics*. And no sooner was this book in proofs than he began outlining a new one, a discourse on his psychoanalytic method. But he was naively unprepared for the uncomprehending responses to his book, to say nothing of the negative reviews, and he buckled under their cumulative weight. In February 1929, during a series of lectures he gave at New York's New School for Social Research, he broke down. He stumbled several times and then stopped, unable to go on. He forswore writing and retired once again into a cranky isolation, applying his method ever more stringently. After a while, he took up his paintbrushes again.

Until 1933 he and Nina spent part of the year in Settignano and part in Paris; they kept an apartment there because Nina couldn't bear the seclusion of an Italian village year-round. But Leo could never tolerate such a public life for long; he would pine for the rectitude of his new Settignano home, the Villino Rosa, nestled among cypresses on a ridge overlooking the Arno valley. The move back and forth became an emblem of his ambivalence; he remained half in and half out of the game, dogged by an ever-worsening deafness.

He was comfortable among the villagers, who liked the tall, thin, well-kempt American who came to town wearing a velour jacket. When his hearing aid worked, he was rather gregarious and sat affably talking about art to whoever would listen. Then he would return to the small villa he'd bought in the early twenties. Over time, he sold off most of his collection—much more than Gertrude had sold—to pay for living expenses and, some said, to offset losses incurred after the stock market crash. Drawings by Picasso and paintings by Renoir, lithographs by Toulouse-Lautrec, Manguins and Matisses, his compact Delacroix—all were slowly dispersed, many long before the market collapsed. In 1921 he offered his remaining Renoirs to Durand-Ruel for sale and that same year parted with Cézanne's apples. Apart, neither he nor Gertrude had bought paintings with the same verve or insight; despite the good canvases she had acquired from Juan Gris, Sir Francis Rose had become her passion. Ottakar Coubine was Leo's.

By the late thirties, Leo had little left; he and Nina gave up the Paris apartment and in 1939 sold the villa. Howard Gans, the painter Edward Bruce, Etta Cone, and Maurice Sterne arranged to buy Leo's paintings every year to make sure he and Nina had enough to eat. Leo began to think of America. Pressed by the threat of war, even Michael and Sarah—though not Allan and his wife—had returned to California in 1935 with their young grandson. Leo booked passage on a liner out of Lisbon, but Nina, who had always resisted the journey, took ill. He sold their tickets. When they began to pack once more, it was too late; the last boat evacuating Americans from Italy had already sailed.

No communication passed between brother and sister, nor did any during World War II, when each, still in Europe, experienced the war quite differently. An ardent supporter of Henri Pétain, Gertrude retired with Alice to their summer home in Bilignin, in eastern France, where they lived protected by friends of the Vichy regime. In 1941 she began to translate Pétain's speeches, appending her own laudatory preface in an attempt to waken her American compatriots to the virtues of the Maréchal, whom she compared with George Washington: "first in war first in peace and first in the hearts of his countrymen." But after 1943 her enthusiasm waned. Whether the change had to do with the roundup and deportation of some 13,000 French Jews in the sum-

mer of 1942 is hard to say, but it seems to have coincided with being advised
to flee France lest she and Toklas endure the same fate. Stein never directly
mentioned what being Jewish meant to Toklas or herself during these years.
Nor did she ever speak about the tragic plight of European Jewry, although it
seems to be the subtext of *Wars I Have Seen,* her chronicle of the war years
begun in late 1942 or early 1943. She and Toklas did not leave France, and they
remained unharmed. Even their apartment in Paris, vacant during the war,
suffered little disturbance.

In Italy, Leo spent most of his time tending Nina, sick and bedridden
with rheumatism. He cooked, carried water, ran errands. Painting out of doors
had been forbidden. After the "ugly days of '42," frequent fatigue, constant interruption, cold, darkness (the Germans knocked out the electricity), and the
need to hide in a cellar with a dozen others for months made any routine living impossible. The batteries in his hearing aid had long since run down. The
Villa Gamberaia was bombed and burned, and a mass of smoke hung blankly
over Florence. Most of the anti-Semitic legislation in Italy seemed to exempt
those over seventy; no one bothered Leo or his French wife, but his friend
and neighbor the painter Rudolf Levy, a German Jew, had been arrested. Nina
was terrified, Leo heartbroken. "Some pious Catholic friends thought I ought
to be grateful to God because I had during the German occupation and the
fascist republic escaped all perils. I said to them that there had been 6,000,000
Jews murdered. Was I to be grateful to God that only 6,000,000 had been murdered and not 6,000,001?"

In 1945, in a letter to a cousin, Gertrude wondered what had happened
to Leo; she had not heard of him since before the war. The cousin sent the
letter to another cousin, who gave it to Howard Gans. He sent a curt note to
Gertrude—apparently he too had been snubbed—and enclosed a copy of a
letter he had recently received from Leo. That was all. When Gertrude died,
Leo read about it in the newspapers.

GERTRUDE'S LAST YEARS are well documented. After the libera-
tion, she and Alice returned to Paris, where she fully enjoyed the role of a literary light and all the attendant publicity. With grace and hospitality and a
renewed taste for public life, she replaced the *littérateurs* of the twenties with
the GIs of the forties, teasing them, scolding them, and encouraging their literary aspirations. She remained a stolid, supportive reader of young writers'
prose—as long as her own work was treated with seriousness and respect.

She herself had continued to write, to experiment, to struggle with language in ways discussed and deciphered, then and now. Recognition increased along with age, never quite sating her appetite, even though publicity
and fame so disturbed her after publication of the immensely popular *Auto-*

biography of Alice B. Toklas that she composed several extended meditations on the blow success had dealt her sense of self. Yet at the same time, some of her writing seemed to become clearer—pandering to a popular audience, huffed skeptics. Virgil Thomson acutely observed that if the last outposts of cubist prose were pure abstraction, on the one hand, and naturalism, on the other, then Stein in effect chose both. The surface intelligibility of works such as *The Geographical History of America* and *The Mother of Us All* in no way diminished their force; neither did the playful ambiguity of *Patriarchal Poetry, Ida,* or *Stanzas in Meditation.* In fact, Stein's best work was always an extended meditation on the conditions under which representation occurred, what Wallace Stevens called "the poem of the mind in the act of finding / What will suffice." Egotistical as she was, Stein was not entirely wrong in supposing, as she said, that "in this epoch the only real literary thinking has been done by a woman."

Although she still rooted her work in her love of the present, in her pleasure in the materiality of words and the things of this world, more and more the past and the yearnings that followed her from girlhood—about knowing and being known, about sexuality and death, about the lonely miracle of consciousness—leavened much of the prose that would have otherwise been flat, reductive, and unfeeling, or solipsistic. Nonetheless, Stein's work would continue to be extolled in terms of its relative opacity, and perhaps because some of her experiments were neglected for so long, and published posthumously more or less en masse, they stupefied critics into fulsome silence or a too lavish praise. As a consequence, too few differentiated between her unique achievements and those writings which simply missed the mark. Stein became part cult figure, part buffoon, and for many remained the Mother Goose of Montparnasse, her work fat, sloppy, and infantile. Yet its marvels continued to intrigue, provoke, and challenge writers bent on writing, and for better or worse, in her own lifetime Stein became the success that she, like any good American reared on the idea of success, had hoped to become.

In the summer of 1946, weary and thin and planning another trip to her native country, she underwent a fatal operation for cancer. She had been ill on and off since the spring, hoping for the best, even though, as a former medical student, she must have been aware of the gravity of her complaint. But by the time she entered the American Hospital at Neuilly in July, her physicians feared she was too weak and the cancer too far advanced for surgery. Drawing herself up furiously—quite like the old days, said Toklas, when someone disparaged her work—Stein demanded something be done immediately. After the operation, on the afternoon of July 27, she sank into a coma. At her bedside were her sister Bertha's son, Daniel Raffel, and of course Alice.

Leo Stein
at seventy-five

Alice stayed on alone, as she was wont to say, for the next twenty-one years. Pursued by poverty, blindness, baldness, and a crippling arthritis, she ushered Stein's unpublished work into print and generally kept her beloved's memory alive, not just in herself but in others. In 1957, fleeing both her Jewish past and events of recent memory, she made her confession, took Holy Communion, and declared she'd been baptized as a child. She entered the Catholic Church for many reasons, but chiefly, it seems, because she felt she might see Gertrude sooner on the other side.

LEO DIED one year after his sister, the American failure par excellence who had never been able to bind curiosity to ambition and hurl them toward a single-minded objective. Except perhaps once.

As if liberated, ironically, by age and war, Leo in his last years had been writing constantly, pounding out on his ancient portable Corona a slim semi-autobiographical volume about poetry, prose, and painting in an accessibly warm and witty style. It was a "little debauch," he said, "in the realm of ideas" that claimed aesthetic values still mattered, perhaps more than ever, even if art and the hullabaloo made of it did not. Light-handed, concrete, wry, and plainly intelligent, the book belied his reputation as a crotchety philistine, for as conservative as some of his taste had become, his notions remained heretical, uncategorizable, even bold. Art, he maintained, was "intimately connected with everything else—even with things that are all wrong, like murder and sudden death." Art was part of culture, part of society, it was a democracy to be found everywhere, in all our vital interests, in food, in the landscape, in the remote and unexpected; every artistic enterprise was a gamble and not the province of idolaters, Great Books, or conventional cant. "Leo was a liberal leader by nature," Alice Toklas tartly told Elizabeth Sprigge. "If he had been English he would have been on the *Manchester Guardian.*"

Everything *The A-B-C of Aesthetics* was not (including very well received), *Appreciation: Painting, Poetry and Prose* was published by Crown in the summer of 1947, a few weeks before Leo was set to undergo a second round of surgery for colon cancer. The first had been during the winter and was followed by radium treatments paid for by the sale of one of the last of his Picasso drawings. In July he was scheduled for a regimen of two more operations. The heat hovered around forty degrees Centigrade and the best clinic in Florence had suddenly closed for repairs, but Leo was in excellent spirits. He'd been eating well, he still walked into Florence from Settignano with a bounce in his step, and despite the bitter winter, with unusual amounts of snow and ice and the pain of a protracted recuperation, there were books he still wanted to write. "My situation is tragic in a way," he had written Howard Gans, "to have come to the foot of the ladder, and such a long ladder at so late a date. I can now imagine a beautiful future of ten or twelve years devoted to the perfecting of things well begun and the perfecting of an art of saying . . . but for years I have months, and these are things that one can't hurry."

One of these was a book about Gertrude and himself, a study in opposites, he said. Perhaps he imagined it as the kind of reunion made possible only by her death and his seventy-five years of age. "Gertrude is the person who takes herself completely for granted," he explained to friends, referring to his dead sister in the present tense. "She always took what she wanted! She could always talk her way into anything!" he told Alfred Kazin. "I never could." "The contrast is extreme," he concluded. And interesting.

Indeed it was; but so of course was the resemblance: both of them proud, introspective, and passionately self-involved; both profoundly competitive; and both intensely cerebral, intellectualizing their emotions while insisting they did the contrary; both could also be unselfish and kind, or arrogant and peremptory; and each in his or her iconoclastic way ambivalently courted the favor of the world, hoping at the same time to leave on it some mark. And they may have been alike in yet another, ironic way, one that Gertrude had already guessed: their demonstration that those qualities which made for success in America also made for failure.

Even if the unspoken could now be spoken or the sundered made whole, Leo probably couldn't have resisted a book in which he emerged victorious at last, if only by dint of longevity.

Days before his second operation, he was sketching out his plans. Gertrude was evidently very much on his mind. And now, in the summer of 1947, of the two sisters and three brothers, Leo was the sole survivor. Simon had died at forty-five, "still fat and fishing," Gertrude had later written with cruel humor; Bertha, a diabetic, had died in 1924; and Michael had succumbed to cancer in 1938.

In the hospital in Florence, as Leo waited patiently for his room to be ready, he scanned a stack of morning mail. He was warmed by letters brimming with praise for *Appreciation,* and his eyes fell on one of the first major reviews of his book. It was from the *New York Herald Tribune,* and bore the title "Leo, Known as Gertrude's Brother, Stein." Everyone is so obsessed with Gertrude, he observed with feeling.

But this time there were satisfactions. The review, like all those to come, offered unstinting praise for his book, "the discourse of a wise, original, engaging thinker whose frame of reference is exceptionally wide, whose genuine enthusiasm is infectious, and whose genial skepticism is tonic." A letter from Albert Barnes was even more to the point. "Your *Appreciation* is a knockout!"

In the final days of July, Leo underwent the first of the two planned surgeries. Afterward, wheeled back to his room, he looked drowsily at Nina. "So far, so good," he said smiling. But infection brooded in the wound, and six days later, on July 29, Leo Stein was dead of peritonitis.

Nina never recovered. Although Leo's American friends and family offered her refuge in New York and Leo's editor, Hiram Haydn, encouraged her to write her memoirs, nothing and no one could replace her darling Steiney. For two years she tasted only grief. Then, in August 1949, not long after her own brother's death, she decided to put her affairs in order. She sent a cable to a friend in France and, her hands aching with arthritis, wrote several letters, sealed them, and arranged them on her bed. She turned on the gas and lay down to rest.

At the last, she regretted she hadn't been able to do as much for Leo as Alice Toklas had for Gertrude. But before she buried her husband in the pretty flowered cemetery of Settignano, she had made sure that Leo Stein would sleep comfortably in his grave, gently placing in his hands a copy of his hard-won book. She also had his signature cut deep into a marble headstone and added beneath it the word inhabited by his sister: *Scrittore.* Writer.

APPENDIX
ACKNOWLEDGMENTS
NOTES
BIBLIOGRAPHY
INDEX

APPENDIX

I found the following essay in a nondescript folder tucked among the miscellaneous papers of Mary Mackall Gwinn Hodder. Eight pages long, typed on legal-sized paper, and titled "Degeneration in American Women," the piece was written probably for publication, perhaps in the *Journal of the American Medical Association*. It is anonymous, but its clean, legible corrections are unmistakable: they are the handiwork of Gertrude Stein.

The essay was neither signed nor dated. Its typeface, however, does correspond to that of an 1899 Stein paper, "The Value of College Education for Women" (also unsigned), which Claribel Cone had the courtesy to identify and date for posterity. Mamie Gwinn Hodder was not so inclined. She presumably loathed "Degeneration in American Women" and, for reasons of her own, kept it.

Although telling, corrections written in Gertrude Stein's hand do not in themselves prove the paper her brainchild. Nor does our knowledge that Mamie Gwinn was in possession of an article by Gertrude Stein, given to her by Alfred Hodder in early 1902. (The story of how that article came into Gwinn's possession is told in chapter 8 of this book.) And if Hodder's description of Stein's article sounds a good deal like "Degeneration," as it does, this too proves nothing. Yet if we take these facts into consideration with some striking internal evidence, there is little room for doubt: Gertrude Stein wrote "Degeneration in American Women," which is a very early exhibition of her ideas—and of the distinctive way in which she expressed them.

Moreover, as any reader of this book—and certainly anyone familiar with Stein's biography—will know, Stein had easy access to George J. Engelmann's "The Increasing Sterility of American Women," which is the catalyst for "Degeneration." Engelmann's essay appeared in the October 5, 1901, issue of the *Journal of the American Medical Association,* a publication known to Stein, who had not yet completely jettisoned her career in medicine or denied her interest in it. Indeed, the ideas presented in "Degeneration" on women, assimilation, America, and class all conform to Stein's general thinking at the time, as demonstrated in "The Value of College Education for Women" or the manuscript "Fernhurst."

Probably written sometime between October 1901, the date of Engelmann's article, and early 1902, when Hodder first mentioned Stein's essay, "Degeneration" contains several allusions, in addition to the medical ones, that lead directly back to her. The mention of Jasper Petulengro's affirmation of life is a reference to George Borrow's picaresque *Lavengro,* a tale whose impact on Stein is a subject in itself. For now, though, suffice it to say that Stein informed Neith Boyce and Hutchins Hapgood in 1903 that she intended to write something "Borrowesque" (this was shortly before she began "Q.E.D.") and that as late as 1939 she still cited Borrow as a major influence. And true to Borrow, Stein's early writing—as well as much of her later work—drew unabashedly on personal experience. In this, "Degeneration" differs little.

Furthermore, the preoccupation with maternity that dominates "Degeneration" runs throughout Stein's early writing. "The Value of College Education for Women" defends higher education against the charge that it will squelch motherhood; aborted motherhood lurks behind the scenes of "The Good Anna," and motherhood kills the main character in "The Gentle Lena." In a sense, motherhood also killed Stein's medical career, when she flunked obstetrics in her fourth year at Johns Hopkins. There are other parallels. In "Degeneration," the author provides an anecdote about a woman who has induced two miscarriages; such a charge was leveled against Stein's own cousin Bird Sternberger. Stein's medical training included obstetrical calls in the black community of Baltimore as well as work in the dispensary, where she may well have heard the "old negress" quoted in "Degeneration." And as students of Stein's work attest, her self-identification with the black community culminates in "Melanctha."

A nascent love of art surfaces in "Degeneration," which alludes to the prominent, if banal, painting by George de Forest Brush, *Mother and Child.* Stein could easily have seen it at the Boston Museum of Fine Arts—long before she cultivated a taste for Picasso. The painting is a sentimentalized rendition of maternity in which a careworn woman sacrifices herself for the greater goods of procreation and race. Although Stein was never one to countenance deferred gratification for herself, this painting, like "Degeneration" generally, captures the orthodoxy she so spiritedly, and ironically, embraced.

Throughout *Sister Brother,* I elaborate several of these themes while only hinting at the significant stylistic evidence that links the "Degeneration" manuscript to Gertrude Stein. Yet this is the evidence that clinched, for me, the identity of the author, for through it one unambiguously confronts the early preoccupation with rhythm that developed, almost unexpectedly, into startling literary experiment: the habit of omitting punctuation, particularly commas; the breathless string of independent clauses and repetitive structures looped with the connective "and." "It is this point," writes the author of the essay, "that cannot be too much insisted upon that this condition does not prevail among the better classes alone but that it is true of every class of the American population and that there is in no portion of the community that lives its fair quota of population except the foreign and this virtue is lost by the first generation born in America." Even the author's tendency to run words together anticipates Stein's later, more deliberate rhythmic signature. And the leitmotif of *The Making of Americans* is virtually rehearsed in "Degeneration": the notion of "right living," and the celebration of the "normal functions of living, walking, talking, thinking, being, eating and drinking." In fact, one might also say, a bit adventurously, that "Degeneration" marks the first known example of Stein's passion for participles.

Such markers as these, and those I have mentioned elsewhere in *Sister Brother,* reveal a Gertrude Stein speaking to us from the distance of almost a century. The voice is young, fresh, untried—and very much hers. It is my hope that this voice, now recognized, will fuel future scholarship—to say nothing of pleasure and debate.

Degeneration in American Women

In an article published in the Journal of the American Medical Association October 5, 1901, Dr. Engellman [*sic;* the spelling of Engelmann's name varies throughout] discusses the alarming increase in sterility among American women. He finds that in the United States there is a higher sterility and a lower fecundity than in any other country outside of France and for the native American population the condition is worse than in France. The data that he uses are his own experience in private practice and in the dispensaries of St. Louis consisting of 1700 cases, series of carefully compiled statistics from Boston, Massachusetts and Michigan and the census records.

The facts are as follows:

The normal rate of sterility in foreign countries is eleven percent. In America over twenty percent of the women are childless. The highest fecundity among American born is to be found in St. Louis and that consists of 2.1 children to a marriage a lower rate of fecundity than than [*sic*] is to be found anywhere outside of Paris. In Boston the fecundity is 1.7 & in Michigan it is in the last few years 1.8. It has been slowly decreasing in every state in the union. This can be profitably contrasted with Franklin's estimate for his contemporaries of eight children to a normal marriage and Malthus's estimate of 5.2 children to a marriage in America.

In private practice in St. Louis Engelmann finds among the Americans of American parentage 1.7 children to a marriage and Americans of foreign parentage 1.9 children to a marriage. Among college women the results are still worse the average number of children to a marriage being 1.3 children to 1.6 while the non college woman of the same class and in the same city gives a record of 2.1. In England we find the same result among college women the average college woman's marriage producing 1.5 children while the non-college women in the same class of society average 4.2 children to a marriage.

Engelmann divides his cases among the laboring classes into those of foreign birth and those born in America. Among the foreign population the percent of sterility is 17 while in one generation of residence in America it rises to 26 percent and in the second generation becomes the apparent normal percentage for the modern American that is about 23 percent. In private practice in St. Louis he finds it to be about 23 percent and for college graduates 25. In Massachusetts we find the same discrepancy between the foreign and the native born population. The foreign born portion of the community shows 13.3 percent of the women sterile while the native population shows a percentage of 20.3 which in Boston runs up to 23.7. Now let us contrast these figures with those of foreign countries. In Paris the percentage of sterility is 27.3, in Berlin the sterility among the higher classes is 25.7 while among the laboring classes it is only 15 percent. These figures are rather appalling for these two cities have always been considered the most complete type of degeneration from the standpoint of fecundity and yet Berlin shows a better percent and Paris only a slightly worse one than obtains throughout America among the native population. From England we get the following figures, among the higher classes 16.4 percent among villagers 9.6 percent and among college alumnae 27.6 percent.

About 25 percent of all this sterility can be attributed to disease caused by the male for the rest as Dr. Engellman concludes the barrenness in the large majority of cases is independent of physical causes as evidenced by the astonishing increase in sterility in this country with the marked increase in progress of gynecology which should control sterility were it due to disease and physical causes. Instead of that we have passed to a fecundity less and a sterility greater than any country except France. In considering the question of the causes for the marked increase in sterility among American women one fact cannot be too often dwelt upon. The fact that the normal period of fertility for a woman is from her eighteenth to her forty fifth year and that unless labor has so to speak cleared a passage, from her twenty fifth year on there is a gradual hardening of all her genitalia making conception rarer, miscarriages more frequent and labor much more dangerous. The first labor of a woman at thirty is always a much more serious matter than in the case of a young woman. This fact is one that must be kept constantly in mind when one is considering the causes of sterility among American women.

In considering the causes of sterility it is best to divide them into two classes,

1. Physiological sterility.
2. Voluntary sterility.

These two classes must again be divided into

A. Absolute sterility by which we mean women who have never conceived.

B. Relative sterility that is women who have never come to term. The causes of phisiological [sic] sterility of the absolute variety are the impotence on the part of the male, anatomical malformation on the part of the female, gonnorheal [sic] infection of the female and gynecological operations. The relative physiological sterility is due either to a syphilitic infection of the female or to congenital weakness. All these causes together with miscarriages due to obscure puerperal infections combine to make up the eleven percent sterility that one may call the normal sterility among civilised races and which is known as Simpson's law of sterility. In addition to these causes for physiological sterility which we may perhaps call the normal causes of sterility among civilized peoples there are a set of causes bringing about physiological sterility both of the absolute and relative type which are due to the education and habits of life that obtain among the American women of to day.

The first point is that of the prevailing tendency to delay marriages until a woman's period of fertility is almost half over and the dangers and difficulties of conception and labor have become markedly increased. The second point is that in our modern system of education the heaviest mental strain is put upon the girl when her genitalia is making its heaviest physical demand and when her sexual desires are being constantly stimulated without adequate physiological relief, a condition that obtains to a very considerable extent in our average American college life. All these causes induce of necessity a weakening of the genitalia and a consequent increase of absolute and relative physiological sterility. The third point is the incessant strain and stress that the modern woman endeavoring to know all things, do all things and enjoy all things undergoes. This condition of life must of necessity lead to weakness and inadequacy of the genitalia as the whole physical scheme of the woman is directed toward fitness for propagation.

If these conditions only obtained among the upper classes in this country one might deplore but one could afford to disregard them for after all a nation never depends upon its upper classes but as will be noted in the statistics given by Engellmann there is not that immense difference in the percentage of sterility and fecundity in this country between the upper and lower classes that we find in all European countries. In America what the upper classes do the middle classes do and what is true of the middle class holds for the laboring classes and so we find in this country a uniform sterility and lack of fecundity varying very little from the top to the bottom.

The second and more important class of sterility is the voluntary type. It is this kind of sterility and lack of fecundity that that [sic] is so markedly increasing in America among all classes of the population. This type of sterility is of course all due to moral causes and these are so numerious [sic] that one can hardly do more than give the headings.

Voluntary sterility consists first of the absolute type that due to methods of prevention of conception and the relative type that of the criminal abortion. As both these types of sterility are due to the same moral causes they may be considered together.

Two classes of the community I imagine are chiefly responsible for the increased knowledge of methods of prevention among the laboring classes. On the one hand the charity workers with misdirected zeal and false ideals have spread as far as in them lay the knowledge of methods of prevention. The constantly increasing use of the dispensaries and the knowledge there obtained has helped to spread this feeling that prevention should be indulged in. As one old negress put it, "I had twenty children I would not do that now any more I know too much." Let us now consider a few of the causes that have led to the disrepute into which the ideal of maternity has fallen and see what can be said for them.

In the first place among the educated classes in this country, that is among the educated women and among the pseudo educated women there is a strong tendency to what we may call the negation of sex and the exaltation of the female ideal of moral and methods and a condemnation and abhorrence of virility.

By this statement is meant the tendency of the modern American woman to mistake her education her cleverness and intelligence for effective capacity for the work of the world. In consequence she underestimates the virile quality because of its apparent lack of intelligence. In the moral world she also finds herself the superior because on account of the characteristic chivalry of the American man the code of morality which her sheltered life has developed seems adequate for the real business of life and it is only rarely that she learns that she never actually comes in contact with the real business and that when she does the male code is the only possible one. All this of course leads to a lack of respect both for the matrimonial and maternal ideal for it will only be when women succeed in relearning the fact that the only serious business of life in which they cannot be entirely outclassed by the male is that of child bearing that they will once more look with respect upon their normal and legitimate function. Of course it is not meant that there are not a few women in every generation who are exceptions to this rule but these exceptions are too rare to make it necessary to subvert the order of things in their behalf and besides if their need for some other method of expression is a real need there is very little doubt but that the opportunity of expression will be open to them.

Another very important cause for the low rate of fecundity lies in the modern morbid responsibility for offspring. This is true in America for both parents. There is a foolish conviction abroad that the parents can raise one or two children better than half a dozen can raise themselves. This fallacy is due to the same cleverness of the American woman which has just ben [sic] mentioned and makes her mistake a knowledge of facts for training in method and makes her believe it possible for her to learn by a few lectures the things one only gets after years spent day after day in the daily round of working, listening and waiting. This conviction produces the type that is the terror to the trained professional mind, the intelligent mother. When this generation learns over again the truth that the training of children should on the one hand consist of a back ground in the home of a tradition that stands for honesty and right living and that for the rest it should in the hands of the trained professional the morbid responsibility, for the offspring will dissappear [sic]. On the paternal side the responsibicity [sic] takes the form of the onviction [sic] that one should bear children only when you can remove them as far as humanly possible from the normal conditions of a struggle for existence.

The prevailing pessimism that characterizes the modern community and carries with it a ceaseless desire for amusement and a consequent incrnase [*sic*] in the expense of living is another of the important causes for the marked increase in sterility. The American population seems to have completely lost sight of the fact that the exercise of ones [*sic*] normal functions of living, walking, talking, thinking, being, eating and drinking is an endless joy of a healthy human being. As Jasper Petulengro puts it in answer to Lavengro's melancholy "There's night and day brother both sweet things, sun moon and stars brother all sweet things, there is likewise the wind on the heath. Life is very sweet brother who would wish to die." No in the developement [*sic*] of the play instinct and the feeling of joy in the world one must look for a counteracting force against the prevailing pessimism and the consequent voluntary sterility. Another important element to be considered is the characteristic inefficiency in household matters of the lower class American woman. She is incapable for the most part of cooking sewing or any of the household duties for which her European sisters are famous. Her housekeeping is expensive and the food she supplies her family is not for the most part nutritious. Besides she does not want to increase her labors by her normal maternal functions. Just to cite one case that is extremely characteristic. A woman the wife of a railroad conductor and a very worthy person has been married for five years. Her husband is very fond of children and wants them the woman however refuses on account of the bother. She has within the last two years voluntarily brought about two miscarriages. This is not an isolated case but can be matched in any street and house in any city in the union. It is this point that cannot be too much insisted upon that this condition does not prevail among the better classes alone but that it is true of every class of the American population and that there is in no portion of the community that lives its fair quota of population except the foreign and this virtue is lost by the first generation born in America.

To conclude: unless the American woman can be made once more to realize that the ideal of maternity is the only worthy one for her to hold, until she can be made to realize that no work of hers can begin to compensate for the neglect of that function we are going the same way as France except that with true American push we are going France considerably better and a few years are showing a worse record than she has after ages of degenerative civilization. In discussing this subject one inevitably thinks of the picture of Brush in the Boston museum that of the mother with the lusty child in her arms. She is worn and weary but the vigorous struggling baby in her arms transfigures her weariness and changes it from a sacrifice to the purest pride.

ACKNOWLEDGMENTS

This book has depended on the kindness—and generosity—of strangers and friends.

I am very grateful to the John Simon Guggenheim Memorial Foundation for the liberal fellowship awarded me during the 1991–1992 academic year to support the research and writing of this book; to the Lilly Library, Indiana University, which granted me its Ball Foundation Fellowship in 1993; and to the Indiana University Institute for Advanced Study, which named me a Visiting Fellow of the Institute during my stay in Bloomington.

I am indebted also to the Beinecke Rare Book and Manuscript Library, Yale University, and its inestimable director, Ralph Franklin, for my appointment as the Donald C. Gallup Senior Fellow in American Literature, 1991–1992; the title alone is an honor, for not only does the Beinecke house the most comprehensive collection of Gertrude Stein and Leo Stein papers and related material, largely because of Donald Gallup, but everyone connected to this fine institution is eminently helpful and well informed. I thank Patricia C. Willis, curator of American literature at the Beinecke, who has supported this book every step of the way with her stimulating friendship. I am obliged too to Bob Babcock and the outstanding staff at the Beinecke service desk, who treated every query—and there were many—with due seriousness. Thanks in particular to Steve Jones, Lori Misura, Kate Sharp, Rick Hart, and Bill Hemmig.

I obtained material also from other research institutions, where I am grateful to more people than I can name. These include the staffs at the following archives and libraries, and the individuals named here: American Philosophical Society; Amherst College Library; Elizabeth Joffrion and Judy Throm, Archives of American Art; Leo Baeck Institute; Sylvan Feit, Archivist, Baltimore Hebrew Congregation; Baltimore Museum of Art; Richard J. Wolfe, Curator of Rare Books and Manuscripts, Francis A. Countway Library of Medicine, Boston and Harvard Medical Libraries; Giuseppe Bisaccia, Curator of Manuscripts, Boston Public Library; Boston University; Caroline Rittenhouse, College Archivist, and Leo M. Dolenski, Canaday Library, Bryn Mawr College; California Historical Society Library; Anthony S. Bliss, Curator, Rare Books & Literary Manuscripts, and Richard Ogar, The Bancroft Library, University of California, Berkeley, and William M. Roberts, University Archivist, and Jodie Collins, Registrar's Office; Anne Caiger, University of California, Los Angeles Library; Nancy Zinn, former head of Special Collections, The Library and Center for Knowledge Management, University of California, San Francisco; Rutherford W. Witthus, Head of Archives,

Auraria Library, University of Colorado at Denver; Rare Book and Manuscript Library, Butler Library, Columbia University; Ronald J. Grele, Director, Oral History Collection, Columbia University; Olin Library, Cornell University; University of Delaware Library; Frick Art Reference Library; Getty Center for the History of Art and the Humanities; Houghton Rare Book and Manuscripts Library, Harvard University; Patrice Donoghue, Danielle Green, and James W. McCarthy, Harvard University Archives; Historical Society of Western Pennsylvania, Pittsburgh; Dale Reed, Hoover Institution Archives; Saundra Taylor, Curator of Manuscripts, The Lilly Library, Indiana University; Virginia Duvall North, Head Archivist, Jewish Historical Society of Maryland; Gerard Shorb, research associate, and Nancy McCall, Head Archivist, The Alan Mason Chesney Medical Archives of the Johns Hopkins Medical Institutions; Milton S. Eisenhower Library, Johns Hopkins University; James Stimpert, Head Archivist, and Brian Harrington, Ferdinand Hamburger, Jr., Archives, Johns Hopkins University; John F. Kennedy Library, Boston; Marine Biological Laboratory, Woods Hole, Massachusetts; Maryland Historical Society; Gail Stavitsky, Curator of American Art, The Montclair Museum of Art, Montclair, New Jersey; Rona Roob, Museum Archivist, and Janis Ekdahl, Acting Director of the Library, The Museum of Modern Art; Alyson Jeffrey, Archivist, The National Museum of the American Indian; Nebraska Jewish Historical Society staff; University of Nebraska Archives; New York City Surrogates Court Hall of Records; New York Public Library, Astor, Lenox, and Tilden Foundations, Berg Collection; Robert J. Bertholf, Curator, Poetry / Rare Books Collection, State University of New York, Buffalo; Newberry Library; William W. Sturm, Oakland History Room, Oakland Public Library; Robert A. Tibbetts, Curator of Rare Books & Manuscripts, Ohio State University Library; Nancy Shawcross, Curator of Manuscripts, Van Pelt Library, University of Pennsylvania; Frank Zabriskie, Hillman Library, University of Pittsburgh; John Sondheim, Enoch Pratt Free Library, Baltimore; Don Skemer, Curator, Department of Rare Books and Special Collections, Princeton University Libraries; Jane Knowles, College Archivist, Radcliffe College; Arthur and Elizabeth Schlesinger Library on the History of Women, Radcliffe College; University of Rochester; Judy Harvey Sahak, The Ella Strong Denison Library, Scripps College of the Claremont Colleges; Amy Hague and Karen Kukil, Sophia Smith Collection, and Maida Goodwin, Archives, Smith College; Linda Long, Stanford University Library Department of Special Collections; Syracuse University Library Department of Special Collections; Fiorella Superbi, Villa I Tatti; Linda Ashton, Assistant Curator, and Carlton Lake, Curator, Harry Ransom Humanities Research Center French Collections, and Cathy Henderson, Harry Ransom Humanities Research Center, The University of Texas at Austin; Courtney Page, Tulane University Library; Vassar College Library; Alderman Library, University of Virginia; Sharon Snow, Curator of Rare Books, Wake Forest University Library; Ruth Rafael, former Head Archivist, and Tova Gazit, Head Archivist, Western Jewish History Center, Judah Magnes Museum, Berkeley, California; State Historical Society of Wisconsin; University of Wisconsin–Madison Archives; Stanley Mallach, Golda Meir Library, University of Wisconsin–Milwaukee; and Judith Ann Schiff, Chief Research Archivist, Yale University Library.

I am obliged also to the many people who over the years granted interviews and answered my letters, telephone calls, e-mail—and the sometimes frantic requests that arrived anytime of the day or night: William Agee, Joseph Barry, Alan Bass, Avis Berman, Ellen Bloom, Barbara Boyer, Barbara Braun, Edward Burns, Robert L. Chapman, Edward T. Cone, the late Arthur Cullman, Carol De Boer–Langworthy, Frederick J. Dockstader, Betty Eckhaus, Alfred Luke Faust, Louise Goldman, Irene

Gordon, George E. Gross, Judith Gutman, Robert Bartlett Haas, Barbara Strachey Halpern, Richard Hamburger, Elizabeth Hardwick, Gilbert A. Harrison, Helen Lefkowitz Horowitz, Philip Kahn, Jr., Louise J. Kaplan, Alfred Kazin, Alice Lowenthal, Joan Mellen, Thomas C. Mendenhall, Cesare Scheggi Merlini, Paul Padgette, Barbara Gans Powell, Janeth Putzel, Rosalie Raffel, Rose Raffel, Henry M. Reed, Brenda Richardson, Walter Rideout, Elizabeth Rigby, Jean C. Roché, Ernest Samuels, Linda Simon, Joseph Solomon, Fred M. Stein, Jr., Julian S. Stein, Jr., Robert Stein, Samuel Steward, the late Virgil Thomson, Don Thurston, the late Elinor Ulman, Tony Vevers, Richard Wattenmaker, and Michael Wreszin.

I consistently imposed on a number of exceptional people who consistently greeted my impositions with patience, hospitality, and friendship: I owe the late Kay Boyle and the late Mary Frances Kennedy Fisher more than I can say. Likewise, the friendship of Sybille Bedford has been a rare privilege, as has that of Richard Howard, who, with his characteristic gift for giving, loaned me volume after Stein volume. The uncommon consideration shown me by Cecilia Stein Cullman, Ellen Hirschland, Donald C. Gallup, Betty Stein, and Daniel M. Stein has made the writing of this book conceivable, even when I feared it was not: they are a special, and specially knowledgeable, group. I am grateful also in this regard to the late Danny Robbins, who, in his final years, unstintingly gave of himself and his expertise on cubism whenever he could. Calman A. Levin, executor of the Gertrude Stein estate, deserves special mention for his attentive and thoughtful support.

I have profited enormously from the voluminous and stimulating Stein scholarship, some of which is mentioned in this book, and from those Stein scholars who have been helpful to me throughout. Among them, I thank Catharine R. Stimpson for her unflagging encouragement, her humor, and her brilliant expositions of the work of Gertrude Stein. I also thank Ulla E. Dydo for her lively attention to detail; she has mined the Stein archive with conscientious devotion. I am equally grateful to James Mellow, who answered my questions with the courtesy and accuracy that distinguish his writing. Their support has been essential to this project.

So has that of various colleagues and students at Union College. I am grateful to the administration for the leaves of absence granted me during the last six years and for several Humanities Faculty Development grants. Thanks also are due two former chairs of the English Department: Adrian Frazier, for enthusiasm, and Peter Heinegg, who, among other things, solved many problems of translation with the erudition for which he is justly known. I also thank the Interlibrary Loan staff and the librarians of Shaffer Library.

The zealous and talented students of my 1994 Gertrude Stein seminar provided one of my best teaching experiences at Union. My gratitude goes as well to former students such as Lori Barth Choudhury, who rescued me from despair in Pittsburgh when she located Norm Smith of Westview Cemetery and Harold Fate of Troy Hill Cemetery in Reserve Township, Pennsylvania. I am beholden for all she did, and did so well. Also at Union College, Peter Tobiessen and the Dana Scholarship Fund assisted my research with the very able and efficient Dana scholars Michael McLaughlin, Katherine Ambrosio, and Jennifer Manna. I am grateful for their precise handling of all manner of tasks. Thanks too to Tiphaine Le Duc, who painstakingly copied Nina Stein's letters into readable French. The ministrations of Thora Girke, English Department secretary, have been legion, critical, and kind; I am the lucky beneficiary of her skill. To all the student aides under her watch, I am likewise grateful.

I owe other colleagues a particular debt of gratitude for setting themselves and others unflinchingly high standards: thanks to my friends William M. Murphy and Merton M. Sealts. My colleagues at the New York University Biography Seminar have proved helpful, and I appreciate the comments that clarified my thinking when I read an early version of chapter 6 to them. Special thanks to Kenneth Silverman, codirector of the seminar, for inviting me to read this chapter and, more generally, for his dependably sensitive, cheering, and intelligent friendship. I also thank him and Frederick R. Karl for appointing me, along with them, seminar codirector. And I am very grateful to the talents of Herbert Leibowitz, who generously read three chapters of this book and offered wise and witty counsel.

For equally wise friendship, I thank Susan Yankowitz. Other friends, tried and true, include Erica Schoenberg, Jane Mallison, and Howard Tharsing and James Cooper, whose hospitality during one of my trips to Oakland was boundless. For providing, still after all these years, a room of my own in Schenectady, and for their unstinting thoughtfulness, I thank the entire Heinegg family. My agent, Elise Goodman, has been a fierce champion, and I am grateful to both her and her husband, Arnold. And to my in-laws, Julia and Angelo Dellario, for their consistent interest.

At Putnam, I am very fortunate to have been surrounded by ability, devotion, and talent. First and foremost, I thank the editor par excellence, Faith Sale; hers is a name to conjure with, rightly so. For her professional skill, her zest, her deep love of language and of the world, I salute her. And for exhibiting, at all times, true grace under pressure. Not surprisingly, an able coterie has gathered about her, including the excellent and unfaltering assistant editor Laura Gaines, and the copy editor supreme, Anna Jardine. For their wonderful diligence and support, I am deeply obliged. I also thank Karen Mayer and Gina Anderson for carefully attending to legal questions.

Last, I thank the one person who has remained advisor, editor, friend, lover, colleague, and confidant: my husband, Michael Dellaira, who makes possible more than I had ever dared dream.

Permissions

The author gratefully acknowledges permission from the following to reprint material in their control:

Archives of American Art, Smithsonian Institution, for material from the Andrew Dasburg and Grace Mott Johnson papers, Walter Pach papers, and Aline and Eero Saarinen papers, all owned by the Archives; from the Manierre Dawson papers; and from the Fanette Reider Meyers Morton Schamberg papers, owned by Murray Makransky and Morton Meyers

The Baltimore Museum of Art, Cone Archives, for unpublished writings and correspondence

The Bancroft Library, University of California, Berkeley, for published and unpublished manuscripts and correspondence

Edward Burns, for Alice B. Toklas material

University of California, Los Angeles, University Research Library, Department of Special Collections, for various writings

University of California, San Francisco, The Library and Center for Knowledge Management, Special Collections/University Archives, for correspondence

Columbia University, Butler Library, Rare Book and Manuscript Library, for writings and correspondence in the Manuel Komroff Papers, Random House Papers, Schaffner Papers, and Lincoln Steffens Papers

Columbia University, Oral History Research Office Collection, for Mahonri Young and Max Weber materials

Crown Publishers, for excerpts from *Appreciation: Painting, Poetry and Prose* by Leo Stein, copyright © 1947 by Leo Stein; and *Journey into the Self* by Leo Stein, edited by Edmund Fuller, copyright © 1950 by the Estate of Leo Stein

Mrs. Arthur W. Cullman for manuscripts, published and unpublished writings, and correspondence of Leo Stein

Alfred Luke Faust, for unpublished Neith Boyce and Hutchins Hapgood materials to be found at the Villa I Tatti or in the Yale Collection of American Literature, Beinecke Rare Book and Manuscript Library, Yale University

Donald Gallup, for Carl Van Vechten and Alfred Stieglitz materials and correspondence

Barbara Strachey Halpern, for Mary Berenson material

Harvard University Archives, for material from the student files of Leo D. Stein and Leon Mendez Solomons

The Johns Hopkins Medical Institutions, The Alan Mason Chesney Medical Archives, for correspondence

The Johns Hopkins University, Ferdinand Hamburger, Jr., Archives, for material on Michael Stein, and Record Group 13.010 of the Registrar, for Leo Stein application files

Lilly Library, Indiana University, Bloomington, for material from the Hannah Whitall Smith papers

The Montclair Art Museum, Montclair, New Jersey, Morgan Russell Archives, for Leo Stein–Morgan Russell correspondence

The Museum of Modern Art Archives, New York, for unpublished writings from the Alfred H. Barr, Jr., papers and the Margaret Potter papers

The Museum of Modern Art Library, New York, Morgan Russell Papers, for an autobiographical fragment of 1947

Princeton University Libraries, Department of Rare Books and Special Collections, Manuscripts Division, Hodder Papers, for correspondence and "The Degeneration of American Women"

Radcliffe College Archives, for unpublished material and correspondence

Random House, Inc., for excerpts from *Everybody's Autobiography* by Gertrude Stein, copyright © 1937 and renewed 1963 by Alice B. Toklas; *Lectures in America* by Gertrude Stein, copyright © 1935 and renewed 1963 by Alice B. Toklas; and *Selected Writings of Gertrude Stein* by Gertrude Stein, edited by Carl Van Vechten, copyright © 1946 by Random House, Inc.

Harry Ransom Humanities Research Center, Carlton Lake Collection, The University of Texas at Austin, for unpublished writings and correspondence

Jean C. Roché, for material from the papers of Henri-Pierre Roché

Estate of Annette Rosenshine, Paul Padgette, Literary Trustee, for excerpts from the unpublished autobiography "Life's Not a Paragraph" by Annette Rosenshine

Schlesinger Library, Radcliffe College, for excerpts from the Mildred Aldrich autobiography and material from the Inez Haynes Irwin Papers

Sophia Smith Collection, Smith College, Northampton, Massachusetts, for material from the Margaret Sanger Papers, Florence Sabin Papers, and Dorothy Reed Mendenhall Papers

Estate of Gertrude Stein, for manuscripts, published and unpublished writings (including "The Degeneration of American Women"), and correspondence

Estate of Ettie Stettheimer, Joseph Solomon, Executor, for a quotation from Stettheimer

Yale Collection of American Literature, Beinecke Rare Book and Manuscript Library, Yale University, for material from the Gertrude Stein papers, Leo Stein papers, Neith Boyce Hapgood and Hutchins Hapgood Collection, Marsden Hartley Collection, Mabel Dodge Luhan Collection, Henry McBride papers, Maurice Sterne papers, Ettie and Florine Stettheimer Collection, Alfred Stieglitz Archive, and Carl Van Vechten papers

Yale University Library, Manuscripts and Archives, Trigant Burrow Papers, for Trigant Burrow correspondence

The author likewise acknowledges the following for permission to reproduce photographs and artwork (referred to by page numbers) in their control:

The Bancroft Library: 42, 266; The Baltimore Museum of Art: 188, 220, 232 (Cone Collection), 356 (Cone Collection); George Eastman House: 277; Harvard University Archives: 68, 105; The Johns Hopkins Medical Institutions, The Alan Mason Chesney Medical Archives: 144; The Lilly Library: 161; Marine Biological Laboratory Archives: 100; The Metropolitan Museum of Art: 366; The Museum of Modern Art: 347; Princeton University Libraries: 134, 139; Réunion des Musées Nationaux: 275; Kate Sharp: 215, 216; Daniel M. Stein: 18 top, 30, 70, 129; University of Wisconsin–Madison Archives: 76; Yale Collection of American Literature, Beinecke Rare Book and Manuscript Library, Yale University: 6, 13, 18 bottom, 25, 35, 41, 47, 52, 54, 64, 84, 110, 114, 116, 121, 122, 156, 170, 172, 197, 198, 200, 208, 227, 236, 244, 248, 251, 254, 273, 286, 289, 294, 304, 323, 330, 331, 338, 376, 390, 391, 393 (copyright Carl Van Vechten), 404; Private collection: 309

Notes

Abbreviations for frequently cited books by Gertrude Stein, Leo Stein, and others are listed in the bibliography, as are full citations of partially cited works.

The following abbreviations are used for frequently cited names:

GS	Gertrude Stein	EC	Etta Cone
LS	Leo Stein	CC	Claribel Cone
NAS	Nina Auzias [Stein]	HH	Hutchins Hapgood
ABT	Alice B. Toklas	NBH	Neith Boyce Hapgood
SS	Sarah Stein	AH	Alfred Hodder
MS	Michael Stein	MMG	Mary Mackall Gwinn [Hodder]
FS	Fred Stein	MDL	Mabel Dodge [Luhan]
BB	Bernhard Berenson	MFW	Mabel Foote Weeks
MCB	Mary Costelloe Berenson	BW	Brenda Wineapple

For frequently cited libraries or collections, the following abbreviations are used:

AAA	Archives of American Art
AMC-JHM	The Alan Mason Chesney Medical Archives of The Johns Hopkins Medical Institutions
Bancroft	The Bancroft Library, University of California, Berkeley
BMA-CC	The Baltimore Museum of Art, Cone Archives
Butler	Butler Library, Columbia University
Claremont	Addison Metcalf Collection, The Ella Strong Denison Library, Scripps College of the Claremont Colleges, Claremont, California
COHC	Oral History Collection of Columbia University
FH-JHU	Ferdinand Hamburger, Jr., Archives, Johns Hopkins University
Houghton	Houghton Rare Book and Manuscripts Library, Harvard University
HRHRC	Harry Ransom Humanities Research Center, The University of Texas at Austin
HUA	Harvard University Archives
I Tatti	Harvard University Center for Renaissance Studies, Settignano, Italy
Lilly	The Lilly Library, Indiana University
MoMA	The Museum of Modern Art, New York City

PU   Special Collections, Princeton University
Schlesinger   Arthur and Elizabeth Schlesinger Library on the History of Women,
                     Radcliffe College
Smith   Sophia Smith Collection, Smith College
Sterling   Manuscripts and Archives, Sterling Memorial Library, Yale University
UCSF   Special Collections, The Library and Center for Knowledge Manage-
                     ment, University of California, San Francisco
YCAL   Yale Collection of American Literature, Beinecke Rare Book and Manu-
                     script Library, Yale University

     When quoting Gertrude and Leo Stein, I have followed the original text. Gertrude
Stein never used accents when writing French, and she developed her own style of
punctuation and spelling. I have left her texts as I found them. Where a word or phrase
was illegible in manuscripts, I have given my interpretation, if possible, in brackets;
if indecipherable, I have noted as such. I have avoided such devices and "[sic]" wherever possible, resorting to them only for purposes of clarity.
     While I was researching and writing *Sister Brother,* the voluminous Gertrude Stein
collection at the Beinecke Rare Book and Manuscript Library had not been recata-
logued and much of the Leo Stein collection remained unprocessed. As a consequence, some of my notations, especially of Leo Stein materials, may be unfamiliar
to the new researcher, who will no doubt profit greatly from the current reclassifica-
tion and processing of Gertrude Stein and Leo Stein papers.

Prologue

"Gertrude I never": LS to Annette Rosenshine, Feb. 12, 1947, Bancroft.
Alice Toklas remembered it: There are two similar versions of Toklas's story: Duncan,
     p. 115, and *WIR*, pp. 105–6.
"compounded of": Samuel Steward to BW, March 28, 1992.
"a place where": Marsden Hartley to GS, [Oct. 18, 1913], YCAL.
"possibly the most": Alfred H. Barr, Jr., *Matisse: His Art and His Public,* p. 57.
"There had never been": ABT to William Rogers, Aug. 10, 1947, YCAL.
"one we don't see!": Natalie Barney to GS, [June 1940], YCAL.
"declines further acquaintance": Quoted in James Mellow, *Charmed Circle,* p. 344.
"How She Bowed to Her Brother": The piece is dated 1931 in *P&P,* and there titled "She
     Bowed to Her Brother" (pp. 236–39). The manuscript itself is dated 1930 and called
     "How She Bowed to Her Brother"; the title makes the piece more a defense of her
     actions:
        "They were. There. That is to say. They were. Passing there. They were passing
     there. But not. On that day. And with this. To say. It was said. She bowed. To her
     brother. Which was. A fact.
        "If she bowed. To her brother. Which was. A fact. That is. If she bowed. Which.
     If she bowed. Which she did. She bowed to her brother.
        "Which she did. She bowed to her brother. Or rather. Which she did. She bowed
     to her brother. Or rather which she did she bowed to her brother.
        "She could think. Of how she was. Not better. Than when. They could say. Not.
     How do you do. To-day. Because. It is an accident. In suddenness. When there is.
     No stress. On their. Address. They do not address you. By saying. Rather. That they
     went by. And came again. Not. As. Or. Why."

Alice Toklas once remarked: ABT to Donald Sutherland, Sept. 21, 1951, YCAL.

"lioness" on the "crest": NBH to MCB, Dec. 10, 1927, I Tatti.

"what makes"; "the success": LIA, p. 172; MOA, p. 278.

1. Bes Almon

On the warm sunny morning: Amelia Stein, diary, June 16, 1884, Bancroft. Harry Stein was born in May 1866 and died the following autumn. The daughter was born in the autumn of 1869.

"It is now a bank": Amelia Stein, diary, June 16, 1884, Bancroft.

"If two little ones": EA, pp. 115, 133. See also, MOA, p. 743: "Mr. Hersland had always intended to have three children and as I was saying there had been two and these two had not gone on being living and so David Hersland came to be living and sometime later in some way he heard this thing when he was still quite a young one and he had it in him then to be certain that being living is a very queer thing, he being one being living and yet it was only because two others had not been ones going on being living. It was to him then that he was certain then that being living was a queer thing."

"We bought as many": EA, p. 146.

When their sixteen-year-old: Amelia Stein, diary, June 8, 1884, Bancroft.

They were going with their sister: See EA, p. 147, and GS to Robert Bartlett Haas, [Oct. 29, 1942], YCAL.

The highlight, for Gertrude: GS to Robert Bartlett Haas, [Oct. 29, 1942], YCAL.

For at ten: See ABT, p. 75. See also Duncan, p. 29, where Alice Toklas remarks that Gertrude Stein "had a happy childhood, an extraordinarily happy childhood, and even in East Oakland until a few years before she left, and then she said she had adolescence pains and it was frightful." In the same interview, Toklas recalls Stein's asking her whether she'd gone through the same painful thing. "Not I," answered Toklas. "Lucky you," Stein replied.

"Anyway we came home": EA, p. 147.

"unwell": Amelia Stein, diary, Nov. 5, 1884, Bancroft.

"What's the use": See EA, p. 75.

"the kind of people": EA, p. 75.

He was self-critical: LS, notebook [7], YCAL. While this biography was being written and prepared for publication, Leo Stein's notebooks had not yet been catalogued or numbered. The numbering system I have used here reflects only the numbers I gave to the notebooks during the course of my research. Where possible, I have indicated internal dates; I have indicated also that at least two of Stein's notebooks were given to YCAL apart from the original bequest, by a different source and at a later date. At the time of this writing, those notebooks were filed separately in a miscellaneous category.

"I remember my mother": LS, "Religion," unpublished lecture, YCAL.

"insignificant": LS to Trigant Burrow, June 9, 1941, Sterling.

"Grief can become": LS, notebook [7], YCAL.

"It is hard": Quoted in "Stein, Bergman and Cohn Families 1787–1954," p. 3.

"Yes, it was she": MOA, pp. 36, 37.

tens of thousands: See Arthur Hertzberg, *The Jews in America*, p. 103.

Articles pensively discussed: See Naomi W. Cohen, *Encounter with Emancipation*, p. 18, and Jacob R. Marcus, *United States Jewry, 1776–1985*, p. 21.

Baltimore was a convenient port: See Philip Kahn, Jr., *A Stitch in Time*, p. 20, and Adolf Guttmacher, *History of the Baltimore Hebrew Congregation*, p. 22.

The oldest son . . . "store-prince": See Isaac M. Wise, *Reminiscences,* p. 38.

The Baltimore Street location: Courtesy Philip Kahn, Jr.

"the prominent Jewish": Wise, *Reminiscences,* p. 182.

Union contracts: "Solomon Stein," *New York Herald Tribune,* June 17, 1902, p. 9.

But the war that brought: See William J. Evitts, *A Matter of Allegiances,* pp. 172–80.

"My mother used to": EA, pp. 147–48; WIHS, p. 6.

It is likely: BW interview with Janeth Putzel, Feb. 2, 1991.

"did not consider": EA, pp. 231, 145.

"Our family was among": LS to NAS, [1924], YCAL.

"old bourgeois Jews": See Marcus, *United States Jewry,* p. 27.

The Keysers appeared: See, for example, MOA, pp. 57ff.

"talent for money making": Rachel Keyser to GS, May 3, 1911, YCAL.

"originality of personality": See GS, notebooks B, 9, YCAL. "B" and "9," which refer to some early notebooks for *The Making of Americans,* are designations used by Leon Katz, who examined the notebooks and created a labeling system for them. I adhere to his system, used also in his 1963 dissertation, "The First Making of *The Making of Americans*: A Study Based on Gertrude Stein's Notebooks and Early Versions of Her Novel (1902–1908)," and in the typed transcriptions of the notebooks (available at YCAL).

Evidently sympathetic: Isaac M. Fein, "Baltimore Jews During the Civil War," p. 68.

they had mercantile: See, for example, Rachel Keyser to [MS], April 10, 1875, courtesy Mrs. A. Raffel: "It seems millinery business is the same trouble everywhere; while we were at the millinery store, a bonnet that had been sent to a lady to see, was sent back and not wanted. . . . This reminded me of the old days in Norfolk; but I don't think they bring so much old trash to be made over, although I can not judge from the little I've seen." See also Duncan, p. 41: "They had cousins who married to the far South, the deep South, with the exception of one branch of the family which was in North Carolina."

"The war broke out": Marcus, *Memoirs,* vol. 1, p. 299.

Daniel Stein "was Northern": JIS, p. 187.

Gertrude suggests her parents': See, for example, MOA, p. 43.

Moreover, the well-insulated: EA, p. 229.

At night: Quoted in *Pittsburgh: Its Industry and Commerce,* p. 118. Lincoln Steffens so liked the image that he used it in *Shame of the Cities.*

the town of Allegheny: Percy F. Smith, *Memory's Milestones,* p. 23. See also Jacob S. Feldman, *The Early Migration and Settlement of the Jews in Pittsburgh, 1754–1894,* p. 17.

to total at least $60,000: Allegheny census, 1870.

he loaned Meyer Hanauer: See Allegheny City Land Records, book 257, June 13, 1870, p. 257.

Leo . . . was born; "I was born and raised": The times of birth for Leo and Gertrude Stein are taken from miscellaneous uncatalogued notes, YCAL, and "Gertrude Stein Arrives and Baffles Reporters by Making Herself Clear," *The New York Times,* Oct. 25, 1934.

"I was born in Allegheny": GS to Harriet Lane Levy, n.d., YCAL.

"to correct a mistake": Allegheny City Land Records, book 302, Nov. 20, 1872, p. 90.

Daniel's great-grandson; "the two sisters-in-law": BW interview with Daniel M. Stein, July 9, 1992; ABT, p. 71.

Milly "forgave": GS, notebook 6, YCAL.

They were bound for Vienna: Rachel Keyser to family, March 1, 1875, courtesy Mrs. Rose Raffel.

"To the psychoanalyst": LS to Trigant Burrow, Oct. 31, 1927, Sterling.
when Gertrude claimed: GS to Marie Claire (*sic*), n.d., miscellaneous papers, YCAL.
That was how: LS to Trigant Burrow, n.d., Sterling.
"You can almost": Rachel Keyser to family, April 6, 1875, courtesy Mrs. Rose Raffel.
"getting along bravely": Rachel Keyser to family, Jan. 10, 1876, courtesy Mrs. Rose Raffel.
Milly and Rachel outfitted: Rachel Keyser to family, May 9, 1875, courtesy Mrs. Rose Raffel.
"as big and as gay": Rachel Keyser to family, March 10, 1875, courtesy Mrs. Rose Raffel.
"She can say something": Rachel Keyser to family, March 1 and 10, 1875, courtesy Mrs. Rose Raffel.
"Mikey['s] whole time": Quoted in Elizabeth Sprigge, "Journal in Quest of Gertrude Stein," unpublished typescript, p. 5, YCAL.
"learn something useful": Rachel Keyser to family, March 1, 1875, courtesy Mrs. Rose Raffel.
"a microscope": ABT, p. 72.
"baby . . . tries": Rachel Keyser to family, Feb. 25, 1876, courtesy Mrs. Rose Raffel.
Leo, himself becoming: JIS, p. 186.
"delighted that you had": Rachel Keyser to family, Feb. 1, 1875, courtesy Mrs. Rose Raffel.
"So you are a big gun": Daniel Stein to Hannah Keyser, April 10, 1875, courtesy Mrs. Rose Raffel.
"real April": Amelia Stein diary, March 29, 1879, Bancroft.
Even on days when rain: Amelia Stein, diary, July 13, 1879, Bancroft.
"a couple of novels": See JIS, p. 187.
"Of course Gertrude": Duncan, p. 2.
"big as all outdoors": See, for example, MOA, p. 142.
his relatives engulfed: BW interview with Mrs. Rose Raffel, April 30, 1992.
"hard up for money": Testimony of Solomon Stein, March 16, 1896, *Sternberger vs. Sternberger*, BB 2061, vol. 6, p. 899, Records Division, New York State Surrogates Court.
Probably he had been: Alice Toklas believed that the Steins visited Los Angeles and San Jose, which Daniel Stein did not like, before settling in Oakland. See Duncan, p. 31.
"rang the emergency bell": ABT, p. 73.
"How far is": "Oakland: The Athens of the Pacific," p. 17.
With its sunny: Mary McLean Olney, "Oakland, Berkeley, and the University of California, 1880–1895," p. 69.
"one of the most desirable": Oakland and Surroundings, Illustrated and Described, p. 118.
"Her father having taken": ABT, p. 74.
"It was very joyous": MOA, p. 90.
The generations after her: BW interview with Daniel M. Stein, July 9, 1992.
Leo said Daniel admired; "deep thinker": JIS, p. 187; MS to P. G. Byrne, [1934], YCAL.
In 1884 he listed: Oakland voting register, seventh ward, 1884, 1886, 1888, Oakland Public Library.
"In Uncle Tom's Cabin": LIA, p. 113.
"And then there was": LIA, p. 113.
"Quite a crowd": Amelia Stein, diary, May 11, 1884, Bancroft.
"My brother and myself": EA, p. 70.
When she wanted to win: ABT, p. 76.
A small clump of scrub oak: JIS, p. 205.
One of Gertrude's most pleasant: GS mentions the excursion in EA, pp. 293–94; the

story is reproduced in Rosalind Miller, *Gertrude Stein*, pp. 133–36. Miller notes erroneously that Stein had no brother named Harry.

"I receive $300.": Amelia Stein, diary, undated entry, 1881, Bancroft.

A jealous younger sister: MS, application to Johns Hopkins University, Sept. 18, 1893, FH-JHU. GS, notebook MA. In this entry, Stein describes the Hersland family, modeled on her own. She writes: "Fanny Hersland his [David Hersland / Daniel Stein] wife. little gentle woman always goes in closet to see Alfred's [Alfred Hersland / composite portrait that includes Michael Stein] clothes while he is in the East loves Alfred the best."

"In The Making": EA, pp. 69, 138.

"rich right" . . . *"She had"*: MOA, p. 133.

But Gertrude also describes: See, for example, GS, notebooks 5, 8, and *MOA*, pp. 252–65.

"Always then": MOA, p. 252. The governess in question was apparently a young woman named Mary Wiedersheim Gruenhagen, called Madeleine Weiman in Stein's notes for her novel and renamed Madeleine Wyman in the final version.

"When my mother died": EA, p. 138. An earlier, similar statement appears in *MOA*, p. 135, modulated by the assertion (p. 134) that Mrs. Hersland's children, husband, and servants forgot her "when all the troubles came to all of them in their later living . . . they all soon forgot that she had ever been important to them as a wife, a mother, a mistress living among them."

"The exercise": [GS], "Degeneration in American Women," [1902], PU. See Appendix.

"I always wanted": GS to Bennett Cerf, n.d. (copy sent to Carl Van Vechten), YCAL.

For their first cross-country: GS, *ABT*, manuscript, vol. 5, YCAL.

"was a very hearty eater": MS to Meyer Stein, Jan. 28, 1891, YCAL.

He suffered constantly: JIS, p. 188; see also LS, miscellaneous notes and fragments, YCAL.

For Leo's chronic: Amelia Stein, diary, Nov. 11, 20, and 23, 1882, private collection. Gertrude's notes for *The Making of Americans* and the book itself suggest that Daniel Stein experimented with all forms of "doctoring."

"I kick you": LS, miscellaneous notes and fragments, YCAL. See also *JIS*, p. 198.

So did the more aggressive: EA, p. 136.

"Of course my feelings": The quotation is taken from LS, miscellaneous notes and fragments, YCAL; a more polished and less personal version of the anecdote is in *JIS*, p. 132.

"this or that . . . I commonly": LS, miscellaneous notes and fragments, YCAL.

"I once met": LS, miscellaneous notes and fragments, YCAL.

To avoid meeting: JIS, p. 198.

"Dancing with Sadie Hardy": LS, notebook [2], YCAL.

"I managed": JIS, p. 188.

In a school English examination: LS to Trigant Burrow, June 9, 1941, Sterling.

"I do feel": GS to François Lachenal, [1943–1944], YCAL.

Although Gertrude and Leo liked: Amelia Stein, diary, March 18, 1885, Bancroft.

As the treatments: Amelia Stein, diary, Dec. 6, 27, and 21, 1885, Bancroft.

The next summer: Oakland Enquirer, July 19, 1887, p. 3.

2. Tempers We Are Born with

"Friends came": GS, notebook 11, YCAL.

"Their father": Elizabeth Sprigge, interview with MFW, "Journal in Quest of Gertrude Stein," unpublished typescript, p. 114, YCAL.

"They had a great influence": Duncan, p. 37.

They concocted: EA, pp. 281–82; JIS, pp. 190, 185.

"It is rare": LS to NAS, [1924], YCAL.

He was like a German Jewish: BW interview with Daniel M. Stein, July 9, 1992; Daniel Stein, "Mike's Portrait," unpublished typescript, Claremont.

"party—sitting around": Grace Davis Street to GS, Aug. 13, 1933, YCAL.

Simon was the child: Elizabeth Sprigge, *Gertrude Stein*, p. 5; Rachel Keyser to family, March 3, 1876, courtesy Mrs. Rose Raffel.

"There always was": EA, p. 136.

His parents considered: Amelia Stein, diary, May 19, 1882, courtesy Mrs. Rose Raffel.

"You may rest assured": Daniel Stein to Simon Stein, June 13, 1890, YCAL.

"Simon I liked": EA, p. 137.

She told Bertha's son: BW interview with Mrs. Rosalie Raffel, Jan. 6, 1991.

Alice Toklas remembered: ABT to Robert Bartlett Haas, March 18, 1952, YCAL.

But the story: GS, notebook B, YCAL.

"definitely sub-normal": LS to NAS, [1924], YCAL.

Relatives remember her: BW interview with Mrs. Rosalie Raffel, Jan. 6, 1991; with Daniel M. Stein, July 9, 1992.

In the summer of 1890: Oakland *Enquirer*, June 13, 1890, p. 2.

Years later: See, for example, Matilda Brown to GS, Dec. 6 and Jan. 30, 1896, YCAL.

"Hersland feels": GS, notebook MA, YCAL; *EA*, pp. 135, 137.

"grinds her teeth": GS, notebook C, YCAL; *EA*, p. 135.

"pure female": GS, notebook J, YCAL.

"The sexual character": GS, notebook DB, YCAL.

"Gertrude said she had": Duncan, p. 40.

"In the Red Deeps": The story includes also a suggestive reference to Shelley's *The Cenci*. For an early, and unsurpassed, treatment of the incest theme in Stein's story, see Richard Bridgman, *Gertrude Stein in Pieces*, pp. 24–26.

As she lies in bed: GS, "In the Red Deeps," Oct. 10, 1894, YCAL; see also Rosalind Miller, *Gertrude Stein*, p. 109. In *ABT*, p. 75, Stein notes that the subject of this story, her first, is the turmoil she experienced during adolescence.

"my sister she is not": "Mrs. Emerson," *Reflection*, p. 44.

"Her old sense": Hortense Sanger first appears in "In the Library," March 22, 1895, YCAL, described as the "first chapter of a connected work." See also chapters 1 and 3 of this book.

Simultaneously excited: GS, theme 14, May 8, 1895, YCAL; Miller, *Gertrude Stein*, p. 151.

He dreamed of Bertha: JIS, p. 224.

"I could not give": LS, notebook [5], YCAL.

Not until adulthood: LS, notebook [5], YCAL.

Years after they had: Grace Davis Street to GS, April 23, 1914, YCAL.

"eating fruit": EA, p. 86.

"It was no longer": EA, p. 87.

"definitely a brighter": LS to the editor, *Time*, May 12, [1933], draft, YCAL.

"Did Leo write": Matilda Brown to GS, April 25, 1910, YCAL.

"The jew stuff": LS to HH, [1939], YCAL.

In 1886 . . . Frank Collins: William M. Kramer, "The Emergence of Oakland Jewry," Oct. 1978, p. 79.

"Oh, those damned": JIS, p. 199.

"Luna, lunae": Matilda Brown to GS, July 2, 1933, YCAL.

she and Leo devoured: ABT, p. 74.

Since Daniel: MS to P. G. Byrne, [1934], YCAL; *ABT*, p. 74; *App*, p. 141.

"found a good many books": EA, p. 72.

"three years' ": JIS, p. 216; LS, "Statement of Previous Education," HUA.

"student at large": William M. Roberts to BW, April 7, 1992. For his courses at Berkeley, see Leo Stein's transcript, University of California, 1889–1892, courtesy Jodie Collins, Verification, Registrar's Office, University of California, Berkeley. See also LS, "Statement of Previous Education," HUA.

Not only did he read: LS, notebook [12], YCAL.

But it is unlikely: Alice Toklas said Stein attended Oakland High School for only one year (see Duncan, p. 36), but Stein in *EA*, p. 87, mentions a second year there. Stein probably did not attend more than two years, if that. Although she did not graduate from Oakland High, there is no reason to suppose she stopped attending school altogether, as Toklas claimed.

No reliable record exists of Stein's education after high school and before college. In *MOA*, p. 128, she writes of the Hersland children that "sometimes one or the other stopped going to school to try some other way of education that their father then thought would be good then for that one of them."

"dark and dreadful": WIHS, p. 14; *SW*, p. 70; *EA*, p. 138.

Using an autobiographical incident: "In the Library," March 22, 1895, YCAL; Miller, *Gertrude Stein*, pp. 141–42. See also *EA*, p. 116: "In the bath this morning I was drumming on the side of the bathtub, I like moving around in the water in a bathtub, and I found myself drumming the Chopin funeral march and I might have stopped doing it but I went on because they used to play it on Golden Gate Avenue in San Francisco and I was worrying then about identity and memory and eternity."

"Our daddy's way": GS, notebook 11, YCAL.

"that was no way": See *MOA*, p. 423.

"My father whenever": WIHS, 3.

"Fathers are depressing": EA, pp. 150, 132.

"Mike stands up": GS, notebook 2, YCAL.

"Daddie [was] lending": GS, notebook 6, YCAL.

When a friend of Gertrude's: See GS, notebook 12, YCAL.

so Gertrude's notebooks suggest: GS, miscellaneous notes and fragments for *MOA*, 91, YCAL.

It was primarily Michael: GS, notebook 12, YCAL. See also GS, notebook 2, YCAL: "Fred's father [Solomon Stein] attempt to remarry   Mrs. Meininger helps him but he dies before it is completed   scenes like ours   Fred speaks to him as Mike did. Bird works on him as I did." The character Herman Dehning was based largely on Solomon Stein, Daniel's brother, who died before his wife. The attempted remarriage seems to refer to Daniel's; see also GS, notebook MA, YCAL.

Angry with Gertrude: GS, notebooks 11, MA, YCAL; *EA*, p. 158.

"A hell of a hoe": LIA, p. 65.

"For hammering": LS, notebook [16], YCAL.

One Saturday: See "Death of a Capitalist Residing in East Oakland," *Oakland Enquirer*, Jan. 26, 1891, p. 2, in which one daughter, presumably Gertrude, is missing from the count of Daniel Stein's survivors. Evidently she was not at home when the reporters prepared the story.

Leo went upstairs: "Oakland News: Death of Daniel Stein," *San Francisco Chronicle*, Jan. 25, 1891, p. 18.

"Problem of nutrition": GS, notebook C, YCAL.

"many prominent men": MS to Meyer Stein, Jan. 28, 1891, YCAL.

Everything would be divided: "A Peculiar Will," *Oakland Enquirer,* Jan. 31, 1891, p. 7. See also "Large Estate," *Oakland Enquirer,* July 8, 1891, p. 5.

There was also a pair: Will of Daniel Stein, notes by Elizabeth Sprigge, Claremont. See also SS to GS, Sept. 22, 1895, YCAL.

"a man who frightened": GS, notebook J, YCAL; *EA,* p. 150.

"Later in their life": MOA, p. 51.

"Once an angry man": The anecdote, which introduces the published *Making of Americans,* is based on a similar one in the sixth chapter of Aristotle's *Nicomachean Ethics.* See *MOA,* p. 3, and Aristotle, *Nicomachean Ethics,* trans. Martin Ostwald (Indianapolis: Bobbs-Merrill, 1962), p. 191.

According to Gertrude's: EA, p. 143.

Before they left: Grace Davis Street to GS, Aug. 13, 1933. Although Street ties the story to the 1885 move to Tenth Street, Milly Stein never mentioned in her diary a Stein brother's visit, an event so unusual and disruptive she surely would have noted it in her daily entries of March and April 1885. Street herself does not mention Milly Stein at all. The incident took place probably after Daniel Stein's death, the only other time when the Steins moved, and a fitting occasion for a visit from a Stein relative. (Gertrude Stein alludes to such visits but suggests they occurred after the move to San Francisco; see *EA,* p. 144.) Since the event in question could not reasonably have taken place before Daniel's death, I assume Grace Street confused Michael Stein with his father; I include her account of the event here to show what were commonly held assumptions about the older male Steins.

Gertrude, however, felt: See Duncan, p. 38.

"hangs down out": Miller, *Gertrude Stein,* p. 133. The passage comes from a composition written in March 1895 and corresponds to the following, written more than forty years later: "It was frightening when the first comet I saw made it real that the stars were worlds and the earth only one of them, it is like the Old Testament, there is God but there is no eternity. . . . Then there was the fear, of dying, anything living knows about that" (*EA,* p. 115).

"She would go": GS, notebook 10, YCAL, identifies the incident as experienced by Stein. See also *MOA,* pp. 414, 424.

But as he explained: LS, application, Committee of the Faculty of Arts and Sciences on Special Students in Harvard College, HUA.

Two former professors: Alexis Lange to Harvard College, May 17, 1892, and Thomas Bacon to Harvard College, May 17, 1892, HUA.

Leo declined: LS to W. M. Davis, June 25, 1892, HUA.

By the middle of June: San Francisco directory, 1892, 1893; LS to W. M. Davis, June 25, 1892, HUA.

As Gertrude would put it: GS, "In the Library," March 22, 1895, YCAL; see Miller, *Gertrude Stein,* p. 142.

In an extravagant: Oakland Enquirer, June 2, 1892, p. 2.

Bertha Stein said: BW interview with Mrs. Rose Raffel, April 30, 1992.

"ugliest man": Isidor Blum, *The Jews of Baltimore,* p. 199; *EA,* p. 153.

"Baltimore, sunny": GS, composition, March 21, 1895, YCAL; Miller, *Gertrude Stein,* p. 139.

Gertrude and Leo, more than: BW interview with Mrs. Rosalie Raffel, Jan. 6, 1991.

"was very Californian": Duncan, p. 8.

When these little aunts: Manuscript pages for *ABT,* YCAL; a version of this incident appears also in GS, *Ida, A Novel* (1941; rpt. New York: Vintage), p. 12.

Again they felt: GS, notebook 2, YCAL.

This community: BW interview with Mrs. Rosalie Raffel, Jan. 6, 1991.
Ambivalent about the standard: LS, miscellaneous notes and fragments, YCAL.

3. Too Darn Anxious to Be Safe

"Eastern colleges": GS, notebook 11, YCAL.
"Yesterday I saw": LS to MS, Sept. 12, 1892, YCAL.
"Can't you please": LS to MS, Sept. 12, 1892, YCAL.
"Our relationship": FS, unpublished reminiscences, YCAL.
Reciting his Omar Khayyám: LS to FS, Dec. 20, 1894, YCAL.
"nothing special": LS, *JIS*, p. 205; LS to FS, Jan. 6, 1893, YCAL.
"Groups are like": Samuel Eliot Morison, *Three Centuries of Harvard*, p. 343.
Leo did well: Daniel Gregory Mason, "At Harvard in the Nineties," p. 62.
"various degrees": FS, unpublished reminiscences, YCAL.
Together, he and Leo: FS, unpublished reminiscences, YCAL.
"Jews are better off": Marcia G. Synott, *A Social History of Admissions at Harvard, Yale, and Princeton, 1900–1930*, p. 247.
"seldom or never"; was Jewish: William James, "The True Harvard," *Memories and Studies*, p. 353; Nitza Rosovsky, *The Jewish Experience at Harvard*, p. 72.
"Of course I'm only": AH to MMG, Jan. 24, 1899, PU.
"The bad manners": AH, autobiographical writings, PU.
"slight smell"; Wendell . . . Norton: George Santayana, *Character and Opinion in the United States*, p. 61; Van Wyck Brooks, *New England*, p. 420.
"I went to college": LS, "It is common for believers . . . ," unpublished lecture, p. 3, YCAL.
"not much to tell": LS to FS, n.d., YCAL.
Reasonably comfortable; "prettiest": ABT, p. 75; Rachel Keyser to GS, May 3, 1911, YCAL.
"once loaned": GS, manuscript notebook for *EA*, vol. 8, YCAL.
Dubbed "the Dowager": Hortense Guggenheimer Moses to GS, Jan. 8, [1905], YCAL.
"In swished": Harriet Lane Levy to ABT, Aug. 4, 1911, YCAL.
Aunt Pauline beheld: GS, notebook MA, YCAL; *ABT*, p. 172.
"bravest and strongest": GS, postscript, LS to FS, July 19, 1896, YCAL.
that arrogant Gertrude: Lillian Wing Smith, Mabel Earle, and Louise Earle, "In Memoriam: Gertrude Stein," p. 21; see also Dorothy Elia Howells, *A Century to Celebrate*, p. 43.
Rather, by the spring: See also, for example, Inez Cohen to GS, [June 1896], YCAL.
Gertrude wanted: Smith et al., "In Memoriam," p. 21.
Downstairs in the reception: Radcliffe College yearbook, 1898, Radcliffe College Archives.
"not uniformly beautiful": *Boston Sunday Journal*, Nov. 6, 1898.
"living in a boarding house": EA, p. 154.
"everybody was New England": EA, p. 154.
"intolerance": GS, composition, Dec. 1, 1894, YCAL; quoted in Rosalind Miller, *Gertrude Stein*, p. 119.
Adele and Ben: After graduation, Adele Oppenheimer went to Columbia for her master's degree and then on to research in bacteriology for the U.S. Department of Health; Ben Oppenheimer took a medical degree from the Columbia College of Physicians and Surgeons, where he became clinical professor of medicine.
"Ruddy": Leo Friedman to GS, Oct. 28, 1895, and Feb. 14, 1896, YCAL.

"the most brilliant"; "rational": LS to FS, Dec. 20, 1894, YCAL; GS, notebook B, YCAL.

"to identify" . . . *"to be a Jew"*: Third Forensic, March 7, 1896, YCAL.

"before I had become": MFW, "Foreword," *JIS*, typescript, [1949], YCAL.

"A Jew admitted": Third Forensic, March 7, 1896, YCAL.

For she always: See, for example, Elizabeth Sprigge, "Journal in Quest of Gertrude Stein," unpublished typescript, p. 66, YCAL.

Later she would associate: See Leon Solomons to GS, Jan. 4, 1898, YCAL. For the association of Jews with a special form of cerebration, see GS, notebook C, YCAL, and chapter 17 of this book.

"Miss Stein spoke": Carl Van Vechten, "At Gertrude Stein's with Fania Marinoff," uncatalogued notes, July 5, 1914, YCAL.

"was given by": Santayana, *Character and Opinion*, pp. 59–60.

"Clever and ingenious": Hugo Münsterberg, *American Traits*, p. 130.

His attitude: Hugo Münsterberg to GS, June 10, 1895, YCAL.

She explained such quantity: Smith et al., "In Memoriam," p. 21.

And so Gertrude spent: Records, 1897–1898, Radcliffe College Archives.

Left more or less: Mabel Vaughn Pugh, "In the Fall of 1893," *Radcliffe Quarterly*, 31, no. 3 (Aug. 1947), pp. 6–7.

"the part of English": GS to Robert Bartlett Haas, Jan. [23], 1938, YCAL.

Recently arrived; "an extraordinarily": Rollo Walter Brown, *Harvard Yard in the Golden Age*, p. 49; William James to Josiah Royce, June 22, 1892, quoted in Phyllis Keller, *States of Belonging*, p. 26.

But he felt that: Münsterberg's background and this allegation are discussed in Keller, *States of Belonging*, especially pp. 68–118.

The laboratory: For an overview of Münsterberg's psychological and philosophical theories, see Bruce Kuklick, *The Rise of American Philosophy*, Cambridge, Massachusetts, pp. 198–209. For a discussion of parallelism, see Nathan G. Hale, *Freud and the Americans*, vol. 1, pp. 54–55.

"degenerates": Hugo Münsterberg, *Psychology and Life*, p. 34.

James thought: Herbert Pope, class notes, "Professor James' Psychology," [1894], Harvard University Archives; Brown, *Harvard Yard*, p. 49.

Students sat: Hugo Münsterberg, "The New Psychology and Harvard's Equipment for Teaching It," pp. 201–09.

"affable"; "a man of deep": Knight Dunlap, in Carl Murchison, ed., *A History of Psychology in Autobiography*, vol. 2, p. 41; Mary Whiton Calkins, in Murchison, ed., *History of Psychology*, vol. 1, p. 33.

"friendly, comradely": Calkins, in Murchison, ed., *History of Psychology*, vol. 1, p. 33.

"The Corporation": Quoted in Kuklick, *Rise of American Philosophy*, p. 590. Calkins commented: "My natural regret at the action of the Corporation has never clouded my gratitude for the incomparably greater boon which they granted me—that of working in the seminaries and the laboratory of the great Harvard teachers. My debt, both academic and personal, to these men, to James, Royce, Palmer, and Münsterberg, may be acknowledged but can never be repaid." See Calkins, in Murchison, ed., *History of Psychology*, vol. 1, p. 35.

"I do still": GS to Robert Bartlett Haas, Jan. [23], 1938, YCAL.

"natural believer": EA, pp. 243, 242.

"Then I went": LIA, p. 137.

"She had": Quoted in Elizabeth Sprigge, "Gertrude Stein's American Years," p. 49.

"neither flesh": GS, composition, Nov. 22, 1894, YCAL; quoted in Miller, *Gertrude Stein*, pp. 115–16.

"was absolutely" . . . "until it became" . . . "What set": Smith et al., "In Memoriam,"
    p. 21.
"wise"; "habit of taking": Porter Sargent to LS, May 7, 1947, YCAL; Howard Gans to
    LS, March 6, 1946, YCAL.
"rich and poor": "The Wendell Phillips Club," *Boston Daily Traveller,* Oct. 16, 1893,
    HUA.
Leo spoke often: Minutes, Wendell Phillips Club, Nov. 3, 1893–April 20, 1894, HUA.
"I've got lots": LS to FS, [fall 1893], YCAL.
"I very rarely"; "with tolerable": LS to FS, [1893–1894], YCAL; LS to FS, Jan. 23, 1894,
    YCAL.
"As a young man": MFW, "Foreword," *JIS,* p. vii.
"a new Annex girl": LS to FS, [Feb.–March 1894], YCAL.
"midyears": LS to FS, Jan. 23, 1894, YCAL.

4. To Know Thyself

In San Francisco: Harriet Lane Levy, "Reminiscences," unpublished memoir, Bancroft.
"She jumped": "The Great Enigma," Dec. 29, 1894, YCAL; quoted in Rosalind Miller,
    Gertrude Stein, p. 124.
Gertrude and Leo first met: Elizabeth Sprigge, "Journal in Quest of Gertrude Stein,"
    unpublished typescript, YCAL, p. 134.
"You & I": SS to GS, Oct. 29, [1893], YCAL.
"He certainly": SS to GS, Oct. 20, [1899], YCAL.
"Tell Leo": SS to GS, Oct. 11, [1893], YCAL.
"must not forget": SS to GS, Oct. 11, [1893], YCAL.
"difficult" . . . "temerity": SS to GS, Sept. 28, 1896, YCAL.
"I know it will": SS to GS, Oct. 11, [1893], YCAL.
"Mike is exceedingly": SS to GS, March 9, 1895, YCAL.
"Why don't": Rachel Keyser to GS, Dec. 7, 1912, YCAL.
Sarah and Michael's: Records were destroyed by the 1906 earthquake. Michael Stein
    gives 1894 as the date of his marriage to Sarah Samuels in a Johns Hopkins alumni
    questionnaire, FH-JHU. In a letter to Fred Stein, Leo mentions that "Mike and
    Sarah are going to be married on the first of March instead of June" (Jan. 23, 1894,
    YCAL).
"Her elder brother's": ABT, p. 52.
"Gertrude is deep": LS to FS, Dec. 20, 1894, YCAL.
"Hardly a law": William James, *The Will to Believe and Other Essays in Popular Psy-
    chology,* pp. 55, 60, 56.
"Is life": GS, composition, April 25, 1895, YCAL; quoted in Miller, *Gertrude Stein,*
    p. 146.
"bass-note": James, *Will to Believe,* p. 32.
"The students of English 22": Franklin Walker, *Frank Norris,* p. 93.
"Are we really": GS, "The Temptation," May 22, 1895, YCAL; quoted in Miller, *Gertrude
    Stein,* pp. 152–55. Originally dated May 14, 1895, the story was rewritten; it seems
    to be a continuation of Stein's March 22, 1895, composition "In the Library."
"Somehow": SS to GS, [late fall 1894], YCAL.
Or at least: See Vern L. Bullough and Martha Voght, "Homosexuality and Its Confu-
    sion with the 'Secret Sin' in Pre-Freudian America," pp. 143–55.
"It seems": SS to GS, [late fall 1894], YCAL.
"simple honest": LS, notebook [6]; quoted in *JIS,* p. 125. See also Nancy Cott, "Pas-
    sionlessness," pp. 219–36.

"in our modern system": [GS], "Degeneration in American Women," [1902], PU. See Appendix.

"I know": GS, composition, Dec. 20, 1894, YCAL; quoted in Miller, *Gertrude Stein,* p. 122.

"Cambridge atmosphere": Laura Oppenheimer and Inez Cohen to GS, Sept. 13, 1895, YCAL.

"Do send me": SS to GS, June 15, [1896], YCAL.

"one of our chief": Arthur Lachman, "Gertrude Stein As I Knew Her," unpublished manuscript, YCAL.

"She loved discussion": Lillian Wing Smith, Mabel Earle, and Louise Earle, "In Memoriam: Gertrude Stein," p. 21.

"seemed to charge": LS to FS, April 4, 1895. GS, notes appended to "In the Library," March 22, 1895, YCAL; quoted in Miller, *Gertrude Stein.* p. 140.

"as well as" . . . *"I've got"*: LS to FS, Dec. 3, 1894, YCAL.

"I hope": Hugo Münsterberg to GS, June 10, 1895, YCAL.

He emphatically: Hugo Münsterberg to Mary Coes, July 18, 1895, Radcliffe College Archives.

"With best regards": Hugo Münsterberg to GS, June 10, 1895, YCAL.

"a definite mark": ABT, p. 77.

"The lad": Jacob Voorsanger, "Leon Mendez Solomons (1873–1900)," p. 142.

Leon's great-grandfather: N. Taylor Phillips, "The Levy and Seixas Families of Newport and New York," p. 206.

"I do not need": Leon Mendez Solomons, application for fellowship in the Graduate School, academic year 1897–1898, HUA.

"a man of unusual": Lachman, "Gertrude Stein."

"I regard": Quoted in Voorsanger, "Solomons," p. 143.

"one of the five": Quoted in Voorsanger, "Solomons," p. 143.

minor surgery: An appendectomy best fits the profile of the operation discussed in the various newspaper articles and eulogies written after Solomons's death. Stein herself never mentioned the cause but did plan that one character in an early version of *The Making of Americans* would die of appendicitis. See GS, notebook MA, YCAL.

Ill for five: See Voorsanger, "Solomons," p. 144, and "Leon Mendez Solomons," *American Israelite*, March 1, 1900, p. 5; *Nebraska State Journal,* Feb. 3, 1900, p. 6; and *San Francisco Chronicle,* Feb. 6, 1900, p. 7. On the basis of his reading of Gertrude Stein's notebooks, Leon Katz attributed Solomons's death to cancer, misinterpreting "cancer" for what seems more probably the word "career," which makes sense in the following sentence, GS, notebook 2, YCAL: "Use for Leon the part about 29 years old when he decided on career [cancer] ultimately separates him from Bird ultimately kills himself, through operation like Leon's." Moreover, there is no evidence suggesting that Solomons in any way "willed" his own death, or that Stein believed as much.

However, his friend: Arthur Lachman to Donald C. Gallup, Aug. 4, 1952, courtesy Donald C. Gallup.

Stunned: Report of Special Committee on Resolutions concerning the death of Dr. Leon M. Solomons, n.d., University Archives, University of Nebraska at Lincoln.

"Ever since": William James to GS, Oct. 17, 1900, YCAL.

"when he gets": GS, notebook 2, YCAL.

It was an offer: See Francis Pollak to GS, [summer 1895], YCAL.

But Leo: See LS to GS, Aug. 19, 1895, YCAL.

"Even if": Laura Oppenheimer to GS, Sept. 8, 1895, YCAL.

"I can see": Leslie W. Hopkinson, in A. W. W. Allen, SC 1935, folder 10, Radcliffe
    College Archives.
As secretary: See Harvard Graduate Magazine (1895–1896), p. 599, HUA. See also
    George Santayana to GS, n.d., YCAL; Charles C. Everett to GS, Nov. 19 and 29,
    1895, YCAL; G. Stanley Hall to GS, Jan. 14, 1896, YCAL; Josiah Royce to GS, March
    27, 1896, YCAL.
Gertrude nonetheless shared: See, for example, Leon Solomons to GS, April 5, 1897,
    YCAL, in response to a recent letter from her: "Am not surprised that [James] Lough
    liked Metaphysics. His paper on intensity before the Congress showed a strong lean-
    ing that way. If his Thesis is in the same spirit I imagine it will be enthusiastically
    received by the department. Shouldn't wonder but what they make him a profes-
    sor on the spot. Was glad to see Witmer kick for a separation of Metaphysics and
    Psychology in the Society."
"Metaphysics!": Boris Sidis, "The Nature and Principles of Psychology," p. 55.
"Sidis was": EA, p. 265.
"That in order": Josiah Royce, Outlines of Psychology, pp. 267–68.
"This is a purely": Leon Solomons, "The Saturation of Colors," p. 55.
"To call": Leon Solomons to GS, Oct. 26, [1896], YCAL.
For her part: See Howard Gans to GS, Feb. 13, 1896, YCAL.
their next major project: See Leon Solomons, "Discrimination in Cutaneous Sensa-
    tions." GS may have been one of his subjects.
"alternate personality": William James, Manuscript Lectures, p. 71.
"Who shall": James, Manuscript Lectures, p. 83.
"post-hypnotic": William James, Memories and Studies, pp. 155–56.
"The phenomena": Alfred Binet, Alterations of Personality, p. 191.
"What the upper": William James, "The Hidden Self," p. 369.
Not as intrigued: See Lachman, "Gertrude Stein."
"Never reject": Robert Bartlett Haas, "Gertrude Stein Talking—A Transatlantic Inter-
    view," 9 (Winter 1964), p. 47.
"I am a victim": Quoted in Ralph Barton Perry, The Thought and Character of William
    James, vol. 2, p. 207.
"Professor James": Harvard Advocate, 58 (1894–1895), p. 16.
"It was suggested": EA, pp. 266–67.
"If he [the subject]": Leon Solomons and Gertrude Stein, "Normal Motor Automatism,"
    p. 503.
"I did not think": EA, p. 267.
"to reproduce": Solomons and Stein, "Normal Motor Automatism," p. 493.
"we may both": Solomons and Stein, "Normal Motor Automatism," p. 510–11.
"If the object": Francis Pollak to GS, [June 1897], YCAL.
"Solomons reported": EA, p. 267.
"Much obliged": SS to GS, [Nov. 1896], YCAL.
an old high school friend wrote: Matilda Adler to GS, Dec. 6, 1896, YCAL.
"Leon like me": GS, notebooks 11, 2, YCAL.
"Likes imitate": GS, notebook B, YCAL.
"characteristically unpleasant": GS, notebook 2, YCAL.
"His not thin": GS, notebook I, YCAL.
"Dear Professor James": ABT, p. 79.
"women were": Quoted in Sprigge, "Journal in Quest of Gertrude Stein," p. 29.
When asked: Mary Coes to William James, Nov. 16, 1896, and William James to Mary
    Coes, n.d., Radcliffe College Archives.

"Now for philosophy": *ABT*, p. 80.

"Imagine": LS to Ettie Stettheimer, Jan. 18, 1934, YCAL; quoted in *JIS*, p. 135.

"How happy": Margaret Sterling Snyder to GS, April 29, 1896, YCAL.

Gertrude Stein would go: SS to GS, April 18, [1896], YCAL.

5. The Feminine Half

"One can understand": LS to MFW, Aug. 28, 1904.

"Three days!": LS to Bird Sternberger, June 27, 1895, YCAL.

"in spite of"; "you really": LS to Solomon and Pauline Stein, Aug. 17, 1895, YCAL; LS to GS, July 30, 1895, YCAL.

"No more": LS to GS, July 30, 1895, YCAL.

"My interest": App, pp. 140–42; *JIS*, p. 205; *LIA*, p. 65.

"There were": App, pp. 141, 102.

"trying to get": LS to GS, July 30, 1895, YCAL.

"you've got": LS to Bird Sternberger, Aug. 30, 1895, YCAL.

"level-headed": LS to Bird Sternberger, Aug. 30, 1895, YCAL.

"services": Quoted in Ernest Samuels, *Bernard Berenson: The Making of a Connoisseur*, p. 101. I retain the pre–World War I spelling of Berenson's first name.

Notice: LS to FS, July 18, 1896, YCAL.

"It is one": LS to Bird Sternberger, Aug. 30, 1895, YCAL.

"perhaps the greatest": App, p. 128.

"I'd rather"; "a durn fool": LS to Bird Sternberger, Aug. 30, 1895, YCAL.

"made of color"; prepared him: LS to BB or MCB, [1907], I Tatti; App, p. 145.

Two months: LS to Bird Sternberger, Aug. 30, 1895, YCAL.

"I saw it": App, p. 144–45.

"I spend": LS to GS, Sept. 7, 1895, YCAL.

To his sister: LS to GS, Sept. 7, 1895, YCAL.

Michael Stein: See MS, postscript, SS to LS, May 29, 1896, YCAL.

"when they have": EA, p. 145. The incident is recorded also in Gertrude Stein's notebooks.

"He wants Fred": LS to GS, Aug. 19, 1895, YCAL.

"For goodness sakes": LS to GS, Sept. 7, 1895, YCAL.

Solomon's daughter: Testimony of Louis Sternberger, *Sternberger vs. Sternberger*, BB 2061, vol. 1, pp. 783–84, Records Division, New York State Surrogates Court.

a trial date: See testimony of Solomon Stein, March 16, 1896, *Sternberger vs. Sternberger*, BB 2061, vol. 4, p. 960, Records Division, New York State Surrogates Court.

"Do you remember": LS to GS, Sept. 7, 1895, YCAL.

Writing chipper letters . . . "perfect, warm": LS to Solomon and Pauline Stein, Nov. 15, 1895, YCAL.

"topsy-turviness": LS to Solomon and Pauline Stein, Nov. 15, 1895, YCAL.

"I always felt": FS, unpublished reminiscences, YCAL.

Fred and Leo: See also LS to FS, Jan. 6, 1893, YCAL.

Americans had known: Van Wyck Brooks, *Fenollosa and His Circle*, p. 23.

"I had": App, p. 142. Stein may well have seen Fenollosa's popular first exhibit, *Hokusai and His School*, which ran at the Boston Museum of Fine Arts from the summer of 1892 to the following April, during Stein's first year at Harvard. And in the spring of 1895, before he left Cambridge, he may have heard Fenollosa's far-reaching and popular lectures on the history of Japanese art, given in Boston.

"From a purely": LS to Solomon and Pauline Stein, Feb. 3, 1896, YCAL.

"*There is no*": LS to Solomon and Pauline Stein, Feb. 3, 1896, YCAL.

"*on a different*": LS to MFW, Aug. 28, 1904, YCAL.

"*the more*": LS to FS, n.d., YCAL.

"*the Poor*": LS to FS, n.d., YCAL.

"*So we became*": LS to FS, n.d., YCAL.

"*The fellows*": HH to MCB, Dec. 22, 1895, I Tatti.

"*pursued God*": MDL, *Movers and Shakers*, p. 45.

he wandered: LS to FS, n.d., YCAL.

"*Leo at that*": HH, *A Victorian in the Modern World*, p. 120.

He lost: LS to FS, n.d., YCAL.

"*genuinely desired*": HH, *Victorian*, p. 120.

"*Every time*": LS to Solomon and Pauline Stein, Jan. 2, 1896, YCAL.

"*everything is*": LS to GS, Dec. 22, 1895, YCAL.

"*so thick*": LS to Solomon and Pauline Stein, Jan. 2, 1896, YCAL.

"*A gallant*": LS to GS, Dec. 22, 1895, YCAL.

"*a product*": LS, miscellaneous notebook [2], YCAL.

"*A European*": LS to Solomon and Pauline Stein, Feb. 3, 1896, YCAL.

The last: LS to MS, Dec. 24, 1895, YCAL.

"*as pretty*": HH to MCB, Dec. 22, 1895, I Tatti.

"*The only*" . . . "*the vilest*": LS to GS, Dec. 22, 1895, YCAL.

"*Tanaguchi*": LS to FS, n.d., YCAL.

"*We went*" . . . "*of course*": HH, *Victorian*, pp. 122–23.

"*I always*": LS, notebook [5], YCAL.

"*the answer*": LS, notebook [15], YCAL.

"*If the development*": LS, miscellaneous notebook [2], YCAL.

But Japan; "*It was the only*": LS to FS, n.d., YCAL; HH, *Victorian*, p. 123.

"*it was a time*": LS to Solomon and Pauline Stein, Jan. 25, 1896, YCAL.

Leo didn't like: LS to FS, n.d., YCAL.

"*I've reached*": LS to GS, March 13, 1896, YCAL.

"*In Egypt*": LS to Solomon and Pauline Stein, April 22, 1896, YCAL.

This time: LS to FS, July 7, 1896, YCAL.

By his own admission: AH to MMG, Sept. 28, 1901, PU.

"*He is*" . . . "*But this*": LS to GS, March 13, 1896, YCAL.

"*I am taking*": GS, postscript, LS to FS, July 11, 1896, YCAL.

"*After all*" . . . "*Well when*": EA, p. 71.

"*Gertrude & I*": LS to FS, July 10, 1896, YCAL.

"*the Court*": "Cannot Have Her Children," *The New York Times,* July 2, 1896, p. 2.

"*Its useless*": GS, postscript, LS to FS, July 19, 1896, YCAL.

"*young eyes*": GS, notebook J, YCAL.

"*I am also*": GS, postscript, LS to FS, July 19, 1896, YCAL.

"*I am at present*": GS, postscript, LS to FS, July [20], 1896, YCAL.

"*They've got*": LS to FS, July [20], 1896, YCAL.

"*one night*" . . . "*She admired*": HH, *Victorian*, p. 131.

Gertrude had gone: SS to GS, June 15, [1896], YCAL; LS to Solomon Stein, Aug. 17, 1895, YCAL.

Leo . . . *confessed* . . . *Leo was anxious*: LS to FS, [Sept. 11, 1896], YCAL.

6. Evolution

"*It's too bad*": SS to GS, Jan. 20, 1897, YCAL.

"*But the Samuels*": SS to GS, Sept. 22, 1895, YCAL.

Gertrude was deeply: See SS to GS, Oct. 8, 1895, YCAL.

"mare's nest": JIS, p. 192.

"Until some one": LS to HH, Feb. 20, [1936], YCAL.

"most historical": JIS, p. 192.

one friend: Leon Solomons to GS, Jan. 19, 1897, YCAL: "So Leo is going to study History at Johns Hopkins."

"Don't you think": Leon Solomons to GS, April 5, 1897, YCAL.

"he is my ideal": MFW, "Foreword," JIS, typescript, [1949], YCAL.

She showed: SS to LS, Nov. 16, 1896, YCAL.

In a desultory: Aline Saarinen interview with Elise Haas, Aline Saarinen papers, AAA.

Sarah not only: SS to LS, Nov. 16, 1896, YCAL.

"Do you know": SS to LS, Nov. 16, 1896, YCAL.

"I spoke": LS, notebook [1], YCAL.

"I hope": Leon Solomons to GS, Oct. 26, 1896, YCAL.

"greater or less" . . . *"In Type II"*: GS, "Cultivated Motor Automatism; A Study of Character in Its Relation to Attention," pp. 299, 295, 299, 297, 298, 305.

It didn't help: Leon Solomons to GS, Feb. 27, 1898, YCAL.

"the nervous": GS, "The Value of College Education for Women," 1899, BMA-CC.

"Please don't": Francis Pollak to GS, March 13, 1897, YCAL.

"began specializing": GS to Robert Bartlett Haas, Jan. [23], 1938, YCAL.

in the scientific community: See Robert M. Young, *Mind, Brain, and Adaptation in the Nineteenth Century*, p. 4, and William Coleman, *Biology in the Nineteenth Century*, pp. 12ff.

Modern zoology: See Mary P. Winsor, *Reading the Shape of Nature*, p. 215.

"Evolution": WIHS, p. 61.

"Permanence": WIHS, p. 144.

"Naturally": WIHS, p. 62.

"I do not think": Leon Solomons to GS, Jan. 4, 1898, YCAL.

"What do you": SS to GS, Jan. 20, 1897, YCAL.

"Wherefore": Francis Pollak to GS, [June 1897], YCAL.

"I have heard": Leon Solomons to GS, April 5, 1897, YCAL.

"the real study": Lillian Wing Smith, Mabel Earle, and Louise Earle, "In Memoriam: Gertrude Stein," p. 21.

"She wrote": Smith et al., "In Memoriam," p. 21.

"Thinking": GS to William Welch, [spring–summer 1897], AMC-JHM.

"she has": William Welch, notes, July 24, 1897, AMC-JHM.

"circular": LS, inquiry to Johns Hopkins University, May 21, 1897, FH-JHU.

"the whole policy": Quoted in Frank R. Lillie, *The Woods Hole Marine Biological Laboratory*, p. 38.

"not a station": Quoted in Lillie, *Woods Hole*, p. 39.

possibly Gertrude: See Grace Lyman to GS, July 27, 1911, YCAL.

At Mrs. Coombs's: See [first name indecipherable] Berlin to GS, Oct. 9, 1897, YCAL.

"The ardor": Henry Fairfield Osborn, "A Sea-Shore Laboratory," p. 554.

"the relations": LS, notebook [6], YCAL.

Rewarding patience: Philip J. Pauly, "Summer Resort and Scientific Discipline: Woods Hole and the Structure of American Biology, 1882–1925," in Ronald Rainger, ed., *The American Development of Biology*, p. 126.

"spoke very highly": SS to GS, Oct. 20, [1899], YCAL.

"For us": See Winterton C. Curtis, "Good Old Summer Times and the M.B.L." and "Rhymes of the Woods Hole Shores," *Falmouth Enterprise*, Aug. 12, 19, and 26, and Sept. 2 and 9, 1955, reprint in the Marine Biological Laboratory Archives.

Overall, the courses: Lillie, *Woods Hole,* p. 117.

"property values": See chapter 5.

Gertrude informed: GS to William Welch, Sept. 27, 1897, AMC-JHM.

"Human kind": Lilian Welsh, *Reminiscences of Thirty Years in Baltimore,* p. 44; Elinor Bluemel, *Florence Sabin,* p. 40.

Almost fifty percent: M. Carey Thomas, "The Education of Women," p. 37.

to the wider public: Mary Roth Walsh, *"Doctors Wanted: No Women Need Apply,"* p. 184.

"To be addressed": Mary Putnam Jacobi, "Woman in Medicine," in Annie Meyer, ed., *Women's Work in America,* p. 161n.

Welch argued: Donald Fleming, *William H. Welch and the Rise of Modern Medicine,* p. 98.

"embarrassments": Simon Flexner and James Thomas Flexner, *William Henry Welch and the Heroic Age of American Medicine,* p. 231.

"Opposition": Jacobi, "Woman in Medicine," p. 196.

"Mr. Gilman": M. Carey Thomas to Simon Flexner, June 23, 1934, William Welch Library, Johns Hopkins University. Quoted in Flexner and Flexner, *Welch,* p. 217.

"Pres. Gilman": Flexner and Flexner, *Welch,* p. 218.

"under the inspiration": Welsh, *Reminiscences,* p. 35.

welcomed Gertrude Stein: Admissions Committee, minutes, Oct. 2, 1897, AMC-JHM.

"a pipe": Adele Oppenheimer to GS and LS, Dec. 15, 1897, and Ben Oppenheimer to GS and LS, Feb. 8, 1898, YCAL.

"you could make": SS to GS, June 12, 1897, YCAL.

"I should not think": MS, postscript, SS to GS, June 12, 1897, YCAL.

"There is certainly": SS to GS, June 12, 1897, YCAL.

7 . Respectability

"Baltimore Jewish": LS to MFW, Dec. 30, 1901, YCAL.

soulless and inane: LS to FS, May 30, [1900], YCAL.

"There is nothing": GS, "The Value of College Education for Women," 1899, BMA-CC.

"you people": GS, "The Value of College Education."

"Mind you": GS, "The Value of College Education."

"an amiable": LS to FS, May 30, [1899], YCAL.

"Respectability": LS, "Society and Art," p. 4.

"Well we have": LS to GS, Feb. 3, [1901], YCAL.

"Hortense never": CC to EC, Sept. 20, 1910, BMA-CC.

Claribel Cone: Barbara Pollack, *The Collectors,* p. 31; Ellen Hirschland, "The Cone Sisters and the Stein Family," in Margaret Potter, ed., *Four Americans in Paris,* p. 82.

fascinating but difficult: Edna Lichtenfels to Elinor Ulman, Oct. 22, 1957, Aline Saarinen papers, AAA.

"that people do": CC to EC, June 30, 1910, BMA-CC.

"as magnificent": Emma Lootz Erving to GS, May 7, 1914, YCAL.

when she was standing: Edna Lichtenfels to Elinor Ulman, Oct. 22, 1957, Aline Saarinen papers, AAA.

She bought two: BW interview with Edward T. Cone, Jan. 3, 1991. See also Edward Cone, "The Miss Etta Cones, the Steins, and M'sieu Matisse: A Memoir," pp. 441–49.

"I hate": EC to GS, Jan. 7, 1908, YCAL.

"hateful": EC to GS, Feb. 24, 1908, YCAL.

She credited: BW interview with Edward T. Cone, Jan. 3, 1991.

she was once described: Hirschland, "Cone Sisters," p. 78.

"Etta seems": Hortense Guggenheimer Moses to GS, Dec. 26, 1910, YCAL.

"You have": CC to EC, June 30, 1910, BMA-CC.

"Throughout life": CC to EC, Aug. 25, 1910, BMA-CC.

"Go on": See GS, "Two Women," holograph manuscript, YCAL. See also chapter 18
   of this book for the dating of the manuscript.

"Aunt Etta": BW interview with Edward T. Cone, Jan. 3, 1991.

Mall was: See Donald Fleming, *William H. Welch and the Rise of Modern Medicine,*
   pp. 160–65.

Once when Mall noticed: Florence Rena Sabin, *Franklin Paine Mall,* p. 177.

"Doctor Mall": ABT, p. 81.

"Do you think": Quoted in Elizabeth Sprigge, *Gertrude Stein,* p. 41.

A former classmate: Elizabeth Sprigge, "Journal in Quest of Gertrude Stein," unpublished typescript, p. 110, YCAL.

"the dirtiest": Edmund Wilson, *Upstate,* p. 61.

"excellent occupation" . . . *" 'research' ":* JIS, p. 148.

"I want to know": Alan Frank Guttmacher, "Recollections of John Whitridge Williams,"
   pp. 26–27.

"couldn't stand": Dorothy Reed Mendenhall, unpublished autobiography, Smith.

"This was not": Charles Winne, Jr., to J. M. D. Olmsted, Aug. 14, 1947, UCSF.

"Fat, awkward": Warfield T. Longcope to J. M. D. Olmsted, Aug. 13, 1947, UCSF.

"She was stout": Charles Winne, Jr., to J. M. D. Olmsted, Aug. 14, 1947, UCSF.

"As a thinker": Mendenhall, unpublished autobiography, Smith.

"her technique": C. S. Bunting to J. M. D. Olmsted, Aug. 13, 1947, UCSF.

"I can truthfully": H. D. Bloombergh to J. M. D. Olmsted, Aug. 20, 1947, UCSF.

Gertrude herself: ABT, holograph manuscript, YCAL.

She disdained: GS, notebook B, YCAL.

"own vigorous self": Marian Walker Williams to GS, June 28, 1928, YCAL.

"I am sure": H. D. Bloombergh to J. M. D. Olmsted, Aug. 20, 1947, UCSF.

" 'Have you ever heard' ": Warfield T. Longcope to J. M. D. Olmsted, Aug. 13, 1947, UCSF.

"I should like": Marion Walker Williams to GS, June 28, 1928, YCAL.

"extremely interesting": Warfield T. Longcope to J. M. D. Olmsted, Aug. 13, 1947,
   UCSF.

"Bring down": FS to GS, Dec. 21, 1897, YCAL.

a student picnic: GS, "The Value of College Education."

"I suppose" . . . *"The experiment":* Leon Solomons to GS, Feb. 27, 1898, YCAL.

"it is a natural": Leon Solomons to GS, Feb. 27, 1898, YCAL.

"I have often": Lewellys F. Barker, *Time and the Physician,* p. 60.

Sabin graduated: GS, notebooks C, B, E; see Elinor Bluemel, *Florence Sabin,* p. 45.

"good deal": ABT, p. 81.

"And the moon": GS to Alexander Woollcott, n.d., Houghton.

Gertrude's hands: Elizabeth Sprigge, "Questing Gertrude Stein," typescript, Claremont.

"all your slides": Arthur Lachman to GS, Dec. [1898], YCAL.

recalled, with admiration: Florence Sabin to J. M. D. Olmsted, Aug. 13, 1947, UCSF;
   Florence Sabin to Mary Sabin, April 20, 1900, Smith.

Gertrude's dedication: See Dolene G. Stein to GS, [1907], YCAL; Sprigge, "Journal in
   Quest of Gertrude Stein," unpublished typescript, YCAL, p. 12; MFW, "Foreword,"
   JIS, typescript, [1949], YCAL.

According to a neighbor: Hortense Federleicht, unpublished memoir, Maryland Jewish Historical Society; GS to Louis Bromfield, [1930s], Ohio State University.

"tell Leo": Leo Friedman to GS, Feb. 2, 1898, YCAL.

"felt sure": Adele Oppenheimer to GS and LS, Feb. 8, 1898, YCAL.

"In a biological": LS, notebooks, [1914], YCAL.

"Your letter": Margaret Lewis Nickerson to LS, Nov. 15, 1897, YCAL.

"The latter": LS to FS, March 22, 1898, YCAL.

"a type then rare": Florence Sabin to J. M. D. Olmsted, Aug. 13, 1947, UCSF.

Leo decided: LS to FS, May 16, 1898, YCAL.

"inexpressibly glad": SS to GS, March [1898], YCAL.

"By comparison": SS to GS, Dec. 9, [1899], YCAL.

"I must sit": SS to GS, Nov. 10, 1897, YCAL.

"if you will pardon": Adele Solomons Jaffa to GS, n.d., YCAL.

"The normal": ABT, p. 83.

Sarah hoped: SS to GS, July 25, 1897, YCAL.

"The Spanish-American": WIHS, p. 48.

Dr. William Osler: William Osler, "The Natural Method of Teaching the Subject of Medicine," p. 1675; Harvey Cushing, *The Life of Sir William Osler,* vol. 1, p. 552.

"as rich": CC, "Making Ward-Rounds with 'Dr. Osler,' " 1927, BMA-CC.

"The whole art": Osler, "Natural Method," p. 1674.

"She thought": Sprigge, "Questing Gertrude Stein," typescript, p. 18, Claremont.

"I did not like": EA, p. 264.

"crude and superficial" . . . One incident: Charles Winne, Jr., to J. M. D. Olmsted, Aug. 14, 1947, UCSF.

She was pleased: See Lewellys F. Barker, *The Nervous System and Its Constituent Neurones,* pp. 721, 725: "Miss Gertrude Stein, who is now studying a series of sagittal sections through this region from the brain of a babe a few weeks old, describes the nucleus of Darkschewitsch as follows: 'The nucleus is more or less conical in shape. It lies dorso-medial from the red nucleus, being about as thick in a dorso-ventral direction as is the dorsal capsule of the red nucleus in which it lies. At this period of medullation the commissura posterior cerebri, considered simply topographically (that is, as a medullated fibre-mass without particular reference to the course of the fibres), appears as a dorso-ventral bundle, solid in the middle, subdivided dorsally into an anterior (proximal) portion and a posterior (distal) portion, while ventrally it expands in the form of a hollow pyramid, which rests directly upon the nucleus of Darkschewitsch.' "

"The gross fact": LS, miscellaneous manuscripts, YCAL.

article on the Jew: LS, "The Jew in Fiction," p. 8.

"ghastly dining": LS to MFW, Dec. 20, 1901, YCAL.

He enjoyed: Pollack, *The Collectors,* pp. 29, 40, 45.

This woman of clarity: MFW, "Foreword," *JIS,* typescript, [1949], YCAL.

"he wanted to talk": MFW, "Foreword," *JIS,* typescript, [1949], YCAL.

"as two quite": MFW to GS, Nov. 8, 1910, YCAL.

"Gertrude's personality": MFW, "Foreword," *JIS,* typescript, [1949], YCAL.

"And you Leo": MFW to LS, n.d., YCAL.

"I'm all too": LS to GS, Dec. 20, 1900, YCAL.

"when I couldn't": See LS to GS, Nov. 9, [1900], YCAL; LS to GS, Dec. 20, 1900, YCAL.

"Only one week": LS to FS, May 30, [1900], YCAL.

8. New Americans

Gans had urged: LS to Lincoln Steffens, April 19, 1932, Butler.
"It was a longer": LS, notebook [2]; LS to Howard Gans, Sept. 3, 1945, YCAL.
"I have never": HH, *A Victorian in the Modern World*, p. 166.
He had spent: AH, notes on William Travers Jerome, box 2, PU.
" 'Take it' ": AH, "A Fight for the City: The Story of a Campaign of Amateurs," Jan. 24, 1903, p. 208.
eight-page newspaper: Moses Rischin, *The Promised Land*, p. 228.
"He had the laughing": HH, *Victorian*, p. 164.
"He had a very brilliant": Bertrand Russell, *The Autobiography of Bertrand Russell*, p. 132.
This would enable: AH to MMG, Jan. 8, 1902, PU.
"she had hated": AH to MMG, Nov. 22, 1901, PU.
"We hate": AH to MMG, Nov. 22, 1901, PU.
Matrimony and maternity: [GS], "Degeneration in American Women," [1902], PU. See Appendix.
Mass civilization: MCB to Hannah Whitall Smith, Sept. 16, 1900, Lilly.
For they had spent: See AH to MMG, [Sept. 1900], PU.
Weeks said: See MFW to GS, Jan. 2, 1901, YCAL.
"for it was": MFW, "Foreword," *JIS*, typescript, [1949], YCAL.
asked a sculptress: Estelle Rumbold [Kohn] to GS, [winter 1901], YCAL.
"sort of irregular": LS to GS, Dec. 20, 1900, YCAL.
"that is too": LS to GS, Dec. 20, 1900, YCAL.
"gone so far": LS to GS, Feb. 2, 1901, YCAL.
she wanted to consult: GS to Adolf Meyer, Dec. 13, 1900, AMC-JHM.
"True medical": Quoted in Jacques M. Quen and Eric T. Carlson, *American Psychoanalysis*, pp. 24–25.
"My dear Meyer": Stewart Paton to Adolf Meyer, Dec. 20, 1990, AMC-JHM.
During their stint: Elinor Bluemel, *Florence Sabin*, p. 46.
"Don't you think": MFW to GS, Dec. 21, 1900, YCAL.
"an intern": Duncan, p. 43.
"justly celebrated" . . . *"and since":* Alan Frank Guttmacher, "Recollections of John Whitridge Williams," p. 22.
Nor did she earn: Elizabeth Sprigge, "Journal in Quest of Gertrude Stein," unpublished typescript, p. 110, YCAL.
"relearn the fundamental": GS, "Fernhurst," manuscript, YCAL.
"What is all": LS to GS, Feb. 2, 1901, YCAL.
On the day: GS, notebook MA, YCAL.
Long afterward: Natalie Barney to GS, Aug. 1, 1939, YCAL.
"As the graduation": ABT, p. 82.
"It is all false": JIS, p. 147.
Edith Hamilton: Sprigge, "Journal in Quest of Gertrude Stein," p. 121.
Most friends: Estelle Rumbold [Kohn] to GS, [Feb. 1901], YCAL.
one friend had bought: Sprigge, "Journal in Quest of Gertrude Stein," p. 121.
"Shown in the picture": Johns Hopkins school of medicine, photograph of class of 1901, key, AMC-JHM.
a faculty committee: Medical Faculty, vol. B, p. 196, AMC-JHM.
"My dear Mr. Meyer": GS to Adolf Meyer, June 15, 1901, AMC-JHM.
"Miss Stein failed": Franklin Paine Mall to Lewellys Barker, Aug. 14, 1901, AMC-JHM.

"Miss Stein will": Franklin Paine Mall to Lewellys Barker, Oct. 11, 1901, AMC-JHM.

The first section: Oddly enough, although Leon Katz—bolstered by Alice Toklas's secondhand version of events and an interview with Emma Lootz Erving he conducted in the 1950s—reads Stein's life literally in terms of the text of "Q.E.D.," he misreads the date of this transatlantic crossing, setting it in the summer of 1902 rather than 1901. In his dissertation he says he was told that the Bookstaver affair took place during Stein's last year at Hopkins, which he understood to mean her last official year in medical school, not the last year she spent in Baltimore, when she was also working at Hopkins. See Leon Katz, "The First Making of *The Making of Americans*," p. 17.

Katz's pivotal work is not unflawed. Unfortunately, however, to date it has remained unchallenged, its conclusions taken at face value. Other scholars, accepting Katz's mistaken inference, have assumed the Stein–Bookstaver affair began before the summer of 1901; still others have asserted the transatlantic crossing never took place—an unlikely possibility, since Leo Stein himself met his sister's boat when it docked in Italy in July 1901. It should be kept in mind that any chronology of the affair is a reconstruction; veracity, or the approximation of it, depends on the evidence assembled. The more substantial and numerous the relevant documents, the more valid the inferences. From the new evidence I have unearthed, I conclude that the chronology of "Q.E.D." closely follows that of the affair, which, whatever its origin or ramifications, apparently did not bloom until the winter of 1901–1902—*after* Stein failed her medical school examinations.

"a succession": "Q.E.D.," *EW*, pp. 53, 61.

"long emotional": Notes for "Q.E.D.," YCAL; "Q.E.D.," *EW*, p. 61.

They also bore: Recognizing Thomas's zeal as well as her long-standing commitment to women's intellectual fulfillment, Gertrude Stein later portrayed her as an autocrat who was indifferent "to any consideration but expediency in the actual working out of her ideal" (see "Fernhurst," *EW*, p. 18).

"in all ways": Russell, *Autobiography,* p. 131; AH, autobiographical notes, box 1, PU.

"So long": M. Carey Thomas, "Should the Higher Education of Women Differ from That of Men?" p. 4.

Their lives were: Russell, *Autobiography,* p. 131.

when Bertrand Russell: MCB, diary, Oct. 20, 1900, I Tatti; MMG to Alys Russell, Sept. 6, 1899, PU.

women including: Although no record of Lounsbery's attendance exists, the alumnae notes in the April 21, 1899, edition of Bryn Mawr's student newspaper *The Fortnightly Philistine* (Bryn Mawr College Archives) reported that Lounsbery was enrolled at Johns Hopkins. No record of Lounsbery's attendance at Hopkins would exist if she had left the program early, as she suggested she may have, because she disapproved of vivisection. See also Sprigge, "Journal in Quest of Gertrude Stein," p. 66.

the uncouth Stein: Katz, "The First Making," p. 19.

"I found her": Lounsbery interview, Sprigge, "Journal in Quest of Gertrude Stein," p. 66.

"American version" . . . *"watching the swallows"*: "Q.E.D.," *EW*, pp. 54, 104, 59, 60, 68.

"Oh why": GS to MFW, July 10, 1901, YCAL.

"agreeing and": "Q.E.D.," *EW*, p. 67.

"I love": GS to MFW, July 10, 1901, YCAL.

"It really": LS to MFW, July 10, 1901, YCAL.

"They slept": App, pp. 149–50; EC, diary, Aug. 29, 1901, BMA-CC.

Etta Cone had come: EC, diary, May 21, 1901, BMA-CC.

"far more interesting": EC, diary, May 27, 1901, BMA-CC.

Gertrude thought: See EC, Sept. 2, 4, 10, 13, 14, 17, and 19, 1901, BMA-CC.

"Talked with": EC, diary, Sept. 14, 1901, BMA-CC.

Aboard ship: It is also possible that the source of the shipboard romance in "Q.E.D." was an affair with Etta Cone, not May Bookstaver, and that the affair with May Bookstaver had yet to happen.

"My vanity": EC, diary, Oct. 8, 1901, BMA-CC. See also Brenda Richardson, *Dr. Claribel & Miss Etta*, pp. 63–64, where Richardson interprets the passage as "an oblique reference to some kind of emotional attachment on Etta's part to Gertrude, an attribution which is only fortified by her apparently later attribution of these feelings to her 'vanity.'"

"everything was": See LS to GS, [1900], YCAL; Elizabeth Sprigge, *Gertrude Stein*, p. 38.

"We women": Florence Sabin to J. M. D. Olmsted, Aug. 13, 1947, UCSF.

"Dr. Mall": Edmund Wilson, *Upstate*, p. 63.

"Miss Stein": Franklin Paine Mall to Lewellys Barker, Nov. 7, 1901, AMC-JHM.

"Dr. Mall, who": Florence Sabin to J. M. D. Olmsted, Aug. 13, 1947, UCSF.

"Gertrude successfully": MFW, "Foreword," *JIS*, p. viii.

"you might": Lewellys Barker to GS, Jan. 30, 1902, YCAL.

"Professor Mall": Writer unknown to Lewellys Barker, April 7, 1902, AMC-JHM.

According to Florence: Dorothy Reed Mendenhall, unpublished autobiography, Smith; Florence Sabin to J. M. D. Olmsted, Aug. 13, 1947, UCSF.

"The game": "Q.E.D.," *EW*, pp. 87, 88, 95.

"This was not" . . . *"I suggested"*: AH to MMG, Jan. 5, 1902, PU.

an essay she had written: In *WIR*, Alice Toklas contended that Stein wrote the "papers" that Bird Sternberger, "an early social worker," read at the meetings of her "mother classes" (p. 49). Sternberger did partake in a women's discussion group that focused on child-rearing literature, and later became the founder of the New York City Child Study Association. Stein may have contributed the "Degeneration" paper or a similar one to the group for discussion, but it is unlikely that Sternberger passed any of them off as her own, as Toklas suggested, or that the views expressed were not Stein's own. Primary sources of the time indicate otherwise.

recent article: See George J. Engelmann, "The Increasing Sterility of American Women," pp. 890–97.

"is of course" . . . *"also finds"*: [GS], "Degeneration." See Appendix.

"Don't talk": Marian Walker Williams to GS, [late fall 1901], YCAL.

Mamie Gwinn, on reading: MMG to AH, [Feb. 1902], PU.

"sentence by sentence" . . . *"he has backed"*: AH to MMG, Feb. 26, 1902, PU.

9. Gilded Cages

"We shall go": *The Fortnightly Philistine*, Feb. 27, 1896, pp. 2–3, Bryn Mawr College Archives.

"not at least": AH to MMG, Sept. 28, 1901, PU.

"But art": LS to GS, Dec. 20, 1900, YCAL.

"As for literary": LS to GS, Nov. 9, 1900, YCAL.

Hanging on the walls: LS to MFW, Oct. 9, 1900, YCAL.

These were: BW interview with Cesare Scheggi Merlini, Sept. 5, 1991.

"Florence is": LS to GS, Oct. 11, 1900, YCAL; quoted in *JIS*, p. 4.

He spent: LS to GS, Feb. 2, 1901, YCAL.

"The mere fact": LS to GS, [Nov.? 1900], YCAL; quoted in *JIS*, p. 8.

"Well I": LS to GS, [Nov.? 1900], YCAL; quoted in *JIS*, p. 8.

"exchanged": HH to BB, July 24, 1900, I Tatti.

"entire activity": BB, *Sketch for a Self-Portrait*, p. 59.

"classify": MCB, signing as Mary Logan, "The New Art Criticism," p. 263.

"kind of vital": Helen Thomas Flexner, *A Quaker Childhood*, p. 287.

Tall and radiant: Flexner, *A Quaker Childhood*, p. 206.

He wasn't particularly: AH to MMG, Oct. 20, 1900, PU; LS to GS, Oct. 9, 1900, YCAL.

For her part: MCB to Hannah Whitall Smith, Jan. 12 and March 19, 1901, Lilly.

"colossal I": LS to MFW, Nov. 7, 1900, YCAL.

"He says": LS to GS, Oct. 9, 1900, YCAL; quoted in *JIS*, p. 3.

"But there's no": LS to GS, Oct. 11, 1900, YCAL.

"It's like": LS to MFW, Nov. 7, 1900, YCAL.

"the laws which": MCB, signing as Mary Logan, "The New Art Criticism," p. 268.

"the painter": BB, *The Italian Painters of the Renaissance*, p. 40.

"serious doubts": LS to Horace Ainsworth Eaton, July 15, 1901, UCLA.

"I got": BB to MCB, April 16, 1901, I Tatti.

Commanding magnificent: MCB to Alys Russell, Dec. 1, 1900, Lilly.

a typical group: LS to MFW, Nov. 7, 1900; LS to GS, [Nov.? 1900], YCAL, quoted in *JIS*, p. 7.

"Virgins": LS to MFW, Nov. 7, 1900, YCAL; MCB, diary, June 14, 1900, I Tatti.

although Bernhard: See NBH, diary, typescript, [Dec. 1907], YCAL.

"Indeed, I": MCB to BB, Aug. 26, 1908, I Tatti.

One night: MCB, diary, Sept. 28, 1907, I Tatti.

"He seemed": MCB, diary, Oct. 20, 1900, I Tatti.

"there will be": LS to MFW, Dec. 2, 1900, YCAL.

He accompanied: Barbara Pollack, *The Collectors*, p. 45; EC, travel diary, May 27 and June 2 and 8, 1901, BMA-CC.

"It is marvelous": EC, travel diary, June 5, 1901, BMA-CC.

"Hyde unacknowledged": LS, notebook [5], YCAL. This is the same terminology Gertrude used in her Radcliffe composition "In the Red Deeps."

"the full tide": LS, notebook [5], YCAL.

"permanent memorial": Sigmund Freud, "Fetishism," in *Sexuality and the Psychology of Love*, p. 216.

"had very little": LS, notebook [5], YCAL. See Freud, "Fetishism," p. 217.

Did an adult: See Louise J. Kaplan, *Female Perversions*, pp. 34–77, for a cogent, nonreductive discussion of fetishism.

"The shoe": LS, notebook [15], dated 1921, YCAL.

"an exaggerated": LS, notebook [15], dated 1921, YCAL.

"For me": LS, notebook [15], dated 1921, YCAL.

"I defended": LS, notebook [15], dated 1921, YCAL.

"Sexual identification": LS, miscellaneous notebook, filed among miscellaneous papers and internally dated 1921, YCAL.

"terrific" . . . *"not real"*: See LS to Trigant Burrow, June 20, 1933, and Nov. 1934, Sterling; LS, notebook [identified by its response to Mary Calkins], YCAL.

"I must": JIS, p. 94.

"I have never": LS to Trigant Burrow, Oct. 24, 1926, Sterling.

"interpretation": Quoted in *JIS*, pp. 94, 92.

"I must simply": LS, notebook [5], YCAL.

Gertrude once boasted: GS, notebook 2, YCAL.

He later: JIS, p. 185.

"freaks": See LS to GS, [Nov.? 1900], YCAL; quoted in *JIS*, p. 7.

"I had a perfect": LS to GS, Oct. 25, 1901, YCAL; quoted in *JIS*, p. 9.

"the world": MCB to Hannah Whitall Smith, Oct. 12, 1901, Lilly.

She accepted: MCB to Hannah Whitall Smith, April 11, 1902, Lilly.

"When in Florence": *App*, p. 150.

"to have them": LS to GS, Oct. 9, 1900, YCAL.

"Once my brother": *JIS*, p. 187.

"men who were": LS, "Practice—Nirvana," miscellaneous papers, YCAL.

In December: LS to MFW, Dec. 20, 1901, YCAL.

By March . . . "Spring &": LS to MFW, March 15, 1902, YCAL.

"I blow": LS to GS, Feb. 3, 1901, YCAL. See also LS to MFW, Sept. 19, 1902, YCAL.

Mary Berenson was dismayed: MCB, diary, Oct. 20, 1900, I Tatti.

"A fat": MCB, diary, May 13, 1902, I Tatti.

"so brilliant": LS to MFW, Sept. 19, 1902, YCAL; quoted in *JIS*, p. 10.

"a black contingent": Logan Pearsall Smith, *Unforgotten Years*, p. 83.

"The more" . . . "Some day": LS to MFW, Sept. 19, 1902, YCAL; quoted in *JIS*, pp. 11, 13.

"Your parent's": GS, "Why Do Americans Live in Europe?" *transition*, 14 (Fall 1928), pp. 97–98.

10. Brother Singular

"You fat": GS, notebook 10, YCAL.

"Don't forget": MS to GS, Jan. 2/9, 1901, YCAL. The Haig diet, brainchild of Alexander Haig, was based on his popular publication *Diet and Food: Considered in Relation to Strength and Power of Endurance, Training and Athletics*. In his preface to the fifth edition (1904), Haig set forth his philosophy: "Mind is a function of the body, and the body is dependent on the material at its disposal for the purposes of stability and renewal." Health was a matter of nutrition, strength, and endurance, Haig said, and his diet attempted to rid the system of "poisonous xanthins and uric acid," and thereby restore individual and even social well-being.

"something as essentially": *ABC*, p. 19.

Gertrude suffered: See LS to GS, Dec. 14, 1919, YCAL; quoted in *JIS*, p. 78.

Yet if descriptions: For an insightful overview of Stein's changing relation to the body, see Catharine R. Stimpson, "The Somagrams of Gertrude Stein."

All good-natured: Simon Stein to GS, Jan. 10, 1908, YCAL.

"both mentally": Warfield T. Longcope to J. M. D. Olmsted, Aug. 13, 1947, UCSF.

"Since I": GS, miscellaneous notes and fragments for *MOA* [32], YCAL, as Stein copied them; flyleaf of "A Long Gay Book," holograph manuscript, YCAL. See also Geoffrey Chaucer, "Merciles Beaute: A Triple Roundel"; the lines are the refrain in the third section, "Escape": "Sin I from Love escaped am so fat, / I never thenk to ben in his prison lene." Thanks to Carroll Hilles for her copy of this poem.

"Toasted susie": "Preciosilla," *SW*, p. 550; "Miguel (Collusion). Guimpe. Candle," *BTV*, p. 38; "Lifting Belly," *BTV*, p. 81.

But especially: [GS], "Degeneration in American Women," [1902], PU. See Appendix.

Only her enormous: NBH, diary, June 24, 1903, YCAL.

both Gertrude and Leo Stein said: LS to MFW, Nov. 2, 1902, YCAL.

"[Robertson] has": LS to MFW, Sept. 19, 1902, YCAL; quoted in *JIS*, p. 11.

"A discoverer": LS, notebooks 16, 4, YCAL. The comments seem to have been written in the mid-1920s and early 1930s.

Was genius: LS, notebook [17], YCAL; see also William James, *Manuscript Lectures,* pp. 79–83, and *The Principles of Psychology,* vol. 2, pp. 110, 360–61.

"most men": LS, miscellaneous notebook, [circa 1921], YCAL; LS, notebook [6], YCAL.

Perhaps not: LS, notebook [6], YCAL.

"If you stop": EA, p. 77.

"A man of genius": GS, "A Man," manuscript, YCAL.

Maleness might: GS, notebooks A and C, YCAL.

"So often": GS, notebook A, YCAL.

synonymous with maleness: For a fuller discussion of Gertrude Stein's assumptions about and use of gender, see Catharine R. Stimpson, "Gertrice/Altrude: Stein, Toklas, and the Paradox of the Happy Marriage," pp. 123–39; "Gertrude Stein and the Transposition of Gender," pp. 1–18; and "The Mind, the Body, and Gertrude Stein," pp. 489–506.

Hodder admired: AH to MMG, [Sept. 5, 1898], PU.

" 'reformed' ": LS to MFW, Nov. 24, 1902, YCAL.

She frequented: ABT, p. 83.

Interspersed: It is difficult to ascertain whether Stein wrote in this notebook during the fall of 1902 while in London, or shortly after her return to New York, or both (as seems likeliest). In any case, the notebook represents Stein's interests during late 1902 and early 1903.

"The dead weight": "Q.E.D.," EW, p. 100.

"it was very bad"; "the dismalness": GS to MFW, [fall 1902], YCAL; ABT, p. 84.

"a little vacation": GS to MFW, [fall 1902], YCAL.

"It happens": "Fernhurst," EW, p. 29.

"First it was": "Fernhurst," EW, p. 30.

seventy-three-page manuscript: The unfinished holograph manuscript entitled "The Making of Americans Being the History of a Family's Progress," appears to have been written before "Q.E.D.," although not necessarily before "Fernhurst." For the dating of the former manuscript by internal evidence, see Leon Katz, "The First Making of *The Making of Americans,*" pp. 33–40ff. After reviewing his argument and the extant evidence, I too conclude that this manuscript probably (but not necessarily) precedes "Q.E.D." in composition—*if* written during the late winter/early spring of 1903. However, because some of the phrases used in the manuscript are scattered among the various drafts of "Q.E.D." and in the miscellaneous papers relating to that novel, it is still possible that Stein began playing with the idea of a family history while writing "Q.E.D." in the fall of 1903 and did not actually start writing it until the fall / early winter of 1903–1904, in the United States, or even later. The fact that the manuscript was written in copybooks bought in England proves nothing; these could have been purchased as late as 1905 when the Steins went to London.

    The dating of "Fernhurst" is similarly complex, and its composition occurred probably earlier than once supposed. Katz's introduction to the text dates the work according to Toklas's loose recollection: Stein "wrote the Hodder story probably a year or so after it happened." Katz then assumes "late 1904 or early winter of 1905" as "the only possible dates." But why not before, especially since extensive research shows how involved the Stein family was with Hodder. Moreover, "Fernhurst" rewrites "Degeneration in American Women"; it rehearses the Bookstaver–Haynes–Stein triangle, concluding just as Haynes (Mrs. Redfern?) learns of Bookstaver and Stein's relationship; it serves as an epilogue to the entire experience of college and medical school—which was on Stein's mind in the winter of 1903, when she must have become as fascinated with the Hodder story as she was with Hodder. Internal evidence, in fact, suggests that the text was originally incomplete, ending just as Mrs. Redfern confronts her husband with evidence of his infidelity. This first section could have been started as early as winter/ spring 1903, in the United States, when Stein first learned of the Hodder–Gwinn affair, possibly from Howard Gans, one of Hodder's few confidants, or from Smith family gossip at the real Fernhurst during the autumn of 1902. (Stein reported the gossip to Neith Boyce Hapgood the following summer.) The final section of the manuscript, undoubtedly added after news of Alfred Hodder's death in 1907, is a kind of coda to his short life. (This section also refers to William James's denunciation of Hodder, which became more well known when James's wife, Alice, involved herself in the bigamy suit filed in 1906 by Jessie Donaldson Hodder, who alleged she was still Hodder's wife at the time of his marriage to Gwinn.)

I therefore reiterate that the dating of these early manuscripts is not conclusive, and that nothing can be settled conclusively without more evidence. However, one can say with certainty that "Fernhurst," "Q.E.D.," and the first draft of *The Making of Americans* were all written before *Three Lives*. It is reasonable to conjecture that "Fernhurst" and the first draft of *The Making of Americans* were both begun before "Q.E.D."; it is also useful to assume "Fernhurst" was written in stages. Unfortunately, no early drafts or notes for the manuscript have survived, nor do Hodder's letters to Leo Stein. I propose that the story was begun in New York (when Stein would have had no such letters), finished while she was still there or later, and copied over into ink even later, when the last section was added.

No doubt hearing: The affair was well known to members of the Smith and Berenson circles. See MMG to Alys Russell, Sept. 6, 1899, PU; see also MCB, diary, Oct. 20, 1900, I Tatti. "Redfern," Hodder's pseudonym, was taken probably from the name of the Smith family dressmaker or clothier.

"I am for" . . . *Stein suspected* . . . *"We the generation"* . . . *"Had I been":* "Fernhurst," *EW,* pp. 5, 7–8.

so naive, said: NBH, diary, holograph, Aug. 28, 1903, YCAL.

"preferred" . . . *"instinct"* . . . *She could lose* . . . *"straight"* . . . *"had her evidence"* . . . *"Naive realism":* "Fernhurst," *EW,* pp. 30, 25, 17, 20, 39, 45, 44.

Mabel Weeks reminisced: Elizabeth Sprigge, "Journal in Quest of Gertrude Stein," unpublished typescript, p. 113, YCAL.

"He never": "Fernhurst," *EW,* p. 49.

When Alfred Hodder: See *Sternberger vs. Sternberger,* BB 2061, vols. 5–9, Records Division, New York State Surrogates Court.

"a very vigorous": GS, "The Making of Americans Being the History of a Family's Progress," manuscript, pp. 20, 37, YCAL; "The Making of Americans," *EW,* pp. 153, 154.

"Be doubly": "The Making of Americans," manuscript, pp. 50–51, YCAL; "The Making of Americans," *EW,* pp. 161–62.

Henry Hersland—the name: Henry Hersland becomes Alfred Hersland in *The Making of Americans.*

"We are misplaced": See *MOA,* p. 21; "The Making of Americans," manuscript, p. 33; "The Making of Americans," *EW,* p. 153.

Quite mannered: "The Making of Americans," *EW,* pp. 144, 162, 163.

"a simple novel"; "a record": "The Making of Americans," manuscript, p. 16; *EW,* p. 144.

"The old people": "The Making of Americans," *EW,* p. 137.

"It has always": "The Making of Americans," *EW,* p. 137.

"fever" . . . *"call of elegance":* "The Making of Americans," *EW,* p. 141.

Abraham Dehning: Bird Sternberger apparently knew a family named Dehning, who spent their summers in Maine.

"Well it won't": "The Making of Americans," *EW*, pp. 143, 142.

"It is a dreary": "The Making of Americans," *EW*, p. 147. See also *MOA*, p. 3, and Aristotle, *Nicomachean Ethics*, trans. Martin Ostwald (Indianapolis: Bobbs-Merrill, 1962), p. 191.

friends perceived: See Sprigge, "Journal in Quest of Gertrude Stein," p. 29, and *JIS*, p. 187.

"In the eighteenth": "The Making of Americans," *EW*, p. 147.

"Opposition": "The Making of Americans," *EW*, p. 170.

"had never gotten": *ABT*, p. 71.

"Perhaps she": "The Making of Americans," *EW*, p. 146.

"like a large": "The Making of Americans," *EW*, p. 160.

"all the respectable": See GS, "The Value of College Education for Women," 1899, BMA-CC; for the comment about the "well trained and scientific doctor," later deleted, see "The Making of Americans," manuscript, p. 72; *EW*, pp. 171–72.

"well dressed": "The Making of Americans," *EW*, p. 152.

11. Quod Erat Demonstrandum

Relenting: *App*, p. 151.

"One could": *App*, p. 150.

No one else: See MCB, diary, Nov. 14, 1900, I Tatti.

"saddle-back": William James, *Psychology*, p. 245.

"republican": William James, *The Will to Believe and Other Essays in Popular Psychology*, p. 270.

"metaphysician": AH, *The Adversaries of the Skeptic*, p. 246.

"including": GS, "Composition as Explanation," *SW*, p. 519.

"a sense": *LIA*, pp. 159, 161. See also chapters 16 and 19.

"suggested": LS to GS, [Nov. 1900], YCAL.

"The argument": AH to MMG, Oct. 20, 1900, PU.

Reading William James's: LS to MFW, Sept. 19, 1902, YCAL; quoted in *JIS*, p. 12.

"A letter": AH to MMG, Dec. 29, 1902, PU. Again, Hodder had been deeply influenced by his teacher William James, whose *Principles of Psychology*, vol. 2, pp. 471–72, emphatically outlines this position.

"For example": LS to Horace A. Eaton, Jan. 16, 1906, UCLA. Stein amplifies these ideas in *ABC*, pp. 105–7.

"is essentially": LS to Horace A. Eaton, Jan. 16, 1906, UCLA.

"is not what": LS, *App*, p. 10.

To demonstrate: *JIS*, p. 195.

"it became": *JIS*, p. 195; see also *ABC*, p. 76.

"The point": LS to Horace A. Eaton, Jan. 17, 1906, UCLA.

"A good thing": LS to Horace A. Eaton, Jan. 16, 1906, UCLA.

"Only things" . . . *"It doesn't"*: LS to MFW, Sept. 19, 1902, YCAL; quoted in *JIS*, p. 12.

"Not that": LS to MFW, April 8, 1903, YCAL; quoted in *JIS*, p. 14.

He said he told: *JIS*, p. 203. This version of the story, published posthumously, was evidently a draft for the more polished version that appears in *App*, p. 151, where Stein says he told Casals he felt himself "growing into an artist."

Leo remembered: *JIS*, p. 203.

Established in 1860: Catherine Fehrer and Robert and Elizabeth Kashey, *The Julian Academy*, p. iv.

The tolerant: See Catherine Fehrer, "New Light on the Académie Julian and Its Founder (Rudolphe Julian)," p. 210.

Some, however: Maurice Sterne, autobiographical notes, YCAL.

Gertrude told: NBH, diary, holograph, Aug. 28, 1903, YCAL.

"I don't see": Andrew Green to LS, Aug. 23, 1903, YCAL.

Rents in the district: Mildred Aldrich, "Confessions of a Breadwinner," unpublished autobiography, p. 130, Schlesinger.

Some speculated: Therese Ehrman Jelenko, unpublished reminiscences, 1965, Bancroft.

"Now everything": LS to MFW, April 8, 1903, YCAL; quoted in *JIS*, p. 14.

"Imagine": LS to MFW, April 8, 1903, YCAL; quoted in *JIS*, p. 14.

"I only started": LS to MFW, April 12, [1903/1904], YCAL.

"often as marked": LS, "Interest in Art," miscellaneous lecture, p. 6, YCAL; see also *App*, p. 199.

"Leo was": Interview with Mahonri Young, 1956, p. 64, COHC.

Stein one day: Interview with Mahonri Young, 1956, p. 65, COHC.

"I couldn't": *JIS*, p. 203.

"It is what": LS to Horace A. Eaton, Jan. 16, 1906, UCLA.

"I don't any": LS to MFW, Nov. 29, 1908, YCAL.

"he had sat": Stanton Macdonald-Wright to James Mellow, June 10, 1971, courtesy James Mellow.

"there was something": Edward T. Cone, "The Miss Etta Cones, the Steins, and M'sieu Matisse: A Memoir," p. 458.

"one of the real": EC to GS, n.d., YCAL. Evidently this note accompanied a gift from Etta Cone.

"It's great": EC, diary, June 21, 1903, BMA-CC.

"It was great": EC, diary, June 22, 1903, BMA-CC.

Stein spent: EC, diary, June 23, 1903, BMA-CC.

"Gertrude has": EC, diary, July 5, 1903, BMA-CC.

Etta nonetheless: EC, diary, June 26, 1903, BMA-CC.

"The Western"; she walked: "The Making of Americans," *EW*, p. 138; EC, diary, June 26, 1903, BMA-CC.

"Had a good": EC, diary, June 28 and 26, 1903, BMA-CC.

For the next: EC, diary, June 22, 1903, BMA-CC.

"beginning with": NBH, diary, holograph, June 22, 1903, YCAL.

"Not usual": NBH, diary, holograph, June 23, 1903, YCAL.

"& a lot": NBH, diary, holograph, June 19/20, 1903, YCAL.

"We enjoyed": NBH, diary, holograph, Aug. 28, 1903, YCAL.

Having donned: NBH, diary, holograph, June 24, 1903, YCAL.

"deepest love": EC to GS, n.d., YCAL.

"I have neither": "Q.E.D.," *EW*, p. 97.

"Nothing but": "Q.E.D.," *EW*, p. 97.

Moreover, if Stein: Elizabeth Sprigge, "Journal in Quest of Gertrude Stein," unpublished typescript, p. 113, YCAL.

"No I am": "Q.E.D.," *EW*, p. 108. Passing mention is made in "Q.E.D." of a character, Jane Fairfield, in whose apartment one of the most overtly sexual encounters between Adele and Helen Thomas takes place. Jane, a friend of Helen's, is not at home when Helen and Adele visit. (While waiting for her to return, Adele "found herself at the end of a passionate embrace.") Initially, Jane may have been slated for a larger role in the story. Among Stein's notes for the novel is a letter, evidently from May Bookstaver, which she copied, changing to Jane the name of a woman

mentioned in it: "You ask about Jane. We do not speak and apparently are further now than ever toward our former relations. Jane makes it evident to almost strangers that we are not on terms and I have come to feel very hard and careless on the subject. We meet frequently in charity & social meetings and naturally people notice and speak of our coolness to each other. I resent her behavior very much. I have always been polite and passed the time of the day on meeting her, but she does not do the same to me so I shall quit." The woman behind "Jane Fairfield" may be Georgiana King, Bryn Mawr 1896, M.A. 1897, who in 1903 was living in New York at 400 West 57th Street, in an apartment she described in terms similar to the ones Stein used; see Georgiana Goddard King, *Bryn Mawr Alumnae Bulletin,* 14, no. 5 (May 1934), p. 2.

"Whole Roman": Miscellaneous papers, "Q.E.D." box, YCAL.

"I did look": Emma Lootz Erving to GS, Aug. 10, 1903, YCAL.

To them: NBH, diary, typescript, Aug. 21, 1903, YCAL.

It was too beautiful: NBH, diary, typescript, Aug. 25, 1903, YCAL.

Stein gave: NBH, diary, holograph, Aug. 28, 1903, YCAL.

As for herself: HH to GS, [1905/1906], YCAL. Stein quotes from George Borrow's *Lavengro* in her "Degeneration in American Women." See also GS, "My Debt to Books," p. 307, and Appendix.

"Gertrude's visit": NBH, diary, typescript, Aug. 25, 1903, YCAL.

"Oscar Wildean": Leon Katz, "The First Making of *The Making of Americans,*" p. 55.

These persisted: Emma Lootz Erving to GS, Sept. 6, 1903, YCAL.

"What a lot" . . . *"Write"*: Miscellaneous papers, "Q.E.D." box, YCAL. Among the miscellaneous papers associated with "Q.E.D." is an early draft of the character based on May Bookstaver (in *EW,* p. 55), which revises part of the letter to Bookstaver: "Courageous and yet fearful, fire in nature and yet capable of abject submission. Not . . . cowed by her imagination, because the imagination was not a [illegible] quality but because after all these things in her that made for successful evil were only [hard?] sustained bluff. Brave duplicities that could not hold their own against a real attack." Sections of the letter appear in the final pages of "Q.E.D." (in *EW,* pp. 132–33). The letter was revised several times; three versions can be found among Stein's papers, YCAL.

The reference to Isabel concerns one of the main characters in Alfred Hodder's *The New Americans* (p. 252): "She possessed indomitable pluck; which is to say, she was incapable of changing her plan of life; she did not possess imagination enough. She wanted what she wanted, simply." Ironically, according to Hodder, the character of Isabel was based partly on M. Carey Thomas.

"the actual": "Q.E.D.," holograph, YCAL.

"How often": Miscellaneous papers, "Q.E.D." box, YCAL.

"Can't she": "Q.E.D.," *EW,* p. 133.

"Good God": Miscellaneous papers, "Q.E.D." box, YCAL.

"The things": Andrew Green to GS, Sept. 28, 1909, YCAL.

"Keep up": Emma Lootz Erving to GS, Oct. 6 and 29, 1903, YCAL.

"I hope": Emma Lootz Erving to GS, Jan. 14, 1904, YCAL.

Stein's later claim: "Q.E.D.," *EW,* p. 74.

She and her friends: See, for instance, Emma Lootz Erving to GS, Dec. 13, 1904, Jan. 14, 1905, and Jan. 25, 1905, YCAL; and MFW to GS, Aug. 27, 1909, YCAL.

long sections: The two longest passages are copied more or less verbatim from volume 1, book 2, chapter 2, and volume 1, book 6, chapter 3, respectively, of *The Wings of the Dove:*

" 'I quite suspect her of believing that, if the truth were known, she likes me literally better than—deep down—you yourself do: wherefore she does me the honour to think I may be safely left to kill my own cause. . . . I'm not the sort of stuff of romance that wears, that washes, that survives use, that resists familiarity. Once in any degree admit that, and your pride and prejudice will take care of the rest!— the pride fed full, meanwhile, by the system she means to practice with you . . . [will make me] come off badly. She likes me, but she'll never like me so much as when she has succeeded . . . in making me look wretched. For then you will like me less.'

"It told a story that made poor Denscher again the least bit sick: it marked so something which Kate habitually and consummately reckoned. That was the story that she was always for her beneficent dragon under arms; living up every hour but especially at festal hours to the value Mrs. Lowder had attached to her. High and fixed, this estimate ruled, in each occasion at Lancaster Gate the social scene; so that our young man now recognized in it something like the artistic idea, the plastic substance imposed by tradition, by genius, by criticism in respect to a given character on a distinguished actress. As such a person was to dress the part, to walk, to look, to speak in every way to express the part, so all this was what Kate was to do for the character she had undertaken, under her aunt's roof to represent. It was made up the character of definite elements and touches—things all perfectly ponderable to criticism; and the way for her to meet criticism was evidently at the start to be sure her make up exact and that she looked at least no worse than usual."

"I don't believe": LS to GS, Dec. 20, 1900, YCAL.
"lacks all": LS to GS, [March 5, 1901], YCAL; quoted in JIS, pp. 7–8.
"the stuff": LS to MFW, Feb. 6, [1934], YCAL; quoted in JIS, p. 137.
Leo considered: See JIS, p. 274; LS to MFW, n.d., YCAL, quoted in JIS, p. 142.
"hidden": "Here. Actualities," PL, p. 12.
"anybody reliable": GS to Louis Bromfield, [summer 1932], Ohio State University.
"There are": Louis Bromfield to GS, [1931/1932], YCAL.
"without manners": NBH, diary, holograph, Aug. 20 and Oct. 17, 1903, YCAL.
"nasty": Hannah Whitall Smith to Alys Russell, Aug. 29, 1903, Lilly.
"black": Hannah Whitall Smith to Alys Russell, Sept. 2, 1903, Lilly.
"the splendid" . . . "was all": NBH, diary, typescript, Oct. 17, 1903, YCAL.
"She was intolerant": "The Great Enigma," Dec. 29, 1894, YCAL; quoted in Rosalind
    Miller, Gertrude Stein, pp. 124–25.

12. Toward a More Quintessential Method

"I am beginning": CC to EC, Sept. 2, 1924.
"I often used": LS, notebook, [dated 1941–1945], Jan. 5, 1944, YCAL.
"We is doing": GS to MFW, [Oct./Nov. 1903], YCAL. An excerpt from this letter
    (quoted in Irene Gordon, "A World Beyond the World: The Discovery of Leo Stein,"
    in Margaret Potter, ed., Four Americans in Paris) is dated consistently as having been
    written in 1905. It is also the evidence consistently cited to place Leo Stein's purchase of Cézanne's Madame Cézanne with a Fan in early 1905. (Gordon herself is
    more circumspect, noting "it was probably [italics mine] during the first half of 1905
    that he [Leo] and Gertrude also acquired their . . . Portrait of Mme Cézanne";
    p. 26). Together with Stein's memoirs, written forty years after the events he recounts, the letter is generally offered to prove that Stein first encountered Cézanne's
    work in the spring of 1904.

Close inspection of the original letter, however, in its entirety, unquestionably dates it to the *fall of 1903*. First, Gertrude refers in the letter to Michael and Sarah's brief stay in New York, which preceded their departure for Paris, slated for December 31, 1903; they arrived in Paris early in 1904. Second, Gertrude mentions her upcoming visit to New York and asks Weeks to meet her on March 11 at the North German Lloyd dock. This was the last visit Stein would make to the United States for almost thirty years; she made no such visit in 1905. Third, Stein says she is "writing a lovely story"—presumably "Quod Erat Demonstrandum," which was written in the fall of 1903. Fourth, Leo Stein's postscript includes an introduction to the artist Paul Dougherty, soon to return to the United States. Leo says that he and Dougherty had a good time in Venice the year before; Weeks met Dougherty in 1904 and by 1905 knew him fairly well.

The significance of the earlier date is not a matter of pedantry. It sets Leo's acquaintance with Cézanne earlier than previously assumed. Moreover, this earlier acquaintance is confirmed by Stein himself. In an older version of a part of *Appreciation* (pp. 154ff), written around 1937 as part of a planned series of lectures in the United States, Stein talks about his introduction to Cézanne via Berenson. In the lecture "The Masterpiece, Art, and Communication" (YCAL), Stein writes: "When I went to Paris in 1902, I began to look around at what in contemporary art might be interesting and found the Société Nouvelle to which Simon and Cottet and Henri Martin and Blanche and one or two others belong. This seemed to be good but when I saw their work a year after it didn't seem so good in fact it had become unimportant. I knew of nothing in the contemporary world except Renoir that was interesting and this was rather an isolated thing. My friend Bernard Berenson happened to be in Paris that spring and I told him of my difficulty. He said do you know Cézanne. I said no where does one see him. He said at Vollard's, so I went to Vollard's. Like others who were rather intensively nourished by Florentine art I took to Cézanne at once. Then I began to look further into the Independants, the Autumn Salon [1903] which was just beginning." This seems a more reliable version of events than the one in the published *Appreciation,* and it accords with other documents. See also note at *Stein told* below.

"Amico di Sandro": See Ernest Samuels, *Bernard Berenson: The Making of a Connoisseur,* p. 325.

"cause it's": GS to MFW, [Oct./Nov.] 1903, YCAL.

"I wanted": App, p. 154.

"livelier": App, p. 153.

Stein told: App, p. 154. Stein's retrospective account packs the Société Nouvelle exhibition, his meeting with Berenson, and his viewing Vollard's and Charles Loeser's Cézannes (see note at *Day after day* below) into a single narrative occurring, it seems, in the spring/summer of 1904. Documents of the time, though, suggest that Berenson's mention of Cézanne came in the spring/summer of 1903; if Berenson visited Paris on his way to Friday's Hill in the summer of 1903, then the meeting may have taken place in person. The Société Nouvelle exhibit to which Stein refers took place probably in 1903. It appears likely that Leo Stein bought his Cézanne that fall, 1903; it is to this purchase that Gertrude refers in her letter (see note at *"We is doing"* above). If, however, as Leo recalled many years later, he bought his first Cézanne in the spring, it was probably during 1903, and he purchased another in the fall.

And since Mantegna's: The relationship between Cézanne and the Italian Renaissance was also of concern to Roger Fry, who apparently met Leo Stein briefly at Friday's Hill. They had similar backgrounds: both were painters before they were critics, both studied at the Académie Julian, both were influenced by Florentine art, and both stressed the formal aspects of Cézanne's art.

If this was Stein's first Cézanne purchase, it was made probably in the spring of 1903; the Cézanne mentioned in Gertrude Stein's letter (see note at *"We is doing"* above) would be another addition to the collection.

Day after day: App, p. 155. Again, Leo Stein telescopes events. He says that after the Cézanne "debauch" he attended the newly formed Autumn Salon. This places his viewing of Loeser's Cézannes in the summer of 1903 and further corroborates dating Gertrude's letter about the Cézanne purchase to 1903. See note at *"We is doing"* above.

When he returned: App, p. 156. See also Therese Ehrman Jelenko, unpublished reminiscences, 1965, Bancroft.

"It was an incredible": ABT, p. 30.

"one of those": ABT, p. 31.

"In the years": LS, unpublished manuscript, [1925–1928], YCAL. The fragment is so closely related to the last pages of *ABC* that it appears it was written as either a first draft or an elaboration, to be given as a lecture shortly after the publication of *ABC*.

more Cézannes than: John Rewald, *Cézanne, the Steins and Their Circle*, pp. 11–13.

"Great mind": LS to MFW, [1905], YCAL; quoted in *JIS*, p. 16.

"fixed his mind" . . . "a man oppressed": LS, "Cézanne," p. 297.

But during a recent: Lucille M. Golson, "The Michael Steins of San Francisco," in Margaret Potter, ed., *Four Americans in Paris*, pp. 37–38; Harriet Lane Levy, "Reminiscences," unpublished memoir, Bancroft.

Living on the proceeds: Therese Ehrman Jelenko, unpublished reminiscences, 1965, Bancroft.

"Salon-lady": SS to GS, Oct. 20, [1899], YCAL.

She was fated: Aline Saarinen interview with Alice Toklas, 1956, Aline Saarinen papers, AAA.

"really intelligently": Henri Matisse, "Testimony Against Gertrude Stein," *transition*, 23, no. 1 (Feb. 1935), p. 3.

"Mike and Sarah": LS to MFW, April 12, 1904, YCAL.

Unaffordable: Therese Ehrman Jelenko, unpublished reminiscences, 1965, Bancroft. Jelenko remembered the figure involved as $8,000, one completely out of line with Leo Stein's characteristic expenditures. The greater value of her recollection lies in its allegation that Stein was about to embark on unusual purchases, which were made probably in the autumn with the windfall of 8,000 francs. See note at *The windfall* below.

"The salon": LS to MFW, April 12, 1904, YCAL.

"no one really": JIS, p. 321.

"was so taken" . . . "give stability": LS to MFW, Aug. 28, 1904, YCAL. The notion that Cézanne was able to eliminate the inessential seems to anticipate aspects of Roger Fry's discussion of the artist. See, for example, Fry, *Cézanne*, p. 42.

"With practice" . . . A china": LS, "Cézanne," p. 297.

"The effect": LS, unpublished, untitled lecture, [1927], YCAL.

"I was a Columbus": App, pp. 156–57.

"I went" . . . "though not": App, p. 157.

"an imp": LS to MFW, [early 1905], YCAL; quoted in *JIS*, p. 17.

"They frequently": ABT, p. 32.

"cubist Picasso": LS to Albert C. Barnes, Oct. 30, 1934; quoted in *JIS*, p. 148.

"is for you": ABT to Alfred H. Barr, Jr., March 17, 1951, Alfred H. Barr, Jr., papers, MoMA Archives.

"*My old[er] brother*": LS, autobiographical notes and fragments, n.d., YCAL.

"*You people*": Emma Lootz Erving to GS, Nov. 20, 1904, YCAL.

The windfall: App, p. 194–95. See Irene Gordon's pioneering "A World Beyond the World," p. 31. I have tried the best I could to reconstruct the major purchases in the Stein collection—a daunting task, in which I have been assisted enormously by the extensive materials collected by Margaret Potter for the Museum of Modern Art's magnificent 1970 show *Four Americans in Paris,* and by all departments at the museum, as well as by various archives, collectors, galleries, individuals, and by the photographs at the Museum of Modern Art and the Beinecke Library at Yale. But because the Stein collection was changeable, because there are only a scant paper trail and an incomplete catalogue raisonné, because Leo dispersed his share of the collection at different and undocumented times, and because, finally, the doors of the Barnes Foundation archives have remained so firmly closed that a complete accounting of Barnes's Renoir purchases is impossible (this also inhibited Margaret Potter), much of the record remains sketchy; nonetheless, I hope that whatever new information I have been able to provide will help guide future research.

They did not: LS to MFW, [early 1905], YCAL; quoted in *JIS,* p. 15.

"*You must*": Emma Lootz Erving to GS, Dec. 13, 1904, YCAL.

"*got an idea*": *App,* p. 195.

He returned: LS, autobiographical notes and fragments, n.d., YCAL.

"*was enthusiastic*": *App,* p. 195.

Vollard, who had: Ambroise Vollard, *Recollections of a Picture Dealer,* p. 137.

Under its influence: ABT, p. 34.

"*To make*" . . . "*the most robust*": LS to MFW, [early 1905], YCAL; quoted in *JIS,* pp. 15–16.

"*In fact*": LS to MFW, [early 1905], YCAL; quoted in *JIS,* pp. 16–17.

"*They take*": MFW to LS, March 25, 1905, YCAL. Weeks was speaking to Estelle Rumbold and Robert Kohn, a sculptress and an architect, respectively.

"*from the point*": LS to MFW, [spring 1905], YCAL.

"*At the beginning*": *App,* p. 201.

"*interested*": Maurice Sterne, *Shadow and Light,* p. 43.

"*Cézanne's 'style'* ": Sterne, *Shadow and Light,* p. 43; Maurice Sterne to LS, Aug. 3, 1909, YCAL.

Across the street: Barbara Rose, "The Price of Originality," in William C. Agee and Barbara Rose, *Patrick Henry Bruce, American Modernist,* p. 90.

The artist Max Weber: Interview with Max Weber, 1958, p. 57, COHC.

The same was: Andrew Dasburg to Grace Mott Johnson, April 24, 1910, AAA; see also Gail Levin, "Andrew Dasburg," p. 129.

"*Yesterday*": Andrew Dasburg to Grace Mott Johnson, April 24, 1910, AAA.

"*This is to compare*": Morgan Russell to LS, Aug. 18, 1910, YCAL.

Without irony: Sterne, *Shadow and Light,* p. 48.

"*So you don't*": MFW to GS, March 14, 1905, YCAL.

She had transcribed: From Lootz's letter of July 13, 1903 (YCAL), Stein copied a characterization of their medical school colleague Marian Walker Williams: "She does want a good deal for one little woman. She was [*sic;* wants] Alan and a practice and babies and its really asking a good deal." These fragments, among the papers for "Q.E.D.," also contain the following, later worked into "The Good Anna": "There are some natures capable of making even the face of the almighty look smutty." Originally, for "smutty," Stein had used the word "sordid." In the finished version of the story, the sentence reads: "She could somehow make even the face of the Almighty seem pimply and a little coarse" (*TL,* p. 32).

"the great master": GS, notebook A, YCAL.

"Everything I have": WAM, p. 98.

"Flaubert has": GS, notebook 13, YCAL.

"realism": WAM, p. 98.

"bodiless": William James, *The Varieties of Religious Experience*, p. 57. See also GS to Robert Bartlett Haas, Oct. 29, 1942, YCAL, for her discussion on the disembodied, or abstract, style in American writing.

"as real": James, *Varieties of Religious Experience*, p. 58.

"Cézanne wanted": App, p. 75.

In its initial: GS, miscellaneous notes and fragments for *MOA*, 195, YCAL.

Gertrude used: GS, notebook 2, YCAL.

"The busted twins": GS, miscellaneous notes and fragments for *MOA*, 195, YCAL.

Originally named: GS, notebook, n.d., YCAL.

"There is always": GS, notebook, n.d., YCAL.

"A German woman": GS, miscellaneous notes and fragments, n.d., YCAL.

"She needs you": Hortense Guggenheimer Moses to GS, May 7, 1905, YCAL.

In "The Good Anna": TL, pp. 6, 11, 10.

A midwife: TL, p. 43.

Mrs. Lehntman, the wise: TL, pp. 43, 34.

"In friendship" . . . *"friendship"*: TL, p. 36.

several of Herbert Giles's: MFW to GS, March 14, 1905, YCAL.

In later years: For Stein's cursory mention of Crane, in this case *The Red Badge of Courage*, see WIHS, p. 43.

"Jack London": LS to MFW, Dec. [11], 1905, YCAL. The postscript by Gertrude Stein to this letter has often been used, retrospectively and out of context, to prove that Leo scorned her work. See the following note.

"Leo he said": GS, postscript, LS to MFW, Dec. [11], 1905, YCAL.

Her penchant: Elizabeth Sprigge, "Journal in Quest of Gertrude Stein," unpublished typescript, p. 113, YCAL; ABT, p. 75; EA, p. 139.

"I suppose": Leo Friedman to GS, Oct. 28, 1907, YCAL.

"I'd hate": MFW to GS, March 14, 1905, YCAL.

Sometime after: GS, postscript, LS to MFW, Dec. [11], 1905, YCAL.

Other purchases: Rewald, *Cézanne, the Steins*, p. 13; Gordon, "A World Beyond the World," p. 26.

The latter: LS, autobiographical notes and fragments, and notebook [1], YCAL. See also LS to EC, May 13, 1937, BMA-CC.

"It is a long": App, p. 198.

"I went through"; *"Manet for the impecunious"*: App, p. 158; ABT, p. 50.

Vallotton's "naked": Margrit Hahnloser-Ingold, "Affirmation and Debate: Vallotton's Critics and Collectors," in Sasha M. Newman, ed., *Felix Vallotton*, p. 239.

"Young and I": Alfred Maurer to LS, Aug. 5, [1905], YCAL.

"that makes": LS, autobiographical notes and fragments, n.d., YCAL.

"Vollard said": ABT, p. 33.

"the nastiest": App, pp. 158, 156.

13. In the Thick of It

"This I mention": The passage from Swift is included with a draft of Gertrude Stein's "Melanctha."

"Please if": EC to GS, April 28 and May 16, 1906, YCAL.

"It seems": GS to EC, [winter 1904/1905], BMA-CC.

"Have just": GS to EC, Jan. 18–March 3, 1905, BMA-CC.

"I can't afford": Interview with Mahonri Young, 1956, p. 68, COHC.

"Gee, don't": Quoted in James Mellow, *Charmed Circle*, p. 101.

When asked: BW interview with Edward T. Cone, Jan. 3, 1991.

"the walls": CC, notes, courtesy Ellen B. Hirschland. A smooth version is quoted in Brenda Richardson, *Dr. Claribel & Miss Etta*, p. 89.

"The visitors"; "People were": App, p. 158; *ABT*, p. 35.

Although Gertrude: ABT, p. 35.

Sarah remembered: Quoted in Fiske Kimball, "Matisse: Recognition, Patronage, Collecting," p. 37.

She and Leo: Henri Matisse, "Testimony Against Gertrude Stein," *transition*, 23, no. 1 (Feb. 1935), p. 3.

Therese Ehrman later: Therese Ehrman Jelenko, reminiscences, March 20, 1962, Margaret Potter papers, folder 4, MoMA Archives.

But in 1908: Inez Haynes Irwin, "Adventures of Yesterday," unpublished autobiography, p. 261, Schlesinger.

Not until 1915: MS to GS, Feb. 12, 1915, YCAL.

Leo recalled: App, p. 159.

Gertrude heard: App, pp. 158–59.

"Oh no, said": ABT, pp. 39–40.

To augment: ABT, "Some Memories of Henri Matisse, 1907–1922," manuscript, 1955, Alderman Library, University of Virginia.

"the ugliest": App, p. 157.

"Decisive": App, p. 158.

"Matisse was": App, p. 159.

"He showed": LS, autobiographical notes and fragments, n.d., YCAL.

Leo continued: App, p. 160.

"he couldn't make": LS, autobiographical notes and fragments, n.d., YCAL. See Jack Flam, *Matisse*, pp. 227–32.

He watched his new: LS, autobiographical notes and fragments, n.d., YCAL.

When it was finished: LS, postscript, GS to MFW, [May 1906], YCAL.

Initially dubious: See Albert C. Barnes and Violette de Mazias, *The Art of Henri Matisse*, p. 368.

Leo deemed: Leo Steinberg, in *Other Criteria*, p. 8, comments thus on the "expanding, rhythmical system" of *Le Bonheur*: "The analogue in nature to this kind of drawing is not a scene or stage on which solid forms are deployed; a truer analogue would be a circulatory system, as of a city or of the blood, where stoppage at any point implies a pathological condition, like a blood clot or a traffic jam."

"painted with": LS, autobiographical notes and fragments, n.d., YCAL.

"because he": App, p. 166.

"Rhythm is": App, pp. 162, 164.

"The static": LS, autobiographical notes and fragments, n.d., YCAL.

"always believed": LS, "A New Salon in Paris," p. 273.

"The Matisse": LS to Albert C. Barnes, Oct. 20, 1934; *JIS*, p. 147.

"perfectly natural": ABT, p. 35.

"Matisse not": GS, notebook H, YCAL.

In addition, her appraisal: GS, notebook A, YCAL.

"critical interest": JIS, p. 298.

"recurring element": Leroy C. Breunig, ed., *Apollinaire on Art*, p. 37.

"will certainly": GS to MFW, [May 1906], YCAL.

Originally titled: The first page of the story identifies the relative as a cousin, but later in the story the cousin turns out to be Lena's aunt, Mrs. Haydon. Her description resembles that of Milly Dehning in the first version of *The Making of Americans.* This character, according to the notebooks, was modeled on Gertrude's Aunt Pauline.

"This place": TL, p. 171.

"real experience": TL, p. 66.

Stein in fact appropriated: MFW to GS, April 23, 1908, YCAL. Evidently Alice Toklas destroyed all of the May Bookstaver correspondence when she learned of the affair in the early 1930s. See Leon Katz, "The First Making of *The Making of Americans,"* p. 16.

Leo also recognized: LS to MFW, Feb. 6, 1934, YCAL; quoted in *JIS,* p. 137. Early on, the astute critic Richard Bridgman took issue with the critical assessments of "Melanctha" that overlooked Stein's "condescending and false" treatment of African-Americans; see Bridgman, *Gertrude Stein in Pieces,* p. 52. Critical analyses of *Three Lives* still abound.

"where no one": GS, composition, March 21, 1895, YCAL; quoted in Rosalind Miller, *Gertrude Stein,* p. 139.

In a college theme: GS, composition, April 27, 1895, YCAL; quoted in Miller, *Gertrude Stein,* p. 148.

During her medical: LS to GS, Dec. 20, 1900, YCAL.

linked the black: For a discussion of this connection, see Sander L. Gilman, "Black Bodies, White Bodies: Toward an Iconography of Female Sexuality in Late Nineteenth-Century Art, Medicine, and Literature," pp. 218, 226.

"it looks like": GS to EC, [winter 1904/1905], BMA-CC.

"complex, desiring": TL, p. 149.

"the earth-born": TL, pp. 60, 148.

Stein's attitude: Stein's racism is not inconsistent with her use of race to subvert standard moral and aesthetic conventions; see Gilman, "Black Bodies, White Bodies," p. 239, n. 16. On the modernist use of primitivism in the arts, see Patricia Leighten, "The White Peril and *L'Art nègre*: Picasso, Primitivism, and Anticolonialism," pp. 609–30. From this perspective, "Melanctha" is one of the texts that symbolically incorporate current events. There is no direct evidence, however, that Gertrude or Leo Stein read such publications as the special issue of *L'Assiette au Beurre* in 1904 devoted to King Leopold's abuses in the Congo, but doubtless both were aware of the widely reported scandals. Similarly, they would have been aware of the political indignation expressed by such figures as Charles Péguy, whose work Gertrude decidedly admired.

"And Jeff": TL, p. 109. See also William Gass, "And," pp. 101–25, for a brilliant discussion of "and," which focuses partly on sections of Stein's "Melanctha."

"It was a struggle" . . . "never can": TL, pp. 108, 128.

"just living" . . . "Dr. Campbell": TL, pp. 118, 81–82.

"Sometimes": TL, p. 97. This echoes Adele's diagnosis of Helen in "Q.E.D." as a double personality.

"everything" . . . "You always": TL, p. 121.

"Always she wanted": TL, p. 151. See also pp. 65, 162. Despite biographical inaccuracies and some unsubstantiated historical assumptions, Corinne E. Blackmer's argument in "African Masks and the Arts of Passing in Gertrude Stein's 'Melanctha' and Nella Larsen's *Passing,"* is significant in stating (p. 245): "For Stein, Melanctha's inability to articulate her desires coherently symbolizes the problems of con-

structing an adequate language of lesbian sexuality in the absence of a historical record of lesbian community."

"Melanctha was": TL, p. 166.

Fond of sharing: Maurice Sterne, "First Visit to Picasso," holograph, YCAL. Sterne gives the date as spring 1905, but Etta Cone was not in Paris then. The actual date was probably fall 1905 or spring 1906; in her account books, Cone noted that she bought one picture, an etching, from Picasso on November 2, 1905, for 120 francs, and eleven drawings and seven etchings on March 11, 1906, for 117.50 francs.

Leo recalled . . . "a man apart": App, p. 172.

"This was the real": App, p. 169.

Guillotine the feet: ABT, p. 43.

"Now you've spoiled": App, p. 173.

"a born liaison": App, p. 169.

"seemed neither": App, p. 180.

The man's gift: LS, autobiographical notes and fragments, n.d., YCAL.

"Gertrude loved": Harriet Lane Levy, "Reminiscences," unpublished memoir, Bancroft.

"Something had been": "Picasso," P&P, p. 17.

She and Leo: Roland Penrose, *Picasso*, p. 102.

"made a real pair": See Fernande Olivier, *Picasso and His Friends*, pp. 82–83, quoted in Pierre Daix and George Boudaille, *Picasso: The Blue and Rose Periods*, p. 284. The latter is a slightly different English translation of Olivier's original French text.

The meeting: John Richardson, with Marilyn McCully, *A Life of Picasso: 1881–1906*, vol. 1, p. 413.

"There was no": App, p. 171.

"As different": Olivier, *Picasso and His Friends*, p. 84.

"The homes": App, p. 170.

"Picasso sat": Picasso's most recent biographer, John Richardson, observed that the artist had trouble finishing the portrait because of Stein's oppressive presence, but also possibly because he had just met Matisse. See Richardson, with McCully, *A Life of Picasso*, vol. 1, pp. 410–11.

"lazy typewriter": EC to GS, Oct. 6, 1906, YCAL. Etta Cone typed the "Three Histories" manuscript probably before she left Paris in the spring of 1906; she may have visited Gertrude in Italy that summer, and typed the manuscript then, but for her to do so, the Steins would have had to bring the typewriter with them. Also, by April, Gertrude had sent Hutchins Hapgood her manuscript, no doubt typed; see HH to GS, April 22, [1906], YCAL.

Two years later: GS, notebook DB, YCAL.

"Completely self-centered": GS, notebook J, YCAL.

"Another world": Levy, "Reminiscences."

"Our collection": App, p. 195.

"The walls": LS to MFW, Dec. [11], 1905, YCAL.

"art students": Interview with Max Weber, 1958, p. 71, COHC.

"outsiders might": Ambroise Vollard, *Recollections of a Picture Dealer*, p. 137.

"Lo and behold": Mrs. Oppenheimer to GS, May 4, 1908, YCAL.

The Steins, said: Daniel-Henry Kahnweiler, "Introduction," PL, p. x; Elizabeth Sprigge, "Journal in Quest of Gertrude Stein," unpublished typescript, p. 43, YCAL. See also Breunig, ed., *Apollinaire on Art*, p. 29.

"But they could": Breunig, ed., *Apollinaire on Art*, p. 29.

"Gertrude had": MDL, *European Experiences*, pp. 324, 321.

"They are not": Mary Cassatt to Ellen Mary Cassatt, March 26, [1913?], quoted in Nancy Mowll Mathews, *Cassatt and Her Circle*, p. 310.

"*They, immigrants*": Jacques-Émile Blanche, *Portraits of a Lifetime*, p. 275.
"*Our collection*": App, p. 197.
"*Of course Gertrude*": Sprigge, "Journal in Quest of Gertrude Stein," p. 69.
"*Neither, so far*": Clive Bell, *Old Friends*, p. 173.
"*calm*" . . . "*trenchant*": Sprigge, "Journal in Quest of Gertrude Stein," p. 69; Daniel-Henry Kahnweiler, "Introduction," *PL*, p. x; Sprigge, "Journal in Quest of Gertrude Stein," p. 77.
"*Never in*": Sterne, *Shadow and Light*, p. 48.
"*totally sincere*" . . . "*dressed*": Stanton Macdonald-Wright to James Mellow, June 10, 1971, courtesy James Mellow.
"*People came*": LS, untitled lecture, [1928], YCAL.
"*I was in*": App, p. 201.
Those offended: Levy, "Reminiscences."
"*The center*": Agnes E. Meyer, *Out of These Roots*, p. 81.
Leo nervously: LS, autobiographical notes and fragments, notebook [1], YCAL.
one of the last Picasso: See Pablo Picasso to GS, Nov. 1908, YCAL. Leo Stein evidently bought a Renoir landscape from Bernheim-Jeune on December 14, 1908, and *Washerwoman and Child* earlier the same year. See Margaret Potter papers, box 3, folder 11, MoMA Archives.

14. Quarreling

Gertrude asked; But painting: MFW to GS, March 27, 1906, YCAL; GS to MFW, postscript from LS, [May 1906], YCAL.
And his main: LS to Horace A. Eaton, Jan. 16, 1906, UCLA.
"*I think*": Therese Ehrman Jelenko, unpublished reminiscences, p. 5, Bancroft.
"*You will*": Hortense Federleicht to GS, May 11, 1906, YCAL.
"*I am afraid*": GS, postscript, LS to MFW, [Dec. 11, 1905], YCAL.
"*I am now*": GS to MFW, [May 1906], YCAL.
"*I was particularly*": MFW to GS, Nov. 13, 1906, YCAL.
"*The Russians*": GS to EC, [winter 1904/1905], AAA.
"*absolutely insulting*": Quoted in Howard Gans to GS, [1906], YCAL.
Bird hadn't: Quoted in Howard Gans to GS, [1906], YCAL.
"*terrible*": GS, miscellaneous notes and fragments for *MOA*, YCAL.
"*Since you*": Howard Gans to GS, [1906], YCAL; GS, miscellaneous notes and fragments for *MOA*, YCAL.
"*I am done*": LS to Howard Gans, draft, n.d., among GS, miscellaneous notes and fragments for *MOA*, YCAL.
"*but that she*": Howard Gans to LS, Dec. 1906, YCAL.
"*I pounded*" . . . "*[If] Bird*": GS, miscellaneous notes and fragments for *MOA*, YCAL. These statements were written on separate pages of an unmarked notebook containing notations for *The Making of Americans*.
But as Gans: Howard Gans to GS, [1906], YCAL.
" '*Gertrude Stein*' ": Hortense Guggenheimer Moses to GS, postscript from Jacob Moses, March 1906, YCAL. The insensitive anecdote was intended to flatter both Stein and Hortense Moses. Jacob Moses continued: "A dread silence fell upon the assembled company as each strained her ear for the answer to these most pertinent queries. At this point an individual, far superior to the others in intellect, judgment, insight and discrimination, stepped forward and saved the day. 'Look at Hortense Moses, and then pass judgment on Gertrude Stein!' "
"*The deep joy*": GS, miscellaneous notes and fragments for *MOA*, YCAL.

"responsive": GS, notebook J, YCAL. This sentiment was incorporated almost directly into *The Making of Americans* (p. 647): "Mostly every one was feeling in her that she was needing to be feeling learning everything because anything could feed her."

"I did not": Bird Sternberger to GS, Oct. 16, 1907, YCAL.

"admired and depended": GS, notebook J, YCAL.

"It takes": MOA, p. 463; see also p. 647.

"Remember"; "Begin": GS, notebook MA, YCAL; GS, miscellaneous notes and fragments for *MOA*, YCAL.

The Herslands: The families were described as "German"; in later revisions, "German" was excised and "middle class" substituted. See GS, miscellaneous notes and fragments for *MOA*, [110], YCAL.

"The real drama": GS, notebook 2, YCAL.

As Stein reconceived: GS, notebook 9, YCAL.

"yes I say": GS, notebook 1, YCAL.

"Clang": GS, notebook MA, YCAL.

"To be dead": GS, notebook 3, YCAL.

"Complete disillusionment": MOA, p. 485.

"after failing": MOA, p. 483.

In the spring of 1906: MS to GS, May 10, 1906, YCAL.

Below stretched: Mildred Aldrich, "Confessions of a Breadwinner," unpublished autobiography, p. 84, Schlesinger.

"A most fearful": MCB to Hannah Whitall Smith, May 24, 1906; quoted in Barbara Strachey and Jayne Samuels, eds., *Mary Berenson*, p. 130.

"Angry Saxon": Harold Acton, *More Memoirs of an Aesthete*, p. 71.

The habits: MCB, diary, Nov. 23, 1902, I Tatti.

"They are people": MCB, diary, June 17, 1907, I Tatti.

After a short visit: Hortense Guggenheimer Moses to GS, Oct. 4, 1906, YCAL.

When Gertrude and Leo: See, for example, Algar Thorold to BB, July 25, [1906], I Tatti.

"There is a lovely": Algar Thorold to BB, July 25, [1906], I Tatti.

"Her figure": NBH to MCB, July 22, 1906, I Tatti.

Gertrude half joked: MFW to GS, June 20/24, 1906, YCAL.

"Full of reality": HH to GS, April 22, [1906], YCAL.

"Where one": Pitts Duffield to GS, Aug. 14, 1906, YCAL.

But at least one: Paul Chalfin to LS, March 30, 1907, YCAL.

He had an intelligent: MCB to Hannah Whitall Smith, Oct. 2, 1906, Lilly.

The two men: NBH to MCB, July 22, 1906, I Tatti.

"in an ecstatic": HH, *A Victorian in the Modern World*, p. 220.

"Sometimes men": "Men," *Two*, p. 310.

And sometimes one: Maurice Sterne, *Shadow and Light*, pp. 193–94.

Regardless, Edstrom: Harriet Lane Levy, "Reminiscences," unpublished memoir, Bancroft.

Anticipating: HH to GS and LS, Dec. 14, 1906, YCAL.

"feeling the drawbacks": HH to MCB, [1906], YCAL.

Hapgood later: HH, *Victorian*, p. 121.

Nonetheless Hapgood: Levy, "Reminiscences."

But when Hapgood: MCB, diary, Feb. 1, 1907, I Tatti.

"sweeter": HH to NBH, [1907], YCAL.

"He has neglected": HH to MCB, June 19, [1911], I Tatti.

"I can't remember": HH to LS, April 14, [1939], YCAL.

The Edstrom affair: HH to NBH, Feb. 15, [1907], YCAL.

"He fools": GS, notebook DB, YCAL.

"It was very": MCB to Hannah Whitall Smith, Sept. 21, 1907, I Tatti.

Briefly humbled: BB to MCB, Sept. 28, 1907, I Tatti.

"capable of": HH, *Victorian*, p. 219.

"I shall save": SS to GS, May 10, 1906, YCAL.

Years later: Annette Rosenshine, "Life's Not a Paragraph," unpublished memoir, p. 36, Bancroft.

Sarah reluctantly: SS to GS, Oct. 8, 1906, YCAL.

"A human": Rosenshine, "Life's Not a Paragraph," p. 70.

"I was very": LIA, p. 136.

"I was crushed": Rosenshine, "Life's Not a Paragraph," p. 70.

She also respected: GS, notebooks B, C, YCAL. See also Rosenshine, "Life's Not a Paragraph," pp. 142, 161.

"successor": EC to GS, Feb. 6, 1907, YCAL.

"knowing that": Rosenshine, "Life's Not a Paragraph," p. 82.

"sex was": Rosenshine, "Life's Not a Paragraph," p. 76.

"a permanent": Otto Weininger, *Sex and Character,* p. 83.

Weininger argued . . . "A woman's demand": Weininger, *Sex and Character,* pp. 46, 50, 64.

"Never before": Charlotte Perkins Gilman, *The Critic,* 48 (May 1906), p. 414.

And probably: GS, notebooks A, DB, YCAL.

But of course: See chapter 8 and Appendix.

Shortly after Sex: Andrew Green to LS, June 6, [1906], YCAL.

Soon Leo: Henri-Pierre Roché, journals, Jan. 21, 1907, HRHRC.

"Everybody looks": GS, notebook 3, YCAL.

Use Weininger: GS, miscellaneous notes and fragments for *MOA,* [75], YCAL.

She figured: GS, notebook DB, YCAL. See also notebooks 8, A, B, C, E, H, I, J.

"The Diagram Book": GS, notebook DB, YCAL.

"Keyser on top": GS, notebook DB, YCAL.

Picasso was a Bazarov: GS, notebook C, YCAL.

"The conception": GS, notebook C, YCAL.

"Impulsive": GS, notebook B, YCAL.

"Ask Leo": See GS, notebooks A, B, C, E, J, M, YCAL.

She pushed: See MFW to GS, Feb. 9, 1908, YCAL; Emma Lootz Erving to GS, Dec. 4, 1908, YCAL.

"By the way": Marian Walker Williams to GS, June 11, 1909, YCAL.

"I stays": GS, miscellaneous notes and fragments for *MOA,* [36], YCAL.

15. Banquets

Her father: ABT to Annette Rosenshine, April 17, 1949, Bancroft; quoted in Edward Burns, ed., *Staying On Alone,* p. 156.

In her youth: GS to Lloyd Lewis, [1939], Harrison Collection, UCLA.

In San Francisco: Annette Rosenshine, "Life's Not a Paragraph," pp. 32, 34, Bancroft.

This was a woman: Elizabeth Sprigge, "Journal in Quest of Gertrude Stein," unpublished typescript, p. 83, YCAL.

she volunteered: Rosenshine, "Life's Not a Paragraph," p. 33.

Her small-framed: Duncan, p. 46.

Toklas's father: Duncan, p. 47.

She insisted: Duncan, pp. 25, 61, 64, 74.

in a house steeped: Rosenshine, "Life's Not a Paragraph," p. 30.
Ferdinand Toklas began: ABT, *WIR,* early draft, Butler.
Each spring: Harriet Lane Levy, *920 O'Farrell Street,* p. 26.
The San Francisco earthquake: Duncan, pp. 87–88; *WIR,* p. 12; *ABT,* p. 4.
It might be: Harriet Lane Levy, "Reminiscences," unpublished memoir, Bancroft.
But Alice needed: ABT, *WIR,* early draft, Butler.
"stripping yourself": MFW to GS, April 21, 1907, YCAL.
"She considers": MFW to GS, April 28, 1907, YCAL.
Georgiana King read: MFW to GS, July 10, 1907, YCAL.
Although the Bobbs-Merrill: Editor, Bobbs-Merrill, to GS, Nov. 7, 1907; quoted in
     MFW to GS, n.d., YCAL.
"Stinker": Rosenshine, "Life's Not a Paragraph," pp. 82–83, 235.
Gertrude was there: See *WIR,* pp. 22–23.
"I thought": WIR, p. 23.
This kind of worship: GS, miscellaneous notes and fragments for *MOA,* [46], YCAL.
"She is docile": GS, notebook DB, YCAL.
"No one": ABT, *WIR,* early draft, HRHRC.
Gertrude calmed: ABT, *WIR,* early draft, HRHRC.
"I impressed": GS, miscellaneous notes and fragments for *MOA,* [46], YCAL.
"In people": GS, notebook B, YCAL.
"not without intention": GS, notebook DB, YCAL.
"It is interesting": GS, notebook B, YCAL.
"Glorieuse": GS, notebook B, YCAL.
an old-maid mermaid: GS, notebooks DB, B, YCAL.
"Now Leo": Levy, "Reminiscences."
"We may even": Levy, "Reminiscences."
arranging for Fernande: Fernande Olivier to GS, Oct. 8, 1908, YCAL.
It was unsuitable: WIR, pp. 33–34.
Sarah Stein referred: Rosenshine, "Life's Not a Paragraph," p. 77. See also GS, mis-
     cellaneous notes and fragments for *MOA,* [1], YCAL; SS to GS, [late spring 1908],
     YCAL.
Levy recalled: Levy, "Reminiscences."
When Picasso needed: Pablo Picasso to LS, Aug. 17, 1906, YCAL.
"Monstrous": Gelett Burgess, "The Wild Men of Paris," p. 408. Burgess visited the stu-
     dio in the spring of 1908.
And although: See William Rubin, "From Narrative to 'Iconic' in Picasso: The Buried
     Allegory in *Bread and Fruitdish on a Table* and the Role of *Les Demoiselles d'Avi-
     gnon,"* p. 628.
"horrible mess": App, p. 175.
"a man of talent": App, p. 178.
"little by little": Picasso, p. 18. "Tschoukine" is the Russian collector Sergei Shchukin.
"Picasso said": Picasso, pp. 9, 14. See also GS, "Composition as Explanation," *The Dial,*
     81, no. 4 (Oct. 1926), p. 328: "The creator of the new composition in the arts is an
     outlaw until he is a classic." The essay is variously reproduced; see, for example,
     SW, pp. 511–24, and Ulla E. Dydo, ed., *A Stein Reader,* pp. 493–503.
"Leo turned": Levy, "Reminiscences."
Leo "looked" . . . Leo showed off: Lee Simonson, *Portrait of a Lifetime,* pp. 14–15.
He carried himself: David Edstrom, *The Testament of Caliban,* p. 239.
When the Matisses: Jack Flam, *Matisse,* p. 207.
"doing 'Rodin' ": Andrew Green to LS, June 6, [1906], YCAL.

Unsurpassed: LS to Morgan Russell, June 26, 1910, AAA.

"The Cézanne": LS to GS, [circa 1913], YCAL; quoted in *JIS*, p. 57.

"forced deformations": App, p. 192.

And both Matisse and Picasso: LS, miscellaneous notes and fragments, YCAL. See Rosenshine, "Life's Not a Paragraph," p. 85. Rosenshine said she kept notes on Leo's theories; she evidently lost or destroyed them.

she invited Hans Purrmann: Hans Purrmann, n.d., Alfred H. Barr, Jr., papers, MoMA Archives.

"Where did these": ABT, p. 66.

But the group: See Alfred H. Barr, Jr., *Matisse, His Art and His Public*, p. 116; Flam, *Matisse*, p. 221. Leo and Gertrude knew Palme through Edstrom.

Annette Rosenshine reminded: Rosenshine, "Life's Not a Paragraph," pp. 102–4.

"This manner": "Matisse Speaks to His Students, 1908: Notes by Sarah Stein," in Barr, *Matisse*, p. 552.

Max Weber: Interview with Max Weber, 1958, p. 256, COHC.

"The antique": "Matisse Speaks to His Students," p. 550.

"You must": Hans Purrmann, "From the Workshop of Henri Matisse," p. 34.

Leo Stein also: Rosenshine, "Life's Not a Paragraph," p. 101; Carl Palme to Alfred H. Barr, Jr., March 28, 1951, Barr papers, MoMA Archives.

"could pick out": Inez Haynes Irwin, "Adventures of Yesterday," unpublished autobiography, p. 263, Schlesinger.

This was his forte: GS, notebook I, YCAL.

"He had only": Irwin, "Adventures of Yesterday," p. 264.

"It is the distinction": LS, "William James," p. 68.

Suggesting that: See Ralph Barton Perry, *The Thought and Character of William James*, vol. 2, p. 475.

"What we here": Quoted in Perry, *Thought and Character*, vol. 2, p. 479.

"The pragmatic": LS to MFW, Oct. 6, 1909, YCAL; quoted in *JIS*, p. 20.

"No consequence": Levy, "Reminiscences."

"Pills for": Morton Schamberg to Walter Pach, Nov. 5, 1908, AAA.

"since Matisse": Walter Pach to Alice Klauber, March 9, 1908, AAA.

"must have wanted" . . . *"I wonder"*: Irwin, "Adventures of Yesterday," pp. 267, 268.

Gertrude lampooned: GS, notebook B, YCAL. Her valuation of Matisse at this time (circa 1909) echoes an earlier assessment by the critic Louis Vauxcelles in "Le Salon d'Automne," *Gil Blas*, Sept. 30, 1907, p. 3. See also Flam, *Matisse*, pp. 214–15, and chapter 13 of this book.

"There was a mutual": LS to NAS, April 29, 1914, YCAL; quoted in *JIS*, p. 59.

when he subsequently: On the quarrel between Gertrude Stein and Matisse, see Janet Flanner's April 4, 1951, letter to Natalia Murray, in Natalia Murray, ed., *Darlinghissima: Letters to a Friend* (New York: Random House, 1985), p. 142: "Alice Toklas can give me some [Matisse material], but she is so inaccurate because she and Gertrude quarreled with Matisse, and so she warps events." Toklas's account of Matisse's refusal to make an arrangement with the Steins is reported in Leon Katz, "The First Making of *The Making of Americans*," p. 123. The account, however, avoids mention of the source of the story and of the reason it is told in the first place. Sarah and Michael Stein continued to collect Matisses, and their friendship with the artist remained virtually untroubled.

Gertrude thought: GS, notebook C, YCAL.

During the past year: GS, notebook 8, YCAL, which contains what seems a draft of a letter to Matisse.

"Brutal egotism": GS, notebook A, YCAL.

Inez Haynes sensed: Irwin, "Adventures of Yesterday," pp. 267–68.

"I lived": Levy, "Reminiscences."

"I had known": WIR, p. 54. In this volume, Toklas generally collapses the years 1907, 1908, and 1909 into one. The flirtation took place probably during the winter/spring after Toklas's arrival, before Leo Stein became seriously involved with Nina Auzias.

Observing that Toklas: SS to GS, [late spring 1908], YCAL.

But both Gertrude: SS to GS, [July 1908], YCAL.

"my pet": EC to GS, Jan. 7, 1908, YCAL.

Toklas herself: WIR, p. 48.

With Etta: CC to EC, Aug. 31, 1910, BMA-CC.

Gertrude didn't: MCB, diary, June 21, 1908, I Tatti.

"showed evidence": Aline Saarinen interview with BB, June 1956, Aline Saarinen papers, AAA.

Gertrude recommended: MCB, diary, June 14, 1908, I Tatti.

"Fletcherize": Harriet Lane Levy to Annette Rosenshine, July 22, 1908, YCAL.

Fletcherizing: See Horace Fletcher, "How I Made Myself Young at Sixty," *Ladies' Home Journal,* 26 (Sept. 1909), pp. 9–10.

"He spared": MCB, diary, June 14, 1908, I Tatti; MCB to Hannah Whitall Smith, June 15, 1908, I Tatti.

He was willing: Edward Steichen to Aline Saarinen, Oct. 8, 1957, AAA.

The spectacle of the fall: See Roger Shattuck's fine summation in *The Banquet Years,* pp. 66–71.

Leo's retrospective account: App, p. 191.

Both the food: Levy, "Reminiscences"; *ABT,* pp. 103–7.

"The feeling": ABT, p. 64.

"Poor, patient": Burgess, "The Wild Men," p. 403.

"I sometimes": GS, notebook A, YCAL.

"emotional practical" . . . hands—heavy: GS, notebooks B, C, YCAL.

"the tenacity": GS, notebook DB, YCAL.

"walks in the light": GS, notebook 13, YCAL.

"When Mat & Pablo": GS, fragment tucked into notebook 8, YCAL.

"Little cubes": See Pierre Daix, "The Chronology of Proto-Cubism: New Data on the Opening of the Picasso/Braque Dialogue," in William Rubin, ed., *Picasso and Braque,* pp. 306–21.

16. I Could Be So Happy

Nina of Montparnasse: Maurice Sterne, *Shadow and Light,* p. 50; NAS, autobiographical notes, YCAL, quoted in *JIS,* p. 27.

"What a salty": HH, *A Victorian in the Modern World,* p. 468.

Maurice Sterne recalled: Sterne, *Shadow and Light,* p. 50.

Nina said she first: NAS, autobiographical notes, YCAL; quoted in *JIS,* p. 25.

Arriving at the Steins': This episode and the account of their meeting are taken from NAS, autobiographical notes, YCAL; much of the material is quoted in *JIS,* p. 26.

"Her looking": LS to MFW, Feb. 15, 1910, YCAL; quoted in *JIS,* p. 23.

Meanwhile, he pressed: HH, *Victorian,* p. 247.

Trembling, she went: NAS, autobiographical notes, YCAL; quoted in *JIS,* p. 27.

Leo said he thought: See Andrew Green to LS, [1909], YCAL.

"In the summer": MOA, p. 36.

"had no imagination"; "the enigma": MOA, p. 365; GS, "The Gradual Making of The Making of Americans," *LIA,* p. 142.

"Early just being": GS, notebook 14, YCAL. For a retrospective account of Stein's discovery that "there were civilizations that had completely disappeared from this earth," see *EA,* pp. 11–12, 115–21.

"discourse on immortality": GS, notebook 6, YCAL.

"without religious": LS to MFW, Oct. 6, 1909, YCAL.

"I want sometime": MOA, p. 574.

She seems to be: Aware of the confusion in her use of the word "repetition"—implying the rise and fall of civilizations on the one hand, and "the inevitable repetition in human expression" on the other—Stein attempted to clarify her terms later in life; see, for example, *LIA,* pp. 168ff. She used the term "insistence" to explain that there was no such thing as repetition, philosophically, but that people continuously communicated their personalities in their spoken expression. This discussion, it must be remembered, was written in retrospect.

Stein initially: MOA, pp. 175, 5.

"There are many": MOA, p. 115.

To Stein, the individual: MOA, pp. 336, 152. The sources for the undertaking were complex. They were related initially, as we have seen, to Stein's scientific training and her immersion in biology, and then to her medical education, which, she reminded herself in her notebooks, taught that "individuals less important life important" (notebook MA, YCAL). Her notion of the individual as both unique and representative bears comparison with Ruth Leys's fine discussion of Adolf Meyer, in "Types of One: Adolf Meyer's Life Chart and the Representation of Individuality," especially pp. 2–7. I am grateful to Eva Moskowitz for drawing my attention to this article.

she devised another system: See GS, notebooks E, F, YCAL.

"[Series] of human": GS, notebook 6, YCAL.

And true to her: GS, notebook DB, YCAL.

But all of these: GS, notebook E, YCAL.

"To begin": MOA, pp. 343–44, 347, 349.

But she determined: GS, notebook C, YCAL.

"A great many": MOA, pp. 605, 606.

"Realising": GS, notebook 14, YCAL. See also note at *She seems to be* above.

"When Leo said": GS, notebook D, YCAL. The date of the entry is probably around 1908. While it is easy to assume that Stein was reading *The Tempest,* she was undoubtedly referring to Shakespeare's Caliban via David Edstrom, who was himself nicknamed Caliban and with whose aesthetic ideas Stein evidently sympathized. The last line of the passage "Sterne gave me the right feeling of it" indicates that she credited Maurice Sterne as well as Edstrom for these insights.

When Stein clearly invokes Shakespeare's Caliban, she does so in a derogatory sense, as when calling Claribel Cone and Harriet Levy "moral Calibans" in notebook DB and in miscellaneous notes for *MOA.*

"Loving repeating": MOA, p. 295.

Alfred Hodder had: AH, *The Adversaries of the Skeptic,* p. 211.

"They are all": MOA, p. 305.

With repetition: GS, notebook 14, YCAL.

"I could be": See MOA, p. 611.

"Always I am": MOA, pp. 337, 338.

"I am all unhappy": MOA, p. 348.

"categories that once": MOA, p. 440.

"Perhaps no one": MOA, pp. 445, 458.

"the most wonderful": MFW to GS, Jan. 28, 1910, YCAL. By this time, Weeks was sent perhaps as many as the first two sections of the novel, which probably took her to MOA, p. 477.

could not stand solitude: GS, notebook B, YCAL.

whose rhythms, she said: ABT to Henry McBride, Aug. 6, 1960, AAA.

"By the time": WIR, p. 44.

Annette Rosenshine and others suspected: See James Lord, "Where the Pictures Were," p. 169.

"Alice was capable": Annette Rosenshine, "Life's Not a Paragraph," unpublished memoir, p. 83, Bancroft.

"giving people": GS, notebook DB, YCAL.

Other friends: BW telephone interview with Linda Simon, Feb. 1992.

But theirs: Esther Arthur to Elizabeth Sprigge, April 1954; Francis Rose to Elizabeth Sprigge, May 1954; Sylvia Beach to Elizabeth Sprigge, May 1954; Pavel Tchelitchew to Elizabeth Sprigge, May 1954; Louise Taylor to Elizabeth Sprigge, July 1954; quoted in Sprigge, "Journal in Quest of Gertrude Stein," unpublished typescript, pp. 29, 38, 42, 59, 83, YCAL.

"She's a sort": LS to MFW, June 1, 1920, YCAL.

Toklas might be: GS, notebook DB, A, YCAL.

"Sexual base": GS, notebook B, YCAL.

Harriet, on the other: GS, notebook B, YCAL.

"Shuts Alice's": GS, notebook B, YCAL.

"Harriet arms": GS, notebook DB, YCAL.

"Aunt Pauline": GS, notebooks D, C, YCAL.

"Always a forward": GS, notebook C, YCAL.

"From the way": GS, notebook H, YCAL.

Stein, wary: GS, notebooks I, C, M, YCAL.

"the vulgar": GS, notebook DB, YCAL.

"Alice at last": Rosenshine, "Life's Not a Paragraph," p. 83.

"I shall do": Frederick Hitchcock to GS, April 9, 1909, YCAL.

By the fall; "Tell her": HH to MCB and BB, Nov. 9, 1909, I Tatti; MFW to GS, Feb. 28, 1910, YCAL.

quipped Michael; Sarah immediately: MS to GS, Aug. 7, 1909, YCAL; SS, postscript.

It stirred: EC to GS, Jan. 19, 1910, YCAL.

" 'Melanctha' is": Hortense Guggenheimer Moses to GS, Nov. 2, 1909, YCAL.

"The theme": MCB to GS, Dec. 19, 1909, YCAL.

"a fine new": William James to GS, May 25, 1910, YCAL.

Of these, only Wells: H. G. Wells to GS, postmarked Jan. 7, 1913, YCAL.

Mabel Weeks also: GS to Henri-Pierre Roché, postmarked Dec. 23, 1909, HRHRC; MFW to GS, Sept. 2, 1909, YCAL.

"I was a New Englander": MFW, "Foreword," JIS, typescript, [1949], YCAL.

"You can imagine": MFW to GS, July [27], 1909, YCAL.

She appeared: MFW to GS, Sept. 2, 1909, YCAL.

But Weeks's report: MFW to GS, Aug. 1909, YCAL.

Mabel was deeply: MFW to GS, [Aug. 1909], YCAL; see also MFW to GS, Aug. 3, 1909, YCAL.

As he later: LS, miscellaneous writings and notebook [2], YCAL.

"Your love": LS to NAS, [Feb. 1910], YCAL.

"in a perfect": LS to MFW, Feb. 15, 1910, YCAL; quoted in *JIS*, p. 23.

He professed: LS to NAS, [May 1910], YCAL.

"Nina I love": LS to NAS, [March 1910], YCAL.

"You are for me": LS to NAS, [winter 1910], YCAL. Leo's letters to Nina are written in French. Unless otherwise noted, they are translated by BW.

as he once told: LS to NAS, Feb. 22, 1910, YCAL.

Her notebooks and letters: See, for example, in addition to the *MOA* notebooks, MFW to GS, Sept. 2, 1909, YCAL.

"decidedly": LS to NAS, Feb. 20, 1910, YCAL.

Berenson quickly: BB to MCB, Sept. 17, 1909, I Tatti.

It was a conversation: Weeks remembered the conversation as occurring in 1906.

"There is no": MFW, "Foreword," *JIS*, typescript, [1949], YCAL.

Financially independent: See W. G. Rogers to Elizabeth Sprigge, Oct. 1954, quoted in Sprigge, "Journal in Quest of Gertrude Stein," p. 96; Robert Dole, "Alfred North Whitehead's Daughter Recollects Gertrude Stein," typescript, p. 6, YCAL.

Perhaps they regarded: LS to FS, Sept. 12, 1919, YCAL.

Leo, who began: LS to FS, Feb. 8, 1920, YCAL.

He had an odd: LS to NAS, [1920s], YCAL.

"many things": NAS to Hiram Haydn, [spring/summer 1948], YCAL.

17. A Fine Frenzy

"Writing books": GS, notebook 6, YCAL.

Painful: ABT, p. 22. For a pivotal discussion of the role the painting played in Picasso's development, see William Rubin, "Cézannisme and the Beginnings of Cubism," in Rubin, *Cézanne*, pp. 184–88.

historic Three Women: See Judith Cousins, "Documentary Chronology," in William Rubin, *Picasso and Braque: Pioneering Cubism*, p. 359.

A story long: See Janet Flanner, "The Surprise of the Century—I," *The New Yorker*, March 9, 1957, p. 38.

"aimed to rival": LS, "Art and Common Sense," p. 14.

A jealous, precocious: LS, "Pablo Picasso," pp. 229–30. See also Leo Steinberg, "Resisting Cézanne: Picasso's 'Three Women,'" pp. 115–33, in which Steinberg—albeit arguing to a different end—fully elaborates a similar point of view, that Picasso had to resist Cézanne.

"At last": LS, "Art and Common Sense," p. 14.

There were nonformal: Stein rarely discussed the painting's sources, for example African sculpture; he did note that Picasso's primitivism was another kind of abstraction through which he tried to arrive at essentials. See LS, notebook [7], YCAL.

When he and Matisse: Cousins, "Documentary Chronology," p. 355, where the canvas in question is identified as probably *Bust of a Woman* (1908). The letter, however, is dated June 12, 1912, and presents a retrospective view of Leo Stein—after he had fallen out of favor. See Isabelle Monod-Fontaine, *Donation Louise et Michel Leiris: Collection Kahnweiler-Leiris*, p. 168.

"faithful disciple": App, p. 178.

"Leo's trenchant": Daniel-Henry Kahnweiler, "Introduction," *PL*, p. x.

"Picasso and Braque": App, p. 183.

represented the position: Daniel-Henry Kahnweiler, *The Rise of Cubism*, p. 8.

"Cubism differs": Guillaume Apollinaire, "The Cubist Painters," in Edward Fry, *Cubism*, p. 116.

Later he would say: App, p. 187.

And that summer: Pablo Picasso to LS, [1910], YCAL. See Gelett Burgess, "The Wild Men of Paris," pp. 401–14, and Pablo Picasso to GS and LS, Thursday [spring 1910], YCAL.

Leo was not impressed: App, p. 186.

"As long as": App, p. 187.

Leo remembered: The anecdote is found in App, p. 176.

"I would explain": App, p. 176.

"You have no": App, p. 187.

"Breathing life": App, p. 181.

Bernhard Berenson had found: BB to MCB, Sept. 17, 1909, I Tatti.

when he castigated: LS, "On Teaching Art and Letters," p. 48. See Roger Fry, "An Essay in Aesthetics" (1909), in *Vision and Design*, pp. 16–38, for the earlier essay.

But to speak . . . "mainly in the complexity": LS to MFW, Feb. 15, 1910, YCAL.

"If I don't": LS to NAS, May 20, 1910, YCAL.

"It might seem": LS to NAS, May 24, 1910, YCAL.

It had worked: Sinclair first extolled the benefits of fasting in the popular article "Starving for Health's Sake," in the May 1910 issue of *Cosmopolitan*. The fact that Stein's preoccupation with fasting began at this time suggests that he may have seen this or related articles.

It is easy to suppose: See Emily Dawson to GS, April 13, 1910, YCAL.

although sales: Frederick Hitchcock to GS, Feb. 28, 1910, YCAL.

"quite extraordinary": "Three Lives. By Gertrude Stein," *The Nation*, 90 (Jan. 20, 1910), p. 65.

"the characters"; "At first": *Boston Morning Herald*, Jan. 8, 1910; *Kansas City Star*, Dec. 18, 1909.

"with a novel": Manierre Dawson, journal, Nov. 2, 1910, AAA.

"they would say": LS to Ettie Stettheimer, Sept. 8, 1924, YCAL.

By May, Leo: LS to NAS, May 20, 1910, YCAL.

Privately, he told: LS to NAS, July 9, 1910, YCAL.

Yet it was Leo: Morgan Russell, autobiographical fragment, MoMA Library.

insisted he wasn't: LS to NAS, [May/June 1910], YCAL.

Gertrude disapproved: BW interview with Edward T. Cone, Jan. 3, 1991; Mrs. Rosalie Raffel to BW, Jan. 6, 1991.

Nina would continue: GS, notebooks H, I, YCAL.

"this one": "Elise Surville," *Two*, p. 316.

In a few days: LS to NAS, Sunday [June 1910], YCAL.

"I am more": LS to NAS, July 22, 1910, YCAL.

"Nina's letters": LS to GS, [June 1910], YCAL.

"I hope": LS to NAS, Sunday [June 1910], YCAL.

"The two fundamental": LS to MFW, Aug. 8, 1910, YCAL; quoted in JIS, p. 35, but misdated in that volume.

"This much": LS to Morgan Russell, July 23, 1910, The Montclair Art Museum, Montclair, New Jersey.

"I don't much": App, p. 107.

"and if you're": LS to GS, July 26, 1910, YCAL.

"comes only": Writer unknown (identified only as "LS" or "LT") to Morgan Russell, Sept. 19, [1910], The Montclair Art Museum. The writer was probably Lee Simonson, whom Stein visited in Dachau; see LS to NAS, July 27, 1910, YCAL.

"perched himself": Writer unknown ("LS" or "LT") to Morgan Russell, Sept. 19, [1910], The Montclair Art Museum. See the preceding note.

"The collections": LS to GS, Aug. 9, 1910, YCAL.

He would stay: LS to NAS, July 30, 1910, YCAL.

Aldrich then worked: Henry McBride to Otto [unidentified surname], June 8, 1910, AAA.

"writes plays": GS to EC, [Jan. 1905], YCAL.

Aldrich liked: See Mildred Aldrich to Henry McBride, July 19, 1923, AAA.

"I had known": Mildred Aldrich, "Confessions of a Breadwinner," unpublished autobiography, pp. 141–47, Schlesinger.

He could be: See Howard Gans to HH, Jan. 17, 1942, YCAL.

He had integrity; "even after all": Aline Saarinen interview with Bernhard Berenson, July 1956, Aline Saarinen papers, AAA; Stanton Macdonald-Wright to James Mellow, June 10, 1971, courtesy James Mellow.

"you did": Adele Wolman to LS, [1930s], YCAL.

"Perhaps he was": Ettie Stettheimer to Henry McBride, Aug. 14, [1950], AAA.

And during the summer: LS to MFW, Aug. 8, 1910, YCAL.

Freud's Interpretation; *Leo later:* Annette Rosenshine, "Life's Not a Paragraph," unpublished memoir, p. 77, Bancroft; see also LS, journals, n.d., YCAL, and LS to Manuel Komroff, June 15, 1937, Butler. Stein said in retrospect that he first heard of Freud in 1909. This may be true, but it was in the summer of 1910, when in Germany, that he first reported having bought and read Freud's work; see LS to MFW, Aug. 8, 1910, YCAL.

"the richest & deepest": LS to MFW, Aug. 8, 1910, YCAL.

"Gertrude Stein never": ABT, p. 79.

Nonetheless, privately: GS to Thornton Wilder, postmarked Sept. 25, 1935, YCAL. Stein went on to say that Freudian theory "is completely based on human and animal nature it is not at all interesting. There is no knowledge in human nature." To her, human knowledge implied the creative consciousness; human nature was, more or less, raw instinct. See in particular *GHA*.

"Suppressed" . . . *"At present"* . . . *"with discussion"*: LS to MFW, Aug. 8, 1910, YCAL; quoted and misdated in *JIS*, p. 36.

"I had never": LS to GS, [Aug./early Sept. 1910], YCAL.

"I'm quite": LS to GS, Monday [late Aug./early Sept. 1910], YCAL; quoted in *JIS*, p. 42.

"I am beginning": LS to NAS, [late Aug./early Sept. 1910], YCAL; partially quoted in *JIS*, p. 44.

"I didn't see": LS to GS, [Aug./early Sept. 1910], YCAL; quoted in *JIS*, p. 43.

"as I don't": LS to GS, Tuesday [early Sept. 1910], YCAL.

"At last he has": BB to MCB, Oct. 26, 1910, I Tatti.

"Miss Stein came": MCB to Hannah Whitall Smith, June 17, 1910, Lilly; quoted in Barbara Strachey and Jayne Samuels, eds., *Mary Berenson*, p. 160. The letter contains the misspelling of Toklas's name.

"tribe of queer": BB to Isabella Stewart Gardner, Aug. 27, 1909; quoted in Rollin Van N. Hadley, ed., *The Letters of Bernard Berenson and Isabella Stewart Gardner*, p. 454.

"turned tail": BB to MCB, Sept. 28, 1909, YCAL.

Not only did: BB to MCB, Oct. 9, 1908, I Tatti; BB, "De Gustibus," *The Nation*, 87 (Nov. 12, 1908), p. 461.

"Where & when": BB to MCB, Sept. 24, 1909, I Tatti.

"I do not know": BB to MCB, Sept. 28, 1909, I Tatti.

"Could not tolerate": BB, diary, April 26, 1950, I Tatti.

"infested": MCB to Hannah Whitall Smith, May 20, 1910, Lilly.

"pretended omniscience": MCB to BB, Sept. 1909, I Tatti.

She paid little: MCB to Hannah Whitall Smith, May 20, 1910, Lilly.

Neither Gertrude; she had: AH to MMG, Oct. 20, 1900, PU; GS, notebooks DB, C, YCAL.

"mostly run": GS, notebook A, YCAL.

"have good": GS, notebook A, YCAL.

"pretty great": GS, notebook A, YCAL.

"Alice runs": GS, notebook DB, YCAL.

"I think Alice": GS, notebook B, YCAL.

"feel passionate": GS, notebook D, YCAL. See also Lisa Ruddick, *Reading Gertrude Stein*, pp. 184–86; Ruddick relates Stein's buried feelings toward her mother with her attraction to Alice Toklas.

"Your news": Mildred Aldrich to GS, July 12, 1910, YCAL.

"I am a person": Elizabeth Sprigge, interview with ABT in "Journal in Quest of Gertrude Stein," unpublished typescript, p. 11, YCAL.

They were married: In a short piece originally titled "Harriet Making Plans," *P&P*, pp. 105–06, Gertrude expressed her exasperation about Harriet's interference, especially that summer: "She had not made plans for the summer and she had not made plans for the following winter. She had not made plans for the winter and so to those who were interested in hearing what her plans were for the winter she told that she had not made plans for the summer she told them that she had not made plans for the summer and they had asked what were her plans for the winter." Alice Toklas dated the piece, correctly it seems, as 1910, in her notations on the manuscripts, YCAL. In Stein's notes on the manuscript, she refers to Harriet as Toklas's "ma-in-law."

"I am still": LS to GS, Tuesday [Sept. 1910], YCAL.

"It suddenly": LS, "Interest in Art," unpublished lecture, YCAL.

"Appreciation": LS, notebook [9], YCAL.

"a bad": LS to MFW, Oct. 12, 1911, YCAL.

"To use": JIS, p. 201. See also LS to Trigant Burrow, Sunday [received Nov. 28, 1934], Sterling.

"It seemed": LS, notebook [16], YCAL.

"Earliest sense": Journal entries quoted in LS to Trigant Burrow, Feb. 11, 1937, Sterling.

"a metaphysics": LS to MFW, Aug. 5, 1911, YCAL.

"nothing more": LS to MFW, Oct. 12, 1911, YCAL.

"everything": LS to MFW, Oct. 3, 1911, YCAL.

Some two years: LS to MFW, Feb. 7, 1913, YCAL.

"It separates": App, p. 77.

18. Myself and Strangers

While in California: SS to GS, [Oct.? 1910]; also SS to GS [1910], YCAL.

"Doesn't Alice": Harriet Lane Levy to GS, July 23, 1911, YCAL.

"I do not think": MFW to GS, Nov. 21, 1909, YCAL.

"I don't like": MFW to GS, June 3, 1910, YCAL.

She claimed . . . "Ada": ABT, pp. 113–14.

This was definitely: Stein sent a group of her early portraits to Harriet Levy; "Ada" was not among them. Levy received "Ada" in a second batch, which included a portrait of the painter Arthur B. Frost, Jr., and the portrait "Miss Furr and Miss Skeene." See Harriet Lane Levy to GS, June 10, 1911, YCAL.

Among the loose pages associated with notebook N, one contains this list: "Leo

Friedman et Co., Then the short sketches in the order done. / Claribel / Mildred / Old Maids / David et al. / Italians." The holograph manuscript suggests that "Leo Friedman et Co." is "Five or Six Men"; "Old Maids" may have been the original title for "Two Women" or "A Kind of Woman," whose notes read "Dora & Annette, Making of an old maid"; "David et al." may have been "Four Proteges" or "Men." There are no extant manuscripts that correlate to "Claribel" or "Mildred," unless the former is "Two Women" (doubtful) and the latter is "A Family of Perhaps Three." This evidence of course does not date "Ada," but it does raise the question as to whether the claim that it was the first written was a literary conceit.

Dating the early portraits is a nightmarish enterprise. Because much of the chronology has depended on Alice Toklas, I advise caution. She had a gift for accuracy but, like anyone else, forgot much over the years and dated pieces and events psychologically. Moreover, she (and often Stein; see P&P) tended to predate works and events, as if to make themselves seem more precocious. For instance, insisting to Janet Flanner that "Ada" was Stein's first portrait, Toklas dated it to the winter of 1908–1909, a very remote possibility (see Flanner, "Introduction," Two, p. x). Surprisingly, Toklas's dating is often assumed to be accurate.

The most extensive list of probable dates for Stein's compositions can be found in Richard Bridgman's Gertrude Stein in Pieces, although the early dating needs much reworking. Subsequent scholarship, particularly by Jayne Walker, Marianne DeKoven, and Ulla Dydo, is therefore indispensable. Cyrena Pondrom ("Notes on Contents and Dates of Composition," G&P) offers a summation of the variously proposed dates for the pieces in G&P but no new or independent evidence. Much work therefore remains to be done, especially since too many critics quote each other, ignore primary sources, and/or rely on Leon Katz's obsolete if interesting work (which itself relies heavily on interviews with Toklas); others are determined to posit stylistic continuity where there may in fact be disruptions, overlaps, and much trial and error. I've added, where I think it useful, corrections or suggestions.

Stein did not begin mentioning her portrait sketches in her correspondence with friends until December 1910. There is no compelling evidence to suggest any was completed earlier than that date.

"charming" . . . "Trembling": "Ada," G&P, pp. 15–16. For a discussion of the importance of collaboration and dialogue in Stein, see Harriet Scott Chessman, The Public Is Invited to Dance, especially chapter 2.

"Dearest," Stein: "Rue de Rennes," holograph manuscript on loose sheets, YCAL.

"Dearest, I wish": "Bon Marche Weather," holograph manuscript, YCAL.

She hadn't read: See Harriet Lane Levy to GS, Dec. 31, [1910], YCAL.

the same gibe: ABT, p. 53.

"Two Women," written around the same time: Internal evidence suggests this date. See also CC to EC, Sept. 20, 1910, BMA-CC. Claribel Cone visited Paris in the fall of 1910, during which time she discussed with Stein a series of photographs she'd had taken of herself. Dismayed that her family did not like the same pictures she did, Cone listened carefully to Gertrude's theory about them. "She assumed that I 'must have looked like that before I became older and more aggressive.' " Stein mentions photographs in her notes to "Two Women," and includes in the portrait a juxtaposition of how the sisters look at younger and older ages. In addition, the fact that the name "Ada" is used for both Etta and Alice suggests parallels in the various sets of relationships. See, for example, Brenda Richardson, Dr. Claribel & Miss Etta, p. 50, and James Mellow, Charmed Circle, p. 132.

Ada was also the name of Nellie Joseph's sister, whom Toklas knew well.

"To aid": "Didn't Nelly and Lilly Love You," AFAM, p. 230.

"bared their souls": Quoted in Hortense Guggenheimer Moses to GS, n.d., YCAL.

"men . . ."; "quite regularly": "Men," Two, p. 310; "Miss Furr and Miss Skeene," G&P, p. 20. "Gay" did not, evidently, refer to homosexuality as it does today, although it is difficult to read a piece such as "Miss Furr and Miss Skeene" without assuming so, or at least assuming Stein's prescience, for here she does link "being gay" with sexuality.

"that one": "Ada," holograph manuscript on loose sheets, YCAL. See also an early, untitled typed version in the Mitchell Kennerley papers, Vassar College.

"The line": ABT, p. 90. Edmund Wilson, in The Shores of Light, was the first to associate Stein's hermeticism with the wish to conceal her lesbianism (see Wilson, p. 581). Richard Bridgman, in Gertrude Stein in Pieces, underlines Wilson's point, noting that Wilson admitted he may have exaggerated the significance of "lesbian sentiments" (see Bridgman, p. 106). More recently, critics consider—rightly, I think—indirection a deliberate literary strategy, albeit connected to sexuality, more than a simple defense. See, for instance, Catharine R. Stimpson, "The Mind, the Body, and Gertrude Stein," pp. 489–506, and Karen M. Cope, "Publicity Is Our Pride," pp. 123–36.

I am indebted also to Alexandra Kreisler for her suggestions in this area.

"completely a real": "Picasso," P&P, p. 19. See also MOA, pp. 538–39, for a full statement of Stein's method of characterization; for example: "I tell about the living in them from the living they have had in them I cannot ever construct action for them to be doing, I have certainly constructive imagination for being in them, sometimes with very little watching I have pretty complete realization of pretty nearly all the being in them."

The portraits . . . And wasn't: See MFW to GS, [spring 1911], for Weeks's response to what must have been a discussion by Stein about her style.

anecdote about the Matisses: "Storyette: H.M.," P&P, p. 40, is included in MOA notebook N, YCAL. The incident serving as the basis for the "storyette" took place in November 1910, around the time of Matisse's departure for Spain. For a discussion of portraiture generally and of Stein's referential/aesthetic literary equivalent, see Wendy Steiner, Exact Resemblance to Exact Resemblance, especially pp. 1–63.

"Sometimes I like": For Stein's own explanation of her vocabulary, see MOA, pp. 539–40: "It is really a very difficult thing to me to be using a word I have not yet been using in writing. . . . in talking I use many more of them of words I am not living but talking is another thing, in talking one can be saying mostly anything, often then I am using many words I never could be using in writing." According to correspondence, these sections of MOA were composed around the end of 1910.

"Making for success": GS, notebook DB, YCAL.

"was not"; "certainly"; "some were": "Julia Marlowe," Two, p. 329; "Purrmann," Two, p. 335; "Russell," Two, p. 337.

Stein immediately sent: In notebook 13, YCAL, Stein lists what must be projected submissions. She sends or intends to send to McClure "Frost," "The Four Proteges of Mrs. Whitney," and "Miss Mars"; to the American, "Alice"; and to Harriet, "Alice," "Nadelman," and "Frost." Other notes suggest that she is writing or planning to write "Russell" and "Matisse" at this time.

friends, who were in turn: MFW to GS, Jan. 1, 1911; Alice Woods Ullman to GS, [March 1911]; Harriet Lane Levy to GS, Feb. 10, [1911], YCAL.

"the nearest": GS to H. H. McClure, [spring 1911], draft, YCAL. Stein received his response rejecting the manuscript on May 1, 1911.

contacted the publisher George Doran: GS to George Doran, [Feb. 1911] draft, YCAL. Doran's answer is dated March 2, 1911. We can assign at least two portraits to this period: having spent several afternoons with Isadora Duncan, Stein apparently wrote her Duncan sketch, "Orta, or One Dancing," that winter, and her portrait of Henri-Pierre Roché was dated March 1911 by him and April 11, 1911, by Toklas.

"It is not such": MOA, p. 521.

"I am a rare": GS, notebook I, YCAL; *MOA,* pp. 565, 573.

Leo meanwhile: Katherine M. Jaeger to LS, April 30, 1911, YCAL.

"The basic change": LS to NAS, March 22, 1911, YCAL; quoted in *JIS,* p. 46.

"Elan vital": LS to MFW, Oct. 3, 1911, YCAL.

"all that kind": LS to MFW, Oct. 3, 1911, YCAL.

Leo spoke animatedly: Henri-Pierre Roché, carnet 55, [spring 1911], HRHRC.

She was a champion: See MFW to GS, [March/April 1911], YCAL.

"But in fact": ABC, p. 116.

Moreover, the abstractions: LS, notebooks [14], [17], YCAL.

"same stunt": LS to GS, June 8, 1911, YCAL.

"Cubism may": LS to MFW, Feb. 4, 1913, YCAL; quoted in *JIS,* p. 49.

"because metaphysical": LS, "A New Salon in Paris," p. 272.

"the genuine": LS, notebook [6], YCAL.

"the slightest": LS, notebook [6], YCAL. Sections in this notebook seem to have been written circa 1914–1920.

What annoyed: Eugene Berman to James Mellow, Aug. 1, 1972, and Stanton Macdonald-Wright to James Mellow, July 17, 1971, both courtesy James Mellow. See also Elizabeth Sprigge, interview with Gabrielle Picabia in "Journal in Quest of Gertrude Stein," unpublished typescript, p. 69, YCAL.

"was expressing": Picasso, p. 16.

"became as brother": There are several versions of this statement, evidently intended as a publicity blurb. See miscellaneous undated and uncatalogued typescripts, YCAL. This one was written probably to promote the publication of *Tender Buttons* (1914), just after Leo Stein left the rue de Fleurus for good; several versions of similar copy were drafted for the publisher Claire-Marie.

"clearly expressing" . . . *"not greatly":* "Matisse," *P&P,* pp. 12, 16. Stein is echoing Leo's formulation ("Leo says Matisse's esthetic quality is clarity," she wrote in notebook 13, YCAL), as well Matisse's own (see Jack Flam, *Matisse on Art,* pp. 32–46); she concludes that "Matisse is clear in his emotional power, that has a clarity and pushes through all obstacles and the more the resistance [*sic*] the difficulties the more vivid the expression" (notebook H, YCAL).

These portraits were composed apparently in the spring of 1911, and sent to publishers; they were rejected by *New English Review* in August 1911. See also Pablo Picasso to Henri-Pierre Roché, April 7, 1911, HRHRC.

"Matisse not": GS, notebook H, YCAL.

"This one was": "Picasso," *P&P,* p. 18.

His work was: "Picasso," *P&P,* p. 18.

"I have the eye": "Farragut or A Husband's Recompense," [1915], UK, p. 13.

"a beginning": "Ada," *G&P,* p. 16.

Reflecting later: Narr, pp. 23, 24, 25.

"Pablo and I": GS, notebook A, YCAL.

"Our initiative": GS, notebook B, YCAL.

"a certain immediacy": LS to Morgan Russell, July 9, 1910, The Montclair Art Museum, Montclair, New Jersey.

"Does the reality": GS, notebooks A, B, YCAL.

"He truly": GS, notebook A, YCAL.

"Keep your eye": LS to Horace A. Eaton, Jan. 16, 1906, UCLA; *App*, p. 143. See also chapter 11.

Etta Cone, who revered: EC to GS, June 25, 1911, YCAL.

"It's probable": LS to NAS, March 22, 1911, YCAL.

Tactlessly, he: MCB to [Hannah Whitall Smith], June 19, 1911, I Tatti.

When Baltimore: EC to GS, Jan. 29, 1911, YCAL.

"Tell the worried": LS to GS, Aug. 17, 1911, YCAL.

When she and Alice . . . After the age: MCB to Hannah Whitall Smith, June 1, 1911, Lilly.

"the definitive fast": LS to Henri-Pierre Roché, July 6, 1911, HRHRC.

What would Sally: MFW to GS, July 24, 1911, YCAL.

That summer: Austin Harrison, *New English Review*, to GS, Aug. 25, 1911, YCAL. These included the portraits of Matisse and Picasso and a reaction to the new art movement, titled "You and Me."

Grafton Press: Editor, Grafton Press to GS, May 4, 1911, YCAL.

She packaged: GS to Harper & Company, n.d., draft, YCAL.

"have a sea" . . . "Quantity": Henri-Pierre Roché to GS, Feb. 12, 1912, draft, HRHRC.

"I made": GS to Henri-Pierre Roché, [Feb. 6, 1912], HRHRC.

"He also may": GS to Mrs. Charles Knoblauch [May Bookstaver Knoblauch], n.d. (with unmailed envelope), HRHRC.

"I know that Leo": Stanton Macdonald-Wright to James Mellow, June 10, 1971, courtesy James Mellow.

"What I need": LS, notebook fragment, Aug. 25, 1911, YCAL.

"mother complex": Maurice Sterne, autobiographical notes, YCAL.

"enjoyed an enlightenment": LS to MFW, Oct. 3, 1911, YCAL.

"I believe": LS to MFW, Oct. 12, 1911, YCAL.

19. Two

"a study in opposites": LS to MFW, Jan. 27, 1947, YCAL.

"not . . . that I am": LS to GS, [Feb. 1912], YCAL.

"Everybody found": ABT, p. 125.

"There was no": LS, notebook [6], YCAL.

"brought a bunch": GS to MDL, [Feb. 1912]; quoted in MDL, *Movers and Shakers*, p. 33.

when the Polish: GS to MDL, [Feb. 1912]; quoted in MDL, *Movers and Shakers*, p. 33.

Nadelman had been: BB to MCB, April 24, 1909, I Tatti; BB to LS, [April 1909], YCAL.

who at first credited: GS, notebooks 8, C, D, YCAL.

"the light would be": GS, notebook C, YCAL.

And like Leo: Lincoln Kirstein, *The Sculpture of Elie Nadelman*, p. 9. On the information elicited from Alice Toklas, see Lincoln Kirstein to ABT, Sept. 4, 1947, YCAL.

The analytic Nadelman: GS, notebook H, YCAL.

"When he is a scientist": GS, notebook D, YCAL.

"Repetition in Leo": GS, miscellaneous notes and fragments for *MOA*, [26], YCAL.

"one of those": LS to GS, n.d., YCAL.

"two knowing": MOA, p. 746.

"It was a thing": MOA, p. 751.

"one clearly": MOA, p. 889.

"Any one": MOA, p. 907.

"Much Leo": GS, miscellaneous notes and fragments for *MOA*, [106], YCAL.

"They were regular": "Miss Furr and Miss Skeene," *G&P*, p. 20.

"In this book": GS, miscellaneous notes and fragments for *MOA*, [23], YCAL.

"I began": LIA, p. 150.

"the aspect": GS, notebook B, YCAL.

"everlasting feeling": "A Long Gay Book," *GMP*, p. 14.

"more broken": "A Long Gay Book," *GMP*, p. 15.

She might never: Harriet Lane Levy, "Reminiscences," unpublished memoir, Bancroft.

Surely she: Polly Jacobs to ABT, Dec. 18, 1910, and Jan. 8, 1911, YCAL.

Gertrude's evaluation: GS, notebook A, YCAL.

Her passions: GS, notebook H, YCAL.

"transform[ing]": GS, notebooks H, G, YCAL.

"Alice is the only": GS, notebook M, YCAL.

"I can fancy": MFW to GS, July 12, 1912, YCAL.

"I have always": MFW to GS, [1912], YCAL.

Originally titled "Two": Published after her death, the text was then called *Two: A Portrait of Gertrude Stein and Her Brother*. This title appears added in Stein's hand on a typescript, evidently long after the fact; perhaps Stein forgot the original subject of the portrait or, more likely, wanted aspects of it suppressed. Moreover, she was in a coded way trying to explain her views of Leo after having excised him from *The Autobiography*. See holograph notes for "Two," HG-35, YCAL, and GS to MDL, [Feb. 1912], quoted in MDL, *Movers and Shakers*, p. 32.

"After making": GS, miscellaneous notes and fragments for *MOA*, [29], YCAL.

Leo did not have: GS, notebook I, YCAL.

"He has the power": GS, notebook M, YCAL.

"Great thinkers": GS, notebook N, YCAL.

"It is because": GS, notebook N, YCAL.

"He's not as good": "Possessive Case," *AFAM*, p. 117.

"the beginning": EA, p. 76.

"There insomnia": Djuna Barnes, *Camera Work*, 47 (July 1914), p. 30.

Stieglitz's roots: MDL to Alfred Stieglitz, n.d., YCAL.

"He hasn't": Morton Schamberg to Walter Pach, Dec. 29, 1910, AAA.

"He's a good": MFW to GS, Dec. 12, 1912, YCAL.

Enthralled by a conversation: Alfred Stieglitz, "Leo Stein," unpublished manuscript, YCAL.

"I am sure": Alfred Stieglitz to Sadakichi Hartmann, Dec. 22, 1911, YCAL.

"They interest me": Alfred Stieglitz to GS, Feb. 26, 1912, YCAL.

"You have undoubtedly": Alfred Stieglitz to GS, Feb. 26, 1912, YCAL.

"I am genuinely": GS to MDL, [Feb. 1912]; quoted in MDL, *Movers and Shakers*, p. 32.

But pleased: GS to Alfred Stieglitz, March 6, 1912, YCAL.

Alice preferred: ABT, p. 116.

From Paris, Leo and Michael: MS to GS, May 25, [1912]; LS to GS, May 29, [1912]; MS to GS, June 19, [1912], YCAL.

Gertrude was certain: ABT, p. 111.

She settled: See Daniel-Henry Kahnweiler to GS, April 1, 1912, YCAL.

fifteen or so people: LS to GS, May 21, 1912, YCAL.

Leo hadn't: MS to GS, June 19, [1912], YCAL.

He long remembered the night: JIS, p. 19.

"fine as [any]": LS to GS, Aug. 29, [1912], YCAL.

"pictures were": LS, *App,* early draft, YCAL. It is impossible to calculate Stein's Renoir purchases exactly, but the total is between twenty and thirty. He brought sixteen with him to Settignano (see chapter 21), and in 1921 offered fifteen for sale through Durand-Ruel, evidently all that were left of his Renoirs. Many had already been sold to Albert C. Barnes, who was not interested in these fifteen.

Writing of him in 1918: LS, "Renoir and the Impressionists," p. 260.

Renoir's women looked: Stieglitz, "Leo Stein."

"that Stieglitz": LS to GS, May 29, [1912], YCAL.

"Gertrude by long": LS to MFW, Feb. 7, 1913, YCAL; quoted in *JIS,* p. 52.

Gertrude had finished: See Georgiana King to GS, June 17, [1912], YCAL.

"good middle class": See LS to GS, June 6, 1912, YCAL, and GS's response in the holograph manuscript of "Two," YCAL: "His strikes . . . at May about Roosevelt." The passage in question includes the following: "If he says that any one saying that the thing that has happened means something that is mistaken he says that the one saying what that one is saying is showing that that one is not grasping what that one cannot grasp." The passage is not entirely critical, and is followed by one called "his integrity."

"sound coming" . . . the way: "Two," *Two,* pp. 2, 7.

"Sound is coming": "Two," *Two,* p. 1.

"He being": "Two," *Two,* p. 39.

The male is: See "Two," *Two,* p. 31.

"Thinking being": "Two," *Two,* p. 50.

The female character: "Two," *Two,* p. 51.

"did not talk" . . . "he felt seeing": "Two," *Two,* pp. 122, 130.

"One can be": "Two," *Two,* p. 55.

comments in the form: Miscellaneous uncatalogued, unidentified fragments, YCAL.

"No artist": ABT, p. 235.

"He can say": "Two," *Two,* p. 91.

"She smiling": "Two," *Two,* p. 107.

"A distant": "Two," *Two,* p. 107.

"Sweet pinky": ABT, miscellaneous uncatalogued, undated fragments, filed in area II, range 61, section II, shelf 4, YCAL.

Plump, flirtatious: ABT, p. 129.

When she read: MDL to GS, [April 1911], YCAL.

"Gertrude Stein": MDL, *European Experiences,* p. 324.

"nothing is any more": MDL, *European Experiences,* p. 325.

"Why are there": MDL to GS, [June 1911], YCAL.

"There are things": MDL to GS, [April 1911], YCAL.

"And your palate": MDL to GS, [April 1911], YCAL.

Leo had been: LS to GS, Aug. 29, 1912, YCAL.

"All he wanted": MDL, *European Experiences,* p. 326.

"Neither makes": LS to MFW, Feb. 7, 1913.

"The light yellows": LS to GS, Aug. 29, 1912.

"A bottle" . . . "There was": "Portrait of Mabel Dodge at the Villa Curonia," *P&P,* pp. 99, 101.

"What they see": MDL to GS, n.d., YCAL.

"sexually emotional life": MFW to GS, Jan. 21, 1913, YCAL.

"I have read": Florence Blood to GS, [1912–1913], YCAL.

"on the Portrait": ELE to GS, Dec. 9, 1912, YCAL.

"And many people": MCB to Alys Russell, Nov. 21, 1912, Lilly.

"Her Post-Impressionist": Logan Pearsall Smith to MCB, Feb. 19, 1913; quoted in John Russell, *A Portrait of Logan Pearsall Smith Drawn from His Letters and Diaries*, p. 90.

"I can't understand": LS to MFW, Feb. 7, 1913, YCAL; quoted in *JIS*, p. 53.

"Creating is not": Samuel Steward, "A Love Letter to Gertrude and Alice," p. 41, Bancroft.

"There was not": LS to MFW, Feb. 7, 1913, YCAL; quoted in *JIS*, p. 53.

"The crucial matter": LS, miscellaneous notebooks, Jan. 11, [1943], YCAL; quoted in *JIS*, pp. 229-30.

"Liquidation": LS to MFW, Feb. 4, 1913, YCAL; quoted in *JIS*, p. 49.

She reported: GS to MDL, [Jan./Feb. 1913]; quoted in MDL, *Movers and Shakers*, p. 33.

"I loved": Harriet Lane Levy to GS, Jan. 19, 1913, YCAL.

"destroyed him": EA, p. 76.

20. The Disaggregation

"He was as timely": ABT to Carl Van Vechten, July 10, 1950, YCAL; quoted in Edward Burns, ed., *Staying On Alone*, p. 196.

"She really had": ABT to Carl Van Vechten, July 4, 1950, YCAL; quoted in Burns, ed., *Staying On Alone*, p. 195.

"He was a very generous": Duncan, p. 115.

"He continued": EA, p. 72.

Tempers blazed: GS to MDL, [Dec. 1912]; quoted in MDL, *Movers and Shakers*, p. 30.

"You will be": Pablo Picasso to GS, Dec. 23, 1912, YCAL.

"Miss Gertrude Stein": GS, miscellaneous uncatalogued material, box F, YCAL.

"His being": GS to MDL, [Jan./Feb. 1913]; quoted in MDL, *Movers and Shakers*, p. 34.

"I have read": Frank Palmer to GS, Jan. 27, 1913, YCAL.

"Under ordinary": Editors, Sidgwick & Jackson, to GS, Jan. 29, 1913, YCAL.

From Paris, Leo reported: LS to GS, Feb. 3, 1913, YCAL.

"A prophet": LS to MFW, Feb. 7, 1913, YCAL; quoted in *JIS*, p. 52.

"Gertrude . . . hungers": LS to MFW, Feb. 7, 1913, YCAL; quoted in *JIS*, p. 52.

"For I have come": LS to MFW, Feb. 7, 1913, YCAL; quoted in *JIS*, p. 51.

"I don't suppose": LS to MFW, Feb. 4, 1913, YCAL.

"Consciousness for me": LS to MFW, Feb. 4, 1913, YCAL.

And of course: LS to MFW, Feb. 4, 1913, YCAL. See also *JIS*, p. 50.

said an onlooker: Aline Saarinen, miscellaneous notes, Aline Saarinen papers, AAA.

For Gertrude, consciousness: See, in particular, *GHA*, pp. 53-54, 59, 68, 74-78, 85-86, 104, 142-43; 183-84.

"always works": Quoted in MDL, *Movers and Shakers*, p. 28.

"The human mind" . . . "with sorrow": GHA, pp. 105, 67.

"Probably the worst": LS, miscellaneous uncatalogued fragments, YCAL.

"society on the rock": ABC, p. 237.

"science was an abstraction": ABC, pp. 21-22.

"to lost simplicities": ABC, p. 27.

"sad and mistaken": See ABT to Carl Van Vechten, July 10, 1950, and ABT to Donald C. Gallup, July 31, 1950, both quoted in Burns, ed., *Staying On Alone*, pp. 196, 199. See also Elizabeth Sprigge, "Journal in Quest of Gertrude Stein," unpublished type-

script, pp. 2, 36, YCAL. Toklas reputedly said that Ezra Pound was mistaken but not sad.

"Everybody can see": LS to Lee Simonson, Oct. 11, 1913, YCAL.

"I'm a rank": LS to MFW, Feb. 4, 1913, YCAL; quoted in *JIS,* p. 49.

"the fairly definite": LS to MFW, Feb. 7, 1913, YCAL; quoted in *JIS,* p. 52.

"You people": LS to MFW, Feb. 4, 1913, YCAL; quoted in *JIS,* p. 48.

"I wouldn't be": LS to MFW, Feb. 7, 1913, YCAL; quoted in *JIS,* p. 54.

"We are going": Walter Pach to MS, March 20, 1913, YCAL.

"This thing": Kenyon Cox, "The 'Modern' Spirit in Art," *Harper's Weekly,* 57 (March 15, 1913), p. 10.

"Pink tea adjunct": Alfred Stieglitz to Sadakichi Hartmann, Jan. 16, 1913, YCAL.

"& it is of the same": MDL to GS, Jan. 24, [1913], YCAL.

"Well, you believe": Quoted in MDL to GS, Jan. 24, [1913], YCAL.

"Every one in NY": MDL to GS, Feb. 18, 1913, YCAL.

"The name": MDL to GS, [March 1913], YCAL.

"Hurrah": GS to MDL, [March 1913]; quoted in MDL, *Movers and Shakers,* p. 35.

"I called": Quoted in Milton W. Brown, *The Story of the Armory Show,* p. 111.

"You are": MFW to GS, May 4, 1913, YCAL.

"Stiffen": Mildred Aldrich to GS, April 16, 1913, YCAL.

the two Picassos: One was *Green Bowl and Black Bottle* (1908); the other was *Vase, Gourd, and Fruit on a Table* (1909).

"Dear Mary": GS to Mary and Louis Bromfield, n.d., Ohio State University.

"telling about": EA, pp. 68–69.

How she lorded: Alfred Kazin, "From an Italian Journal," p. 557.

Like Picasso: LS to MFW, [1934], YCAL; quoted in *JIS,* p. 142.

"Gertrude and I": Quoted in *JIS,* p. 149.

"gnarled New England": MDL, manuscripts filed with correspondence to Stieglitz, YCAL.

"I hardly expected": Marsden Hartley to GS, [Oct. 18, 1913], YCAL.

"There was a door": Marsden Hartley, "Gertrude Stein," unpublished manuscript, YCAL.

"There was more": Virgil Thomson, "Remembering Gertrude," p. 10.

Etta Cone and the writer Virgil Geddes: See Virgil Geddes, "Leo and Gertrude Stein," p. 16.

Gertrude was furious: Elizabeth Sprigge, interview with MFW in "Journal in Quest of Gertrude Stein," p. 114.

Mabel Dodge accused; The painter Maurice Grosser: See MDL, *European Experiences,* pp. 332–33; Maurice Grosser, "Visiting Gertrude and Alice," p. 37.

"about the only": LS to MFW, Feb. 7, 1913, YCAL; quoted in *JIS,* p. 53.

"Gertrude really": BB to MCB, July 3, 1913, I Tatti.

That spring, 1913: See Judith Cousins, "Documentary Chronology," in William Rubin, *Picasso and Braque: Pioneering Cubism,* p. 418. While there is no evidence that the appraisal is related specifically to Gertrude and Leo's upcoming division of the household, it probably is related to their estrangement. Kahnweiler calculated that the Steins owned thirty-three oils, three gouaches, fifty-nine drawings and other items, and two sculptures, and estimated the value of everything at 158,550 francs. See Isabelle Monod-Fontaine, *Donation Louise et Michel Leiris: Collection Kahnweiler-Leiris,* p. 170.

"because I don't want": GS to MDL, [circa early Feb. 1913]; quoted in MDL, *Movers and Shakers,* p. 33.

"stress of poverty": GS to MDL, [circa Feb. 1913]; quoted in MDL, *Movers and Shakers*, p. 31.

She had been working: GS to MDL, [Feb./March 1913]; quoted in MDL, *Movers and Shakers*, p. 35. On the basis of this letter and two (albeit contradictory) statements made in *ABT*, Jayne L. Walker dates *Tender Buttons* as in the process of being written, if not finished, by this time; see Walker, *The Making of a Modernist*, p. 161. The evidence, however, is scant. The voluminous contemporary correspondence at the Beinecke Library suggests that *Tender Buttons* was written during and after Stein's second trip to Spain in the summer of 1913.

"words began": Robert Bartlett Haas, "Gertrude Stein Talking," 8 (Summer 1962), p. 10.

"The trouble": LIA, p. 188.

"there is no remembering": GHA, p. 117.

"There is no use": "Tender Buttons," *SW*, p. 479.

"language to induce": Mabel Dodge [Luhan], "Speculations, or Post-Impressionism in Prose," p. 6.

"It is genuinely": GS to Alfred Stieglitz, [Nov. 1913], YCAL.

"creating" . . . *"Union"* . . . *"The music"* . . . *"Resembling"*: "G.M.P.," *GMP*, pp. 203, 250, 252, 260.

"Tooth cake": "G.M.P.," *GMP*, p. 278.

But these: ABT, p. 119.

"a chocolate" . . . *"There is"*: "G.M.P.," *GMP*, pp. 253, 256, 258.

"It's such": ABT, miscellaneous uncatalogued, undated fragments filed in area II, range 61, section II, shelf 4, YCAL. Toklas is unquestionably referring to *The Architect's Table*, in which "Ma Jolie" looks like "La Jolie." Roger Fry's second postimpressionist exhibition opened at the Grafton Galleries, London, on October 5, 1912.

"We are having": GS to CC, postmarked July 27, 1913, BMA-CC.

"Susie Asado". . . : *"Preciosilla,"* *SW*, pp. 549–51. Accounts vary as to whether these poems were composed in Spain during the summer of 1912 or 1913. Stein and Toklas saw the singer Preciosilla perform in Madrid evidently in 1912; they may have visited Madrid also in 1913 before going on to Barcelona.

"Nuts" . . . *"Rose"* . . . *"Cow"*: "Sacred Emily," *G&P*, pp. 186, 187, 181.

And it is virtually: Again, accounts vary, especially when Stein and Toklas confuse or collapse the two trips to Spain. But correspondence of the time strongly suggests that *Tender Buttons* was not composed earlier than this summer, and certain manuscript notes link it to other works written during this time, notably "Miguel (Collusion). Guimpe. Candle."

These were: See Haas, "Gertrude Stein Talking," 8 (Summer 1962) p. 10.

"Please pale": "Tender Buttons," *SW*, p. 496.

"Asparagus" . . . *"This makes"*: "Tender Buttons," *SW*, p. 491.

"The care": "Tender Buttons," *SW*, p. 509.

"A white hunter": Haas, "Gertrude Stein Talking," 9 (Spring 1963), p. 44.

"I began": LIA, p. 191.

"I was making": "Poetry and Grammar," *LIA*, p. 236.

"to describe": "Bee Time Vine," *BTV*, p. 35.

"Leaves in grass": "Tender Buttons," p. 492.

"Why is a feel" . . . *"Rub her coke"*: "Tender Buttons," *SW*, pp. 495, 476.

"Aider, why aider": "Tender Buttons," *SW*, p. 476.

she mailed a small: William James to GS, May 25, 1910, YCAL.

"Kandinsky's intentions": Arnold Rönnebeck to GS, April 1, 1913, YCAL.

"The sister": "Tender Buttons," *SW*, p. 499.

"He said": *EA*, p. 76.

"The Saturday": "Tender Buttons," *SW*, p. 479.

"our changeless ideal": MDL to LS, [early fall 1913], YCAL.

"I shall soon" . . . *"the next few"* . . . *"inanities"* . . . *"I don't expect"*: LS to Lee Simonson, [Sept. 1913] (copy sent to Alfred Stieglitz, Oct. 11, 1913), YCAL.

"One wonders": Marsden Hartley to Andrew Dasburg, [1913], AAA.

"Stupendous": Lee Simonson to Alfred Stieglitz, Sept. 29, 1913, YCAL.

"I do": MDL to LS, Nov. 13, [1913], YCAL.

"some power": MDL to LS, Nov. 13, [1913], YCAL.

"Things you": Albert C. Barnes to LS, Feb. 27, [1914], YCAL.

"Yes and so": *GHA*, p. 187.

"If you are": *ABT*, p. 246.

"I was very pleased": Florence Blood to GS, Oct. 11, 1913, YCAL.

"You have seen": Mildred Aldrich to Henry McBride, [Nov. 1913], AAA.

McBride rushed: Henry McBride, "What Is Doing in World of Art, Artists and Art Dealers," *The Sun* (New York), Nov. 30, 1913, p. 2.

"So far as": LS to GS, penciled note, n.d., YCAL; quoted in *JIS*, pp. 50–51.

Toklas recalled: James Lord, "Where the Pictures Were," p. 166.

"I'm afraid": LS to GS, [1913–early 1914], YCAL; quoted in *JIS*, p. 56.

Toklas was bitter: See Lord, "Where the Pictures Were," p. 166; see also Aline Saarinen, notes from interview with ABT, n.d., Aline Saarinen papers, AAA.

"It would appear" . . . *"We are"* . . . *"I very much"*: LS to GS, [1913–early 1914], YCAL; quoted in *JIS*, p. 56.

Years later, Picasso: Aline Saarinen interview with Walter Pach, Feb. 1956, Aline Saarinen papers, AAA.

21. Of Having a Great Many Times

Gertrude immediately: Daniel-Henry Kahnweiler to GS, Oct. 17, 1913, YCAL.

Picasso promised . . . Then: See Marsden Hartley to GS, Oct. 23, 1913, YCAL; Emily Dawson to GS, Feb. 2, 1914, YCAL; GS to CC, Jan. 14, 1914, BMA-CC.

The Steins sold: *Great French Paintings from the Barnes Foundation*, p. 308. See also Albert C. Barnes to LS, March 30, 1913, YCAL, and a scrap of paper itemizing two paintings by Matisse, one of which is called simply "Still Life." According to this note, Barnes paid 3,500 francs for this painting, which included 80 francs for the frame.

both were ardent: GS to MDL, [Dec. 1912]; quoted in MDL, *Movers and Shakers*, p. 29. BW discussion with Richard Wattenmaker, June 15, 1994.

"Mother with child": Albert C. Barnes to LS, Feb. 9, 1914, YCAL.

But Leo had already: Albert C. Barnes to LS, Feb. 27, [1914], YCAL; LS to NAS, [spring 1914], YCAL.

Of the Picassos: Pierre Assouline, *An Artful Life*, p. 109.

The Renoir filled: LS to NAS, [spring 1914], YCAL.

"Someone told me": LS to NAS, April 29, 1914, YCAL; quoted in *JIS*, p. 59.

"I have been": GS to CC, Jan. 2, 1914, BMA-CC.

section titled "Rooms": Stein wrote that she finished this section after returning from Spain, but said also that it was composed after the first trip to Spain, not the second. However, in *ABT*, she tends to collapse three trips into two; see *ABT*, p. 156.

"This made": "Tender Buttons," *SW*, p. 500.

"A table": "Tender Buttons," *SW*, p. 500.

"There was a whole": "Tender Buttons," *SW*, p. 501.

"This shows" . . . *"Giving"*: "Tender Buttons," *SW*, pp. 500, 501, 503. For another vantage point, see James Mellow's persuasive reading of the latter quotation as a reference to Albert Barnes and his incredulity that Picasso did not sell Stein her portrait but gave it to her (see Mellow, *Charmed Circle*, p. 178, and GS, *Picasso*, p. 8). It is true, though, that Stein's commentary is a recollection long after the fact.

"A plain hill": "Tender Buttons," *SW*, p. 502.

"Act so": "Tender Buttons," *SW*, p. 498.

Walter Pach recalled: Aline Saarinen, notes from interview with Walter Pach, Feb. 1956, Aline Saarinen papers, AAA.

"quite interesting": William Sanger to Margaret Sanger, Jan. 5, 1914, Smith.

"complete retirement": Alvin Langdon Coburn to GS, July 27, 1914, YCAL. James's response is filed with this letter.

all came back: Robert Sterling Yard to GS, April 14, 1914, YCAL. The rejection from *Everybody's* came in June; see Trumball White to GS, June 15, 1914, YCAL.

"never applied": Florence Bradley to GS, Oct. 12, 1913, YCAL.

Stein herself . . . *"what could be"*: ABT, p. 132; *LIA*, p. 119. See Marc Robinson, "Gertrude Stein, Forgotten Playwright," for an excellent discussion of the plays. I am indebted to Herbert Leibowitz for bringing this article to my attention.

"I do not": GS to MDL, n.d., YCAL.

Leo thought: NBH, diary, typescript, Aug. 14, 1914, YCAL.

"he laughed": MDL, *Movers and Shakers*, p. 38. See also MDL, *European Experiences*, p. 333.

"very ordinary": Quoted in Carl Van Vechten, "At Gertrude Stein's with Fania Marinoff," July 5, 1914, uncatalogued notes, YCAL; substantially repeated in NBH, diary, typescript, Aug. 14, 1914, YCAL.

"I cabled": MDL to GS, [March 29, 1914], YCAL.

"I am sending": GS to Donald Evans, draft, n.d., uncatalogued material, box F, YCAL.

In fact, Evans: Donald Evans to GS, April 15, 1914, YCAL.

"Mabel finally" . . . *"Perhaps"*: Quoted in Carl Van Vechten, "At Gertrude Stein's."

she never denied: See MDL to Carl Van Vechten, [Oct.] 6, 1951, YCAL.

"How many cases": "A History of Having a Great Many Times Not Continued to Be Friends," *AFAM*, p. 291.

"I agree": Miriam Price to GS, [spring 1912], YCAL.

"I'm the only": Quoted in Elizabeth Sprigge, "Journal in Quest of Gertrude Stein," unpublished typescript, p. 99, YCAL.

"In short": ABT, p. 142.

"It all becomes": LS to NAS, [April/May 1914], YCAL.

He unpacked: LS to MS, April 8, 1914, YCAL. Leo Stein itemized the Renoirs in a reminiscence in notebook [1], YCAL.

One reviewer . . . *eggbeater*: "Contributors' Club," *The Atlantic Monthly*, 115 (Sept. 1914), p. 432.

Her friends, however: See Harriet Lane Levy to GS, [1914], YCAL.

"Lovely snipe": Quoted in Carl Van Vechten, "How to Read Gertrude Stein," p. 557. The section in question can be found in "Tender Buttons," *SW*, p. 479.

"You see": Quoted in Van Vechten, "How to Read," p. 556.

"I tried": Quoted in Van Vechten, "At Gertrude Stein's."

Alice Toklas wore: Van Vechten, "At Gertrude Stein's."

"Mr. Stein's phrase": Van Vechten, "How to Read," p. 556.

"First define": Quoted in MDL, *Movers and Shakers,* pp. 224–25.

"I sat": Van Vechten, "How to Read," p. 554.

"Mabel [Dodge]": NBH, diary, typescript, Aug. 14, 1914, YCAL.

Leo said "Alice was": MDL, *European Experiences,* p. 327.

Albert Barnes's memory: Albert C. Barnes to LS, Nov. 2, 1934, YCAL. The remark is recorded also in Carl W. McCardle, "The Terrible Tempered Dr. Barnes," April 4, 1942, p. 19. McCardle goes on to write that Gertrude Stein observed the same thing of her brother: "When Barnes next saw Gertrude, he said, 'I hear Leo's going to Italy to live.' 'That's fine,' said Gertrude. 'You know, Leo's crazy.'"

"I believe": "One Sentence," AFAM, p. 75. The piece may have been begun in 1914 and concluded sometime in early 1915.

"We went": "No," AFAM, p. 64. The piece seems to have been written in 1914.

"Guillaume Apollinaire": In *A Stein Reader,* Ulla E. Dydo provides an excellent introduction to this portrait as well as to some of Stein's more difficult pieces, pp. 278–79.

puns; "rest less": "In," BTV, pp. 50, 44; "Carry," BTV, p. 41.

One of Stein's: Richard Bridgman, *Gertrude Stein in Pieces,* p. 141. This book is an excellent, comprehensive, and insightful introduction to Stein's entire work.

"Little sweet": "A New Happiness," PL, p. 155. This piece seems to have been written late in 1914.

"Your brother-in-law": "Possessive Case," AFAM, pp. 125, 130.

"I innocently meant": "Painted Lace," PL, p. 1. This piece seems to have been written in 1914.

"To-night bore" . . . variations: "One Sentence," holograph, manuscript notebook, HG 104, YCAL.

"A young deaf": "One Sentence," AFAM, p. 73.

"We have decided": "One Sentence," AFAM, pp. 77, 99, 105, 70.

"Haven't you heard?": Edith Wharton, *A Backward Glance* (New York: Scribner, 1964), p. 336.

"We can understand": "We Have Eaten Heartily and We Were Alarmed," PL, p. 40.

"We are nervous": "We Have Eaten Heartily," p. 40.

"quite handsome": NBH to MCB and BB, Nov. 12, [1914], YCAL.

He confided: See LS to MFW, Oct. 4, 1914, and LS to MFW, Jan. 10, 1915, YCAL.

"Everyone's son": ABT to Harriet Lane Levy, [Oct.] 1914, Bancroft.

"though being": LS to MFW, Oct. 4, 1914, YCAL.

"would be the triumphant": LS to MFW, Oct. 4, 1914, YCAL.

"lead to a development": LS to MFW, Jan. 10, 1915, YCAL; quoted in JIS, p. 61.

Leo appears indifferent: LS to NAS, Feb. 6, 1915, YCAL. Stein dates the letter 1914; internal evidence suggests the correct date is 1915.

writing her again: See for example LS to NAS, Feb. 6, 1915, YCAL.

Leo did not know: LS to NAS, Feb. 2, 1915, YCAL.

"Brother brother": "Names of Flowers," BTV, p. 217. The piece is alternately dated 1914–1915 and 1920.

Epilogue

"When a thing": See Elizabeth Sprigge, "Journal in Quest of Gertrude Stein," unpublished typescript, pp. 52, 60, YCAL. Sprigge quotes Pavel Tchelitchew, who remembered the remark. Virgil Thomson recalled something similar, in *An Autobiography,* p. 180.

"I could only": LS to MFW, April 13, 1915, YCAL.

while there he may have amassed: As of this writing, I have not been able to ascertain the date of the purchases. According to Barbara Braun, who courteously examined photographs of many of the pieces, the collection was sold to Leo Stein probably as one lot. She suggested also that the purchase could have been made in Paris circa 1912 from a dealer such as Joseph Brummer, whom Stein in fact knew. If this is the case, however, evidence of the purchase would have appeared either in his correspondence or in photographs of the rue de Fleurus, but it does not. Nor is the collection itemized among the possessions he subsequently moved to Settignano.

While it is possible that Stein bought the collection and then stored it in a vault in Paris, it is peculiar that he would have amassed such a large collection just when he was beginning to divest himself of many of his pieces. Further muddying the waters is an entry in the 1928–1929 annual report of the National Museum of the American Indian, which mentions "a fine collection presented by her [Thea Heye] from Mexico, made over 40 years ago by Mr. Leo Stein" (p. 70). The unclear syntax could suggest that Stein made the purchase forty years before (as a lad of sixteen), or that the collection itself had been amassed forty years earlier, and then came into Stein's possession at a later date. One item in the collection, the black granite votive axe, was described and illustrated by a Mexican scholar in 1887— "when it was in private hands" (see *Indian Notes,* 6, no. 3, p. 271).

The notion that Leo Stein—or more likely, Daniel Stein—owned these pieces before settling in France is intriguing, for it indicates that many of the painters in and out of the rue de Fleurus may have seen parts of this marvelous collection. I myself am dubious. If Daniel owned the collection, why wasn't it jointly owned, after his death, by his children? Why is no mention ever made of it? Why is it not part of the photographic archive? It is possible, on the other hand, that Leo Stein bought the collection just before moving to Settignano, which would account for its curious absence from the record. But this too seems doubtful to me.

The matter is far from settled. And perhaps it was its impenetrability that kept the able Margaret Potter, who knew of the collection's existence, from exhibiting any portion of it in the 1970 Museum of Modern Art show *Four Americans in Paris.* But this mystery confirms yet again the wide and deep range of Stein's taste, as well as its high quality; his eye was discerning and his appetite unsated, and aesthetics and ownership were both significant for him.

Stein sold the collection for 10,000 gold marks to George Heye (see George Heye to LS, Nov. 7, 1928, courtesy the National Museum of the American Indian; the collection is still found in that museum). I am grateful to Barbara Braun and Frederick J. Dockstader for their ready assistance in evaluating this collection and suggesting avenues of research.

"the first to recognize": Albert C. Barnes and Violette de Mazias, *The Art of Henri Matisse,* dedication.

"Long ago": LS to GS, Feb. 15, 1916, YCAL; quoted in *JIS,* p. 71.

"I wish you'd": MDL to GS, Jan. 14, 1917, YCAL.

"He speaks": MCB to HH, May 19, 1920, YCAL.

"I sent you": LS to GS, Dec. 14, 1919; quoted in *JIS,* pp. 77–78. A month before writing this letter, Leo Stein sent his sister a friendly postcard announcing his plans to return to Europe: "I'm sailing today for Italy. It's quite a thrilling idea. Whether I'll get to Paris or not depends on lots of things. Perhaps whether I get to Florence also. Mike [Stein] reports that you've [mained lionhood] at last—& Howard [Gans] tells me that you're to have a new pump. I've been trying for 4 years to get new tires but I reckon I've only gotten tired. Regards to Alice" (LS to GS, Nov. 11, 1919, YCAL).

He wrote . . . Alice quickly: LS to GS, [1920], YCAL; LS to ABT, April 13, 1920, YCAL.

By the next March: ABT to Harriet Lane Levy, [1915], Bancroft.

"the well-sieved": Solita Solano, "The Hotel Napoleon Bonaparte," in John Broderick, "Paris Between the Wars: An Unpublished Memoir by Solita Solano," *Quarterly Journal of the Library of Congress,* Oct. 1977, p. 309.

"standing there": Sherwood Anderson, "Four American Impressions: Gertrude Stein, Paul Rosenfeld, Ring Lardner, Sinclair Lewis," *The New Republic,* Oct. 11, 1922, p. 171.

"If they were": William Carlos Williams, *The Autobiography of William Carlos Williams,* p. 254.

"There is the eternal": Robert Bartlett Haas, "Gertrude Stein Talking," 9 (Winter 1964), p. 47.

She was not returning: See, for instance, GS to Carl Van Vechten, n.d. (copy sent to Bennett Cerf, June 25, 1946), Butler.

"the same fine": Andrew Turnbull, ed., *The Letters of F. Scott Fitzgerald* (New York: Scribner, 1963), p. 518.

Mabel Weeks was deeply: MFW to LS, Nov. 18, [1934], YCAL.

"to build something": LS to Albert C. Barnes, Oct. 20, 1934; quoted in *JIS,* p. 146.

"That her long": LS to MFW, [June 1934], YCAL; quoted in *JIS,* p. 142.

"There is not enough": "Gertrude Stein Will Visit America," *New York Herald Tribune,* Oct. 6, 1934, p. 9.

"radically" . . . "Ah well": LS to MFW, June 25, [1939], YCAL.

"Like a Jewish": Alfred Kazin, "From an Italian Journal," p. 556.

"It's important": Kazin, "From an Italian Journal," p. 555.

"But God what": LS to MFW, Dec. 28, 1933, YCAL; quoted in *JIS,* p. 134.

"You can have": LS to NAS, [1919], YCAL; quoted in part in *JIS,* p. 82. The letter appears to have been written during Stein's return voyage to Europe.

"I have played": LS to Trigant Burrow, May 15, 1926, Sterling.

he had undertaken: See LS to Joseph Asch, [1925], Francis A. Countway Library of Medicine, Boston.

"to how great": LS to Trigant Burrow, May 15, 1926, Sterling.

"Practical Solipsism": See *ABC,* chapter 10, especially p. 102, for an early formulation of his theory.

"It is about time": LS to Morgan Russell, [1914], The Montclair Art Museum, Montclair, New Jersey.

all were slowly dispersed: BW interview with Mrs. Rosalie Raffel, Jan. 6, 1991.

In 1921, he offered: Among the Renoirs handled by Durand-Ruel were *Mother and Child, Pears, Head of a Child, The Summer Hats, The Bay of Douarnenez, Young Woman in a Blue Blouse, Bather,* two landscapes, and *Woman Darning.* See Margaret Potter papers, MoMA Archives, for the best account of this sale and Stein's Renoir holdings in general.

"first in war": GS, introduction to the speeches of Maréchal Pétain, typescript, Random House Collection, Butler.

"Some pious": App, p. 69.

if the last outposts: Virgil Thomson, *An Autobiography,* p. 174.

"the poem of the mind": "Of Modern Poetry," in Wallace Stevens, *The Collected Poems* (New York: Knopf, 1981).

"in this epoch": GHA, p. 218.

Drawing herself up: ABT to Carl and Fania Van Vechten, [July 31, 1946], YCAL; see Edward Burns, ed., *Staying On Alone,* p. 4.

She entered the Catholic: See ABT to William Alfred, Aug. 26, 1958, Houghton. See also Thomson, *Autobiography,* p. 378.

"little debauch": App, p. 8.

"intimately connected": App, p. 8.

"Leo was": Elizabeth Sprigge, "Journal in Quest of Gertrude Stein," unpublished type-script, p. 8, YCAL.

"My situation": LS to Howard Gans, Sept. 3, 1945, YCAL.

a study in opposites: LS to Annette Rosenshine, Feb. 12, 1947, Bancroft.

"Gertrude is the person": LS to MFW, Jan. 27, [1947], YCAL. See also LS to FS, Jan. 28, 1947; quoted in *JIS*, p. 283.

"She always took": Quoted in Kazin, "From an Italian Journal," p. 557.

"The contrast": LS to MFW, Jan. 27, [1947], YCAL. See also LS to FS, Jan. 28, 1947; quoted in *JIS*, p. 283.

"still fat": EA, pp. 151–52.

"the discourse": Lloyd Morris, "Leo, Known as Gertrude's Brother, Stein," *New York Herald Tribune,* July 20, 1947, p. 3.

"Your Appreciation": Albert C. Barnes to LS, July 3, 1947, YCAL.

Nina never . . . She turned: Richard Guggenheimer to EC, Aug. 24, 1949, University of North Carolina at Greensboro; BW interview with Cesare Scheggi Merlini, Sept. 5, 1991.

BIBLIOGRAPHY

Selected Bibliography

Editions of works by Gertrude Stein cited frequently in the text; in parentheses, the abbreviations used in the notes:

Alphabets and Birthdays. Introduction by Donald Gallup. New Haven, CT: Yale University Press, 1957. (*AB*)

As Fine as Melanctha. Foreword by Natalie Clifford Barney. New Haven, CT: Yale University Press, 1954. (*AFAM*)

The Autobiography of Alice B. Toklas. New York: Vintage, 1990. (*ABT*)

Bee Time Vine and Other Pieces. Preface and notes by Virgil Thomson. New Haven, CT: Yale University Press, 1953. (*BTV*)

"Cultivated Motor Automatism: A Study of Character in Its Relation to Attention." *Psychological Review,* 5, no. 3 (May 1898), pp. 295–306.

Everybody's Autobiography. New York: Cooper Square, 1971. (*EA*)

Fernhurst, Q.E.D., and Other Early Writings. Introduction by Leon Katz. New York: Liveright, 1971. (*EW*)

The Geographical History of America. Introduction by William H. Gass. New York: Vintage, 1973. (*GHA*)

Geography and Plays. Introduction by Cyrena Pondrom. Madison: University of Wisconsin Press, 1993. (*G&P*)

Lectures in America. New York: Vintage, 1975. (*LIA*)

The Making of Americans. New York: Something Else, 1966. (*MOA*)

Matisse Picasso and Gertrude Stein [G.M.P.]. New York: Something Else, 1972. (*GMP*)

"My Debt to Books." *Books Abroad,* 13 (Summer 1939), pp. 307–08.

Narration. Introduction by Thornton Wilder. Chicago: University of Chicago Press, 1935. (*Narr*)

Painted Lace and Other Pieces. Introduction by Daniel-Henry Kahnweiler. New Haven, CT: Yale University Press, 1955. (*PL*)

Paris France. New York: Liveright, 1970. (*PF*)

Picasso. Boston: Beacon, 1969.

Portraits and Prayers. New York: Random House, 1934. (*P&P*)

Reflection on the Atomic Bomb, vol. 1 of *The Previously Uncollected Writings of Gertrude Stein,* ed. Robert Bartlett Haas. Los Angeles: Black Sparrow, 1973. (*Reflection*)

Selected Writings of Gertrude Stein. Introduction by Carl Van Vechten. New York: Random House, 1962. (*SW*)

Three Lives. Introduction by Ann Charters. New York: Viking Penguin, 1990. (*TL*)

Two: Gertrude Stein and Her Brother and Other Early Portraits. Foreword by Janet Flanner. New Haven, CT: Yale University Press, 1951. (*Two*)

Useful Knowledge. New York: John Lane, 1929. (*UK*)

Wars I Have Seen. New York: Random House, 1945. (*WIHS*)

What Are Masterpieces? Foreword by Robert Bartlett Haas. New York: Pitam, 1940. (*WAM*)

Readers seeking a selection of Stein's work should see also Ulla E. Dydo, ed., *A Stein Reader* (Evanston, IL: Northwestern University Press, 1993) or Richard Kostelanetz, ed., *The Yale Gertrude Stein* (New Haven, CT: Yale University Press, 1980).

Works by Leo Stein frequently cited in the text, with the abbreviations used in the notes, followed by the only bibliography of his work to date (arranged chronologically):

The A-B-C of Aesthetics. New York: Boni & Liveright, 1927. (*ABC*)

Appreciation: Painting, Poetry and Prose. New York: Crown, 1947; rpt. Lincoln: University of Nebraska Press, 1956. (*App*)

Journey into the Self, ed. Edmund Fuller. New York: Crown, 1950. (*JIS*)

"The Jew in Fiction." *The Jewish Comment,* 11, no. 5 (May 18, 1900), pp. 6–7.

"Society and Art." *The Jewish Comment,* 11, no. 7 (June 1, 1900), pp. 3–4.

"Cézanne." *The New Republic,* Jan. 22, 1916, pp. 297–98.

"New Return to Nature." *The New Republic,* March 18, 1916, pp. 179–81.

"Zuloaga." *The New Republic,* Dec. 23, 1916, pp. 210–12.

"Meanings." *The Seven Arts,* Feb. 1917, pp. 402–05.

"William M. Chase." *The New Republic,* March 3, 1917, pp. 133–34.

"Introductory to the Independent Show." *The New Republic,* April 7, 1917, pp. 288–90.

"Art and Common Sense." *The New Republic,* May 5, 1917, pp. 13–15.

"American Optimism." *The Seven Arts,* May 1917, pp. 72–92.

"Degas and Draughtsmanship." *The New Republic,* Nov. 3, 1917, pp. 13–14.

"The Painting of Arthur B. Davies." *The New Republic,* Jan. 19, 1918, p. 338.

"Rembrandt's Etchings in the Public Library." *The New Republic,* March 2, 1918, pp. 137–38.

"Renoir and the Impressionists." *The New Republic,* March 30, 1918, pp. 259–60.

"If Rubens Were Born Again." *The New Republic,* June 1, 1918, pp. 143–45.

"Aesthetic Fundamentals." *The New Republic,* March 1, 1919, pp. 138–40.

"Arch in New York City." *The New Republic,* Jan. 11, 1919, pp. 303–05.

"Art Versus Its Estimation." *The New Republic,* Feb. 1, 1919, pp. 18–20.

"The Defeat of John Ruskin." *The New Republic,* Feb. 8, 1919, pp. 51–53.

"Pablo Picasso." *The New Republic,* April 23, 1924, pp. 229–30.

"A New Salon in Paris." *The New Republic,* July 30, 1924, pp. 271–73.

"Tradition and Art." *The Arts,* 7, no. 5 (May 1925), pp. 265–67.

"Renoir." *The Arts,* 12, no. 4 (Dec. 1925), pp. 311–13.

"On Teaching Art and Letters." *The New Republic,* March 3, 1926, pp. 47–48.

"Knowing and Feeling." *The New Republic,* March 17, 1926, pp. 102–03.

"Art and the Frame." *The New Republic,* March 24, 1926, pp. 143–44.

"Personality and Identification." *The New Republic,* March 31, 1926, pp. 172–73.

"Integrity and Integration." *The New Republic,* April 7, 1926, pp. 196–97.
"William James." *The American Mercury,* 9, no. 33 (Sept. 1926), pp. 68–70.
"Distortions." *The Dial,* July 1927, pp. 28–32.
"Reality," *The Dial,* Sept. 1927, pp. 201–07.
"Letter." *The New Yorker,* 11, no. 14 (May 18, 1935), p. 91.
"Ritual and Reality." *The American Scholar,* 16 (Summer 1947), pp. 140–47.

Texts frequently cited in the notes, with their abbreviations:

Alice B. Toklas, *What Is Remembered.* San Francisco: North Point, 1985. (*WIR*)
Roland E. Duncan. Interview with Alice B. Toklas, Nov. 28–29, 1952. The Bancroft
     Library, University of California, Berkeley. (Duncan)

Other Works Consulted

Acton, Harold. *Memoirs of an Aesthete.* London: Methuen, 1948.
———. *More Memoirs of an Aesthete.* London: Methuen, 1970.
Adler, Cyrus. *I Have Considered the Days.* Philadelphia: Jewish Publication Society of
     America, 1941.
Agee, William C. *Synchromism and Color Principles in American Painting.* New York:
     Knoedler, 1965.
———, and Barbara Rose. *Patrick Henry Bruce, American Modernist: A Catalogue
     Raisonné.* New York: Museum of Modern Art, 1979.
Allen, Mary. "Gertrude Stein's Sense of Oneness." *Southwest Review,* 66, no. 1 (Win-
     ter 1981), pp. 1–10.
Assouline, Pierre. *An Artful Life: A Biography of D. H. Kahnweiler,* trans. Charles Ruas.
     New York: Grove Weidenfeld, 1990.
Barker, Lewellys F. *The Nervous System and Its Constituent Neurones.* New York:
     D. Appleton, 1899.
———. *Time and the Physician.* New York: Putnam, 1942.
Barnes, Albert C., and Violette de Mazias. *The Art of Henri Matisse.* New York: Scrib-
     ner, 1933.
———. *The Art of Renoir.* New York: Minton, Balch, 1935.
Barr, Alfred H., Jr. *Matisse, His Art and His Public.* New York: The Museum of Mod-
     ern Art, 1951.
Baxandall, Michael. *Patterns of Intention: On the Historical Explanation of Pictures.*
     New Haven, CT: Yale University Press, 1985.
Beirne, Francis F. *The Amiable Baltimoreans.* Baltimore: Johns Hopkins University
     Press, 1984.
Bell, Clive. *Old Friends.* Chicago: University of Chicago Press, 1973.
Benjamin, Jessica. *The Bonds of Love: Psychoanalysis, Feminism, and the Problem of
     Domination.* New York: Pantheon, 1988.
Berenson, Bernard. *The Italian Painters of the Renaissance.* Ithaca, NY: Cornell Uni-
     versity Press, 1980.
———. *Sketch for a Self-Portrait.* New York: Pantheon, 1949.
Bergson, Henri. *Creative Evolution.* New York: Modern Library, 1949.
———. *The Creative Mind.* New York: Citadel, 1946.
Binet, Alfred. *Alterations of Personality* and *On Double Consciousness,* in Daniel Robin-
     son, ed., *Significant Contributions to the History of Psychology,* vol. 5. Washington,
     DC: University Publications of America, 1977.

Birmingham, Stephen. *"Our Crowd": The Great Jewish Families of New York.* New York: Harper & Row, 1967.

Blackmer, Corinne E. "African Masks and the Arts of Passing in Gertrude Stein's 'Melanctha' and Nella Larsen's *Passing.*" *Journal of the History of Sexuality,* 4, no. 2 (Oct. 1993), pp. 230–63.

Blake, Nancy. "Everybody's Autobiography: Identity and Absence." *Recherches Anglaises et Américaines,* 15 (1982), pp. 135–45.

Blanche, Jacques-Émile. *Portraits of a Lifetime.* London: Dent, 1937.

Bloom, Ellen F. "Three Steins: A Very Personal Recital." *Texas Quarterly,* Summer 1970, pp. 15–22.

Bloom, Harold, ed. *Gertrude Stein.* New York: Chelsea House, 1986.

Bluemel, Elinor. *Florence Sabin.* Boulder: University of Colorado Press, 1959.

Blum, Isidor. *The Jews of Baltimore.* Baltimore: Historical Review, 1910.

Brandt, David E. "Separation and Identity in Adolescence." *Contemporary Psychoanalysis,* 13, no. 4 (Oct. 1977), pp. 507–18.

Breunig, Leroy C., ed. *Apollinaire on Art: Essays and Reviews 1902–1918,* trans. Susan Suleiman. New York: Da Capo, 1972.

Bridgman, Richard. *Gertrude Stein in Pieces.* New York: Oxford University Press, 1970.

Brinnin, John Malcolm. *The Third Rose.* Boston: Little, Brown, 1957.

Brooks, Van Wyck. *Fenollosa and His Circle.* New York: Dutton, 1962.

———. *New England: Indian Summer 1865–1915.* New York, Dutton: 1940.

Brown, Milton W. *The Story of the Armory Show.* New York: Joseph H. Hirshhorn Foundation, 1963.

Brown, Rollo Walter. *Harvard Yard in the Golden Age.* New York: Wyn, 1948.

Buck, Paul, ed. *The Social Sciences at Harvard: 1860–1920.* Cambridge, MA: Harvard University Press, 1965.

Bullough, Vern L., and Martha Voght. "Homosexuality and Its Confusion with the 'Secret Sin' in Pre-Freudian America." *Journal of the History of Medicine,* 28 (April 1973), pp. 143–55.

Burgess, Gelett. "The Wild Men of Paris." *Architectural Record,* 27, no. 5 (May 1910), pp. 401–14.

Burke, Carolyn. "Gertrude Stein, the Cone Sisters, and the Puzzle of Female Friendship." *Critical Inquiry,* 8, no. 3 (Spring 1982), pp. 543–64.

Burnham, John C. "Psychiatry, Psychology and the Progressive Movement." *American Quarterly,* 12 (1960), pp. 457–65.

Burns, Edward, ed. "Gertrude Stein Issue." *Twentieth Century Literature,* 24, no. 1 (1978).

———. *The Letters of Gertrude Stein and Carl Van Vechten,* 2 vols. New York: Columbia University Press, 1986.

———. *Staying On Alone: Letters of Alice B. Toklas.* New York: Liveright, 1973.

Chessman, Harriet Scott. *The Public Is Invited to Dance: Representation, the Body, and Dialogue in Gertrude Stein.* Stanford, CA: Stanford University Press, 1989.

Chisolm, Lawrence W. *Fenollosa: The Far East and American Culture.* New Haven, CT: Yale University Press, 1963.

Cochin, Henri. "Quelques Reflexions sur les Salons." *Gazette des Beaux-Arts,* 19 (1903), pp. 441–64; 20 (1903), pp. 20–52.

Cohen, Naomi W. *Encounter with Emancipation: German Jews 1830–1914.* Philadelphia: Jewish Publication Society, 1984.

Coleman, William. *Biology in the Nineteenth Century.* Cambridge, England: Cambridge University Press, 1977.

Collins, Douglas. *Photographed by Bachrach: 125 Years of American Portraiture.* New York: Rizzoli, 1992.

Cone, Edward T. "The Miss Etta Cones, the Steins, and M'sieu Matisse: A Memoir." *The American Scholar,* Summer 1973, pp. 441–60.

Cope, Karen M. "Publicity Is Our Pride: The Passionate Grammar of Gertrude Stein." *Pre/Text,* 13, no. 4 (Fall 1992), pp. 123–36.

Cott, Nancy. "Passionlessness: An Interpretation of Victorian Sexual Ideology, 1790–1850." *Signs,* 4, no. 2 (Winter 1978), pp. 219–36.

Cushing, Harvey. *The Life of Sir William Osler,* vol. 1. Oxford: Clarendon, 1925.

Daix, Pierre. *Picasso: Life and Art.* New York: HarperCollins, 1994.

———, and George Boudaille. *Picasso: The Blue and Rose Periods.* Greenwich, CT: New York Graphic Society, 1967.

———, and Joan Rosellet. *Picasso: The Cubist Years, 1907–1916.* Boston: New York Graphic Society, 1979.

Daulte, François. *Auguste Renoir: Catalogue Raisonné de l'Oeuvre,* vol. 1. Lausanne, Switzerland: Durand-Ruel, 1971.

Davidson, Abraham. *Early American Modernist Painting, 1910–1935.* New York: Harper & Row, 1981.

Degler, Carl. *At Odds: Women and the Family from the Revolution to the Present.* New York: Oxford University Press, 1980.

———. *In Search of Human Nature.* New York: Oxford University Press, 1991.

DeKoven, Marianne. *A Different Language: Gertrude Stein's Experimental Writing.* Madison: University of Wisconsin Press, 1983.

———. "Gertrude Stein's Landscape Writing." *Women's Studies: An Interdisciplinary Journal,* 9, no. 3 (1982), pp. 221–39.

de Lauretis, Teresa. *The Practice of Love: Lesbian Sexuality and Perverse Desire.* Bloomington: Indiana University Press, 1994.

D'Emilio, John, and Estelle B. Freedman. *Intimate Matters: A History of Sexuality in America.* New York: Harper & Row, 1988.

DeZayas, Marius. "Pablo Picasso." *Camera Work,* April–July 1911, pp. 65–67.

Dodge, Mabel [Mabel Dodge Luhan]. "Speculations, or Post-Impressionism in Prose." *Arts and Decoration,* 3 (1913), pp. 172–74.

Dubnick, Randa. *The Structure of Obscurity: Gertrude Stein, Language, and Cubism.* Urbana: University of Illinois Press, 1984.

Dydo, Ulla. "Landscape Is Not a Grammar: Gertrude Stein in 1928." *Raritan,* 7, no. 1 (Summer 1987), pp. 97–113.

———. "*Stanzas in Meditation*: The Other Autobiography." *Chicago Review,* 35, no. 2 (Winter 1985), pp. 4–20.

Edstrom, David. *The Testament of Caliban.* New York: Funk & Wagnalls, 1937.

Eisler, Benita. *O'Keeffe and Stieglitz.* New York: Penguin, 1991.

Elderfield, John. "The Language of Pre-Abstract Art." *Art Forum,* Feb. 1971, pp. 46–51.

———. *Matisse: A Retrospective.* New York: Museum of Modern Art, 1992.

Eliot, Charles W. *Harvard Memories.* Cambridge, MA: Harvard University Press, 1923.

Engelmann, George J. "The Increasing Sterility of American Women." *Journal of the American Medical Association,* 37, no. 14 (Oct. 5, 1901), pp. 890–97.

Evitts, William J. *A Matter of Allegiances: Maryland from 1850–1861.* Baltimore: Johns Hopkins University Press, 1974.

Faderman, Lillian. *Odd Girls and Twilight Lovers: A History of Lesbian Life in Twentieth-Century America.* New York: Penguin, 1989.

Fehrer, Catherine. "New Light on the Académie Julian and Its Founder (Rudolphe Julian)." *Gazette des Beaux-Arts,* May–June 1984, pp. 207–16.

———, and Robert and Elizabeth Kashey. *The Julian Academy: Paris, 1868–1939.* New York: Shepherd Gallery, 1989.

Fein, Isaac M. "Baltimore Jews During the Civil War." *American Jewish Historical Quarterly,* 2 (Dec. 1961), pp. 67–96.

Feldman, Jacob S. *The Early Migration and Settlement of the Jews in Pittsburgh, 1754–1894.* Pittsburgh: United Jewish Federation, 1959.

Fellman, Anita Clair. *Making Sense of Self: Medical Advice Literature in Late Nineteenth Century America.* Philadelphia: University of Pennsylvania Press, 1981.

Fenichel, Otto. *The Collected Papers of Otto Fenichel,* 2nd ser. New York: Norton, 1954.

Fifer, Elizabeth. "In Conversation: Gertrude Stein's Speaker, Message, and Receiver in Painted Lace and Other Pieces." *Modern Fiction Studies,* 34 (Autumn 1988), pp. 465–80.

———. "Is Flesh Advisable? The Interior Theatre of Gertrude Stein." *Signs,* 4, no. 3 (Spring 1979), pp. 472–83.

———. "Rescued Readings: Characteristic Deformations in the Language of Gertrude Stein's Plays." *Texas Studies in Literature and Language: A Journal of the Humanities,* 24, no. 4 (Winter 1982), pp. 394–428.

Finney, J. M. T. *A Surgeon's Life.* New York: Putnam, 1940.

Flam, Jack. *Matisse: The Man and His Art, 1869–1918.* Ithaca, NY: Cornell University Press, 1986.

———. *Matisse on Art.* London: Phaidon, 1956.

Fleming, Donald. *William H. Welch and the Rise of Modern Medicine.* Boston: Little, Brown, 1954.

Flexner, Helen Thomas. *A Quaker Childhood.* New Haven, CT: Yale University Press, 1940.

Flexner, Simon, and James Thomas Flexner. *William Henry Welch and the Heroic Age of American Medicine.* New York: Viking, 1941.

Flower, Elizabeth, and Murray G. Murphey. *A History of Philosophy in America.* New York: Putnam, 1977.

Frankfort, Roberta. *Collegiate Women: Domesticity and Career in Turn of the Century America.* New York: New York University Press, 1977.

Freud, Anna. "Adolescence." *The Psychoanalytic Study of the Child,* 12 (1958), pp. 255–77.

Freud, Sigmund. *General Psychological Theory.* New York: Macmillan, 1963.

———. *Sexuality and the Psychology of Love.* New York: Collier, 1963.

Fry, Edward. *Cubism.* New York: McGraw-Hill, 1966.

———. "Picasso, Cubism, and Reflexivity." *Art Journal,* 47, no. 4 (Winter 1988), pp. 296–310.

Fry, Roger. *Cézanne: A Study of His Development.* New York: Noonday, 1968.

———. *Vision and Design.* New York: Brentano's, 1924.

Furman, Edna. "On Trauma: When Is the Death of a Parent Traumatic?" *The Psychoanalytic Study of the Child,* 41 (1986), pp. 191–208.

Gallup, Donald. "The Pleasure of Their Company." *Review,* 9 (1987), pp. 53–65.

———, ed. *The Flowers of Friendship: Letters Written to Gertrude Stein.* New York: Knopf, 1953.

Gass, William. "And," in Allen Wier and Don Hendrie, eds., *Voicelust: Eight Contemporary Fiction Writers on Style.* Lincoln: University of Nebraska Press, 1985.

———. "Gertrude Stein: Her Escape from Protective Language." *Accent,* Autumn 1958, pp. 233–44.

Geddes, Virgil. "Leo and Gertrude Stein." *Lost Generation Journal,* 2 (Winter 1974), pp. 16–17.

Gilman, Sander L. "Black Bodies, White Bodies: Toward an Iconography of Female Sexuality in Late Nineteenth-Century Art, Medicine, and Literature." *Critical Inquiry*, 12 (Autumn 1985), pp. 204–42.

———. *Difference and Pathology: Stereotypes of Sexuality, Race, and Madness.* Ithaca, NY: Cornell University Press, 1985.

Gilot, Françoise. *Life with Picasso.* London: Virago, 1990.

———. *Matisse and Picasso: A Friendship in Art.* Garden City, NY: Doubleday, 1990.

Glanz, Rudolf. *The Jews of California: From the Discovery of Gold Until 1880.* New York: Waldon, 1960.

Golding, John. *Cubism: A History and an Analysis.* New York: Wittenborn, 1959.

Gosling, Francis. *Before Freud: Neurasthenia and the American Medical Community, 1870–1910.* Urbana: University of Illinois Press, 1987.

Great French Paintings from the Barnes Foundation. New York: Knopf, 1993.

Greenberg, Rose. *The Chronicle of the Baltimore Hebrew Association.* Baltimore: Baltimore Hebrew Association, 1976.

Grosser, Maurice. "Visiting Gertrude and Alice." *The New York Review of Books,* 33, no. 17 (Nov. 6, 1986), pp. 36–38.

Guttmacher, Adolf. *History of the Baltimore Hebrew Congregation.* Baltimore: Lord Baltimore, 1905.

Guttmacher, Alan Frank. "Recollections of John Whitridge Williams." *Bulletin of the Institute of the History of Medicine,* 3 (1935), pp. 19–30.

Haas, Robert Bartlett. "Gertrude Stein Talking—A Transatlantic Interview." *UCLAn Review Magazine,* 8 (Summer 1962), 2–11; 9 (Spring 1963), pp. 40–48; 9 (Winter 1964), pp. 44–48.

Hadley, Rollin Van N., ed. *The Letters of Bernard Berenson and Isabella Stewart Gardner, with Correspondence by Mary Berenson.* Boston: Northeastern University Press, 1987.

Hale, Nathan G. *Freud and the Americans: The Beginnings of Psychoanalysis in the United States, 1876–1917,* vol. 1. New York: Oxford University Press, 1971.

Handlin, Oscar. *Adventure in Freedom: Three Hundred Years of Jewish Life in America.* New York: McGraw-Hill, 1954.

Hapgood, Hutchins. *A Victorian in the Modern World.* New York: Harcourt, Brace, 1939.

Hertzberg, Arthur. *The Jews in America.* New York: Simon & Schuster, 1989.

Hindus, Milton. "Ethnicity and Sexuality in Gertrude Stein." *Midstream,* 20 (Jan. 1974), pp. 69–76.

Hodder, Alfred. *The Adversaries of the Skeptic, or The Specious Present: A New Inquiry into Human Knowledge.* New York: Macmillan, 1901.

———. "A Fight for the City: The Story of a Campaign of Amateurs." *Outlook,* 73 (Jan. 17, 1903), pp. 159–208; (Jan. 24, 1903), pp. 203–08; (Jan. 31, 1903), pp. 251–88; (Feb. 14, 1903), pp. 393–400; (Feb. 21, 1903), pp. 419–21.

———. *The New Americans.* New York: Macmillan, 1901.

Hoffman, Michael J. *Critical Essays on Gertrude Stein.* Boston: Hall, 1986.

———. *The Development of Abstractionism in the Work of Gertrude Stein.* Philadelphia: University of Pennsylvania Press, 1965.

———, ed. *Critical Essays on Gertrude Stein.* Boston: Hall, 1986.

Hollander, J. H. *The Financial History of Baltimore.* Baltimore: Johns Hopkins University Press, 1899.

Homer, William Innes. *Alfred Stieglitz and the American Avant-Garde.* Boston: New York Graphic Society, 1977.

Horowitz, Helen Lefkowitz. *The Power and Passion of M. Carey Thomas*. New York: Knopf, 1994.

Howells, Dorothy Elia. *A Century to Celebrate: Radcliffe College 1879–1979.* Cambridge, MA: Radcliffe College Alumnae Association, 1978.

Hubly, Erlene. "Gertrude Stein: 'When This You See, Remember Me . . .' " *North American Review*, 271, no. 3 (Sept. 1986), pp. 65–75.

Hughes, H. Stuart. *Consciousness and Society*. New York: Vintage, 1977.

Hyland, Douglas K. S. "Agnes Ernst Meyer, Patron of American Modernism." *The American Art Journal*, 12, no. 1 (Winter 1980), pp. 64–81.

James, William. "The Hidden Self." *Scribner's Magazine*, 7 (1890), pp. 361–73.

———. *Manuscript Lectures*. Cambridge, MA: Harvard University Press, 1988.

———. *Memories and Studies*. London: Longmans, 1912.

———. *The Principles of Psychology*, 2 vols. New York: Holt, 1890.

———. *Psychology: Briefer Course*. Cambridge, MA: Harvard University Press, 1984.

———. *The Varieties of Religious Experience*. New York: Vintage Library of America, 1990.

———. *The Will to Believe and Other Essays in Popular Psychology*. New York: Dover, 1956.

Jensen, Jens. "Collector's Mania." *Acta Psychiatry Scandinavia*, 39, no. 4 (1963), pp. 606–18.

Kahn, Philip, Jr. *A Stitch in Time*. Baltimore: Maryland Historical Society, 1989.

Kahnweiler, Daniel-Henry. *Juan Gris: His Life and Work*, trans. Douglas Cooper. New York: Valentin, 1947.

———. *My Galleries and Painters*, trans. Helen Weaver. New York: Viking, 1971.

———. *The Rise of Cubism*, trans. Henry Aronson. New York: Wittenborn, Schulz, 1949.

Kaplan, Louise J. *Female Perversions*. New York: Anchor Doubleday, 1991.

Karp, Abraham J. *Haven and Home: History of the Jews in America*. New York: Schocken, 1985.

Katz, Leon. "The First Making of *The Making of Americans*." Doctoral dissertation, Columbia University, 1963.

Kazin, Alfred. "From an Italian Journal." *Partisan Review*, 15, no. 5 (May 1948), pp. 550–67.

Keller, Phyllis. *States of Belonging: German-American Intellectuals and the First World War*. Cambridge, MA: Harvard University Press, 1979.

Kellner, Bruce. *Carl Van Vechten and the Irreverent Decades*. Norman: University of Oklahoma Press, 1968.

———. *A Gertrude Stein Companion*. New York: Greenwood, 1988.

Kett, Joseph F. *Rites of Passage: Adolescence in America, 1790 to the Present*. New York: Basic Books, 1977.

Kimball, Fiske. "Matisse: Recognition, Patronage, Collecting." *Philadelphia Museum Bulletin*, 43, no. 217 (March 1948), pp. 35–47.

Kirstein, Lincoln. *The Sculpture of Elie Nadelman*. New York: Museum of Modern Art, 1948.

Kostelanetz, Richard. *Gertrude Stein Advanced: An Anthology of Criticism*. Jefferson, NC: McFarland, 1990.

Kramer, William M. "The Emergence of Oakland Jewry." *Western States Jewish Historical Quarterly*, 10, no. 2 (Oct. 1977), pp. 99–125; no. 3 (April 1978), pp. 238–59; no. 4 (July 1978), pp. 353–73; 11, no. 1 (Oct. 1978), pp. 69–86; no. 2 (Jan. 1979), pp. 173–86; no. 3 (April 1979), pp. 265–78; no. 4 (July 1979), pp. 364–76.

Kuklick, Bruce. *The Rise of American Philosophy, Cambridge, Massachusetts: 1860–1930.* New Haven, CT: Yale University Press, 1977.

Kushner, Marilyn S. *Morgan Russell.* New York: Hudson Hill, 1990.

Lake, Carlton, and Linda Ashton. *Henri-Pierre Roché: An Introduction.* Austin, TX: Harry Ransom Humanities Research Center, 1991.

Laughlin, James. "About Gertrude Stein." *Yale Review,* 77, no. 4 (Summer 1988), pp. 528–36.

Lears, T. J. Jackson. *No Place of Grace: Anti-Modernism and the Transformation of American Culture.* New York: Pantheon, 1981.

Leibowitz, Herbert. *Fabricating Lives.* New York: Knopf, 1989.

Leighten, Patricia. *Re-ordering the Universe: Picasso and Anarchism.* Princeton, NJ: Princeton University Press, 1989.

———, "The White Peril and *L'Art nègre*: Picasso, Primitivism, and Anticolonialism." *Art Bulletin,* 72, no. 4 (Dec. 1990), pp. 609–30.

Levin, Gail. "Andrew Dasburg: Recollections of the Avant-Garde." *Arts Magazine,* 52, no. 10 (June 1978), pp. 126–30.

———. "Kandinsky and the American Literary Avant-Garde." *Criticism,* 21, no. 4 (Fall 1979), pp. 347–55.

Levy, Harriet Lane. *920 O'Farrell Street.* Garden City, NY: Doubleday, 1947.

Leys, Ruth. "Types of One: Adolf Meyer's Life Chart and the Representation of Individuality." *Representations,* 34 (Spring 1991), pp. 1–28.

Lillie, Frank R. *The Woods Hole Marine Biological Laboratory.* Chicago: University of Chicago Press, 1944.

Logan, Mary [Mary Costelloe Berenson]. "The New Art Criticism." *The Atlantic Monthly,* 76 (Aug. 1895), pp. 263–70.

Lord, James. "Where the Pictures Were." *Prose,* 7 (1973), pp. 133–87.

Lowe, Sue Davidson. *Stieglitz.* New York: Farrar, Straus & Giroux, 1983.

Luhan, Mabel Dodge. *European Experiences.* New York: Harcourt, Brace, 1935.

———. *Movers and Shakers.* Albuquerque: University of New Mexico Press, 1985.

McCardle, Carl W. "The Terrible Tempered Dr. Barnes." *The Saturday Evening Post,* 214 (March 28, 1942), pp. 20–21, 78, 80–81; (April 4, 1942), pp. 18–19, 34–35, 38; (April 11, 1942), pp. 20–21, 64, 66, 68.

Maienschein, Jane. *100 Years Exploring Life, 1888–1988: The Marine Biological Laboratory at Woods Hole.* Boston: Jones & Bartlett, 1989.

Mall, Franklin P. "The Anatomical Course and Laboratory of the Johns Hopkins University." *Bulletin of The Johns Hopkins Hospital,* 7, nos. 62–63 (May–June 1896), pp. 85–100.

———. "What Is Biology?" *Chautauquan,* 18 (1894), pp. 411–14.

Marcus, Jacob R. *Memoirs of American Jews, 1775–1865,* 3 vols. Philadelphia: Jewish Publication Society, 1953–1955.

———. *United States Jewry, 1776–1985.* Detroit: Wayne State University Press, 1989.

Marrus, Michael. *The Politics of Assimilation: A Study of the French Jewish Community at the Time of the Dreyfus Affair.* New York: Oxford University Press, 1974.

Mason, Daniel Gregory. "At Harvard in the Nineties." *New England Quarterly,* 9 (1936), pp. 43–70.

Mathews, Nancy Mowll. *Cassatt and Her Circle: Selected Letters.* New York: Abbeville, 1984.

Mellow, James. *Charmed Circle: Gertrude Stein and Company.* New York: Praeger, 1974.

Merrill, Cynthia. "Mirrored Image: Gertrude Stein and Autobiography." *Pacific Coast Philology,* 20, nos. 1–2 (Nov. 1985), pp. 11–17.

Meyer, Agnes E. *Out of These Roots: The Autobiography of an American Woman.* Boston: Little, Brown, 1953.

Meyer, Annie Nathan, ed. *Women's Work in America.* New York: Holt, 1891.

Meyer, Martin A. *The Jew in California.* San Francisco: Emanu-El, 1916.

Miller, Rosalind. *Gertrude Stein: Form and Intelligibility.* New York: Exposition, 1949.

Milner, John. *The Studios of Paris.* New Haven, CT: Yale University Press, 1988.

Miner, Earl. *The Japanese Tradition in British and American Literature.* Princeton, NJ: Princeton University Press, 1958.

Mizejewski, Linda. "Gertrude Stein: The Pattern Moves, the Woman Behind Shakes It." *Women's Studies: An Interdisciplinary Journal,* 13, nos. 1–2 (1986), pp. 33–47.

Monod-Fontaine, Isabelle. *Donation Louise et Michel Leiris: Collection Kahnweiler-Leiris.* Paris: Centre Georges Pompidou, Musée National d'Art Moderne, 1984.

Morelli, Giovanni. *Italian Masters in German Galleries.* London: Bell, 1883.

Morison, Samuel Eliot. *Three Centuries of Harvard.* Cambridge, MA: Harvard University Press, 1936.

Mosse, George. "The Mystical Origins of National Socialism." *Journal of the History of Ideas,* 22, no. 1 (Jan.–March 1961), pp. 81–96.

———. *Toward the Final Solution.* New York: Fertig, 1978.

Muensterberger, Werner. *Collecting: An Unruly Passion.* Princeton, NJ: Princeton University Press, 1994.

Münsterberg, Hugo. *American Traits.* Boston: Houghton Mifflin, 1901.

———. "The New Psychology and Harvard's Equipment for Teaching It." *The Harvard Graduates Magazine,* 1, no. 2 (Jan. 1893), pp. 201–09.

———. *Psychology and Life.* Boston: Houghton Mifflin, 1899.

———. *Science and Idealism.* Boston: Houghton Mifflin, 1906.

Murchison, Carl, ed. *A History of Psychology in Autobiography,* vol. 1, Worcester, MA: Clark University Press, 1930; vol. 2, New York: Russell & Russell, 1961.

Muscatine, Doris. *Old San Francisco: The Biography of a City.* New York: Putnam, 1975.

Nagera, Humberto. "Children's Reactions to the Death of Important Objects." *The Psychoanalytic Study of the Child,* 25 (1970), pp. 360–99.

Neuman, Shirley, and Ira Nadel, eds. *Gertrude Stein and the Making of Literature.* Houndmills, England: Macmillan, 1988.

Newman, Sasha M., ed. *Félix Vallotton.* New Haven, CT: Yale University Art Gallery, and New York: Abbeville, 1991.

"Oakland: The Athens of the Pacific." Oakland: Loofbourow, 1897.

Oakland and Surroundings, Illustrated and Described. Oakland: Elliott, 1885.

Olivier, Fernande. *Picasso and His Friends,* trans. Jane Miller. New York: Appleton-Century, 1965.

Olney, Mary McLean. "Oakland, Berkeley, and the University of California, 1880–1895." Interview conducted by William Klug Brown, 1963. The Bancroft Library, University of California, Berkeley.

Osborn, Henry Fairfield. "A Sea-Shore Laboratory." *Harper's Magazine,* 104 (1902), pp. 552–58.

Osler, William. "The Natural Method of Teaching the Subject of Medicine." *The Journal of the American Medical Association,* 36, no. 24 (June 15, 1901), pp. 1673–79.

Pach, Walter. *Queer Thing, Painting.* New York: Harper, 1938.

Parke, Catherine N. "Simple Through Complication: Gertrude Stein Thinking." *American Literature,* 90 (Dec. 1988), pp. 554–73.

Penrose, Roland. *Picasso: His Life and Work.* Berkeley: University of California Press, 1981.

Perloff, Marjorie. *The Poetics of Indeterminacy.* Princeton, NJ: Princeton University Press, 1981.

Perry, Ralph Barton. *The Thought and Character of William James,* 2 vols. Boston: Little, Brown, 1935.

Phillips, N. Taylor. "The Levy and Seixas Families of Newport and New York." *Publications of the American Jewish Historical Society,* 4 (1895), pp. 189–214.

Pittsburgh: Its Industry and Commerce. Pittsburgh: Barr & Myers, 1870.

Pollack, Barbara. *The Collectors: Dr. Claribel and Miss Etta Cone.* Indianapolis: Bobbs-Merrill, 1962.

Pondrom, Cyrena. "Gertrude Stein: From Outlaw to Classic." *Contemporary Literature,* 27, no. 1 (1986), pp. 98–114.

Potter, Margaret, ed. *Four Americans in Paris: The Collections of Gertrude Stein and Her Family.* New York: Museum of Modern Art, 1970.

Preston, John Hyde. "A Conversation." *The Atlantic Monthly,* 156 (Aug. 1935), pp. 81–97.

Pugh, Mabel Vaughn. "In the Fall of 1893." *Radcliffe Alumnae Quarterly,* 21, no. 3 (Aug. 1947), pp. 6–7.

Purrmann, Hans. "From the Workshop of Henri Matisse." *The Dial,* July 1922, pp. 32–40.

Quen, Jacques M., and Eric T. Carlson. *American Psychoanalysis: Origins and Development, The Adolf Meyer Seminars.* New York: Brunner/Mazel, 1978.

Rainger, Ronald, ed. *The American Development of Biology.* Philadelphia: University of Pennsylvania Press, 1988.

Raymond, Janice G. *A Passion for Friends: Toward a Philosophy of Female Affection.* Boston: Beacon, 1986.

Reed, Helen Leah. "Radcliffe College." *The New England Magazine,* Jan. 1895, pp. 609–23.

Retallack, Joan. "The High Adventure of Indeterminacy." *Parnassus,* 11, no. 1 (Spring–Summer 1983), pp. 231–63.

Rewald, John. *Cézanne and America: Dealers, Collectors, Artists, and Critics, 1891–1921.* Princeton, NJ: Princeton University Press, 1989.

———. *Cézanne, the Steins and Their Circle.* New York: Thames & Hudson, 1987.

Richardson, Brenda. *Dr. Claribel & Miss Etta.* Baltimore: Baltimore Museum of Art, 1985.

Richardson, John, with Marilyn McCully. *A Life of Picasso,* vol. 1, *1881–1906.* New York: Random House, 1991.

Rischin, Moses. *The Promised Land: New York's Jews, 1870–1914.* Cambridge, MA: Harvard University Press, 1977.

Robbins, Daniel. "Abbreviated Historiography of Cubism." *Art Journal,* 47, no. 4 (Winter 1988), pp. 277–83.

Robinson, Daniel, ed. *Significant Contributions to the History of Psychology, 1750–1920,* vol. 5. Washington, DC: University Publications of America, 1977.

Robinson, Marc. "Gertrude Stein, Forgotten Playwright." *South Atlantic Quarterly,* 91, no. 3 (Summer 1992), pp. 620–43.

Rönnebeck, Arnold. "Gertrude Was Always Giggling." *Books Abroad,* 17, no. 1 (Oct. 1944), pp. 3–7.

Rosenberg, Charles E. "Sexuality, Class, and Role in Nineteenth-Century America." *American Quarterly,* 25 (May 1973), pp. 131–53.

Rosenblum, Robert. *Cubism and Twentieth-Century Art.* New York: Abrams, 1976.

Rosenfeld, Paul. *By Way of Art.* Freeport, NY: Books for Libraries, 1967.

Rosovsky, Nitza. *The Jewish Experience at Harvard.* Cambridge, MA: Harvard University Press, 1986.

Rossiter, Margaret W. *Women Scientists in America: Struggles and Strategies to 1940.* Baltimore: Johns Hopkins University Press, 1982.

Royce, Josiah. *Outlines of Psychology.* New York: Macmillan, 1903.

Rubin, William. *Cézanne: The Late Work.* New York: Museum of Modern Art, 1977.

———. "From Narrative to 'Iconic' in Picasso: The Buried Allegory in *Bread and Fruitdish on a Table* and the Role of *Les Demoiselles d'Avignon.*" *Art Bulletin,* 65, no. 4 (Dec. 1983), pp. 615–49.

———. "Pablo and Georges and Leo and Bill." *Art in America,* 67, no. 2 (March–April 1979), pp. 128–47.

———. *Picasso and Braque: Pioneering Cubism.* New York: Museum of Modern Art, 1989.

———, ed. *Picasso and Braque: A Symposium.* New York: Museum of Modern Art, 1992.

———. *Picasso in the Collection of the Museum of Modern Art.* New York: Museum of Modern Art, 1972.

Ruddick, Lisa. *Reading Gertrude Stein: Body, Text, Gnosis.* Ithaca, NY: Cornell University Press, 1990.

Russell, Bertrand. *The Autobiography of Bertrand Russell.* Boston: Little, Brown, 1967.

Russell, John, ed. *A Portrait of Logan Pearsall Smith Drawn from His Letters and Diaries.* London: Dropmore, 1950.

Sabin, Florence Rena. *Franklin Paine Mall.* Baltimore: Johns Hopkins University Press, 1934.

Salmon, André. *Souvenirs sans Fin.* Paris: Gallimard, 1956.

Samuels, Ernest. *Bernard Berenson: The Making of a Connoisseur.* Cambridge, MA: Harvard University Press, 1979.

———, with Jayne Newcomer Samuels. *Bernard Berenson: The Making of a Legend.* Cambridge, MA: Harvard University Press, 1987.

Santayana, George. *Character and Opinion in the United States.* New York: Scribner, 1920.

Schapiro, Meyer. "Mr. Berenson's Values." *Encounter,* 16 (1961), pp. 57–65.

———. *Modern Art.* New York: Braziller, 1982.

Schmitz, Neil. *Of Huck and Alice: Humorous Writing in American Literature.* Minneapolis: University of Minnesota Press, 1983.

Schneider, Pierre. *Matisse.* New York: Rizzoli, 1984.

Sears, Hal D. *The Sex Radicals: Free Love in High Victorian America.* Lawrence: Regents Press of Kansas, 1977.

Secor, Cynthia. "The Question of Gertrude Stein," in Fritz Fleischmann, ed., *American Novelists Revisited: Essays in Feminist Criticism.* Boston: Hall, 1982.

Shattuck, Roger. *The Banquet Years.* New York: Vintage, 1968.

Shiff, Richard. *Cézanne and the End of Impressionism.* Chicago: University of Chicago Press, 1986.

Shyrock, Richard Harrison. *The Development of Modern Medicine.* Philadelphia: University of Pennsylvania Press, 1936.

Sicherman, Barbara. "The Uses of a Diagnosis: Doctors, Patients, and Neurasthenia." *Journal of the History of Medicine,* 32 (Jan. 1977), pp. 33–54.

Sidis, Boris. "The Nature and Principles of Psychology." *American Journal of Insanity,* 56 (July 1899), pp. 41–52.

Simon, Linda. *The Biography of Alice B. Toklas.* Lincoln: University of Nebraska Press, 1991.

Simonson, Lee. *Portrait of a Lifetime.* New York: Duell, Sloan and Pearce, 1942.

Sinclair, Upton. "Starving for Health's Sake." *Cosmopolitan,* 48 (May 1910), pp. 739–46.

Skinner, B. F. "Has Gertrude Stein a Secret?" *The Atlantic Monthly,* Jan. 1934, pp. 50–57.

Smith, Lillian Wing, Mabel Earle, and Louise Earle. "In Memoriam: Gertrude Stein." *Radcliffe Alumnae Quarterly,* 30, no. 3 (Aug. 1946), p. 21.

Smith, Logan Pearsall. *Unforgotten Years.* Boston: Little, Brown, 1939.

Smith, Percy F. *Memory's Milestones.* Pittsburgh: Smith, 1918.

Smith-Rosenberg, Carroll. *Disorderly Conduct: Visions of Gender in Victorian America.* New York: Oxford University Press, 1985.

Solomons, Leon. "The Alleged Proof of Parallelism from the Conservation of Energy." *The Philosophical Review,* 8, no. 2 (1899), pp. 146–65.

———. "Automatic Reactions." *Psychological Review,* 6 (July 1899), pp. 376–94.

———. "Discrimination in Cutaneous Sensations." *Psychological Review,* 4 (May 1897), pp. 246–50.

———. "A New Explanation of Weber's Law." *Psychological Review,* 7 (May 1900), pp. 234–40.

———. "The Saturation of Colors." *Psychological Review,* 3 (Jan. 1896), pp. 50–56.

———, and Gertrude Stein. "Normal Motor Automatism." *Psychological Review,* 3 (Sept. 1896), pp. 492–512.

Sprigge, Elizabeth. *Gertrude Stein: Her Life and Work.* New York: Harper, 1957.

———. "Gertrude Stein's American Years." *The Reporter,* 13, no. 2 (Aug. 11, 1955), pp. 46–52.

"Stein, Bergman and Cohn Families 1787–1954." Baltimore: Ida Charles Wilkins Foundation, 1954.

Steinberg, Leo. *Other Criteria: Confrontations with Twentieth-Century Art.* New York: Oxford University Press, 1972.

———. "Resisting Cézanne: Picasso's 'Three Women.'" *Art in America,* 66, no. 6 (Nov.–Dec. 1978), pp. 114–33.

Steiner, Wendy. *Exact Resemblance to Exact Resemblance: The Literary Portraiture of Gertrude Stein.* New Haven, CT: Yale University Press, 1978.

Sterne, Maurice. *Shadow and Light: The Life, Friends, and Opinions of Maurice Sterne,* ed. Charlotte Leon Mayerson. New York: Harcourt, Brace, 1962.

Stimpson, Catharine R. "Gertrice/Altrude: Stein, Toklas, and the Paradox of the Happy Marriage," in Ruth Perry, ed., *Mothering the Mind: Twelve Studies of Writers and Their Silent Partners.* New York: Holmes & Meier, 1984.

———. "Gertrude Stein and the Lesbian Lie," in Margo Culley, ed., *American Women's Autobiography: Fea(s)ts of Memory.* Madison: University of Wisconsin Press, 1992.

———. "Gertrude Stein and the Transposition of Gender," in Nancy K. Miller, ed., *The Poetics of Gender.* New York: Columbia University Press, 1986.

———. "The Mind, the Body, and Gertrude Stein." *Critical Inquiry,* 3, no. 3 (Spring 1977), pp. 489–506.

———. "The Somagrams of Gertrude Stein." *Poetics Today,* 6, nos. 1–2 (1985), pp. 67–80.

Strachey, Barbara, and Jayne Samuels, eds., *Mary Berenson: A Self-Portrait from Her Diaries and Letters.* New York: Norton, 1983.

Suleiman, Susan Rubin, ed. *The Female Body in Western Culture.* Cambridge, MA: Harvard University Press, 1986.

Sutherland, Donald. "Alice and Gertrude and Others." *Prairie Schooner,* Winter 1971–1972, pp. 284–99.

———. "The Conversion of Alice B. Toklas." *Colorado Quarterly,* Autumn 1968, pp. 129–41.

———. *Gertrude Stein: A Biography of Her Work*. New Haven, CT: Yale University Press, 1951.

———. "A Wicked Alice in Wonderland." *Denver Quarterly*, Spring 1974, pp. 80–83.

Synott, Marcia G. *A Social History of Admissions at Harvard, Yale, and Princeton, 1900–1930*. Ann Arbor: UMI, 1980.

Tate, Allen. "Miss Toklas' American Cake." *Prose*, Fall 1971, pp. 137–61.

"Testimony Against Gertrude Stein." *transition*, 23, no. 1, supp. (Feb. 1935), pp. 2–15.

Thomas, M. Carey. "The Education of Women," in Nicholas Murray Butler, ed., *Monographs of Education in the United States*, vol. 7 (Department of Education for the United States Commission to the Paris Exposition of 1900). Albany, NY: Lyon, 1899.

———. "Should the Higher Education of Women Differ from That of Men?" *Education Review*, 21 (Jan. 1901), pp. 1–10.

Thomson, Virgil. *An Autobiography*. New York: Dutton, 1966.

———. "Remembering Gertrude." *Columbia Library Columns*, 31, no. 2 (Feb. 1982), pp. 3–17.

Van Vechten, Carl. "How to Read Gertrude Stein." *The Trend*, 7, no. 5 (Aug. 1914), pp. 553–57.

Vollard, Ambroise. *Recollections of a Picture Dealer*, trans. Violet Macdonald. Boston: Little, Brown, 1936.

Voorsanger, Jacob. "Leon Mendez Solomons (1873–1900)." *Western States Jewish Historical Quarterly*, 10, no. 2 (Jan. 1978), pp. 138–45.

Walker, Franklin. *Frank Norris: A Biography*. New York: Russell & Russell, 1963.

Walker, Jayne L. *The Making of a Modernist: Gertrude Stein, from Three Lives to Tender Buttons*. Amherst: University of Massachusetts Press, 1984.

Walsh, Mary Roth. *"Doctors Wanted: No Women Need Apply": Sexual Barriers in the Medical Profession, 1835–1975*. New Haven, CT: Yale University Press, 1977.

Weininger, Otto. *Sex and Character*. New York: AMS, 1975.

Welsh, Lilian. *Reminiscences of Thirty Years in Baltimore*. Baltimore: Norman, Remington, 1925.

White, Ray Lewis. *Gertrude Stein and Alice B. Toklas: A Reference Guide*. Boston: Hall, 1984.

Wiebe, Robert. *The Search for Order, 1877–1920*. New York: Hill & Wang, 1967.

Williams, William Carlos. *The Autobiography of William Carlos Williams*. New York: New Directions, 1951.

Wilson, Edmund. *Axel's Castle*. New York: Scribner, 1931.

———. *The Shores of Light*. New York: Farrar, Straus and Young, 1952.

———. *Upstate: Records and Recollections of Northern New York*. New York: Farrar, Straus & Giroux, 1971.

Winsor, Mary P. *Reading the Shape of Nature: Comparative Zoology in the Agassiz Museum*. Chicago: University of Chicago Press, 1991.

Winterstein, Alfred. "Der Sammler (The Collector)," trans. Peter Heinegg. *Imago*, 7 (1921), pp. 180–94.

Wise, Isaac M. *Reminiscences*, ed. David Philipson. New York: Arno, 1973.

Wolfenstein, Martha. "The Image of the Lost Parent." *The Psychoanalytic Study of the Child*, 28 (1973), pp. 433–56.

———. "Loss, Rage, and Repetition." *The Psychoanalytic Study of the Child*, 24 (1969), pp. 432–60.

Young, Robert M. *Mind, Brain, and Adaptation in the Nineteenth Century*. Oxford: Clarendon, 1970.

INDEX

Page numbers in italics refer to illustrations.